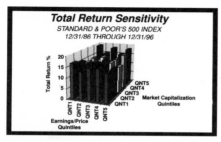

Atlas contains robust performance diagnostic tools enabling the analyst to identify significant factors driving returns over time.

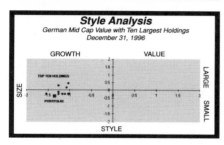

Atlas' powerful risk models allow the manager to identify structural bets and explicitly control the resulting return variance of the portfolio relative to the benchmark over time.

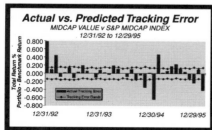

Wilshire's new global style analysis allows managers to monitor the impact of individual stocks on the total portfolio style orientation.

W I L S H I R E

Now in Windows™ 95 and NT

For more information please contact:

Santa Monica
T 310.451.3051
F 310.458.0520

London
T 44.171.814.7355
F 44.171.814.6611

www@wilshire.com
e-mail: quantum@ wilshire.com

or leave a voice message at:
310.319.2501

Handbook of Portfolio Management

Edited by

Frank J. Fabozzi, CFA
Adjunct Professor of Finance
School of Management
Yale University

Published by Frank J. Fabozzi Associates

© 1998 By Frank J. Fabozzi Associates
New Hope, Pennsylvania

ISBN: 1-883249-41-4

Printed in the United States of America

Table of Contents

Contributing Authors

Roger G. Clarke	Analytic/TSA Global Asset Management
David F. DeRosa	DeRosa Research and Trading, Inc. and Yale University
Harindra de Silva	Analytic/TSA Global Asset Management
Chris P. Dialynas	Pacific Investment Management Company
Lev Dynkin	Lehman Brothers
Mark Edwards	Plexus Group
David Eichhorn	J.P. Morgan Investment Management
Frank J. Fabozzi	Yale University
Sergio Focardi	The Intertek Group
James P. Garland	The Jeffrey Company
Benjamin J. Gord	Miller Anderson & Sherrerd, LLP
James L. Grant	Simmons College
Francis Gupta	J.P. Morgan Investment Management
William J. Hurley	The Royal Military College of Canada
Jay Hyman	Lehman Brothers
Bruce I. Jacobs	Jacobs Levy Equity Management
David M. Jones	Aubrey G. Lanston & Co. Inc.
Frank J. Jones	Guardian Life Insurance
Ronald N. Kahn	BARRA
Vadim Konstantinovsky	Lehman Brothers
Robert C. Kuberek	Wilshire Associates Incorporated
Kenneth N. Levy	Jacobs Levy Equity Management
John S. Loftus	Pacific Investment Managment Company
Luis R. Luis	Scudder, Stevens & Clark
J. Hank Lynch	BankBoston
Jack Malvey	Lehman Brothers
Greg M. McMurran	Analytic/TSA Global Asset Management
Thornton L. O'Glove	
Leonard J. Peltzman	Guardian Life Insurance
Ellen Rachlin	Aubrey G. Lanston & Co. Inc.
Shrikant Ramamurthy	Prudential Securities Incorporated
Scott F. Richard	Miller Anderson & Sherrerd, LLP
John C. Ritchie Jr.	Temple University
Mary Rooney	Merrill Lynch
David M. Stein	Parametric Portfolio Associates
Christopher B. Steward	Putnam Investments
Kara Tan Bhala	Merrill Lynch Asset Management
Jane Tripp Howe	Pacific Investment Management Company
Kenneth E. Volpert	The Vanguard Group, Inc.
Wayne H. Wagner	Plexus Group

List of Advertisers

BARRA

Capital Access International

Derivative Solutions

Wall Street Analytics

Wilshire

Section I:

Background Information

Chapter 1

Overview of Portfolio Management

Frank J. Fabozzi, Ph.D., CFA
Adjunct Professor of Finance
School of Management
Yale University

INTRODUCTION

There are several terms used to describe the process of managing funds: portfolio management, investment management, or money management. The individual or team of individuals who manage a portfolio of investments is referred to as a portfolio manager, an investment manager, a money manager, or, simply, a manager. In industry jargon, the manager "runs money." The purpose of this book is to describe the process of portfolio management — that is, how managers run money. This process requires an understanding of the various investment vehicles, the way these investment vehicles are valued, and the various strategies that can be used to select the investment vehicles that should be included in a portfolio in order to accomplish investment objectives. Our focus in this book is on the two major asset classes in which individual and institutional managers invest — common stock and fixed income securities.

This chapter provides an overview of the portfolio management process. This is a useful starting point for our journey, since it allows us to see the key steps involved in managing a portfolio and therefore the significance of the chapters that follow in this book. This process involves the following five steps: (1) setting investment objectives; (2) establishing investment policy; (3) selecting a portfolio strategy; (4) selecting the assets; and (5) measuring and evaluating performance. We conclude the chapter with a discussion of ethics in investment management.

SETTING INVESTMENT OBJECTIVES

The first step in the portfolio management process, setting investment objectives, begins with a thorough analysis of the objectives of the entity whose money is being managed. These entities can be classified as individual investors and institutional investors. Within each of these broad classifications is a wide range of investment objectives.

3

The objectives of an individual investor may be to accumulate funds to purchase a home or other major acquisition, to have sufficient funds to be able to retire at a specified age, or to accumulate funds to pay for college tuition for children. An individual investor may engage the services of a financial advisor/consultant in establishing investment objectives.

Institutional investors include pension funds, depository institutions (i.e., commercial banks, savings and loan associations, and credit unions), insurance companies (i.e., life companies and property and casualty companies), mutual funds, endowments, and foundations. In general we can classify institutional investors into two broad categories — those that must meet contractually specified liabilities and those that do not. We can classify those in the first category as institutions with *liability-driven objectives* and those in the second category *non-liability driven objectives*. We will discuss the nature of liabilities faced by the first category of institutions below. For the second category, the objective is to outperform some designated benchmark that may be either a market benchmark or a customized benchmark. Even within the same institutional investor group, there are situations where both liability and non-liability objectives may be found.

Regardless of whether the assets are liability driven or not, an institutional investor must remain solvent. Solvency is measured by the institution's surplus (or stockholders' equity) and is the difference between its assets and liabilities. Sounds like a simple concept; however, because of the accounting requirements for assets and liabilities by different institutions as determined by generally accepting accounting principles (GAAP) and regulatory accounting principles (RAP), there can be a significant difference between the computed surplus. Moreover, neither GAAP nor RAP may be a good measure of the true economic difference between the institution's assets and liabilities.

Below we will discuss the nature of liabilities faced by institutional investors, and the different types of surplus measures. Then, we take a brief look at the objectives of the major institutional investors.

Nature of Liabilities

A *liability* is a cash outlay that must be made at a specific time to satisfy the contractual terms of an issued obligation. An institutional investor is concerned with both the amount and timing of liabilities, because its assets must produce the cash flow to meet any payments it has promised to make in a timely way. In fact, liabilities are classified according to the degree of certainty of their amount and timing as shown in Exhibit 1. This exhibit assumes that the holder of the obligation will not cancel it prior to any actual or projected payout date.

The description of cash outlays as either "known" or "uncertain" are undoubtedly broad. When we refer to a cash outlay as being uncertain, we do not mean that it cannot be predicted. There are some liabilities where the "law of large numbers" makes it easier to predict the timing and/or amount of cash outlays. This work is typically done by actuaries, but even actuaries have difficulty predicting natural catastrophes such as floods and earthquakes.

Exhibit 1: Classification of Liabilities of Institutional Investors

Liability Type	Amount of Cash Outlay	Timing of Cash Outlay
Type I	known	known
Type II	known	uncertain
Type III	uncertain	known
Type IV	uncertain	uncertain

A Type-I liability is one for which both the amount and timing of the liabilities are known with certainty. An example would be a liability where an institution knows that it must pay $8 million six months from now. Banks and thrifts know the amount that they are committed to pay (principal plus interest) on the maturity date of a fixed-rate deposit, assuming that the depositor does not withdraw funds prior to the maturity date. Another example is a product offered by a life insurance company — a *guaranteed investment contract*, popularly referred to as a GIC. The obligation of the life insurance company under this contract is that it will guarantee an interest rate up to some specified maturity date.

A Type-II liability is one for which the amount of cash outlay is known, but the timing of the cash outlay is uncertain. The most obvious example of a Type-II liability is a basic life insurance policy. There are many types of life insurance policies, but the most basic type provides that, for an annual premium, a life insurance company agrees to make a specified dollar payment to policy beneficiaries upon the death of the insured.

A Type-III liability is one for which the timing of the cash outlay is known, but the amount is uncertain. A 2-year floating-rate certificate of deposit offered by a depository institution where the interest rate resets quarterly based on a market interest rate is an example.

A Type-IV liability is one where there is uncertainty as to both the amount and the timing of the cash outlay. There are numerous insurance products and pension obligations in this category. Probably the most obvious examples are automobile and home insurance policies issued by property and casualty insurance companies. When, and if, a payment will have to be made to the policyholder is uncertain. Whenever damage is done to an insured asset, the amount of the payment that must be made is uncertain.

Measuring an Institution's Surplus

As noted above, the surplus is the difference between an institution's assets and liabilities. There are three types of surpluses that may be computed: economic, accounting, and regulatory.

Economic Surplus

The *economic surplus* of any entity is the difference between the market value of all its assets and the market value of its liabilities. That is,

Economic surplus = Market value of assets − Market value of liabilities

While the concept of a market value of assets may not seem unusual, one might ask: What is the market value of liabilities? This value is simply the present value of the liabilities, where the liabilities are discounted at an appropriate interest rate. A rise in interest rates will therefore decrease the present value or market value of the liabilities; a decrease in interest rates will increase the present value or market value of liabilities. Thus, the economic surplus can be expressed as:

Economic surplus = Market value of assets − Present value of liabilities

Accounting Surplus

Institutional investors must prepare periodic financial statements. These financial statements must be prepared in accordance with GAAP. GAAP for assets is governed by Statement of Financial Accounting Standards No. 115, more popularly referred to as FASB 115. However, it does not deal with the accounting treatment for liabilities.

For assets, there are rules for determining whether an asset's value will be based on amortized cost (historical cost) or market value, despite the fact that an asset's real cash flow is the same regardless of the accounting treatment. Specifically, the accounting treatment required for a security depends on how the security is classified. There are three classifications of investment accounts: (1) held to maturity, (2) available for sale, and (3) trading. The definition of each account is set forth in FASB 115.

Regulatory Surplus

Institutional investors that are regulated at the state or federal levels must also provide financial reports to regulators based on RAP. These accounting principles are not necessarily the same as set forth in FASB 115 (i.e., GAAP). Liabilities may or may not be reported at their present value, depending on the type of institution and the type of liability. The surplus as measured using RAP is called *regulatory surplus*, and, as in the case of accounting surplus, may be materially different from economic surplus.

Overview of Investment Objectives of Institutional Investors

Below we provide an overview of the investment objectives of insurance companies, pension funds, investment companies, depository institutions, and endowment funds.

Insurance Companies

Insurance companies are financial intermediaries that, for a price, will make a payment if a certain event occurs. They function as risk bearers. There are two types of insurance companies: life insurance companies ("life companies") and property and casualty insurance companies ("P&C companies"). The principal event that the former insures against is death. Life insurance protection is not the only financial product sold by these companies; a major portion of the business of life companies is in the area of providing retirement benefits. In contrast, P&C companies insure against a wide variety of occurrences. Two examples are automobile and home insurance.

The key distinction between life and P&C companies lies in the difficulty of projecting whether a policyholder will be paid off and, if so, how much the payment will be. While this is no simple task for either type of insurance company, from an actuarial perspective it is easier for a life company. The amount and timing of claims on P&C companies are more difficult to predict because of the randomness of natural catastrophes and the unpredictability of court awards in legal cases. This uncertainty about the timing and amount of cash outlays to satisfy claims affects the investment strategies used by the managers of the P&C companies' funds.

There are fundamental characteristics of the insurance industry that are shared by life companies and P&C companies. An *insurance policy* is a legally binding contract for which the policyholder (or owner) pays *premiums* in exchange for the insurance company's promise to pay specified sums contingent on future events. The company is said to *underwrite* the owner's risk, and acts as a buffer against the uncertainties of life. Premiums can be paid in a single payment, or, more commonly, in a regular series of payments. If the owner fails to pay premiums, the policy is said to *lapse*, or *terminate*. Unless both parties renew the contract, the company loses the future stream of premiums, and the owner loses the protection the policy had promised.

Since the accounting treatment of both assets and liabilities is established by state statutes covering an insurance company, regulatory surplus must be computed. Regulatory surplus, more popularly referred to as *statutory surplus*, is important because regulators view this as the ultimate amount that can be drawn upon to pay policyholders. The growth of this surplus for an insurance company will determine how much future business it can underwrite.

The overall profit or loss of an insurance company can be divided into two parts: investment income and underwriting income. *Investment income* is basically the revenue from the insurance company's portfolio of invested assets. *Underwriting income* is the difference between the premiums earned and the costs of settling claims.

Life Insurance Companies The liabilities of an insurance company are the insurance policies that it has underwritten. Here we will review a few of the major products. Many of the products are interest-rate sensitive. The interest rate offered on an investment-type insurance policy is called the *crediting rate*. If the crediting rate of a policy is not competitive with market interest rates or rates offered by other life companies, an owner may allow the policy to lapse or, if permissible, may borrow against the policy. In either case, this will result in an outflow of cash from the life insurance company.

Term life insurance is a contract that provides a death benefit but no cash build-up; it has no investment component. Further, the premium charged by the insurance company remains constant only for a specified term of years. Most policies are automatically renewable at the end of each term, but at a higher rate. When an insurance company issues this type of contract, it knows the amount of the liability it may have to pay, but does not know the date. However, using actuarial data, the timing of the liability can be reasonably estimated for a pool of insured individuals. The premium that the insurance company charges is usually such that, no matter what happens to interest rates, the life company will have sufficient funds to meet the obligation when policyholders die.

Whole life insurance is a policy with two features: (1) it pays off a stated amount upon the death of the insured and (2) it accumulates a cash value. The first feature is an insurance protection feature — the same feature that term insurance provides. The second is an investment feature because the policy accumulates value and at every point in time has a *cash surrender value*, an amount the insurance company will pay, if the policyholder ends the policy. The policyholder has the option to borrow against the policy and the amount that can be borrowed is called the *loan value*. The interest rate at which the funds can be borrowed is specified in the policy. The objective of investing the premiums for a whole life insurance policy is to earn a return on its investments greater than its policies' crediting rate. This would result in a decline in the life insurance company's surplus. Offering a lower crediting rate on a whole life policy than competitors may reduce the risk that the crediting rate will not be earned, but increases the likelihood that the owner will borrow against the policy or allow it to lapse.

Universal life is a whole life product where the policyholder pays a premium for insurance protection and for a separate fee can invest in a vehicle that pays a competitive interest rate rather than the below-market crediting rates typically offered on a whole life policy. For a policyholder, the advantage of this investment alternative relative to the direct purchase of a security is that under the current tax code, the interest rate earned is tax deferred. The risk that the insurer faces is that the return earned is not competitive with those of other insurance companies, resulting in policy lapses. There are policies where the rate is based on the performance of equities. For such policies, there is no fixed dollar liability. Instead, the payout is dependent on the performance of the equity portfolio. However, there may be a minimum value set for an equity-linked policy should the policyholder die.

An *annuity* is a regular periodic payment made by the insurance company to a policyholder for a specified period of time. There are policies with fixed payments and there are variable annuities (i.e., annuities whose value will depend on a portfolio of securities, typically equities). A *guaranteed investment contract* is a pure investment product. In a GIC, a life company agrees, for a single premium, to pay the principal amount and a predetermined annual crediting rate over the life of the investment, all of which is paid at the maturity date.

From the description of the products above, it can be seen that for some types of life insurance policies the objectives are liability driven. For the variable rate or equity-linked products, there is a minimum liability in terms of a payout at the termination of the policy or in the case of death. Any payout above the minimum liability depends on the performance of the underlying portfolio of securities.

Property and Casualty Insurance Companies P&C insurance companies provide a broad range of insurance protection against loss, damage, or destruction of property, loss or impairment of income-producing ability, claims for damages by third parties because of alleged negligence, loss resulting from injury or death due to occupational accidents. The amount of the liability coverage is specified in the policy. The premium is invested until the insured makes a claim on all or part of the amount of the policy, and that claim is validated. For some lines of business, the P&C company will know immediately that it has incurred a liability from a policy it has underwritten; however, the amount of the claim and when it will have to be paid may not be known at that time. P&Cs also have lines of business where a claim is not evident until several years after the policy period.

The liabilities of P&C companies have a shorter term than life companies and varies with the type of policy. As noted earlier, the exact timing and amount of any liability are unknown. However, the maximum amount of the liability cannot exceed the amount of the coverage specified in the policy.

Unlike many life insurance products, P&C liabilities are not interest-rate sensitive, but some are inflation sensitive.

Pension Funds

A *pension plan* is a fund that is established for the payment of retirement benefits. The entities that establish pension plans — called the *plan sponsors* — are private business entities acting for their employees; state and local entities on behalf of their employees; unions on behalf of their members (called Taft-Hartley funds); and individuals for themselves.

There are two basic and widely used types of pension plans: defined contribution plans and defined benefit plans. In a *defined contribution plan*, the plan sponsor is only responsible for making specified contributions into the plan on behalf of qualifying participants. The amount contributed is typically either a percentage of the employee's salary or a percentage of profits. The plan sponsor does not guarantee any specified amount at retirement. The payments that will be made to qualifying participants upon retirement will depend on the growth of the plan assets; that is, payment is determined by the investment performance of the assets in which the funds are invested. Therefore, in a defined contribution plan the employee bears all the investment risk

In a *defined benefit plan*, the plan sponsor agrees to make specified dollar payments to qualifying employees at retirement (and some payments to beneficiaries in case of death before retirement). The retirement payments are determined by a formula that usually takes into account the length of service of the employee and the recent earnings of the employee. The pension obligations are effectively the debt obligation of the plan sponsor, who assumes the risk that plan assets will not be sufficient to satisfy the contractual payments that must be made to retired employees. Thus, unlike a defined contribution plan, in a defined benefit plan, all the investment risks are borne by the plan sponsor.

With a defined contribution plan, the plan sponsor's liability stops with the payment to the employee. The employee then allocates those funds among the various investment vehicles offered by the plan (for example, company stock, mutual funds, GICs). In contrast, for a defined benefit plan the plan sponsor assumes a liability. The liability is the projected payments that must be made to The plan assets are invested so as to earn the rate of return necessary to satisfy the project liabilities. Hence, this is the investment objective of a defined benefit plan.

Investment Companies

Investment companies sell shares to the public and invest the proceeds in a diversified portfolio of securities. Each share that they sell represents a proportionate interest in a portfolio of securities. The securities purchased could be restricted to specific types of assets such as common stock, government bonds, corporate bonds, or money market instruments. The investment strategies followed by investment companies range from high-risk active portfolio strategies to low-risk passive portfolio strategies.

There are two types of actively managed investment companies — open-end funds and closed-end funds. An *open-end fund*, more popularly referred to as a *mutual fund*, continually stands ready to sell new shares to the public and to redeem its outstanding shares on demand at a price equal to an appropriate share of the value of its portfolio, which is computed daily at the close of the market. A mutual fund's share price is based on its net asset value (NAV), which is found by subtracting from the market value of the portfolio the mutual fund's liabilities and then dividing by the number of mutual fund shares outstanding.

In contrast to mutual funds, *closed-end funds* sell shares like any other corporation and usually do not redeem their shares. Shares of closed-end funds sell on either an organized exchange or in the over-the-counter market. The price of a share in a closed-end fund is determined by supply and demand, so the price can be below or above the NAV.

Every prospectus for a fund must include a statement about the *investment objectives* that the manager of the fund seeks to accomplish and the *policies* that the manager will follow to meet the investment objectives. The investment objectives can only be changed by vote of a majority of the outstanding shares of the fund. The statement about policies indicates in broad terms the type of strategy that the fund manager will pursue and the asset classes in which the fund manager may invest.

There is a wide range of investment objectives. There are common stock funds whose objective may be income or capital gain. There are bond funds that specialize in different types of bonds and with various objectives. For example, a bond fund might have as its objective capital preservation and modest income, while another fund might have an objective of high income through capital appreciation and high coupon income. There are a few bond funds called *target term trusts*. The objective of these funds is to return a specified dollar amount to the shareholders at some specified future date. Unlike other investment companies, these funds are not perpetual. That is, they have a finite life.

With the exception of target terms trusts, the investment objectives of mutual funds are not liability driven.

Depository Institutions

Depository institutions are financial intermediaries that accept deposits. They include commercial banks (or simply banks), savings and loan associations (S&Ls), and credit unions. It is common to refer to the depository institutions other than banks as "thrifts." Depository institutions are highly regulated and supervised because of the important role that they play in the financial system.

A depository institution seeks to earn a positive spread between the assets it invests in (loans and securities) and the cost of its funds (deposits and other sources). This difference between income and cost is referred to as *spread income* or *margin income*. The spread income should allow the institution to meet operating expenses and earn a fair profit on its capital. The objective of a depository institution is to earn a specified spread income.

Endowment Funds

Endowment funds include colleges, private schools, museums, hospitals, and foundations. The investment income generated from the funds invested are used for the operation of the entity. In the case of a college, the investment income is used to meet current operating expenses and capital expenditures (i.e., the construction of new buildings and sports facilities). The board of trustees of the endowment fund specifies the investment objectives. The primary investment objective is typically the safe-guarding of principal. The second goal, and an important one, is to generate a stream of earnings that allows the endowment to meet its projected cash distributions.

ESTABLISHING INVESTMENT POLICY

The second step in the investment management process is establishing policy guidelines to satisfy the investment objectives. Setting policy begins with the *asset allocation decision*. That is, a decision be made as to how the institution's funds should be distributed among the major classes of assets in which it may invest. The major asset classes typically include stocks, bonds, real estate, and foreign securities. Asset allocation models are commercially available for assisting those individuals responsible for making this decision. Chapter 4 describes one such model.

In the development of investment policies, the following factors must be considered: client constraints, regulatory constraints, and accounting and tax issues. Examples of client-imposed constraints would be restrictions that specify the types of securities in which a manager may invest and concentration limits on how much or little may be invested in a particular asset class or in a particular issuer. Where the objective is to meet the performance of a particular market or customized benchmark, there may be a restriction as to the degree to which the manager may deviate from some key characteristics of the benchmark. For example, in later chapters of this book the concept of the beta of a common stock portfolio and a duration of bond portfolio will be discussed. These risk measures provide an estimate of the exposure of a portfolio to changes in key factors that affect the portfolio's value — the market overall in the case of a portfolio's beta and the general level of interest rates in the case of a portfolio's duration. Typically, a client will not set a specific value for the level of risk exposure. Instead, the client restriction may be in the form of a maximum on the level of the risk exposure or a permissible range for the risk measure relative to the benchmark. For example, a client may restrict the portfolio's duration to be +0.5 or −0.5 of the client-specified benchmark. Thus, if the duration of the client-imposed benchmark is 4, the manager has the discretion of constructing a portfolio with a duration between 3.5 and 4.5.

There are many types of regulatory constraints. These involve constraints on the asset classes that are permissible and concentration limits on investments. Moreover, in making the asset allocation decision, consideration must be given to any risk-based capital requirements. For depository institutions and insurance companies, the amount of statutory capital required is related to the quality of the assets in which the institution has invested. There are two types of risk-based capital requirements: credit risk-based capital requirements and interest rate-risk based capital requirement. The former relates statutory capital requirements to the credit-risk associated with the assets in the portfolio. The greater the credit risk, the greater the statutory capital required. Interest rate-risk based capital requirements relate the statutory capital to how sensitive the asset or portfolio is to changes in interest rates. The greater the sensitivity, the higher the statutory capital required.

Tax consideration are important for several reasons. First, certain institutional investors such as pension funds and endowments are exempt from federal income taxation. Consequently, the assets in which they will invest will not be those that are tax advantaged investments. Second, there are tax factors that must be incorporated into the investment policy. For example, while a pension fund might be tax-exempt, there may be certain assets or the use of some investment vehicles in which it invests whose earnings may be taxed.

GAAP and RAP are important considerations in developing investment policies. An excellent example is a defined benefit plan for a corporation. FASB 87 specifies that a corporate pension fund's surplus is equal to the difference between the market value of the assets and the present value of the liabilities. If the surplus in negative, the corporate sponsor must record the negative balance as a liability on its balance sheet. Consequently, in establishing its investment policies, recognition must be given to the volatility of the market value of the fund's portfolio relative to the volatility of the present value of the liabilities. Consider this. In 1994 the return on the S&P 500 and the Lehman Brothers Aggregate Bond Index was 1.29% and −2.92%, respectively. Interest rates rose in 1994. In 1995, the return on the S&P 500 was 37.52% and 18.47% on the Lehman Brothers Aggregate as a result of a decline in interest rates. Most pension plans allocate most of their funds to common stocks and bonds. Which was the best year for pension funds? It would seem that 1995 was the best year. Yet, The Pension Benefit Guaranty Corp. stated that underfunding by pension funds increased in 1995 but decreased in 1994.[1] The reason is that the decline in rates increased the present value of liabilities in 1995 and decreased liabilities in 1994 due to a rise in interest rates. Thus, it is not just the performance of the assets that affects the performance of a pension fund but the relative performance of assets versus liabilities.

SELECTING A PORTFOLIO STRATEGY

Selecting a portfolio strategy that is consistent with the objectives and investment policy guidelines of the client or institution is the third step in the investment management process. Portfolio strategies can be classified as either active or passive. An *active portfolio strategy* uses available information and forecasting techniques to seek a better performance than a portfolio that is simply diversified broadly. Essential to all active strategies are expectations about the factors that could influence the performance of an asset class. For example, with active common stock strategies this may include forecasts of futures earnings, dividends, or price-earnings ratios. With bond portfolios that are actively managed, expectations may involve forecasts of future interest rates and sector spreads. Active portfolio strategies involving foreign securities may require forecasts of local interest rates and exchange rates.

A *passive portfolio strategy* involves minimal expectational input, and instead relies on diversification to match the performance of some market index. In effect, a passive strategy assumes that the marketplace will reflect all available information in the price paid for securities. Between these extremes of active and passive strategies, new strategies have sprung up that have elements of both. For example, the core of a portfolio may be passively managed with the balance actively managed.

In the bond area, several strategies classified as *structured portfolio strategies* have been commonly used. A structured portfolio strategy is one in which a portfolio is designed to achieve the performance of some predetermined liabilities that must be paid out. These strategies are frequently used when trying to match the funds received from an investment portfolio to the future liabilities that must be paid.

---

[1] "Underfunding of Pension Plans Had More than Doubled in 1995," *Investor's Business Daily* (December 13, 1996).

Given the choice among active, structured, or passive management, which should be selected? The answer depends on (1) the client's or money manager's view of how "price-efficient" the market is, (2) the client's risk tolerance, and (3) the nature of the client's liabilities. By *marketplace price efficiency* we mean how difficult it would be to earn a greater return than passive management would, after adjusting for the risk associated with a strategy and the transaction costs associated with implementing a strategy.

SELECTING THE ASSETS

Once a portfolio strategy is selected, the next step is to select the specific assets to be included in the portfolio. This requires an evaluation of individual securities. In an active strategy, this means trying to identify mispriced securities. It is in this phase that the portfolio manager attempts to construct an efficient portfolio. An *efficient portfolio* is one that provides the greatest expected return for a given level of risk, or equivalently, the lowest risk for a given expected return.

In recent years, there has been greater emphasis on structuring efficient portfolios to match a benchmark using factor models. The basic principle is that the value of a security is driven by a number of systematic factors (or, equivalent, risk exposures) plus a component unique to a particular company or industry. In selecting the securities to be included in a portfolio for which a manager is seeking to outperform or match a benchmark, these models allow the optimal matching of the risk characteristics of the portfolio constructed to that of the benchmark. Selecting securities that intentionally cause the characteristics of the portfolio to differ from that of the benchmark is the way a manager makes an active bet. Indexing means matching the characteristics. Enhanced indexing basically means that the assets selected for the portfolio do not cause the characteristics of the portfolio constructed to depart materially from the characteristics of the benchmark.

MEASURING AND EVALUATING PERFORMANCE

The measurement and evaluation of investment performance is the last step in the investment management process. Actually, it is misleading to say that it is the last step since the investment process is an ongoing process. This step involves measuring the performance of the portfolio and then evaluating that performance relative to some benchmark.

Although a portfolio manager may have performed better than a benchmark portfolio, this does not necessarily mean that the portfolio satisfied the client's needs. For example, suppose that a financial institution established as its objective the maximization of portfolio return and allocated 75% of the fund to stocks and the balance to bonds. Suppose further that the manager responsible for the stock portfolio realized a 1-year return that was 150 basis points higher than the established benchmark portfolio. Assuming that the risk of the portfolio was similar to that of the benchmark portfolio, it would appear that the manager outperformed the benchmark portfolio. However, suppose that in spite of this performance, the financial institution cannot meet its liabilities. Then the failure was in establishing the investment objectives and setting policy, not the failure of the manager.

ETHICS IN INVESTMENT MANAGEMENT

The investment industry is a highly competitive business that offers individuals and the organization for which they are employed the potential to realize high income. There are brokers/dealers, the "sell side of the business," who execute orders for customers (individual/retail investors and institutional investors). In providing that service, brokers/dealers generate income from commissions and spreads (the difference between the offer price and bid price). Portfolio managers, referred to as the "buy side of the business," invest funds for individuals and institutions, generating income from investment advisory fees. The fee can be in the form of a percentage of the amount of money under management and/or a fee based on performance. The former is the more common form of compensation. Money managers are the provider of services for individuals and institutions. But they are also the clients of brokers and dealers.

In the process of carrying out their responsibilities, there are many instances in which a conflict between the interests of the provider of services (brokers/dealers and money managers) and a client will arise. A client of a service provider expects that the provider will act ethically and resolve any such conflict in the best interest of the client. A client should not be surprised that a service provider will face a conflict of interest. Such a conflict is not unethical. What the client expects is that the service provider's ethics will prevail when faced with a conflict of interest.

The first line of defense that a client has against a service provider acting in its self interest is the ethics of the individual providing the service and the firm that employs that individual. The second line of defense for a client is industry-wide policies or self-regulatory policies that set forth rules or guidelines as to the proper way to handle a conflict of interest. For brokers and dealers, rules are set forth by the various exchanges and the National Association of Securities Dealers (NASD). For all service providers in the investment management industry there are ethical and professional standards set forth by the Association of Investment Management Research (AIMR) which are published in that organization's *Standards of Practice Handbook*.

Service providers who violate the rules of the exchanges or the NASD can be stripped of the right to transact on the exchange or NASD. Moreover, in the legal cases in which a service provider is found to violate such rules, the trier of fact (court or arbitration panel) can require that the violating party compensate the client for any monetary damages that are determined to have resulted. Moreover, the trier of fact can require the service provider to pay punitive damages.

For members of the AIMR who have earned the highly regarded designation of Chartered Financial Analyst (CFA), the right to use that designation can be taken away. None of the self-policing organizations have the authority to sentence violators to a term in prison.

In many situations, how a service provider acts will be dictated by laws governing such situations. The genesis of much regulation in the United States with regard to the securities industry and banking is the abusive practices of service providers who placed self-interest over the interest of clients. For example, the dominant enforcement agency in the United States is the Securities and Exchange Commission (SEC). The SEC was created in the early 1930s because of well publicized abuses. Service providers who violate security laws can be fined.

Chapter 2

Monetary Policy: How the Fed Sets, Implements, and Measures Policy Choices

David M. Jones, Ph.D.
Chief Economist and Vice Chairman
Aubrey G. Lanston & Co. Inc.

Ellen Rachlin
Co-Head IBJI Agent Department
Aubrey G. Lanston & Co. Inc.

INTRODUCTION

A significant element of competitive and successful equity and fixed income portfolio management is to understand and anticipate the effect of interest rate changes on asset prices. This chapter outlines the key components of the interest rate policy process undertaken by the Federal Reserve, the policy making body that sets short-term interest rates. Although the Federal Reserve publicly announces its policy decisions, it is extremely useful for the portfolio manager to anticipate policy shifts. The portfolio manager who can anticipate policy shifts can more accurately anticipate changes in asset valuations. In order to anticipate policy shifts, the portfolio manager must not only understand the dynamics of the Fed's decision making process but must watch the key economic indicators that the Fed watches.

Monetary policy is the U.S. government's most flexible policy tool. It is controlled by the Federal Reserve which acts independently of government interference. The Federal Reserve since early 1994 immediately announces policy decisions and communicates forthcoming policy intentions through venues such as Congressional testimony and public speeches. Other government policy instruments that influence economic activity include fiscal policy (taxes and spending), trade, foreign exchange, and other regulatory practices. But none of these government policy tools are as flexible as monetary policy.

We wish to thank Lee R. Youngdahl (Vice President, Aubrey G. Lanston & Co. Inc.) and Alan Levenson (Senior Vice President and Director of Research, Aubrey G. Lanston & Co. Inc.) for their comments.

Since the Federal Reserve's inception in 1913, it has had the primary task of ensuring that financial conditions are supportive of sustainable, non-inflationary economic growth. The Fed has several tools it can employ to influence demand growth and price behavior. But, as will be discussed later, all of the Fed policy tools directly influence short-term interest rates and only indirectly influence long-term rates.

The effectiveness of any Fed policy on achieving the goal of price stability is limited to the influence of that policy on both short- and long-term interest rates, real and nominal. Price stability is the primary prerequisite for steady long-term economic growth. Low inflation rates enable businesses to increase their investment in infrastructure including new machinery and high-tech equipment. Therefore, a low inflationary environment brighten the prospects for future increases in productivity and an improved standard of living.

In the short term, the Fed must juggle the simultaneous objectives of stable prices and maximum employment (sustainable growth). Although the President appoints the Fed Chairman, by legislative decree, the Federal Reserve is an independent agency and is accountable to the public only through the legislative branch of the U.S. government. If the Fed were not an independent agency, the Fed could be subject to political influences promoting economic growth over price stability.

Fed-induced price stability and the absence of consumer and business inflationary expectations are essential to containing speculation and allowing the capital markets to efficiently allocate funds in support of sustainable growth. Generally speaking, capital markets efficiently allocate funds to the sectors of the economy promising the highest risk-adjusted returns. This process is absolutely crucial to the wealth-creating success of modern capitalism. But, as we will discuss later, at times excesses of capital allocation can occur. Capital markets may allocate capital to countries where the risks of debt default or likely debt downgrades appears quite high, such as Mexico in 1995 and southeast Asia in 1997, as these participants have confidence central bankers will successfully stave off defaults. This exaggerated if not misplaced faith that somebody will bail them out of bad investment or lending decisions, called the moral hazard of central banking, is one of the few downside effects to the central bankers' role of lender of last resort.

KEY ECONOMIC INFLUENCES ON FED POLICY

Monetary policy is more art than science. In essence, Fed policy is a process of trial and error, observation and adjustment. The Fed's policies are often counter-cyclical to the business cycle. At best, Fed policymakers can hope to smooth the peaks and troughs of business cycles. In pursuit of this counter-cyclical policy approach, when real economic growth is excessive and potentially inflationary, Fed officials will lean in the direction of more restraint in their policy stance.

They will tend to increase interest rates, eventually slowing real economic activity to a more sustainable and potentially less inflationary pace. Conversely, when real economic growth falters and recession threatens, Fed officials will tilt their policy stance in the direction of greater ease, lowering interest rates. Lower interest rates serve to boost economic activity and lessen the threat of recession. A word of caution: Fed officials must feel their way along after implementing policy shifts because the effects from policy shifts are long, variable, and often unpredictable. The Fed enacts policy shifts based on economic forecasts. Economic forecasting is almost as uncertain as the effect of the policy shifts themselves.

One can develop an idea of the Fed's next policy objective by paying careful attention to various indicators of current economic activity. The key economic releases which serve as the Fed's intermediate policy indicators and that should be followed carefully include: non-farm payrolls, NAPM supplier deliveries, industrial production, housing starts, motor vehicle sales, durable good orders, and commodity prices. Exhibit 1 gives the release cycles of these figures. Consistent and meaningful changes in these economic indicators will signal changes in the business cycle and in Fed policy.

Non-farm payrolls are released monthly and detail the previous month's changes in the complexion of the workforce including numbers employed, hourly pay changes and hours worked. *Supplier deliveries* are part of the National Association of Purchasing Management's monthly survey. This report reflects survey results of the purchasing managers of hundreds of industrial corporations. The survey reports on the lead time between orders placed with suppliers and delivery of those orders. The greater the lead time, the stronger the economy and the lesser the lead time, the weaker the economy.

Industrial production, released monthly, measures the collective output of factories, utilities, and mines. If final demand is high and inventory stockpiles are rapidly shrinking, future industrial production, employment, and income will be boosted as inventories are restocked, thereby stimulating economic activity. If, in contrast, final demand growth is slowing and inventory growth is excessive, future industrial production, employment, and income will weaken as inventories are trimmed, thereby depressing economic activity.

Exhibit 1: Significant Economic Releases

Payroll Employment	Monthly — 1st Friday
Housing Starts	Monthly — 3rd-4th week
Industrial Production	Monthly — 3rd week
NAPM (Supplier Deliveries)	Monthly — 1st business day
Motor Vehicle Sales	Monthly — 1st-3rd business day
Durable Goods Orders	Monthly — 4th week
Commodity Prices	Continuously Released

Housing starts, published monthly, are the number of new single- and multi-family housing units begun for construction in the previous month. Housing starts, which are financed, are highly sensitive to interest rate changes. If housing starts slow dramatically, this signals that interest rates are high enough in the current economic environment to choke off demand. Conversely, if housing starts are increasing, this signals that interest rates are low enough in the current economic environment to promote demand.

Motor vehicle sales, released monthly, are a key reflection of consumer confidence and income. Motor vehicle sales are strongly positively correlated to both income levels and consumer confidence.

Durable goods orders, released monthly, are new orders placed by consumers with manufacturers of "large ticket" consumer goods, expected to last three or more years. These items may include appliances or business machinery.

Commodity prices, for which the market receives continual input, are important indicators of future price rises in both producer and subsequently consumer prices. The most influential prices are those of raw goods and materials such as oil, lumber, metals, and agricultural commodities. Consistent, sympathetic, and significant price increases in these raw goods and materials will signal higher future prices in finished consumer goods.

It is extremely difficult to recognize meaningful and consistent changes in these economic variables: non-farm payrolls, industrial production, housing starts, motor vehicle sales, durable good orders, and commodity prices. Even if changes in these variables appear consistent and meaningful, it is difficult to predict whether the changes in the economic variables are temporary or if left unchecked will be longer lasting.

If the Fed believes the changes in key economic variables are consistent and potentially longer lasting, they will take measures to influence the availability of credit in the economy. The Fed's most frequently employed policy tools include open market operations and changes to the discount rate. Less frequently, the Fed will employ changes in bank reserve requirements or verbal persuasion aimed at influencing bank behavior with respect to the supply of credit to consumer and business borrowers, and even more rarely, the Fed may change margin requirements on stocks.

Through open market operations, the purchase or sale of U.S. government securities, the Fed either adds liquidity or funds into the market or subtracts liquidity or funds from the system. By changing the discount rate, the Fed changes the rate it charges depository institutions for the privilege of borrowing funds at the discount window. The combination of these tools can either make the cost of funds, i.e. interest rates, cheaper or dearer. Open market operations work on the principles of supply and demand while changes in the discount rate directly alter the interest charged on funds. Discount rate changes are proposed by the Board of Directors of one or more district Reserve Banks for the approval by the Board of Governors of the Federal Reserve. Open market operations are conducted by the Federal Open Market Committee (FOMC) in a manner consistent with decisions made at the periodic FOMC meetings. The FOMC consists of the seven members of the Board of Governors plus five voting Bank Presidents.

Exhibit 2: Fed Policy Objectives, Intermediate Indicators and Alternative Open Market Operating Procedures

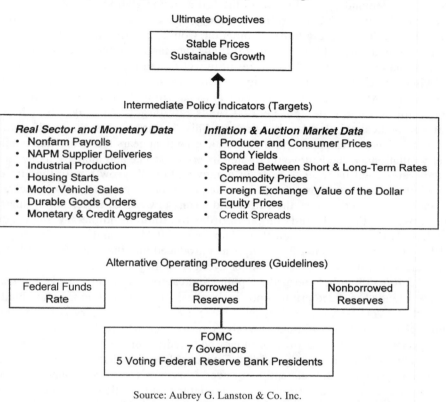

Ultimate Objectives

Stable Prices
Sustainable Growth

Intermediate Policy Indicators (Targets)

Real Sector and Monetary Data
- Nonfarm Payrolls
- NAPM Supplier Deliveries
- Industrial Production
- Housing Starts
- Motor Vehicle Sales
- Durable Goods Orders
- Monetary & Credit Aggregates

Inflation & Auction Market Data
- Producer and Consumer Prices
- Bond Yields
- Spread Between Short & Long-Term Rates
- Commodity Prices
- Foreign Exchange Value of the Dollar
- Equity Prices
- Credit Spreads

Alternative Operating Procedures (Guidelines)

Federal Funds Rate

Borrowed Reserves

Nonborrowed Reserves

FOMC
7 Governors
5 Voting Federal Reserve Bank Presidents

Source: Aubrey G. Lanston & Co. Inc.

The other two policy tools, changes in the reserve requirements and verbal persuasion, are tools infrequently used to reinforce stated Fed policy aims and they are used to complement policy changes already enacted through open market operations. Discount rate changes are more commonly used to put into effect Fed policy aims implemented through open market operations. These tools are employed by the Federal Reserve Board of Governors to underscore a policy of easing or tightening. Exhibit 2 attempts to simplify the decision making and policy implementation process of the Federal Reserve's Open Market Committee.

Historically, the Federal Reserve under different chairmen has introduced two contrasting techniques for implementing open market operations (see Exhibit 2). Initially, the Fed has used as its operating procedures (guidelines) a rigid Federal fund rate target, generally in effect from the late 1920s through the late 1970s. More recently, Fed officials have introduced a more flexible Federal funds rate target. When the Fed uses a rigid Federal funds rate target, Fed open market operations tend to have pro-cyclical results. That is, during economic expansions, the Fed's use of a rigid Federal funds rate target, in the face of increasing money and credit demands, would result in the full accommodation of these demands, thereby triggering an acceleration in money and credit growth, excessive real growth, and the mounting threat of inflation. Conversely, during economic downturns, the Fed's use of a rigid Federal funds rate target, in the face of declining money and credit demands, would result in weakening money and credit growth, slowing real growth, and lessening inflation pressures. Fed Chairman William McChesney Martin Jr., who was Fed Chairman from 1951 to 1970, started the transition to a more flexible Federal funds rate target. He sought to achieve counter-cyclical effects when he introduced his "leaning against the wind" policy approach. Under this approach, if economic growth appears too strong and potentially inflationary, the Fed would tighten its policy stance and increase its Federal funds rate target in order to restrain money and credit growth with the aim of slowing real economic growth and lessening inflationary pressures. Conversely, if economic growth weakens, the Fed would "lean" towards an easier policy stance and lower its Federal funds target in order to stimulate monetary and credit growth. Under Fed Chairmen Paul Volcker (1979-1987) and Alan Greenspan (1987-present) still greater flexibility was introduced into the Fed's Federal funds rate target in order to enhance "counter-cyclical" policy actions.

Regarding the intermediate policy indicators in Exhibit 2, Fed Chairman Volcker tended to place primary policy emphasis on curtailing money and credit growth. In Volcker's own words, "[a] basic premise of monetary policy is that inflation cannot persist without excessive monetary growth, and it is our view that appropriately restrained growth of money and credit over the longer run is critical to achieving the ultimate objectives of reasonably stable prices and sustainable economic growth."[1] Subsequently, however, Chairman Greenspan found it necessary to lessen the Fed's emphasis on monetary and credit growth in favor of greater policy emphasis on a wider range of intermediate indicators of the real sector, inflation, and auction (financial) markets. Greenspan feared that owing to globalization, securitization, and, most importantly, financial product innovation such as mutual funds, money and credit growth was no longer a reliable predictor of economic activity and inflation.

IMPLEMENTING MONETARY POLICY: THE TRANSMISSION PROCESS

The monetary policy transmission process has always been a long and variable one. In the past the banking system, the conduit for monetary policy, was the dominant source of credit for consumers and businesses. Typically, it has taken

---

[1] Statement before U.S. Congress, Joint Economic Committee (June 15, 1982).

from six to twelve months for a shift in monetary policy to work its way through the banking system and capital markets to impact real economic activity. It takes even longer for a given policy shift to influence price behavior. Complicating this process in today's world, a declining share of credit is supplied through the banking system and a rising share of credit is supplied through globally integrated capital markets (see Exhibit 3). As a result, the Federal Reserve today more than in the past, must be highly attuned to financial market participants' perceptions of Fed intentions and potential market impact of the Fed's perceived intentions. The banking system remains the point of contact for the Fed when it initiates shifts in policy stance. However, Fed intentions and related market expectations of their intentions remain a critical concern in the transmission of Fed policy shifts. This process results in capital market asset price adjustments that ultimately influence changes in real economic growth and inflation.

Fed authorities began in February 1994 to immediately announce policy decisions. (See Exhibit 4 for policy statements following FOMC meetings.) Today's Fed monetary policy transmission process is a transparent one. Monetary policy transparency easily conveys Fed policy intentions. Typically, Fed officials, through speeches, interviews, and Congressional testimony, will seek to prepare financial market participants for any policy shift that may be in store in upcoming policy meetings. Clear information on current Fed policy helps the monetary policy transmission process operate more effectively.

Exhibit 3: Depository Institutions' Share of Total Nonfinacial Debt (Percent)

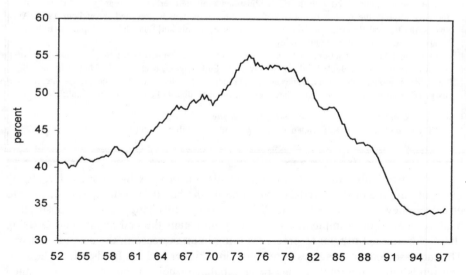

Source: Standard & Poor's DRI

Exhibit 4: Sampling of the Federal Reserve's Official Statements of FOMC Actions, First Half of 1994

Friday, February 4, 1994 at 11:05 a.m. — FOMC meeting
"Chairman Alan Greenspan announced today that the Federal Open Market Committee decided to increase *slightly* the degree of pressure on reserve positions. The action is expected to be associated with a *small* increase in short-term money market interest rates.

The decision was taken to move toward a less accommodative stance in monetary policy in order to sustain and enhance the economic expansion.

Chairman Greenspan decided to announce this action immediately so as to avoid any misunderstanding of the committee's purposes, given the fact that this is the first firming of reserve market conditions by the committee since early 1989."

Tuesday, March 22, 1994 at 2:20 p.m. — FOMC meeting
"Chairman Alan Greenspan announced today that the Federal Open Market Committee decided to increase *slightly* the degree of pressure on reserve positions. This action is expected to be associated with a *small* increase in short-term money market interest rates."

Monday, April 18, 1994 at 10:06 a.m. — FOMC telephone conference call
"Chairman Alan Greenspan announced today that the Federal Reserve will increase *slightly* the degree of pressure on reserve positions. This action is expected to be associated with a *small* increase in short-term money market interest rates."

Tuesday, May 17, 1994 at 2:26 p.m. — FOMC meeting
"The Federal Reserve today announced two actions designed to maintain favorable trends in inflation and thereby sustain the economic expansion.

The Board approved an increase in the discount rate from 3% to 3½%, effective immediately, and the Federal Open Market Committee agreed that this increase should be allowed to show through completely into interest rates in reserve markets.

These actions, combined with the three adjustments initiated earlier this year by the FOMC, substantially remove the degree of monetary accommodation which prevailed throughout 1993. As always, the Federal Reserve will continue to monitor economic and financial developments to judge the appropriate stance of monetary policy.

In taking the discount action, the Board approved requests submitted by the Boards of Directors of eleven Federal Reserve Banks -- Boston, New York, Philadelphia, Richmond, Atlanta, Chicago, St. Louis, Minneapolis, Kansas City, Dallas and San Francisco. The discount rate is the interest rate that is charged depository institutions when they borrow from their district Federal Reserve Bank."

Wednesday, July 6, 1994 at 2:18 p.m. — FOMC meeting
"The meeting of the FOMC ended at 12:35 pm and there will be no further announcement."

Historically, the Fed policy transmission process has worked largely by manipulating the cost of credit as supplied by the banking system. Specifically, to effect a policy shift, the Fed has traditionally begun by changing the composition of bank reserves. For example, more Fed restraint means the Fed manipulates a rising share of borrowed to total reserves, resulting in an increase in the cost of reserves. The increased cost of reserves is reflected in a higher Federal funds rate. (The Federal funds rate is the rate on bank reserve balances held at the Fed that are loaned and borrowed among banks, usually overnight.) Conversely, less Fed restraint (more ease) means the Fed manipulates a declining share of borrowed reserves to total reserves. This action results in a declining cost of reserves that is reflected in a lower Federal funds rate. Borrowed reserves are those reserves that banks borrow temporarily at the Fed's discount window for purposes of adjusting their reserve positions. Banks traditionally try to avoid borrowing at the Fed discount window. There is a perception that such borrowings are a sign of financial weakness. Banks that are forced to borrow temporarily at the discount window will, generally, first turn to other sources of loanable funds such as Federal funds or repo borrowings. Exhibit 2 describes the importance of bank reserves to Fed policy implementation.

Banks, when faced with greater Fed restraint and a rising cost of loanable funds, find their net interest margins narrowing or their profits declining. Under these circumstances, banks will have less of an incentive to increase their investments and loans. This results in a decline in the availability of funds and an increase in the cost of bank credit to consumers and businesses. Therefore, consumers and businesses will cut back on their borrowing and spending. This in turn results in a declining rate of increase in real economic growth and eventually a moderation in inflation pressures. Conversely, a Fed move towards an easier policy posture reduces banks' cost of funds. Banks find their net interest margins widening or profits increasing because the fed funds rate is far more elastic than long-term interest rates. Banks incentive to increase the availability and reduce the cost of credit increases. This stimulates consumer and business borrowing and spending, thereby spurring real economic growth and eventually triggering a rise in inflationary pressures. The only exception to our converse case is in the environment of an inverted yield curve such as the U.S. government bond curve in the early 1980s. Despite the Fed's efforts to ease short term rates in the initial stages, the reduction in the cost of funds to banks may not have a significant impact on potential profit margins if the yield curve is inverted enough. Long term rates may be too low on a relative basis to short term rates to make bank or other financial institutions' extensions of long term credit profitable.

Looking at this monetary transmission process from the investment side, Fed policy shifts set off a chain reaction. For example, in the case of a Fed shift towards a more restrictive policy posture, investors who hold short-term credit market instruments such as Treasury bills or money market mutual funds will find interest rates on their short-term investments moving up to higher and more attractive levels relative to yields on longer-term bonds. Accordingly, investors will shift their investments down the yield curve. They will sell longer-term bonds and place the proceeds in shorter-term money market investments. This process will result in rising longer-term interest rates. Rising longer-term interest rates will, in turn, make the returns on bonds more attractive relative to the return on stocks. As a result, investors will sell stocks, place the proceeds in bonds and stock prices will decline. As capital market expectations of future Fed restrictive intentions are formed, these portfolio asset adjustments between money market investments, bonds, and stocks will be hastened and intensified.

Exhibit 5: Fed Funds and Short-Term Rates

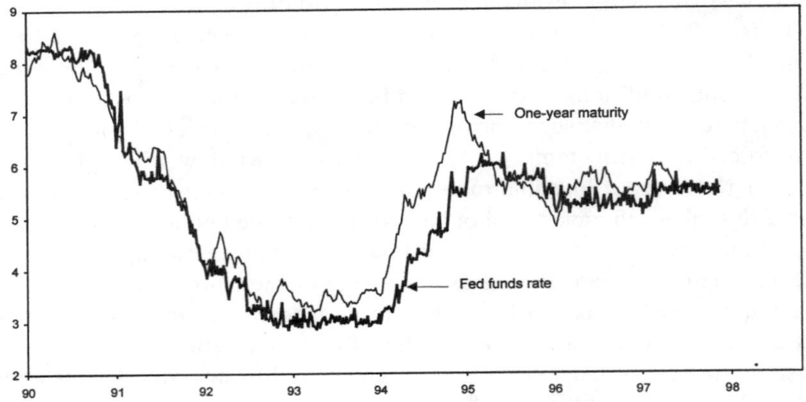

Source: Standard & Poor's DRI

THE IMPACT OF MONETARY POLICY:
ITS DECLINING DIRECT INFLUENCE

Since the mid-1970s, there has been a sharp decline in the proportion of bank credit to total credit available. The bank share of total credit has fallen to 33% in the mid-1990s from 55% in the mid-1970s (see Exhibit 3). The main factors contributing to the declining bank share of total credit has been globalization of credit resources, securitization, and financial product innovation. The result has been a rising share of credit extended directly through the capital markets to consumers and businesses. Among the major new nonbank institutional suppliers of credit through the capital markets are mutual funds, hedge funds, pension funds, finance companies, and insurance companies. Currently, with the advent of the information revolution, these nonbank lenders are in virtually as good a position as bank lenders to assess market and credit risks.

Today, the Fed's policy transmission process works to an increasingly greater extent through capital market asset price adjustments (i.e., bonds, stocks, commodities) than through the availability of funds. As in the past, the Fed initiates a policy shift by changing the composition of bank reserves. As we have previously explained, there is a resulting change in the cost of funds as reflected in a change in the Federal funds rate. The Federal funds rate prompts positively correlated changes in short-term market rates as Exhibit 5 demonstrates. These changing costs of short-term credit, including bank loans made at the prime rate and funds raised in the commercial paper market. The impact on capital market price adjustments work in the following manner: as short-term borrowing costs rise, borrowers will find longer-term borrowing rates relatively more attractive. Eventually, corporate bond and fixed-rate mortgage offerings increase, driving up longer-term interest rates. This impact of Fed policy shifts on short-term and long-term market interest rates is magnified as Fed intentions are recognized by capital market participants. The participants form expectations of further Fed tightening (easing) moves. The effect of capital market participants is reflected in the changing shapes of the yield curve as the Fed funds rate changes as illustrated in Exhibit 6.

Rising longer-term interest rates and declining stock prices will increase the cost of capital. Increasing the cost of capital decreases business investment. Also, higher longer-term rates depress housing activity. In addition, declining financial asset prices depress consumer wealth and consumer spending, resulting in a decline in the pace of real economic activity. This process serves to moderate inflationary pressures. Commodity prices are likely to be falling in such an environment. Moreover, increasing interest rates will generally cause the value of the U.S. dollar to appreciate in the foreign exchange markets relative to other currencies. A stronger U.S. dollar will cause a decline in exports and a rise in imports, all other factors being equal. This rising trade deficit also serves to dampen economic activity.

GLOBAL CREDIBILITY:
THE CENTRAL BANKER'S RESPONSIBILITY

Important influences on the global financial environment include: market deregulation or regulation, financial innovation, integrated global financial markets, and advanced information processing and communications technology. There is a massive pool of mobile capital that relentlessly seeks out countries where business activity generates the highest possible return for a given amount of risk. In order to compete effectively for capital from global investors, countries must pursue disciplined macroeconomic policies and pro-business microeconomic policies including deregulation and privatization. Countries competing for capital must aim for balanced and sustained non-inflationary growth.

Exhibit 6: Yield Curve Shapes for Given Fed Funds Rates

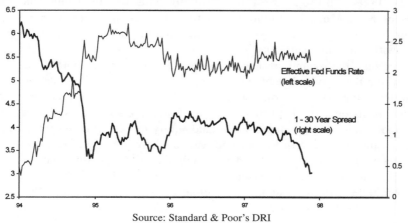

Source: Standard & Poor's DRI

A more sobering lesson for modern-day central bankers is their reduced effectiveness in controlling massive global capital flows and related financial asset price bubbles. At times this has been manifested in capital market participants' overly optimistic view of central bankers' abilities and desire to stave off debt defaults. This may be particularly true in the case of staving off sovereign and quasi-sovereign debt where there is a history of central bankers providing meaningful amounts of liquidity. The legacy was underscored in the Mexican financial crisis in 1995. The U.S. government provided amounts up to $50 billion USD available to the Mexican government, staving off a debt default. The benefits of staving off the Mexican default were not without their drawbacks. This lesson can be found in the Asian financial crisis that began in mid-1997. The Asian financial turmoil began in the rapidly growing economy of Thailand and spread initially to the other Southeastern Asian countries of Malaysia, Indonesia, and the Philippines. These developing countries had benefited from an abundance of foreign liquidity. But the heavy capital inflows eventually resulted in excessive growth, mounting trade deficits, and speculative financial bubbles typically manifested in frenzied local bank-financed speculation in equities and real estate. The currency crisis in these Southeast Asian countries was triggered as escalating trade deficits scared away global money managers, triggering a rapid depreciation in their currencies, with interest rates rising sharply in response. As the bubble burst, real estate and equity prices plummeted. This unforeseen instability posed a major threat to the affected countries' banking systems, as bad debts mounted.

It was not until equity market selling pressures spread to Hong Kong that the rest of the world began to take serious notice. With the return of Hong Kong to Mainland China, the Chinese government kept the Hong Kong dollar pegged to the U.S. dollar as a matter of political principle. Nevertheless, speculators continued to attack the Hong Kong dollar on the assumption that it had to fall in line with other Southeastern Asian currencies in order for Hong Kong to remain competitive. In its effort to fight off the speculative attack on the Hong Kong dollar, the Hong Kong Monetary Authority was forced to sharply increase interest rates, thereby weakening the Hong Kong real estate market and threatening Hong Kong banks with mounting bad debts.

Next, the Asian currency crisis spread to the larger South Korean economy, where the heavily indebted financial system was vulnerable, and ultimately to the huge Japanese economy which was still attempting to recover from the bursting of its own 1980s financial bubble. Then, like a rapidly spreading contagion, the Asian currency depreciation and equity market plunge spread to Latin America and even Eastern Europe and Russia where previously high-performing debt and equity markets registered extremely disorderly declines, and ultimately to declines in the Western European and U.S. stock markets. Exhibit 7 illustrates the magnitude of these Asian market declines.

Exhibit 7: Changing Values in Asian Equities, Bonds, and Currencies

Country	Currency Levels		Equity Index — 6 Month Return Local Currency Terms	Fixed Income Yield Benchmark	
	7/07/97	1/07/98	7/07/97-1/07/98	7/07/97	1/07/98
Malaysia	2.53	4.06	−50.87	T10+63	T10+260
Indonesia	2432	8000	−46.58	T10+118	T10+650
South Korea	883	1650	−47.7	T10+86	T10+525
Philippines	26.41	45.00	−36.53	T30+221	T30+440
Thailand	28.63	52.88	−41.5	T10+82	T10+500
Hong Kong	7.74	7.74	−35.8	T10+73	T10+160
Japan	112.78	131.73	−23.74	T10−371	T10−364

The importance of the Asian financial crisis is that it illustrates the lessening influence that central bankers have on today's globally integrated capital market flows, apart from serving as last-resort lenders of liquidity. The role of last-resort lender, however, should not be minimized. The central bank and supra-led package of loans to Mexico in 1995 staved off a dramatic currency crisis that could have led to a debt default. With the stunning advances in information processing and communications technology so far in the 1990s, global money managers can move capital around the world at virtually the speed of light. This capital, as already noted, seeks out opportunities offering the highest risk-adjusted returns, but it flees from turmoil. The point is that the increasingly efficient global capital markets are linked more tightly than ever before. Apart from maintaining anti-inflation credibility and serving as lenders of last resort, central bankers, including the U.S. Fed Chairman, may in the future have only a marginal influence on these massive global capital market flows and related financial asset price bubbles.

Moreover, on the heels of the Asian currency turmoil, it is the stark power of the global capital markets themselves rather than domestic politicians or central bankers that are forcing major financial system changes in the affected countries, including the desirable privatization of public corporations and large scale banking reform. The only means by which the governments in Japan and elsewhere (or the IMF) can stabilize market forces is to respond by offering larger or more effective financial reform packages than global capital market participants expect. For example, global money managers are demanding that bank reform include provisions for allowing insolvent banks to fail and for the weaker banks to be acquired by healthy domestic or foreign financial institutions. In addition, taxpayer funds, along with deposit insurance, must be used to pay off depositors in failed banks. Also, most importantly, bank reform must make provision for transparency, including full disclosure of bad loans and off-balance sheet items by banks and securities firms.

Huge, global pools of mobile capital may serve to actually discipline national and global macroeconomics policies. If, for example, any developed or emerging country tries to boost growth through overly stimulative macroeconomic policies that are potentially inflationary for political reasons, its trade deficit will worsen and its currency will depreciate. Global institutional investors and money managers will become fearful of the increased inflationary threat and sell bonds, thus pushing long-term interest rates higher and helping to choke off growth in that developing or emerging country.

Accordingly, the best that any country can do for its citizens is to create a favorable economic climate for participation in the world economy. There are many important economic building blocks for positive participation in the world economy. They include deregulation, privatization, free markets, minimal government interference, longer-term productivity-enhancing measures (investment in education, job training, research as well as the implementation of technological innovations, and rewards for savings and investment), and, above all, central bank anti-inflation credibility and consistency. Longer-term price stability creates steady, predictable levels of economic growth. These are the rewards of pursuing a monetary policy that seeks price stability and, thereby, sets the stage for enhanced productivity.

In sum, while central bankers still play a key stabilization role in the effort to ensure that financial conditions are supportive of sustainable economic growth, the ability of central banks to influence massive global flows of mobile capital and related asset price bubbles is diminishing. This raises the spectre of additional currency crises from time to time, not unlike those in Mexico in 1995 and in Southeast Asia in 1997. To be sure, central bankers can help limit the private sector's speculative tendencies by maintaining a high level of anti-inflation credibility. Moreover, central banks can help contain the damage where asset price bubbles break by serving as last-resort lenders of liquidity. But in the final analysis, these central bank influences are marginal compared with today's sheer power of global capital market forces.

Chapter 3

The Changing Framework and Methods of Investment Management

Sergio Focardi, Dr. Ing.
Partner
The Intertek Group

INTRODUCTION

If the power of the theories of physics were similar to that of the theories of economics, all the complex mathematics employed today would allow us — at best — to build modest bridges. In fact, drawing a parallel from physics, general equilibrium theories can be likened to classical physics without a description of the shape of force fields. The entire mathematical apparatus of classical physics, with its all-encompassing Hamiltonians and variational principles, would not have allowed us to send a man to the moon.

Although the past decade witnessed a growing use of sophisticated modeling tools and optimization algorithms in investment management, from a practical standpoint, finance theory is still based on statistical estimates plus some relatively crude local models. This chapter provides a critical appraisal of issues related to today's financial modeling. The shortcomings of classical general equilibrium theories will be examined and avenues that might lead to a more empirically faithful modeling of economic and financial phenomena explored.

MARKET EFFICIENCY

An important question for investment management is if and how information can be used to earn a return by trading, thus exploiting market movements. It was long held that trading in itself could not produce gains as efficient markets wipe out trading profits. This view was later challenged by techniques such as technical analysis and forecasting models. It is now clear that the notion of market efficiency is related to our understanding of risk and uncertainty in a dynamic environment.

Although the fundamental ideas of investment management under uncertainty were laid down in the pioneering work of Markowitz,[1] the explicit consideration and quantification of uncertainty, i.e., risk, is recent. Only in the 1980s did financial firms and fund managers begin to use modeling tools to quantify risk-return trade-offs. It is not surprising, therefore, that the question of how to characterize the risk-return opportunities in the market is still far from being settled.

The question of risk-return opportunities can be considered from several points of view. First, there is the need to understand how the global return from investing in securities is formed. Second, there is the need to understand how this global return is allocated among the various securities. Third, there is the need to ascertain if trading capability might be an additional source of profit. We will begin by exploring if and how a positive return can be obtained by actively trading.

In the 1960s, Samuelson and Fama developed the Efficient Market Hypothesis (EMH) which states that securities are always fairly priced as profit-seeking investors respond without delay to new fundamental information, thereby readjusting prices. This immediate and appropriate response is the key concept of market efficiency.

At about the same time, Muth noted the essential self-reflectivity of the economy,[2] observing that the same level of knowledge must be attributed to agents as to the economist who observes them. This observation imposes coherence between the general findings of economic theory and the processes on which agents actually base their decisions. The notion of rational expectations — which was subsequently to play a fundamental role in economics — was born.

To render these notions precise, economic theory developed an abstract model of agent decision making. The key assumption is: agents act in isolation but the market remains perfectly coordinated. This principle originated the formulation of general equilibrium theories of the market.

General equilibrium theories assume that agents are characterized by utility functions and that the decision-making process of each agent can be represented by the maximization of his/her individual utility function. By equilibrium is meant that actual price processes maximize the utility functions of each agent independently. The global effect of agent behavior can thus be summarized as the effect of a single *representative agent*.

General equilibrium theories are dynamic and forward-looking insofar as utility maximization is carried out on the entire dividend-price process. They explain market price processes through variational principles similar to those used in the physical sciences. In fact, utility maximization is the mathematical condition that determines price processes.

Though general equilibrium assumes the existence of utility maximization functions, it does not prescribe their computation. In addition, as was shown

---

[1] H. Markowitz, "Portfolio Selection," *Journal of Finance* (1952), pp. 77-91.

[2] J.F. Muth, "Rational Expectations and the Theory of Price Movements," *Econometrica* (1961), pp. 315-335.

by Harrison and Kreps,[3] every arbitrage-free dividend-price process can be rationalized as a general equilibrium. General equilibrium per se is a mathematical condition which is fundamentally equivalent to absence of arbitrage.

Assuming general equilibrium, the outstanding questions are: (1) Can the informational efficiency of markets be ascertained? (2) Is it possible to characterize market efficiency and to quantify return opportunities in a simple empirically verifiable way? and (3) Can the randomness and unpredictability of prices be inferred from general equilibrium?

Within the general equilibrium framework, the question of the informational efficiency of markets is conventional. In fact, general equilibrium *is* the formal statement of efficiency conditions. If utility functions could be ascertained empirically, the question of market efficiency would be the question of the validity of general equilibrium models. As the theory is formulated today, however, there is no independent characterization of utility.

Absence of arbitrage is therefore the only general market efficiency condition; markets are efficient if they do not allow unbounded gains. One might still characterize informational efficiency as the deviation of actual price processes from a reference general equilibrium model, but this is a conventional notion of efficiency as the reference general equilibrium model is specified arbitrarily.

The specification of reference models is presently limited in practice as well as in theoretical scope. It might be used to detect mispricings, i.e., to detect if the price of a given security is at odds with the price of other securities. But it is of no use in detecting market trends and global market movements; this would require more analysis.

Market efficiency is not a simple yes/no concept in the sense that it cannot be argued. Efficiency is a quantitative concept, measured by the ability to realize additional gains in the market. An agent makes an independent assessment of market efficiency which is given by the incremental profit that could be realized by buying additional information and/or by better forecasting.

It was long believed that market efficiency implies absence of forecastability in price processes as utility optimization would wipe out the possibility of gains from trading. This, however, cannot generally be established. As any boundedly forecastable arbitrage-free dividend-price process can be rationalized as a general equilibrium, the randomness of price processes is not a consequence of general equilibrium, i.e., of market efficiency.

Nor can the weaker condition that market prices follow martingales, i.e., that expected prices equal actual prices, be generally established. It has, however, been shown that any arbitrage-free dividend-price process can be transformed — by a change in the probability measure — into a martingale price process where prices are always the expected value of future dividends. General equilibrium

---

[3] J.M. Harrison and D. Kreps, "Martingales and Arbitrage in Multiperiod Securities Markets," *Journal of Economic Theory* (1979), pp. 381-408.

implies that, by a transformation of probabilistic coordinates, the price process becomes a martingale.

The above has consequences for investment management. Trading is not a zero-sum game. By trading, agents set prices, thereby "creating" and "destroying" market value. Phenomena of agent aggregation are at work. The classical view that securities have a well defined fundamental value and that any additional profit opportunities due to price predictability are wiped out by market efficiency is too simplistic.

Financial markets — and the economy at large — exhibit complex micro-structure. Though this structure may still be interpreted in terms of utility maximization, the complexity of the risk-return characteristics present in the market must be admitted. The representative agent is an abstract mathematical concept, not an extrapolation of common-sense economic rationality.

STYLIZED FACTS OF STOCK-PRICE PROCESSES

Finance theory in its generality does not say much about price and return processes. Still, the characterization of these processes is essential to investment management. To gain an understanding of price and return processes, we must turn to statistical analysis.

A number of "stylized" or statistical facts about economic time series have been observed with a high degree of persistence and might therefore be considered well established. Some of these stylized facts reveal non-linear characteristics of economic time series that are of importance to investment management.

It was initially hypothesized that stock prices follow a random walk or a Brownian motion in continuous time. First advanced by Bachelier in 1902, this hypothesis has been reproposed many times since. Though random-walk behavior is not a necessary consequence of market efficiency, stock prices might still behave as random walks. It is therefore reasonable to look at stock-price processes to verify their behavior.

Testing the randomness hypothesis is more difficult than might at first appear. Economic time series such as security prices have only one realization. The probabilistic characterization of price processes must therefore be expressed — and empirically tested — through time statistics. But any empirically known series covers only a limited amount of time; no test can therefore be considered conclusive.

Early tests of randomness included tests on sequences, reversals, and runs. These tests were subsequently refined by modern analyses of Markov chains.[4] More recent tests of randomness include the use of filter rules, i.e., trad-

---

[4] D. Aldous, *Probability Approximation via the Poisson Clumping Heuristics* (New York, NY: Springer-Verlag, 1989); and P. Diaconis, *Group Representations in Probability and Statistics* (Hayward, CA: Institute of Mathematical Statistics, 1988).

ing strategies. Tests of this type were performed by several researchers.[5] Lo and MacKinley have provided tests for autocorrelation.[6]

The above and other tests indicate that stock prices do not behave as a random walk, not even in weak forms. Rather it appears that price processes exhibit some level of predictability. Whether this predictability can be exploited for profit, however, requires more careful investigation: the risk-return of a specific forecasting algorithm and trading strategy would have to be tested against objectives.

A second early hypothesis was to represent price processes as the expected value of dividend processes discounted at some fixed rate. Given any dividend process discounted by a fixed rate, the law of iterated expectations (a purely mathematical theorem independent of any price behavior) shows that expected values, though not necessarily random walks, are, nevertheless, martingales. In fact, a martingale is a process whose instantaneous value is always equal to its expected value. The law of iterated expectations states that if we take the expected value of any process, the resulting process is a martingale.

Performing tests of the martingale hypothesis requires assuming some specific model for expected value relationships. Campbell, Lo, and MacKinley provide a synthetic mathematical resume of the many tests performed.[7] Results show that there is no firm evidence that prices behave as martingales. But these tests are of a partial and probabilistic nature; no firm conclusion can be reached by exploring a single segment of the time-series realization.

Another general test of stock behavior investigated recently is the unit root test. This test, which detects linear trends in the data generating process (DGP), has been performed under different conditions and for different sets of stocks. Though it is not possible to reject the unit root test outright, results show no evidence that stock prices exhibit simple linear forecastability.

Among the observed stable non-linearities is the volatility clustering effect. This behavior was explained by the ARCH model introduced by Engel[8] and generalized by the GARCH model developed by Bollerslev.[9] These models impose conditions on the moments of second order. ARCH and GARCH models were subsequently expanded into an entire family of X-ARCH models that capture various aspects of volatility clustering.

---

[5] See, for example, W.A. Brock, J. Lakonishok, and B. LeBaron, "Simple Technical Trading Rules and the Stochastic Properties of Stock Returns," *Journal of Finance* (December 1992), pp. 1731-1764; B. LeBaron, "Technical Trading Rule Profitability and Foreign Exchange Intervention," Working paper 5505, NBER, Cambridge, MA, (1996); and, S. Neftci, "Naive Trading Rules in Financial Markets and Wiener-Kolmogorov Prediction Theory: A Study of 'Technical Analysis,'" *Journal of Business* (1991), pp. 549-572.

[6] A.W. Lo and A.C. MacKinley, "When Are Contrarian Profits Due to Stock Market Over-reaction," *Review of Financial Studies* (1990), pp. 175-208.

[7] J.A. Campbell, A.W. Lo, and A.C. MacKinley, *The Econometrics of Financial Markets* (Princeton, NJ: Princeton University Press, 1997).

[8] R.F. Engle, "Autoregressive Conditional Heteroscedasticity with Estimates of Variance of United Kingdom Inflation," *Econometrica* (1982), pp. 987-1007.

[9] T. Bollerslev, "Generalized Autoregressive Conditional Heteroscedasticity," *Journal of Econometrics* (1986), pp. 307-327.

Another important class of stylized facts that imply the non-linear phenomena of fat tails are the fractal characteristics of time series. Fractal behavior is a long-range phenomenon: it links behavior over vastly different time horizons. The discovery of the fractal behavior of economic time series was made by Mandelbrot who, back in the 1960s, observed similarities in the shape of cotton price evolution at different time scales. Many similar facts have since been observed.

In substance, no conclusion can be reached about the representation of stock prices. But it is unlikely that prices follow simple models such as martingale models of returns or even simple linear models of returns. In this sense, markets are efficient: they do not allow an investor to exploit simple regularities such as linear models.

To improve upon state-of-the-art forecasting, some really clever modeling capability is required. However, no theoretical conclusion allows to propose, in full generality, theoretically sound models. Models are a compromise between risk-return and the ability to test and use the model.

Adding to the difficulty, over the past few years returns generated by buy-and-hold strategies have been high by historical standards. Objectives in investment management have shifted from the search for higher returns to catastrophe management, i.e., how to strategize about possible sudden catastrophic market movements.

It is now clear that markets exhibit complex microstructures and time-dependent trends. These are important to investment management. Though this market behavior is not incompatible with general equilibrium descriptions, it requires additional principles to characterize structure not implied by general equilibrium.

ISSUES IN FINANCIAL MODELING

The only general finance law — the no-arbitrage principle — does not suffice to manage investments. The key tool for asset pricing based on replication (i.e., option pricing) does not allow one to discriminate among investments, a prerequisite for investment management. The no-arbitrage principle is nonetheless a fundamental constraint that must be applied to the modeling of any portfolio of securities as it links the different price processes.

Arbitrage-free modeling has proven successful when payoffs are either contractually determined or imposed as modeling assumptions. With contractually fixed payoffs, derivatives can be modeled provided that a suitable model of the underlying securities can be determined. Assuming a factorization of returns, one again has a mathematical relationship between security prices and factors that must satisfy no-arbitrage conditions which can therefore be used to determine processes.

But absence of arbitrage leaves undetermined a number of fundamental processes (i.e., the risk factors) that require independent modeling. Exhibit 1 represents schematically the technology of investment and risk management. Presently, it is statistics more than theory that allows the modeling of factors.

Exhibit 1: The Technology of Investment and Risk Management

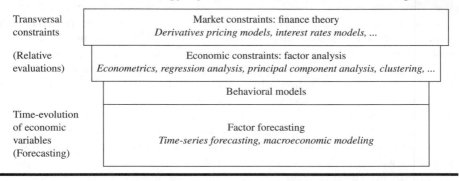

Transversal constraints	Market constraints: finance theory *Derivatives pricing models, interest rates models, ...*
(Relative evaluations)	Economic constraints: factor analysis *Econometrics, regression analysis, principal component analysis, clustering, ...*
	Behavioral models
Time-evolution of economic variables (Forecasting)	Factor forecasting *Time-series forecasting, macroeconomic modeling*

We will now explore some of the key issues in financial modeling. We will begin by considering advances in the modeling of arbitrage-free processes and the related numerical methods, and then go on to explore issues related to the analysis and forecasting of factors. On the modeling side, there are two important areas of innovation: (1) the modeling of interest rates and interest-rate derivatives and (2) the integration of credit and market risk. On the numerical side, there are advances in Monte Carlo methodologies and in the solution of differential equations.

A key question in arbitrage-free modeling is the completeness of markets. If markets are complete, any new security that might be introduced can be replicated by a dynamic portfolio of existing securities. As a consequence, any new security can be priced by no-arbitrage arguments and eventually hedged. Intuitively, the market determines a price for every possible risk.

In complete markets, the mathematical technology of equivalent martingale measures can be applied. Developed in the 1980s by Harrison, Kreps, and Pliska, this technology was an important step forward in the mathematics of dynamic asset pricing. It states that by a suitable change in the probability measures, every price process becomes a martingale after discounting by a suitable interest-rate process.

Making this change in the probability measures, every price process can be expressed as the present expected value of its discounted payoffs; any new security can be priced as the present expected value of its discounted payoffs. Pricing is thereby formally equivalent to pricing in a risk-neutral world. This allows significant simplifications in modeling.

If markets are complete, the change in probability measures is univocally determined. Given the true probability measure, the equivalent martingale measure can also be determined. It is thus possible to conduct statistical estimates of the true probability and to subsequently compute the new equivalent measure. It is therefore convenient to do all the computations in a risk-neutral world, applying appropriate conversions to true statistical estimates.

Although the mathematical details of the equivalent martingale measure transformation in continuous time are complex, the concept of measure transformation is conceptually simple. It states that there are infinite ways to describe mathematically a stochastic process. Under the conditions of absence of arbitrage and market completeness, a martingale representation can always be determined.

Not all markets are complete, however. In incomplete markets, pricing is not necessarily determined by arbitrage arguments as the equivalent martingale measures cannot be univocally determined. Hedging new securities might prove impossible. Holding an option in an incomplete market is a truly risky strategy.

Whether a market is complete or not is an empirical question. Completeness is due to the availability of appropriate securities and the presence of counterparties willing to take both sides of any transaction. Markets can be completed by introducing suitable securities under the condition that there are a sufficient number of trading partners.

Insurance firms typically work in incomplete markets: they assume risks that they might not be able to hedge. Taking insurance risk to the financial markets and completing the insurance risk market is one area of financial innovation. Another is credit risk. Some credit risk markets are already complete; others will most likely follow. We will now explore the modeling challenges involved in integrating market and credit risk from the point of view of investment management.

INTEGRATING MARKET AND CREDIT RISK

The integration of market and credit risk entails a number of distinct steps, with difficulties in the integration process more conceptual than mathematical. The various relationships between credit risk and price processes in a no-arbitrage framework that might include stocks, bonds, and derivatives prices must be understood.

Modeling requires the mathematical representation of credit risk and its pricing; representing credit risk requires introducing uncertainty into an otherwise contractually fixed stream of payoffs. Consider the bond, a contract that promises to pay coupons and repay the principal at fixed dates. If a bond is not risk-free, each coupon and principal payment will be subject to a probability distribution of losses. This concept also applies to derivatives and other securities whose payoffs are subject to credit risk.

Representing credit risk is therefore analogous to representing the stochastic structure of dividend payments. The key difference is that credit risk exhibits only downward risk as fixed payments can be diminished by default but not augmented.

An entire set of possible future scenarios might be imagined, including a subset characterized by default events. Default events, in turn, will be characterized by the time of insolvency and the recovery rate. Modeling the latter involves the mathematical characterization of a complex structure of debt seniority; in most cases a fixed recovery rate or a distribution of recovery rates is assumed.

Consider, for instance, the entire set of future scenarios of a bond portfolio. Each scenario, parameterized by the evolution of interest rates and default events, corresponds to a history of interest rates plus the eventual time of default and recovery rate. If interest rates and defaults are considered independent, the same structure of default time scenarios and recovery rates is associated to each interest-rate scenario; if not, correlations between the two must be considered.

The modeling challenge is to create a single mathematical model that represents both the probabilistic evolution of the time of default and recovery rates plus relevant economic variables. Such a model must be coherent with option theory and suitable for calibration with market data. In particular, it must be reconciled with the practice of assigning credit ratings, a controversial point given the lack of agreement on the interpretation of agency ratings. Often considered an independent summary evaluation of credit risk, these ratings cannot be interpreted as default probabilities.

There are many conceptual schemes for representing default probabilities. The first to be proposed models the causes of default as the primary source of credit risk. The groundwork for this approach to the integration of credit and market risk was laid by Merton in 1974.[10] Merton observed that default occurs when the value of a firm becomes negative. He consequently modeled default time by modeling the firm's value process.

Traditional analysis of the firm relies on accounting data; Merton's analysis relies on market data (i.e., it considers the market value of assets as opposed to their accounting value). Assuming a stochastic process (e.g., a geometric Brownian motion) for the value of the firm, the default time is the first passage through zero of such a process. It is thus easy to show that, assuming a fixed recovery rate, the credit risk of a zero-coupon bond can be represented as an option on the value of the firm. In other words, a risky bond can be represented as the sum of a risk-free bond plus an option on the value of the firm.

If a security such as a bond has many intermediate payments, the mathematical problem is more complex as default must be evaluated for each intermediate date. Geske showed that this problem can be solved as a compound option problem since at each payment date the firm has the option to either default or raise additional capital.[11]

The value-of-the-firm approach has been extended to cover correlations between the value-of-the-firm process and interest rates, and to allow for different assumptions on the probability distributions of recovery rates. In addition, default might occur when the value process hits a specified process and not only zero.

Another approach to the integration of market and credit risk was developed by Jarrow and Turnbull[12] and later extended by Jarrow, Lando, and Turn-

---

[10] R.C. Merton, "On the Pricing of Corporate Debt: the Risk Structure of Interest Rates," *Journal of Finance* (1974), pp. 449-470.

[11] R. Geske, "The Valuation of Corporate Liabilities as Compound Options," *Journal of Finance and Quantitative Analysis* (1977), pp 541-552.

[12] R.A. Jarrow and S. Turnbull, "Pricing Derivatives on Financial Securities Subject to Credit Risk," *Journal of Finance* (March 1995).

bull,[13] Das and Tufano,[14] and Duffie, Schroder, and Skiadas.[15] These models, which are intensity-based, model credit risk as an independent risk process whose first passage through zero gives the default time.

The credit risk process may be quite general in nature. It can be interpreted as the value-of-the-firm process, but it can also represent an independent rating process. Its function is to determine the structure of default time. Adding a stochastic description of recovery rates, credit risk is completely characterized (i.e., the process of payoffs is specified).

From a mathematical point of view, risk processes might be modeled as continuous-time Markov chains characterized by a transition matrix and a distribution of transition times. These continuous-time processes are characterized by a finite number of states with the transition between states occurring at random intervals governed by an exponential distribution. When a transition occurs, the probabilities of transition between any two states are given by a transition probability matrix.

To summarize, the time of default is generally modeled as the random time given by the first passage through zero of some risk process. These risk processes might be interpreted, as in Merton's approach, as the value of the firm and put into relationship with stock market prices. Or they might be considered more general risk processes.

The value-of-the-firm approach is dependent on determining and calibrating a suitable process for the value of the firm. It is generally not easy to have access to all the information that would allow to estimate these processes directly for each counterparty. However, the no-arbitrage principle imposes a relationship between the stock market price processes of a firm and the processes that represent the value of its assets and liabilities. In fact, as Merton showed that the stock price process can be modeled as an option on the value of the firm, this value can be inferred by the market price of stocks.

KMV Corporation pioneered the representation and estimation of value-of-firm processes from market data. Based on the work of Vasicek,[16] the San Francisco-based software company developed a methodology and the computing algorithms for estimating *Expected Default Frequency* for listed firms.

KMV also went one step further, developing a portfolio approach to credit risk. In fact, market data allow one to infer not only the probability of default but also default correlations. Their methodology, which allows one to compute these correlations, was incorporated into J.P. Morgan's CreditMetrics and is a component of software firm CAT*S's CARMA risk management software.

---

[13] R.A. Jarrow, D. Lando, and S. Turnbull, "A Markov Model for the Term Structure of Credit Risk Spreads," *Review of Financial Studies* (1997), pp. 481-523.
[14] S. Das and P. Tufano, "Pricing Credit-Sensitive Debt When Interest Rates, Credit Ratings and Credit Spreads Are Stochastic," Working paper, Harvard Business School (1995).
[15] D. Duffie, M. Schroder, and C. Skiadas, "Recursive Valuation of Defaultable Securities and the Timing of Resolution of Uncertainty," Working paper, Stanford University and Northwestern University (1995).
[16] O. Vasicek, "EDF and Corporate Bond Pricing," KMV Corporation proprietary documentation.

Intensity-based models might be less data-dependent than value-of-the firm models. Specific risk processes can be estimated by market data, as was shown by Jarrow, Lando, and Turnbull. Rating processes such as those supplied by the rating agencies might also be used. In this case, the migration matrix — a statistical estimate — is used. Ratings might, however, have an interpretation that cannot be directly translated into default probabilities.

Evaluating credit risk through a default-time generation process is not the only possible way of interpreting credit risk; credit risk might also be modeled assuming default losses as primary processes. This is the approach espoused by Credit Suisse Financial Products (CSFP) in its recently announced CreditRisk$^+$ approach to measuring and managing credit risk. This methodology uses expected losses and volatility as risk variables. The loss probability distribution function is then inferred by assumptions on the distribution of recovery rates.

The CreditRisk$^+$ methodology makes explicit use of the dependence of default losses on macroeconomic variables. This dependence is modeled making assumptions on how macroeconomic variables selectively influence market segments. Agency data and proprietary data are then used to calibrate processes.

Determining the loss stochastic process is only one step in measuring and managing credit risk. The next crucial steps are pricing and forecasting price changes. In its generality, this is an instance of dynamic asset pricing. Assuming that markets are complete, securities subject to credit risk can be priced in the equivalent martingale measure. This implies that securities are priced as the expected value of their discounted cash flows taking into account the probability structure of default risk.

An active area of research, the mathematical analysis of bond and derivatives pricing was tackled by Das, Duffie, Jarrow, Lando, Turnbull and others under various modeling hypotheses on the correlations between interest rates and credit risk processes. These analyses are generally done directly in the equivalent martingale measure. The underlying assumption is that credit risk markets will develop and be completed where this is not already the case.

Pricing in the equivalent martingale measures yields elegant formal models; but the true market price of risk, embedded in the martingale measure, must be estimated from market data. The observables of the process are market prices of stocks, bonds, and derivatives as well as agency ratings and default events. These observables are also used to calibrate the processes that are assumed to describe prices, ratings and default-time frequency rates.

The relationships implied by option theory should perhaps be summarized. Given a stochastic process for stock prices, the corresponding value process is implied by no-arbitrage conditions. The value process in turn implies the random time of default. Given a process for the recovery rate, the stochastic payoff of a corresponding bond is determined in consequence. When new stock prices are revealed, processes are updated.

The above, however, does not imply bond prices. To determine the latter requires a pricing model (i.e., it is necessary to estimate the market price of risk which allows one to compute the equivalent martingale measure). If this pricing model is complete, any other credit-risk-dependent security is priced by no-arbitrage.

Suppose that the risk process of an intensity-based model is given. This process determines the default random time. Again, assuming a recovery rate process, it completely determines the stochastic process of a bond payoff. Given a pricing model, bond and derivative prices are determined.

Though there is one value process for each firm, there may be fewer risk processes. In the case of an agency rating in particular, there is one rating process for the entire market. Each firm belongs to one of the possible rating categories and the random time of default is the same for all firms in the category.

Assuming a model of the corresponding stock prices, the random default time eventually implied by the risk and stock price processes should be (at least approximately) the same. As a consequence, any significant change in a stock's price should be reflected in the relative rating. If this is indeed the case or not is actively debated given the central role of the rating agencies. It is, however, a difficult question to settle because of the different levels of approximation involved.

In incomplete markets, the above techniques cannot be used. Pricing in incomplete markets might borrow techniques from the actuarial pricing methods used in the insurance sector. Lending to non-listed companies is an instance of pricing in incomplete markets. A number of major banks, including Credit Suisse First Boston, have announced the adoption of actuarial pricing methodologies for their loan portfolios.

INTEREST RATE MODELS

Interest rate risk cannot simply be diversified away, it must be hedged. But interest rate modeling errors are potentially serious and the modeling itself difficult as it involves representing the evolution not only of a single quantity, but of a complete term structure. Hence the considerable interest that models of interest rates have attracted. There are modeling issues.

At any instant, there is an entire term structure of interest rates given by the interest rates at different maturities. These rates are fixed by government bonds of different maturities that can be considered representative of the risk-free interest rate of the corresponding maturities. This term structure can be represented in various ways, for instance by the yields of zero-coupon risk-free bonds of different maturities.

A first problem is due to the fact that, at any given instant, we cannot observe a continuous curve but only a set of discrete points. The fact that most government bonds will not be zero-coupon bonds poses no conceptual problems, but some practical ones in reconstructing hypothetical equivalent zero-coupon risk-free bonds.

Interpolation for missing time points, however, represents a real conceptual problem. Some criteria have to be determined that allow one to assign a yield to maturities for which no yield can be observed. A number of interpolation techniques are available (e.g., polynomial interpolation, spline methods, maximum smoothness methods), but each methodology introduces a bias in the present term structure.

Once the problem of the determination of the present term structure is solved, one has to understand how to model (i.e., to forecast) the future evolution of the curve. In principle, this is a problem of infinite dimensionality. But problems of infinite dimensionality are not tractable. While it is possible to develop the relative mathematics, only a few points for estimates are known. It is therefore assumed that term structures can be subject to only a predetermined set of motions, the simplest assumption being that they can only experience parallel shifts. For each future instant, only one number indicates the displacement of the term structure.

It is, however, known empirically that the shape of the term structure is not fixed but changes. A more faithful modeling of interest rates requires that these changes be taken into account. Studies have shown that most of the variability of the term structure is accounted for by parallel shifts plus changes in steepness and curvature. Hence the term structure does not assume shapes with many ripples; it can therefore be modeled as a smooth curve characterized by a steepness and a curvature factor plus a parallel shift.

These movements can be modeled in various ways. A natural choice, but by no means the only one, is to assume a stochastic process for the short-term interest rate. If we assume a one-factor model for the short-term interest rate, the term structure remains determined in consequence and can only experience parallel shifts.

To model the shape behavior of the term structure, multifactor models are required. For instance, to model parallel shifts plus steepness and curvature changes, three independent risk factors are required. Additional risk factors are needed if more general shape evolutions are to be taken into account.

If one assumes as primitive a multifactor process, the present term structure is consequently fixed. Discrepancies between the observed term structure and the theoretical term structure are perceived as an arbitrage opportunity and must be avoided. It is therefore important to ensure that the computed and observed present term structures coincide.

Heath, Jarrow, and Morton[17] developed a general arbitrage-free theory to model the stochastic evolution of the term structure of interest rates in an arbitrage-free environment with an arbitrary number of parameters. This theory of interest rates establishes general links between the prices of a set of arbitrage-free risk-free bond processes and the short-term interest rates.

There are many ways to represent the stochastic evolution of the term structure of interest rates. Each representation is characterized by the primary risk factors and the constraints to be applied. One possibility is to take a finite number of points of the term structure (i.e., a number of forward rates), and model these directly using a suitable stochastic process. If several points are considered, the

[17] D. Heath, R. Jarrow, and A. Morton, "Bond Pricing and the Term Structure of Interest Rates: A New Methodology," *Econometrica* (1992), pp. 77-105.

number of factors is correspondingly high. At Sakura Global Capital, Jamshidian and Zhu used principal component analysis to reduce the number of factors to three; computational savings were significant.[18]

For investment management, it is important that the model for interest rates not only be arbitrage-free but that it have good forecasting capabilities. In forecasting, the objective is to gain maximum information about the future. The choice of factors in multifactor models plays a fundamental role; adding factors per se does not necessarily improve a model's forecasting ability.

New non-linear methodologies for estimating parameters in continuous-time stochastic processes might find useful application in the forecasting of interest rates. They yield models that can be easily integrated with the current framework of fixed income modeling (see the section below on non-linear forecasting methods).

ADVANCES IN NUMERICAL METHODS

Numerical methods employed in financial modeling fall into two main categories: tree and Monte Carlo methods on the one side, numerical solutions of differential equations on the other. Closed formulas remain useful when applicable, but their importance is reduced by the availability of low-cost high-performance computing power.

Trees and Monte Carlo methodologies produce a large number of representative samples of possible scenarios. From a set of these scenarios, any quantity that is a function of the scenario variables can be easily computed. These methodologies are intuitive as each scenario represents a possible path of the economy, but describing and choosing scenarios might be a complex task.

The key problem with Monte Carlo methodologies is the number of scenarios that need to be explored in order to obtain a good estimate of the relevant parameters. Monte Carlo methods can, in fact, be considered a sampling technique which operates on a set of logical objects. As with statistical sampling, accuracy depends on a large sample.

Despite the substantial computing power available in financial firms, the computational burden of many Monte Carlo simulations might be considered excessive. As calculated by Jamshidian and Zhu,[19] without recourse to compression techniques, a multicurrency problem involving interest-rate scenarios might result in a number of scenarios in excess of 10^{17}, a number that exceeds the computational burden acceptable on even very fast computers.

Intelligent Monte Carlo methodologies are being used to overcome the problem. Different lines of attack have been proposed. Methodologies such as antithetic variables are well known and are used in most simulation environments. More recent methods are based on factor analysis or on the clustering of possible scenarios.

[18] F. Jamshidian and Y. Zhu, "Scenario Simulation: Theory and Methodology," *Finance and Stochastics* (January 1997), pp. 43-67.
[19] Jamshidian and Zhu, "Scenario Simulation: Theory and Methodology."

Factor analysis reduces the number of factors to be considered and, consequently, the number of computations. One example of factor analysis was mentioned above in relationship to interest rate models where Zhu and Jamshidian reduced the number of key rates to be considered in term structure models to three. The number of scenarios to be computed in the resulting Monte Carlo simulation was thereby greatly reduced.

Clustering techniques, on the other hand, reduce the number of paths to be simulated by taking a representative path from each cluster of similar paths. These methodologies might include specific criteria for identifying clusters of similar paths or generalized methods such as Kohonen maps.

Methodologies such as those cited above now are commercially available, either embedded in global risk and investment management software or as middleware. The advanced Monte Carlo algorithms developed by New York-based NumeriX are one such example.

The alternative numerical technique to Monte Carlo simulation consists in solving numerically partial differential equations (PDEs). PDEs arise in two contexts: as a consequence of Ito's lemma and as differential operators associated to stochastic processes. The first is exemplified by the Black-Scholes option pricing methodology whereby option prices are assumed to follow an Ito process which is a function of the underlying Ito processes. The no-arbitrage condition applied to a replication trading strategy translates into a PDE governing the above function.

PDEs also appear in a broader context. A stochastic process, such as an Ito process, starting at a given point can be described by the time-dependent probability distribution function (PDF) associated to its random variables. This PDF is in general governed by a PDE. An infinitesimal operator which determines the corresponding PDF is associated to each process. Correspondence works in both directions: a stochastic process which gives a stochastic solution of the PDE can be associated to each PDE.

There are several numerical methods for the solution of PDEs. The most obvious is the finite difference method. This method creates a grid in the PDE's domain and replaces the PDE with an algebraic difference equation at each point. The PDE is solved approximately, by solving a (generally large) system of algebraic equations. Other methods include the finite element methods and the use of neural networks to approximate the solution of PDEs.

More recently, Monte Carlo methods have been proposed to estimate directly the probability distribution function. Because they consist of independent computations, these methodologies can be easily implemented as parallel algorithms, thus taking advantage of the power of parallel machines. Such an implementation was developed at the Northeast Parallel Architectures Center at Syracuse University.[20]

---

[20] M. Makivic, "Path Integral Monte Carlo Method for Valuation of Derivative Securities," *Neural Network World* (1995), pp. 503-524.

The choice of methods depends on the type of equation to be solved and the boundary conditions to be satisfied. As PDEs are the backbone of mathematical methods in the physical sciences, the relative numerical methods are well known and many proven algorithms are commercially available.

FACTOR ANALYSIS AND FORECASTING

Investment management requires the forecasting of the relevant investment variables, not just the relative evaluation provided by the no-arbitrage principle. Forecasting has to be intended in a probabilistic sense as the evaluation of a probability distribution function at a given time horizon.

There is presently no well developed theory that might allow one to describe the time evolution of primary processes. In the physical sciences, it is generally possible to compute the future evolution of a system starting from a set of initial conditions. Economic and financial forecasting is, however, still far from this stage; it remains based on statistical estimates of parameters that characterize generalized processes.

One could attempt to forecast individually every independent security, but in many instances, looking for additional constraints that bind security price processes is more fruitful. These constraints might be purely mathematical or of a more economic nature. Applying constraints reduces the number of independent risk factors and allows one to both reduce computational complexity and improve one's understanding of the problem at hand. Next we will outline the standard methods of factor analysis and forecasting as applied to stock behavior and then review recent advances in methodology.

MULTIFACTOR MODELS OF STOCK PRICES

State-of-the-art models of stock prices entail fundamental simplifications. A widely used simplification is the assumption of linearity and the use of linear regressions. Among the models are the Capital Asset Pricing Model (CAPM) and the Arbitrage Pricing Theory (APT) multifactor model.

The first general equilibrium model proposed, the standard CAPM, is a one-period model that assumes normally distributed end-of-the-period security returns. It makes the additional assumption that returns can be linearly expressed in terms of a single factor. Each return is thus characterized by a beta which is a measure of its covariance with this factor.

There is a considerable amount of theory behind the CAPM which will not be discussed here. Formulated in the 1960s by Sharpe-Lintner-Mossin, the CAPM was developed as a consequence of the Markowitz mean-variance decision-making model which stated that investors should decide in terms of a trade-off between expected return (mean) and risk as measured by variance. The CAPM models a market where investors follow the mean-variance rule and stock returns are jointly normally distributed.

The single factor of the CAPM is the return of the global *market portfolio* of tradeable assets. A rather elusive concept, this is difficult to ascertain empirically. Practical implementations of the CAPM use some proxy — either an abstractly defined factor or a broad index — for the market factor.

The CAPM has been generalized to take into account multiple factors. Multifactor APT models assume linear regression models for stock returns and adjust parameters through no-arbitrage arguments. They posit that stock returns are determined not by a single factor but by a number of factors. It is assumed that factors and returns are normally distributed and that there is a linear relationship between the two.

The key issues in multifactor models are the determination of factors and the actual estimates of returns through regression coefficients. Factor analysis might follow several avenues. One is pure economic theory by which factors are identified by economic reasoning about the relationship between the performance of a firm and macroeconomic quantities, such as the GNP or the unemployment rate. Returns are then estimated through linear regressions based on historical data.

A second avenue is principal component analysis. Principal component analysis is a technology for reducing the dimensionality of a set of normal variables. It can be performed in various ways. A classical methodology is to diagonalize the variance-covariance matrix by computing its eigenvectors and to consider only the largest variances. This method identifies abstract factors to which it might be difficult to associate an economic meaning.

A third avenue is to select factors through adaptive optimization algorithms such as genetic algorithms or simulated annealing. This methodology is a generalization of principal component analysis. Factors are selected in function of some generalized objective that might be directly related to management objectives. Segmentation algorithms might be used to group together in a single "factor" a set of securities that show similar behavior.

Multifactor models, of which CAPM can be considered an instance, are the workhorse of state-of-the-art stock portfolio management. Most implementations are single-period implementations where returns are evaluated at a given time horizon. There is no theoretical reason for not implementing a multiperiod model, except the complexity of statistical estimates of the relevant parameters.

In practice, multifactor models are periodically recalibrated to adjust the regression parameters of each stock to new information and changing business conditions. Occasionally, the entire structure of factors might need a revision, eventually performed with optimization algorithms.

Linear multifactor models have significant advantages. First and foremost, they allow intuition: managers can project returns over the relevant macroeconomic parameters in simple intuitive terms. Litterman argues that the advantages of intuition offered by linear models, when applicable, should not be underestimated.[21]

---

[21] R. Litterman, "Hot Spots and Hedges," *Journal of Portfolio Management* (December 1996).

While the assumption of linearity and normality is clearly a simplification, it requires evaluation in function of available data and stock behavior. There is no compelling evidence to force a rejection of linear behavior for stock prices as a first approximation. Considering the need to evaluate large portfolios of hundreds or eventually thousands of stocks, linearity might be a good technology trade-off.

NON-LINEAR MODELS OF SECURITY RETURNS

In going from linear to non-linear models of stock returns, we enter a less explored terrain, at least from the point of view of economic theory. Although non-linear models have enjoyed growing popularity in the last decade, most of them are still to be regarded as ad hoc models of economic time series.

Non-linear models of stock returns are, in most cases, mathematical representations of the data generating process (DGP) of time series. They can be either univariate or multivariate, linking current values of a time series with past values of several other time series. Models can be divided into two broad categories: (1) deterministic models of non-linear dynamical systems and (2) purely statistical models.

The theory of non-linear dynamical systems is a mathematical theory that can be applied to any dynamical system, not only to economic time series. Its history began with the discovery that simple dynamical equations could produce very complex behavior where complexity is understood in the sense that very small differences in initial conditions can produce unbounded excursion in future outcomes. As a consequence, the motion of such systems is generally aperiodic, though confined in some region of the parameter space called attractors.

Because their motion appears random, such systems are called chaotic and their behavior deterministic chaos. A notable example of chaotic systems is given by models of the weather. Current models have only short-term forecasting ability due to the chaotic nature of weather phenomena; over long periods of time, however, their statistical behavior is again close to empirical data.

The ability of simple deterministic equations to produce rich behavior gave rise to the hope that the apparent complexity and randomness of economic time series could be explained as deterministic chaos. Were this the case for even short periods of time, it would be possible to build models able to yield excess returns by exploiting hidden non-linearities. For this reason, non-linear dynamics commanded, and still does, interest at the level of theoreticians, practitioners, and management.

Practical applications of chaos theory appeared with the development of a methodology for the analysis of chaotic data. Developed for dynamical systems in general, this methodology is based on a mathematical process of "embedding" in a high-dimensional space which consists in taking sets of points adjacent in time. These vectors design a path in a high-dimensional space from which one might reconstruct the attractor. The interest in this methodology is easy to explain: if it is possible to identify local areas of data described by low-dimensional attractors, then these data can be simulated by relatively simple algorithms.

The interest in non-linear dynamics was extended by the simultaneous development of adaptive computational algorithms able to efficiently search large spaces of possible algorithms. In fact, after identifying a low-dimensional area one still has to determine the algorithm to represent data. Automatic learning methodologies offer a solution. The use of neural networks and similar non-linear approximation methods is essentially based on the possibility of exploiting low-dimensional areas of data through automatic searches.

In fact, the ability to let a low-dimensional neural network learn a path is due to constraints in the complexity of the path. If a path is characterized by a very high dimensionality, no approximation methodology based on simple algorithms is effective. The discovery that the complexity of time series might be only apparent made these approximation methods attractive.

Of the many non-linear adaptive algorithms that have been proposed, a partial list includes:

- *Neural networks* which, as universal function approximators, approximate functions through the output of a trained network. A large variety of topologies, threshold functions, and learning algorithms exist.
- *Wavelet models* are an extension of classical series expansion such as the Fourier or Taylor series. Innovation is in the variety of basis functions and approximation properties.
- *Induction trees and rule-induction systems* that work by performing a cascade of logical tests or by optimizing a set of rules which may be written in plain English.
- *Segmentation algorithms* that work by similarity maximization or like principles. These create clusters of individuals following non-linear classification rules.

The engineering of algorithms has also made significant progress. Perhaps key from the practitioner's point of view is that the engineering of adaptive algorithms has been highly automated thanks to new levels of available computing power and to the diffusion of methodologies such as the Minimum Length Description Principle. The latter helps in choosing the optimal configuration for the algorithm. Commercial implementations such as IBM's Intelligent Miner relieve the user from most mathematical concerns.

The above algorithms are deterministic, which presents several problems. First, the risk involved in using a deterministic data generating process (DGP) might be difficult to evaluate. Second, it might be difficult to integrate these methods with other statistical methods typically used in finance. One might want to create upfront statistical non-linear models; non-linear regressions are classical non-linear statistical methods.

New methodologies allow one to estimate parameters in non-linear stochastic processes. Among these methodologies are the generalized methods of moments (GMM) of Hansen[22] and methods based on the infinitesimal generator of stochastic processes developed by Hansen and Scheinkman.[23] These methodologies are based on the observation that stochastic processes, though time dependent, are described by a deterministic probability distribution. The key idea is to use available data to fit directly the probability distribution function by estimating the coefficients of the deterministic mechanism that govern probability distributions. These statistical methods look promising: they combine the ability to represent non-linearities with an easy-to-integrate statistical framework.

Mention should also be made of a new generation of models that quantify the price impact of large trades. Traditionally difficult to model, this problem has only recently been solved with a significant degree of empirical validation. These models — of which BARRA's Market Impact Model is an example — are non-linear in that there is no assumption of predetermined behavior for price processes. What they model, in fact, is the relationship between the size of a trade and its impact on the market. This problem belongs to the theory of market microstructure. In modeling the price changes induced by trades, such models violate the assumption of the price-taking behavior of agents. The trend towards program trading is behind the requirement for this technology.

The use of non-linear methodologies in stock price modeling has changed. Early implementations were aimed at "beating the market" by stock picking and active trading. But by and large, these implementations underestimated the fact that a deterministic DGP obtained through learning methods might still carry a lot of risk. With a better understanding of these technologies, the accent is shifting from "beating the market" to managing risk and performing financial optimization, eventually in a multiperiod environment.

It is now clear that linearity is the exception, not the rule, a tolerable approximation rather than an empirically faithful description of economic facts. Non-linearities are commonplace when portfolios include even a modest level of optionality. To some extent, they must be taken into consideration. The availability of high-frequency data is providing a wealth of empirical data for training and testing adaptive methods and for understanding general laws.

OPTIMIZING INVESTMENTS

The previous discussion covered some of the modeling issues of investment management. The objective of modeling is, ultimately, the ability to forecast in the

---

[22] L.P. Hansen, "Large Sample Properties of Gneralized Methods of Moments Estimators," *Econometrica* (1982), pp. 1029-1054.
[23] L.P. Hansen and J.A. Scheinkman, "Back to the Future: Generating Moment Implications for Continuous-Time Markov Processes," *Econometrica* (July 1995), pp. 767-804.

sense of estimating or computing probability distributions at some given time horizon. Once the forecast is done, optimal decisions must be taken. Whether made by human judgment or through formal optimizers, the optimality side of investment management is not negotiable; in one way or another, investment decisions must be made using some rule that expresses the optimal trade-offs.

There are two distinct issues in investment management: (1) how to quantify the objectives, and (2) how to attain those objectives. There are theoretical and practical considerations in both instances.

Objectives must be established in some formalized, and if possible quantitative, way. But there are no rules for determining objectives. While it is reasonable to assume that everybody wants the highest possible return, the trade-off between risk and return is judgmental. Some subjective criteria for optimality must be adopted.

Increasingly, investment managers are being requested to articulate their objectives more formally. But it would be misleading to believe that the formalization of objectives simply translates into formulas those objectives established through more intuitive means. Through formalization, the entire decision-making process becomes more articulate.

The most common formalized framework for decision making is the quantification of preferences: a quantity is assigned to each possible choice and one choice is preferred to another if it is identified by a higher level of the quantitative parameter. This is the framework of utility functions.

The mathematical theory of decisions gives a number of conditions under which different choices could be discriminated through single numbers. From a strictly mathematical point of view, the ability to order choices numerically is a restrictive condition. Not every set of decisions can be ordered through utility functions; there are sets of choices that cannot be formalized through utility maximization.

The advantage of a quantitative ordering of preferences through utility functions or similar preference ordering is the ability to feed objectives to an optimizer. An optimizer is a mathematical algorithm that seeks the minimum or maximum of a function in a given domain and subject to constraints. If objectives can be quantified, the entire management process can be seen as an optimization process and automated.

The technology of optimizers is relatively mature and has applications in many fields, from classical operations research to complex engineering problems. In the field of investment management, the key technology is stochastic optimization as problems are typically cast in a probabilistic framework. Stochastic optimization requires defining the deterministic equivalent of the stochastic problem. In one-period investment management, for example, the deterministic equivalent can be expected utility maximization.

The complexity of optimization problems increases significantly in going from one-period to multiperiod optimization. In the latter, optimizing decisions have to be made at each period, eventually in continuous time. The time dimension of the problem has to be taken into account.

Making optimization decisions at each step of a multistep problem might prove to be computationally difficult and call for methodologies to reduce computational complexity. Different multistage stochastic optimization techniques exist; among those commercially available are Toronto-based Algorithmics' scenario optimization methods.

In state-of-the-art implementations, the technology of optimization is applied under two (slightly) different frameworks. In the first, investors seek the maximization of some quantitative objective, for instance the expected utility of some mathematical form, over the forecasted process of security prices. The classical mean-variance quadratic optimization is an instance of this framework.

In the second and more general framework, one process is optimized with respect to another. This involves optimizing some quantity, such as an utility function, defined on the difference between a target process and the forecasted process. This is the classic tracking problem: given an investment objective, for instance a benchmark portfolio plus a target return, the goal is to minimize variation from the target. Most investment management problems can be cast in this framework: mean-variance optimization is tracking of a fixed objective; hedging and immunization problems can be expressed as minimization of tracking errors.

Under these frameworks, the challenge is to establish the target and to identify the most appropriate quantitative measure of utility. There are many choices given the uncertain and probabilistic nature of problems. Expected utility is a common choice in a probabilistic environment. Another is the "regret" function. Developed by the founder of Algorithmics Ron Dembo and IBM researcher Alan King,[24] the regret function allows a general formulation of multistage stochastic optimization.

Optimization methodologies in both single-step and multistage implementations have reached a high level of sophistication and maturity. The key issue today is not the technology itself but the underlying processes. Because optimizers are sensitive to error, they require an accurate evaluation of the underlying processes and careful supervision.

Though optimization is the key to the automation of investment management, the maximization of a quantitative objective is not the only road to automation. Expert systems, for example, have been used to automate investment management by establishing a set of well-defined rules that govern choices. A generic set of rules might not be equivalent to a utility optimization framework. As remarked, the utility optimization framework implies some regularity in the set of available choices; rules might violate these regularities. One solution could be the combination of rule-based systems with formal optimizers to attain the highest possible generality.

---

[24] R.S. Dembo and A.J. King, "Trading Models and the Optimal Regret Distribution in Asset Allocation," *Applied Stochastic Models and Data Analysis* (1992), pp. 151-157.

How far is it possible to automate the investment process? There are currently funds managed automatically by optimizers. Here the role of the fund manager is to make major asset allocation decisions, to establish the objectives to be given to the optimizers, and to supervise the process. Automation changes, not reduces, the role of the investment manager. By requiring a high level of interaction with the algorithms in setting objectives and supervising results, it effectively raises the stakes.

LOOKING AHEAD

Most state-of-the-art investment management technology is still based on linear models similar to those developed 40 years ago. Much progress has been made in the area of derivatives and fixed income securities where the use of mathematics to model relative evaluations of contractually fixed security relationships has proved quite successful. But when it comes to our understanding of the evolution of financial markets in a *causal* sense, progress has been modest. Non-linearities have been found in economic time series. These not only appear because of the optionality of derived processes, they are a fundamental feature of basic risk factors.

The only technology available presently for modeling non-linear risk factors are non-linear adaptive computational methods. Modeling non-linearities through adaptive algorithms has, however, proved difficult and the number of modeling options becomes unmanageably vast if problems are considered in full generality. Nevertheless, the accumulation of empirical data, in particular of high-frequency data, is allowing for better training and testing of adaptive methods. The result is the increasingly faithful modeling of economic and financial phenomena.

There is, however, the need for a firmer theoretical understanding of risk factors and for the ability to model the changing characteristics of financial markets and of the economy at large. What is needed, in fact, is a new understanding of dynamic causal links. Two areas of research that might make a fundamental contribution are: (1) the modeling of market aggregation phenomena and (2) new ideas in the macroeconomy of economic growth.

The power of demand aggregation is becoming increasingly clear. J.M. Keynes used to refer to the "animal spirit" of markets; more recently, neoclassical economists shifted attention to the rationality of markets. Rationality, however, has proved to be an elusive concept. How demand is aggregated is a complex phenomenon that involves an understanding of the web of relationships among economic agents.

Based on the paradigm of the representative agent, neoclassical finance theory is too weak empirically to address the problem of aggregation. Assuming he could be described, the representative agent would be a highly complex entity that rationalizes, in the sense of variational principles, all the aggregation phenomena that take place in the market. Unless the theory is somehow completed, this hypothetical entity is out of empirical reach.

Research efforts are attempting to model the market as a truly interacting, multiagent system using techniques borrowed from statistical mechanics and the theory of complex systems. Results obtained to date are still at a higher level of idealization. Bak, Chen, Scheinkman, and Woodford used the concept of self-organized criticality to show how many small independent shocks might produce fluctuations in the aggregate.[25] At the Santa Fe Institute which pioneered work in complex systems, Holland, Arthur, and LeBaron simulated market activity through intelligent learning agents.[26] Lux showed how ARCH behavior can be explained as the aggregation of two types of agents, fundamentalists and followers.[27]

A general discussion of economic explanations based on interacting agents with bounded rationality is provided by Kirman[28] and Sargent,[29] a pioneer in the development of rational expectations. Much of the research in the line of relaxing rational expectations and adopting a complex systems approach is being done introducing small perturbations away from rational expectations, to allow one to accommodate complex decision making.

The key theoretical obstacle is the self-reflectivity of the economy. Research must start from those phenomena that are not affected by their own explanation. In general terms, however, there must be some sort of coherence between the level of uncertainty of economic theory and the actual possibility to exploit theoretical findings for profit.

Notwithstanding, the modeling of multiagent systems is making progress: different levels of structure are been introduced; applications of non-linear dynamics are being explored; the role of agent learning is being assessed; and explanations have been advanced for a number of stylized facts.

In the area of macroeconomics, we can expect a new understanding of economic growth and inflation. Current macroeconomic theory takes scant account of the internal structure of the economy. Considered a system that produces an output measurable by some agreed-upon physical unit, the economy is handled as a slowly evolving entity that allows the definition of economic growth and inflation.

Modern economies, however, have more structure than is posited by current theory. It is becoming increasingly clear that a simple inflation parameter is questionable in economies characterized by rapid innovation and changes in the creation and distribution of wealth. Consider the information industry, a key component of today's economy. Were information considered part of the industrial output, the economy would be in a highly deflationary period. What we consider output is physical output filtered and reified by the market. This filter, however, adds a large number of variables to the economy.

---

[25] P. Bak, K. Chen, J. Scheinkman, and M. Woodford, "Aggregate Fluctuations from Independent Sectoral Shocks: Self-Organized Criticality in a Model of Production and Inventory Dynamics," *Ricerche Economiche* (March 1993), pp. 3-30.

[26] Sergio Focardi and Caroline Jonas, *Modeling the Market: New Theories and Techniques* (New Hope, PA: Frank J. Fabozzi Associates, 1996).

[27] T. Lux, "Time-Variation of Second Moments from a Multi-Agent Noise Trader Model of Financial Markets," *Second International Conference on Computing in Economics and Finance* (Geneva: 1996).

[28] A.P. Kirman, "Economies with Interacting Agents," Working Paper G & WII, University of Bonn (1995).

[29] T.J. Sargent, *Bounded Rationality in Macroeconomics* (Oxford: Claredon Press, 1993).

Exhibit 2: The Neoclassical and Modern Concepts of Macroeconomics

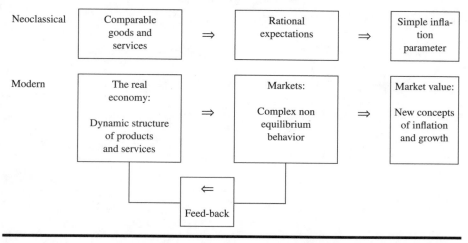

Exhibit 2 illustrates the difference between the two concepts — neoclassical and the modern — of macroeconomics. The modeling of these systems is related to our understanding of complex, self-reflective systems with a rich internal structure. The theory of multiagent systems under uncertainty might prove helpful also in this broad macroeconomic context.

Understanding agent interaction will be a factor of growing importance for investment management. Ultimately, returns are related to the wealth-producing capabilities of the economy. If wealth is increasingly market value projected by financial markets over physical products with rapidly changing rules, the fundamentals require redefinition.

Chapter 4

Mean-Variance Optimization for Practitioners of Asset Allocation

Francis Gupta, Ph.D.
Associate
Strategic Investment Advisory Group
J.P. Morgan Investment Management

David Eichhorn
Analyst
Strategic Investment Advisory Group
J.P. Morgan Investment Management

INTRODUCTION

Asset allocation is the core of portfolio management. In its simplest form, it pertains to the allocation of a portfolio across different asset classes. The basic premise of asset allocation is derived from the fact that the returns on various asset classes are not perfectly correlated. As a consequence, investors can hold portfolios that diversify optimally across asset classes. Because the optimally diversified portfolios result in the maximum possible return for different levels of risk, the portfolios are efficient.

This chapter has two objectives. The first is to provide a concise, in-depth description of asset allocation vis-à-vis mean-variance optimization. This will be of help not only to the novice, but will also assist the avid practitioner to reiterate some of the finer points of mean-variance optimization that over time are taken for granted.

Second, we will outline the problem of arriving at a non-intuitive or unreasonable efficient frontier. This problem is so common that it has given rise to a dilemma faced by all practitioners of asset allocation. More specifically, the portfolios that comprise the efficient frontier are heavily weighted in one or two asset classes. In most cases, practitioners of mean-variance optimization circumvent this problem by arbitrarily constraining the shares of certain asset classes during optimization, until the portfolios that fall on the frontier align to their perceptions.[1] In this chapter we will formalize the costs and benefits of using con-

---

[1] In particular, practitioners impose a lower bound on an asset class with which they are comfortable, and therefore force a minimum of that asset class to be included in the efficient portfolios, and/or they impose an upper bound on an asset class with which they are "uncomfortable," and therefore force a maximum of that asset class to be included in the efficient portfolios.

straints in an optimization. As a result, practitioners will be able to gain a clearer understanding of the implications of using constraints in an optimization.

The appendix to this chapter provides readers with information on some of the optimizers available today. These products save investors from the tedious and time-consuming task of determining the efficient frontier and the composition of the efficient portfolios.

A REVIEW OF MEAN-VARIANCE OPTIMIZATION

Modern portfolio theory as formalized by Markowitz,[2] together with today's readily available computing power, is an extremely useful combination for an investor making asset allocation decisions. The theory says that if the returns on the various asset classes are normal, then to obtain the set of efficient portfolios, the investor simply needs to compile the expected returns, standard deviations, and correlations of the asset classes. These data are then fed as inputs into an asset allocation/optimization software package and, assuming that certain conditions are met,[3] the investor is able to generate the efficient frontier (i.e., the set of portfolios which maximizes expected return for given levels of risk).

It should be kept in mind that because returns are assumed to be (jointly) normal, the asset allocations implied by mean-variance optimization are efficient. Therefore, accepting mean-variance optimization as efficient is the equivalent to accepting that the returns of the various asset classes are distributed as jointly normal, and vice versa.[4]

Constructing the Inputs

Before the vendor supplied software can determine the efficient frontier and optimal portfolio allocations, the investor must supply the information contained in the first two moments of the joint distribution of the asset classes to be included in the portfolio. This information is summarized by the expected returns, standard deviations, and correlations among the returns of those assets classes.

Generally, practitioners construct the expected returns, volatilities, and correlations for the various asset classes using historical returns. There is one major problem with this approach: the future does not mimic the past. Or stated otherwise, past performance is no guarantee of future results. As a consequence, the portfolios constructed using these expected returns and volatilities may not perform as expected. But if investors believe that historical returns provide the most reliable information on expected returns, then they may be justified in using past returns. Of course, depending on the asset class and investors' expectations

---

[2] Harry M. Markowitz, *Mean-Variance Analysis in Portfolio Choice and Capital Markets* (New York: Basil Blackwell, 1967).

[3] In particular, the variance-covariance matrix of the assets must be invertible.

[4] This is important because some investors believe that the returns of some "alternative" asset classes are not normal. In this case, mean-variance optimization generally will not yield an efficient asset allocation.

regarding its performance, they may want to alter the implied historical returns and volatilities accordingly.[5] Further, investors may want to use only certain historical periods — the ones they believe are more relevant to the future.[6]

In this vein, Exhibit 1 presents the expected returns, volatilities and correlations for three asset classes — U.S. Fixed Income, U.S. Large Caps, and Emerging Markets (EM) Equity. Though the approach is applicable to as many asset classes, for ease of exposition, we restrict our attention to three.

The returns, variances, and correlations are computed using the historical returns for the Ibbotson U.S. Long-Term Corporate Bond Index, the S&P 500, and IFCI Emerging Composite, respectively. These estimates will be used as inputs in the mean-variance optimization example that follows. Note that in this case, the estimates are historical and have not been altered in any way to reflect personal or market beliefs about the future performance of these asset classes.

The Efficient Frontier or the Set of Optimal Portfolios

Having constructed the inputs, the next step is simple: the inputs are fed into a vendor-supplied optimizer which computes both the efficient frontier and the composition of the efficient portfolios.[7]

Exhibit 2 illustrates three efficient frontiers; the "unconstrained" frontier, which allows the optimizer to freely choose the allocations to the three asset classes, and two frontiers that constrain the allocation to EM Equity. The "moderately constrained" frontier restricts the maximum exposure to EM Equity to 25% of the portfolio, while the "constrained" frontier restricts the maximum exposure to EM Equity to 10% of the portfolio. The exhibit also illustrates three equally risky portfolios — a, b, and c — that have volatilities of 11% and lie on the three frontiers.

Exhibit 1: The Inputs: Historical Expected Returns, Standard Deviations and Correlations of Asset Classes

Asset Class	Expected Return	Standard Deviation	1	2	3
1 U.S. Fixed Income	9.7%	9.6%	1.00		
2 U.S. Large Cap	13.4%	15.2%	0.42	1.00	
3 Emerging Markets Equity	17.3%	20.0%	0.11	0.40	1.00

Source: Ibbotson. All numbers are calculated using nominal, historical monthly returns which are annualized. The benchmarks for the three asset classes are the Ibbotson U.S. Long-Term Corporate Bond Index, S&P 500, and IFCI Emerging Composite, respectively. EM Equity uses data starting January 1987 and ending October 1997. Data for the other two asset classes goes back to January 1970.

[5] We will return to this in the next section.

[6] For example, U.S. fixed income managers generally argue that the period after 1970 is a more realistic reflection of the present. Therefore, they ignore the history of that asset class prior to that year. We do the same in this example. In another example, while performing asset allocation in different scenario analyses regarding different inflation regimes, practitioners concentrate on the periods corresponding to the scenario of interest.

[7] At each level of risk, the efficient portfolio is unique.

Exhibit 2: The Unconstrained Efficient Frontier Lies Above the Constrained Efficient Frontiers

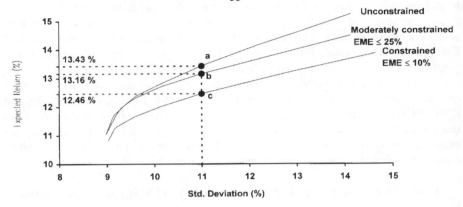

Exhibit 3: Compositions of the Unconstrained Efficient Portfolios

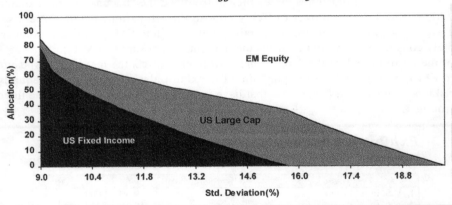

REASONS FOR CONSTRAINING THE ALLOCATION TO AN ASSET CLASS

Initially, it may seem that the EM Equity has been constrained arbitrarily in frontiers depicted in Exhibit 2. However, there are a number of justifications as to why investors may deem it necessary to constrain an asset class. Before expositing the reasons for constraining EM Equity, let us take a look at the composition of the unconstrained efficient frontier. Exhibit 3 displays the composition of the portfolios that comprise the unconstrained efficient frontier.

It is clear that as the total risk — as measured by the standard deviation — of the portfolios increases, the allocations to U.S. Fixed Income and U.S. Large Cap decline rapidly. Portfolios with volatilities greater than 16% contain no U.S. Fixed Income. Also notice that for even moderate total risk levels the portfolios are heavily weighted in EM Equity.[8] These extreme or large allocations in a subset of the asset classes may cause some investors to become uncomfortable. Consequently, investors may want to limit their exposure to EM Equity. This is one reason why investors may be willing to use constraints in an optimization.

It should be clarified that constraining EM Equity increases the allocations to the other asset classes. For example, the share of U.S. Large Cap increases in the portfolios.[9] Therefore, frontiers similar to those that are constrained could be obtained by introducing constraints that force a minimum allocation to U.S. Large Cap, thereby penalizing EM Equity.

As mentioned at the beginning of this chapter, investors circumvent the problem of obtaining non-sensical portfolios that are inconsistent with intuition by introducing constraints into the optimization. In doing so, investors may be implicitly (and rather subjectively) revealing a preference for certain asset classes. In the following sections of this chapter, we make a case that it is possible to interpret these constraints as the relative confidence that investors have in the accuracy of the risk/return estimates of the asset classes.

The fact that in most cases efficient portfolios that comprise the unconstrained efficient frontier are heavily invested in one or two asset classes does not mean that there are problems with the mean-variance method. However, those cases do raise questions about the precision of the risk, return, and correlation estimates of the asset classes. It is possible that the discomfort that investors feel when their portfolios are heavily exposed to EM Equity may be mapped into the subjective confidence that investors place in the risk/return characteristics of that asset class.

Confidence in the risk/return estimates for different asset classes may vary for a number of reasons. Differences in the confidence of the estimates may arise due to the variation in the lengths of time the asset classes have traded. From a statistical point of view, it is reasonable to imagine that investors exhibit a higher confidence in the risk/return characteristics for U.S. Large Cap, which are constructed using trading information generated over more than two decades (in this case), than the estimates for EM Equity, which are compiled over one decade only.[10]

---

[8] As mentioned, this is one of the most common problems encountered by practitioners of asset allocation. Even at relatively low risk levels, portfolios have significant allocations to the more risky asset classes (for example, EM Equity in this case, and EAFE if it is included in the analysis). Perhaps most problematic is the fact that asset classes that are generally thought to form the backbone of a sensible portfolio (U.S. Large Cap, for example) are either excluded or receive small allocations in most of the portfolios that lie on the frontier.

[9] Constraining EM Equity may also be interpreted as revealing a preference for U.S. Large Cap and U.S. Fixed Income.

[10] Statistically, the precision of estimates using more information is greater than or equal to those that use less information.

Exhibit 4: Compositions of Equally Risky Portfolios on the Unconstrained and Constrained Efficient Frontiers

Asset Class	Unconstrained	Moderately Constrained EM Equity ≤ 25%	Constrained EM Equity ≤ 10%
	a	b	c
U.S. Fixed Income	40%	33%	37%
U.S. Large Cap	22%	42%	53%
Emerging Markets Equity	38%	25%	10%
Expected Return	13.43%	13.16%	12.46%
Std. Deviation	11.00%	11.00%	11.00%
Cost of Constraint	+0 bps	+27 bps	+97 bps

Furthermore, in comparison to economies that are still growing, developed economies have more efficient capital markets (due mainly to a faster flow of information), are more politically stable and historically have exhibited more successful monetary and fiscal policies. As a result, investors may place greater confidence in the asset classes of developed economies as compared to those of developing markets.

A final reason for variations in the confidence investors place in different asset classes is founded in the behavioral finance literature. It has been noted that ambiguity in the odds of a lottery makes individuals more risk averse (i.e., they prefer to avoid the gamble).[11] Therefore, ambiguity about the risk/return estimates of "foreign" or unfamiliar asset classes makes them less attractive to investors in comparison to asset classes with which they are familiar. This is because familiar risks seem "less" risky than unfamiliar risks. As a consequence of this subjective confidence, it is generally the case that investors consider the asset classes with which they are most familiar as anchors to their portfolios.[12]

THE COST OF CONSTRAINING AN ASSET CLASS

Exhibit 4 shows the compositions of the three equally risky portfolios (a, b, and c) which have standard deviations of 11%. The differences in the expected returns of the portfolios demonstrate the cost of constraining the optimizer. The constraint that dictates EM Equity to be a maximum of 25% of the portfolio has little effect on efficiency. Portfolio b which lies on the frontier has a 27 basis points lower expected return than portfolio a, the equally risky portfolio that lies on the unconstrained frontier (13.43% versus 13.16%). Stated differently, the investor pays a cost of 27 basis points for decreasing the allocation to EM Equity from 38% to 25% and increasing the exposure to U.S. Large Cap from 22% to 42%.

[11] Daniel Ellsberg, "Risk, Ambiguity and the Savage Axioms," *Quarterly Journal of Economics* (1961), pp. 643-669.
[12] This is sometimes revealed as a "domestic asset class bias" by investors.

Exhibit 5: Forgone Returns Depend on the Constraint and the Volatility of the Portfolio

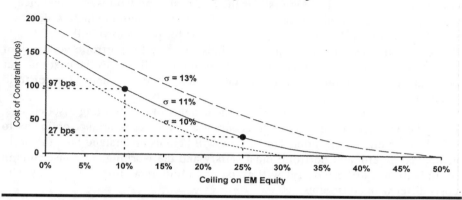

On the other hand, the constraint that limits the allocation of EM Equity to a maximum of 10% costs more in terms of expected returns. Portfolio c, which has a volatility of 11%, results in an expected return that is 97 basis points lower than portfolio a, the portfolio with the same volatility that lies on the unconstrained frontier. In exchange, the investor now has an exposure of only 10% to EM Equity, while the optimal share of U.S. Large Cap has more than doubled (from 22% to 53%). In addition, the share of U.S. Fixed Income declines by 3% only (37% versus 40%). A trade-off like this one, which lowers expected return but results in allocations with which individuals are comfortable, may be worthwhile for investors who place more confidence in the risk/return estimates of U.S. Large Cap relative to those of EM Equity.

The cost of constraining an asset class differs by the severity of the constraint and with the volatility of the total portfolio. Exhibit 5 displays the total cost of different constraints for portfolio with volatilities of 10%, 11%, and 12%, respectively.

First, notice that the cost of the constraint decreases as it becomes more lax. For example, a constraint that excludes EM Equity from the allocation (i.e., sets the maximum allocation to zero) costs more than any constraint that allows a positive allocation to EM Equity. The reason for this is simple: the more severe the constraint, the faster it binds and, therefore, the more it costs in forgone returns. For even a relatively risky portfolio with a standard deviation of 13%, a constraint that allows an allocation of more than 50% to EM Equity does not bind and, therefore, costs nothing in terms of forgone returns.[13]

Second, because EM Equity is an asset class with high risk/return characteristics, investors that hold more aggressive portfolios pay more for constraining

---

[13] In addition, notice that the curves are convex and thus the marginal cost of constraining decreases as the constraint becomes less severe.

this asset class in comparison to conservative investors. This is because the frontier allocates more of EM Equity to more aggressive portfolios. Therefore, if a constraint does bind, it binds first for the aggressive portfolios. For instance, a constraint that limits the allocation of EM Equity to no more than 30% does not bind for portfolio volatility of 10%, barely binds for portfolio volatility of 11%[14] (the cost being less about 15 bps), and binds severely for portfolio volatility of 13%[15] (the cost being about 60 bps). The exhibit also illustrates the cost that our constraints — EM Equity $\leq$ 10% and EM Equity $\leq$ 25% — impose for portfolio volatility of 11%.

Before we proceed to highlight the benefits of constraining asset classes, it may be beneficial to review the procedure used by a mean-variance optimizer to solve for the efficient frontier. This review will help us understand both the properties that an efficient portfolio must satisfy and the workings of constraints in optimization. Furthermore, it will assist us in understanding the reasons why costs differ with constraints.

THE ROLE OF ASSET CLASS CONSTRAINTS IN AN OPTIMIZATION

Though the efficient frontier is presented in the risk/return space, it will be illuminating to perform the analysis in the asset allocation space as outlined by the axes in Exhibit 6. The horizontal axis, w_{EM}, represents the proportion of the portfolio allocated to EM Equity and the vertical axis, w_{LC}, represents the proportion allocated to U.S. Large Cap. Therefore, for any given point in this plane, the allocation to U.S. Fixed Income is determined by the constraint that sets the sum of the allocations to 100%. For example, the portfolio defined by the point where w_{EM} equals 0.5 and w_{LC} equals 0.25, implies a 25% allocation to U.S. Fixed Income.[16]

We know that the expected return of any portfolio R_P is given by the weighted average of the returns of the individual asset classes, where the weights represent shares of the asset classes in the portfolio, i.e.,

$$R_P = w_{FI}R_{FI} + w_{LC}R_{LC} + w_{EM}R_{EM} \tag{1}$$

where w_I is the allocation to asset I in the portfolio and R_I is the return on asset I. Note, that the weights of the asset classes in equation (1) should sum to 100%. The variance of the portfolio is given by

---

[14] We know from Exhibit 4 that the unconstrained allocation of an efficient portfolio with a volatility of 11% is 38%.

[15] The unconstrained allocation to the efficient portfolio with a volatility of 13% is 38%. The reader may get an idea of this from Exhibit 3.

[16] For simplicity, we refrain from using weights that are negative or greater than one. But all the analyses presented here are applicable when allowing for selling short or buying long.

Exhibit 6: The Composition of Efficient Portfolios are Determined by Tangencies of Isoreturn Lines and Isovariance Ellipses

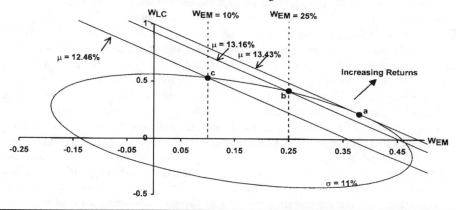

$$\text{Var}(R_P) = w_{FI}^2\text{Var}(R_{FI}) + w_{LC}^2\text{Var}(R_{LC}) + w_{EM}^2\text{Var}(R_{EM})$$
$$+ 2w_{FI}w_{LC}\text{Cov}(R_{FI}, R_{LC}) + 2w_{LC}w_{EM}\text{Cov}(R_{LC}, R_{EM})$$
$$+ 2w_{FI}w_{EM}\text{Cov}(R_{FI}, R_{EM}) \tag{2}$$

For any given portfolio we can compute the expected return from equation (1). Using the expected returns for the asset classes given in Exhibit 1, the expected return on the composite portfolio made up of $w_{FI} = 0.5$, $w_{LC} = 0.25$, and $w_{EM} = 0.25$ is 12.5%. However, this is not the only portfolio that corresponds to a expected return of 12.5%. For instance, a portfolio with an allocation of 35% to U.S. Fixed Income, 55% to U.S. Large Cap, and 10% to EM Equity also has an expected return of 12.5%. In fact, there are an infinite number of portfolios which have an expected return of 12.5%. A line that passes through all portfolios that yield the same expected return is called an *isoreturn line*.[17] Because the expected return of a portfolio is a linear combination of asset class returns, isoreturn lines are straight.

Exhibit 6 illustrates three isoreturn lines corresponding to expected returns of 13.43%, 13.16%, and 12.46%, respectively. Portfolios *a*, *b*, and *c*, reported in Exhibit 4, must lie on these isoreturn lines, respectively. Higher expected return isoreturn lines lie parallel to and northeast of the lines shown.[18]

The method used with expected returns can be applied to variances as well. By substituting the values of the weights of the asset classes, and their variances and covariances from Exhibit 1 in equation (2), we can obtain the variance of any com-

---

[17] From *isos*, Greek for equal.

[18] Since any point to the north-east implies a higher allocation to EM Equity and U.S. Large Cap and, therefore, a lower allocation to U.S. Fixed Income, it must have a higher expected return and therefore lie on a higher isoreturn line.

posite portfolio. Just as many portfolios have the same expected return, there are many different portfolios with identical variances. However, unlike with isoreturn lines, portfolios with the same variances do not lie on a straight line. Instead, because the formula for the variance includes square terms (w_x^2) and cross-product terms ($w_x w_y$), they form ellipses. These are called *isovariance ellipses*. Exhibit 6 depicts the isovariance ellipse for portfolios with a standard deviation of 11%.[19]

The maximum-returning portfolio for a given variance is the portfolio that lies at the tangent of the isovariance ellipse (which represents all the portfolios that have the given variance) and an isoreturn line.[20] A mean-variance optimizer looks for these tangencies. For example, the point *a* is a tangency between the isovariance ellipse with a standard deviation of 11% and the isoreturn line with an expected return of 13.43%. The implied standard deviations and expected returns of all such tangencies when plotted in the risk-return space is referred to as the efficient frontier.

All portfolios defined by points falling to the left of the dotted lines satisfy the constraints defined by those lines. As an illustration, consider the dotted line along which EM Equity is held constant at 25%. The portfolios that satisfy the constraint that the maximum share of EM Equity not exceed 25% of the portfolio must lie between the y-axis and the dotted line. Furthermore, the portfolio with a volatility of 11% must lie on the part of the ellipse that is bounded by the y-axis and the dotted line. Because returns are increasing in the northeast direction, portfolio *b*, the one that falls on the intersection of the dotted line and the isovariance ellipse (therefore it satisfies the EM Equity constraint and has a volatility of 11%), is the efficient portfolio and results in the maximum expected return at that level of risk.[21] Its return is given by the isoreturn line that passes through that point, (i.e., 13.16%). Portfolio *b* will lie on the efficient frontier that constrains the share of EM Equity to a maximum of 25% of the portfolio.

Similarly, portfolio *c* will lie on the efficient frontier that constrains the share of EM Equity to a maximum of 10%. Notice that portfolio *c* lies on the intersection of the constraint that set EM Equity to 10% (the dotted line), the isovariance ellipse that defines the set of portfolios with a volatility of 11%, and the isoreturn line that defines the set of portfolios that have an expected return of 12.46%.

BENEFITS OF CONSTRAINING AN ASSET CLASS

For the purposes of illustration, we will hypothesize that investors are not confident about the estimate of the standard deviation of EM Equity.[22] In particular, they believe that the standard deviation is estimated with error. Exhibit 7 illus-

---

[19] In our example, lower-variance isovariance ellipses will lie within those with higher variance.

[20] This isoreturn line will be unique.

[21] If there exisits a tangency to the left of the dotted line that defines the constraint, the constraint would be satisfied and would not be binding.

[22] We could also choose to make the estimate for the expected return uncertain.

trates an example of an investor's, beliefs regarding three possible scenarios. The investor believes the standard deviation of EM Equity have a value of 20%, 25%, and 30% with probability p,q, and $1-p-q$, respectively.[23] In a more complex example, we might have assumed that the true standard deviation could be anywhere between 20% and 30% with a continuous density.

Exhibit 8 depicts the efficient frontiers in scenarios A, B, and C. Because EM Equity has a lower standard deviation in scenario A than in scenario B, any given portfolio (that has EM Equity) has a lower volatility in scenario A than in scenario B. As a consequence, the frontier in scenario A lies above the frontier in scenario B. Similarly, the frontier, in scenario B lies above the frontier in scenario C. Generalizing this approach, if an investor's beliefs were continuous over different values in the interval [20%,30%], one can imagine a family of efficient frontiers lying between the two extreme frontiers. Therefore, assuming estimation error, the efficient frontier would be more accurately represented as an "efficient band."

Finally, it should be noted that because the compositions of portfolios a, b, and c do not change, they result in the same expected return under all three scenarios.[24] As a result, the portfolios do not move in the north/south directions in the risk/return space. Because their volatilities change (in particular, they increase), they do move along the x-axis, the one that measures the standard deviation.

Exhibit 7: An Example of Investors' Beliefs on the Standard Deviation of EM Equity

Scenario	Outcome	Probability
A	Std Dev (R_{EM}) = 20%	p
B	Std Dev (R_{EM}) = 25%	q
C	Std Dev (R_{EM}) = 30%	$1-p-q$

Exhibit 8: The "Efficient Band"

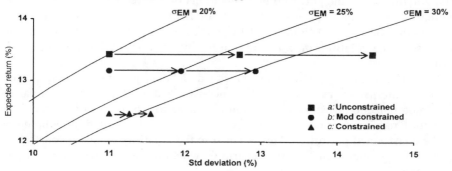

---

[23] Given the wide swings in EM Equity returns in 1997, this is not an outrageous example.

[24] Recall from equation (1) that the return on a portfolio depends on asset class weights and the returns on the asset classes — not on variances.

Exhibit 9: The Volatilities of the Unconstrained and Constrained Portfolios in the Three Scenarios

Scenario	Unconstrained	Moderately Constrained EME ≤ 25%	Constrained EME ≤ 10%
	a	b	c
A: Std Dev (R_{EM}) = 20%	11.00%	11.00%	11.00%
B: Std Dev (R_{EM}) = 25%	12.72%	11.95%	11.27%
C: Std Dev (R_{EM}) = 30%	14.46%	12.93%	11.55%

Constraints May Assist in Containing Volatility

The volatilities of the unconstrained and constrained portfolios will depend on the volatilities of EM Equity in the different scenarios. These volatilities are presented in Exhibit 9. In scenario A, we know that each of three portfolios (a, b, and c) have a volatility of 11%. In scenario B, a's volatility goes from 11.00% to 12.72% — an increase of 172 bps. Portfolio b's volatility increases to 11.95% — an increase of 95 bps, and portfolio c's volatility, at 11.27%, experiences the smallest increase, of 27 bps.[25]

The reason for the difference in the moves among the three portfolios is simple. Portfolio a's allocation to EM Equity, at 38%, gives the highest exposure to the asset class, and therefore to the uncertainty in its volatility. As a consequence, its volatility takes the strongest beating. It now makes a little more sense as to why investors may want to limit the exposure to asset classes with which they are less confident. The benefit of limiting exposure are clearly realized if scenario B is the true state of the world.

Portfolio a takes an even bigger beating if scenario C is realized. In other words, if the true volatility of EM Equity is given by 30%, the volatility of a, the unconstrained portfolio, increases by 346 basis points. Portfolios b and c, the constrained portfolios, are less sensitive to increases in the volatility of EM Equity. The volatility of b, the portfolio that constrains the share of EM Equity to 25%, increases by 193 basis points, while the volatility of c, the portfolio that constraints the share of EM Equity to 10%, increases by only 55 basis points. The increase in the volatility of a, b, and c in the different scenarios is presented in Exhibit 10.

The fact that constrained portfolios do a better job at containing volatility under alternative scenarios than the unconstrained portfolio may be of particular importance to investors who exhibit high aversion to risk. For instance, if an investor's maximum appetite for risk is 13%, then he should definitely hold one of the constrained portfolios. This is because the volatility of the unconstrained portfolio is greater than 13% in scenario C, which has a positive probability of occurring.

---

[25] The volatilities of portfolios a, b, and c may be calculated directly by substituting the weights, variances, and covariances into equation (2).

Exhibit 10: Additional Volatilities of the Unconstrained and Constrained Portfolios in the Three Scenarios

		Unconstrained	Moderately Constrained EM Equity ≤ 25%	Constrained EM Equity ≤ 10%
Scenario	Outcome	a	b	c
A	Std Dev (R_{EM}) = 20%	0	0	0
B	Std Dev (R_{EM}) = 25%	+172 bps	+95 bps	+27 bps
C	Std Dev (R_{EM}) = 30%	+346 bps	+193 bps	+55 bps

Exhibit 11: Forgone Returns for the Unconstrained and Constrained Portfolios in the Three Scenarios

		Unconstrained	Moderately Constrained EM Equity ≤ 25%	Constrained EM Equity ≤ 10%
Scenario	Outcome	a	b	c
A	Std Dev (R_{EM}) = 20%	0	27 bps	97 bps
B	Std Dev (R_{EM}) = 25%	13 bps	2 bps	35 bps
C	Std Dev (R_{EM}) = 30%	40 bps	4 bps	9 bps

Constraints May Decrease Inefficiency

In scenarios B and C, not only do the frontiers shift (see Exhibit 8), but also the composition of the portfolios that make up the frontiers change. Therefore, relative to the frontiers under scenarios B and C, the constrained portfolios will not be as inefficient as they were under scenario A. Because the volatilities of both the unconstrained and constrained portfolio increase under scenarios B and C, the question we are interested in answering is: how inefficient are the portfolios relative to their new volatilities? Exhibit 11 answers this question.

Recall from Exhibit 4 that the constrained portfolios paid a price, in terms of forgone returns, for constraining their allocations to EM Equity. For scenario A, the cost paid is shown in the first row of the exhibit. If the volatility of EM Equity is 20%, portfolio a is efficient (and therefore pays no penalty), while portfolios b and c have an expected return that is lower by 27 and 97 basis points, respectively.

However, if scenario B is realized, we know that: (1) the efficient frontier moves (see Exhibit 8), and (2) the volatilities of the three portfolios (a, b, and c) increases to 12.72%, 11.95%, and 11.27%, respectively (see Exhibit 9). To evaluate how inefficient a, b, and c are relative to the new efficient frontier, we simply compare the expected returns of a, b, and c to the expected returns of portfolios with the same volatility as a, b, and c, but which lie on the efficient frontier. The answers under scenarios B and C are presented in rows 2 and 3 of Exhibit 12.

Notice that portfolio a, which was efficient under scenario A, is inefficient under scenarios B and C. In particular, the efficient portfolios with the same volatility as portfolio a under those scenarios have returns that are 13 and 40 basis points greater than portfolio a's return.[26] In contrast, portfolio b, the one that constrains EM Equity to a maximum of 25%, looks relatively efficient in scenarios B and C. In those scenarios, portfolio b's return is only 2 and 4 basis points lower than the equally risky efficient portfolios. Finally, portfolio c, the one which constrains EM Equity to a maximum of 10%, and looks relatively inefficient under scenario A, also looks significantly better under scenarios B and C. The equally risky portfolios have an expected return of 35 and 9 basis points greater than the return on portfolio c.

Constraints May Limit Downside Risk or Probability of Shortfalls

Mean-variance optimization in its simplest form solves for the set of portfolios that maximize returns for different levels of risk. However, investors frequently have objectives other than obtaining the greatest expected return for the risk that they undertake. For example, institutional investors may be interested in controlling the variability of returns across time, or minimizing the probability of a certain predetermined loss. The recent focus on risk management with an emphasis on "Value at Risk" models (VaR) provides sufficient evidence of this hypothesis. Research in behavioral finance suggests that individual investors also have other objectives. Principal preservation is one such major goal.

Mean-variance optimization essentially solves one specific static problem and is not equipped to address more complicated, dynamic objectives. Consequently, given the objectives above, the implied portfolios may not be "efficient" from an investor's perspective. This may be another reason why investors choose to constrain the allocations of certain asset classes in the portfolios they hold.

To illustrate how constraints may be used to achieve other objectives, we simulated the returns on the three asset classes used in our example to obtain estimates for the downside and the probability of shortfalls for the portfolios. For the purposes of exposition, we ignore scenario B and present these estimates for scenarios A and C in Exhibit 12.[27] In other words, the estimates pertain to the scenarios in which the standard deviation of EM Equity is 20% and 30%, respectively.

Because the returns on the asset classes is identical in scenarios A and B, the expected returns for the three portfolios are the same in the two scenarios. But the 27 bps cost of constraining EM Equity to a maximum allocation of 25% in the moderately constrained portfolio translates into $1 less in returns over a 1-year period, for every $100 invested. Over 10 years, the moderately constrained portfolio provides $12 less than the unconstrained portfolio ($344 versus $356). Similarly, the 97 bps cost of constraining EM equity to a maximum allocation of 10% in the constrained portfolio results in $2 and $34 less than the unconstrained portfolio over 1-year and 10-year periods, respectively.

---

[26] Keep in mind that the returns of a, b, and c are unchanged.

[27] One could imagine that scenario B has a zero probability of occurrence.

Exhibit 12: Risk/Return and Downside Shortfall Over One and Ten Years for a $100 Initial Investment

(All Figures in Dollars Except Where Indicated)

Portfolio Characteristic	Scenario A Std Dev (R_{EM}) = 20%		Scenario C Std Dev (R_{EM}) = 30%	
a: Unconstrained	1 year	10 years	1 year	10 years
Expected return	$114	$356	$114	$356
Standard deviation	11	113	15	151
5th percentile	96	207	91	171
Prob[end balance < principal]	11.2%	0%	17.2%	0.1%
b: Moderately constrained, EME≤25%	1 year	10 years	1 year	10 years
Expected return	$113	$344	$113	$344
Standard deviation	11	107	13	126
5th percentile	95	201	93	181
Prob[end balance < principal]	12.3%	0%	15.1%	0%
c: Constrained, EME≤10%	1 year	10 years	1 year	10 years
Expected return	$112	$322	$112	$322
Standard deviation	11	101	11	106
5th percentile	94	187	94	182
Prob[end balance < principal]	12.8%	0%	12.4%	0%

Note. For the investment horizon of 10 years, the portfolios are rebalanced annually.

The benefits of limiting exposure to EM Equity can be seen by comparing the standard deviations, 5*th* percentiles and the probability that the 1-year and 10-year balances will fall short of the principal across the three portfolios. In scenario A, all the portfolios have a standard deviation of $11 over a 1-year period. But over a 10-year period, portfolios *b* and *c* have a lower standard deviation. This is a consequence of compounding annual expected returns.[28] Under scenario C, the volatility of portfolio *a* increases by $4 and $38 over 1- and 10-year periods (it was $11 and $113 under scenario A). Given the differences in exposure to EM Equity for portfolios *a*, *b*, and *c*, these increases were inevitable. As expected, the constrained portfolios do a better job at controlling the overall volatility.

In scenario A, the 1- and 10-year 5*th* percentiles are $96 and $207 for portfolio a. In the same scenario, 5*th* percentiles of portfolio *b* are $95 and $201, while those of portfolio *c* are even lower.[29] However, in scenario C, the 1- and 10-year 5th percentiles fall to $91 and $171 for portfolio *a* — declines of $5 and $36, respectively. In comparison, the 1- and 10-year declines for portfolio *b* are $2 and $20, respectively. But the 5*th* percentile for portfolio *c* remains unchanged over one year and falls by only $5 over ten years. Now the unconstrained portfolio *a* has lower 5*th* percentiles than the constrained portfolios, *b* and *c*.

---

[28] The variance of a distribution that is a product of log-normals is increasing in the mean of the log-normals.

[29] This is an artifact of the different expected returns on these portfolios. A distribution that has a lower return with the same variance as another will have a lower 5*th* percentile.

Exhibit 13: Ten-Year Standard Deviations for a Range of Beliefs Over Scenarios A and C

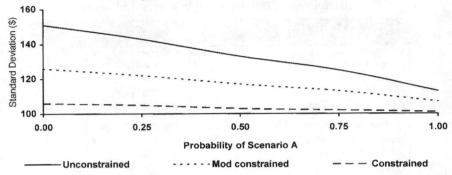

Exhibit 14: Probability of Loss in One Year for a Range of Beliefs Over Scenarios A and C

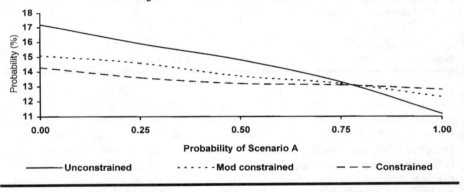

For individual investors, perhaps the greatest benefit of constraining are revealed by the probabilities that their balances will fall short of their original principals.[30] In scenario A, over a 1-year period, portfolios *b* and *c* have a slightly higher probability that the year-end balance will fall below the principal than portfolio *a* (12.3% and 12.8% versus 11.2%). But in scenario C, portfolios *b* and *c* have a significantly lower probability of loss than portfolio *a* (15.1% and 12.4% versus 17.2%). Furthermore, over a 10-year period, under any of the scenarios, the portfolios that limit exposure to EM Equity have virtually no chance of resulting in balances smaller than their principals. But the unconstrained portfolio has a 0.1% chance of resulting in a balance smaller than its principal.

Given beliefs regarding the likelihood of scenarios A and C occurring, how does an investor choose from a set of portfolios that trade off expected return for lower volatility and more downside protection? Exhibits 13 and 14 illustrate,

---

[30] Keep in mind, everything is measured in nominal terms.

for a range of beliefs, the volatilities for the three portfolios over ten years, and the probability that the 1-year ending balance will be less than the principal.[31]

For both statistics, the values for portfolio a, the unconstrained portfolio, are the most sensitive to investor beliefs concerning the two scenarios. Portfolio b, the one that constrains the share of EM Equity to a maximum of 10%, is less sensitive. However, portfolio c, the portfolio that constrains the share of EM Equity to a maximum of 30%, is virtually insensitive to investor beliefs regarding the two scenarios.

The 10-year standard deviations for portfolio a range from a low of $113 in the case where scenario A occurs with certainty to a high of $151 in the case that scenario C occurs with certainty — a range of $38. In comparison, for portfolio b this range, at $19, is not only smaller, but its endpoints are also lower. The range falls to $5 only for portfolio c.

The probability that the year-ending balance falls below the principal also exhibits the same pattern. However, if investors believe that scenario A has an 80% chance of occurring (with scenario C having a 20% chance of occurring), they will essentially be indifferent when choosing from among portfolios a, b, and c with respect to the probability of loss. For probabilities of scenario A that are greater than 80%, an investor prefers the unconstrained portfolios. Alternatively, for a probability of A that is less than 80%, the constrained portfolios are better at reducing the chances of a loss. Thus if probability of shortfall is an investors main concern, they must be very confident in their estimate of the volatility of EM Equity to choose the unconstrained portfolio.

The differences in portfolio expected returns, and the associated risks under alternative beliefs over asset class risk/return estimates (in this case the risk estimate for EM Equity), allow investors to evaluate the trade-offs of using constraints in the optimization in a systematic fashion. The portfolios chosen by investors should reflect their relative preferences for return and appetites over risk — volatility and probability of shortfalls — under alternate scenarios, as well as their confidence in the risk/return assumption.

CONCLUSIONS

By introducing uncertainty in the risk/return estimates, we derive the benefits that arise from a lower (expected) volatility of the constrained portfolios. Another benefit of the constrained portfolios over the unconstrained one was that in the "high volatility" outcome they had a lower probability of a shortfall. On the other hand, the cost of constraining was a lower expected return.

It is difficult to make a case for constraining the allocations to asset classes if investors have equal confidence in the risk/return estimates used as the

---

[31] The probability that the 10-year ending balance is less than the principal is virtually zero for all three portfolios.

inputs in an optimization. We have shown that one easy answer as to why investors constrain certain asset classes may be the differences in the relative "confidence" that investors place in the precision of the inputs.

This chapter formalizes guidelines for investors to use while making asset allocation decisions. In particular, it has laid out a framework for evaluating the cost and benefits associated with constraining an optimization. As a consequence, investors are able to ensure that the portfolio chosen is the least sensitive to alternative realizations of risk/return estimates.

APPENDIX

Now that we understand the underlying theory and the problems of implementation, it would be useful to take a look at the availability of commercial asset allocation software. The table below lists alphabetically the companies and names of their products. The information on these products, and in some cases the demo versions, can be obtained from each of the company's sites on the World Wide Web.

Company	Asset Allocation Software Name	Web Site/Phone Number/E-Mail
BARRA	World Markets	http://www.barra.com
Frontier Analytics Inc.	Allocation Master	Ph. (619) 552-1268
Ibbotson Associates	Encorr	http://www.ibbotson.com
Northfield Information Services Inc.	PACO	http://www.northinfo.com
Sponsor-Software Systems, Inc.	Expert Allocator	Sponsorsi@aol.com
Wilshire Associates Inc.	Horizon	http://www.wilshire.com
Wilson Associated International	Power Optimizer	http://www.wilsonintl.com

Chapter 5

Foreign Exchange Hedging by Managers of International Fixed Income and Equity Portfolios

David F. DeRosa, Ph.D.
President
DeRosa Research and Trading, Inc.
and Adjunct Professor of Finance
Yale School of Management

INTRODUCTION

Foreign exchange risk has serious implications for successful investing in international equity and bond markets. Leading academic authorities have published opinions giving every possible kind of advice on how investors should manage foreign exchange risk. Yet today no single view prevails about whether portfolios should be hedged. International fixed income managers focus a great deal on currency hedging decisions. Their attention is understandable because currency risk has been a large component of fixed income investment performance. In most circles, currency risk management is also considered to be an important part of managing international equity portfolios. But here professionals are remarkably divided in their opinions about what kind of hedging, if any at all, can be expected to add value. In recent years, a style of currency risk management called "overlay" has spread in popularity among institutional investors. Overlay is a process whereby the responsibility for currency risk is delegated to a specialized currency funds manager who works apart from the individuals, who make security and country allocation decisions.

FOREIGN EXCHANGE RISK IN INTERNATIONAL FIXED INCOME PORTFOLIOS

In the case of fixed income, it should be clear that the exchange rate is an integral part of investment performance. This stems from the fact that a bond is a fixed nominal claim. A U.S. dollar-based investor who maintains an unhedged position in a German government bond is at risk to fluctuations in the U.S. dollar/German mark exchange rate. The investor will benefit when the dollar falls against the mark and suffers when the dollar rises against the mark.

75

Exhibit 1: Total Returns on Salomon Brothers World Government Bond Indices
Unhedged and Currency Hedged, 1985-1996

	World Ex-Germany		World Ex-Japan		World Ex-USA	
	Hedged Into DEM	Unhedged DEM	Hedged Into JPY	Unhedged JPY	Hedged Into USD	Unhedged USD
1985	12.49%	−1.98%	15.66%	−1.00%	11.14%	35.01%
1986	10.74%	−3.57%	11.18%	−6.51%	11.40%	31.35%
1987	2.17%	−3.69%	1.06%	−14.15%	9.27%	35.15%
1988	4.29%	18.63%	3.83%	8.13%	9.12%	2.34%
1989	6.55%	−0.50%	5.77%	27.58%	4.11%	-3.41%
1990	6.20%	−1.74%	5.58%	6.40%	3.32%	15.29%
1991	16.85%	18.63%	15.11%	5.29%	11.11%	16.21%
1992	14.39%	12.47%	8.50%	4.37%	8.03%	4.77%
1993	18.15%	22.19%	11.70%	−1.29%	13.42%	15.12%
1994	−2.47%	−9.43%	−6.25%	−9.77%	−4.02%	5.99%
1995	16.28%	9.18%	11.93%	25.80%	17.92%	19.55%
1996	6.37%	12.06%	2.79%	19.55%	11.82%	4.08%
Compound Annual Return	9.16%	5.53%	7.06%	4.61%	8.75%	14.45%
Standard Deviation of Returns	6.48%	10.70%	6.38%	13.34%	5.63%	13.14%

Notes: Currency-hedged returns calculated on the basis of rolling one-month forwards.
Source: Salomon Brothers. Compound annual return and standard deviation of annual returns calculated by author. Reprinted from David F. DeRosa, *Managing Foreign Exchange Risk* (Burr Ridge, IL: Irwin Professional Publishing, 1996).

Exhibit 1 presents evidence on the impact of foreign exchange movements on global bond portfolio returns. The data are the Salomon Brothers world government bond index returns. These particular indexes focus attention on exchange rate risk in that they represent non-domestic fixed income investments from the point of view of an investor. For example, the "world excluding Germany" data represent the returns to a German mark-based investor from owning the ex-Germany portion of the Salomon index. The table shows similar data for the world excluding Japan, representing a yen-based investor, and the world excluding the United States, representing a U.S. dollar-based investor.

Each category is presented twice, once as the index hedged back to the home country currency and once as the index with no hedging. A hedged index return was constructed by combining the unhedged index return with the return on 1-month rolling forward contracts. These forwards constitute the foreign exchange hedge; they deliver foreign currency and receive domestic currency. The differences traceable to the hedging decision are large. Hedged index returns differ from unhedged returns by 363, 245, and 570 basis points of compound annual return over the period 1985-1996 for marks, yen, and dollars, respectively. There are substantial differences in the standard deviations of returns as well — the decision to hedge or not to hedge can as much as double or half the volatility of returns.

Bond portfolio mangers fall into three general camps with respect to currency risk management. A few managers espouse the dogmatic view that currency risk should never be hedged. This view has to be difficult when the home currency of the investor is appreciating against the currencies that are represented in the portfolio.

Of the opposite view are a small group that believes that currency risk should be hedged fully all of the time. This would leave the investment manager with one less degree of freedom in making portfolio decisions. Absent exchange rate risk, success or failure would depend on choices involving issuer selection, anticipation of interest rate movements, and portfolio duration and convexity.

The most prevalent strategy for international bond managers is to do at least some discretionary hedging. This seems to be a natural choice of strategy because fixed income specialist are usually deeply involved in fundamental macro-economic research, making it likely that they would be comfortable in forming simultaneous views on both currency and interest rates.

FOREIGN EXCHANGE RISK IN INTERNATIONAL EQUITY PORTFOLIOS

Exhibit 2 shows that foreign exchange risk has a dramatic effect on the performance of international equity portfolios. Nonetheless, knowing what to do about foreign exchange risk in managing international equity portfolios is far less clear than in the case of fixed income investing. Moreover, the literature from academicians and practitioners contains no shortage of advice on what should be done about the foreign exchange risk associated with international equity portfolio management. Unfortunately, no one generally accepted view has emerged from the debate.

A large part of what has been written addresses the question of whether or not foreign exchange risk should be permanently — or "statically" — hedged as a rule. Here there are three prominent opinions.

The first comes from Perold and Schulman who believe that foreign exchange risk should be hedged 100%, all of the time.[1] They reach this conclusion based in part on the proposition that foreign currency hedging has no risk premium. Perold and Schulman present evidence that currency hedging can materially reduce the risk of investing in assets denominated in a foreign currency. They examine the volatility of hedged and unhedged quarterly real U.S. dollar rates of return over the decade ending December 1987 for investments made in the stock and bond markets of Japan, the United Kingdom, and Germany. The volatility of hedged returns are significantly and uniformly lower than the volatility of unhedged returns. Given their no risk-premium assertion, they conclude that currency hedging is a "free lunch."

---

[1] Andre Perold and Evan C. Schulman, "The Free Lunch in Currency Hedging: Implications for Investment Policy and Performance Standards," *Financial Analysts Journal* (May/June 1988), pp. 45-50.

Exhibit 2: Total Returns on FT/S&P-Actuaries World Stock Market Indices
Unhedged and Currency Hedged, 1986-1996

	World Ex-Germany		World Ex-Japan		World Ex-USA	
	Hedged Into DEM	Unhedged DEM	Hedged Into JPY	Unhedged JPY	Hedged Into USD	Unhedged USD
1986	42.34%	12.82%	28.17%	0.39%	39.81%	66.55%
1987	11.35%	-2.29%	5.05%	-18.97%	-0.52%	26.25%
1988	24.05%	38.62%	13.83%	19.68%	34.50%	27.93%
1989	23.49%	11.44%	23.30%	49.03%	26.09%	12.17%
1990	-22.25%	-27.03%	-11.73%	-8.71%	-30.38%	-23.12%
1991	19.54%	21.96%	24.63%	14.84%	4.85%	13.32%
1992	1.24%	1.43%	4.22%	2.25%	-11.03%	-13.06%
1993	22.24%	30.91%	20.17%	8.84%	26.25%	32.25%
1994	0.43%	-5.47%	-7.28%	-10.26%	-0.75%	8.36%
1995	18.62%	10.56%	19.75%	32.69%	10.74%	10.45%
1996	15.69%	21.71%	17.69%	37.84%	13.71%	6.50%
Compound Annual Return	13.03%	8.92%	11.77%	9.74%	8.35%	13.04%
Standard Deviation of Returns	16.69%	18.38%	13.24%	21.58%	20.86%	23.74%

Notes: Currency-hedged returns calculated on the basis of rolling 1-month forwards and include effect of bid-ask spread. Hedged returns for Thailand, Brazil, S. Africa and Mexico are actually Unhedged returns for lack of forwards data, but these countries are a minuscule part of the indices.

Sources: The returns are calculated by Goldman, Sachs & Co. and are derived from the FT/S&P-Actuaries World Indices which are owned by FT-SE International Limited, Goldman, Sachs & Co. and Standard & Poors. The indices are compiled by FT-SE International and Standard and Poors. In conjunction with the Faculty of Actuaries and the Institute of Actuaries. NatWest Securities Ltd. was a co-founder of the Indices.
Compound annual return and standard deviation of annual returns calculated by the author.
Reprinted from David F. DeRosa, *Managing Foreign Exchange Risk* (Burr Ridge, IL: Irwin Professional Publishing, 1996).

A second view comes from Black who advises that although some hedging is desirable, investors in international equities should retain some exposure to foreign exchange risk.[2] Black derives an optimal hedge ratio (meaning the fraction of exchange rate exposure that needs to be hedged) which rests in part on a somewhat obscure mathematical principle called Siegel's paradox (or to a related concept known as Jensen's inequality). The paradox concerns the asymmetrical effect of a movement in exchange rates as considered by consumers whose wealth and income are denominated in opposite sides of an exchange rate. For example, a decline in dollar/ mark from 1.5000 to 1.4500 would represent a loss of 3.33% in foreign purchasing power for dollar-based consumers but a gain of 3.44% in foreign purchasing power for mark-based consumers. Black argues that this seemingly paradoxical asymmetry represents an exploitable profit opportunity if some portion of one's foreign exchange exposure were left unhedged. The optimal hedge ratio is "universal" because, in his words,

---

[2] Fischer Black, "Universal Hedging: How to Optimize Currency Risk and Reward in International Equity Portfolios," *Financial Analysts Journal* (July/August 1989), pp. 16-22; and, Fischer Black, "Equilibrium Exchange Rate Hedging," *Journal of Finance* (July 1990), pp 899-907.

The formula applies to every investor who holds foreign securities. It applies to a U.S. investor holding Japanese assets, a Japanese investor holding British assets, and a British investor holding U.S. assets.

A third opinion comes from Froot who studied long-term movements of exchange rates.[3] Froot argues that the benefits from currency hedging are short-term in nature. Over longer periods, he finds that there is either no benefit or actually a cost to hedging. His argument hinges on his empirical finding that real exchange rates are mean-reverting, a condition which would explain why hedging appears to be so different in the short- and long- runs. Froot writes:

> I argue ... that currency hedges have very different properties at long horizons compared with short horizons. ... The properties of currencies hedges vary with horizon in part because hedge returns at different horizons are driven by very different factors. At relatively short horizons, hedge returns are dominated by changes in real exchange rates, i.e. in the purchasing power of one currency compared with another. However, mean reversion in the real exchange rates implies that these purchasing powers tend toward parity, so that real exchange rates over time remain roughly constant. At long horizons, hedge returns are instead dominated by fluctuations in cross-country differences in unexpected inflation and real interest differentials. The importance of this latter component grows the longer the hedge remains in place.

An entirely different group of opinions are based on the assumed existence of exploitable inefficiencies in foreign exchange. Kritzman argues that currency returns are non-random on the grounds of variance ratio tests.[4] He argues that central bank activity in the market induces serial dependence in exchange rates that can be exploited by what he terms convex investment strategies. Convex strategies are basically trend-following investment rules. They buy or add to a position in a currency as its exchange rate increases and sell or reduce a position it as its exchange rate declines. In a similar line, Levich and Thomas propose that non-randomness in currency futures prices can be exploited with an agglomeration of filter rules and moving-average crossover rules.[5]

---

[3] Kenneth A. Froot, "Currency Hedging over Long Horizons," Working paper No 4355, National Bureau of Economic Research, May 1993.

[4] Mark Kritzman, "Serial Dependence in Currency Returns: Investment Implications," *Journal of Portfolio Management* (Fall 1989), pp 96-101.

[5] Richard Levich and Lee Thomas, "The Merits of Active Currency Risk Management: Evidence from International Bond Portfolios," *Financial Analysts Journal* (September/October 1993), pp. 63-70.

Kritzman calls attention to another potentially exploitable market anomaly which has to do with the forward exchange rate.[6] In some circles, classical economic theory is believed to postulate that the forward exchange rate is an unbiased estimator of the future spot exchange rate — the so-called uncovered interest parity theorem. Yet the body of empirical evidence roundly rejects this notion. Kritzman develops a normative approach for currency hedging that takes advantage of the supposed forward rate bias. Hazuka and Huberts take it one step further.[7] They recommend an approach that prefers currencies with comparatively high real interest rates. Their empirical work gives evidence of outperformance of their alternative method of favoring high nominal interest rate, meaning discount, currencies.

What characterizes the work of Levich and Thomas, Kritzman, and Hazuka and Huberts is the belief that there is no optimal, static hedging policy. Each advocates implementation of decision rules that are based on market anomalies.

Finally, it should be recognized that none of the above mentioned research stands in the way of active management of currency hedging to express views on the future direction of exchange rates.

WHAT IS MEANT BY CURRENCY RISK IN OVERLAY PROGRAMS

Many of the most sophisticated institutional investors rely on the expertise of specialized currency overlay managers to protect their equity portfolios from exchange rate risk. The presumption behind currency overlay is that it is possible to manage currency risk apart from the investment management processes that determine country allocation and security selection. Because movements in foreign exchange rates affect international investments in many ways, it is necessary to be precise about the definition of "currency risk."

In the context of overlay, the term means the risk of currency translation gains or losses that an investment might experience from the conversion of the local currency of the investment to the home currency of the investor. All other ways that exchange rates affect international investments are classified as "local market risks." Local market risks also include such things as strikes, changes in the cost of raw materials, shifts in world demand, technological change, and revision of government policies. Consider the following two cases:

1. A dollar-based investor buys a French government bond. The price of the bond, quoted in French francs, remains stable but the value of the franc falls by 10% against the dollar. This is an example of exchange rate risk as it applies to currency overlay.

---

[6] Mark Kritzman, "The Optimal Currency Hedging Policy with Biased Forward Rates," *Journal of Portfolio Management* (Summer 1993), pp94-100.
[7] Thomas B. Hazuka and Lex C. Huberts, "A Valuation Approach to Currency Hedging," *Financial Analysts Journal* (March/April 1994), pp. 55-59.

2. A dollar-based investor buy shares in a French pharmaceutical company that exports a major portion of its output to Australia. The French franc is stable against the dollar but rises in value by 10% against the Australian dollar. This adversely affects the value of the shares but nonetheless is classified as a local market risk.

The Separation Rule

The distinction between market risk and currency risk in overlay leads to a useful decomposition of investment return. Define the holding period return on an investment bought at the end of period 1 and held until the end of period 2, R_2^{local}, measured in local currency as

$$R_2^{local} = \frac{(P_2 + d_2)}{P_1} - 1$$

where P_1 and P_2 are the prices of the investment at the end of two successive periods (1 and 2) in the currency of the local market. The amount of any dividends or other cash distributions paid during the second period is d_2.

To calculate the total return in the investor's home currency, it is necessary to convert prices and dividends using the prevailing spot exchange rate. The total return in the domestic currency, R_2^{home}, is

$$R_2^{home} = \frac{\frac{P_2}{S_2} + \frac{d_2}{S_2}}{\frac{P_1}{S_1}} - 1$$

which equals

$$R_2^{home} = \frac{S_1}{S_2} \times \frac{P_2 + d_2}{P_1} - 1$$

where S_1 and S_2 are the spot exchange rates at the ends of periods 1 and 2, quoted in terms of the number of units of foreign currency equal to one unit of domestic currency. Dividends and other cash distributions are converted to the home country currency at the end of the second period. The first term in brackets on the right-hand side of the latter equation is the portion of the total return generated by exchange rate movements. The second term in brackets is the portion due to local market performance.

For example, suppose that the shares of a hypothetical Japanese company sell for 1,000 yen today and that the exchange rate is 100 yen to one U.S. dollar. Over the next year, the stock pays no dividends but rises to 1,200 yen. At the end of the year, the exchange rate is 95 yen per dollar. Then

$$R_2^{local} = \frac{1,200}{1,000} - 1 = 20.00\%$$

$$R_2^{\text{home}} = \frac{100}{95} \times \frac{1,200}{1,000} - 1 = 26.32\%$$

Note that the rise in share price in yen compounds the effect of the rise in the value of the yen.

This decomposition points to what overlay managers call the separation rule:

Currency risk can be managed separately from local market risk, with the latter confined to country and security selection.

The separation rule postulates that currency risk can be managed apart from individual security selection. Decentralization of the investment process makes it possible to think about hedging sterling, for example, regardless of whether the currency exposure derives from ownership of shares in a British bank, a British automobile manufacturer, or for that matter, any other investment denominated in pounds.

Under the separation rule the equity portfolio gets long the exposure to a foreign currency at the time that the foreign currency is acquired to pay for the purchase of foreign shares. Likewise, the exposure to exchange rate risk associated with an equity position ceases when a trade is executed to dispose of the foreign currency proceeds from the sale of shares.

HEDGING CURRENCY RISK: A BRIEF INTRODUCTION TO THE FOREIGN EXCHANGE MARKET

Foreign exchange hedging transactions for institutional portfolios are normally executed in the inter-bank currency market. Some material that briefly describes this market will now be presented in anticipation of the sections below that discuss hedging procedures.

Foreign exchange is the largest of all of the financial markets. Some estimates of the size of the trading volume are reported in parallel surveys undertaken during the month of April 1995 in cooperation by the Bank for International settlements (BIS)[8] and the New York Federal Reserve Bank. Earlier surveys were undertaken in April 1992 and April 1989. According to the 1992 survey, the global net turnover in the world's foreign exchange markets was estimated to have been some $1,230 billion dollars per business day. This figure was adjusted for virtually all double-counting, as well as for estimated gaps in reporting. The comparable numbers for 1992 and 1989 were $880 billion and $620 billion. The majority of transactions occur in the inter-bank market in the form of spot and forward deals. There is also a nontrivial dollar amount of trading done in listed futures contracts on a few of the major exchange rates, although the survey estimate is that they account for only 1% of total volume.

---

[8] Bank for International Settlements, "Survey of Foreign Exchange Market Activity," Basle, 1993.

Foreign exchange is traded by a wide international network of dealers, most of whom are commercial banks and investment banking firms. London, New York, and Tokyo are the three largest centers for foreign exchange, by respective volume of trading. But dealing institutions are located in many other cities throughout Asia, Europe, and America. The center of trading rotates around the globe throughout the day. New Zealand and Australia open the day in what is known as the Austral-Asian trading time zone. Six A.M. Sydney time is the official start of the foreign exchange day. Japan, Hong Kong, and Singapore join in a few hours later. Next, the center moves to the European trading time zone. Trading takes place mainly in London but Zurich, Frankfurt, and Paris are also important along with many other European cities. In the American trading time zone, New York dominates but Chicago, Los Angeles, Toronto, and Montreal are also sizable participants. Finally, trading for the day closes at five o'clock in the afternoon New York time.

Spot and forward exchange are traded in an over-the-counter market where money center banks act as the dealers. Usually, a bank is on the "other side" of every trade. Foreign exchange is a dealer's market. By definition, a dealer is a principal party who "makes a market" — that is, provides two-way quotes, both bid and offer, on foreign exchange in meaningful size (which is usually a minimum of $10 million worth of currency). As a principal, the dealer buys and sells for his own account (called his "book") by taking the other side of trades. When a counterparty buys, the dealer sells and when counterparty sells, the dealer buys.

The spot exchange rate is a quote for the exchange of two currencies in two business days (except in the case of the Canadian dollar versus the U.S. dollar, where delivery is in one business day). The spot rate is normally given as a bid-ask quotation. For example, a quote on the Japanese yen of 150.00/10 means that a dealer is willing to sell yen for dollars at 150.00 yen per dollar or buy yen for dollars at the rate of 150.10 yen per dollar. Unfortunately, two conventions for the quotation of spot and forward rates have evolved. In the American convention, currency is quoted in terms of U.S. dollars per unit of foreign exchange (i.e., one British pound equals $1.50). The British pound, Australian dollar, New Zealand dollar, and ECU are quoted American. All the other currencies are quoted European, which means as the number of units of foreign currency equal to one dollar (i.e., 150 yen per one U.S. dollar or 1.70 German marks per one U.S. dollar).

FORWARD FOREIGN EXCHANGE TRANSACTIONS

The forward exchange rate is a quote for settlement (or "value") at a more distant date in the future than spot settlement. A forward rate can be negotiated for any settlement date, but indications are usually given for one month, three months, six months, or one year in the future. Forward transactions are the workhorse of foreign exchange hedging.

The forward exchange rate, also called the outright, is sometimes quoted in two parts, one being the spot bid or ask, and the other part called the forward points. Forward points are either added or subtracted from the spot rate to arrive at the forward exchange rate. For example, if the forward points on yen for settlement in one year are quoted −2.97/−2.95, the outright would be 147.03/147.15, using 150.00/10 as the spot rate. Note that the negative sign indicates that the forward points should be subtracted from the spot bid or ask.

Forward points originate from a well know relationship called the interest parity theorem which links the forward exchange rate and interest rates. The basic concept is that the market sets the forward rate in relation to spot in order to absorb the interest rate differential between two currencies (known as the interest rate spread). This is a "no free lunch" idea: You cannot hop between currencies, picking up yield advantage, and lock up a guaranteed profit by using the forward market. The forward rate acts as the "spoiler."

For example, suppose that a U.S. dollar-based investor were attracted by a substantial yield spread offered by the British pound over the U.S. dollar. If the investor were to convert dollars to pounds for the purpose of investing in high yielding sterling paper, there would be no guarantee of any yield pick up because the future level of the spot exchange rate is unknown — that is, the rate at which the investor would later have to exchange pounds back into dollars. The future spot might be higher than the initial spot, in which case the investor would make an even greater profit; or lower than the initial spot, in which case some or all of the yield differential would be lost. In fact, if the spot exchange rate were to fall by a great enough amount, the investment might even suffer a negative return in dollars, meaning that the exchange rate loss had been greater than the interest earned on the pounds.

The exchange rate risk could be hedged by selling the future value of the pounds versus the dollar in the forward market. But at what forward rate? If there were a 500 basis point spread between pound and dollar 1-year interest rates and if the spot exchange rate were $1.80 per pound, then the only 1-year forward rate that would make economic sense would be $1.72. At any other rate, riskless arbitrage would be possible. To see this, take the example of $100.00. This converts to 55.56 British pounds at the spot rate. This sum invested at say 13% would become 62.78 pounds in one year. Comparing this to the alternative of keeping the funds in dollars, say at 8%, and compounding to $108 after one year, we see that the forward rate must be

$$\frac{108.00\,USD}{62.78\,GBP} = 1.7200\,USD/GBP$$

The interest parity theorem tells portfolio managers that they must "pay" to hedge currencies that have interest rates above the home country currency. Likewise, investors receive value for hedging currencies that have lower interest rates than the home country currency.

CURRENCY OPTIONS

Foreign exchange risk management programs sometimes use currency options together with or in place of forward foreign exchange contracts.

The foreign exchange option market is the second largest option market. Only the option market for fixed income securities and their derivatives is thought to be larger. The largest portion of the currency option market is the inter-bank market. But there are also listed, meaning exchange traded, currency options. The Philadelphia Stock Exchange lists options on actual foreign currency. The Chicago Mercantile Exchange's International Monetary Market lists options on currency futures, which are referred to as futures options.

Currency options are either calls or puts. A currency call is the right but not the obligation to buy a sum of foreign currency at a fixed exchange rate, called the strike, on or before the option's expiration date. A put is an option to sell a sum of foreign exchange. Take the example of a dollar-mark call struck at 1.5400 on a face amount of ten million dollars. This option grants the right but not the obligation to buy 10 million dollars against 15.4 million marks. It is a call on dollars but it is also a put on marks. To minimize the chance of what could be a costly misunderstanding, the convention is to mention both currencies, tagging each with a call or a put identifier. The correct and unambiguous name for the option is "dollar-call/mark put." European style exercise options can be exercised only on the exercise date but American style options can be exercised at any time before or on expiration date.

The inter-bank currency option market trades 24 hours per day right along side spot and forward foreign exchange. All of the top-tier foreign exchange dealers make markets in currency options for their customers and for other dealing institutions. Most of the trading is done in options on the major currencies but practically any exchange rate can be traded as an option. The majority of trading is done in European exercise calls and puts. There is also a brisk and rapidly growing interest in exotic currency options, meaning options with non-standard features, such as knock-outs, average rate options, and compound options.

THE BASICS OF FOREIGN EXCHANGE HEDGING

This section concerns some of the basic hedging techniques that are applied by investment portfolio managers. Hedging programs attempt to immunize an exposure to currency movements, up or down. Hedging programs can be bilateral, where there is exposure to a single foreign currency, or multicurrency (also called multilateral), where there are exposures to several foreign currencies. Bilateral hedges can be implemented with forward contracts or with currency futures. Multicurrency hedges are more complicated. One version, called a matched hedge, calls for each foreign currency to be bilaterally hedged on a stand-alone basis.

Many times, especially in international portfolio management, there are exposures to 10, 20, or even more currencies. This is where an alternative to the matched hedge, called the *basket hedge*, becomes economical. The basket consists of three or four major currencies that are held in proportions designed to closely track the exposure to the greater number of currencies.

Another topic for discussion will be proxy hedging, a tool of active currency management which involves hedging an exposure to one exchange rate by taking a position in another exchange rate. This method has proved to be effective at times — but in other instances has been disappointing, if not outright disastrous.

BILATERAL HEDGING WITH FORWARD CURRENCY FORWARDS

International equity and fixed income portfolio managers use forwards as part of their currency hedging strategies. Take the example of a manager who is long one billion yen worth of Japanese equities and who is concerned that the value of the yen might deteriorate over the next two months. A direct step would be to sell one billion yen forward for two months against dollars. This hedging transaction is called an "opening transaction." At a two month outright equal to 84.25, the trade would consist of a commitment to deliver one billion yen in two months and receive dollars in the amount equal to $11,869,436.20 since

$$\frac{1\ billion\ JPY}{84.25} = \$11,869,436.20$$

Forward contracts generate no cash flow before their value date.

The portfolio manager must make some decisions once the forward hedge is in place. Since portfolio hedgers rarely enter into forward contracts intending to make delivery of currencies, the hedge must be closed or rolled prior to settlement. A forward hedge can be closed anytime before the forward value date by means of a closing transaction. This is accomplished by reversing the original hedge with a second transaction that has the same original value date as does the opening transaction. In the example, the hedge might be closed one month later, day 30, by buying one billion yen for settlement on day 60. The new forward rate would be a 1-month rate because only one month would now remain until day 60. Suppose that the spot rate now is 84.00/10 and that the forward points are −26/−25. The outright for value in 30 days would be 83.74/85. The closing transaction would be a purchase of one billion yen against 11,926,058.44 dollars at a rate of 83.85. If the opening and closing trades were done with two different banks, they would have to be settled in the usual way: to settle the opening trade, the portfolio manager must deliver one billion yen to the first bank and receive dollars on day 60; to settle the second trade, the portfolio manger must receive one billion yen from the second bank and receive dollars on day 60. However, the portfolio manager might be permitted to take net settlement in cases where both the opening and closing transactions have been done with the same bank. In the example, the net loss on the hedge is $56,622.24:

	Dollars	Yen
Opening Trade 84.25	$11,869,436.20	(1,000,000,000)
Closing Trade 83.85	($11,926,058.44)	1,000,000,000
	($56,622.24)	0

Under net settlement, this amount would have to be wired directly to the portfolio manager's dealer counterparty on day 60 to complete settlement of both the opening and closing trades.

On the other hand, the portfolio manager might wish to keep the yen hedge in place indefinitely. In a technique called *rolling forwards*, the manager would do a spot transaction on day 58 to take care of the original forward transaction that settles on day 60 plus simultaneously re-establish the hedge with a new two month forward trade. Gains or losses would be settled each time the hedge is rolled.

The time when the hedge is rolled is an ideal moment to re-scale the currency hedge to match any movement in the size of the underlying securities portfolio. The size of the portfolio naturally expands and contracts with movements in the prices in the securities markets. Correctly matching the size of the hedge to the value of the portfolio can be difficult. To the extent that the size of the hedge and the size of the portfolio drift apart, the residual overhang represents a naked bet on an exchange rate. For this reason, risk managers are apt to re-scale the size of the currency hedging program anytime that there has been a large move in the underlying markets.

The choice of the term of the forward contracts used to hedge currency risk is a decision with subtle implications. Most hedgers automatically elect for 1- or 3-month forward contracts without considering the consequences. In fact, the term decision is actually a bet on the interest rate spread between the two currencies. Depending on how much the spread moves, a 6-month hedge, for example, might do better or worse than a pair of consecutive 3-month hedges. If the spread does not change in the course of the hedging program, the choice of the forward terms can be shown to have been irrelevant. But if the spread does change, the hedger may wish after the fact to have chosen a longer or shorter term forward.

HEDGING WITH CURRENCY OPTIONS

Currency options are trickier to use in hedging programs than are forwards but they offer greater flexibility. The straightforward advantage to option hedging is that the risk management objectives can be achieved at a fixed premium cost without sacrificing the entire upside gains from currency appreciation if the foreign currency value of the portfolio appreciates. The disadvantage is that options fluctuate in price — sometimes they are cheap and at other times expensive.

The basic hedge is to buy a home currency call/foreign currency put. The face value of the option is set to match the size of the currency exposure in the underlying securities portfolio. In most cases, the option is struck at the market level forward outright.

Option hedgers face some of the same problems that exist for forward hedgers The term decision is even more complex because it involves not only the spread between interest rates but also the term structure of option implied volatility. The scaling problem is identical to what faces forward hedgers. Here too there is no magic answer to how the size of the option hedge can be kept in order to match the value of the underlying securities portfolio.[9]

HEDGING MULTICURRENCY EXPOSURE

The previous section considered hedging a single foreign currency exposure using forward contracts. The discussion now turns to the management of not one but multiple foreign currency exposures, a situation that is more relevant to international portfolio managers. One popular benchmark index is the FT-Actuaries World index for international equities. Because benchmark indices are capitalization-weighted, concentration is developed in a handful of the major markets and currencies. This fact naturally leads to an application of portfolio theory and quadratic programming called *basket hedging*.

Matched Hedging

Matched hedging is a simple idea: maintain a separate bilateral hedge for each currency exposure. This certainly works well in the case where the portfolio is exposed only to a small number of currencies. But if the number of currencies is large, a match hedge probably is not efficient. A large number of separate hedges can be cumbersome to manage, and opening a closing forward contracts on minor currencies can be expensive. Matched hedging is mentioned here to show how a sledge hammer can be used to open the currency hedging nut. It is meant to increase appreciation for basket hedging.

Basket Hedging

Basket hedging is an important tool in currency risk management. Two, three, or four major currencies, usually, the dollar, the mark, sterling, and the yen are combined to make a basket that tracks the currency exposure of the entire portfolio. The latter is usually referred to as the *index*. The objective is to minimize the forecast tracking error which is defined as the difference between the currency return on the index and the basket.

---

[9] An exotic currency option called a "quantos option" solves the problem in that it features a floating face value that is linked to the foreign currency value of the portfolio.

Exhibit 3: Basket Hedge for FT-Actuaries World Index Ex-USA, as of March 31, 1995

BARRA World Markets Model (5.0a). Database March 1995, Market Prices April 12, 1995
Index (As of December 30, 1994)

Country	Percentage
Australia	2.43%
Austria	0.22%
Belgium	1.10%
Canada	2.51%
Denmark	0.58%
Finland	0.48%
France	5.59%
Germany	5.74%
Hong Kong	2.79%
Ireland	0.25%
Italy	2.25%
Japan	46.48%
Malaysia	1.70%
Mexico	0.87%
Netherlands	3.07%
New Zealand	0.32%
Norway	0.18%
Singapore	0.96%
Spain	1.55%
Sweden	1.45%
Switzerland	3.81%
Thailand	0.35%
U.K.	15.31%
Total	99.99%

Basket

Currency	Raw Weight	Scaling	Adjusted Weight	Spot	Forward Points	Outright	Give-up Pick-up
GBP/USD	31.17%	0.9926	30.94%	0.6289	0.0047	0.6336	−0.74%
USD/DEM	16.39%	0.9926	16.27%	1.4040	−0.0218	1.3822	1.58%
USD/JPY	52.44%	0.9926	52.05%	83.77	−4.03	79.74	5.05%
Total	100.00%		99.26%		Weighted Average		2.68%

Estimated Tracking Error: 1.044%

The goal is to produce a set of weightings for two, three, or four currencies to make a basket that tracks the portfolio's currency exposure as close as possible. It is assumed that the expected rates of return on all currencies are zero and that the problem is to minimize the variance of the tracking error between the basket and the portfolio's currency exposure (i.e., the index).

Exhibit 3 shows the basket hedge for a U.S. dollar-based investor's perspective for the FT-Actuaries World non-USA Index. The basket is composed of sterling, marks, and yen. The basket was constructed using the BARRA World

Markets Model™. The FT-Actuaries World Index non-USA basket hedge is concentrated in yen which should be expected given the weight that Japan has in the index. The projected tracking error is 1.044% (annualized). In constructing the actual basket hedge, the three currencies are sold forward one year against dollar. Two of these currencies, marks, and yen happened to be at premium to the dollar on April 12, 1995 when this exhibit was constructed. The result is that the basket hedge has a net forward pickup equal to 2.68% (annualized). Of course, if the basket currencies were at discount to the dollar, there would be a yield give-up instead of a pickup.

Basket hedging is not without its limitations. Basket hedging optimization depends on an assumed correlation matrix and a set of standard deviations; these are the Achilles heel of basket hedging. If the correlation matrix is accurate as well as stable, optimization will produce a good basket hedge. This is more likely when the portfolio is dominated by exposures to the currencies of the larger, more stable economies. Otherwise, if the portfolio is heavily invested in unstable countries with rapidly changing economic environments, the correlation matrix is not likely to be at all indicative of the future currency interrelationships. Basket hedging might be quite off the mark.

Implementation of a basket hedge can be accomplished using either forward contracts or currency options.

PROXY HEDGING

Proxy hedging refers to a technique wherein a short position in a stable, low interest rate currency is employed to hedge an exposure to a high interest rate currency. Inter-bank dealers and proprietary traders have used proxy hedging strategies for some time. To take an example, suppose that a dollar/Swiss dealer is long dollars and short Swiss. One strategy would be to sell the position immediately in the inter-bank market. But conditions might not be opportune at that moment to make a sale. An alternative is to sell dollar/mark in the full dollar amount of the position. This would leave the trader approximately hedged with a net long position in the relatively stable mark/Swiss cross exchange rate.

Proxy hedging is fundamentally different from any of the hedging that has been discussed. In reality, it is a form of active currency management. Where the idea of proxy hedging proved disastrous was in the two Exchange Rate Mechanism (ERM) crises of September 1992 and August 1993. A substantial market position had developed in what came to be known as the "convergence play." This assumed that interest rates among the European Monetary System currencies would converge with exchange rates enjoying the protection of the ERM. When the ERM failed, the ensuing flight to marks obliterated any apparent but illusory yield advantage to holding the high interest rate currencies.

CONCLUSIONS

The decision about whether and how to hedge foreign exchange risk should be viewed as an integral part of the investment management process. A variety of views have be expressed about what investors should do about currency exposure — but no one conclusive course of action dominates. Nonetheless, a variety of hedging programs are available, some that use currency forwards and others that use currency options.

Chapter 6

Investment Management for Taxable Investors

David M. Stein, Ph.D.
Managing Director
Parametric Portfolio Associates

James P. Garland, CFA
President
The Jeffrey Company

INTRODUCTION

Much of the practice of investment management has evolved to suit the needs of tax-exempt institutional pension funds. There is an increasing realization, however, that many of the paradigms suitable for tax-exempt investing need to be modified for taxable investing.

Taxes matter a great deal. Taxes represent a very large performance drag, often larger than transaction costs, management fees, or inflation. The popular sentiment is that investors should not allow their investment decisions to be dominated by tax considerations. While it is true that tax considerations should not *dominate* investment decisions, tax considerations do significantly *influence* investment returns, and investors would be well advised to consider taxes in their investment decisions. Failing to do so can be expensive, particularly if investors allow taxes to erode their returns over the long term.

Taxes complicate decision-making in many ways. Here are a few key examples:

1. *Asset allocation*, one of the most important investment decisions, is complicated not only by the particular tax rates that investors face, but also by their investment horizons and by the unrealized appreciation in their portfolios.
2. There are *many different tax rates*, even for the same type of taxable investor. Federal rates differ for long-term capital gains, for short-term capital gains, and for dividend income. Many states tax gains and dividends as well. For most taxable investors the tax rate on dividends is much higher

93

than on capital gains, yet for some the opposite is true. Tax laws are complex and change frequently. This makes tax-sensitive investing more difficult.

3. In the presence of taxes, *portfolio valuation* becomes a more complex subject. The value of a taxable portfolio depends in large part on what happens to it in the future. The calculation of returns is difficult and idiosyncratic, and is dependent not only on tax rates but also on the sequence of cash flows into and out of the portfolio. A good manager before taxes can become a poor one after taxes. Finally, there is no single benchmark or even set of benchmarks that apply to all taxable investors.

4. Taxes affect the *investment strategy* chosen. Many indexed strategies are very attractive to taxable investors because they naturally have low turnover. Taxes complicate both the search for superior returns and the task of rebalancing portfolios.

5. Taxes affect the choice of *investment vehicle*. Many commingled vehicles, which are attractive to tax-exempt investors because of their returns to scale, are unattractive to taxable investors. Separate accounts provide customized and flexible tax management.

6. Taxes change the *risk characteristics* of portfolios, insofar as risk is a function of the portfolios' return volatility.

In this chapter we shall discuss some of these issues in greater depth. We shall focus primarily on portfolios of publicly traded *equities,* but shall address other investment topics as well.

Taxes are a liability, intricately connected to the investment asset. We take the position that this liability is best managed in co-ordination with the asset. To deal successfully with taxes, managers must change their tax-exempt investment processes. Managers who understand after-tax performance measurement will naturally prefer certain investment styles (e.g., relatively passive approaches). Clever tax management methods can enhance after-tax returns.

INVESTMENT DECISIONS IN THE PRESENCE OF TAXES

Types of Taxes

We shall discuss three broad classes of taxes in this chapter: the taxation of capital gains, dividends, and estates.

Taxes on Capital Gains

Capital gains taxes are incurred whenever securities are sold. The tax rate depends on the holding time and generally decreases with age. Current Federal tax rates on realized capital gains vary widely, e.g., from as little as 10% (for individuals with little other income) to as much as 35% (for corporations) or roughly 40% (for individuals with short-term gains and significant other income). Most states tax realized capital gains as well.

From the portfolio managers' point of view, capital gains taxes are a hurdle that they must overcome to justify trading a security. When considering the sale of a security, managers must compute the tax due and evaluate whether the benefit of selling the security would warrant the realization of the gain. Often the answer will be no. Investment managers should be particularly cautious about realizing short-term gains if the tax rate on short-term gains is much higher than that on long-term gains. In most situations investors have the option not to realize unrealized gains. Deferring gain realization is one of the easiest and most direct ways to improve after-tax performance.

Taxes on Dividends

Individual investors generally pay taxes on dividends at the same rate as ordinary income, often twice the rate of capital gains. Reducing the dividend component of investment returns can thereby increase these investors' after-tax returns — as long, of course, as aggregate total returns are not reduced by such an effort. The common way to accomplish this is by investing in a portfolio of "growth" stocks with low dividend yields, rather than "value" stocks with high dividend yields.

Corporations pay a lower tax on dividends, due to the so-called Dividends Received Deduction,[1] than they do on realized capital gains. This encourages corporations to seek investments whose returns are tilted in favor of dividends rather than capital gains. There is no free lunch, however. Carrying out a successful, tax-efficient, higher-yield investment strategy can be both difficult and risky.

Taxes on Estates

Estate taxes themselves are beyond the scope of this chapter, but note that these taxes have important consequences for individual investors. Investors' estates pay no capital gains taxes. Their securities' costs are stepped up to their market values at the valuation date used in the estate appraisal (generally the date of death).[2] This fact has the effect of giving elderly and terminally ill investors a life insurance policy for their appreciated securities. The policy pays off when those investors die,

---

[1] The United States taxes dividends twice, once as part of a corporation's pre-tax profits, and a second time when that profit is distributed to shareholders. In one situation it is even possible for dividends to be taxed three times. Suppose Corporation A owns shares of Corporation B. Corporation B earns a profit and pays a tax. It then pays a dividend to Corporation A, which pays a second tax. Corporation A then pays a dividend to its shareholders, who pay a third tax. To reduce this tax burden slightly, Congress allows Corporation A to exclude 70% of the dividends it receives from its taxable income. The Dividends Received Deduction reduces the tax rate on the dividends paid by Corporation B and received by Corporation A to 10.5% (30% times 35%).

[2] While it may seem odd that living investors pay capital gains taxes while dead ones do not, we have heard that this is because Congress has long had a policy of taxing an event only once. Apparently even Congress balks at applying *both* estate taxes and capital gains taxes upon an investor's death.

but disappears if they sell their stocks beforehand.[3] This option-like feature complicates investment decisions by making it worthwhile to continue to hold appreciated securities even when their long-term outlook may be unattractive.

After-Tax Performance Measurement

The Association for Investment Management and Research (AIMR) has promulgated a set of standards for measuring investment returns. The second edition of those standards[4] presents a method for measuring after-tax returns. These standards were designed primarily for investment managers' use when presenting historical returns to potential clients. Nevertheless, the standards provide a useful starting point for calculating and evaluating individual portfolio returns.

The basic formula is:

$$\text{After-tax return} = [\text{Realized gains} \times (1 - \text{Capital gains tax rate})$$
$$+ \text{Increase in unrealized gains} + \text{Taxable income}$$
$$\times (1 - \text{Income tax rate})$$
$$+ \text{Tax free income}]/\text{Starting asset value}$$

The standards use simplifying assumptions such as the absence of state taxes and a uniform (maximum) Federal tax rate for all clients. They also provide guidelines for adjusting returns for client-ordered withdrawals.

Managers' aggregate after-tax return data have a somewhat limited utility. Individual taxable investors' performance is idiosyncratic. Well managed, tax-efficient portfolios within a single firm will necessarily have different holdings with different cost bases. The firm's clients may have significant differences in their income and capital gains tax rates. Unlike the case for tax-exempt managers, where a low dispersion in returns is desirable, a tax sensitive manager who treats each client individually will have a relatively high dispersion of returns.

After-Tax Performance Evaluation

Performance measurement requires measuring the change in value of a portfolio from one period to the next. In calculating after-tax returns, the AIMR standard (and industry practice) is to deduct taxes paid on dividends and on *realized* capital gains. Morningstar measures the tax efficiency of mutual funds in this same manner. This gives an incomplete picture. What is missing is an attempt to evaluate the *unpaid* tax liability.

Stein discusses the question of portfolio valuation in depth and provides a more accurate and generally more useful method of measuring current value.[5] Two simple estimates of portfolio value are:

---

[3] James P. Garland, "Taxable Portfolios: Value and Performance," *Journal of Portfolio Management* (Winter 1987).

[4] See the *AIMR Performance Presentation Standards Handbook*.

[5] D.M. Stein, "Measuring and Evaluating Portfolio Performance After Taxes," *Journal of Portfolio Management* (Winter 1998).

Exhibit 1: Equations for Determining the Cost Basis and Market Value of the Portfolio Over Time

Let us assume an investment horizon of N periods at which point the portfolio will be liquidated and any unrealized taxes will be paid. Under assumptions on return (r), dividend rate (d), dividend tax rate (t_d), capital gains tax rate (t_g), and the rate at which gains are realized (g), we can compute the final after-tax value of the portfolio. Let V_I and C_I be the market value and cost basis respectively of the portfolio at the start of period I. Then taxes are due on dividends dV_I at the end of the period, and the capital gain realized is $g[(1 + r - d)V_I - C_I]$. Dividends and capital gains are re-invested, and taxes paid from the portfolio. For simplicity we allow capital losses, and credit the portfolio with the value of the tax saving. Then, at the start of period $I + 1$,

$$C_{I+1} = C_I + (1 - t_d)dV_I + g(1 - t_g)[(1 + r - d)V_I - C_I]$$

$$V_{I+1} = (1 + r)V_I - t_d dV_I - t_g g[(1 + r - d)V_I - C_I]$$

The final liquidation value after N periods is $V_N - t_g(V_N - C_N)$

The two difference equations provide the cost basis and market value of the portfolio at each stage in time.

Market value (V_m): Market value is used by AIMR, Morningstar, and the industry in general. This overstates true value. At any time a security is sold for a gain and taxes paid, V_m will be reduced.

Liquidation value (V_l): At the other extreme, consider if we were to liquidate the portfolio immediately at the tax rate t_g.[6] This understates true value for investors with no desire to liquidate. If we define the cost basis as V_c, then the liquidation value V_l is:

$$V_l = V_m - t_g(V_m - V_c)$$

Both of these valuations are limited because they over-simplify the tax liability. If the portfolio remains invested into the future, we need to be more precise. Exhibit 1 shows two difference equations that can be used to compute the cost basis and market value of the portfolio over time.

Consider an example. Assuming an initial market value of $100 and cost basis $50, let the portfolio evolve over 20 years. Assume also an annual price appreciation of 7%, a dividend rate of 3%, an annual capital gain realization rate of 5%, and a tax rate on dividends of 40% and capital gains of 20%. Exhibit 2 shows how this investment will evolve over time.

This computation now allows us a more careful evaluation of the tax liability. To value the portfolio currently, we ask the following question. What current cash value will result in terminal wealth equal to the liquidation value ($437.34) under the same investment assumptions? We term this the *full cost equivalent* (FCE) *value* of the portfolio. If $V_c < V_m$, the FCE value lies between the market value and liquidation value. It turns out that the FCE value is $95.7 for this example.

---

[6] For simplicity here, t_g is the tax rate on both long- and short-term capital gains.

Exhibit 2: Evolution of a Portfolio over 20 Years

Assumptions:

Initial market value	= $100	Annual capital gain realization rate	=	5%
Cost basis	= $50	Tax rate on dividend	=	40%
Annual price approach	= 7%	Capital gains tax rate	=	20%
Dividend rate	= 3%			

	Year				
	1	2	3	...	20
Starting market value	$100.00	$108.23	$117.14		$449.24
Starting cost basis	50.00	54.08	58.50		223.50
Ending market value, before taxes & dividends	107.00	115.81	125.34		480.69
Dividends	3.00	3.25	3.51		13.48
Gain (unrealized)	57.00	61.73	66.84		257.19
Realized gain	2.85	3.09	3.34		12.86
Taxes paid	1.77	1.92	2.07		7.96
Reinvestment	4.08	4.42	4.78		18.37
Ending cost basis	54.08	58.50	63.28		241.87
Ending value	108.23	117.14	126.78		486.20
Liquidation value					437.34

This valuation depends on the following parameters:

- the investment horizon
- the final disposition of the assets (some investors receive a step-up in tax basis on a bequest to heirs)
- future tax rates
- future returns — both capital appreciation and dividends (through investment returns on unrealized taxes)
- the rate at which capital gains will be realized over the period

Stein shows that the FCE valuation V_f can be written as:[7]

$$V_f = V_m - f\, t_g (V_m - V_c) \tag{1}$$

or

$$V_f = (1 - f)V_m + fV_1 \tag{2}$$

for some value of f, $0 \le f \le 1$. Comparing with the definition of liquidation value V_l, equation (1) allows us to think of the FCE value as a liquidation value, but with the modified tax rate $f t_g$ the factor f adjusts the actual tax rate downwards. Equation (2) allows us to think of V_f as a weighted average of the market value V_m and the liquidation value V_l. For the numeric example in Exhibit 2, f is equal to 0.43.

---

[7] Stein, "Measuring and Evaluating Portfolio Performance After Taxes."

A simple method for portfolio valuation, then, is to compute a liquidation value of the portfolio, but to use as the tax rate on capital gains a fraction f of the true tax rate. The value of the fraction depends on the investor, the horizon, tax rates, return expectation, and gain realization rate. Or, one can similarly compute a weighted average of the liquidation value and market value, where f is the weight of the liquidation value.

Performance Benchmarking

In evaluating portfolio performance, the benchmark is key. It would be misleading to compare after-tax returns from a portfolio with pre-tax returns from a benchmark; consequently, the benchmark must be taxed as well. However, only a few firms publish after-tax benchmark returns.

For a portfolio that starts not from cash but from a pre-existing set of appreciated holdings, one useful benchmark would be the unchanged initial portfolio, held into the future. A good manager must provide additional after-tax value to this base case.[8]

On the other hand, starting with cash, an ideal benchmark would be an indexed portfolio with cash flows identical to those of the portfolio. Investment flows affect both portfolio performance and benchmark performance since taxes depend on the cost basis at which the securities were acquired.

Stein determines the historical after-tax return of an S&P 500 indexed portfolio by computer simulation and explores the effect of the start date on after-tax return.[9] These simulations are complex, but simplifications can be made. For example, one can treat an investment in the S&P 500 as a single security and, using the actual S&P 500 turnover level each month, apply the difference equations shown in Exhibit 1 to estimate how the cost basis and value of the benchmark change over time. A further simplification can be made, if necessary, by applying a uniform annual turnover rate to the benchmark index. Jeffrey and Arnott[10] and Dickson and Shoven,[11] for instance, found that turnover of the S&P 500 during the 1980s averaged around 3% per year. In any case, the after-tax returns of the benchmark index depend upon the basis of the securities in the index and therefore on the starting date of the analysis. For example, the after-tax benchmark returns for the S&P 500 during 1996 would be different (and lower) for an investor who began investing in 1990 than for one who began investing in 1996.

After-Tax Risk

One of the basic goals of investment management is to control risk by diversification. Here we define risk as the volatility of return or as the "tracking error" from

---

[8] The authors are indebted to Keith Ambachtsheer and Jean L. P. Brunel for this insight.

[9] Stein, "Measuring and Evaluating Portfolio Performance After Taxes."

[10] Robert H. Jeffrey and Robert D. Arnott, "Is Your Alpha Big Enough To Pay Its Taxes?" *Journal of Portfolio Management* (Spring 1993), pp 15-25.

[11] J.M. Dickson and J.B. Shoven, "A Stock Index Mutual Fund Without Net Capital Gains Realizations," *National Bureau of Economic Research*, Working Paper No. 4717 (1994).

a benchmark.[12] The presence of taxes changes the nature of risk. Let us consider a few aspects of this premise.

With respect to diversification, a common pragmatic concern is the following: how much is it worth paying now (because of the immediate taxation of capital gains) in order to diversify a portfolio of low-basis holdings? Once again, there is no easy answer, and the solution depends on the expected horizon, the expected return of the proposed assets, the expected return of the existing assets, the tax rate, and risk tolerance of the investor. However, thoughtful tradeoffs based on analysis as in Exhibit 1 can provide useful insight.

Tax-exempt investors often monitor the tracking error of their portfolios with respect to their benchmarks. The typical concern is the risk that the active manager takes relative to a broadly diversified benchmark in seeking the active return. Taxable investors concerned with this issue need to specify the base against which the tracking error is to be measured. A pre-tax benchmark is inappropriate if it requires a taxable turnover. In practice, it is often worthwhile to incur tracking error risk relative to a pre-tax benchmark if this reduces taxes.

To illustrate that the nature of risk changes in the presence of taxes, let us work through a simple model. Consider two stocks, A and B, with the same expected return but different degrees of volatility as shown in Exhibit 3. At time t_0, we have two stocks each with a purchase price of $1. Each stock has two, equally likely, pre-tax return outcomes at time t_1 and the expected return for each stock is 10%. However, stock A has less volatility than stock B.

To simplify further, assume that subsequent to time t_1, the two stocks behave the same, each with a return of 10% per year for 20 years. After this, the investment will be liquidated. We assume a tax rate of 20% on capital gains and 40% on dividends. We also assume that the investor has external capital gains at time t_1, and there are no capital loss limitations (i.e., the investor can productively exploit any losses).

Exhibit 3: Illustration of the Nature of Risk Changes in the Presence of Taxes

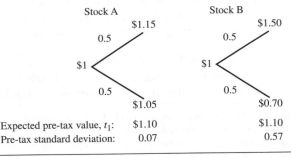

	Stock A	Stock B
Expected pre-tax value, t_1:	$1.10	$1.10
Pre-tax standard deviation:	0.07	0.57

---

[12] Richard C. Grinold and Ronald N. Kahn, *Active Portfolio Management* (Homewood, IL: Richard D. Irwin, Inc., 1995).

Using our FCE value above, our parameters define the f value at time t_1 as 0.43 and we use this to determine the value of each stock at t_1. If stock A rises to $1.15 at t_1, its FCE value is $1.137. If stock A rises to value $1.05, its FCE value is $1.046. Stock A therefore has an expected FCE value at period 1 of $1.09. The after-tax risk, measured by the standard deviation of return at 0.06, is lower than the pre-tax risk.

Similarly, consider stock B. If stock B rises to $1.50 at t_1, its FCE value at t_1 is $1.457. If, however, stock B falls to value $0.70 we can realize a loss, and obtain a tax saving. The value is $0.70 + (0.2)(0.3) = $0.76. Stock B therefore has an expected FCE value at t_1 of $1.11. The after-tax risk is 0.49.

Note that stock B, with higher volatility, has a higher after-tax expected return because of the way in which losses are realized. In addition, the nature of risk is asymmetrical. While losses are never desirable, losses that do occur can be exploited to the investor's advantage, and the degree of loss can be alleviated. As a result, taxable investors should be more willing than tax-exempt investors to endure high-volatility pre-tax returns.[13]

After-Tax Asset Allocation

After-tax asset allocation is a particularly complex subject that has received minimal industry attention. While some publications have addressed aspects of the topic, we know of no truly pragmatic and general work. We consider a detailed discussion of the subject beyond the scope of this chapter.

Perhaps the simplest initial way of addressing after-tax asset allocation is to pursue a mean-variance study, but to adjust the returns for taxes. The first basic observation is that tax-free bonds have an important place in a portfolio.[14]

But, harder issues remain. Given an initial starting portfolio, its cost basis is critical, and will affect decisions. Brunel discusses this subject briefly, and presents a conceptually difficult three-dimensional efficient frontier, where the third dimension is the portfolio's cost basis.[15] The practical choice of an operating solution is not easy. In general, the investment horizon and expected turnover within the component asset classes will affect the decision.

Once an allocation has been made, the issue of re-balancing appears. While recommendations are often made to keep the allocation tightly within bounds, doing this now comes at a tax cost. Some have suggested that the re-balancing trigger points must be wider for taxable investors.

---

[13] This phenomenon is essentially a result of the optionality of capital gains taxes. The investor has the option of choosing when to realize his capital gains. This option has a value, and is more valuable when the underlying security has higher volatility. The risk and return profile of an option is asymmetrical. (See George M. Constantinides, "Optimal Stock Trading with Personal Taxes," *Journal of Financial Economics* (1984), pp. 65-89.)

[14] J.P. Meecham, D. Foo, and H.G. Fong, "Taxable Asset Allocation with Varying Market Risk Premiums," *Journal of Portfolio Management* (Fall 1995), pp 79-87

[15] Jean L.P. Brunel, "The Upside-Down World of Tax-Aware Investing," *Trusts & Estates* (February 1997), pp. 34-42.

The implementation of an asset allocation strategy is different in the presence of taxes. It is now inefficient to use derivative securities to gain *underlying* exposure to the asset classes. Any appreciation of a futures contract (for example) is taxed each year, 40% at the short-term rate and 60% at the long-term rate. If one wishes to pursue a strategy of tactical allocation, taxes are due on any gains realized. Jeffrey and Arnott make the point that an efficient way to implement a tactical strategy is to let the base portfolio accumulate its unrealized gains as long as possible, and to re-balance with a futures *overlay*.[16]

Individual investors have the ability to accumulate tax-deferred (e.g., 401K) savings accounts. While these are powerful tax-saving tools, issues arise as to how to construct a balanced total portfolio with sensible choices on where the different asset classes reside, and where the active strategies are pursued. For example, a tax-efficient approach is to invest a core passive equity portfolio in the taxable component, and to pursue very aggressive active decision-making in the tax-free component. The liquidation of tax-free savings accounts comes with a substantial tax penalty as gains are taxed at income tax rates.

This subject is in its infancy.

Investment Vehicle

An important issue that taxable investors face is whether to use a separate account or a commingled account as the vehicle for investing in equities. Separate accounts offer particular advantages and commingled vehicles suffer disadvantages for the taxable investor.

Separate accounts offer the best opportunity to manage capital gains taxes. Maintaining records of individual tax lots can be used to substantial advantage. An investor has additional flexibility with respect to the ultimate disposition of the assets, and can select which assets to bequeath to his heirs and which to donate to a charitable remainder trust.

Commingling also offers some advantages. Indeed, some tax-managed indexed mutual funds are attractive investment options for many people.[17] The costs for commingled accounts are generally lower than for separate accounts. A more subtle advantage is that commingled accounts may have fewer problems with diversification. The cash flows — both in and out of the account — can be directed towards diversification. Many tax-sensitive separate accounts develop a handful of concentrated, highly appreciated holdings after many years.

On the other hand, commingled accounts present several problems. One is that investors who join a commingled fund may be buying shares or units of a pool whose average basis is lower than its current market value. Taxes will ultimately have to be paid on this liability. Ironically, this problem is worse for low-turnover funds.

---

[16] Jeffrey and Arnott, "Is your Alpha Big Enough to Pay Its Taxes?"

[17] James P. Garland, "The Advantage of Tax Managed Index Funds," *Journal of Investing* (Spring 1997), pp13-20.

The major problem with commingled funds is more severe. It is possible for one investor to receive a tax liability that was caused by another investor's action. In fact, it is possible for the same realized gain to create two tax liabilities.

We can explain this most easily with an example. Suppose investor A and investor B each invest $100 in a new mutual fund, of which they are the only shareholders. Their $200 investment doubles to $400. Investor A decides to liquidate his holding. The manager sells half of the fund to produce $200 cash for investor A, and this sale triggers a $100 realized capital gain within the fund. At the end of the year, the fund manager will declare a $100 capital gain distribution, which will be taxable to the only remaining shareholder, investor B. Thus, at the end of the year, the total realized gain, in the eyes of the IRS, will be the following:

Investor A: $100 in realized capital gain
Investor B: $100 in capital gains distributions

Investor A's withdrawal creates a tax liability for investor B, and the total tax liability is for $200 of realized gains, double the fund's actual realization.[18]

While this example is extreme, the problem is real. Investors do not eliminate it by avoiding the purchase of mutual funds shares just preceding the year-end capital gains distributions. The problem is a perennial one. Investors in commingled funds can experience tax liabilities that in a rational world would belong to other investors.

PORTFOLIO MANAGEMENT SOLUTIONS

Taxes complicate investment decision-making. Portfolio managers who understand the effect of taxes on performance will be driven in the direction of certain investment styles. Additionally, careful tax management can enhance after-tax returns. While this is a complex subject, it has received little formal attention in the literature.

Taxable portfolio managers need to put in place portfolios that they will be comfortable with for a long time. Ideally, such portfolios will be broadly diversified and will realize capital gains at an extremely low rate. The managers may want to tilt their portfolios to suit the tax situations of their clients: individual investors may prefer capital appreciation to dividend yield, while corporations may prefer dividend yield. The portfolio must also outperform a suitable after-tax benchmark.

The Power of Passive Investing

We first focus on capital gains. Taxes on turnover are effectively a transaction cost. Jeffrey and Arnott[19] show that long-term benefits accrue to managers

---

[18] This story can become even more extreme if investor B wishes to receive his capital gains distribution in cash. In this case, the manager will need to liquidate the entire fund's holdings.

[19] Jeffrey and Arnott, "Is your Alpha Big Enough to Pay Its Taxes?"

who can reduce the realization rate to the lowest levels possible.[20] This benefit derives essentially from the reinvestment of the deferred tax liability, and implies a very passive approach, with very few gains realized each year.[21]

This is not as hard as it sounds. A capitalization-weighted indexed portfolio[22] is a suitable starting point because it needs action only when index constituents change or when dividends are to be reinvested. If there are no constituent changes and no corporate actions, a portfolio that is indexed at the start will still be indexed in the future, independent of the movement of the constituent stock prices.

In most developed markets an indexed portfolio has the added benefits of being extremely well diversified and of having median pre-tax performance. It is close to "efficient" in the sense that it is the consensus expectation of a large number of market participants.

While a passive indexed portfolio is hard to beat for tax-exempt investors, it is even more powerful for taxable investors. One way of seeing this is to evaluate the "hurdle" that an active portfolio manager must overcome before taxes in order to justify realizing capital gains. Using the difference equations in Exhibit 1 and under simple assumptions, we evaluate this hurdle in Exhibit 4.

A number of studies (Jeffrey and Arnott, Dickson and Shoven) have explored the after-tax performance of populations of mutual funds.[23] All have concluded that indexed portfolios are consistently superior performers after taxes and fees. With an average turnover rate of over 70% a year, there are very few managers who are able to deliver the consistent pre-tax excess return required by Exhibit 4.

Exhibit 4: Pre-Tax Hurdle (Alpha, Percent) as a Function of Market Return and Rate of Realization of Capital Gains

Market Return	Rate of realization of capital gains										
	5%	10%	20%	30%	40%	50%	60%	70%	80%	90%	100%
8%	0.5	0.6	0.8	1.0	1.2	1.4	1.6	1.8	2.0	2.3	2.5
10%	0.5	0.7	1.0	1.3	1.6	1.8	2.1	2.5	2.8	3.1	3.5
12%	0.5	0.7	1.1	1.5	1.9	2.3	2.7	3.1	3.6	4.0	4.5

Assumptions: 10% total return per year, of which 5% is dividends; liquidation after 20 years; tax rates are 40% on dividends and short term (less than 1 year) capital gains, 20% on long term capital gains; at turnover (gain realization) rate of $T\%$, a fraction $(1-T)$ is short-term gain and T is long term gain. We also assume an additional 50bp management fee for the active portfolio.

[20] Reducing the rate of gain realization each year from, say, 70% to 30% does not provide much value. The real benefits accrue at very low rates, those below 10%.

[21] The term "passive" has two common investment meanings. First, a passive portfolio remains fixed, does not buy and sell securities, and realizes gains only when withdrawals are made. In a second meaning, a passive portfolio is one that does not engage in "active" stock selection to try and beat the benchmark. Efficient tax management requires passive in the first sense. Portfolios that are indexed to a cap-weighted benchmark are passive in the second sense as well.

[22] For example, the S&P 500 or the Frank Russell Company's Russell 3000.

[23] See, for example, Jeffrey and Arnott, "Is Your Alpha Big Enough to Pay Its Taxes?" and J.M. Dickson and J.B. Shoven, "Ranking Mutual Funds on an After-Tax Basis," *Center for Economic Policy Research*, Publication No, 344, Stanford University, 1993.

Taxation of Dividends

For individual investors, the dividend tax rate is higher than the capital gains tax rate. Individual investors would therefore prefer return in the form of long-term capital appreciation rather than as dividend income.

If the portfolio has a very high turnover rate, then capital gains are taxed at the short-term rate as well, and there is no preference for low dividend yield. At the other extreme, if turnover is low, then the taxation of dividends becomes very important. In this latter case, if dividends are taxed at the 40% rate, then reducing the dividend rate from 4% to 2% (while keeping total return constant) can improve after-tax return by up to 0.8% per year.

For most individual investors, a tilt towards a "growth" style, with a lower dividend yield, is then preferable. One cost of adopting a growth stock strategy is a reduction of diversification and increased risk relative to the market as a whole. Style indexes are common (e.g., Russell and S&P/Barra Value and Growth indexes), but these have relatively high annual turnover rates of 15%-20% per year. Investing in portfolios that are indexed to these styles is not always a good idea. For taxable investors, an alternative passive definition of style, one with lower turnover, would be more suitable.

Conversely, most tax-exempt and corporate investors prefer a "value" style. Some researchers have argued in the absence of taxes that value stocks, with a higher dividend yield, outperform growth stocks over the long run.[24] But, note that "value" stock investing may generate more turnover due to the less stable nature of some of their businesses and therefore realize higher capital gains.

Active Tax Management

Investment managers can enhance after-tax performance with careful tax management. Dickson and Shoven[25] discuss the benefits of tax lot accounting and show that these are substantial.

Some simple methods of loss management work well.[26] In diversified portfolios, losses on individual holdings typically occur, even when the portfolio as a whole does very well. Such losses have value to the investor if they are realized immediately. A portfolio manager who acts as "Maxwell's Demon,"[27] realizing losses when they occur and letting gains ride, can obtain a non-trivial after-tax advantage for the investor.[28]

Whenever the portfolio is rebalanced or optimized, taxes must be considered. There is typically a tradeoff between risk (i.e., tracking error) and the realization of capital gains. For indexed taxable investors, it is often beneficial to hold

---

[24] J. Lakonishok, A. Schleifer, and R.W. Vishny, "Contrarian Investment, Extrapolation and Risk," *Journal of Finance* (December 1994), pp. 1541-1578.

[25] Dickson and Shoven, "Ranking Mutual Funds on an After-Tax Basis."

[26] N.L. Jacob, "Tax-Efficient Investing: Reduce the Tax Drag, Improve Asset Growth," *Trusts & Estates* (May 1995), pp. 25-33.

[27] In thermodynamics, an idealized demon of Maxwell opens a trap door between two chambers of air, separating low-energy molecules from high-energy molecules, and so creates an efficient engine.

[28] Stein, D.M., "The value of active tax management," in preparation.

onto securities that leave the index if selling them would realize a capital gain. This will result in a tracking difference from the index.

Active Stock Selection

The challenge for tax-sensitive active equity managers is to find securities that they will be willing to hold for extremely long periods of time. They need to be extremely confident about their stock selections. Apelfeld, Fowler, and Gordon[29] discuss the challenges of active equity management. They make two strong points. First, a tax sensitive optimization process is important, with the risk/return impact of each trade carefully evaluated. Second, their value-based strategies tend to perform better over the long haul than their momentum-based strategies.

The most difficult challenges to active portfolio management appear after portfolios have been in place for many years and some securities have accrued large unrealized gains. At this time it is necessary to "refresh" the portfolio, but the tax cost of doing so is very high. To exchange existing securities for others that are expected to outperform over the long haul is extremely difficult. This need to refresh a portfolio can be delayed by diversification.

Active portfolio management is a complex subject. The community of active portfolio managers must still prove its mettle in an appropriately measured taxable world.

CONCLUSION

Tax-exempt investors are used to thinking of equity investing in two key dimensions, those of risk (volatility) and return. In this chapter, however, we have argued that taxable investors face many more issues. The additional dimensions of taxable investing include portfolio cost-basis, investment horizon, and turnover. These additional dimensions influence portfolio valuation, benchmarks, asset allocation, tactical decisions, and the investment vehicle.

The practice and theory of taxable investing is immature. Most of the citations in this chapter are recent. While the industry has identified many problems, some of which we have discussed here, solutions are still far from complete.

Taxes must be an important consideration for investors. The bad news is that taxable investing is both idiosyncratic and difficult. Investment managers are only slowly integrating tax sensitivity into their investment processes. The good news is that investors, investment managers, and the academic community are becoming increasingly aware of the burden of taxes and the benefits to managing them. With this increased interest will come increased tax sensitivity and eventually improved after-tax returns. While tax-sensitive investing offers intellectual challenges, it also offers that most basic of tangible rewards — more money in one's pocket. It is an effort worth pursuing.

---

[29] Roberto Apelfeld, Gordon B. Fowler Jr., and James P. Gordon Jr., "Tax-Aware Equity Investing," *Journal of Portfolio Management* (Winter 1996), pp. 18-27.

Section II:

Equity Portfolio Management

Chapter 7

Investment Management: An Architecture for the Equity Market

Bruce I. Jacobs, Ph.D.
Principal
Jacobs Levy Equity Management

Kenneth N. Levy, CFA
Principal
Jacobs Levy Equity Management

INTRODUCTION

Anyone who has ever built a house knows how important it is to start out with a sound architectural design. A sound design can help ensure that the end product will meet all the homeowner's expectations — material, aesthetic, and financial. A bad architectural design, or no design, offers no such assurance and is likely to lead to poor decision-making, unintended results, and cost overruns.

It is equally important in building an equity portfolio to start out with some framework that relates the raw materials — stocks — and the basic construction techniques — investment approaches — to the end product. An architecture of equity management that outlines the basic relationships between the raw investment material, investment approaches, potential rewards and possible risks, can provide a blueprint for investment decision-making.

We provide such a blueprint in this chapter. A quick tour of this blueprint reveals three building blocks — a comprehensive core, static style subsets, and a dynamic entity. Investment approaches can also be roughly categorized into three groups — passive, traditional active, and engineered active. Understanding the market's architecture and the advantages and disadvantages of each investment approach can improve overall investment results.

The authors thank Judith Kimball for her editorial assistance.

Exhibit 1: Equity Market Architecture

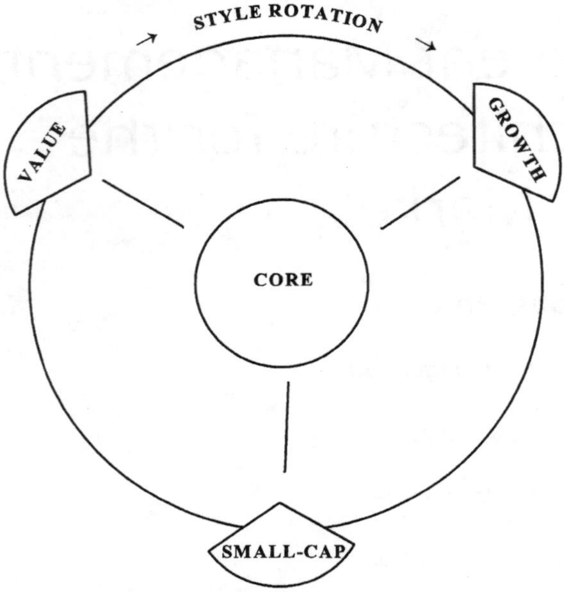

AN ARCHITECTURE

Exhibit 1 provides a simple but fairly comprehensive view of the equity market.[1] The heart of the structure, the core, represents the overall market. Theoretically, this would include all U.S. equity issues. (Similar architectures can be applied to other national equity markets.) In line with the practice of most equity managers, a broad-based equity index such as the S&P 500 or (even broader) the Russell 3000 or Wilshire 5000, may proxy for the aggregate market.

For both equity managers and their clients, the overall market represents a natural and intuitive starting place. It is the ultimate selection pool for all equity strategies. Furthermore, the long-term returns offered by the U.S. equity market have historically outperformed alternative asset classes in the majority of multi-year periods. The aim of most institutional investors (even those that do not hold core investments per se) is to capture, or outdo, this equity return premium.

The core equity market can be broken down into subsets that comprise stocks with similar price behaviors — large-cap growth, large-cap value, and small-cap stocks. In Exhibit 1, the wedges circling the core represent these style subsets. The aggregate of the stocks forming the subsets equals the overall core market.

---

[1] See also Bruce I. Jacobs and Kenneth N. Levy, "How to Build a Better Equity Portfolio," *Pension Management* (June 1996), pp. 36-39.

Exhibit 2: Small-Cap Stocks May Outperform Large-Cap in Some Periods and Underperform in Others

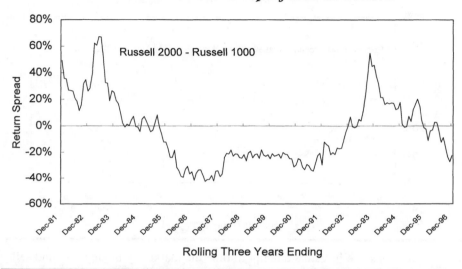

One advantage of viewing the market as a collection of subsets is the ability it confers upon the investor to "mix and match." Instead of holding a core portfolio, for example, the investor can hold market subsets in market-like weights and receive returns and incur risks commensurate with those of the core. Alternatively, the investor can depart from core weights to pursue returns in excess of the core market return (at the expense, of course, of incremental risk). Investors who believe that small-cap stocks offer a higher return than the average market return, for example, can overweight that subset and underweight large-cap value and growth stocks.

Over time, different style subsets can offer differing relative payoffs as economic conditions change. As Exhibit 2 shows, small-cap stocks outperformed large-cap stocks by 60 percentage points or more in the rolling 3-year periods ending in mid-1983 and by 45 to 55 percentage points in late 1993. But small cap underperformed by 20 to 40 percentage points in the rolling 3-year periods between early 1986 and December 1991.[2] Exhibit 3 shows that large-cap growth stocks outperformed large-cap value stocks by 30 to 40 percentage points in the rolling 3-year periods from mid-1991 to mid-1992 but underperformed by 20 to 35 percentage points in every rolling 3-year period from mid-1983 through 1986.[3]

---

[2] Exhibit 2 uses the Frank Russell 1000 (the largest stocks in the Russell 3000) as the large-cap index and the Russell 2000 (the smallest stocks in the Russell 3000) as the small-cap index.

[3] Exhibit 3 uses the Russell 1000 Growth and the Russell 1000 Value as the growth and value indexes; these indexes roughly divide the market capitalization of the Russell 1000. Results are similar using other indexes, such as the Wilshire and S&P 500/BARRA style indexes.

Exhibit 3: Large-Cap Growth Stocks Outperform Large-Cap Value in Some Periods and Underperform in Others

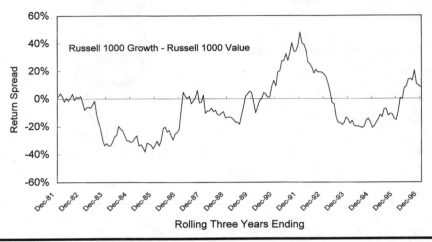

Just as some investors attempt to time the market by buying into and selling out of equities in line with their expectations of overall market trends, investors can attempt to exploit the dynamism of style subsets by rotating their investments across different styles over time, in pursuit of profit opportunities offered by one or another subset as market and economic conditions change.[4] The curved lines connecting the style wedges in Exhibit 1 represent this dynamic nature of the market.

The equity core and its constituent style subsets constitute the basic building blocks — the equity selection universes — from which investors can construct their portfolios. Another important choice facing the investor, however, is the investment approach or approaches to apply to the selection universe. Exhibit 4 categorizes possible approaches into three groups — traditional, passive, and engineered. Each of these approaches can be characterized by an underlying investment philosophy and, very generally, by a level of risk relative to the underlying selection universe.

TRADITIONAL ACTIVE MANAGEMENT

Traditional investment managers focus on "stock picking." In short, they hunt for individual securities that will perform well over the investment horizon. The search includes in-depth examinations of companies' financial statements and investigations of companies' managements, product lines, facilities, etc. Based on the findings of these inquiries, traditional managers determine whether a particular firm is a good "buy" or a better "sell."

---

[4] See Bruce I. Jacobs and Kenneth N. Levy, "High-Definition Style Rotation," *Journal of Investing* (Fall 1996), pp. 14-23.

Exhibit 4: Equity Investment Approaches

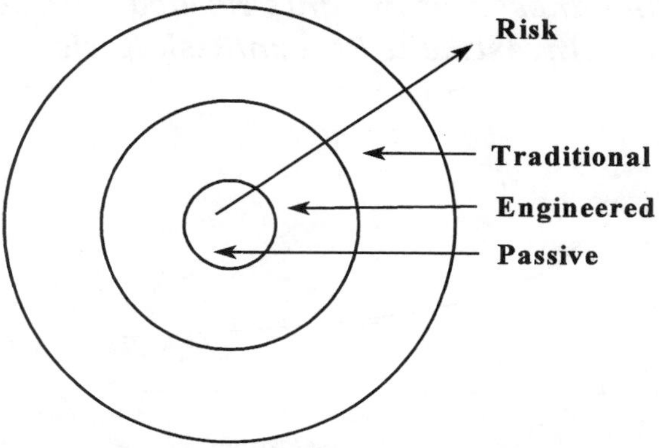

Risk

Traditional

Engineered

Passive

The search area for traditional investing may be wide — the equivalent of the equity core — and may include market timing that exploits the dynamism of the overall market. Because in-depth analyses of large numbers of securities are just not practical for any one manager, however, traditional managers tend to focus on subsets of the equity market. Some may hunt for above-average earnings growth (growth stocks), while others look to buy future earnings streams cheaply (value stocks); still others beat the grasses off the trodden paths, in search of overlooked growth and/or value stocks (small-cap stocks). Traditional managers have thus fallen into the pursuit of growth, value, or small-cap styles.

Traditional managers often screen an initial universe of stocks based on some financial criteria, thereby selecting a relatively small list of stocks to be followed closely. Focusing on such a narrow list reduces the complexity of the analytical problem to human (i.e., traditional) dimensions. Unfortunately, it may also introduce significant barriers to superior performance.

Exhibit 5 plots the combinations of breadth and depth of insights necessary to achieve a given investment return/risk level.[5] Here the breadth of insights may be understood as the number of independent insights — i.e., the number of investment ideas or the number of stocks. The depth, or goodness, of insights is measured as the *information coefficient* — the correlation between the return forecasts made for stocks and their actual returns. Note that the goodness of the insights needed to produce the given return/risk ratio starts to increase dramatically as the number of insights falls below 100; the slope gets particularly steep as breadth falls below 50.

---

[5] The plot reflects the relationship:

$$IR = IC \times \sqrt{BR}$$

where *IC* is the information coefficient (the correlation between predicted and actual returns), *BR* the number of independent insights, and IR (in this case set equal to one) the ratio of annualized excess return to annualized residual risk. See Richard C. Grinold and Ronald N. Kahn, *Active Portfolio Management* (Chicago, IL: Probus Publishing, 1995), Chapter 6.

Exhibit 5: Combination of Breadth (Number) of Insights and Depth, or "Goodness," of Insights Needed to Produce a Given Investment Return/Risk Ratio

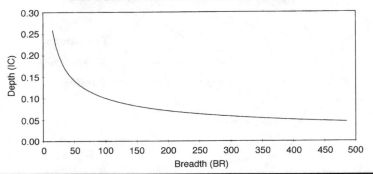

Traditional investing in effect relies on the ability of in-depth research to supply information coefficients that are high enough to overcome the lack of breadth imposed by the approach's fairly severe limitations on the number of securities that can be followed. As Exhibit 5 shows, however, the level of information coefficients required at such constricted breadth levels constitutes a considerable hurdle to superior performance. The insights from traditional management must be very, very good to overcome the commensurate lack of breadth.[6]

Furthermore, lack of breadth may also have detrimental effects on the depth of traditional insights. While reducing the range of inquiry makes tractable the problem of stock selection via the labor-intensive methods of traditional active management, it is also bound to result in potentially relevant (and profitable) information being left out. Surely, for example, the behavior of the growth stocks not followed by traditional growth managers — even the behavior of value stocks outside the growth subset — may contain information relevant to the pricing of those stocks that do constitute the reduced traditional universe.

Another inherent weakness of traditional investment approaches is their heavy reliance on subjective human judgments. An ever-growing body of research suggests that stock prices, as well as being moved by fundamental information, are influenced by the psychology of investors. In particular, investors often appear to be under the influence of cognitive biases that cause them to err systematically in making investment decisions.[7]

---

[6] Market timing strategies are particularly lacking in breadth, as an insight into the market's direction provides only one investment decision. Quarterly timing would produce four "bets" a year — a level of diversification few investors would find acceptable. Furthermore, unless timing is done on a daily basis or the timer is prodigiously skilled, it would take a lifetime to determine whether the results of timing reflect genuine skill or mere chance.

[7] See, for example, Daniel Kahneman and Amos Tversky, "Prospect Theory: An Analysis of Decision Under Risk," *Econometrica* (Number 2, 1979), pp. 263-292, and Richard H. Thaler (ed.), *Advances in Behavioral Finance* (New York, NY: Russell Sage Foundation, 1993).

Kenneth Arrow, for example, finds that investors tend to overemphasize new information if it appears to be representative of a possible future event; thus, if investors perceive a firm's management to be "good," and the firm has recently enjoyed high earnings, they will tend to place more reliance on the higher than the lower earnings estimates provided by analysts.[8] Robert Shiller finds that investors are as susceptible as any other consumers to fads and fashions — bidding up prices of "hot" stocks and ignoring out-of-favor issues.[9] We describe below four common cognitive errors that investors may fall prey to.

Cognitive Errors
Loss Aversion (The "Better Not Take the Chance/ What the Heck" Paradox)

Investors exhibit risk-averse behavior with respect to potential gains: faced with a choice between (1) a sure gain of $3,000 and (2) an 80% chance of gaining $4,000 or a 20% chance of gaining nothing, most people choose the sure thing, even though the $3,000 is less than the expected value of the gamble, which is $3,200 (80% of $4,000). But investors are generally risk-seeking when it comes to avoiding certain loss: faced with a choice between (1) a sure loss of $3,000 and (2) an 80% chance of losing $4,000 or a 20% chance of losing nothing, most people will opt to take a chance. It's only human nature that the pain of loss exceed the glee of gain, but putting human nature in charge of investment decision-making may lead to suboptimal results. Shirking risk leads to forgone gains. Pursuing risk in avoidance of loss may have even direr consequences ("digging a deeper hole"), as recent episodes at Barings and Daiwa have demonstrated.

Endowment Effect (The "Pride in Ownership" Syndrome)

The price people are willing to pay to acquire an object or service is often less than the price they would be willing to sell the identical object or service for if they owned it. Say you bought a stock last year and it's quadrupled in price. If you won't buy more because "it's too expensive now," you should sell it. If you won't sell it because you were so brilliant when you bought it, you're sacrificing returns for pride in ownership.

The Gambler's Fallacy ("Hot Streaks, Empty Wallets")

Is it more likely that six tosses of a coin will come up HTTHTH or HHHTTT? Most people think the former sequence is more typical than the latter, but in truth both are equally likely products of randomness. In either case, the probability of the next flip of the coin turning up heads, or tails, is 50%. Market prices, too, will display patterns. It's easy to interpret such patterns as persistent trends, and tempt-

---

[8] Kenneth J. Arrow, "Risk Perception in Psychology and Economics," *Economic Inquiry* (Number 1, 1982), pp. 1-8.

[9] Robert J. Shiller, "Stock Prices and Social Dynamics," *Brookings Papers on Economic Activity* (Number 2, 1984), pp. 457-510.

ing to trade on them. But if the latest "hot streak" is merely a mirage thrown up by random price movements, it will prove an unreliable guide to future performance.

Confirmation Bias ("Don't Confuse Me with the Facts")

People search for and place more reliance upon evidence that confirms their preconceived notions, ignoring or devaluing evidence that refutes them. Four cards lie on a table, showing A, B, 2, and 3: What is the fewest number of cards you can turn over to confirm or refute that every card with a vowel on one side has an even number on the other side? Most people choose A, then 2. An odd number or a letter on the reverse of A would refute the conjecture. The 2, however, can merely confirm, not refute; the presence of a vowel on the reverse would confirm, but anything else would simply be immaterial. The correct choice is to turn A, 3, and B. A vowel on the reverse of 3 can refute, as can a vowel on the reverse of B. Investment approaches that do not have a method of systematically searching through all available evidence without prejudice, in order to find the exceptions that disprove their rules, may leave portfolios open to blindsiding and torpedo effects.

Investors susceptible to these biases will tend to take too little (or too much) risk; to hold on to an investment for too long; to see long-term trends where none exist; and to place too much reliance on information that confirms existing beliefs. As a result, the performances of their portfolios are likely to suffer.

The reliance of traditional investment management on the judgments of individual human minds makes for idiosyncrasies of habit that work to the detriment of investment discipline, and this is true at the level of the investment firm as well as the individual at the firm. It may be difficult to coordinate the individual mindsets of all analysts, economists, investment officers, technicians, and traders, and this coordination is even harder to achieve when subjective standards for security analysis differ from individual to individual.

Constructing Portfolios

The qualitative nature of the outcome of the security evaluation process, together with the absence of a unifying framework, can give rise to problems when individual insights into securities' performances are combined to construct a portfolio. However on target an analyst's buy or sell recommendations may be, they are difficult to translate into guidelines for portfolio construction. Portfolio optimization procedures require quantitative estimates of relevant parameters — not mere recommendations to buy, hold, or sell.

The traditional manager's focus on stock picking and the resulting ad hoc nature of portfolio construction can lead to portfolios that are poorly defined in regard to their underlying selection universes. While any particular manager's portfolio return may be measured against the return on an index representative of an underlying equity core or style subset, that index does not serve as a "benchmark" in the sense of providing a guideline for portfolio risk. Traditional portfolios' risk-return profiles may thus vary greatly relative to those of the underlying selection universe.

As a result, portfolios do not necessarily fit into the market's architecture. A traditional value manager, for example, may be averse to holding certain sectors, such as utilities. Not only will the portfolio's returns suffer when utilities perform well, but the portfolio will suffer from a lack of "integrity" — of wholeness. Such a portfolio will not be representative of the whole value subset. Nor could it be combined with growth and small-cap portfolios to create a core-like holding.

Because the relationship between the overall equity market and traditional managers' style portfolios may be ambiguous, "value" and "growth," "small-cap" and "large-cap" may not be mutually exclusive. Value portfolios may hold some growth stocks, or growth portfolios some value stocks. There is no assurance that a combination of style portfolios can offer a market-like or above-market return at market-like risk levels.

Because of their heavy reliance on human mind power and subjective judgment, traditional approaches to investment management tend to suffer from a lack of breadth, a lack of discipline, and a resulting lack of portfolio integrity. Traditional management, while it may serve as well as any other approach for picking individual stocks, suffers from severe limitations when it comes to constructing portfolios of stocks. Perhaps it is for this reason that traditionally managed portfolios have often failed to live up to expectations.

PASSIVE MANAGEMENT

The generally poor performance of traditional investment management approaches helped to motivate the development, in the late 1960s and the 1970s, of new theories of stock price behavior. The efficient market hypothesis and random walk theory — the products of much research — offered a reason for the meager returns reaped by traditional investment managers: stock prices effectively reflect all information in an "efficient" manner, rendering stock price movements random and unpredictable. Efficiency and randomness provided the motivation for passive investment management; advances in computing power provided the means.

Passive management aims to construct portfolios that will match the risk/return profiles of underlying market benchmarks. The benchmark may be core equity (as proxied by the S&P 500 or other broad index) or a style subset (as proxied by a large-cap growth, large-cap value, or small-cap index). Given the quantitative tools at its disposal, passive management can fine-tune the stock selection and portfolio construction problems in order to deliver portfolios that mimic very closely both the returns and risks of their chosen benchmarks.

Passive portfolios, unlike traditional portfolios, are disciplined. Any tendencies for passive managers to succumb to cognitive biases will be held in check by the exigencies of their stated goals — tracking the performances of their underlying benchmarks. Their success in this endeavor also means that the resulting portfolios will have integrity. A passive value portfolio will behave like its underlying selection universe, and a combination of passive style portfolios in market-like weights can be expected to offer a return close to the market's return at a risk level close to the market's.

As the trading required to keep portfolios in line with underlying indexes is generally less than that required to "beat" the indexes, transaction costs for passive management are generally lower than those incurred by active investment approaches. As much of the stock selection and portfolio construction problem can be relegated to fast-acting computers, the management fees for passive management are also modest. For the same reason, the number of securities that can be covered by any given passive manager is virtually unlimited; all the stocks in the selection universe can be considered for portfolio inclusion.

Unlike traditional management, then, passive management offers great breadth. Breadth in this case doesn't count for much, however, because passive management is essentially insightless. Built on the premise that markets are efficient, hence market prices are random and unpredictable, passive management does not attempt to pursue or offer any return over the return on the relevant benchmark. Rather, its appeal lies in its ability to deliver the asset class return or to deliver the return of a style subset of the asset class. In practice, of course, trading costs and management fees, however modest, subtract from this performance.

An investor in pursuit of above-market returns may nevertheless be able to exploit passive management approaches via style subset selection and style rotation. That is, an investor who believes value stocks will outperform the overall market can choose to overweight a passive value portfolio in expectation of earning above-market (but not above-benchmark) returns. An investor with foresight into style performance can choose to rotate investments across different passive style portfolios as underlying economic and market conditions change.

ENGINEERED MANAGEMENT

Engineered management recognizes that markets are reasonably efficient in digesting information and that stock price movements in response to unanticipated news are largely random. It also recognizes, however, that significant, measurable pricing inefficiencies do exist, and it seeks to deliver incremental returns by modeling and exploiting these inefficiencies. In this endeavor, it applies to the same company fundamental and economic data used by traditional active management many of the tools that fostered the development of passive management, including modern computing power, finance theory, and statistical techniques — instruments that can extend the reaches (and discipline the vagaries) of the human mind.

Engineered approaches use quantitative methods to select stocks and construct portfolios that will have risk/return profiles similar to those of underlying equity benchmarks but offer incremental returns relative to those benchmarks, at appropriate incremental risk levels. The quantitative methods used may range from fairly straightforward to immensely intricate. In selecting stocks, for example, an engineered approach may use something as simple as a dividend discount model. Or it may employ complex multivariate models that aim to capture the complexities of the equity market.[10]

The engineered selection process can deal with and benefit from as wide a selection universe as passive management. It can thus approach the investment problem with an unbiased philosophy, unhampered, as is traditional management, by the need to reduce the equity universe to a tractable subset. At the same time, depending upon the level of sophistication of the tools it chooses to use, engineered management can benefit from great depth of analysis — a depth similar to that of traditional approaches. Multivariate modeling, for example, can take into account the intricacies of stock price behavior, including variations in price responses across stocks of different industries, economic sectors, and styles.

Because engineered management affords both breadth and depth, the manager can choose a focal point from which to frame the equity market, without loss of important "framing" information. Analysis of a particular style subset, for example, can take advantage of information gleaned from the whole universe of securities, not just stocks of that particular style (or a subset of that style, as in traditional management). The increased breadth of inquiry should lead to improvements in portfolio performance vis-a-vis traditional style portfolios.

Engineering Portfolios

Engineered management utilizes all the information found relevant from an objective examination of the broad equity universe to arrive at numerical estimates for the expected returns and anticipated risks of the stocks in that universe. Unlike the subjective outcomes of traditional management, such numerical estimates are eminently suitable for portfolio construction via optimization techniques.[11]

The goal of optimization is to maximize portfolio return while tying portfolio risk to that of the underlying benchmark. The portfolio's systematic risk should match the risk of the benchmark. The portfolio's residual risk should be no more than is justified by the expected incremental return. Risk control can be further refined by tailoring the optimization model so that it is consistent with the variables in the return estimation process.

The quantitative nature of the stock selection and portfolio construction processes imposes discipline on engineered portfolios. With individual stocks defined by expected performance parameters, and portfolios optimized along those parameters to provide desired patterns of expected risk and return, engineered portfolios can be defined in terms of preset performance goals. Engineered managers have little leeway to stray from these performance mandates, hence are

---

[10] See Bruce I. Jacobs and Kenneth N. Levy, "Investment Analysis: Profiting from a Complex Equity Market," Chapter 2 in this book.

[11] See also Bruce I. Jacobs and Kenneth N. Levy, "Engineering Portfolios: A Unified Approach," *Journal of Investing* (Winter 1995).

less likely than traditional managers to fall under the sway of cognitive errors. In fact, engineered strategies may be designed to exploit such biases as investor overreaction (leading to price reversals) or investor herding (leading to price trends).

The discipline of engineered management also helps to ensure portfolio integrity. The style subset portfolios of a given firm, for example, should be non-overlapping, and the style subset benchmarks should in the aggregate be inclusive of all stocks in the investor's universe. Value portfolios should contain no growth stocks, nor growth portfolios any value stocks. The underlying benchmarks for value and growth portfolios, or large and small-cap portfolios, should aggregate to the equity core.

Engineering should reduce, relative to traditional management, portfolio return deviations from the underlying core or subset benchmark, while increasing expected returns relative to those available from passive approaches. While judicious stock selection can provide excess portfolio return over a passive benchmark, optimized portfolio construction offers control of portfolio risk.

Exhibit 6 compares the relative merits of traditional, passive, and engineered approaches to portfolio management. Traditional management offers depth, but strikes out with lack of breadth, susceptibility to cognitive errors, and lack of portfolio integrity. Passive management offers breadth, freedom from cognitive error, and portfolio integrity, but no depth whatsoever. Only engineered management has the ability to construct portfolios that benefit from both breadth and depth of analysis, are free of cognitive errors, and have structural integrity.

MEETING CLIENT NEEDS

A broad-based, engineered approach offers investment managers the means to tailor portfolios for a wide variety of client needs. Consider, for example, a client that has no opinion about style subset performance, but believes that the equity market will continue to offer its average historical premium over alternative cash and bond investments. This client may choose to hold the market in the form of an engineered core portfolio that can deliver the all-important equity market premium (at the market's risk level), plus the potential for some incremental return consistent with the residual risk incurred.

Exhibit 6: Comparison of Equity Investment Approaches

	Traditional	Passive	Engineered
Depth of Analysis	Yes	No	Simple — No Complex — Yes
Breadth of Analysis	No	Yes	Yes
Free of Cognitive Error	No	Yes	Yes
Portfolio Integrity	No	Yes	Yes

Alternatively, the client with a strong belief that value stocks will outperform can choose from among several engineered solutions. An engineered portfolio can be designed to deliver a value-benchmark-like return at a comparable risk level or to offer, at the cost of incremental risk, a return increment above the value benchmark. Traditional value portfolios cannot be designed to offer the same level of assurance of meeting these goals.

With engineered portfolios, the client also has the ability to fine-tune bets. For example, the client can weight a portfolio toward value stocks while retaining exposure to the overall market by placing some portion of the portfolio in core equity and the remainder in a value portfolio, or by placing some percentage in a growth portfolio and a larger percentage in a value portfolio. Exposures to the market and to its various subsets can be engineered. Again, traditional management can offer no assurance that a combination of style portfolios will offer the desired risk-return profile.

Expanding Opportunities

The advantages of an engineered approach are perhaps best exploited by strategies that are not constrained to deliver a benchmark-like performance. An engineered style rotation strategy, for example, seeks to deliver returns in excess of the market's by forecasting style subset performance. Shifting investment weights aggressively among various style subsets as market and economic conditions evolve, style rotation takes advantage of the historical tendency of any given style to outperform the overall market in some periods and to underperform it in others. Such a strategy uses the entire selection universe and offers potentially high returns at commensurate risk levels.

Allowing short sales as an adjunct to an engineered strategy — whether that strategy utilizes core equity, a style subset, or style rotation — can further enhance return opportunities. While traditional management focuses on stock picking — the selection of "winning" securities — the breadth of engineered management allows for the consideration of "losers" as well as "winners." With an engineered portfolio that allows shorting of losers, the manager can pursue potential mispricings without constraint, going long underpriced stocks and selling short overpriced stocks.

In markets in which short selling is not widespread, there are reasons to believe that shorting stocks can offer more opportunity than buying stocks. This is because restrictions on short selling do not permit investor pessimism to be as fully represented in prices as investor optimism. In such a market, the potential candidates for short sale may be less efficiently priced, hence offer greater return potential, than the potential candidates for purchase.[12]

Even if all stocks are efficiently priced, however, shorting can enhance performance by eliminating constraints on the implementation of investment

---

[12] See, for example, Bruce I. Jacobs and Kenneth N. Levy, "20 Myths About Long-Short," *Financial Analysts Journal* (September/October 1996).

insights. Consider, for example, that a security with a median market capitalization has a weighting of approximately 0.01% of the market's capitalization. A manager that cannot short can underweight such a security by, at most, 0.01% relative to the market; this is achieved by not holding the security at all. Those who do not consider this unduly restrictive should consider that placing a like constraint on the maximum portfolio overweight would be equivalent to saying the manager could hold, at most, a 0.02% position in the stock, no matter how appetizing its expected return. Shorting allows the manager free rein in translating the insights gained from the stock selection process into portfolio performance.

Long-Short Portfolios

If security returns are symmetrically distributed about the underlying market return, there will be fully as many unattractive securities for short sale as there are attractive securities for purchase. Using optimization techniques, the manager can construct a portfolio that balances equal dollar amounts and equal systematic risks long and short. Such a long-short balance neutralizes the risk (and return) of the underlying market. The portfolio's return — which can be measured as the spread between the long and short returns — is solely reflective of the manager's skill at stock selection.[13]

Not only does such a long-short portfolio neutralize underlying market risk, it offers improved control of residual risk relative even to an engineered long-only portfolio. For example, the long-only portfolio can control risk relative to the underlying benchmark only by converging toward the weightings of the benchmark's stocks; these weights constrain portfolio composition. Balancing securities' sensitivities long and short, however, eliminates risk relative to the underlying benchmark; benchmark weights are thus not constraining. Furthermore, the long-short portfolio can use offsetting long and short positions to fine-tune the portfolio's residual risk.

In addition to enhanced return and improved risk control, an engineered long-short approach also offers clients added flexibility in asset allocation. A simple long-short portfolio, for example, offers a return from security selection on top of a cash return (the interest received on the proceeds from the short sales). However, the long-short manager can also offer, or the client initiate, a long-short portfolio combined with a position in derivatives such as stock index futures. Such an "equitized" portfolio will offer the long-short portfolio's security selection return on top of the equity market return provided by the futures position; choice of other available derivatives can provide the return from security selection in combination with exposure to other asset classes. The transportability of the long-short portfolio's return offers clients the ability to take advantage of a manager's security selection skills while determining independently the plan's asset allocation mix.

---

[13] See Bruce I. Jacobs and Kenneth N. Levy, "The Long and Short on Long-Short," *Journal of Investing* (Spring 1997), pp. 73-86.

THE RISK-RETURN CONTINUUM

The various approaches to investment management — as well as the selection universes that are the targets of such approaches — can be characterized generally by distinct risk-return profiles. For example, in Exhibit 1, risk levels tend to increase as one moves from the core outward toward the dynamic view of the market; expected returns should also increase. Similarly, in Exhibit 4, risk can be perceived as increasing as one moves from passive investment management out toward traditional active management; expected returns should also increase.

Where should the investor be along this continuum? The answer depends in part on the investor's aversion to risk. The more risk-averse the investor, the closer to core/passive the portfolio should be, and the lower its risk and expected return. Investors who are totally averse to incurring residual risk (that is, departing from benchmark holdings and weights) should stick with passive approaches. They will thus be assured of receiving an equity market return at a market risk level. They will never "beat" the market.

Less risk-averse investors can make more use of style subsets (static or dynamic) and active (engineered or traditional) approaches. With the use of such subsets and such approaches, however, portfolio weights will shift away from overall equity market weights. The difference provides the opportunity for excess return, but it also creates residual risk. In this regard, engineered portfolios, which control risk relative to underlying benchmarks, have definite advantages over traditional portfolios.

The optimal level of residual risk for an investor will depend not only on the investor's level of aversion to residual risk, but also on the manager's skill. Skill can be measured as the manager's information ratio, or IR — the ratio of annualized excess return to annualized residual risk. For example, a manager that beats the benchmark by 2% per year, with 4% residual risk, has an IR of 2%/4%, or 0.5.

Grinold and Kahn formulate the argument as follows:[14]

$$\omega^* = \frac{IR}{2\lambda}$$

where ω^* equals the optimal level of portfolio residual risk given the manager's information ratio and the investor's level of risk aversion, λ. Increases in the manager's IR will increase the investor's optimal level of residual risk and increases in the investor's risk-aversion level will reduce it.

Exhibit 7 illustrates some of the trade-offs between residual risk and excess return for three levels of investor aversion to residual risk and two levels of manager skill. Here the straight lines represent the hypothetical continuum of portfolios (defined by their residual risks and excess returns) that could be offered

---

[14] Grinold and Kahn, *op. cit.*

by a highly skilled manager with an *IR* of 1.0 and a good manager with an *IR* of 0.5.[15] The points H, M, and L represent the optimal portfolios for investors with high, medium, and low aversions to residual risk. The point at the origin, P, with zero excess return and zero residual risk, may be taken to be a passive strategy offering a return and a risk level identical to the benchmark's.

Several important observations can be made from Exhibit 7. First, it is apparent that greater tolerance for risk (a lower risk aversion level) allows the investor to choose a portfolio with a higher risk level that can offer a higher expected return. Second, the more highly skilled the manager, the higher the optimal level of portfolio residual risk, and the higher the portfolio's expected excess return, whatever the investor's risk-aversion level. In short, higher excess returns accrue to higher-risk portfolios and to higher-*IR* managers.

Exhibit 7: Risk and Return Change with Investor Risk and Manager Skill

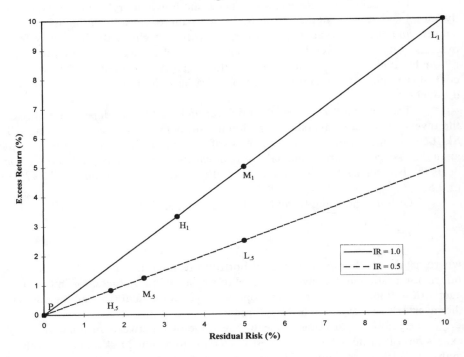

---

[15] In reality, no manager will offer a strategy for each possible risk/return combination. Furthermore, although *IR* is a linear function of residual risk when liquidity is unlimited and short selling unrestricted, in the real world *IR* will begin to decline at high levels of residual risk.

Exhibit 8: Sacrifice in Return from Overestimating Investor Risk Aversion

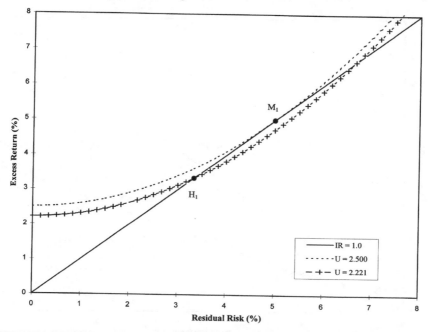

Within this framework, an investor who takes less than the optimal level of residual risk or who selects less than the best manager will sacrifice return.[16] Exhibit 8, for example, shows the decrease in return and utility (U) that results when an investor overestimates risk aversion. Here, an investor with a highly skilled manager, who actually has a medium level of risk aversion (M_1), chooses a portfolio suitable for an investor with a high level of risk aversion (H_1). The investor give-up in return can be measured as the vertical distance between M_1 and H_1. In somewhat more sophisticated terms, the higher-risk portfolio corresponds to a certainty-equivalent return of 2.500% and the less risky portfolio to a certainty-equivalent return of 2.221%, so the investor who overestimates his or her level of risk aversion and therefore chooses a suboptimal portfolio sacrifices 0.279 percentage points.

Exhibit 9 illustrates the return give-up that results when an investor with medium risk aversion uses a less skilled manager (*IR* of 0.5) rather than a higher-skill manager (*IR* of 1.0). Here the give-up in certainty-equivalent return between portfolio M_1 and portfolio $M_{.5}$ amounts to 1.875 percentage points. Choice of manager can significantly affect portfolio return.

---

[16] See also Bruce I. Jacobs and Kenneth N. Levy, "Residual Risk: How Much is Too Much?" *Journal of Portfolio Management* (Spring 1996).

Exhibit 9: Sacrifice in Return from Using Less Skillful Manager

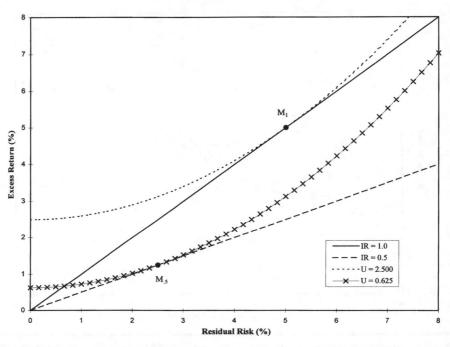

Suppose an investor finds a highly skilled manager ($IR = 1$), but that manager does not offer a portfolio with a risk level low enough to suit the investor's high level of risk aversion. A less skilled ($IR = 0.5$) manager, however, offers portfolios $H_{.5}$ and $M_{.5}$, which do provide about the right level of residual risk for this investor.

The investor might try to convince the $IR = 1$ manager to offer a lower-risk portfolio. If that fails, however, is the investor constrained to go with the less skilled manager? No. The investor can instead combine the highly skilled manager's H_1 portfolio with an investment in the passive benchmark portfolio P, reducing risk and return along the $IR = 1$ manager frontier. Such combination portfolios will offer a higher return than the portfolios of the less skilled manager, at a level of residual risk the investor can live with.

Finally, the manager's investment approach may affect the investor's optimal level of portfolio risk. Because engineered strategies control portfolio systematic and residual risk relative to the benchmark and take only compensated risks, they offer more assurance than traditional active strategies of achieving a return commensurate with the risk taken. Investors may feel more comfortable taking more risk with engineered portfolios, where risk and expected return are rigorously and explicitly assessed, than with traditional active portfolios.

THE ULTIMATE OBJECTIVE

The ultimate objective of investment management, of course, is to establish an investment structure that will, in the aggregate and over time, provide a return that compensates for the risk incurred, where the risk incurred is consistent with the investor's risk tolerance. The objective may be the equity market's return at the market's risk level or the market return plus incremental returns commensurate with incremental risks incurred.

This may be accomplished by focusing on the core universe and a passive representation or by mixing universes (core and static subsets, for example) and approaches (e.g., passive with traditional active or engineered). Whatever the selection universe and investment approach chosen, success is more likely when investors start off knowing their risk-tolerance levels and their potential managers' skill levels. The goal is to take no more risk than is compensated by expected return, but to take as much risk as risk-aversion level and manager skill allow.

Success is also more likely when equity market architecture is taken into account. Without explicit ties between portfolios and the underlying market or market subsets (and thus between market subsets and the overall market), managers may be tempted to stray from their "fold" (core, value, or growth investing, say) in search of return. If value stocks are being punished, for example, an undisciplined value manager may be tempted to "poach" return from growth stock territory. An investor utilizing this manager cannot expect performance consistent with value stocks in general, nor can the investor combine this manager's "value" portfolio with a growth portfolio in the hopes of achieving an overall market return; the portfolio will instead be overweighted in growth stocks, and susceptible to the risk of growth stocks falling out of favor. The investor can mitigate the problem by balancing non-benchmark-constrained, traditional portfolios with engineered or passive portfolios that offer benchmark-accountability.

When investors set goals in terms of return only, with no regard to equity architecture, similar problems can arise. Consider an investor who hires active managers and instructs them to "make money," with no regard to market sector or investment approach. Manager holdings may overlap to an extent that the overall portfolio becomes overdiversified and individual manager efforts are diluted. The investor may end up paying active fees and active transaction costs for essentially passive results.

Equity architecture provides a basic blueprint for relating equity investment choices to their potential rewards and their risks. It can help investors construct portfolios that will meet their needs. First, however, the investor must determine what those needs are in terms of desire for return and tolerance for risk.

Then the investor can choose managers whose investment approaches and market focuses offer, overall, the greatest assurance of fulfilling those needs.

We believe that engineered management can provide the best match between client risk-return goals and investment results. An engineered approach that combines range with depth of inquiry can increase both the number and goodness of investment insights. As a result, engineered management offers better control of risk exposure than traditional active management and incremental returns relative to passive management, whether the selection universe is core equity, static style subsets, or dynamic style subsets.

Chapter 8

Investment Analysis: Profiting from a Complex Equity Market

Bruce I. Jacobs, Ph.D.
Principal
Jacobs Levy Equity Management

Kenneth N. Levy, CFA
Principal
Jacobs Levy Equity Management

INTRODUCTION

Scientists classify systems into three types — ordered, random, and complex. Ordered systems, such as the structure of diamond crystals or the dynamics of pendulums, are definable and predictable by relatively simple rules and can be modeled using a relatively small number of variables. Random systems like the Brownian motion of gas molecules or white noise (static) are unordered; they are the product of a large number of variables. Their behavior cannot be modeled and is inherently unpredictable.

Complex systems like the weather and the workings of DNA fall somewhere between the domains of order and randomness. Their behavior can be at least partly comprehended and modeled, but only with great difficulty. The number of variables that must be modeled, and their interactions, are beyond the capacity of the human mind alone. Only with the aid of advanced computational science can the mysteries of complex systems be unraveled.[1]

The stock market is a complex system.[2] Stock prices are not completely random, as the efficient market hypothesis and random walk theory would have it.

---

[1] See, for example, Heinz Pagels, *The Dreams of Reason: The Computer and the Rise of the Sciences of Complexity* (New York, NY: Simon and Schuster, 1988).

[2] See, for example, Bruce I. Jacobs and Kenneth N. Levy, "The Complexity of the Stock Market," *Journal of Portfolio Management* (Fall 1989).

The authors thank Judith Kimball for her editorial assistance.

129

Some price movements can be predicted, and with some consistency. But nor is stock price behavior ordered. It cannot be successfully modeled by simple rules or screens such as low price/earnings ratios or even elegant theories such as the Capital Asset Pricing Model or Arbitrage Pricing Theory. Rather, stock price behavior is permeated by a complex web of interrelated return effects. A model of the market that is complex enough to disentangle these effects provides opportunities for modeling price behavior and predicting returns.

This chapter describes one such model, and its application to the stock selection, portfolio construction, and performance evaluation problems. We begin with the very basic question of how one should approach the equity market. Should one attempt to cover the broadest possible range of stocks, or can greater analytical insights be garnered by focusing on a particular subset of the market or a limited number of stocks? As we will see, each approach has its advantages and disadvantages. Combining the two, however, may offer the best promise of finding the key to market complexity and unlocking investment opportunity.

AN INTEGRATED APPROACH TO A SEGMENTED MARKET

While one might think that U.S. equity markets are fluid and fully integrated, in reality there exist barriers to the free flow of capital. Some of these barriers are self-imposed by investors. Others are imposed by regulatory and tax authorities or by client guidelines.

Some funds, for example, are prohibited by regulation or internal policy guidelines from buying certain types of stock — non-dividend-paying stock, or stock below a given capitalization level. Tax laws, too, may effectively lock investors into positions they would otherwise trade. Such barriers to the free flow of capital foster market segmentation.

Other barriers are self-imposed. Traditionally, for example, managers have focused (whether by design or default) on distinct approaches to stock selection. Value managers have concentrated on buying stocks selling at prices perceived to be low relative to the company's assets or earnings. Growth managers have sought stocks with above-average earnings growth not fully reflected in price. Small-capitalization managers have searched for opportunity in stocks that have been overlooked by most investors. The stocks that constitute the natural selection pools for these managers tend to group into distinct market segments.

Client preferences encourage this Balkanization of the market. Some investors, for example, prefer to buy value stocks, while others seek growth stocks; some invest in both, but hire separate managers for each segment. Both institutional and individual investors generally demonstrate a reluctance to upset the apple cart by changing allocations to previously selected "style" managers. Several periods of underperformance, however, may undermine this loyalty and motivate a flow of capital from one segment of the market to another (often just as the out-of-favor segment begins to benefit from a reversion of returns back up to their historical mean).

In the past few decades, a market segmented into style groupings has been formalized by the actions of investment consultants. Consultants have designed style indexes that define the constituent stocks of these segments and have defined managers in terms of their proclivity for one segment or another. As a manager's performance is measured against the given style index, managers who stray too far from index territory are taking on extra risk. Consequently, managers tend to stick close to their style "homes," reinforcing market segmentation.

An investment approach that focuses on individual market segments can have its advantages. Such an approach recognizes, for example, that the U.S. equity market is neither entirely homogeneous nor entirely heterogeneous. All stocks do not react alike to a given impetus, but nor does each stock exhibit its own, totally idiosyncratic price behavior. Rather, stocks within a given style, or sector, or industry tend to behave similarly to each other and somewhat differently from stocks outside their group.

An approach to stock selection that specializes in one market segment can optimize the application of talent and maximize the potential for outperformance. This is most likely true for traditional, fundamental analysis. The in-depth, labor-intensive research undertaken by traditional analysts can become positively ungainly without some focusing lens.

An investment approach that focuses on the individual segments of the market, however, presents some severe theoretical and practical problems. Such an approach may be especially disadvantaged when it ignores the many forces that work to integrate, rather than segment, the market.

Many managers, for example, do not specialize in a particular market segment but are free to choose the most attractive securities from a broad universe of stocks. Others, such as style rotators, may focus on a particular type of stock, given current economic conditions, but be poised to change their focus should conditions change. Such managers make for capital flows and price arbitrage across the boundaries of particular segments.

Furthermore, all stocks can be defined by the same fundamental parameters — by market capitalization, price/earnings ratio, dividend discount model ranking, and so on. All stocks can be found at some level on the continuum of values for each parameter. Thus growth and value stocks inhabit the opposite ends of the continuums of P/E and dividend yield, and small and large stocks the opposite ends of the continuums of firm capitalization and analyst coverage.

As the values of the parameters for any individual stock change, so too does the stock's position on the continuum. An out-of-favor growth stock may slip into value territory. A small-cap company may grow into the large-cap range.

Finally, while the values of these parameters vary across stocks belonging to different market segments — different styles, sectors, and industries — and while investors may favor certain values — low P/E, say, in preference to high P/E — arbitrage tends to counterbalance too pronounced a predilection on the part of investors for any one set of values. In equilibrium, all stocks must be owned. If too many investors want low P/E, low-P/E stocks will be bid up to higher P/E levels, and some investors will step in to sell them and buy other stocks deserving of higher P/Es. Arbitrage works toward market integration and a single pricing mechanism.

A market that is neither completely segmented nor completely integrated is a complex market. A complex market calls for an investment approach that is 180 degrees removed from the narrow, segment-oriented focus of traditional management. It requires a complex, unified approach that takes into account the behavior of stocks across the broadest possible selection universe, without losing sight of the significant differences in price behavior that distinguish particular market segments.

Such an approach offers three major advantages. First, it provides a coherent evaluation framework. Second, it can benefit from all the insights to be garnered from a wide and diverse range of securities. Third, because it has both breadth of coverage and depth of analysis, it is poised to take advantage of more profit opportunities than a more narrowly defined, segmented approach proffers.[3]

A COHERENT FRAMEWORK

To the extent that the market is integrated, an investment approach that models each industry or style segment as if it were a universe unto itself is not the best approach. Consider, for example, a firm that offers both core and value strategies. Suppose the firm runs a model on its total universe of, say, 3000 stocks. It then runs the same model or a different, segment-specific model on a 500-stock subset of large-cap value stocks.

If different models are used for each strategy, the results will differ. Even if the same model is estimated separately for each strategy, its results will differ because the model coefficients are bound to differ between the broader universe and the narrower segment. What if the core model predicts GM will outperform Ford, while the value model shows the reverse? Should the investor start the day with multiple estimates of one stock's alpha? This would violate what we call the "Law of One Alpha."[4]

Of course, the firm could ensure coherence by using separate models for each market segment — growth, value, small-cap — and linking the results via a single, overarching model that relates all the subsets. But the firm then runs into a second problem with segmented investment approaches: To the extent that the market is integrated, the pricing of securities in one segment may contain information relevant to pricing in other segments.

For example, within a generally well integrated national economy, labor market conditions in the U.S. differ region by region. An economist attempting to

---

[3] See, for example, Bruce I. Jacobs and Kenneth N. Levy, "Engineering Portfolios: A Unified Approach," *Journal of Investing* (Winter 1995).

[4] See Bruce I. Jacobs and Kenneth N. Levy, "The Law of One Alpha," *Journal of Portfolio Management* (Summer 1995).

model employment in the Northeast would probably consider economic expansion in the Southeast. Similarly, the investor who wants to model growth stocks should not ignore value stocks. The effects of inflation, say, on value stocks may have repercussions for growth stocks; after all, the two segments represent opposite ends of the same P/E continuum.

An investment approach that concentrates on a single market segment does not make use of all available information. A complex, unified approach considers all the stocks in the universe — value and growth, large and small. It thus benefits from all the information to be gleaned from a broad range of stock price behavior.

Of course, an increase in breadth of inquiry will not benefit the investor if it comes at the sacrifice of depth of inquiry. A complex approach does not ignore the significant differences across different types of stock, differences exploitable by specialized investing. What's more, in examining similarities and differences across market segments, it considers numerous variables that may be considered to be defining.

For value, say, a complex approach does not confine itself to a dividend discount model measure of value, but examines also earnings, cash flow, sales, and yield value, among other attributes. Growth measurements to be considered include historical, expected, and sustainable growth, as well as the momentum and stability of earnings. Share price, volatility, and analyst coverage are among the elements to be considered along with market capitalization as measures of size.[5]

These variables are often closely correlated with each other. Small-cap stocks, for example, tend to have low P/Es; low P/E is correlated with high yield; both low P/E and high yield are correlated with DDM estimates of value. Furthermore, they may be correlated with a stock's industry affiliation. A simple low-P/E screen, for example, will tend to select a large number of bank and utility stocks. Such correlations can distort naive attempts to relate returns to potentially relevant variables. A true picture of the variable-return relationship emerges only after "disentangling" the variables.

DISENTANGLING

The effects of different sources of stock return can overlap. In Exhibit 1, the lines represent connections documented by academic studies; they may appear like a ball of yarn after the cat got to it. To unravel the connections between variables and return, it is necessary to examine all the variables simultaneously.

[5] At a deeper level of complexity, one must also consider alternative ways of specifying such fundamental variables as earnings or cash flow. Over what period does one measure earnings, for example? If using analyst earnings expectations, which measure provides the best estimate of future real earnings? The consensus of all available estimates made over the past six months? Only the very latest earnings estimates? Are some analysts more accurate or more influential? What if a recent estimate is not available for a given company? See Bruce I. Jacobs, Kenneth N. Levy, and Mitchell C. Krask, "Earnings Estimates, Predictor Specification, and Measurement Error," *Journal of Investing* (Summer 1997), pp. 29-46.

Exhibit 1: Return Effects Form a Tangled Web

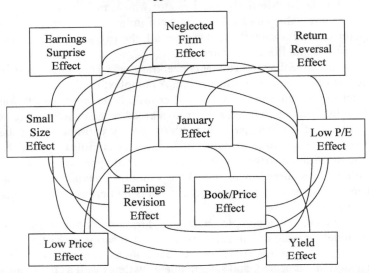

For instance, the low-P/E effect is widely recognized, as is the small-size effect. But stocks with low P/Es also tend to be of small size. Are P/E and size merely two ways of looking at the same effect? Or does each variable matter? Perhaps the excess returns to small-cap stocks are merely a January effect, reflecting the tendency of taxable investors to sell depressed stocks at year-end. Answering these questions requires disentangling return effects via multivariate regression.[6]

Common methods of measuring return effects (such as quintiling or univariate — single-variable — regression) are "naive" because they assume, naively, that prices are responding only to the single variable under consideration — low P/E, say. But a number of related variables may be affecting returns. As we have noted, small-cap stocks and banking and utility industry stocks tend to have low P/Es. A univariate regression of return on low P/E will capture, along with the effect of P/E, a great deal of "noise" related to firm size, industry affiliation and other variables.

Simultaneous analysis of all relevant variables via multivariate regression takes into account and adjusts for such interrelationships. The result is the return to each variable separately, controlling for all related variables. A multivariate analysis for low P/E, for example, will provide a measure of the excess return to a portfolio that is market-like in all respects except for having a lower-than-average P/E ratio. Disentangled returns are "pure" returns.

---

[6] See Bruce I. Jacobs and Kenneth N. Levy, "Disentangling Equity Return Regularities: New Insights and Investment Opportunities," *Financial Analysts Journal* (May/June 1988).

Exhibit 2: Naive and Pure Returns to High Book-to-Price Ratio

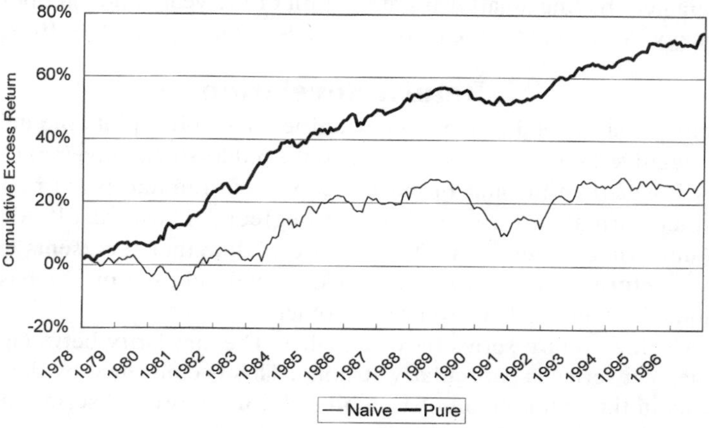

Noise Reduction

Exhibit 2 plots naive and pure cumulative excess (relative to a 3,000-stock universe) returns to high book-to-price ratio.[7] The naive returns show a great deal of volatility; the pure returns, by contrast, follow a much smoother path. There is a lot of noise in the naive returns. What causes it?

Notice the divergence between the naive and pure return series for the 12 months starting in March 1979. This date coincides with the crisis at Three Mile Island nuclear power plant. Utilities such as GPU, operator of the Three Mile Island power plant, tend to have high-B/Ps, and naive B/P measures will reflect the performance of these utilities along with the performance of other high-B/P stocks. Electric utility prices plummeted 24% after the Three Mile Island crisis. The naive B/P measure reflects this decline.

But industry-related events such as Three Mile Island have no necessary bearing on the book/price variable. An investor could, for example, hold a high-B/P portfolio that does not overweight utilities, and such a portfolio would not have experienced the decline reflected in the naive B/P measure in Exhibit 2. The naive returns to B/P reflect noise from the inclusion of a utility industry effect. A pure B/P measure is not contaminated by such irrelevant variables.

Disentangling distinguishes real effects from mere proxies and thereby distinguishes between real and spurious investment opportunities. As it separates high B/P and industry affiliation, for example, it can also separate the effects of firm size from the effects of related variables. Disentangling shows that returns to small firms in January are not abnormal; the apparent January seasonal merely proxies for

[7] In particular, naive and pure returns are provided by a portfolio having a book-to-price ratio that is one standard deviation above the universe mean book-to-price ratio. For pure returns, the portfolio is also constrained to have universe-average exposures to all the other variables in the model, including fundamental characteristics and industry affiliations.

year-end tax-loss selling.[8] Not all small firms will benefit from a January rebound; indiscriminately buying small firms at the turn of the year is not an optimal investment strategy. Ascertaining true causation leads to more profitable strategies.

Return Revelation

Disentangling can reveal hidden opportunities. Exhibit 3 plots the naively measured cumulative excess returns (relative to the 3,000-stock universe) to portfolios that rank lower than normal in market capitalization and price per share and higher than normal in terms of analyst neglect.[9] These results derive from monthly univariate regressions. The "small-cap" line thus represents the cumulative excess returns to a portfolio of stocks naively chosen on the basis of their size, with no attempt made to control for other variables.

All three return series move together. The similarity between the small-cap and neglect series is particularly striking. This is confirmed by the correlation coefficients in the first column of Exhibit 4. Furthermore, all series show a great deal of volatility within a broader up, down, up pattern.

Exhibit 3: Naive Returns Can Hide Opportunities: Three Size-Related Variables

—Small Cap —— Neglect ····· Price

Exhibit 4: Correlations between Monthly Returns to Size-Related Variables*

Variable	Naive	Pure
Small Cap/Low Price	0.82	−0.12
Small Cap/Neglect	0.87	−0.22
Neglect/Low Price	0.66	−0.11

* A coefficient of 0.14 is significant at the 5% level.

---

[8] See Bruce I. Jacobs and Kenneth N. Levy, "Calendar Anomalies: Abnormal Returns at Calendar Turning Points," *Financial Analysts Journal* (November/December 1988).

[9] Again, portfolios with values of these parameters that are, on average, one standard deviation away from the universe mean.

Exhibit 5: Pure Returns Can Reveal Opportunities: Three Size-Related Variables

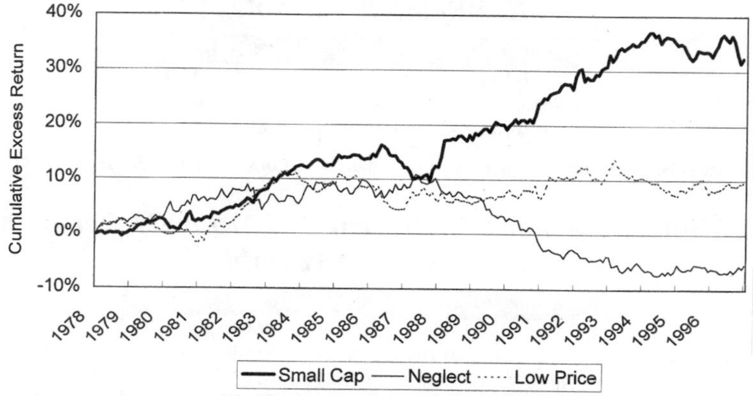

Exhibit 5 shows the pure cumulative excess returns to each size-related attribute over the period. These disentangled returns adjust for correlations not only between the three size variables, but also between each size variable and industry affiliations and each variable and growth and value characteristics. Two findings are immediately apparent from Exhibit 5.

First, pure returns to the size variables do not appear to be nearly as closely correlated as the naive returns displayed in Exhibit 3. In fact, over the second half of the period, the three return series diverge substantially. This is confirmed by the correlation coefficients in the second column of Exhibit 4.

In particular, pure returns to small capitalization accumulate quite a gain over the period; they are up 30%, versus an only 20% gain for the naive returns to small cap. Purifying returns reveals a profit opportunity not apparent in the naive returns. Furthermore, pure returns to analyst neglect amount to a substantial loss over the period. Because disentangling controls for proxy effects, and thereby avoids redundancies, these pure return effects are additive. A portfolio could have aimed for superior returns by selecting small-cap stocks with a higher-than-average analyst following (i.e., a negative exposure to analyst neglect).

Second, the pure returns appear to be much less volatile than the naive returns. The naive returns in Exhibit 3 display much month-to-month volatility within their more general trends. By contrast, the pure series in Exhibit 5 are much smoother and more consistent. This is confirmed by the standard deviations given in Exhibit 6.

The pure returns in Exhibit 5 are smoother and more consistent than the naive return responses in Exhibit 3 because the pure returns capture more "signal" and less noise. And because they are smoother and more consistent than naive returns, pure returns are also more predictable.

Exhibit 6: Pure Returns are Less Volatile, More Predictable: Standard Deviations of Monthly Returns to Size-Related Variables*

Variable	Naive	Pure
Small Cap	0.87	0.60
Neglect	0.87	0.67
Low Price	1.03	0.58

* All differences between naive and pure return standard deviations are significant at the 1% level.

Exhibit 7: Market Sensitivities of Monthly Returns to Value-Related Variables

Variable	Naive	(t-stat.)	Pure	(t-stat.)
DDM	0.06	(5.4)	0.04	(5.6)
B/P	−0.10	(−6.2)	−0.01	(−0.8)
Yield	−0.08	(−7.4)	−0.03	(−3.5)

Predictability

Disentangling improves return predictability by providing a clearer picture of the relationship between stock price behavior, fundamental variables, and macroeconomic conditions. For example, investors often prefer value stocks in bearish market environments, because growth stocks are priced more on the basis of high expectations, which get dashed in more pessimistic eras. But the success of such a strategy will depend on the variables one has chosen to define value.

Exhibit 7 displays the results of regressing both naive and pure returns to various value-related variables on market (S&P 500) returns over the 1978-1996 period. The results indicate that DDM value is a poor indicator of a stock's ability to withstand a tide of receding market prices. The regression coefficient in the first column indicates that a portfolio with a one-standard-deviation exposure to DDM value will tend to outperform by 0.06% when the market rises by 1.00% and to underperform by a similar margin when the market falls by 1.00%. The coefficient for pure returns to DDM is similar. Whether their returns are measured in pure or naive form, stocks with high DDM values tend to behave procyclically.

High book-to-price ratio appears to be a better indicator of a defensive stock. It has a regression coefficient of −0.10 in naive form. In pure form, however, B/P is virtually uncorrelated with market movements; pure B/P signals neither an aggressive nor a defensive stock. B/P as naively measured apparently picks up the effects of truly defensive variables — such as high yield.

The value investor in search of a defensive posture in uncertain market climates should consider moving toward high yield. The regression coefficients for both naive and pure returns to high yield indicate significant negative market sensitivities. Stocks with high yields may be expected to lag in up markets but to hold up relatively well during general market declines.

Exhibit 8: Forecast Response of Small Size to Macroeconomic Shocks

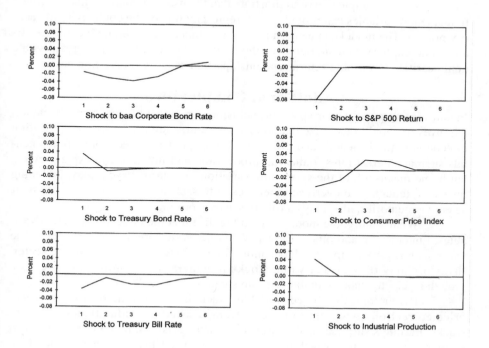

These results make broad intuitive sense. DDM is forward-looking, relying on estimates of future earnings. In bull markets, investors take a long-term outlook, so DDM explains security pricing behavior. In bear markets, however, investors become myopic; they prefer today's tangible income to tomorrow's promise. Current yield is rewarded.[10]

Pure returns respond in intuitively satisfying ways to macroeconomic events. Exhibit 8 illustrates, as an example, the estimated effects of changes in various macroeconomic variables on the pure returns to small size (as measured by market capitalization). Consistent with the capital constraints on small firms and their relatively greater sensitivity to the economy, pure returns to small size may be expected to be negative in the first four months following an unexpected increase in the BAA corporate rate and positive in the first month following an unexpected increase in industrial production.[11] Investors can exploit such predict-

[10] See also Bruce I. Jacobs and Kenneth N. Levy, "On the Value of 'Value'," *Financial Analysts Journal* (July/August 1988).

[11] See Bruce I. Jacobs and Kenneth N. Levy, "Forecasting the Size Effect," *Financial Analysts Journal* (May/June 1989).

able behavior by moving into and out of the small-cap market segment as economic conditions evolve.[12]

These examples serve to illustrate that the use of numerous, finely defined fundamental variables can provide a rich representation of the complexity of security pricing. The model can be even more finely tuned, however, by including variables that capture such subtleties as the effects of investor psychology, possible nonlinearities in variable-return relationships, and security transaction costs.

Additional Complexities

In considering possible variables for inclusion in a model of stock price behavior, the investor should recognize that pure stock returns are driven by a combination of economic fundamentals and investor psychology. That is, economic fundamentals such as interest rates, industrial production, and inflation can explain much, but by no means all, of the systematic variation in returns. Psychology, including investors' tendency to overreact, their desire to seek safety in numbers, and their selective memories, also plays a role in security pricing.

What's more, the modeler should realize that the effects of different variables, fundamental and otherwise, can differ across different types of stocks. The value sector, for example, includes more financial stocks than the growth sector. Investors may thus expect value stocks in general to be more sensitive than growth stocks to changes in interest rate spreads.

Psychologically based variables such as short-term overreaction and price correction also seem to have a stronger effect on value than on growth stocks. Earnings surprises and earnings estimate revisions, by contrast, appear to be more important for growth than for value stocks. Thus Intel shares can take a nose dive when earnings come in a penny under expectations, whereas Ford shares remain unmoved even by fairly substantial departures of actual earnings from expectations.

The relationship between stock returns and relevant variables may not be linear. The effects of positive earnings surprises, for instance, tend to be arbitraged away quickly; thus positive earnings surprises offer less opportunity for the investor. The effects of negative earnings surprises, however, appear to be more long-lasting. This nonlinearity may reflect the fact that sales of stock are limited to those investors who already own the stock (and to a relatively small number of short-sellers).[13]

Risk-variable relationships may also differ across different types of stock. In particular, small-cap stocks generally have more idiosyncratic risk than large-cap stocks. Diversification is thus more important for small-stock than for large-stock portfolios.

---

[12] See, for example, Bruce I. Jacobs and Kenneth N. Levy, "High-Definition Style Rotation," *Journal of Investing* (Fall 1996), pp. 14-23.

[13] See Bruce I. Jacobs and Kenneth N. Levy, "Long/Short Equity Investing," *Journal of Portfolio Management* (Fall 1993).

Return-variable relationships can also change over time. Recall the difference between DDM and yield value measures: high-DDM stocks tend to have high returns in bull markets and low returns in bear markets; high-yield stocks experience the reverse. For consistency of performance, return modeling must consider the effects of market dynamics — the changing nature of the overall market.

The investor may also want to decipher the informational signals generated by "informed agents." Corporate decisions to issue or buy back shares, split stock, or initiate or suspend dividends, for example, may contain valuable information about company prospects. So, too, may insiders' (legal) trading in their own firms' shares.

Finally, a complex model containing multiple variables is likely to turn up a number of promising return-variable relationships. But are these perceived profit opportunities translatable into real economic opportunities? Are some too ephemeral? Too small to survive frictions such as trading costs? Estimates of expected returns must be combined with estimates of the costs of trading to arrive at realistic returns net of trading costs.

CONSTRUCTING, TRADING, AND EVALUATING PORTFOLIOS

To maximize implementation of the model's insights, the portfolio construction process should consider exactly the same dimensions found relevant by the stock selection model. Failure to do so can lead to mismatches between model insights and portfolio exposures.

Consider a commercially available portfolio optimizer that recognizes only a subset of the variables in the valuation model. Risk reduction using such an optimizer will reduce the portfolio's exposures only along the dimensions the optimizer recognizes. As a result, the portfolio is likely to wind up more exposed to those variables recognized by the model — but not the optimizer — and less exposed to those variables common to both the model and the optimizer.

Imagine an investor who seeks low-P/E stocks that analysts are recommending for purchase, but who uses a commercial optimizer that incorporates a P/E factor but not analyst recommendations. The investor is likely to wind up with a portfolio that has a less than optimal level of exposure to low P/E and a greater than optimal level of exposure to analyst purchase recommendations. Optimization using all relevant variables ensures a portfolio whose risk and return opportunities are balanced in accordance with the model's insights. Furthermore, the use of more numerous variables allows portfolio risk to be more finely tuned.

Insofar as the investment process — both stock selection and portfolio construction — is model-driven, it is more adaptable to electronic trading venues. This should benefit the investor in several ways. First, electronic trading is generally less costly, with lower commissions, market impact, and opportunity costs.

Second, it allows real-time monitoring, which can further reduce trading costs. Third, an automated trading system can take account of more factors, including the urgency of a particular trade and market conditions, than individual traders can be expected to bear in mind.

Finally, the performance attribution process should be congruent with the dimensions of the selection model (and portfolio optimizer). Insofar as performance attribution identifies sources of return, a process that considers all the sources identified by the selection model will be more insightful than a commercial performance attribution system applied in a "one-size-fits-all" manner. Our investor who has sought exposure to low P/E and positive analyst recommendations, for example, will want to know how each of these factors has paid off and will be less interested in the returns to factors that are not a part of the stock selection process.

A performance evaluation process tailored to the model also functions as a monitor of the model's reliability. Has portfolio performance supported the model's insights? Should some be reexamined? Equally important, does the model's reliability hold up over time? A model that performs well in today's economic and market environments may not necessarily perform well in the future. A feedback loop between the evaluation and the research/modeling processes can help ensure that the model retains robustness over time.

PROFITING FROM COMPLEXITY

It has been said that: "For every complex problem, there is a simple solution, and it is almost always wrong."[14] For complex problems more often than not require complex solutions.

A complex approach to stock selection, portfolio construction, and performance evaluation is needed to capture the complexities of the stock market. Such an approach combines the breadth of coverage and the depth of analysis needed to maximize investment opportunity and potential reward.

Grinold and Kahn present a formula that identifies the relationships between the depth and breadth of investment insights and investment performance:

$$IR = IC \times \sqrt{BR}$$

IR is the manager's information ratio, a measure of the success of the investment process. IR equals annualized excess return over annualized residual risk (e.g., 2% excess return with 4% tracking error provides 0.5 IR). IC, the information coefficient, or correlation between predicted and actual results, measures the goodness of the manager's insights, or the manager's skill. BR is the breadth of

---

[14] Attributed to H.L. Mencken.

the strategy, measurable as the number of independent insights upon which investment decisions are made.[15]

One can increase *IR* by increasing *IC* or *BR*. Increasing *IC* means coming up with some means of improving predictive accuracy. Increasing *BR* means coming up with more "investable" insights. A casino analogy may be apt (if anathema to prudent investors).

A gambler can seek to increase *IC* by card-counting in blackjack or by building a computer model to predict probable roulette outcomes. Similarly, some investors seek to outperform by concentrating their research efforts on a few stocks: by learning all there is to know about Microsoft, for example, one may be able to outperform all the other investors who follow this stock. But a strategy that makes a few concentrated stock bets is likely to produce consistent performance only if it is based on a very high level of skill, or if it benefits from extraordinary luck.

Alternatively, an investor can place a larger number of smaller stock bets and settle for more modest returns from a greater number of investment decisions. That is, rather than behaving like a gambler in a casino, the investor can behave like the casino. A casino has only a slight edge on any spin of the roulette wheel or roll of the dice, but many spins of many roulette wheels can result in a very consistent profit for the house. Over time, the odds will strongly favor the casino over the gambler.

A complex approach to the equity market, one that has both breadth of inquiry and depth of focus, can enhance the number and the goodness of investment insights. A complex approach to the equity market requires more time, effort, and ability, but it will be better positioned to capture the complexities of security pricing. The rewards are worth the effort.

---

[15] Richard C. Grinold and Ronald N. Kahn, *Active Portfolio Management* (Chicago, IL: Probus, 1995).

Chapter 9

Dividend Discount Models

William J. Hurley, Ph.D.
Associate Professor of Business Administration
Department of Business Administration
The Royal Military College of Canada

Frank J. Fabozzi, Ph.D., CFA
Adjunct Professor of Finance
School of Management
Yale University

INTRODUCTION

Several models have been used to identify whether a stock is mispriced. These models fall into two general categories: factor-based models and dividend discount models. Factor-based models are the subject Chapter 6. In this chapter we provide a survey of dividend discount models.

Typically, the dividend discount models used by analysts are *deterministic* in that they make specific assumptions about what future dividends will be. Recently, a new approach to dividend discount modeling has been proposed.[1] This approach models the future dividend stream as *uncertain* or *stochastic*. Since the future dividend stream is uncertain, so too is the resulting valuation. The product of this approach to dividend discount modeling is a probability distribution for the stock's discounted value. An analyst can use this probability distribution to assess whether a stock is sufficiently undervalued or overvalued to justify a buy or sell recommendation. These models that treat the future dividend as uncertain are termed *stochastic models*.

To appreciate the importance of stochastic dividend discount models compared to deterministic dividend discount models, consider an analyst who uses a deterministic model and estimates a stock's value to be $42. Suppose further that the stock is trading at $35. The analyst concludes that the stock is undervalued and recommends purchase. But what confidence does the analyst have that

---

[1] See William J. Hurley and Lewis. D. Johnson, "A Realistic Dividend Valuation Model," *Financial Analysts Journal* (July-August 1994), pp. 50-54; William J. Hurley and Lewis D. Johnson, "Stochastic Two-Phase Dividend Discount Models," *Journal of Portfolio Management* (Summer 1997), pp. 91-98 and, William J. Hurley and Lewis D. Johnson, "Confidence Intervals for Stochastic Dividend Discount Models," forthcoming in *Journal of Portfolio Management* (1998).

his recommendation is a good one? He knows that the actual future dividend stream is unlikely to follow the exact pattern assumed by the deterministic model employed. One way around this problem is to assume that future dividends are uncertain. Given that the analyst is able to specify the nature of this uncertainty, a stochastic dividend discount model produces a probability distribution of discounted values. The distribution, for example, might have a mean (average) value of $42. Given a current market price of $35 and the probability distribution generated, the analyst will be able to assess the probability that there is some chance that the true discounted value exceeds $35. For example, the analyst might conclude that the probability that the stock's value is greater than $35 is 90%. In this case the analyst is confident that a buy recommendation is warranted. As we will see, if an analyst is prepared to make subjective assumptions about the uncertain nature of future dividends, he is then able to translate these beliefs into probabilistic assessments on the relationship between model value and the market price.

Valuation using a dividend discount model (DDM) represents a bottom-up investment management style. In theory, the DDM is unbiased and thus rationally reflects the consensus of market participants for the value of a stock. However, proponents of the DDM argue that market "inefficiencies" such as superior information and market psychology do exist and can be translated by the DDM to reveal overvaluation and undervaluation. The DDM can be used in combination with fundamental security analysis and/or factor models in trying to obtain a fair value for the stock.

DETERMINISTIC DIVIDEND DISCOUNT MODELS

The basis for the *dividend discount model* is simply the application of present value analysis, which asserts that the fair price of an asset is the present value of the expected cash flows.[2] In the case of common stock, the cash flows are the expected dividend payouts. The basic model is:

$$P = \frac{D_1}{(1+r_1)} + \frac{D_2}{(1+r_2)^2} + \dots \tag{1}$$

where

P = the fair value or theoretical value of the stock
D_t = the expected dividend for period t
r_t = the appropriate discount or capitalization rate for period t

We call equation (1) the *general model*. This model has an infinite number of parameters, so various assumptions must be made to make the valuation calculation tractable.

---

[2] John B. Williams, *The Theory of Investment Value* (Cambridge, MA: Harvard University Press, 1938).

The Finite Life General Model

One common approach is to estimate dividends for a finite time period (say N periods), and then assume some terminal value, P_N, intended to capture the future value of all subsequent dividends. The general model then becomes:

$$P = \frac{D_1}{(1+r_1)} + \frac{D_2}{(1+r_2)^2} + \ldots + \frac{D_N}{(1+r_N)^N} + \frac{P_N}{(1+r_N)^N} \tag{2}$$

where

P_N = the expected sale price (or terminal price) at the horizon (period N)
N = the number of periods in the horizon
r_t = the appropriate discount or capitalization rate for period t

Equation (2) is called the *finite-life general model*. The benefit of this model is that the dividend stream to be estimated is finite and within a reasonable forecast horizon (say, a business cycle). However, the model begs the question of how one estimates the terminal value, and still requires estimation of period-specific discount rates.

The first level of abstraction is to assume that the discount rate will be the same for all future periods. This is a fairly innocuous assumption, analogous to those associated with the term structure of interest rates. That is, we know that the year-by-year rate on a 10-year bond is not the same in each period (except for the case of a flat term structure), yet we use the 10-year yield, as a geometrically weighted average of the yearly rates, to describe the yield on that bond. In the same way, we can think of the constant discount rate, r, as being a (very) long-term weighted average of individual period discount rates. Any bias induced by this assumption is liable to be minimal in comparison with the estimation errors inherent in predicting individual period discount rates far into the future. Hence we posit the constant discount rate version of the finite-life model:

$$P = \frac{D_1}{(1+r)} + \frac{D_2}{(1+r)^2} + \ldots + \frac{D_N}{(1+r)^N} + \frac{P_N}{(1+r)^N} \tag{3}$$

For example, suppose that the following data are determined by an analyst for stock XYZ:

$D_1 = \$2.00$ $D_2 = \$2.20$ $D_3 = \$2.30$ $D_4 = \$2.55$ $D_5 = \$2.65$
$P_5 = \$26$ $N = 5$ $r = 0.10$

Given the assumption of a constant discount rate, the fair price of stock XYZ based on the constant discount rate version of the finite-life model given by equation (3) is:

$$P = \frac{\$2.00}{(1.10)} + \frac{\$2.20}{(1.10)^2} + \frac{\$2.30}{(1.10)^3} + \frac{\$2.55}{(1.10)^4} + \frac{\$2.65}{(1.10)^5} + \frac{\$26.00}{(1.10)^5} = \$24.895$$

The constant discount rate version of the finite-life model requires three forecasts as inputs to calculate the fair value of a stock:

1. the expected terminal price (P_N)
2. the dividends up to period N (D_1 to D_N)
3. the discount rate (r)

Thus the relevant question is, How accurately can these inputs be forecasted?

The terminal price is the most difficult of the three forecasts. According to theory, P_N is the present value of all future dividends after N; that is, D_{N+1}, D_{N+2}, ... , D_{infinity}. Also, the discount rate (r) must be estimated. In practice, forecasts are made of either dividends (D_N) or earnings (E_N) first, and then the price P_N is estimated by assigning an "appropriate" requirement for yield, price-earnings ratio, or capitalization rate. Note that the present value of the expected terminal price $P_N/(1 + r)^N$ in equation (3) becomes very small if N is very large. In practice, the value for r is typically generated from the capital asset pricing model (CAPM). Recall that CAPM provides the expected return for a company based on its systematic risk (beta).

Given the fair price derived from a dividend discount model, the assessment of the stock proceeds along the following lines. If the market price is below the fair price derived from the model, then the stock is *undervalued* or *cheap*. The opposite holds for a stock whose market price is greater than the model-derived price. In this case, the stock is said to be *overvalued* or *expensive*. A stock trading equal to or close to its fair price is said to be *fairly valued*.

The DDM tells us the relative value but does not tell us when the price of the stock should be expected to move to its fair price. That is, the model says that based on the inputs generated by the analyst, the stock may be cheap, expensive, or fair. However, it does not tell the analyst that if it is mispriced how long it will take before the market recognizes the mispricing and corrects it. As a result, a manager may hold a stock perceived to be cheap for an extended period of time and may underperform a benchmark during that period.

Moreover, as we pointed out at the outset of this chapter, while a stock may be perceived to be mispriced, an analyst must consider how mispriced it is in order to take the appropriate action (buy a cheap stock and sell or sell short an expensive stock). The stochastic dividend discount model described later in this chapter will allow an analyst to express the degree of confidence he has that a stock is mispriced.

Practitioners rarely use the DDM as given by equation (3). Instead, the specialized deterministic DDMs described below are used.

Deterministic Constant Growth Models

If it assumed there is a constant growth in dividends over the life of the stock, then the finite-life dividend discount model assuming a constant discount rate can be modified further.

Deterministic Geometric Growth Model

Dividend growth can be assumed to be geometric or additive. If future dividends are assumed to grow at an assumed rate (g) and a single discount rate is used, then the dividend discount model given by equation (3) becomes

$$P = \frac{D_1}{(1+r)} + \frac{D_1(1+g)^1}{(1+r)^2} + \frac{D_1(1+g)^2}{(1+r)^3} + \ldots + \frac{D_1(1+g)^N}{(1+r)^N} + \frac{P_N}{(1+r)^N} \qquad (4)$$

and it can be shown that as N approaches infinity, equation (4) reduces to:

$$P = \frac{D_1}{r-g} \qquad (5)$$

Equation (5) is called the *deterministic constant growth model*. It also referred to as the *Gordon model*, named after Myron Gordon who was one of its earliest advocates.[3] An equivalent formulation for the constant growth model is

$$P = \frac{D_0(1+g)}{r-g} \qquad (6)$$

where D_0 is the current dividend and therefore D_1 is equal to $D_0(1+g)$.

Let's apply the model as given by equation (6) to estimate the price of three utilities, Bell Atlantic, BellSouth, and Cincinnati Bell, as of 1994. The discount rate for each telephone utility was estimated using the capital asset pricing model assuming (1) a market risk premium of 5% and (2) a risk-free rate of 6%. The beta estimate for each telephone utility was obtained from Value Line (0.90 for Bell Atlantic, 0.80 for BellSouth, and 0.95 for Cincinnati Bell). The discount rate, r, for each telephone utility based on the CAPM was then:

Bell Atlantic $r = 0.06 + 0.90\,(0.05) = 0.105$ or 10.5%
BellSouth $r = 0.06 + 0.80\,(0.05) = 0.100$ or 10.0%
Cincinnati Bell $r = 0.06 + 0.95\,(0.05) = 0.1075$ or 10.75%

The dividend growth rate can be estimated by using the compounded rate of growth of historical dividends. The dividend history for the three telephone utilities ending in 1994 is shown in Exhibit 1. The data needed for the calculations are summarized below:

	Starting in	Dividend	1994 dividend	No. of years
Bell Atlantic	1984	$1.60	$2.80	10
BellSouth	1984	$1.72	$2.88	10
Cincinnati Bell	1977	$0.22	$0.84	17

---

[3] Myron J. Gordon, *The Investment, Financing and Valuation of the Corporation* (Homewood, IL: Richard D. Irwin, 1952).

Exhibit 1: Annual Dividend and Dividend Changes for Bell Atlantic, BellSouth, and Cincinnati Bell

	Bell Atlantic		BellSouth		Cincinnati Bell	
Year	Dividend	% Change*	Dividend %	Change*	Dividend %	Change*
1977					0.22	
1978					0.27	22.73
1979					0.30	11.11
1980					0.32	6.67
1981					0.33	3.13
1982					0.34	3.03
1983					0.35	2.94
1984	1.60		1.72		0.37	5.71
1985	1.70	6.25	1.88	9.30	0.42	13.51
1986	1.80	5.88	2.04	8.51	0.44	4.76
1987	1.92	6.67	2.20	7.84	0.48	9.09
1988	2.04	6.25	2.36	7.27	0.56	16.67
1989	2.20	7.84	2.52	6.78	0.68	21.43
1990	2.36	7.27	2.68	6.35	0.76	11.76
1991	2.52	6.78	2.76	2.99	0.80	5.26
1992	2.60	3.17	2.76	0	0.80	0
1993	2.68	3.08	2.76	0	0.80	0
1994	2.80	4.48	2.88	4.35	0.84	5.00

* The percent change is found as follows:

$$\frac{\text{Dividend in year } t}{\text{Dividend in year } t-1} - 1$$

The compound growth rate, g, is found using the following formula:

$$\left(\frac{1994 \text{ dividend}}{\text{Starting dividend}}\right)^{1/\text{no. of years}} - 1$$

Substituting the values from the table into the formula we get:

$$g \text{ for Bell Atlantic} = \left(\frac{\$2.80}{\$1.60}\right)^{1/10} - 1 = 0.0576$$

$$g \text{ for BellSouth} = \left(\frac{\$2.88}{\$1.72}\right)^{1/10} - 1 = 0.0529$$

$$g \text{ for Cinc. Bell} = \left(\frac{\$0.84}{\$0.22}\right)^{1/17} - 1 = 0.0820$$

The value of D_0, the estimate for g, and the discount rate r for each electric utility are summarized below:

	D_0	g	r
Bell Atlantic	$2.80	0.0576	0.1050
BellSouth	$2.88	0.0529	0.1000
Cincinnati Bell	$0.84	0.0820	0.1075

Substituting these values into equation (6) we obtain:

$$\text{Bell Atlantic estimated price} = \frac{\$2.80\ (1.0576)}{0.105 - 0.0576} = \$62.47$$

$$\text{BellSouth estimated price} = \frac{\$2.88\ (1.0529)}{0.10 - 0.0529} = \$64.38$$

$$\text{Cinc. Bell estimated price} = \frac{\$0.84\ (1.0820)}{0.1075 - 0.0820} = \$35.64$$

A comparison of the estimated price and the actual price is given below:

	Estimated price	Actual price
Bell Atlantic	$62.48	$61
BellSouth	$64.38	$60
Cincinnati Bell	$35.64	$22

Notice that the simple constant growth model gives a decent estimate of price for Bell Atlantic and BellSouth, but is considerably off the mark for Cincinnati Bell. The reason can be seen in Exhibit 1 which shows the annual percentage change in dividends for the three utilities. The dividend growth pattern for none of the three utilities appears to suggest a constant growth rate. However, the Bell Atlantic and BellSouth appear to be more in conformity with a constant growth than Cincinnati Bell. We'll return to this issue later in this chapter when we look at a more realistic DDM that can handle dividend patterns such as those of Cincinnati Bell.

Deterministic Additive Growth Model

It is also possible that dividend growth follows an additive process. For instance, suppose the current dividend is D_0 and the dividend in one period's time is $D_0 + d$ where d is the dollar change in dividends. The dividend in two period's time is $D_0 + 2d$, the dividend in three period's time is $D_0 + 3d$, and so on, *ad infinitum*. The present value of this dividend stream is

$$P = \frac{D_0 + d}{r} + \frac{d}{r^2} \tag{7}$$

Equation (7) is termed the *deterministic additive growth model*.

More Complex Growth Models

Most multiperiod dividend growth models try to model the life cycle concept. In the simplest case, a model may recognize a finite period of accelerated growth followed by a more stable growth phase. An extension to this approach is to allow for a period of transition between the high and stable growth phases. These approaches are called the *two-phase model* and *three-phase model*, respectively.

Two-Phase Model

The two-phase geometric growth model recognizes that high growth rates can only be sustained for a finite period (say until the end of period N), and then the firm will face more stable growth prospects from period $N + 1$ to infinity. Hence we suppose that dividends grow at a geometric rate g_1 over the first N periods and, thereafter, at a geometric rate g_2. Under this assumption, the present value of future dividends can be shown to be:[4]

$$P = \frac{D_1}{r - g_1}\left[1 - \left(\frac{1 + g_1}{1 + r}\right)^N\right] + \frac{1}{(1 + r)^N}\left(\frac{D_N(1 + g_2)}{r - g_2}\right) \tag{8}$$

where $D_N = D_1(1 + g_1)^{N-1}$

The first term in equation (8) gives the value of the dividends paid during the high growth phase, while the second term gives the value of the dividends paid from period $N+1$ to infinity.

Three-Phase Model

A simple variation of the two-phase model incorporates a transition phase in recognition of the fact that changes in growth rates are gradual and not abrupt. This is the three-phase growth model. Hence, suppose that dividends grow at a high geometric rate g_1 over the first N periods, at a geometric rate g_2 over the next M periods, and, thereafter, at a long-run steady state geometric rate g_3. Under this assumption, the present value of future dividends is[5]

$$P = \frac{D_1}{r - g_1}\left[1 - \left(\frac{1 + g_1}{1 + r}\right)^N\right] + \frac{1}{(1 + r)^M}\left(\frac{D_N(1 + r)^N}{r - g_2}\right)\left(1 - \frac{(1 + g_2)^M}{1 + r}\right)$$

$$+ \frac{1}{(1 + r)^{N + M}}\left(\frac{D_{N + M}(1 + r)^N}{r - g_3}\right) \tag{9}$$

where

$$D_N = D_0(1 + g_1)^N$$
$$D_{N+M} = D_0(1 + g_1)^N(1 + g_2)^M$$

The three-phase model is reasonably intuitive if one recognizes that the first term in equation (9) grosses up the original dividend at the high growth rate, the second term (the transition period) increases the dividend at a decreasing rate, and the third term is again the constant growth model discounted back to the present.

---

[4] This model and its derivation are from Eric Sorensen and David Williamson, "Some Evidence on the Value of Dividend Discount Models," *Financial Analysts Journal* (November-December 1985),pp. 60-69.

[5] This model, also from Sorensen and Williamson ("Some Evidence on the Value of Dividend Discount Models"), is most closely associated with Nicholas Moldovsky. (See, Nicholas Moldovsky, Catherine May, and Sherman Chattiner, "Common Stock Valuation — Principles, Tables, and Applications," *Financial Analysts Journal* (March-April 1965).)

Different companies are assumed to be at different phases in the three-phase model. An emerging growth company would have a longer growth phase than a more mature company. Some companies are considered to have higher initial growth rates and hence longer growth and transition phases. Other companies may be considered to have lower current growth rates and hence shorter growth and transition phases.

In the typical investment organization, analysts supply the projected earnings, dividends, growth rates for earnings, and dividend and payout ratios using fundamental security analysis. The growth rate at maturity for the entire economy is applied to all companies. As a generalization, approximately 25% of the expected return from a company (projected by the DDM) comes from the growth phase, 25% from the transition phase, and 50% from the maturity phase. However, a company with high growth and low dividend payouts shifts the relative contribution toward the maturity phase, while a company with low growth and a high payout shifts the relative contribution toward the growth and transition phases.

A three-phase model is used by Salomon Brothers Inc. This organization is a broker/dealer that provides research to clients. The three-phase model that it developed is called the E-MODEL (E for earnings).[6]

STOCHASTIC DDM

As we noted in the illustration of the constant growth model, an erratic dividend pattern such as that of Cincinnati Bell can lead to quite a difference between the estimated price and the actual price. In the case of Cincinnati Bell the estimated price of $35.74 was considerably greater than the actual price of $22, suggesting that this telephone utility was trading significantly below its true value.

William Hurley and Lewis Johnson have suggested a new approach to dividend discounting modeling.[7] Their work differs from conventional dividend discount models discussed earlier in this chapter in that they assume that the future dividend stream follows a stochastic process. They then find the expected discounted value of this random dividend stream.

In this section we analyze the distribution of this discounted value for various assumptions about the stochastic process generating dividends. Processes with a Markov property are employed. This is a reasonable property for time series like dividends. Generally history will be unimportant for the valuation process — we care only about the current dividend and the probabilistic way in which uncertainty will unfold. Hence the memoryless property of Markov processes is suitable.[8]

---

[6] For a discussion of this model, see Eric H. Sorensen and Steven B. Kreichman, "Valuation Factors: Introducing the E-MODEL," Salomon Brothers Inc., May 12, 1987.

[7] Hurley and Johnson, "A Realistic Dividend Valuation Model," and "Confidence Intervals for Stochastic Dividend Discount Models."

[8] In addition, this general assumption gives rise to functional equations which are relatively straightforward to solve.

The models we describe below are divided into two types: *binomial dividend growth models* and *generalized Markov dividend growth models*. For the binomial dividend growth models it is assumed that the dividend will either stay the same in the next period or change in the next period. The change is either an increase or a decrease, but not both. Typically, a dividend increase is assumed. In contrast, for generalized Markov dividend growth models, dividends can stay the same in the next period, increase in the next period, or decrease in the next period.

Furthermore, within each type of stochastic model, the type of dividend change can be specified. As with the deterministic dividend discount models, the dividend can be assumed to follow a geometric growth pattern or an additive growth pattern. In the discussion below, we will begin with a discussion of the binomial stochastic DDMs and then describe the generalized Markov growth stochastic DDMs.

The Binomial Growth Stochastic Model

In the additive version of the binomial growth stochastic model, dividends are assumed to increase by a constant dollar amount or stay unchanged. This formulation of the model is called the *binomial additive growth stochastic model* and expressed as follows:

$$D_{t+1} = \begin{cases} D_t + d \text{ with probability } p \\ D_t \text{ with probability } 1 - p \end{cases} \quad \text{for } t = 1, 2, \ldots$$

where

$\begin{aligned} D_t &= \text{dividend in period } t \\ D_{t+1} &= \text{dividend in period } t{+}1 \\ d &= \text{dollar amount of the dividend increase} \\ p &= \text{probability that the dividend will increase} \end{aligned}$

The expected discounted value of the stock based on the additive stochastic DDM can be shown to be:

$$P = \frac{D_0}{r} + \left[\frac{1}{r} + \frac{1}{r^2}\right] dp \tag{10}$$

For example, consider once again Cincinnati Bell. In the illustration of the constant growth model, we used D_0 of $0.84 and g of 8.2%. For the probability of an increase in dividends, the historical percentage of annual dividend increases can be used. The estimate for d is obtained by calculating the dollar increase in dividend for each year that had a dividend increase and then taking the average dollar dividend increase. For the 15 years in which there was a dividend increase, the average dividend increase was $0.041. Since dividends increased 15 of the 17 years, a value of 15/17 or 88.24% was used. Substituting these values into equation (10), we find the estimated price to be:

$$P = \frac{0.84}{0.1075} + \left[\frac{1}{0.1075} + \frac{1}{(0.1075)^2}\right](0.041)(0.8824) = \$11.28$$

This result is still quite different from the actual price. The reason for this difference is that the additive model still does not reflect the pattern of dividends. We'll return to this point shortly when we discuss a different stochastic DDM.

The additive binomial growth model given by equation (10) assumes that the dividend will either increase or not change. There is also the possibility that the firm goes bankrupt. Given this possibility, a lower bound for the price of the stock (P_L) can be determined as follows. Letting p_B be the probability of bankruptcy then:

$$D_{t+1} = \begin{cases} D_t + d \text{ with probability } p \\ D_t \text{ with probability } 1 - p - p_B \text{ for } t = 1, 2, \ldots \\ 0 \text{ with probability } p_B \end{cases}$$

and it can be demonstrated that the lower bound for the price of the stock is:

$$P_L = \frac{D_0(1 - p_B)}{r} + \left[\frac{1}{r + p_B} + \frac{1}{(r + p_B)^2} \right] dp \tag{11}$$

Now let's look at the corresponding geometric growth model. Letting g be the growth rate, then the geometric dividend stream ignoring the probability of bankruptcy is

$$D_{t+1} = \begin{cases} D_t(1 + g) \text{ with probability } p \\ D_t \text{ with probability } 1 - p \end{cases} \text{ for } t = 1, 2, \ldots$$

The price of the stock is then:

$$P = \frac{D_0(1 + pg)}{r - pg} \tag{12}$$

Let's apply equation (12) to Cincinnati Bell. The growth rate used here is the geometric average of the percentage dividend increases for those years in which dividends increased.[9] Based on the figures reported in Exhibit 1, g is 7.63%. Using a growth rate of 7.63% and the previous values for D_0, r, and p, the estimated price using equation (12) is:

$$P = \frac{0.84[1 + (0.8824)(0.0763)]}{0.1075 - (0.8824)(0.0763)} = \$22.32$$

The estimated price based on a geometric stochastic DDM comes close to the actual price of $22 and is a far superior estimate than that derived from the additive stochastic DDM and the deterministic constant growth model.

Incorporating the probability of bankruptcy into the geometric stochastic DDM allows for the calculation of a lower bound estimate for the price. The formula is:

[9] Letting g_t be the percent change in dividend (in decimal form) and $N+$ the years of years of a dividend increase, then the geometric average is found as follows: $[g_1 \times g_2 \times g_3 \times \ldots \times g_{N+}]^{1/N+}$

$$P_L = D_0\left[\frac{1 + pg - p_B}{r - (pg - p_B)}\right] \tag{13}$$

From the difference in estimates between the additive and geometric stochastic models it can be seen that the selection of the assumed dividend pattern is critical.

Trinomial Markov Growth Model

The binomial stochastic models allow for two possibilities: an increase in dividends and no change in dividends. A lower bound for the stock's value can be determined by allowing for bankruptcy. It is not uncommon for companies to cut dividends temporarily. For example, an examination of the dividend record of the electric utilities industry as published in *Value Line Industry Review* found that in the aggregate firms cut dividends three times over a 15-year period.[10] The generalized Markov growth stochastic dividend discount model can accommodate dividend cuts.

The additive model version of the stochastic DDM is as follows:

$$D_{t+1} = \begin{cases} D_t + d \text{ with probability } p_U \\ D_t - d \text{ with probability } p_D \qquad \text{for } t = 1, 2, \ldots \\ D_t \text{ with probability } 1 - p_C = 1 - p_U - p_D \end{cases}$$

where

p_U = probability that the dividend will increase
p_D = probability that the dividend will decrease
p_C = probability that the dividend will be unchanged

The theoretical value of the stock based on the generalized Markov additive growth stochastic model then becomes:

$$P = \frac{D_0}{r} + \left[\frac{1}{r} + \frac{1}{r^2}\right]d(p_U - p_D) \tag{14}$$

Notice that when p_D is zero (that is, there is no possibility for a cut in dividends), equation (14) reduces to equation (10). Since the model deals with three possibilities for dividends next period, it is called a *trinomial additive growth model*.

Allowing for the possibility of bankruptcy, the lower bound for the theoretical price is determined as follows:

$$P_L = \frac{D_0(1 - p_B)}{r + p_B} + \left[\frac{1}{r + p_B} + \frac{1}{(r + p_B)^2}\right]d(p_U - p_D) \tag{15}$$

where $p_B = 1 - p_U - p_D$.

---

[10] Yulin Yao, "A Trinomial Dividend Valuation Model," *Journal of Portfolio Management* (Summer 1997), 99-103.

For the trinomial geometric stochastic model that allows for a possibility of cuts, we have:

$$D_{t+1} = \begin{cases} D_t(1+g) & \text{with probability } p_U \\ D_t(1-g) & \text{with probability } p_D \\ D_t & \text{with probability } 1 - p_C = 1 - p_U - p_D \end{cases} \quad \text{for } t = 1, 2, \ldots$$

and the theoretical price is:

$$P = \frac{D_0[1 + (p_U - p_D)]}{r - (p_U - p_D)g} \tag{16}$$

Substituting zero for p_D, equation (16) reduces to equation (12) — the binomial version assuming dividends are not cut. The model given by equation (16) is the *trinomial geometric growth model*.

The lower bound price for this version of the generalized Markov growth model allowing for bankruptcy is:

$$P_L = D_0\left[\frac{1 + (p_U - p_D)g - p_B}{r - (p_U - p_D)g + p_B}\right] \tag{17}$$

Application of the Stochastic DDMs

Yulin Yao applied the stochastic DDMs to five electric utility stocks that had regular dividends from 1979 to 1994 and had a temporary reduction of dividends in some periods: Rochester G&E, United Illum., Ohio Edison, Montana Power, and Sierra Pacific.[11] The historical dividends and the beta for each electric utility is reported in Exhibit 2. The discount rate is determined from the capital asset pricing models assuming a market risk premium of 5%, a risk-free rate of 6%, and the beta for the electric utility shown in Exhibit 2. The value for the dollar amount of the dividend change and the growth rate are estimated from the past pattern of dividend changes. The probabilities are based on the number of years of dividend increases, decreases, and no changes.

The results of the estimates are reported in Exhibit 3. For all five electric utility stocks, the trinomial growth stochastic models provide a better estimate of the price than the binomial growth stochastic models. Notice that there was no superiority of the geometric or additive models. In the case of Montana Power, the pattern of dividends reported in Exhibit 2 is best described by a geometric model; the geometric model was the best fit. For Sierra Pacific, the pattern of dividends payments is best described by an additive model and the additive model in fact provided an estimate closer to the actual price.

Confidence Intervals

One of the most useful properties of stochastic DDMs is that the discounted value of dividends is a random variable. Hence we ought to be able to specify a distribution for the discounted value. This then would allow an analyst to use the theory of statistical inference to judge whether a valuation is sufficiently far away from its market price to justify a buy or sell recommendation.

---

[11] Yao, "A Trinomial Dividend Valuation Model."

Exhibit 2: Dividend History and Beta for Five Electric Utilities

Year	Rochester G&E	United Illum.	Ohio Edison	Montana Power	Sierra Pacific
1979	1.33	2.62	1.76	1.03	1.28
1980	1.40	2.68	1.76	1.06	1.43
1981	1.49	2.76	1.76	1.17	1.46
1982	1.75	2.92	1.76	1.27	1.46
1983	1.84	3.08	1.80	1.46	1.50
1984	2.04	2.30	1.84	1.30	1.57
1985	2.20	2.08	1.88	1.00	1.63
1986	2.20	2.32	1.92	1.26	1.69
1987	2.03	2.32	1.96	1.34	1.74
1988	1.50	2.32	1.96	1.35	1.77
1989	1.52	2.32	1.96	1.39	1.81
1990	1.58	2.32	1.73	1.44	1.84
1991	1.62	2.44	1.50	1.50	1.84
1992	1.68	2.56	1.50	1.55	1.48
1993	1.72	2.66	1.50	1.55	1.12
1994	1.76	2.76	1.50	1.59	1.12
Beta	0.60	0.60	0.75	0.75	0.60

Source: Exhibit 2 in Yulin Yao, "A Trinomial Dividend Valuation Model,"
Journal of Portfolio Management (Summer 1997), p. 102.
This copyrighted material is reprinted with permission from Institutional Investor, Inc.
Journal of Portfolio Management, 488 Madison Avenue, New York, NY 10022.

Exhibit 3: Valuation and Actual Prices of Five Electric Utilities Using the Stochastic DDM Ignoring the Probability of Bankruptcy

Company	Actual Price	Ignoring Dividend Cuts		Allowing for Dividend Cuts	
		Additive Model	Geometric Model	Additive Model	Geometric Model
Rochester G&E	$23	$27.91	$40.50	$24.63*	$28.39
United Illum	35	40.63	46.87	36.79*	39.09
Ohio Edison	19	19.74	19.82	18.73	18.74*
Montana Power	24	19.68	33.02	17.40	21.91*
Sierra Pacific	19	21.88	24.60	19.58*	20.27

* Indicates the best fit model.
Source: Adapted from Exhibit 3 in Yulin Yao, "A Trinomial Dividend Valuation Model,"
Journal of Portfolio Management (Summer 1997).
This copyrighted material is reprinted with permission from Institutional Investor, Inc.
Journal of Portfolio Management, 488 Madison Avenue, New York, NY 10022.

Unfortunately, it is not easy to specify the form of this distribution, much less estimate its parameters. Fortunately the technique of Monte Carlo simulation can be used to generate an empirical distribution and estimates of important parameters such as expected discounted value and the variance of expected discounted value. The calculation of a confidence interval can be obtained by making the simplifying assumption that the discounted value is normally distributed. Monte Carlo simulation can also be used to do the same thing.

Assuming that the distribution of discounted value follows a normal distribution, the true value of the stock ought to be in the interval

Expected value ± 3 × standard deviation of stock value

with probability 99.7%

The expected value for the discounted dividends is obtained from the equation above for the specific stochastic DDM. The standard deviations for each stochastic DDM can be derived mathematically.[12] However, obtaining a closed-form solutions for the standard deviation of a discounted Markov dividend stream is tedious, even for the simplest processes.

By way of example, consider a firm which currently pays a dividend of $2.50 ($D_0$) and suppose an analyst has estimated the following parameters for the binomial geometric growth model: $r = 0.15$, $g = 0.10$, and $p = 0.6$. Using equation (12), the expected value is:

$$P = \frac{\$2.50(1 + 0.6 \times 0.10)}{0.15 - 0.6 \times 0.10} = \$29.44$$

The variance for the discounted dividends for the binomial growth model has been derived mathematically and is as[13]

$$Var(P) = \frac{g^2 p(1-p)}{(1+r)^2 - (1+pg)^2 - g^2 p(1-p)} \left[\frac{(1+r)^2 D_0^2}{(r-pg)^2} \right] \tag{18}$$

Using equation (18), the variance in our example can be shown to be equal to 12.46 and therefore the standard deviation is $3.53. An approximate 99.7% confidence interval is then:

[$29.44 − 3 ($3.53) to $29.44 + 3 ($3.53)] = [$18.85 to $40.03]

In fact these results were confirmed with Monte Carlo simulation. Ten thousand random dividend streams consistent with the assumed random process were generated.[14] Each dividend stream consisted of 200 periods. Each of the dividend streams was discounted, and hence, 10,000 random values were generated. The mean value was $29.45 and the sample standard deviation was $3.55 (the theoretical standard deviation is $3.53). Hence the simulation results are consistent with the theory.

However the assumption of a normal distribution does not appear to be justified. In Exhibit 4 a plot of the frequency distribution of the simulation is shown. This distribution is skewed to the right. Hence the calculation of more accurate confidence intervals requires the computation of higher order moments. One way around this problem is to use Monte Carlo simulation. We detail this approach below.

---

[12] See William J. Hurley, "An Introduction to Stochastic Dividend Discount Modeling," unpublished manuscript, July 1997.

[13] The derivation is provided in Hurley, "An Introduction to Stochastic Dividend Discount Modeling."

[14] Hurley, "An Introduction to Stochastic Dividend Discount Modeling."

Exhibit 4: Frequency Distribution for the Binomial Geometric Growth Stochastic Model

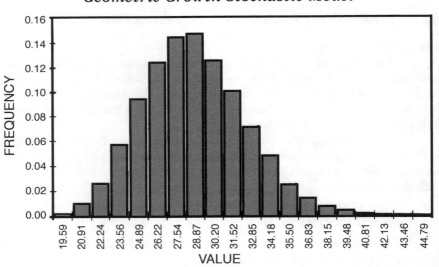

Obtaining Confidence Intervals Using Monte Carlo Simulation

As noted above, it is not simple to obtain a closed-formed solution for the variance of a discounted Markov dividend stream even for the simplest processes. The problem is compounded by the fact that the distribution of the discounted value tends to be non-normal. Hence estimation of confidence intervals will be difficult. A much simpler approach is to simulate the distribution of the discounted value. The following procedure using Monte Carlo simulation can be

1. Generate a truncated random dividend stream according to the assumed stochastic process.
2. Discount this truncated dividend stream to the present.
3. Repeat steps 1 and 2 a large number of times.

In terms of the parameters of the simulation, there are two issues. The first is where to truncate the dividend stream. This will depend on what discount rate is being used, but the experience of one of the authors suggests that truncating at 200 periods will give extremely accurate discounted values. The second is the number of discounted values to generate. Obviously, the more observations, the more accurate the discounted value and associated confidence interval will be. Again, based on the experience of one of the authors, 10,000 observations is more than sufficient.

Exhibit 5: Frequency Distribution for the Trinomial Simulation

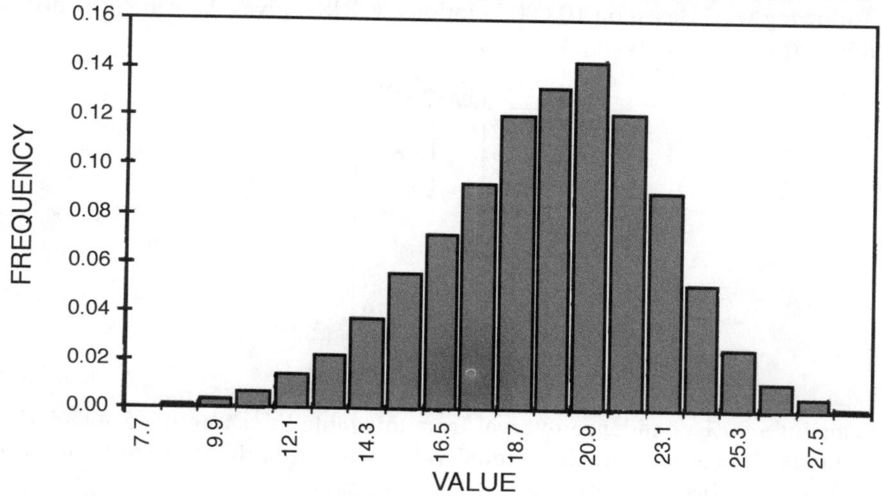

Consider the following example. Given the past dividend history and beliefs about the future, suppose an analyst believes that a firm's dividend stream is subject to the following trinomial process: the current dividend will remain unchanged with a probability of 50%; it will increase by 8% with probability 45%; and there will be a 25% cut with probability 5%. The current dividend is $2.50 and the discount rate is 15%. Based on these beliefs the analyst needs to determine the expected discounted value and its associated confidence interval.

A simulation in an EXCEL spreadsheet using the add-in @RISK was executed.[15] Ten thousand observations of discounted value were generated. This sample gave the following summary statistics:

Mean Observation	$20.23
Standard Deviation	$3.23
Minimum Observation	$7.73
Maximum Observation	$29.72
Skewness	−0.323

A frequency plot of discounted value is shown in Exhibit 5. Note that this distribution is skewed to the left, which is consistent with the sample skewness of −0.323.

---

[15] About the only difficulty in setting up the model is the logic associated with determining the dividend each period. To accomplish this the following nested IF statement was used:

$new = \text{IF}((r < 0.05, \text{old} \times (1 - 0.25), \text{IF}(r < 0.05 + 0.50, \text{old}, \text{old} \times (1 + 0.08)))$

where *new* is the calculated dividend, *r* is a pseudo-random number drawn from a uniform distribution on [0,1], and *old* is the previous dividend.

An empirical confidence interval can be obtained from @RISK output in the following way. Based on 10,000 iterations, @RISK gives the percentile distribution shown in the following table:

	Percentile
5%	14.541
10%	15.821
15%	16.725
.	.
.	.
.	.
85%	23.479
90%	24.153
95%	25.151

We can get a 90% confidence interval from this table by taking the 5% and 95% percentiles. Hence the true discounted value will lie in the interval [$14.54 to $25.15] with probability 90%.

The @RISK percentile output is nice for another reason. It allows the analyst to estimate the probability that a stock is undervalued or overvalued. For instance, in the example above, suppose the stock is trading at $15.80. From the percentile table above we see that 10% of the sample observations of value were less than $15.821. Hence we can conclude that there is approximately a 90% chance that the true stock value is at least $15.80, and hence a 90% chance that the stock is undervalued.

DDM ASSUMPTIONS

We conclude this chapter with a discussion of the implicit assumptions when a DDM is used. The first assumption is that there is no attribute bias. Attribute bias means that stocks preferred by the DDM tend to be biased toward certain equity attributes. Examples of equity attributes are low price-earnings ratios, high dividend yield, high book value ratio, or a particular industry sector. To test for such biases, Jacobs and Levy conducted a study.[16] They analyzed over 1,000 stocks on a quarterly basis for five years (mid-1982 to mid-1987) and estimated the expected return for each stock using a DDM. Given the expected return, they then used multiple regression analysis to estimate the relationship between 25 equity attributes and 38 industry categories and the expected return. What Jacobs and Levy found is that expected returns from a DDM are related to equity attributes such as low price-earnings ratio, book-value-to-price ratio, dividend yield, beta,

---

[16] Bruce I. Jacobs and Kenneth N. Levy, "On the Value of Value," *Financial Analysts Journal* (July-August 1988), pp. 47-62.

and firm size. Thus, while the DDM assumes no attribute bias, this is not supported by empirical research.[17]

Second, the DDM assumes that the investor's horizon matches the time horizon used in the model. In practice, this is often not true. Users of DDMs typically hold stocks for much shorter time periods than those implied by the model. Finally, when applying any quantitative model such as a DDM there is the problem of estimating the required inputs.

---

[17] Another study that has suggested such attribute bias is Richard Michaud, "A Scenario-Dependent Dividend Discount Model: Bridging the Gap Between Top-Down Investment Information and Bottom-Up Forecasts," *Financial Analysts Journal* (November/December 1985), pp. 49-59.

Chapter 10

Factor-Based Approach to Equity Portfolio Management

Frank J. Fabozzi, Ph.D., CFA
Adjunct Professor of Finance
School of Management
Yale University

INTRODUCTION

The theory of asset pricing in terms of factors is well developed in the academic literature and is explained in every textbook on investment management. In this chapter, we will show how factor models can be used to construct equity portfolios and control portfolio risk

TYPES OF FACTOR MODELS

There are three types of factor models being used today to manage equity portfolios: statistical factor models, macroeconomic factor models, and fundamental factor models.[1] We describe these three factor models below.

Statistical Factor Models

In a *statistical factor model,* historical and cross-sectional data on stock returns are tossed into a statistical model. The statistical model used is *principal components analysis* which is a special case of a statistical technique called *factor analysis.* The goal of the statistical model is to best explain the observed stock returns with "factors" that are linear return combinations and uncorrelated with each other.

For example, suppose that monthly returns for 1,500 companies for ten years are computed. The goal of principal components analysis is to produce "factors" that best explain the observed stock returns. Let's suppose that there are six "factors" that do this. These "factors" are statistical artifacts. The objective in a

---

[1] Gregory Connor, "The Three Types of Factor Models: A Comparison of Their Explanatory Power," *Financial Analysts Journal* (May-June 1995), pp. 42-57.

I wish to thank Bruce Jacobs and Kenneth Levy of Jacobs Levy for their helpful comments on an earlier draft of this chapter.

statistical factor model then becomes to determine the economic meaning of each of these statistically derived factors.

Because of the problem of interpretation, it is difficult to use the factors from a statistical factor model for valuation and risk control. Instead, practitioners prefer the two other models described below, which allow them to prespecify meaningful factors, and thus produce a more intuitive model.

Macroeconomic Factor Models

In a *macroeconomic factor model*, the inputs to the model are historical stock returns and observable macroeconomic variables. That is, the raw descriptors are macroeconomic variables. The goal is to determine which macroeconomic variables are pervasive in explaining historical stock returns. Those variables that are pervasive in explaining the returns are then the factors and included in the model. The responsiveness of a stock to these factors is estimated using historical time series data.

Two examples of proprietary macroeconomic factor models are the Burmeister, Ibbotson, Roll, and Ross (BIRR) model[2] and the Salomon Brothers model.[3] Salomon Brothers refers to its model as the "Risk Attribute Model" or RAM. A RAM is built for the United States and other countries

In the BIRR model, there are five macroeconomic factors that reflect unanticipated changes in the following macroeconomic variables:

- Investor confidence (confidence risk)
- Interest rates (time horizon risk)
- Inflation (inflation risk)
- Real business activity (business cycle risk)
- A market index (market timing risk)

Exhibit 1 explains each of these macroeconomic factor risks

In the U.S. version of the Salomon Brothers RAM model, the following six macroeconomic factors have been found to best describe the financial environment and are therefore the factors used:

- change in expected long-run economic growth
- short-run business cycle risk
- long-term bond yield changes
- short-term Treasury bill changes
- inflation shock
- dollar changes versus trading partner currencies

---

[2] Edwin Burmeister, Roger Ibbotson, Richard Roll, and Stephen A. Ross, "Using Macroeconomic Factors to Control Portfolio Risk," unpublished paper. The information used in this chapter regarding the BIRR model is obtained from various pages of the BIRR website (*www.birr.com*).

[3] This model is described in Eric H. Sorensen, Joseph J. Mezrich, and Chee Thum, *The Salomon Brothers U.S. Risk Attribute Model, Salomon Brothers*, Quantitative Strategy, October 1989, and Joseph J. Mezrich, Mark O'Donnell, and Vele Samak, *U.S. RAM Model: Model Update*, Salomon Brothers, Equity Portfolio Analysis, April 8, 1997.

Exhibit 1: Macroeconomic Factor Risks in the BIRR Factor Model

Confidence Risk

Confidence Risk exposure reflects a stock's sensitivity to unexpected changes in investor confidence. Investors always demand a higher return for making relatively riskier investments. When their confidence is high, they are willing to accept a smaller reward than when their confidence is low. Most assets have a positive exposure to Confidence Risk. An unexpected increase in investor confidence will put more investors in the market for these stocks, increasing their price and producing a positive return for those who already held them. Similarly, a drop in investor confidence leads to a drop in the value of these investments. Some stocks have a negative exposure to the Confidence Risk factor, however, suggesting that investors tend to treat them as "safe haven" when their confidence is shaken.

Time Horizon Risk

Time Horizon Risk exposure reflects a stock's sensitivity to unexpected changes in investors' willingness to invest for the long term. An increase in time horizon tends to benefit growth stocks, while a decrease tends to benefit income stocks. Exposures can be positive or negative, but growth stocks as a rule have a higher (more positive) exposure than income stocks.

Inflation Risk

Inflation Risk exposure reflects a stock's sensitivity to unexpected changes in the inflation rate. Unexpected increases in the inflation rate put a downward pressure on stock prices, so most stocks have a negative exposure to Inflation Risk. Consumer demand for luxuries declines when real income is eroded by inflation. Thus, retailer, eating places, hotels, resorts, and other "luxuries" are harmed by inflation, and their stocks therefore tend to be more sensitive to inflation surprises and, as a result, have a more negative exposure to Inflation Risk. Conversely, providers of necessary goods and services (agricultural products, tire and rubber goods, etc.) are relatively less harmed by inflation surprises, and their stocks have a smaller (less negative) exposure. A few stocks attract investors in times of inflation surprise and have a positive Inflation Risk exposure.

Market Timing Risk

Market Timing Risk exposure reflects a stock's sensitivity to moves in the stock market as a whole that cannot be attributed to the other factors. Sensitivity to this factor provides information similar to that of the CAPM Beta about how a stock tends to respond to changes in the broad market. It differs in that the Market Timing factor reflects only those surprises that are not explained by the other four factors.

Business Cycle Risk

Business Cycle Risk exposure reflects a stock's sensitivity to unexpected changes in the growth rate of business activity. Stocks of companies such as retail stores that do well in times of economic growth have a higher exposure to Business Cycle Risk than those that are less affected by the business cycle, such as utilities or government contractors. Stocks can have a negative exposure to this factor if investors tend to shift their funds toward those stocks when news about the growth rate for the economy is not good.

Source: Reproduced from pages of the BIRR website (www.birr.com).

Exhibit 2: Macroeconomic Factors in the Salomon Brothers U.S. Risk Attribute Model

Economic Growth[a]
Monthly change in industrial production as measured concurrently with stock returns.

Business Cycle[b]
The change in the spread between the yield on 20-year investment-grade corporate bonds and 20-year Treasury bonds is used as a proxy for the shorter-term cyclical behavior of the economy. Changes in the spread capture the risk of default resulting from the interaction of earnings cyclicality and existing debt structure.

Long-Term Interest Rates[b]
The change in interest rates is measured by the change in the 10-year Treasury yield. Changes in this yield alters the relative attractiveness of financial assets and therefore induces a change in the portfolio mix.

Short-Term Interest Rates[b]
The change in short-term interest rates is measured by changes in the 1-month Treasury bill rate.

Inflation Shock[a]
Inflation is measured by the Consumer Price Index. The inflation shock component is found by subtracting expected inflation from realized inflation. Expected inflation is measured using a proprietary econometric model.

U.S. Dollar[b]
The impact of currency fluctuations on the market is measured by changes in the basket of currencies. Specifically, a 15-country, trade-weighted basket of currencies is used.

a. Adapted from Joseph J. Mezrich, Mark O'Donnell, and Vele Samak, *U.S. RAM Model: Model Update*, Salomon Brothers, Equity Portfolio Analysis, April 8, 1997, p. 1.
b. Adapted from the discussion on page 4 of Eric H. Sorensen, Joseph J. Mezrich, and Chee Thum, *The Salomon Brothers U.S. Risk Attribute Model*, Salomon Brothers, Quantitative Strategy, October 1989.

In addition, there is another factor called "residual market beta" which is included to capture macroeconomic factors after controlling for the other six macroeconomic factors. Exhibit 2 provides a brief description of each macroeconomic factor.

We'll use the RAM model to explain the procedure for estimating the parameters of the model. For each stock in the universe used by Salomon Brothers (about 3,500) a multiple regression is estimated. The dependent variable is the stock's monthly return. The independent variables are the six macroeconomic factors, the residual market factor, and other market factors. The size and statistical significance of the regression coefficients of each of the macroeconomic factors is examined. Then for all stocks in the universe the regression coefficient for each of the macroeconomic factors is standardized. The purpose of standardizing the estimated regression coefficients is that it makes a comparison of the relative sensitivity of a stock to each macroeconomic factor easier.

The standardization methodology is as follows. For a given macroeconomic factor, the average value and standard deviation of the estimated regression coefficient from all the stocks in the universe are computed. The standardized regression coefficient for a stock with respect to a given macroeconomic factor is then found by calculating the difference between the estimated regression coefficient and the average value and then dividing this value by the standard deviation. The standardized regression coefficient is restricted to a value between −5 and +5.

A stock's standardized regression coefficient for a given macroeconomic factor is then the measure of the sensitivity of that stock to that risk factor. The standardized regression coefficient is therefore the factor sensitivity. If a stock has a factor sensitivity for a specific macroeconomic factor of zero, this means that it has average response to that macroeconomic factor. The more the factor sensitivity deviates from zero, the more responsive the stock is to that risk factor. For example, consider the economic growth factor. A positive value for this macroeconomic factor means that if all other factors are unchanged, a company is likely to outperform market returns if the economy improves. A negative value for the economic growth factor means that if all other factors are unchanged, a company is likely to underperform market returns if the economy improves.

The sensitivity for the factors are estimated so that they are statistically independent. This means that there will be no double counting the influence of a factor.

Fundamental Factor Models

Fundamental factor models use company and industry attributes and market data as raw descriptors. Examples are price/earnings ratios, book/price ratios, estimated economic growth, and trading activity. The inputs into a fundamental factor model are stock returns and the raw descriptors about a company. Those fundamental variables about a company that are pervasive in explaining stock returns are then the raw descriptors retained in the model. Using cross-sectional analysis the sensitivity of a stock's return to a raw descriptor is estimated.

As determined by Jacobs and Levy,[4] many of these descriptors are highly correlated. Adding highly correlated factors to a model neither enhances returns nor lowers risk. Factors that by themselves seem to be important may be unimportant when combined with other factors; factors that by themselves seem not to be important may be important when combined with other factors. A manager must be able to untangle these relationships.

Two commercially available fundamental factor models are the BARRA and the Wilshire models. The BARRA E2 model begins with raw descriptors.[5] It then combines raw descriptors to obtain risk indexes to capture related company attributes. For example, raw descriptors such as debt-to-asset ratio, debt-to-equity ratio, and fixed-rate coverage are measures that capture a company's financial leverage. These measures would be combined to obtain a risk index for financial leverage.

[4] Bruce I. Jacobs and Kenneth N. Levy, "Disentangling Equity Return Regularities: New Insights and Investment Opportunities," *Financial Analyst Journal* (May-June 1988), pp. 18-43.
[5] The BARRA E2 model is BARRA's second generation U.S. equity model. In 1997, BARRA released its third generation U.S. equity model (BARRA E3). The discussion in this chapter and the information provided in Exhibits 3 and 4 are based on the BARRA E2 model. The E3 model closely resembles the E2 model in structure, but with improved industry and risk index definitions. Chapter 32 describes the E3 model.

The BARRA E2 fundamental factor model has 13 risk indexes and 55 industry groups. For 12 of the risk indexes and the 55 industry groups, the model is estimated for BARRA's HICAP universe (1,000 of the largest-capitalization companies plus selected slightly smaller companies to fill underrepresented industry groups) using statistical techniques. The universe has varied from 1,170 to 1,300 companies.

Exhibit 3 reproduces the information about the 13 risk indexes as published by BARRA. Also shown in the exhibit are the raw descriptors used to construct each risk index. For example, the earnings-to-price ratio is a combination of the following raw descriptors: current earnings-to-price ratio, earnings-to-price ratio for the past five years, and IBES earnings-to-price ratio projection. Before each raw descriptor in Exhibit 3 is a plus or minus sign. The sign indicates how the raw descriptor influences a risk index. The 55 industry classifications are shown in Exhibit 4.

Exhibit 3: BARRA E2 Model Risk Index Definitions*

1. Variability In Markets (VIM)

This risk index is a predictor of the volatility of a stock based on its behavior and the behavior of its options in the capital markets. Unlike beta, which measures only the response of a stock to the market, Variability in Markets measures a stock's overall volatility, including its response to the market. A high beta stock will necessarily have a high Variability in Markets exposure. However, a high exposure will not necessarily imply a high beta; the stock may be responding to factors other than changes in the market.

This index uses measures such as the cumulative trading range and daily stock price standard deviation to identify stocks with highly variable prices. BARRA uses different formulas for three categories of stocks.

    a. Optioned stocks — all stocks having listed options.
    b. Listed stocks — all stocks in the HICAP universe that are listed on an exchange but do not have listed options.
    c. Thin stocks — all stocks that are traded over the counter or are outside the HICAP universe, except those with listed options.

Optioned stocks are distinct for several reasons. First, the option price provides an implicit forecast of the total standard deviation of the stock itself. Second, optioned stocks tend to be those with greatest investor interest and with the most effective trading volume. Stock trading volume descriptors understate the effective volume because they omit option volume.

Thin stocks, about ten percent of the basic sample, are broken out because they tend to trade differently from other stocks. Over-the-counter stocks and other thinly traded securities show price behavior inconsistent with efficient and timely prices. Thin stocks are less synchronized with market movements, and exhibit frequent periods in which no meaningful price changes occur as well as occasional outlying price changes that are promptly reversed. These influences cause some indicators of stock price variability to be biased.

In calculating this index, BARRA standardizes the formulas for the three stock categories relative to one another to provide one index for the total population.

    A. Optioned Stock Descriptors
        + Cumulative Range, 12 months
        + Beta * Sigma
        + Option Standard Deviation
        + Daily Standard Deviation

Exhibit 3 (Continued)

B. Listed Stock Descriptors
+ Beta * Sigma
+ Cumulative Range, 12 months
+ Daily Standard Deviation
+ Trading Volume to Variance
− Log of Common Stock Price
+ Serial Dependence
− Annual Share Turnover

C. Thin Stock Descriptors
+ Beta * Sigma
+ Cumulative Range, 12 months
+ Annual Share Turnover
− Log of Common Stock Price
− Serial Dependence

2. Success (SCS)

The Success index identifies recently successful stocks using price behavior in the market (measured by historical alpha and relative strength) and, to a lesser degree, earnings growth information. The relative strength of a stock is significant in explaining its volatility.

+ Relative Strength
+ Historical Alpha
+ Recent Earnings Change
+ IBES Earnings Growth
− Dividend Cuts, 5 years
+ Growth in Earnings per Share

3. Size (SIZ)

The Size index values total assets and market capitalization to differentiate large stocks from small stocks. This index has been a major determinant of performance over the years as well as an important source of risk.

+ Log of Capitalization
+ Log of Total Assets
+ Indicator of Earnings History

4. Trading Activity (TRA)

Trading activity measures the relative activity of a firm's shares in the market, or the "institutional popularity" of a company. The most important descriptors are the share turnover variables. In addition, this index includes the ratio of trading volume to price variability, the logarithm of price, and the number of analysts following the stock, as reported in the IBES database. The stocks with more rapid share turnover, lower price, and signs of greater trading activity are generally the higher risk stocks.

+ Annual Share Turnover
+ Quarterly Share Turnover
+ Share Turnover, 5 years
+ Log of Common Stock Price
+ IBES Number of Analysts
+ Trading Volume to Variance

Exhibit 3 (Continued)

5. Growth (GRO)

The Growth index is primarily a predictor of a company's future growth but also reflects its historical growth. BARRA estimates earnings growth for the next five years using regression techniques on a comprehensive collection of descriptors, all of which are distinct elements of the growth concept. The Growth index includes descriptors of payout, asset growth and historical growth in earnings, the level of earnings to price, and variability in capital structure.

- − Payout, 5 years
- − Earnings to Price Ratio, 5 years
- + Earnings Growth
- + Capital Structure Change
- − Normalized Earnings to Price Ratio
- + Recent Earnings Change
- − Dividend Yield, 5 years
- + IBES Earnings Change
- − Yield Forecast
- + Indicator of Zero Yield
- − Earnings to Price Ratio
- − IBES Earnings to Price Ratio
- + Growth in Total Assets

6. Earnings to Price Ratio (EPR)

The Earnings to Price Ratio measures the relationship between company earnings and market valuation. To compute the Earnings to Price Ratio, BARRA combines measures of past, current, and estimated future earnings.

- + Current Earnings to Price Ratio
- + Earnings to Price Ratio, 5 years
- + IBES Earnings to Price Ratio Projection

7. Book to Price Ratio (BPR)

This index is simply the book value of common equity divided by the market capitalization of a firm.

8. Earnings Variability (EVR)

The Earnings Variability index measures a company's historical earnings variability and cash flow fluctuations. In addition to variance in earnings over five years, it includes the relative variability of earnings forecasts taken from the IBES database, and the industry concentration of a firm's activities.

- + Variance in Earnings
- + IBES Standard Deviation to Price Ratio
- + Earnings Covariability
- + Concentration
- + Variance of Cash Flow
- + Extraordinary Items

9. Financial Leverage (FLV)

The Financial Leverage index captures the financial structure of a firm as well as its sensitivity to interest rates using the debt to assets ratio, the leverage at book value, and the probability of fixed charges not being covered. Bond market sensitivity is included only for financial companies.

Exhibit 3 (Continued)

− Bond Market Sensitivity
+ Debt to Assets Ratio
+ Leverage at Book (Debt to Equity)
+ Uncovered Fixed Charges

10. Foreign Income (FOR)

This index reflects the fraction of operating income earned outside the United States. It is a measure of sensitivity to currency exchange rate changes.

11. Labor Intensity (LBI)

This index estimates the importance of labor, relative to capital, in the operations of a firm. It is based on ratios of labor expense to assets, fixed plant and equipment to equity, and depreciated plant value to total plant cost. A higher exposure to Labor Intensity indicates a larger ratio of labor expense to capital costs and can be a gauge of sensitivity to cost-push inflation.

+ Labor Share
− Inflation-adjusted Plant to Equity Ratio
− Net Plant to Gross Plant

12. Yield (YLD)

The Yield index is simply a relative measure of the company's annual dividend yield.

13. LOCAP

The LOCAP characteristic indicates those companies that are not in the HICAP universe. It permits the factors in the model to be applied across a broader universe of assets than that used to estimate the model. The LOCAP factor is, in part, an extension of the Size index, allowing the returns of approximately 4500 smaller companies to deviate from an exact linear relationship with the Size index.

*In 1997, BARRA released its E3 model which closely resembles the E2 model but with improved risk index definitions.

Source: *United States Equity Model Handbook* (Berkeley, CA: BARRA, 1996), pp. 19-23.

Exhibit 4: BARRA E2 Model Industry Classifications*

The industry classifications in the U.S. Model are:			
1. Aluminum	15. Liquor	29. Photographic, Optical	43. Retail (All Other)
2. Iron & Steel	16. Tobacco	30. Consumer Durables	44. Telephone, Telegraph
3. Precious Metals	17. Construction	31. Motor Vehicles	45. Electric Utilities
4. Misc. Mining, Metals	18. Chemicals	32. Leisure, Luxury	46. Gas Utilities
5. Coal & Uranium	19. Tires & Rubber	33. Health Care (Non-drug)	47. Banks
6. International Oil	20. Containers	34. Drugs, Medicine	48. Thrift Institutions
7. Dom. Petroleum Reserves	21. Producer Goods	35. Publishing	49. Miscellaneous Finance
8. For. Petroleum Reserves	22. Pollution Control	36. Media	50. Life Insurance
9. Oil Refining, Distribution	23. Electronics	37. Hotels, Restaurants	51. Other Insurance
10. Oil Service	24. Aerospace	38. Trucking, Freight	52. Real Property
11. Forest Products	25. Business Machines	39. Railroads, Transit	53. Mortgage Financing
12. Paper	26. Soaps, Housewares	40. Air Transport	54. Services
13. Agriculture, Food	27. Cosmetics	41. Transport by Water	55. Miscellaneous
14. Beverages	28. Apparel, Textiles	42. Retail (Food)	

* In 1997, BARRA released its E3 model which has improved industry classifications.

Source: *United States Equity Model Handbook* (Berkeley, CA: BARRA, 1996), pp. 32.

Exhibit 5: Fundamental Factors and Market Sensitive Factor Definitions for Wilshire Atlas Factor Model

1.Earnings/price ratio	Sum of the most recent four quarters' earnings per share divided by the closing price.
2. Book value/price ratio	Book value divided by common equity shares outstanding.
3. Market capitalization	The natural logarithm of the product of a security's price multiplied by the number of shares outstanding.
4. Net earnings revision	Analysts momentum measure: Net earnings revision, based on I/B/E/S data, measures analysts' optimism of earnings. Net earnings revision is the percentage of analysts who are feeling more optimistic about earnings in the next period. The higher the net earnings revision number, the more optimistic analysts are about an increase in that company's earnings.
5. Reversal	Price momentum measure: Reversal captures the mean reversion tendencies of stocks. It is a measure of the difference between a security's actual return in the last period and the expected return with respect to its beta. If a stock has a positive reversal this means that it had a higher than expected return in the last period given its beta. Thus, this security is expected to have a lower than expected return in the next period so that the returns for this security will conform to the norm expectations over the long run.
6. Earnings torpedo	Earnings momentum measure: Earnings torpedo, based on I/B/E/S data, is a measure of the estimated growth in earnings for a security relative to historical earnings. Earnings torpedo is based on the ratio of next years estimated earnings per share versus its historical earnings per share. The securities in the universe are then ranked by the estimate and given an earnings torpedo score. A security with a high earnings torpedo score is considered to be vulnerable to a large drop in price if earnings do not meet the higher earnings estimates forecasted by analysts in the next period.
7. Historical beta	Classic measure of security volatility. Measured for each security by regressing the past 60 months worth of excess returns against the S&P500. A minimum of 38 months are required for the data to be valid.

Source: Adapted from *U.S. Equity Risk Model* (Santa Monica, CA: Wilshire Associates, July 1997 draft).

As with the macroeconomic factor model, the raw descriptors are standardized or normalized. The risk indices are in turn standardized. The sensitivity of each company to each risk index is standardized.

The Wilshire Atlas model uses six fundamental factors, one market factor sensitivity, and 39 industry factors to explain stock returns. The six fundamental factors and the market factor sensitivity are listed in Exhibit 5, along with their definitions.

The BARRA and Wilshire factor models are commercially available. Now we'll look at a proprietary model developed by a firm for its own use in managing client equity portfolios — Goldman Sachs Asset Management (GSAM). This firm is the investment management subsidiary of Goldman Sachs & Co., a broker/dealer firm. There are nine descriptors used in the GSAM factor model. These descriptors which are the factors in the model are described in Exhibit 6. The factors fall into three categories: (1) value measures, (2) growth and momentum measures, and (3) risk measures.

Exhibit 6: Factor Definitions for the Goldman Sachs Asset Management Factor Model

Factor	Definition
Book/Price	Common equity per share divided by price
Retained EPS/Price	Year-ahead consensus EPS forecast less indicated annual dividend divided by price. One-year forecast EPS is a weighted average of the forecasts for the current and next fiscal years.
EBITD/Enterprise Value	Earnings before interest, taxes and depreciation divided by total capital. Total capital is equity at market plus long-term debt at book.
Estimate Revisions	The number of estimates raised in the past three months, less the number lowered, divided by the total number of estimates.
Price Momentum	Total return over the last 12 months, less the return for the latest month (to adjust for short-term reversals).
Sustainable Growth	The consensus long-term growth forecast.
Beta	The regression coefficient from a 60-month regression of the stock's excess returns (above the T-bill rate) against the market's excess returns.
Residual Risk	The "unexplained" variation from the above regression; the standard error of the regression.
Disappointment Risk	The risk that actual earnings will not meet projections. Stocks with high expected one-year earnings growth have high disappointment potential; stocks with low expectations have less disappointment risk.

Source: Table 4 in *Select Equity Investment Strategy*, Goldman Sachs Asset Management, February 1997, p. 4.

THE OUTPUT AND INPUTS OF A FACTOR MODEL

Now that we have identified the types of factor models, let's look at the output of the model and the inputs to the model after the estimation has taken place. The output of a factor model is found by first multiplying a factor sensitivity by the assumed value for the factor measure (assumed risk factor).[6] This gives the contribution to the model's output from a given risk factor exposure. Summing up over all risk factors gives the output. For a K-factor model this is expressed mathematically as follows:

$$\text{Output} = \text{Beta}_1 \times (\text{Factor}_1 \text{ measure}) + \text{Beta}_2 \times (\text{Factor}_2 \text{ measure}) + \ldots + \text{Beta}_K \times (\text{Factor}_K \text{ measure})$$

Let's look first at the Beta's. These are the factor sensitivities and are estimated statistically. As explained earlier, they are commonly standardized or normalized.

The output varies by model. For example, in the BIRR macroeconomic factor model, the output is the *expected excess return* given the estimated factor sensitivities and the assumed values for the factor measures. The expected excess return is the expected return above the risk-free rate. In contrast, in the Salomon

---

[6] For an example of quantitative estimation of returns to the size factor using economic variables, see Bruce I. Jacobs and Kenneth N. Levy, "Forecasting the Size Effect," *Financial Analysts Journal* (May-June 1989), pp.61-78.

Brothers RAM factor model, the output is a score that is used to rank the outcome given the estimated factor sensitivities and assumed values for the factor measures.

The factor measures vary by model. In the BIRR macroeconomic factor model, for example, a factor measure is the estimated market price of the risk factor expressed in percent per year. For the Salomon Brothers RAM factor model, a factor measure is the normalized value for the factor.

Let's use the two macroeconomic models described earlier to show how the output is obtained. First, the BIRR model. The estimated risk exposure profile for Reebok International Limited and the assumed values for the risk factors (expressed in percent per year) are shown below:

Risk factor	Estimated factor sensitivity	Estimated market price of risk (%)
Confidence risk	0.73	2.59
Time horizon risk	0.77	-0.66
Inflation risk	-0.48	-4.32
Business cycle risk	4.59	1.49
Market timing risk	1.50	3.61

The expected excess return is then found as follows:

$$\text{Expected excess return for Reebok} = 0.73\,(2.59) + 0.77\,(-0.66) + (-0.48)\,(-4.32) + 4.59\,(1.49) + 1.50\,(3.61) = 15.71\%$$

To obtain the expected return, the risk-free rate must be added. For example, if the risk-free rate is 5%, then the expected return is 20.71% (15.71% plus 5%).

In the Salomon Brothers RAM model, the set of forecasts for the factor measures are called *scenario factors*. Based on scenario factors, the sensitivity of a stock to each factor can be calculated. Adding up the sensitivity of a stock to each factor gives a stock's *scenario score*. Recall that in this factor model there are six macroeconomic factors (described in Exhibit 2) and the residual beta. Each factor is expressed in normalized or standardized form. For Pepsico (in October 1989) the factor betas and a factor scenario for a weakening economy are given below:[7]

Risk factor	Estimated factor sensitivity	Factor scenario (Weakening economy)
Economic growth	-1.8	-1.0
Business cycle	-0.9	-0.5
Long rate	0.0	0.5
Short rate	0.1	0.3
Inflation rate	-0.3	0.1
U.S. dollar	0.1	0.3
Residual beta	-1.1	-0.5

[7] Sorensen, Mezrich, and Thum, "The Salomon Brothers U.S. Stock Risk Attribute Model," p. 6.

The scenario score for Pepsico is then:

$$\text{Pepsico scenario score} = -1.8\,(-1.0) + (-0.9)\,(-0.5) + 0\,(0.5) + 0.1\,(0.3)$$
$$+ (-0.3)\,(0.1) + 0.1\,(0.3) + (-1.1)\,(-0.5) = 1.7$$

This scenario score is then compared to the scenario score of other stocks in the universe of purchase or short-sale candidates of a portfolio manager.

PORTFOLIO CONSTRUCTION WITH FACTOR MODELS

Now let's see how factor models are used in portfolio construction. Specifically, based on expectations about the future outcomes of the factors, an active equity manager can construct a portfolio to add value relative to some benchmark should those outcomes be realized.

Portfolio Expected Excess Returns and Risk Exposure Profiles

In factor models in which the output is an expected excess return for a stock, the expected excess return for a portfolio can be easily computed. This is the weighted average of the expected excess return for each stock in the portfolio. The weights are the percentage of a stock value in the portfolio relative to the market value of the portfolio. Similarly, a portfolio's sensitivity to a given factor risk is a weighted average of the factor sensitivity of the stocks in the portfolio. The set of factor sensitivities is then the portfolio's risk exposure profile. Consequently, the expected excess return and the risk exposure profile can be obtained from the stocks comprising the portfolio.

Since a stock market index is nothing more than a portfolio that includes the universe of stocks making up the index, an expected excess return and risk exposure profile can be determined for an index. This allows a manager to compare the expected excess return and the risk profile of a stock and/or a portfolio to that of a stock market index whose performance the portfolio manager is measured against. For example, in the BIRR model, the risk exposure profile for the S&P 500 is shown below, as well as that of Reebok for comparative purposes:

Risk factor	Estimated factor sensitivity for	
	S&P 500	Reebok
Confidence risk	0.27	0.73
Time horizon risk	0.56	0.77
Inflation risk	−0.37	−0.48
Business cycle risk	1.71	4.59
Market timing risk	1.00	1.50

By comparing the risk exposure profile of Reebok to the S&P 500, a portfolio manager can see the relative risk exposure. Using the same assumed values for the risk factors as used earlier for Reebok, the expected excess return for the S&P 500 is 8.09% compared to 15.71% for Reebok.

Exhibit 7: Portfolio Holdings for Manager X

IDENT	NAME	SHARES	PRICE	%WGT	BETA	%YLD	IND
1 FDX	FEDERAL EXPRESS CORP	80700	41.625	3.00	1.15	0.00	AIR
2 NEM	NEWMONT MNG CORP	67500	49.500	2.98	0.76	1.21	GOLD
3 I	FIRST INTST BANCORP	167700	33.000	4.94	1.32	9.09	BANKS
4 HWP	HEWLETT PACKARD CO	126900	43.125	4.89	1.15	0.97	BUS MN
5 IBM	INTERNATIONAL BUS MACH	141400	111.500	14.08	1.01	4.34	BUS MN
6 F	FORD MTR CO DEL	273100	41.500	10.12	0.98	7.17	MOT VH
7 HCSG	HEALTHCARE SVCS GRP IN	93000	24.250	2.01	1.29	0.28	SERVCS
8 TXN	TEXAS INSTRS INC	81500	32.000	2.33	1.41	2.25	ELCTRN
9 S	SEARS ROEBUCK & CO	342900	33.625	10.30	1.09	5.94	RET OT
10 AXP	AMERICAN EXPRESS CO	291900	29.125	7.59	1.20	3.15	FINANC
11 JNJ	JOHNSON & JOHNSON	205800	70.625	12.98	1.02	1.92	HEALTH
12 EK	EASTMAN KODAK CO	324800	38.125	11.06	1.10	5.24	PHOTOG
13 WMX	WASTE MGMT INC	185900	41.375	6.87	1.24	0.86	POLL C
14 PCI	PARAMOUNT COMMUNICATIO	118900	39.500	4.20	1.14	1.77	PUBLSH
15 TAN	TANDY CORP	79800	36.750	2.62	1.26	1.63	RET OT

BARRA Microcomputer Products: Interactive PORCH   Page   1
Portfolio: SAMPLE   Market: SAP500   Pricing Date: 07-31-90

Source: The information in this exhibit is adapted from Figure VI-1 of *United States Equity Model Handbook* (Berkeley, CA: BARRA, 1996), p. 40.

In factor models such as the Salomon Brothers RAM model where the output is a *scenario score*, the risk exposure profile of a portfolio and market index is calculated in the same manner as when the model's output is the expected excess return. However, in scenario score models the portfolio's and market index's output is a ranking.

The power of a factor model regardless of the type of output is that given the risk factors and the factor sensitivities, a portfolio's risk exposure profile can be quantified and controlled. The examples below show how this can be done with a fundamental factor model. This allows managers to avoid making unintended bets.

Assessing the Exposure of a Portfolio

A fundamental factor model can be used to assess whether the current portfolio is consistent with a manager's strengths. In this application of factor models and the one that follows, we will use the BARRA factor model.[8] Exhibit 7 is a list of the holdings of manager X as of July 31, 1990.[9] There are 15 stocks held with a total market value of $111.9 million.

Exhibit 8 assesses the risk exposure of manager X's portfolio relative to the risk exposure of the S&P 500. The boxes in the second column of the exhibit indicate the significant differences in the exposure of manager X's portfolio relative to the S&P 500. There are two risk indices boxed — success and foreign

[8] The illustrations are adapted from Chapter VI of *United States Equity Model Handbook* (Berkeley, CA: BARRA, 1996).
[9] This was an actual portfolio of a BARRA client.

income — and two industry groupings boxed — business machines and miscellaneous finance. Exhibit 3 describes the risk indices. The -0.45 exposure to the success risk index reveals that manager X's portfolio exhibits low relative strength as measured by stock price and earnings momentum — a style characteristic. Consequently, the success risk index indicates an exposure to style. Thus, we can see that manager X is making a style bet. The 0.62 exposure to the foreign income risk index tells manager X that the companies in the portfolio tend to earn a significant portion of their operating income abroad. Consequently, manager X is making an international bet. In terms of industry exposure, manager X is extremely more aggressive in his or her holdings of business machine stocks and miscellaneous finance stocks.

Notice in this example how the manager is able to identify where the bets are made. Manager X has made a style bet, an international bet, and a bet on two industries. If the manager did not intend to make these bets, the portfolio can be rebalanced to eliminate any unintended bets.

Tilting a Portfolio

Now let's look at how an active manager can construct a portfolio to make intentional bets. Suppose that manager Y seeks to construct a portfolio that generates superior returns relative to the S&P 500 by tilting it toward high-success stocks. At the same time, the manager does not want to increase tracking error risk significantly. An obvious approach may seem to be to identify all the stocks in the universe that have a higher than average success risk index. The problem with this approach is that it introduces unintentional bets with respect to the other risk indices.

Instead, an optimization method combined with a factor model can be used to construct the desired portfolio. The input to this process is the tilt exposure sought, the benchmark stock market index, and the number of stocks to be included in the portfolio. The BARRA optimization model also requires a specification of the excess return sought. In our illustration, the tilt exposure sought is high success stocks, the benchmark is the S&P 500, and the number of stocks to be included in the portfolio is 50. While we do not report the holdings of the optimal portfolio here, Exhibit 9 provides an analysis of that portfolio by comparing the risk exposure of the 50-stock optimal portfolio to that of the S&P 500.

Fundamental Factor Models and Equity Style Management

In Chapter 4, we covered equity style management. Notice that the factors used in fundamental factor models such as the BARRA factor model (Exhibit 3), Wilshire factor model (Exhibit 5), and the GSAM factor model (Exhibit 6) are the same characteristics used in style management. Since the factors can be used to add value and control risk, this suggests that factor models can be used in style management for the same purposes.

Exhibit 8: Analysis of Manager X Portfolio's Exposure Relative to the S&P 500

```
Comparison Summary Report                        Date: 07-31-90

Portfolio              SAMPLE
Comparison Port.       SAP500
Market                 SAP500

Number of Assets              15
Port. Value      111,940,087.50
Predicted Yield            3.78
Alpha                      0.00
Utility                   -0.36
Tracking Error             7.25
```

FACTORS	SAMPLE	SAP500	DIFF	MCTE
VARIABILITY IN MARKETS	0.02	-0.06	0.09	0.010
SUCCESS	-0.45	0.01	-0.47	-0.021
SIZE	0.54	0.29	0.26	0.004
TRADING ACTIVITY	0.22	0.00	0.22	-0.002
GROWTH	-0.12	-0.05	-0.07	0.016
EARNINGS/PRICE	0.08	0.01	0.08	0.007
BOOK/PRICE	0.18	-0.02	0.20	0.001
EARNINGS VARIATION	0.00	-0.05	0.05	0.003
FINANCIAL LEVERAGE	0.28	0.03	0.25	-0.001
FOREIGN INCOME	0.62	0.12	0.51	-0.001
LABOR INTENSITY	0.30	0.01	0.29	-0.003
YIELD	0.16	0.02	0.14	0.007
LOCAP	0.02	0.00	0.02	-0.005
ALUMINUM	0.00	0.60	-0.60	0.099
IRON AND STEEL	0.00	0.30	-0.30	0.081
PRECIOUS METALS	1.25	0.42	0.83	0.071
MISC. MINING, METALS	0.54	0.61	-0.07	0.073
COAL AND URANIUM	0.00	0.40	-0.40	0.013
INTERNATIONAL OIL	0.00	4.49	-4.49	-0.033
DOM PETROLEUM RESERVES	0.51	3.46	-2.96	-0.047
FOR PETROLEUM RESERVES	0.69	2.25	-1.56	-0.037
OIL REFINING, DISTRIBUTN	0.00	1.29	-1.29	-0.011
OIL SERVICE	0.00	1.02	-1.02	-0.017
FOREST PRODUCTS	0.00	0.30	-0.30	0.120
PAPER	0.00	2.06	-2.06	0.082
AGRICULTURE, FOOD	0.00	4.99	-4.99	0.047
BEVERAGES	0.00	1.41	-1.41	0.066
LIQUOR	0.00	1.05	-1.05	0.050
TOBACCO	0.00	1.38	-1.38	0.067
CONSTRUCTION	0.00	0.88	-0.88	0.098
CHEMICALS	1.99	3.44	-1.45	0.083
TIRE & RUBBER	0.00	0.10	-0.10	0.101
CONTAINERS	0.00	0.17	-0.17	0.069
PRODUCERS GOODS	0.02	4.49	-4.47	0.086
POLLUTION CONTROL	6.87	1.13	5.75	0.124
ELECTRONICS	2.21	2.39	-0.18	0.126
AEROSPACE	0.00	2.47	-2.47	0.089
BUSINESS MACHINES	19.07	4.80	14.26	0.130
SOAPS, HOUSEWARE	0.00	1.99	-1.99	0.084
COSMETICS	4.54	0.94	3.60	0.096
APPAREL, TEXTILES	0.00	0.77	-0.77	0.080
PHOTOGRAPHIC, OPTICAL	6.75	0.55	6.20	0.114
CONSUMER DURABLES	0.00	0.99	-0.99	0.104
MOTOR VEHICLES	8.91	2.42	6.49	0.114
LEISURE, LUXURY	0.00	0.18	-0.18	0.096
HEALTH CARE (NON-DRUG)	5.06	1.85	3.21	0.070
DRUGS, MEDICINE	5.70	6.81	-1.12	0.066
PUBLISHING	2.10	1.48	0.62	0.090
MEDIA	2.10	1.67	0.43	0.079
HOTELS, RESTAURANTS	0.00	1.75	-1.75	0.094
TRUCKING, FREIGHT	0.00	0.13	-0.13	0.098
RAILROADS, TRANSIT	0.00	0.92	-0.92	0.046
AIR TRANSPORT	3.00	0.59	2.41	0.139
TRANSPORT BY WATER	0.00	0.03	-0.03	0.039
RETAIL (FOOD)	0.00	0.85	-0.85	0.062
RETAIL (ALL OTHER)	6.12	5.19	0.93	0.098
TELEPHONE, TELEGRAPH	0.00	8.26	-8.26	0.036
ELECTRIC UTILITIES	0.00	4.37	-4.37	0.024
GAS UTILITIES	0.00	1.17	-1.17	0.019
BANKS	6.49	2.93	3.56	0.063
THRIFT INSTITUTIONS	0.00	0.28	-0.28	0.073
MISC. FINANCE	10.87	2.20	8.67	0.094
LIFE INSURANCE	0.00	0.92	-0.92	0.061
OTHER INSURANCE	2.37	2.24	0.13	0.059
REAL PROPERTY	0.82	0.19	0.63	0.107
MORTGAGE FINANCING	0.00	0.00	-0.00	0.068
SERVICES	2.01	1.89	0.12	0.070
MISCELLANEOUS	0.00	0.56	-0.56	0.053

Source: The information in this exhibit is adapted from Figure VI-3 of *United States Equity Model Handbook* (Berkeley, CA: BARRA, 1996), p. 42.

Exhibit 9: Analysis of a 50-Stock Portfolio Constructed to be Tilted Toward High Success Stocks

```
Comparison Summary Report                              Date: 07-31-90

Portfolio             SUCCESS
Comparison Port.      SAP500
Market                SAP500

Number of Assets            50
Port. Value      99,999,723.50
Predicted Yield           3.04
Alpha                     0.31
Utility                   0.18
Tracking Error            4.19
```

FACTORS	US50	SAP500	DIFF
VARIABILITY IN MARKETS	0.10	-0.06	0.16
SUCCESS	0.77	0.01	0.76
SIZE	0.24	0.29	-0.05
TRADING ACTIVITY	-0.06	0.00	-0.07
GROWTH	0.10	-0.05	0.15
EARNINGS/PRICE	-0.00	0.01	-0.01
BOOK/PRICE	-0.16	-0.02	-0.14
EARNINGS VARIATION	0.00	-0.05	0.05
FINANCIAL LEVERAGE	-0.16	0.03	-0.19
FOREIGN INCOME	-0.10	0.12	-0.21
LABOR INTENSITY	-0.04	0.01	-0.05
YIELD	-0.11	0.02	-0.13
LOCAP	0.00	0.00	-0.00
ALUMINUM	1.98	0.60	1.38
IRON AND STEEL	0.00	0.30	-0.30
PRECIOUS METALS	0.50	0.42	0.07
MISC. MINING, METALS	0.47	0.61	-0.14
COAL AND URANIUM	0.42	0.40	0.02
INTERNATIONAL OIL	4.36	4.49	-0.13
DOM PETROLEUM RESERVES	2.45	3.46	-1.01
FOR PETROLEUM RESERVES	3.19	2.25	0.94
OIL REFINING, DISTRIBUTN	1.44	1.29	0.15
OIL SERVICE	1.79	1.02	0.77
FOREST PRODUCTS	0.03	0.30	-0.27
PAPER	1.07	2.06	-0.99
AGRICULTURE, FOOD	5.29	4.99	0.30
BEVERAGES	0.00	1.41	-1.41
LIQUOR	0.37	1.05	-0.68
TOBACCO	3.13	1.38	1.75
CONSTRUCTION	2.27	0.88	1.39
CHEMICALS	3.39	3.44	-0.05
TIRE & RUBBER	0.00	0.10	-0.10
CONTAINERS	0.00	0.17	-0.17
PRODUCERS GOODS	4.36	4.49	-0.14
POLLUTION CONTROL	2.38	1.13	1.25
ELECTRONICS	4.24	2.39	1.84
AEROSPACE	3.11	2.47	0.64
BUSINESS MACHINES	1.39	4.80	-3.42
SOAPS, HOUSEWARE	4.79	1.99	2.80
COSMETICS	0.29	0.94	-0.66
APPAREL, TEXTILES	0.98	0.77	0.21
PHOTOGRAPHIC, OPTICAL	0.00	0.55	-0.55
CONSUMER DURABLES	0.73	0.99	-0.27
MOTOR VEHICLES	4.35	2.42	1.94
LEISURE, LUXURY	0.00	0.18	-0.18
HEALTH CARE (NON-DRUG)	2.10	1.85	0.25
DRUGS, MEDICINE	4.60	6.81	-2.21
PUBLISHING	0.00	1.48	-1.48
MEDIA	0.16	1.67	-1.51
HOTELS, RESTAURANTS	0.59	1.75	-1.16
TRUCKING, FREIGHT	0.00	0.13	-0.13
RAILROADS, TRANSIT	0.00	0.92	-0.92
AIR TRANSPORT	0.00	0.59	-0.59
TRANSPORT BY WATER	0.00	0.03	-0.03
RETAIL (FOOD)	4.78	0.85	3.93
RETAIL (ALL OTHER)	9.80	5.19	4.62
TELEPHONE, TELEGRAPH	0.00	8.26	-8.26
ELECTRIC UTILITIES	12.31	4.37	7.95
GAS UTILITIES	1.03	1.17	-0.14
BANKS	0.00	2.93	-2.93
THRIFT INSTITUTIONS	0.00	0.28	-0.28
MISC. FINANCE	2.10	2.20	-0.10
LIFE INSURANCE	1.67	0.92	0.75
OTHER INSURANCE	1.55	2.24	-0.69
REAL PROPERTY	0.23	0.19	0.04
MORTGAGE FINANCING	0.00	0.00	-0.00
SERVICES	0.19	1.89	-1.70
MISCELLANEOUS	0.15	0.56	-0.42

Source: The information in this exhibit is adapted from Figure VI-7 of *United States Equity Model Handbook* (Berkeley, CA: BARRA, 1996), p. 47.

Exhibit 10: Summary of Perfect Foresight Tests Two Strategies Using Factor Models: 12-Month Rolling Value Added (%) from January 1987 to July 1995

Country	Long Stock Strategy			Market Neutral Strategy		
	High	Low	Average	High	Low	Average
United States	82%	39%	55%	195%	75%	138%
United Kingdom	131	52	82	326	50	155
Japan	106	56	74	236	66	121
Canada	91	63	77	—	—	—

Source: Table 15 from David J. Leinweber, Robert D. Arnott, and Christopher G. Luck, "The Many Sides of Equity Style," Chapter 11 in T. Daniel Coggin, Frank J. Fabozzi, and Robert D. Arnott (eds.), *The Handbook of Equity Style Management* (New Hope, PA: Frank J. Fabozzi Associates, 1997).

RETURN PERFORMANCE POTENTIAL OF FACTOR MODELS

It is interesting to see how well a portfolio constructed using a factor model would have performed with perfect foresight. For example, suppose we are examining monthly returns. We look at the actual factor return for the month and use that as our expectation at the beginning of the month. Given the forecasts an optimization model can be used to design the optimal portfolio.

Leinweber, Arnott, and Luck performed this experiment for several countries using the BARRA factor model for those countries — United States, United Kingdom, Japan, and Canada — for the period January 1987 to July 1995.[10] Transaction costs for rebalancing a portfolio each month were incorporated. A 12-month rolling value added return was calculated. A value added return is the return above a broad-based stock index for the country.

Two strategies were followed. One was simply a long position in the stocks. The second was a market neutral long-short strategy.[11] Exhibit 10 reports the results of the perfect foresight tests. With perfect foresight, the BARRA factor model would have added significant value for each country stock portfolio. For example, in the United States even in the worst 12-month rolling period the factor-based model added 39% for the long stock strategy and 75% for the market neutral long-short strategy.

Eric Sorensen, Joseph Mezrich, and Chee Thum performed two backtests of the Salomon Brothers RAM (a macroeconomic factor model) to assess the model. The tests were basically event studies.[12] In the first backtest, these

---

[10] David J. Leinweber, Robert D. Arnott, and Christopher G. Luck, "The Many Sides of Equity Style," Chapter 11 in T. Daniel Coggin, Frank J. Fabozzi, and Robert D. Arnott (eds.), *The Handbook of Equity Style Management* (New Hope, PA: Frank J. Fabozzi, 1997).

[11] See Bruce I. Jacobs and Kenneth N. Levy, "The Long and Short on Long-Short," *Journal of Investing* (Spring 1997), pp. 73-86.

[12] Sorensen, Mezrich, and Thum, *The Salomon Brothers U.S. Risk Attribute Model*.

researchers looked at daily returns following an unexpected announcement regarding an inflation measure. Specifically, on July 14, 1989 the Producer Price Index that was announced was sharply less than anticipated. As a result, the yield on Treasury bills with one month to maturity fell on that day from 8.6% to 8.4%. An optimized portfolio that had a high sensitivity to inflation was constructed. The inflation sensitive tilted portfolio outperformed the S&P 500 by 46 basis points from the day prior to the event (July 13, 1989) through the day after the event (July 15, 1989). This result supports the position that the factor model was an important tool for constructing a portfolio based on expectations.

The second backtest was based on a longer period of time. The event in this case was the movement of the U.S. dollar during the spring of 1989. Specifically, there was an unexpected strengthening (i.e., appreciation) of the U.S. dollar relative to the German mark from May 12 to June 2, 1989. An optimized portfolio was constructed that was tilted towards stocks that benefited from a stronger U.S. dollar. The RAM-based portfolio tilted with this bias outperformed the S&P 500 by 62 basis points.

DIVIDEND DISCOUNT MODELS VERSUS FACTOR MODELS

Another approach used to value common stock is a dividend discount model (DDM). Based on certain assumptions, a DDM gives the expected return for a stock. As explained in this chapter, a factor model also gives the expected return for a stock. Thus both a factor model and a DDM are valuation models. The DDM can be either a stand-alone model or one of several inputs to a factor model.

A study by Bruce Jacobs and Kenneth Levy suggests that simple factor models can outperform a traditional dividend discount model.[13] Specifically, when they compared the contribution of a simple factor model with a traditional dividend discount model they found that less than one-half of 1% of the quarterly average actual returns is explained by the DDM. In contrast, about 43% of the average actual returns is explained by a factor model which includes the DDM and other factors. Thus, in their study the factor model outperformed the DDM hands down.

SUMMARY

There are three types of factor models: statistical factor models, macroeconomic factor models, and fundamental factor models. Statistical factor models use a statistical technique called principal components analysis to identify which raw descriptors best explain stock returns. The resulting factors are statistical artifacts

---

[13] Jacobs and Levy, "On the Value of 'Value'," *Financial Analysts Journal* (July/August 1988).

and are therefore difficult to interpret. Consequently, a statistical factor model is rarely used in practice. The more common factor models are the macroeconomic factor model and the fundamental factor model.

In a factor model, the sensitivity of a stock to a factor is estimated. The risk exposure profile of a stock is identified by a set of factor sensitivities. The risk exposure profile of a portfolio is the weighted average of the risk exposure profile of the stocks in the portfolio. Similarly, the risk exposure profile of a market index can be obtained.

The output of a factor model can be either the expected excess return or a scenario score. The expected excess return of a stock is found by multiplying each factor sensitivity by the assumed value for the risk factor and summing over all risk factors. The expected return is the expected excess return plus the risk-free rate. The expected excess return for a portfolio and a market index is just the weighted average of the expected excess return of the stocks comprising the portfolio or the market index.

The power of a factor model is that given the risk factors and the factor sensitivities, a portfolio's risk exposure profile can be quantified and controlled. Applications of factor models include the ability to assess whether or not the current portfolio is consistent with a manager's strengths and to construct a portfolio with a specific tilt without making unintentional bets. Since many factors in a fundamental model are the same characteristics used in style management, factor models can be used in controlling risk in a style management strategy.

Both dividend discount models and factor models can be used to value common stock. The output of a dividend discount model can be used as a factor in a factor model. One study suggests that factor models have significantly outperformed dividend discount models.

Chapter 11

Review of Financial Statements

Frank J. Fabozzi, Ph.D., CFA
Adjunct Professor of Finance
School of Management
Yale University

Thornton L. O'Glove
Former Publisher of The Quality of Earnings Report

John C. Ritchie Jr., Ph.D.
Professor of Finance
Temple University

INTRODUCTION

A key source of information in analyzing the earnings of a company as well as its economic well being is provided in various financial reports required to be published by the company. In this chapter and the one that follows we look at the factors that an analyst should consider in analyzing the financial statements of a company. Quantitative analysts who rely on fundamental factor models to construct equity portfolios should recognize that the inputs to these models are culled from financial statements and that some of the inputs may be questionable. Unfortunately, quantitative analysts tend to be more concerned with the statistical properties of the resulting models rather than the questionable nature of the inputs.

In this chapter, we focus on financial reporting and financial statements — income statement, balance sheet, and statement of cash flows. In the next chapter, we look at how these financial reports can be used by analysts. What is the distinction between financial reporting and financial analysis? The Financial Accounting Policy Committee (FAPC) of the Association of Investment Management and Research (AIMR) in a 1993 report entitled *Financial Reporting in the 1990s and Beyond* expressed this distinction as follows:

> We believe that financial reporting should be concerned with presenting the economic history of specific economic entities and that it is best done when managements also are willing to disclose and discuss their strategies, proposed tactics and plans, and expected outcomes. It is self-evident that reporting on the past always requires

185

the use of estimates and other assessments of future events; uncollectible receivables, depreciable lives, warranty repair costs, and the like. Forecasts of the future and similar material enhances financial report usefulness, but they must be separated from and not confused with the financial statements themselves. Financial analysts avidly seek management's forecasts as part of the financial reporting process, accompanying but not incorporated in the financial statements.

Financial analysts, in turn, must digest all relevant economic information that can affect an economic entity, including but not limited to its financial reports. The function of analysis is to allow those who participate in the financial markets to form their own rational expectations about future economic events, in particular the amounts, timing, and uncertainty of an enterprise's future cash flows. Through this process, analysts form opinions about the absolute and relative value of individual companies, make investment decisions or cause them to be made, and thereby contribute to the economically efficient allocation of capital and clearing of the capital markets. Allocation decisions are made primarily on the basis of comparisons. Financial reporting and financial analysis cross paths because, ultimately, economic value (wealth) is created by expectations of future inflows of economic benefits, primarily in the form of or the equivalent of cash flows. The amounts and timing of future cash flows are in most cases uncertain to various degrees. It is the function of analysis to deal rationally with that uncertainty. It is the function of financial reporting to provide data useful to analysts making assessments of an enterprise's future cash flows and its value today.[1]

SOURCES OF INFORMATION FOR ANALYZING A COMPANY

There are several sources of information available to analysts. One source of information is documents prepared by the company. The other is information prepared by entities other than the company.

Documents prepared by a company can be divided into three groups: (1) documents that a corporation prepares and files with the Securities and Exchange Commission (SEC), (2) documents that a corporation prepares and distributes to shareholders, and (3) documents that a regulated company must prepare for regulators. A summary of the contents of the first two types of documents is given in

---

[1] *Financial Reporting in the 1990s and Beyond* (Charlottesville, VA: Association for Investment Management and Research, 1993), pp. 18-19. The report was authored by one of the committee members, Peter H. Knutson.

Exhibit 1.[2] The documents in the first group include the 10-K (an annual filing), the 10-Q (a quarterly filing), and the proxy statement. The documents that the corporation prepares and distributes to shareholders include the annual report and the quarterly financial report. The annual report is the principal document used by corporations to communicate with shareholders. It is not an official SEC filing; consequently, companies have significant discretion in deciding on what types of information will be reported and the way it is reported. In addition, when a corporation offers a new security to the public, the SEC requires that the corporation prepare and file a registration statement, and provide a condensed version of this statement, called a prospectus, to potential investors.

Exhibit 1: Summary of Documents that a Corporation Prepares

1. Documents that the corporation must prepare and file with the SEC
a. Document: Form 10-K
When must be filed: 90 days after close of corporation's fiscal year
Contents:
   Part I: Covers business, properties, legal proceedings, principal security holders, and security holdings of management
   Part II: Covers selected financial data, management's discussion and analysis of financial conditions and results of operations, financial statements, and supplementary data
   Part III: Covers directors and executive officers and remuneration of directors and officers
   Part IV: Provides complete, audited annual financial information.
   Part V: Schedule of various items provided.
b. Document: Form 10-Q must be filed 45 days after close of corporation's fiscal quarter.
c. Document: Form 8-Q
When must be filed: 45 days after close of corporation's each fiscal quarter.
Contents:
   Part I: Quarterly financial statements provided.
   Part II: Covers legal proceedings, changes in securities, defaults upon senior securities, changes in amount outstanding of securities or indebtedness, submission of matters to a vote of security holders, and other materially important events.
d. Document: Proxy statement
Contents: Notifies designated classes of stockholders of matters to be voted upon at a shareholders' meeting.

2. Documents that the corporation prepares and distributes to shareholders (not official SEC filings)
a. Document: Annual report to shareholders
Contents: Provides financial information on annual operations and often non-financial information about the business that are not reported elsewhere.
b. Document: Quarterly report to shareholders
Contents: Provides quarterly financial information on operations.

---

[2] At one time, an analyst had to obtain hard copies of these documents from the issuer. Recent filing are now available over the Internet using the SEC's Electronic Data Gathering and Retrieval system (nick-named EDGAR).

The reports filed with the SEC are bland and legalistic. The best place to start the analysis of a corporation would be with the annual report sent to shareholders. One of the reasons companies issue annual reports is to comply with the mandate set down in Rule 14a-3 of the Securities Exchange Act of 1934, which enumerates the specific financial information which must be revealed, but not the form in which it is to be presented. Annual reports contain some basic accounting and statistical data and commentaries. It is in the commentaries that there is a chance that management will include information that can be helpful to the analyst in going beyond the numbers reported in the accounting and statistical sections of the report.

More specifically, in every annual report is the *shareholders' letter*. It is in this section of the annual report where one can often find discussions by management of successful and failed strategies. Also, the shareholders' letter is usually jargon-free. Occasionally an analyst can come across letters which communicate problems and possibilities clearly, in such a way as to simultaneously illuminate the situation at the firm and provide guidance for the probing of the rest of the report which necessarily must follow. In fact, this is the prime purpose of these letters. We'll see examples of this in the next chapter.

In addition to the documents listed in Exhibit 1 that the corporation prepares, there are reports that regulated companies must prepare for the supervising regulatory entity. For example, utilities companies and insurance companies must prepare reports for state regulatory commissions. Banks must fill "call reports" with the U.S. Comptroller of the Currency.

Databases are available from commercial vendors that contain financial data culled from company prepared documents. Compustat, for example, provides financial statistics on more than 10,000 companies in the United States. The National Automated Accounting Retrieval System has a database that includes the actual text of the financial reports of more than 5,000 companies. What is critical for the analyst to understand is whether the service adjusts the reported data and, if so, how the data are adjusted. Compustat, for example, attempts to adjust the data. In this and the next chapter, we will see the flexibility available to corporations in preparing financial statements and therefore the need to adjust data for comparability to not only other firms but to produce a consistent time series of financial data for the same company.

In analyzing the industry or industries in which a company operates, trade association publications or government industry publications are useful sources of information for analysts. The Association of Investment Management and Research periodically publishes the views of experts on specific industries based on its conferences.

The nationally recognized statistical rating organizations (Standard & Poor's Corporation, Moody's Investor Service, Duff & Phelps Credit Rating, and Fitch Investors Service) provide financial data and company and industry commentaries. Specialized research services such as the Value Line Investment Service provide similar information along with recommendations about individual companies.

THE ROLE OF THE AUDITOR

The financial statements of a company are prepared by the firm's management. However, it is the role of the independent auditor, who is paid by the firm being audited, to review its accounting books and issue an opinion as to the veracity of the financial statements. The auditor's opinion is presented in a section of the financial statements called the *auditor's report.*

Financial statements are prepared in accordance with *generally accepted accounting principles (GAAP).* But what exactly is GAAP? Prior to 1964, the pronouncements of the Committee on Accounting Procedure and the Accounting Principles Board (APB) were viewed by the accounting profession as GAAP. But, lacking enforcement power, accountants did not necessarily comply with the recommendations of GAAP. In 1964, the Council of the American Institute of Certified Public Accountants (AICPA) incorporated Rule 203 into its rule of ethics. Rule 203 states:

> A member shall not express an opinion that financial statements are presented in conformity with generally accepted accounting principles if such statements contain any departure from an accounting principle promulgated by the body designated by the Council to establish such principles which has a material effect on the statements taken as a whole, unless the member can demonstrate that due to unusual circumstances the financial statements would otherwise have been misleading. In such cases his report must describe the departure, the approximate effects thereof, if practicable, and the reasons why compliance with the principle would result in a misleading statement.

Since 1973, the Financial Accounting Standards Board (FASB) has been the accounting standard-setting body of the accounting profession. This means that the accounting standards issued by the FASB are GAAP. The FASB is a private entity whose board members are full time and include representatives from the accounting profession, private industry, and financial analysts.

One might think that an auditor who operates under these professional guidelines could certainly be relied upon. That is, if anything in the financial statements is to be accepted at face value, it would be the auditor's report. If the auditor finds items that smack of deceit he or she can — indeed, must — say so in the opinion.

In fact, there are four categories of opinions that might be awarded:

1. a *clean opinion* means that there is an unqualified acceptance by the auditor of the financial statements;
2. a *subject to opinion* means that the auditor accepts the financials statements subject to pervasive uncertainty that cannot be adequately mea-

sured, such as information relating to the value of inventories, reserves for losses, or other matters subject to judgment.

3. an *except for opinion* means that the auditor was unable to audit certain areas of the company's operations because of restrictions imposed by management or other conditions beyond the auditor's control.

4. a *disclaimer of opinion* is a statement from the auditor disclaiming any opinion regarding the company's financial condition.

Most opinions are clean, and disclaimers are rare. The issuance of an opinion would seem to be very scientific, precise, and legalistic. Unfortunately this is not always the case. While the accounting profession maintains that the opinions remain a good indication of the accuracy of financial statements, there have been many shareholder suits alleging that the auditors have not been doing their jobs as well as they might. For example, Baldwin-United, Penn Square Bank, and Continental Illinois all failed. They also have something else in common: all received clean opinions in the most recent report prior to collapse. And these are only the more spectacular cases.[3] That these incidents are out of the ordinary is certainly true, but that can hardly console stockholders in the failed companies who thought the clean auditor's report meant that everything was as represented.

The reason for this is not necessarily incompetence. Rather, its roots are in the unusual relationship between auditors and their clients. The client pays the bill to have an independent audit and will be displeased if the auditor discovers irregularities sufficient to prevent him or her from offering a clean opinion. Putting that in writing may mean the loss of an audit account in an industry marked by intense competition, in which raids for clients and price slashing have become the rule. Moreover, it can close the door for other services and fees.

In 1985, the SEC issued a warning to registrants and independent auditors attempting to engage in "opinion shopping." The practice of *opinion shopping* involves a corporation that attempts to obtain reporting objectives by following questionable accounting principles and a pliable auditor willing to go along with the desired treatment.

While the average investor probably never even looks at the auditor's statement, the professional analyst should consider it carefully and with discretion.

Financial Statements of Non-U.S. Entities

The concern is even greater in dealing with financial statements of non-U.S. reporting entities for several reasons. First, as of this writing, there are no internationally acceptable standards of financial reporting. This includes not only the accounting methods that are acceptable for handling certain economic transactions and the degree of disclosure, but other issues. Specifically, there is no uniform treatment of the frequency of disclosure. Some countries require only annual

---

[3] For additional examples, see Thornton L. O'Glove (with Robert Sobel), *Quality of Earnings* (NY: Free Press, 1987), Chapter 2.

or semiannual reporting rather than quarterly as in the United States. Moreover, there is a major concern with non-U.S. auditors. The enhancement role played by auditors in some countries is far from ideal, with little emphasis on the independence of the auditor and the reporting entity. In fact, in some countries, the nation's security laws may require that the auditor be a member of the governing board of the reporting entity. Even where there is an independent auditor, the education and training of auditors may be inadequate.

The International Accounting Standards Committee (IASC) has attempted to resolve many of these concerns. However, at this time, an analyst should look extremely closely at non-U.S. financial reports, particularly for issuers in emerging markets.

THE INCOME STATEMENT

The *income statement* shows the revenues, expenses, and income (the difference between revenues and expenses) of a corporation over some period of time. Corporations must prepare income statements for its fiscal year and interim periods (quarterly). For many years, major emphasis has been placed on the income statement — not only in the case of common stock analysis — but also in the analysis of bonds and preferred stock. The margin of safety for fixed income security holders is provided by a corporation's earnings and cash flow. The value of the business reflects the amount that can be earned on the invested capital and the cash flow generated by that firm. Therefore, the analyst must determine a true earnings base of recurring earnings from which growth and volatility of earnings and dividends may be projected. All a common stockholder can receive from an investment are dividends and/or capital appreciation. Both are dependent on future earnings — and expectations by investors of future earnings and dividends.

Analysts seek information from the income statement in order to answer the following questions:

1. What is the true recurring earnings base that serves as a starting point for generating useful projections of future performance?
2. How has the company performed over a relatively long time horizon (ten years of data often are studied to encompass a business cycle), and in the recent past? What factors underlie the revenue and cost trends exhibited?
3. Is earnings growth consistent or is the company in decline? Does the earnings pattern from year-to-year display significant variability? If so, what causes this variability?
4. How does the company being analyzed compare with the earnings growth of the economy and the industry in which it participates? How does the company compare with competitors in terms of revenue, cost behavior, and profitability?
5. Does the company appear to have good control of costs?

Exhibit 2: Income Statement for The Home Depot, Inc.: 1991 and 1990 (Dollars in Thousands)

	1991	1990
Net Sales	$3,815,356	$2,758,535
Cost of Goods Sold	2,751,085	1,991,777
Gross Profit	1,064,271	766,758
Operating Expenses	693,657	504,363
General & Admin.	91,664	67,901
Pre-Opening Expense	13,315	9,845
Net Operating Profit	$265,635	$184,649
Interest Expense (Net)	5,807	2,634
Earnings Before Taxes	259,828	182,015
Income Taxes	96,400	70,061
Net Income	$163,428	$111,954

The focal point of common stock analysis is on growth and profitability of the firm. Exhibit 2 provides the income statement appearing in the 1991 Annual Report of The Home Depot, Inc. for its 1991 and 1990 fiscal years.

Matching Revenues and Expenses

The most fundamental accounting principle applied to the income statement is that which requires the matching of revenues and expenses. Revenue is recognized when it is realized, not when the cash is received. The matching concept requires the recognition of all costs that are associated with the generation of the revenue reported in the income statement. For this reason, corporations are required to use accrual accounting. Many subjective judgments are made by accountants in matching costs and revenues, leading to potential limitations of the figures in the income statement and possibly misleading conclusions if not properly considered by the analyst.

Below we discuss the major items in the income statement and note the careful attention required by the analyst. The relationship between items in the income statement usually is explored by means of ratio analysis, which will be discussed in the next chapter.

Revenues

The revenues of a company are its net sales. Sales can be divided into cash sales and installment sales. Cash sales do not present a problem. The major concern of the analyst is installment sales. Many companies recognize the entire profit for an installment sale when the sale is made, assuming the company is reasonably certain it will be paid. Certain types of sales may, however, result in periodic installment payments which could stretch over several years (e.g., a land development company). One could then raise the question as to the number of payments that would have to be received before the buyer has a sufficient stake to make continued payments relatively certain.

The AICPA has issued standards governing the accounting for installment sales, but some companies follow practices that are more conservative than the required standards while other companies follow only the minimally acceptable standards.

Expenses

Any income statements offered by firms today separate the results achieved through regular operations from those produced by nonoperating and/or extraordinary activities of the company. Moreover, expenses often are classified by functions, e.g., the cost to produce and sell goods, selling expenses, administrative expenses, and other expenses. This facilitates year-by-year comparisons of key expense categories and forecasting efforts.

Expenditures for items where the benefits are expected to be received over a period longer than one year typically are *capitalized* (i.e., recorded in asset accounts) and then depreciated or amortized over the life of the asset. Where the benefit is expected to be received within a year, the cost of the item is *expensed* (i.e., directly charged to an expense account) and fully reduces reported profit of that year. Many items are not easily labeled as short or long term, and some companies may capitalize a given item (a liberal policy since it increases reported income), while other companies expense it (a conservative policy since it decreases reported income). This can lead to non-comparability of reported profits among firms.

There are numerous items that a corporation may expense in its tax return but capitalize in its published balance sheet. Many companies have followed such a procedure in regard to advertising and promotional expenses. Analysts are cynical about capitalization and deferral of expense items. When companies defer items that more properly should be currently expensed, the result is higher reported profit. The analyst must make adjustments, increasing reported expenses and decreasing reported profits for these and similar expense items that should be expensed in the current year rather than deferred to later years.

Other items that are capitalized in annual reports, but expensed in tax returns, are intangible drilling costs of oil and natural gas producers and exploration and development expenses of mining companies. These all raise a problem for the analyst attempting to place different companies on a comparable base.

Inventory Valuation Methods and Cost of Goods Sold

At the moment that net income is increased by revenues derived from the sale of a product, it is also decreased by the costs associated with producing that product. Accountants determine the total cost of goods sold for a period by a process of deduction. The value of inventory on hand at the beginning of the period is added to that acquired during the period to determine the *total cost for all goods available for sale*. Those units still on hand at the end of the period obviously were not sold. Accordingly, the value of goods on hand at the end of the period is determined by means of a physical inventory and subtracted from the costs of goods available for sale to determine the cost of goods sold figure used in the income statement.

Exhibit 3: Inventory Purchases and Costs

	Number of Units	Cost Per Unit	Total Cost
Beginning Inventory	140	$12	$1,680
Purchase, February 26	70	18	1,260
Purchase, June 13	70	22	1,540
Purchase, September 28	70	28	1,960
Purchase, December 12	70	35	2,450
Available for Sale	420		$8,890
Units Sold	220		
Units in Ending Inventory	200		

Inventory, in accordance with accounting standards, should be valued "at cost or market, whichever is lower." Application of this rule, however, requires the determination of cost. If prices were constant, the determination of cost of goods sold would be simple. Prices to acquire units of inventory do change, however, and one must determine which particular units were sold to match costs and revenues. How are the units sold and those in ending inventory valued? The two most widely used methods for assigning these costs are *first-in-first-out (FIFO)* and *last-in-first-out (LIFO)*. The specific inventory valuation method used by a corporation is indicated in the footnotes to the financial statements.

To illustrate the problem, assume the inventory data shown in Exhibit 3. The FIFO method is based on the assumption that the first merchandise acquired is the first merchandise sold. The ending inventory, therefore, consists of the most recently acquired goods. The key to calculating the cost of goods sold is determination of the value of the ending inventory of 200 units that was determined by physical count. The value of the ending inventory is $5,730. Calculated as follows:

70 units purchased December 12	$2,450
70 units purchased September 28	1,960
60 units purchased June 13 (@ $22/unit)	1,320
Total: 200 units	$5,730

Cost of goods sold is $3,160 calculated as follows:

Beginning Inventory	$1,680
Plus Purchases	7,210
Cost of Goods Available for Sale	$8,890
Less Ending Inventory	5,730
Cost of Goods Sold	$3,160

Under the LIFO method, the most recently acquired goods are assumed to be sold first, and the ending inventory consists of "old" goods acquired through the earliest purchases. For purposes of measuring income, the flow of costs may be more significant than the actual flow of goods. LIFO seems realistic in this context since costs stated in more current dollars are matched against revenues stated in relatively current dollars.

The value of the ending inventory under the LIFO method is $2,760 calculated as follows:

140 units, Beginning Inventory	$1,680
60 units, February 26 Purchase	1,080
Total: 200 units	$2,760

Cost of Goods Sold is $6,130 calculated as follows:

Beginning Inventory	$1,680
Plus Purchases	7,210
Cost of Goods Available for Sale	$8,890
Less Ending Inventory	2,760
Cost of Goods Sold	$6,130

Assuming that net sales for the period were $13,200, the gross profit as reported under each of the above methods is shown below:

	FIFO	LIFO
Net Sales	$13,200	$13,200
Less Costs of Goods Sold	3,160	6,130
Gross Profit	$10,040	$7,070

As can be seen, the inventory valuation method can have a significant impact on the gross profit during a period of rising profits.

Management has a great deal of flexibility in determining what expenses will be capitalized in the inventory accounts and which expenses will be written off directly as cost of the period. For example, if the personnel department was housed in the building used for administrative staff, the expenses associated with its operation are likely to be written off directly as part of administrative expense. If the personnel department staff were housed in an operating plant, at least part of the expenses of its operation are likely to be capitalized in the inventory account. A liberal interpretation of the question of capitalizing versus expensing such costs could improve reported income for a given period. Moreover, different decisions as to whether to capitalize in the inventory account or directly expense could distort comparability of reported income data between companies or through time.

Current tax laws practically allow any business firm to adopt LIFO, regardless of the actual flow of goods through the firm, and many firms have adopted the method since the 1950s. A firm that uses LIFO for financial reporting purposes must use the same system for tax purposes.

As illustrated above, during a period of rising prices the use of LIFO will result in lower reported profits and, therefore, the firm will incur a lower income tax liability than under FIFO. This is because "old" inventory costs that do not reflect current replacement costs are matched against revenues stated in current dollars. In contrast, during periods of rising prices, FIFO inventory valuation will overstate income. It is important to understand that a significant portion of reported net income of companies using the FIFO method may be inventory profits that will melt away as inventory must be replaced in the future. Furthermore, if prices were to fall, then the firm using FIFO would report the lower profits and higher cost of goods sold.

Profits appear to be more volatile when FIFO rather than LIFO costing is used to determine ending inventory values. This occurs because FIFO accounting tends to cause inventory profits to be added to regular operating profits when prices are rising since current cost is not matched with current revenue. The opposite will occur during a recession, thus increasing volatility. Where selling prices are less flexible than new material prices, however, profits may not be more volatile under FIFO than under LIFO.

Finally, LIFO could show illusory profits if a firm does not replenish inventory in a given year and digs into the "old" cost LIFO reserve to meet sales at current prices. The firm will have to restock eventually at the higher current replacement cost, causing a sharp decline in future profits. This can occur, for example, when a firm faces an extended strike by employees and attempts to continue sales from existing inventory.

Where inventories are not a significant asset, the analyst need not be overly concerned about differences in inventory costing systems. In many cases, however, misleading conclusions may be drawn if the analyst is not careful to adjust when different systems are used.

The footnotes to the financial statements, unfortunately, rarely facilitate an accurate adjustment, unless a company has just switched from one method to the other. Where a company has changed inventory costing methods, they must report the dollar and cents impact on inventory, cost of goods sold, taxes, and profits in the financial report of that year. This data need not be repeated, however, in future annual reports.

FASB Statement No. 33 (*Financial Reporting and Changing Prices*) requires that large corporations disclose what it would cost to replace their inventories at year-end and what their cost of goods sold would be if computed using current replacement cost at the date of sale. This data can help the analyst better frame reasonable adjustments where two companies use different inventory costing systems.

For comparative purposes, either the LIFO or FIFO firm could be adjusted to the system used by the other firm. Our preference is for LIFO reporting on the grounds that this system reports more meaningful profit data. Therefore, it would seem best to adjust the firm using FIFO to the LIFO approach. Unfortunately, an analyst is likely to find that available information facilitates adjusting LIFO to FIFO, using current replacement cost information. When contrasting two companies using different inventory costing methods, the analyst can only subjectively adjust the data of one to the system used by the other company.[4]

---

[4] Sometimes analysts assume that the gross profit margin percentages would have been the same if the companies had used the same inventory costing procedures, to facilitate an adjustment. This is not a useful technique, however, since this will wash out differing efficiencies between companies that the analyst is looking for.

ortant to recognize that the choice of an inventory cost-
le balance sheet. A period of sustained inflation tends to
in the balance sheet at amounts substantially below their
, especially when the LIFO costing system is used. This
is carried at "old" costs to acquire, which deviate more
replacement cost as inflation continues. Accordingly, a
y have a low current ratio (discussed in the next chapter)
ing FIFO.

on facilities would be a cost entering into the determina-
d, but depreciation of sales office space properly would be
se. Depreciation may, therefore, affect the determination
of several major subdivisions of the income statement.

Because the accounting charge for depreciation does not represent a corresponding outlay of cash, some investors and analysts have implied that depreciation is not a real expense by using the terms "cash earnings per share" or "cash
flow earnings per share" and have even substituted these terms for "net earnings
per share." Strong criticism of this position by the AICPA, the New York Stock
Exchange, and the Financial Analysts Federation has sharply reduced the use of
these terms in brokerage houses and annual corporate reports.

Since fixed assets, particularly plant and equipment, represent such a substantial outlay, it would be impractical to write them off entirely as an expense
charged against the income of the year in which they are purchased, especially since
benefits from their use will be received over an extended period. Furthermore, as
soon as it is purchased, a fixed asset begins to depreciate. To ignore this fact would
be to experience a gradual loss of capital without any reflection on the books of
account. Accountants consider the original cost of a fixed asset to be a prepaid
expense that must be amortized during the service life of the asset by regular periodic charges to the depreciation expense account. After deduction of the annual
charge, the remaining amount is the unamortized cost; but in no way, except by
coincidence, does this amount represent the economic value of the asset at that time.

Concern with inflation has led many to advocate a policy of substituting
replacement cost for original cost as the basis for determining depreciation
charges in the income statement. Corporate management has been especially
vocal on this subject. The basic function of depreciation charges is to amortize the
cost of a capital asset over its useful life. Management is concerned with a second
function: providing the funds needed for replacement of assets after they have
worn out or become technologically obsolete. Depreciation charges do not provide a company with cash. However, they are tax deductible and they do protect
cash generated by sales operations from the burden of taxes.

When replacement costs have risen far above original cost, prudent business management must recognize this capital erosion and set aside the additional

funds necessary to continue operating the business. Such funds must be provided from retained earnings, because the income tax laws do not recognize the inflation situation. Income taxes must be paid on the capital lost through inflation, which makes the problem of maintaining a company's capital doubly difficult.

Depreciation Methods Although corporate laws and accounting principles require that corporations make some charge for depreciation, corporate management is permitted numerous alternatives in the manner in which it amortizes the cost of fixed assets over their useful life on its books and in published reports.

The straight-line method provides for the regular distribution of the original cost of fixed assets, less their estimated salvage value, over their estimated service lives. In addition to the straight-line method of depreciation, two other depreciation methods are permitted for financial reporting purposes: the declining-balance method and the sum-of-the-years-digits method. These two methods allow for a faster write off of the asset in the earlier years of the service life and are thus referred to as *accelerated depreciation methods.*

For tax reporting purposes, prior to the Economic Recovery Tax Act of 1981, fixed assets could be depreciated using any of the three methods. The 1981 tax act substantially revised the method of computing depreciation by introducing the Accelerated Cost Recovery System (ACRS), a modified version of which is still used today. Under this system, taxpayers have virtually no choice in selecting a useful life for depreciable property, and salvage value is ignored. The Tax Reform Act of 1986 provided less liberal write-offs, especially of real estate, but retained the ACRS approach. The shorter depreciable lives mandated by ACRS introduce another factor that can cause taxable income to differ from reported accounting income, since different depreciation methods may be used for purposes of preparing financial statements and tax returns.

Since 1954 most corporations have reported publicly on a straight-line basis to stockholders, while taking advantage of the rapid amortization permitted for tax reporting purposes. What this means is that when reporting to shareholders, a lower depreciation expense is taken resulting in higher reported income than if accelerated depreciation is used. In contrast to reporting to shareholders, the objective is to minimize reported income when preparing tax returns. Thus, accelerated depreciated is used, resulting in higher depreciation charges and lower reported income compared to what would be reported if straight line depreciation is used for tax accounting purposes. This practice of reporting to shareholders using straight line depreciation and accelerated depreciation for tax purposes and "flowing through" the lower income taxes actually paid to the financial statement prepared for shareholders is called the *flow-through method.*

Until fiscal 1968, income statements in annual reports of numerous corporations reported depreciation by using the flow-through method. However, other corporations reported depreciation by the *normalizing method*, making a charge in the income account equivalent to the tax savings and thus washing out the benefits of the tax savings as far as final net income in their financial statements to shareholders. In financial statements, the charge for deferred taxes (the difference between the taxes as reported in the income statement prepared for shareholders and the tax return) resulting from the use of the flow-through method usually is included in the total item entitled "Federal Income Taxes."

APB Opinion No. 11 stated categorically that the deferred method of tax allocation should be followed. An exception would be allowed for regulated companies, such as public utilities where particular regulatory authorities may require the use of flow-through accounting.

Those who favor normalizing argue that the use of rapid amortization for tax purposes will result in lower taxes being paid in the earlier years of the life of the assets than under the straight-line method because of higher depreciation charges, but that in later years depreciation will be less than straight-line rates; taxes will therefore be higher than in the earlier years. Total taxes for the entire life of the assets should be the same under either straight-line for tax purposes or rapid amortization for tax purposes. Therefore, tax savings are temporary and deferred until later years of lower depreciation charges. Those holding this viewpoint, including the AICPA and the SEC, therefore wish to eliminate any effect of tax savings on net income in the earlier years of the asset's life.

Those who have advocated the flow-through method, including numerous state public utility commissions (not the SEC), have argued that as long as a company is regularly expanding and purchasing fixed assets, the new assets will have the advantage of rapid amortization, therefore offsetting the declining depreciation on older assets. The lower taxes paid in the earlier years, therefore, are not deferred to later years, but payment will be deferred indefinitely. Therefore, there will be a constantly increasing "deferred taxes" account on the balance sheet.

Although depreciation is a real expense, it does not involve an outlay of cash in the period charged; therefore, the sales revenues allocated to the depreciation charges do represent a tax-protected source of funds to the business enterprise. While the total depreciation charged over the life of the asset is not affected by the method used, the greater amounts of revenues protected in early years by the declining-balance method and sum-of-the-years-digits method have a higher present value than funds that might be protected in later years. Rapid amortization is similar to an interest-free loan from the Treasury Department.

Depreciation charges often are substantial, and the estimates made have a material effect on the reported profits or loss of a given year. Profits are overstated when depreciation charges understate the actual depletion of assets during the productive process. Depreciation charges can be understated by increasing the estimated life of the asset beyond the time that the asset is useful economically, or overstating salvage value. For example, several American airlines extended the depreciable life of their aircraft between 1968 and 1970, thereby reducing annual depreciation expense and increasing reported earnings at a time when airline earnings generally were depressed.

Accountants cannot know in advance how long an asset will last or what its salvage value will be. The depreciation expense charged in the income statement is a rough estimate of cost and does not allow for the effects of inflation. Determining the adequacy of depreciation charges is difficult. The following tests are suggested:

1. The consistency of the rate of depreciation charged over time can be explored by studying depreciation as a percentage of gross plant assets and sales over an extended period of time.
2. Depreciation rates of a given company should be compared to those utilized by similar companies.

Amortization of Intangibles

In addition to the major noncash charges for depreciation in the income statement, the amortization of intangibles such as goodwill, patents, and trademarks represents noncash charges in the income account. The problem of determining the time over which the values recognized for intangibles are consumed is a difficult one, and differing judgments can lead to noncomparability of reported income data by different companies.

Goodwill, and the accounting for goodwill, has become important to analysts with the tremendous merger movement that has occurred since World War II. The costs of acquisitions often have been well in excess of the book value of the assets acquired, and a balancing item of goodwill has been added in the balance sheet. The AICPA requires that the item of goodwill be amortized annually as a charge against income over a period of not more than 40 years. Since firms may write-off using any time span within the 40-year period, profit comparability can be distorted.

Other Expenses

Selling, administrative, other expenses and taxes must be deducted from gross profit, and other income added, to determine net income. These expenses are not identifiable specifically with or assigned to production. Some costs may be included here because they are difficult to allocate; it is, therefore, possible that parts of these expense items should affect production costs.

The main classifications under operating expenses in the income statement are selling, general, and administrative expenses. Expenses related to storing and displaying merchandise for sale, advertising, sales salaries, and delivery costs are the main items included under selling expenses. General and administrative expenses include: costs related to the operation of the general offices, costs of the accounting department, costs of the personnel office, and the costs of the credit and collections departments. Certain expenses may be listed separately under operating expenses, including depreciation, depletion and amortization, maintenance and repair expenses, research and development (R & D) expenses, rental expenses, costs of exploration, and employee benefit payments (mainly pension costs), though they should have been part of the determination of cost of goods sold.

The analyst should calculate each of the listed expenses as a percentage of sales. This will highlight the changing importance of expense items, trend patterns, and how costs relate to sales activity. A useful comparison also can be made between the behavior of individual expense items relative to sales, both over time and with industry composite figures.

Below we describe the various operating expenses.

Maintenance and Repairs The significance of maintenance and repair costs will vary with the amount invested in plant, equipment, and productive activity. These costs typically are composed of both fixed and variable elements. While it is useful to look at their behavior in relation to sales, one should not make much of this comparison — a consistent relationship with sales is not to be expected. Also, it is useful to look at annual maintenance and repair costs in relation to total plant and equipment. Unfortunately, maintenance and repair expense is not always presented separately in the financial statements.

These costs are discretionary and can be postponed within limits. Unfortunately, management may be tempted to postpone needed maintenance and repairs when revenues are falling to maintain the level of income reported to stockholders. This can lead to continued future deterioration in profits. The analyst must make sure that reasonable amounts are being spent to maintain competitive facilities.

Inadequate maintenance and repairs can shorten the useful lives of assets, thereby invalidating depreciation expense charges, which are related to useful life estimates.

Rental Expenses A large number of corporations have chosen to lease rather than purchase assets. Lease rental costs, therefore, can become important expense items. Where a long-term lease is involved, the resulting rental expense can be characterized as a required series of payments over many years that include elements of both principal amortization and interest expense. To an important extent, the payment requirements on a long-term lease are equivalent to fixed charges incurred when debt is utilized to acquire an asset and the fixed charge obligation of a lease can force a company into financial difficulties just as readily as can fixed charges on funded or other debt.

An analyst should determine the future minimum lease payments required, both for capital leases and operating leases, and relate the payment requirements to expected cash flow to ensure that the firm has not over-committed itself.

Pension Costs Pension plans come in two basic forms: defined contribution and defined benefit plans. A defined contribution plan is one in which the firm's contribution rate is fixed. Once a company has made the required contribution, it has no liability for additional payments. The recognition of the required contribution as expense, therefore, assures proper recognition of pension costs in the income account.

A defined benefit plan, by contrast, is one where the benefits are determined by formula and the employer contributions are treated as variable. The estimation of the size of the pension obligation is difficult and subject to great uncertainty in terms of what the company actually will be obligated to pay in the future. Under a defined benefit plan, the employer's commitment is to fund a future benefit. The required annual contribution to the plan is not fixed, but is being redefined constantly in terms of changing wage rates, earnings rates of the fund, and other variables.

When a firm establishes a defined benefit plan, it commits itself to two undetermined costs: (1) past service costs that arise because of contracted obligations to employees for years served before either the founding of a plan or a change in the plan, and (2) current period costs as required by the plan. APB Opinion 8 and FASB Statement No. 87 are the basic guides to accounting for pension costs.

In determining pension costs, there are various assumptions that the actuary who is responsible for calculating these costs must make. One assumption is the interest rate assumption, which represents the annual rate of return that the actuary expects the pension fund assets to earn. Another assumption is the wage assumption, which represents the annual rate at which covered wages are expected to grow. The higher the interest rate assumption and the lower the wage growth assumption, the smaller will be the reported unfunded pension liability and the lower the required company contribution. In actuality, the setting of these assumptions is more art than science, making it difficult to compare pension costs among firms and to judge the adequacy of the costs charged for funding purposes. Therefore, reported profits can be distorted in a comparative sense because of different assumptions used in determining annual charges, both over time and between companies.

Other Employee Benefits Accounting requires the disclosure of the costs of past employment benefits. The costs of health and life insurance benefits are the main components of these costs, and such benefits usually continue after an employee reaches retirement and often include the spouse and children. These costs are potentially large and should receive careful consideration in terms of the liability they create and their impact on future income.

Research and Development Costs Research and development (R&D) costs are difficult to properly account for because (1) the ultimate results are highly uncertain, and (2) the amount of time that can go by between the initiation of a research project and the determination of its ultimate success or failure. Such expenditures are often substantial and must be considered when analyzing current income and forecasting future profits. FASB Statement No. 2 concludes that, subject to certain exceptions, all R&D costs should be charged to expense in the year incurred.

The analyst should attempt to judge the success of past R&D expenditures and the likelihood of future successes when evaluating a firm. It is the future that is of importance when evaluating a common stock, and accounting for R&D expenses is not helpful in this regard. Evaluation of the potential future success generated by R&D outlays requires information on the types of research performed, the outlays by category, the technical feasibility of projects being undertaken, and the quality of the research staff. Moreover, it is useful for the analyst to know the company's success-failure experience in the past.

BALANCE SHEET

A *balance sheet* (also called the *statement of financial condition*) is a technical accounting term. "In this view, a balance sheet may be defined as a tabular statement or summary of balances (debt and credit) carried forward after an actual or constructive closing of books of account kept according to principles of accounting."[5] This is as far as accountants are willing to go. The investor must expect neither more nor less than this. A balance sheet does not purport to list economic or investment values, which are related more to cash flow and earning power of a firm.

Investors must understand what balance sheets demonstrate. One examines a balance sheet to determine the company's current financial position, the amount and nature of invested capital, the sources of invested capital, the proportionate division of corporate capitalization, and, with the income statement, the rate of return earned on total assets, on total capitalization, and on stockholders' equity.

Balance Sheet Values

The word "value" is used in accounting to describe the figure at which an asset or liability is carried in the accounts, although the amount may represent something different than "value" as the word is used ordinarily. Accounting is based predominantly on cost, and assets usually are carried at cost or some modification of cost. For example, accountants report the original cost of fixed assets on the balance sheet, less amortization of that cost over the useful life of the asset. Inventories will reflect the cost to purchase the items included, unless current market value falls below that cost. Accounting values, therefore, are not intended to represent current market value, replacement value, or liquidation value of assets.

Accounting values are book values which signify only the amount at which an item is stated in accordance with the accounting principles related to the item. The term *book value* also is used to represent the total owners' equity shown in the balance sheet; book value per share is the owners' equity divided by the number of shares of common stock outstanding. Book value per share should not be thought of as an indicator of economic worth.

Balance Sheet Information Sought by Analysts

The major types of information that the analyst seeks from the balance sheet are as follows:

---

[5] *Accounting Research Study No. 7* (New York: American Institute of Certified Public Accountants, 1965), p. 226.

1. The sources of funds that have been used to acquire the corporate assets:
   (a) The long-term funds invested by creditors, preferred stockholders, and common stockholders. In the case of common stockholders, it includes earnings retained in the business (not paid out as dividends) and capital in excess of par.
   (b) The short-term funds supplied by banks, commercial paper houses, factors and trade creditors, etc.
   On the basis of the above information, the investor can calculate the proportion of invested capital contributed by creditors, preferred stockholders, and common stockholders and can determine such ratios as long-term debt to stockholders' equity. It is worthwhile for the investor to calculate the market value of the corporation's securities and the ratios of each component to the total capitalization. In this calculation par value often is used for bonds and preferred stock, but market value is used for common stock: hence the term "total capitalization with common at market" (number of shares times market price).

2. The strength of the corporation's working capital position as indicated by the various working capital ratios. These ratios indicate the corporation's assumed ability to meet current liabilities, which are expected to be paid with current assets.

3. The assets of the corporation, which indicate the sources of the corporation's income and the manner in which capital was invested, as well as providing a base for assessing the adequacy of total assets and the mix of assets to support expected levels of operation.

4. Data for an analysis of the balance sheet combined with an analysis of the income statements to indicate: (a) the amount and the rate of return on total long-term capitalization; (b) the rate of return on total assets; (c) the rate of return on the stockholders' equity; and, (d) a check of the retained earnings account in the balance sheet with the earnings reported over a period of years in the income statement. (Retained earnings at the beginning of the period plus earnings (less losses) for the entire period less dividends paid should give the total in the retained earnings account at the end of the period, except for charges or credits made directly to the retained earnings account that may not have been recorded in any income statement but that should have been disclosed in annual reports.) In essence, the balance sheet when combined with income statement data offers a basis for a long-term study of earning power relative to asset mix and financial structure.

We will discuss the ratios mentioned above in much greater detail in the next chapter. Exhibit 4 shows the balance sheet for The Home Depot, Inc. for the fiscal years 1991 and 1990.

Exhibit 4: Balance Sheet for The Home Depot, Inc.: 1991 and 1990 (Dollars in Thousands)

	1991	1990
Assets		
Cash	$137,296	$135,381
Receivables (net)	49,235	38,993
Inventory	509,022	381,452
Other	17,931	10,474
Total Current Assets	$713,574	$566,240
Plant, Prop. & Equip.	963,619	568,690
Less Accumulated Dep.	(84,889)	(54,250)
Net Plant, Prop & Equip	$878,730	$514,440
Other Assets	47,199	36,854
Total Assets	$1,639,503	$1,117,534
Liabilities		
Accounts Payable	$235,267	$172,876
Accrued Liabilities	166,734	118,066
Other Current Liab.	10,706	1,447
Total Current Liabilities	$12,707	$292,389
Long-Term Debt	530,774	302,901
Capital Lease Obligations	12,620	10,115
Shareholder's Equity		
Retained Earnings	439,770	289,177
Paid-in-Capital	264,301	233,458
Other	(26,572)	(10,506)
Tot. Stockholders' Equity	$683,402	$512,129
Total Liab. & Equity	$1,639,503	$1,117,534

Assets Section of the Balance Sheet

In considering assets in the balance sheet as offsets to the liabilities and capital, the analyst must recognize what asset figures really mean. The analyst should not be under the illusion that these offsets to liabilities and capital represent reliable estimates of economic value, except to some extent in the case of current assets; and, even in this case, book figures may be far removed from economic values, especially in the case of inventories.

Current Assets

Current assets of a business (also called *circulating assets* or *working assets*) represent its working capital. For accounting purposes the term current assets is used to designate cash and other assets or resources commonly identified as those that are expected to be realized in cash or sold or consumed during the normal operating cycle of the business. This generally encompasses the following resources: cash available for current operations and items that are the equivalent of cash, inventories, receivables, marketable securities representing the temporary investment of cash, and prepaid expenses. The ordinary operations of a business involve a circulation of capital within the current asset group. Expenditures are accumulated as inventory cost. Inventory costs, on sale of the products, are converted into trade receivables and ultimately into cash again. The average time intervening between the acquisition of materials or services entering this process and the final cash realization constitute an *operating cycle*.

The character of a borrower's working capital has been of prime interest to grantors of credit. Bond indentures, credit agreements, and preferred stock agreements commonly contain provisions restricting corporate actions that would affect a reduction or impairment of working capital (and would impair ability to satisfy debt requirements). Such restrictions can affect future financing possibilities of a firm, growth and dividend paying capacity thereby affecting the common stockholders' interest. Net working capital is represented by the excess of current assets over current liabilities and identifies the relatively liquid portion of total enterprise capital that constitutes a margin or buffer for meeting obligations within the ordinary operating cycle of the business.

Cash equivalent items include temporary investments of currently excess cash in short-term, high-quality investment instruments such as Treasury bills and commercial paper. There is little or no chance of loss in the event that these items have to be liquidated. Sometimes cash and cash equivalent items are segregated arbitrarily and not included in current assets. If such segregated items have been excluded from current assets and if these items are, in fact, subject to the full control of management and not required to be segregated by regulations or contract agreements, the analyst should add them back to the current assets.

Receivables, less any allowance for doubtful accounts, are included as current assets on the grounds that the firm intends to convert them to cash in the ordinary operating cycle of the business. Accordingly, receivables may be included as a current asset when the payment period runs beyond a year, as with installment sales discussed below. This must be kept in mind when judging the firm's ability to pay current liabilities. The analyst must consider the nature of the receivables in terms of the characteristics of the industry and the company's business. The analyst should determine whether the receivables are proportionately larger than normal in respect to current assets for the type of business and whether the deductions for estimated doubtful accounts are reasonable in terms of industry averages and firm experience. Schedule VIII of a firm's 10-K filing with the SEC offers useful information for evaluating the adequacy of the reserve for doubtful accounts of a firm, especially when compared with other firms operating in the same industry.

The estimate for doubtful or uncollectible accounts must be reasonable in relation to receivables in the case of installment sales, and this is true if profits on installment sales are taken into income in the period that the sales are accomplished rather than when receivables are collected. If a corporation sells (or "factors") its installment notes to banks or finance companies, it should note whether they have been sold outright or on a "recourse basis." In the latter case, the corporation has a contingent liability, which usually is not shown in the balance sheet but is included as a footnote. The analyst must consider the size of these contingent liabilities and the likelihood of the contingency materializing in the light of industry and company experience and the character of the receivables.

Inventories are classified as raw materials, work-in-process, and finished goods. In investigating inventory, the analyst must consider the implications of FIFO and LIFO inventory accounting as applied to analysis between companies and over a period of years for the same company if company reports do not provide actual figures indicating the effect of a change from FIFO to LIFO or vice versa. One must be careful to make appropriate adjustments when comparing two firms if one uses LIFO while the other uses FIFO. The firm using LIFO will report a lower profit and inventory than the firm using FIFO, when there are no real differences.

Noncurrent Assets

One of the noncurrent classifications applicable to assets is that of investments. Investments owned by business enterprises include shares of stock, bonds, and other securities, mortgages and contracts receivable, life insurance policies on the lives of officers that designate the company as beneficiary, and special funds to finance plant expansion or to retire long-term debt. Temporary investments are classified as current assets. Only long-term holdings of securities are classified as investments.

A basic accounting position on the reporting of long-term investments and noncurrent assets is quoted below.

> Long-term investments in securities should be carried at the lower of aggregate cost or market. When market quotations are available, the aggregate quoted amounts (and information as to whether aggregate cost or market is the carrying amount) should be disclosed. Investments in affiliates should be segregated from other investments.[6]

Fixed assets consist of land, plant, and equipment reported at cost less depreciation, i.e., amortization of cost. Depreciation is the process of amortization of cost over the estimated life of the asset and is in no sense a process of valuation, as discussed earlier. The economic value of fixed assets is their earning power, which bears no necessary relationship to the amount at which they are carried on the books.

Intangibles that appear in the balance sheet come from two sources: (1) intangible assets purchased outright, and (2) intangible assets initially developed in the regular course of business. Such assets have no physical existence and depend on future anticipated benefits for their value. Intangibles purchased outright are intangibles (such as goodwill) that have been acquired in exchange for an issue of securities, for cash, or for other considerations. The AICPA stated in APB Opinion No. 17 that the costs of all intangible assets, including those arising from a "purchase" type of business combination, should be recorded as assets and

---

[6] Quoted from *Accounting Research Study No. 7*, pp. 259-260, and APB Opinion No. 18, except for changes made by *FASB Statement No. 12* (December 1975).

should be amortized by systematic charges to income over estimated benefit periods, the period of amortization not to exceed 40 years.

Liabilities and Shareholders' Equity of the Balance Sheet

The balance sheet furnishes information on the amount of funds raised from creditors, both short- and long-term obligations, and from owners (including retained earnings). Investors should analyze the long-term capitalization of the corporation (long-term debt plus owners' equity) by means of ratios, to measure the degree of financial leverage being utilized by the corporation and rates of return being earned on capitalization. Short-term obligations should be analyzed in terms of the current assets and cash flow factors from which payment must come.

Current Liabilities

Current liabilities designate obligations that must be paid within one year from the date of the balance sheet. The current liability classification, however, is not intended to include a contractual obligation falling due at an early date that is expected to be refunded, or debts to be liquidated by funds that are carried in noncurrent asset accounts. Liquidation of such liabilities could reasonably be expected to require the use of current assets or the creation of other current liabilities. Current liabilities are therefore related to current assets when assessing the possibility that the firm will experience liquidity problems. The ratios used in such an analysis will be discussed in the next chapter.

Long-Term Debt

This section consists of long-term obligations such as bonds, private placement notes, equipment obligations, and bank loans with a maturity of more than one year. The amounts that appear on the balance sheet generally can be assumed to state accurately the amount of long-term obligations currently outstanding. Notes to financial statements will furnish additional information about the debt contracts, such as restrictive clauses against charges to retained earnings for dividends and officers' salaries. Such restrictions are important to common stockholders, since they can limit financing opportunities to support growth and dividend payments.

In the post-World War II period, leasing has become a major method of financing the use of property and equipment. Leasing differs in technique, although often not in substance, from conventional purchase of assets. FASB Statement No. 13 contains guidelines for classifying leases and accounting and reporting standards for each class of lease. According to FASB Statement No. 13 leases are classified as either (1) capital leases or (2) operating leases. Operating leases are those that the lessor will reacquire to lease again. They are to be accounted for as rental expense to the lessee and as rental income to the lessor. Capital leases must be capitalized by the lessee on the balance sheet as an asset and an obligation. The treatment is as if the firm purchased the asset with borrowed funds. Consequently, each period the capitalized asset is depreciated and the obligation is amortized, giving rise to depreciation expense and interest expense.

When a corporation establishes a pension fund, it accepts two costs: (1) past service costs that have not been funded, and (2) current pension costs based on current payrolls. The problem as far as the balance sheet is concerned is that of past service cost — the unfunded pension costs covering the period prior to the inauguration of the pension plan. These funds were not set aside previously but would have been funded if a pension plan had been in effect. The amount of these unfunded pension costs is often substantial and in the case of large corporations may amount to several billion dollars. These unfunded pension costs are a liability of the corporation. However, many pension fund agreements provide that annual payments to amortize unfunded pension costs may be skipped in years of poor earnings, sometimes for as many as three consecutive years.

However, the Accounting Principles Board of the AICPA stated that a major objective of Opinion No. 8 was to eliminate inappropriate fluctuation in recorded pension costs. It stated that "costs should not be limited to the amounts for which the company has a legal liability." The principles involved are that the pension cost accounting method should be applied consistently from year to year and that the amount recognized for past pension service costs should be relatively stable from year to year.

Preferred Stock

If the corporation has preferred stock outstanding the balance sheet will disclose the number of shares, the par or stated value per share, and the total dollar amount of the preferred stock. In the balance sheet, preferred stock is listed in the shareholders' equity section along with the common stock. Although it is essentially an equity security, it is a strictly limited equity security.

The preferred stock is senior to the common stock. The amount shown on the balance sheet should represent the claim of preferred stock coming ahead of the common stock, but this is not always the manner in which it is reported. If the preferred stock has a par value or a stated value relatively close to its legal claim (for example, liquidating value) ahead of the common stock, then the balance sheet closely reflects the actual situation. However, if the stated value is only a nominal amount and is not close to the claim of the preferred stock, then the preferred stock on the balance sheet (number of shares of preferred stock times the stated value) does not reflect the true situation. If the balance sheet does not reflect the preferred stock's claim properly, the analyst should reconstruct the balance sheet so that it reflects the preferred claims that are senior to the common stock.

In addition, there may be dividend arrears, which, while they are not liabilities of the corporation, do represent a claim senior to the common stock. However, such arrearages usually are not shown on the balance sheet but are disclosed only as a footnote.

Common Stock and Retained Earnings

Common stock is classified as part of shareholders' equity. Because the common stock is the residual claimant to the assets and the earnings of the corporation, the shareholder's equity section of the balance sheet is divided into paid-in-capital and retained earnings. The latter is earnings that have not been distributed to shareholders.

STATEMENT OF CASH FLOWS

A key financial statement that is used in the analysis of an entity's ability to repay its financial obligations and to gain insight into an entity's financing methods, capital investment strategies, and dividend policy, is the *statement of cash flows*.[7] This is because the revenues and expenses reported in the income statement for the reporting period will be different from cash receipts and cash disbursements for that same reporting period.

Reasons Why Cash Flow Differs from Net Income

There are two primary reasons for this difference. First, because the accrual method of accounting is used, revenues and expenses are recognized even though no cash receipts or cash disbursements are made. For example, suppose that a firm sells a product on December 1, 19X1 and the cash payment for that sale is due on January 15, 19X2. Also suppose that the selling firm's fiscal year ends on December 31, 19X1. Then in the preparation of this firm's 19X1 income statement, the sale is recorded in the income statement but there will be no cash receipt until the next year. (On the balance sheet, the credit sale will be recorded as an increase in accounts receivable.) Similarly, a firm can incur a liability from the purchase of merchandize or the accrual of interest but the cash disbursement need not be made until the subsequent reporting period. Expenses such as depreciation or amortization are recorded in the income statement without a corresponding cash disbursement for the reporting period.

The second reason is that the income statement does not recognize the cash receipts or cash disbursements from nonoperating activities. For example, if a firm issues stock or borrows funds, the income statement does not reflect the cash receipts. Nor does the income statement recognize cash disbursements for the acquisition of capital equipment, the acquisition of a business, or the payment of cash dividends.

Sections of the Statement of Cash Flows

Exhibit 5 presents the consolidated statements of cash flows of the Walt Disney Company for fiscal year 1996. We'll use this company to illustrate the sections of the statement of cash flows. For the fiscal year 1996, the ending cash and cash equivalents for this company was $278 million while the beginning balance for this account was $1.077 billion. Therefore, the change in cash and cash equivalents for the 1996 fiscal year was a decline of $799 million. The statement of cash flows shows the reasons for the reduction in this account balance of $799 million.

---

[7] This financial statement replaces the statement of changes in financial position.

Exhibit 5: 1996 Consolidated Statements of Cash Flows for Walt Disney Company

	Year ended September 30, 1996 (in millions)
Net Income	$1,214
Charges to Income Not Requiring Cash Outlays	
Amortization of film and television costs	2,966
Depreciation	677
Amortization of intangible assets	301
Accounting change	300
Other	22
Changes In (including the impact of the ABC acquisition)	
Investments in trading securities	85
Receivables	(426)
Inventories	(95)
Other assets	(160)
Accounts and taxes payable and accrued liabilities	(455)
Unearned royalty and other advances	274
Deferred income taxes	(78)
	3,411
Cash Provided by Operations	4,625
Investing Activities	
Acquisition of ABC, net of cash acquired	(8,432)
Film and television costs	(3,678)
Investments in theme parks, resorts and other property	(1,745)
Purchases of marketable securities	(18)
Proceeds from sales of marketable securities	409
Other	—
	(13,464)
Financing Activities	
Borrowings	13,560
Reduction of borrowings	(4,872)
Repurchases of common stock	(462)
Dividends	(271)
Exercise of stock options and other	85
	8,040
Increase (Decrease) in Cash and Cash Equivalents	(799)
Cash and Cash Equivalents, Beginning of Period	1,077
Cash and Cash Equivalents, End of Period	278
Supplemental disclosure of cash flow information:	
Interest paid	379
Income taxes paid	689

The statement is divided into three sections: (1) cash provided by operations, (2) investing activities, and (3) financing activities. *Cash provided by operations* indicates the cash generated from the sale of goods and services to customers and the payment of obligations to suppliers and employees. The calculation of this section of the statement begins with the net income. This amount is then adjusted to reconcile net income to net cash from operating activities. These adjustments include depreciation and amortization charges. Note also for the Walt Disney Company there was a change in accounting policy that generated a charge of $300 million. The cash provided by operations for Walt Disney Company in 1996 was $4.625 billion — the net income of $1.214 billion plus adjustments of $3.411 billion.

The second section of the statement of cash flows shows the cash flow from investing activities. For Walt Disney Company, the major cash expenditure was for the acquisition of Capital Cities/ABC Inc. ($8.432 billion). The sale of marketable securities generated cash of $409 million. In total, the cash outflow from investing activities was $13.464 billion.

The third section identifies the financing activities and the cash inflow and outflow from such activities. For example, Walt Disney Company borrowed $13.560 billion in 1996. This generates a cash inflow. However, the company paid off $4.872 billion of borrowings as well as repurchased $462 million of common stock. Both of these activities reduced the cash flow. There were cash dividends of $271 million. The net impact on the cash flow from financing activities was to increase cash flow by $8.040 billion.

In summary, for the Walt Disney Company in 1996 the three sections of the statement of cash flows indicated (in millions):

Cash provided by operations	$4,625
Investing activities	(13,464)
Financing activities	8,040
Change in cash and cash equivalents	($799)

This reconciles to the decrease in cash and cash equivalents for the company noted earlier.

SUMMARY

Analysts rely on the financial information prepared by the corporation. Financial statements must be prepared in accordance with generally accepted accounting principles. While financial statements are audited by an independent accountant, there are potential conflicts that may bias the auditor's opinion as to how the financial statements were prepared by management. The shareholders' letter in the annual report occasionally communicates actual and potential problems in a jargon-free manner that can provide guidance to the investor for the probing of the rest of the annual report.

The three financial statements that must be prepared by a corporation are the income statement, the balance sheet, and the statement of cash flows. In this chapter we discussed the key items of these financial statements and how the judgments in preparing financial statements and the accounting policy choices available may make comparison among firms difficult.

Chapter 12

Introduction to Fundamental Analysis

Frank J. Fabozzi, Ph.D., CFA
Adjunct Professor of Finance
School of Management
Yale University

Thornton L. O'Glove
Former Publisher of The Quality of Earnings Report

John C. Ritchie Jr., Ph.D.
Professor of Finance
Temple University

INTRODUCTION

In the previous chapter we reviewed the financial statements prepared by a company. In this chapter we will look at how to analyze these statements. In financial circles, the two measures often used to evaluate common stock are earnings per share and the related ratio of market price to earnings per share, the price/earnings ratio. Accountants and analysts have criticized the undue emphasis often placed on earnings per share, especially when reviewed in isolation without taking into consideration the accounting limitations inherent in its calculation. Moreover, reported net income or earnings per share are not good surrogates for cash flow from operations when considering bill paying capacity and ability to finance company growth and operations.

The three major criticisms of the use of earnings per share figures by themselves are: (1) unless associated with an income statement review and analysis, it can lead to erroneous conclusions; (2) reported earnings per share may be non-comparable over time or between companies; and, (3) it concentrates the investor's attention on a single figure without reference to the corporation as a whole, which would provide information on the sources and the nature of income and provide some basis for a reasonable projection of earnings and dividends. An analyst should carefully review the income statement and adjust where needed to represent economic and comparable income over time and between firms. In this chapter we show how this should be done.

We then turn our focus on the ability of a firm to meet its debt obligations. Traditionally, this has involved the calculation of various ratios that attempt to measure the company's short-term solvency, financial leverage, and debt burden. As we will explain, these ratios may be of limited use as an early warning system for an analyst to identify financial difficulties. Instead, we will explain how the statement of cash flows can provide better information about impending financial difficulties.

Before discussing how to analyze financial statements, let's look at the different types of equity analysts and the potential conflicts that may arise for one particular type of equity analyst.

BUY-SIDE AND SELL-SIDE ANALYSTS

Equity analysts are responsible for analyzing the earnings of companies that they cover. There are *sell-side* (also referred to as "Wall Street") analysts and *buy-side* analysts. Investment management firms that have their own analysts — buy-side analysts — rely on their analysis. Investment management firms that do not have their own analysts, and individual investors, rely on the recommendations of sell-side analysts — analysts employed by brokerage firms — that appear in published reports.

There are several thousand "sell side" securities analysts at work reading financial entrails and interviewing corporate executives. Major houses may carry upward of 50, each assigned to specialized tasks, while the small, regional firms may have only three or four generalists. Why is it necessary to undertake an analysis of earnings if this task is being performed by sell-side analysts? Here's why.

A full-fledged senior Wall Street analyst may receive a salary in excess of $200,000 plus bonuses depending upon performance, with top analysts' earnings in excess of $1 million. Analysts develop contacts with managements, which together with required reports are their main source of information. They attend trade shows, seminars run by the industry covered, and are expected to live, eat, and breathe it. Out of all this will come the familiar company write-ups brokers distribute to clients.

The trouble is the analyst is working for the brokerage firm, not for the investor, and that creates complications and conflicts. For example, an analyst is expected to be on good terms with the managements of companies covered, so he or she can scout for other business for the firm. The analyst can identify which private companies in the industry are contemplating an initial public offering or which public companies might be expected to come to market for funds or might be considering an acquisition or merger. The fees generated from investment banking activities related to this information can be significant and can be used to justify the compensation package of a high profile equity analyst. As commissions have declined significantly in the past decade, it is not the commissions generated from trades that are paying the freight to carry analysts on staff.

It is the potential investment banking business that is critical. Such relationships are not fostered by negative reports or sell recommendations by an analyst. A good write-up and recommendation for that clothing chain, fast-food operation, steel company, or electronics firm might fetch a reward, in the form of its management asking the investment banker to underwrite its next issue of stocks or bonds or perform some other function, such as arranging a merger. Analysts must earn their keep by being on good terms with the firms they cover, and that usually means pressure for supportive commentaries.

A portfolio manager should keep this in mind the next time he receives a glowing report on one or another company, with a disclaimer saying, "The information contained herein is based on sources believed to be reliable, but is neither all-inclusive nor guaranteed by our firm ..." but ends with words like this: "We have been an underwriter, manager, or co-manager, or have previously placed securities of the company within the last three years, or were a previous underwriter of this company." Perhaps that recommendation was honest enough, but one typically observes precious few sells for companies with which the underwriter has such a relationship.

The pressure upon analysts to "be positive," particularly when writing up firms which the investment banking part of the firm is wooing, can be intense. This is especially so when the analyst has earlier been positive on the stock. Being negative makes enemies of managements; switching positions can be murder on the brokers and institutional salesmen, those people and fiduciaries with whom customers deal.

Another problem analysts have to guard against is the tendency to fall in love with the firms they are following. Over the years analysts tend to form close relationships with the executives and public relations people there, who often provide them with tips, hints, or other information which makes the job all that easier and gives them bragging rights in the office. Why jeopardize a good thing with a sell recommendation?

A good example of this view appears in an excellent publication on the media industry based on a 1996 AIMR seminar.[1] In one of the sessions there was a mock interview between a senior equity (sell side) analyst and an investor relations specialist that sought to demonstrate to the audience the art of company interviewing. While the presentation was insightful and clearly illustrated how an analyst should prepare and structure questions for an interview, the final comment in the list of conclusions was:

> The worst thing an analyst can do is say something impolite about management in the press. Even if it is true, mention of it should be avoided in the press. The company may never forgive and never forget. An analyst once wrote a report about a company, and although she thought it was very reasonable and was not trying to be particularly negative, she made a comment on what she

[1] Katrina F. Sherrerd, *The Media Industry* (Charlottesville, VA: Association for Investment Management and Research, 1996).

thought the company's long-term earnings growth would be. It has been five years, and the company's chair has never let her forget it. The fact that she was wrong did not make it any better.[2]

While we agree that being impolite about management in the press is improper, we're not sure whether an analyst's view on earnings prospects being less optimistic than that of management would fall into the area of being impolite. The fact that the analyst's forecast turned out to be wrong is irrelevant.

As Richard Hoey, economist and portfolio manager at Dreyfus Corp. stated: "It's clear that good stock picks aren't responsible for the dominant part of analysts' compensation packages. We need to have unbiased advice."[3] Historically, there have been analysts who have left Wall Street firms to set up firms providing such advice. More recently, an increasing number of investment management firms and plan sponsors have begun to build up their in-house staff of analysts — both in the public and private sectors.[4]

Now we can return to the question we posed at the outset of this section as to why it is necessary to analyze financial statements despite the large number of sell-side analysts who provide this information to clients. Prospecting is basically the way that analysts earn their keep at an investment banking firm, since low commission rates are typically not adequate to support the compensation of analysts.[5]

This conflict of interest is one reason why investors must be careful about blindly accepting sell-side analyst recommendations and probably accounts for the greater number of buy recommendations than sell recommendations in sell-side analysts' reports. Another reason is that analysts are typically reluctant to deviate from what other analysts are saying about a particular company. Renegades are often severely criticized and, in extreme cases, have lost their jobs.

EARNINGS PER SHARE

A corporation's *earnings per share* is calculated by dividing the earnings available to common stockholders (earnings after taxes less any required preferred stock dividends) by the weighted average number of common shares outstanding over the year for which the calculation takes place. That is:

$$\text{Earnings per share} = \frac{\text{Earnings available to common}}{\text{Avg. no. of common shares}}$$

But what if a corporation has issued securities or entered into contracts that may increase the number of outstanding shares of common stock? Such secu-

---

[2] *The Media Industry*, p. 99.

[3] Suzanne McGee, "After Oracle Misfire, Wall Street's Research is Blasted," *The Wall Street Journal* December 11, 1997), p. C1.

[4] McGee, "After Oracle Misfire, Wall Street's Research is Blasted," p. C22.

[5] Claire Makin, "Has the Compensation Bubble Burst?" *Institutional Investor* (December 1984), p. 109.

rities might include convertible securities, options, warrants, or other stock issue agreements. These instruments are referred to as "dilutive securities" because they can dilute the earnings per share since they can increase the number of shares outstanding. When there are dilutive securities that do in fact result in the dilution of earnings per share, generally accepting accounting principles (GAAP) requires that the potential dilutive effects be taken into consideration.

For reporting periods ending on or before December 15, 1997, APB Opinion No. 15 required that companies make two presentations of earnings per share in such instances: (1) *primary earnings per share* and (2) *fully diluted earnings per share*. In calculating the former number, APB Opinion No. 15 required that only dilutive securities classified as "common stock equivalents" must be considered and set forth rules for classifying a dilutive security as a common stock equivalent. In contrast, fully diluted earnings per share takes into account the dilutive effects of all dilutive securities.

The rules for calculating earnings per share changed for periods ending after December 15, 1997. Instead of reporting primary and fully diluted earnings per share, FAS No. 128 ("Earnings Per Share") requires the reporting of *basic earnings per share* and *diluted earnings per share*. In most cases, diluted earnings per share as specified in FAS No. 128 is the same as fully diluted earnings per share as specified by APB Opinion No.15. Basic earnings per share is simply the net income available to common stockholders divided by the average number of shares outstanding. It does not give any recognition to diluitve securities. Thus, basic earnings per share will be greater than primary earnings per share since the latter gives some recognition to dilutive securities.

Closer Examination of Earnings per Share

In the previous chapter we explained the alternative acceptable accounting principles that could be used by a firm to construct its financial statements. Below we focus on factors that the analyst should consider in assessing the quality of reported earnings.

Nonoperating and/or Nonrecurring Income

Two reference standards in the investment community, Standard & Poor's *Stock Reports* and Moody's *Handbook of Common Stocks*, indicated that the earnings per share of Pepsico increased from $2.40 in 1982 to $3.01 in 1983, an increase of 25%. Another standard source of information about earnings per share, *The Value Line Investment Survey*, indicated that the 1982 earnings were $3.24 in 1982 and $3.01 in 1982, for a decline of 7%. This is not a trivial difference. According to S&P and Moody's, the company was growing; by contrast, according to Value Line, the company was stagnating.

The reason for the difference in the earnings reported by these standard references involves the matter of *nonoperating* and/or *nonrecurring income*. The debate on this topic can become quite complex, but the fundamental principles involved are not difficult to comprehend. The issue in some cases can be quite crucial when deciding whether to invest in a company' stock. We use the difference in Pepsi's earnings to illustrate the fundamental principles involved in the debate.

In 1982 Pepsico reported an "unusual charge" relating to the write-down of overseas bottling assets. Previously these facilities had been overvalued due to the application of an improper accounting techniques. The charge amounted to $79.4 million, or $0.84 per share. It would seem that such things are unusual and so might be considered nonrecurring. For this reason, Value Line decided to exclude the item from Pepsico's earnings, and so reported the higher figure. This was not the stance taken by S&P and Moody's who decided to include the charge, and so came up with the lower figure.

At one time, any charge or earnings not resulting from the company's prime business would almost automatically be classified as nonrecurring. The accounting profession reconsidered this position in the 1970s. Pepsi's accountant took the stance that company's have write-offs of assets on a regular basis, which means that write-offs are not extraordinary, and so should not be reported as non-recurring. Another accounting firm might take a different view of the matter.

Most of the time the differences between operating and nonoperating income are quite clear; the problem comes on close calls. One can readily agree that some charges are unusual, such as the expropriation of assets by a foreign government or a loss due to a natural disaster such as a fire when destroyed properties are uninsured. On a more individual level, a million dollars won in a lottery drawing could be seen as nonrecurring.

Take the example of a company that sells a property on which it makes a $15 million profit. Is that nonrecurring? It probably is if the firm is a small manufacturer of electronic parts moving to a new location after a couple of decades in one place. However, what about a real estate operator who engaged in this transaction on a regular basis? What is unusual for the electronics firm is bread-and-butter for a real estate operator.

Not only is the distinction difficult to make, but unlike many other items we will be discussing, there is no single place in the annual report or quarterly financial statements in which the items are isolated and analyzed in just these terms. Investors have to be prepared to ferret the information out of the shareholders' letter, the management and discussion segment, and footnotes, as well as the income statement. Occasionally an analyst can learn of developments which impact upon whole industries or individual corporations from the front pages or business sections of the daily press.

Shareholder Reporting Versus Tax Reporting

Corporations legitimately keep two sets of books: one for shareholders and one for tax purposes. The earnings reported are those that are prepared for shareholders. Only substantial shareholders can receive a copy of the tax filings, IRS Form 1120, which is the official designation for the U.S. Corporation Tax Return. The tax code classifies a substantial investor as one who owns at least 1% of the outstanding stock. Many fiduciaries do own 1% or more of a particular stock which may be of only minuscule size in comparison to a Fortune 500 company. Such a stock position is sufficient for a money manager to secure the actual IRS corporate tax report of his holding.

In just about all annual reports there is a section entitled "Income Taxes," which provides information that an analyst can use to assess the difference between a corporation's tax books and shareholder books. Below we provide an example to demonstrate how an analyst can gain insight into the ways and means of unraveling the differences.

Consider the case of DSC Communications, a manufacturer of digital telephone switching systems. DSC's earnings had been growing rapidly; in 1984 they increased to $1.40 per share, compared with $0.89 in 1983 and only $0.23 in 1982 — the very model of a modern major growth company. But as is so often the case, there was more to it than met the eye. In this instance, it was the growing gap between shareholder and tax reporting. DSC's accounting policies were as follows:

> Revenue is generally recognized on switching systems when the Company has completed all manufacturing to customer's specifications, factory testing has been completed and accepted by the customer and the system has been delivered to the designated location.

> Revenue is recognized on transmission and terminal products generally when the products are shipped to the customer, except that certain revenue from long-term contracts in years prior to 1984 was recognized using the percentage-of-completion method.

Reproduced below is an excerpt from the DSC 1984 Annual Report pertaining to the company's provision for deferred income taxes.

	1984	1983	1982
Revenue recognition difference between book and tax return*	$31,403	$14,051	$2,648
Excess of tax over book depreciation	1,316	1,439	297
Excess of tax overbook employee benefit costs	662	1,830	—
Warranty costs accrued	(1,710)	(1,149)	—
Inventory reserves	(1,009)	(130)	7
DISC	128	1,368	—
Tax credits	—	(1,929)	—
Other	1,270	(580)	101
	$32,060	$14,900	$3,053

* Emphasis added.

As we have seen, for reporting purposes, DSC recorded earnings totaling $1.40 a share in 1984, $0.89 in 1983, and $0.23 in 1982. During the same years, the company recognized an additional $31.4 million equal to $0.77 a share, $14 million equal to $0.37 a share, and $2.6 million equal to $0.09 a share in reference to revenue recognition for shareholder reporting purposes versus tax reporting purposes. (For simplicity's sake, these figures have been calculated on the basis of a 50% tax rate.)

Hence, it was evident that a goodly portion of DSC's earnings were the result of faster revenue recognition for book reporting than for tax reporting. This phenomenon is not necessarily unusual in the case of fast-growing high tech firms, but there is an added risk involved in investing in this kind of situation because of the growing gap between tax reporting and shareholder reporting in the area of revenue recognition. DSC does not have to spell everything out in fine detail, but shareholders and investors should be aware that the company is quite legally keeping two sets of books, one for shareholders, the other for the IRS.

On October 3, 1985, DSC announced it was restating its 1984 financial statement and its first and second quarter statements for 1985. It related that the previously reported earnings of $1.40 a share for the year ended December 31, 1984, were being restated downward to $1.08 per share, and that the 1986 six months earnings totaling $0.68 a share would be reduced to a loss of $0.11.

DSC informed shareholders that the restatement was being made:

> to exclude previously reported revenues and earnings from ship-ments of current switching expansion ports for which a customer is now denying any obligation. Our restatements in 1985 exclude revenue and earnings attributable to sales switching systems to the customer which were reflected in the first quarter of 1985 and because of a recent change made by the Company in its rev-enue recognition policy for financial reporting in 1985.

In summary, DSC commented that:

> the weakness in the long distance switching market, which became significant earlier in 1985, has caused the Company to change its revenue recognition policy for financial reporting in 1985. The policy as changed reflects current conditions wherein customer installation plans and programs are being changed or delayed frequently and provides that revenue from sales of the Company's equipment is reflected in its financial reporting only when the equipment has been shipped to the customer's final installation site.

A few days after this announcement, two shareholders filed separate class action lawsuits against the company alleging that its financial reports for 1984 and 1985 were "materially false and misleading." According to a newspaper report,

> The action was taken because of an accounting change and a customer dispute over a contract for long-distance switching

equipment. The Company said one of the suits also names as a defendant three of DSC's principal officers and its auditor, Arthur Andersen & Company. DSC said it intends to defend itself against the suits.[6]

If there is a moral to this for analysts it is that a careful examination of DSC's reports, available for all to see, would have revealed a very wide gap between DSC's tax and shareholder books with reference to revenue recognition. Astute analysts need not have worked out all of the figures: what was required was a knowledge that, of the two methods of calculating profits, DSC was utilizing the one that made it appear most favorable.

Differential Disclosure

Differential disclosure refers to the possibility that what the company says in one document is markedly different from what it says in another. Or, there may be more complete information on a particular topic. Here we are not referring to press releases and interviews by reporters, but rather to those in the annual and quarterly reports and the 10-Ks and 10-Qs.

An analyst should exercise caution when encountering any significant divergences between annual and quarterly financial statements and the reports mandated by the SEC. The reason for differential disclosure is that the annual reports and quarterly financial statements are meant to be read by stockholders, most of whom, in the opinion of managements, tend to be more impressed by glossy presentations and hyped writing than statistics and footnotes. The 10-Ks and 10-Qs are official reports filed with the SEC. No chief executive officer will go to jail if, in the face of declining business and stiffer competition, he predicts a rosy future in the stockholders' letter. But he could be in trouble if the 10-K and 10-Q do not conform to SEC guidelines. Generally speaking, the narrative portion of annual reports is put together with the assistance of public relations experts whereas the financial part of the annuals is compiled by the accounting staff of the company and reviewed by the external auditors. The 10-K is the direct responsibility of accountants and lawyers.

If this is the case, why should an analyst bother reading the annual reports and quarterly financial statements at all? Why not go straight to the 10Ks and 10-Qs, if that is where one can get more accurate statements? The answer is that only in the stockholders' letter can one discover the ideas and rationale behind management's actions and decisions. It is there that CEOs talk about their strategies, defend past actions, and, possibly disclose plans. Moreover, a comparative study of all these statements can indicate their credibility.

A prime example of differential disclosure can be found in Procter & Gamble's 1984 Annual Report. For the fiscal year ended June 30, 1984, P&G

---

[6] *Wall Street Journal* (October 9, 1985), p. 46.

earned $5.35 per share versus $5.22 in 1983, hardly an earthshattering increase. Moreover, the company revealed that part of the improvement came from changes in its corporate tax rate, which declined to 37.6% from 44.1% in 1983 (the equivalent of $0.56 per share). Finally, the 1984 figure included an $0.18 per share special item, compared with one of $0.10 in 1983, both resulting from swaps of stock for debt. So the company actually experienced an operating earnings decline in 1984, a fact which is noted elsewhere in the "Analysis and Discussion" section — located in the back of the report.[7]

In the letter, management explained that the "modest earnings increase ... reflects the cost of broadening the Company's product base and augurs well for the long-term health and vitality of the business." So it would appear that P&G believed it would reap a bountiful harvest from the investment in new products somewhere down the line. All's well and good, for this is a sign of vigor and health. In some new product areas increased marketing expenses can be an indication that better bottom-line results are in the offing. But this was not the case at the time.

Changes in family structure had something to do with it. Says an advertising executive who once worked at P&G, "There is no way the traditional housewife, who is generally a smart shopper, is going to go for something like a toothpaste pump. Today's consumer will [go for such gimmicks], however, and that's the kind of thing P&G might not see."

Given the breakdown of the nuclear family, two-job families, and related social changes, men do more of the shopping than they used to. Studies show that husbands select different brands than their wives 43% of the time. So it was that P&G's Crest toothpaste, long an industry leader, was being seriously challenged by Colgate. Tide was threatened by Wisk, and Pampers, which once had 75% of the disposable diaper market, was down to less than 33% in 1985.

Increased advertising budgets, which in the past had enabled P&G to increase market share, were also not working well. None of these basic problems are discussed in the P&G annual report — we would not expect them to be. But in the analysis and discussion section we encounter this explanation: In addition to the aggressive investment program there was "the highly competitive climate faced by many of the Company's established brands in the U.S. consumer business." Which is another way of saying that rivals have turned in a remarkable job of "catch up." That this would be a long-term problem could be seen in the fact that for the fiscal year ended June 30, 1985, P&G's earnings dropped for the first time in three decades.

Convergent Technologies (CVGT), once one of the hottest stocks of the microcomputer age, also offers a good example of differential disclosure. For 1983 the company reported earnings of $0.40 a share compared with $0.42 in 1982. CVGT's Annual Report and letter were both optimistic, but the 10-K provided a somewhat different picture.

[7] Procter & Gamble, *1984 Annual Report,* pp. 2-5; *Quality of Earnings Report* (September 25, 1984), p. 116.

Among CVGT's more important products were multiprocessor supermin-icomputers known as the NGEN work stations and the MegaFrame, upon which the company had pinned much of its hopes. The letter to stockholders in the annual report started out by noting that "1983 was a year of progress and challenge for Convergent Technologies." Now this word "challenge" should put an analyst on guard; corporate management often use "challenge" to mean "trouble."

Although the rest of the letter was relatively upbeat, there were exceptions. For example, NGEN shipments were below expectations and costs were above expectations. The reason: "Slow manufacturing start up and disappointing performance by some suppliers." There were words of praise for WorkSlate, a powerful portable microcomputer which can also function as a terminal. "These machines were sent as 'high tech stocking stuffers' to initial customers ordering through the American Express Christmas catalog," with a good reception.[8]

Some of the numbers looked great, but some were not at all pleasing. Revenues rose from $96.4 million to $163.5 million, net income went from $11.9 million to $14.9 million, but CVGT earned only $0.40 per share compared with $0.42 in 1982 due to a substantial increase in the number of shares outstanding.[9] Despite this, the letter ended on a note of triumph. "Upon reflection, 1983 was a year of investment and a year of rewards... We have retained our tough operating culture and entrepreneurial spirit, and will continue to set demanding goals for ourselves."[10]

The 10-K presented quite a different picture, one of the clearest examples of differential disclosure. In that document we learn that there was only one supplier for the advanced microprocessor upon which MegaFrame is based, and one for the disk drives. "To date the disk drives have been manufactured in limited quantities and the microprocessor is on allocation from its manufacturer." The report went on to claim that this had no material impact upon the business, but later in the 10-K we read that "with the increased demand for certain components in the computer system industry the Company believes that there is a greater likelihood that the Company will experience such delays." Further, "some of these new components have yet to be manufactured in volume by their suppliers. The Company's ability to manufacture these products may be adversely affected by the inability of the Company's vendors to supply high quality components in adequate quantities."[11] A similar situation existed for the company's other product, WorkSlate.

Changes in Discretionary Expenses

There are scores of examples by which earnings are increased or decreased through one-time changes in discretionary expenses, and others in which earnings remain the same, but the quality can be altered. Examples of discretionary expenses are maintenance repair costs, the cost of replacement of obsolete equipment, advertis-

---

[8] Convergent Technologies, *1983 Annual Report Commission*, pp. 2-3.

[9] Ibid., p. 19.

[10] Ibid., p. 3.

[11] Convergent Technologies, *1983 10-K Report to the Securities & Exchange Commission*.

ing costs, and the costs of training programs. Changes in these expenditures are the result of business decisions made by management, not accounting decisions.

By either cutting a discretionary cost or postponing it to a future accounting period a company can favorably impact earnings in the current period but have a detrimental affect on future earnings. For example, consider the case where a company in the last month of its fiscal year decides to cut advertising expenditures for the remainder of the fiscal year and in future years. The immediate effect might be to improve earnings in the current fiscal year. But future earnings will be adversely affected if the reduction in advertising reduces future sales by a greater amount.

Changes in discretionary expenses could also have the opposite effect: it could decrease earnings but result in a favorable impact on earnings in future periods. An increase in advertising or the acquisition of more efficient capital equipment are examples of positive discretionary expenses.

In summary, an analyst must read all the publications of a corporation, and be alert to unusual charges and sources of income, changes and large differences in changes in discretionary expenses, and differences in information disclosed. By reading between the lines, the astute analyst can uncover issues that corporate managers may be asked to address.

PROFITABILITY ANALYSIS

Profitability ratios are utilized to explore the underlying causes of a change in earnings per share. They show the combined effects of liquidity and asset and debt management on the profitability of the firm. These ratios break earnings per share into its basic determinants for purposes of assessing the factors underlying the profitability of the firm. They help to assess the adequacy of historical profits, and to project future profitability through better understanding of its underlying causes.

Standards for a given ratio will vary according to operating characteristics of the company being analyzed and general business conditions; such standards cannot be stated as fixed and immutable. Experience plays an important role in setting such standards.

It is assumed that the analyst has made all adjustments deemed necessary to reflect comparable and true earning power of the corporation before calculating the ratios discussed below. It is important to stress that ratios are utilized to raise significant questions requiring further analysis, not to provide answers. Ratios must be viewed in the context of other ratios and other facts, derived from sources other than the financial statements.

Determinants of Earnings Per Share

The analyst must relate earnings to total assets and common stockholders' equity to avoid being misled. For example, assume a firm with 1,000,000 common shares outstanding earned $1,000,000 after taxes. Earnings per share, assuming only that class of equity outstanding, would be $1 per share. Now assume the company could earn an additional $500,000 after taxes by utilizing the funds raised through selling an additional 1,000,000 common shares. While total earnings would increase, this would not be advantageous to the stockholder. There are now 2,000,000 shares outstanding, and since earnings would be $1,500,000 after taxes, earnings per share would fall to $0.75 per share. Return on the total owners' investment also would fall. This suggests concentrating at least initially, on earnings per share and its determinants rather than earnings after taxes.

The two basic determinants of earnings per share are the return on stockholders' equity and the book value per share, as shown by the equation below:

$$\text{Earnings per share} = \frac{\text{Earnings available to common}}{\text{Avg. no. of common shares}}$$

$$= \frac{\text{Earnings available to common}}{\text{Stockholders' equity}} \times \frac{\text{Stockholders' equity}}{\text{Avg. no. of common shares}}$$

The first ratio is the *return on stockholders' equity*

$$\text{Return on stockholders' equity} = \frac{\text{Earnings available to common}}{\text{Stockholders' equity}}$$

The second ratio is *book value per share*

$$\text{Book value per share} = \frac{\text{Stockholders' equity}}{\text{Avg. no. of common shares}}$$

To illustrate, the calculation of the ratios above and other ratios discussed in this chapter, we use the 1991 and 1990 balance sheet and income statement of The Home Depot, Inc.[12] We presented these two financial statements in the previous chapter. Exhibit 1 reproduces the income statement and Exhibit 2 the balance sheet. (The last two columns in both exhibits will be discussed later in this chapter.) Exhibit 3 shows the calculation of the various financial measures discussed throughout this chapter.

Growth in Book Value Per Share

As can be seen from the partitioning of the earnings per share measure earlier, all other things being equal, a higher book value per share ratio is better than a low one. How can a firm get growth in book value per share? There are three basic ways.

First, the company can retain earnings. By doing so, stockholders' equity increases, but there is no change in the number of common shares outstanding. This assumes that the retained earnings can be utilized as effectively as past owners' equity has been; in other words, that the return on stockholders' equity is at least maintained.

---

[12] The source of the data on Home Depot is a research report by Christopher E. Vroom of Alex. Brown & Sons, Inc. dated September 5, 1991.

Exhibit 1: Income Statement for The Home Depot, Inc.: 1991 and 1990 (Dollars in Thousands)

	1991	1990	Common Size Analysis(*) 1991	Common Size Analysis(*) 1990
Net Sales	$3,815,356	$2,758,535	100.00%	100.00%
Cost of Goods Sold	2,751,085	1,991,777	72.11	72.20
Gross Profit	$1,064,271	$766,758	27.89	27.80
Operating Expenses	$693,657	$504,363	18.18	18.28
General & Admin.	91,664	67,901	2.40	2.46
Pre-Opening Expense	13,315	9,845	0.35	0.36
Net Operating Profit	$265,635	$184,649	6.96	6.69
Interest Expense (Net)	$5,807	$2,634	0.15	0.10
Earnings Before Taxes	$259,828	$182,015	6.81	6.60
Income Taxes	96,400	70,061	2.53	2.54
Net Income	$163,428	$111,954	4.28	4.06

(*) All items expressed as a percentage of net sales.

Exhibit 2: Balance Sheet for The Home Depot, Inc.: 1991 and 1990 (Dollars in Thousands)

	1991	1990	Common Size Analysis(*) 1991	Common Size Analysis(*) 1990
Assets				
Cash	$137,296	$135,381	8.37%	12.11%
Receivables (net)	49,235	38,993	3.00	3.49
Inventory	509,022	381,452	31.05	34.13
Other	17,931	10,474	1.09	0.94
Total Current Assets	$713,574	$566,240	43.52%	50.67%
Plant, Prop. & Equip.	963,619	568,690	58.78	50.89
Less Accumulated Dep.	(84,889)	(54,250)	(5.18)	(4.85)
Net Plant, Prop & Equip	$878,730	$514,440	53.60%	46.03%
Other Assets	47,199	36,854	2.88	3.30
Total Assets	$1,639,503	$1,117,534	100.00%	100.00%
Liabilities				
Accounts Payable	235,267	172,876	14.35%	15.47%
Accrued Liabilities	166,734	118,066	10.17	10.56
Other Current Liab.	10,706	1,447	0.65	0.13
Total Current Liabilities	$412,707	$292,389	25.17	26.16
Long-Term Debt	530,774	302,901	32.37	27.10
Capital Lease Obligations	12,620	10,115	0.77	0.91
Stockholder's Equity				
Retained Earnings	439,770	289,177	26.82	25.88
Paid-in-Capital	264,301	233,458	16.12	20.89
Other	(26,572)	(10,506)	(1.62)	(0.94)
Tot. Stockholders' Equity	$683,402	$512,129	41.68	45.83
Total Liab. & Equity	$1,639,503	$1,117,534	100.00	100.00

(*) All items expressed as a percentage of total assets.

Exhibit 3: Calculation of Financial Ratios for
The Home Depot, Inc.: 1991 and 1990

The balance sheet and income statement are shown in Exhibits 1 and 2, respectively. Additional information:

Average number of shares of common stock outstanding: 1991 = 181,252,000; 1990 = 177,472,000
Year end 1989 accounts receivable = $17,614,000
Year end 1989 inventory = $294,274,000
Since there is no preferred stock in the capital structure, Net Income = Earnings Available to Common

Financial Measure	1991	1990
Earnings Per Share:		
$\dfrac{\text{Earnings available to common}}{\text{Average number of common shares}}$	$\dfrac{\$163,428,000}{181,252,000} = \$0.90$	$\dfrac{\$111,954,000}{177,472,000} = \$0.63$
Return on Stockholders' Equity:		
$\dfrac{\text{Earnings available to common}}{\text{Stockholders' equity}}$	$\dfrac{\$163,428,000}{\$683,402,000} = 23.91\%$	$\dfrac{\$111,954,000}{\$512,129,000} = 21.86\%$
Book Value Per Share:		
$\dfrac{\text{Stockholders' equity}}{\text{Average number of common shares}}$	$\dfrac{\$683,402,000}{181,252,000} = \$3.77$	$\dfrac{\$512,129,000}{\$177,472,000} = \$2.88$
Return on Total Assets:		
$\dfrac{\text{Earnings available to common}}{\text{Total assets}}$	$\dfrac{\$163,428,000}{\$1,639,503,000} = 9.97\%$	$\dfrac{\$111,954,000}{\$1,117,534,000} = 10.02\%$
Asset/Equity Ratio:		
$\dfrac{\text{Total assets}}{\text{Stockholders' equity}}$	$\dfrac{\$1,639,503,000}{\$683,402,000} = 2.40$	$\dfrac{\$1,117,534,000}{\$512,129,000} = 2.18$
Gross Profit Margin:		
$\dfrac{\text{Gross profit}}{\text{Net sales}}$	$\dfrac{\$1,064,271,000}{\$3,815,356,000} = 27.89\%$	$\dfrac{\$766,758,000}{\$2,758,535,000} = 27.80\%$
Net Operating Margin:		
$\dfrac{\text{Net operating income}}{\text{Net sales}}$	$\dfrac{\$265,635,000}{\$3,815,356,000} = 6.96\%$	$\dfrac{\$184,649,000}{2,758,535,000} = 6.69\%$
Before-Tax Profit Margin:		
$\dfrac{\text{Net income before taxes}}{\text{Net sales}}$	$\dfrac{\$259,828,000}{\$3,815,356,000} = 6.81\%$	$\dfrac{\$182,015,000}{\$2,758,535,000} = 6.60\%$
After-Tax Profit Margin:		
$\dfrac{\text{Net income}}{\text{Net sales}}$	$\dfrac{\$163,428,000}{\$3,815,356,000} = 4.28\%$	$\dfrac{\$111,954,000}{\$2,758,535,000} = 4.06\%$
Total Asset Turnover:		
$\dfrac{\text{Net sales}}{\text{Total assets}}$	$\dfrac{\$3,815,356,000}{\$1,639,503,000} = 2.33$	$\dfrac{\$2,758,535,000}{\$1,117,534,000} = 2.47$

Exhibit 3 *(Continued)*

Financial Measure	1991	1990
Accounts Receivable Turnover:		
$\dfrac{\text{Net sales}}{\text{Average accounts receivable*}}$	$\dfrac{\$3,815,356,000}{\$44,114,000} = 86.49$	$\dfrac{\$2,758,535,000}{\$28,303,500} = 97.46$
Days Sales in Accts Receivable:		
$\dfrac{360 \text{ days}}{\text{Average accounts receivable turnover}}$	$\dfrac{360}{86.49} = 4.2 \text{ days}$	$\dfrac{360}{97.46} = 3.7 \text{ days}$
Inventory Turnover:		
$\dfrac{\text{Cost of goods sold}}{\text{Average inventory**}}$	$\dfrac{\$2,751,085,000}{\$445,237,000} = 6.2$	$\dfrac{\$1,991,777,000}{\$337,863,000} = 5.9$
Days to Sell Inventory:		
$\dfrac{360 \text{ days}}{\text{Inventory turnover}}$	$\dfrac{360}{6.2} = 58 \text{ days}$	$\dfrac{360}{5.9} = 61 \text{ days}$
* Average accounts receivable	($49,235,000 + $38,993,000)/2	($38,993,000 + $17,614,000)/2
** Average Inventory	($509,022,000 + $381,452,000)/2	($381,452,000 + $294,274,000)/2

The growth rate in earnings supported by retained earnings can be calculated by multiplying the rate of return earned on stockholders' equity by the *retention rate* of the firm (retained earnings divided by earnings after taxes). A firm that earns 10% on its stockholders' equity and has a retention rate of 40%, builds a 4% growth rate for earnings per share. To illustrate assume:

        Earnings per share   = $1
        Book value per share = $10
        Retention rate   = 40%

Forty cents will be retained of each $1 earned per share, increasing book value per share to $10.40. If, however, the firm continues to earn 10% on the stockholders' capital ($1/$10), the earnings per share will rise to $1.04, or a 4% growth rate. If the rate earned on stockholders' capital fell because of the added production capacity, earnings per share could fall, even with retention. For example, if the return on stockholders' capital fell to 8%, the earnings per share would be only 83 cents ($0.08 \times \$10.40 = \$0.832$).

The second way to get growth in book value per share is to buy back company stock at a price less than book value per share. The third way is to sell stock at a price above book value per share. Mergers can result in an increase in book value per share for the surviving company, since the book value of the acquired shares may be greater than the book value of the shares given in exchange. While it is true that book value per share has no necessary relationship to market value per share, analysts should follow what happens to book value, since it can be an important determinant of earnings.

Return on Stockholders' Equity

Stockholders are the residual claimants to the profits earned after taxes less any preferred dividends (earnings available to common). The rate earned on the stockholders' equity and the behavior of the basic components determining that return are the key criterion when selecting stocks. The two basic determinants of return on stockholders' equity are the return on total assets and the proportion of assets financed by stockholders, as opposed to creditors. This is demonstrated in the equation below:

$$\frac{\text{Earnings available to common}}{\text{Stockholders' equity}}$$

$$= \frac{\text{Earnings available to common}}{\text{Total assets}} \times \frac{\text{Total assets}}{\text{Stockholders' equity}}$$

The first ratio is the *return on total assets*:

$$\text{Return on total assets} = \frac{\text{Earnings available to common}}{\text{Total assets}}$$

The second ratio, the *asset/equity ratio*, indicates the amount of total assets relative to stockholders' equity:

$$\text{Asset/equity ratio} = \frac{\text{Total assets}}{\text{Stockholders' equity}}$$

The reciprocal of the asset/equity ratio is the percentage of the firm's assets provided by the stockholders.

Most firms have a leverage capitalization, which means that debt has been used as a source of funds. This will cause profits and the return to stockholders to be much more variable than if only equity capital were used to raise funds. The effects of financial leverage are compounded by the effects of operating leverage introduced by fixed operating costs.

The difference between the rate of return on total capital invested and the rate of return on stockholders' equity indicates the effect of financial leverage. Favorable financial leverage means that the rate of return on the total capital invested exceeds the cost of borrowed funds. When this occurs, the rate of return on stockholders' equity will exceed the rate earned on total invested capital.

Return on Total Assets

As explained above, return on total assets is a key determinant of the return earned on stockholders' equity. There are two basic determinants of the return on total assets: (1) the cents of profit generated by each dollar of sales (the margin), and (2) the dollars of sales generated on average for each dollar of assets (the turnover of assets). This is demonstrated in the equation below:

$$\text{Return on total assets} = \frac{\text{Earnings available to common}}{\text{Total assets}}$$

$$= \frac{\text{Earnings available to common}}{\text{Net sales}} \times \frac{\text{Net sales}}{\text{Total assets}}$$

The first ratio is called the *profit margin* and the second the *total asset turnover*; that is:

$$\text{Profit margin} = \frac{\text{Net earnings}}{\text{Net sales}}$$

$$\text{Total asset turnover} = \frac{\text{Net sales}}{\text{Total assets}}$$

Return on total assets and the behavior of its components offers some of the most useful statistics for studying the operating efficiency of a firm

Profit Margin

To aid in studying operating efficiency of a firm, an analyst should calculate and assess each of the following margin ratios.

Gross Profit Margin

Gross profit margin is calculated by dividing gross profit by net sales:

$$\text{Gross profit margin} = \frac{\text{Gross profit}}{\text{Net sales}}$$

This ratio is a useful indicator of the productive efficiency of a firm. It should be analyzed in terms of its trend over time and in relationship to other companies operating in the same industry. As explained in the previous chapter, the method of inventory valuation used by the firm (e.g., LIFO versus FIFO) is important, and the analyst must be sure that the figures used for comparison are, in fact, comparable.

Net Operating Margin

Net operating margin is calculated by dividing net operating income by net sales:

$$\text{Net operating margin} = \frac{\text{Net operating income}}{\text{Net sales}}$$

The net operating margin is the complement of the net operating expense ratio, since the two when added must always equal 100%. This ratio indicates the percentage of sales dollars not used up in the generation of sales. In other words, this is the percentage of sales dollars available to meet finance charges, pay taxes, to pay dividends, and to finance corporate capital needs.

Before-Tax and After-Tax Profit Margins

The *before-tax profit margin* and the *after-tax profit margin* are calculated as shown below:

$$\text{Before-tax profit margin} = \frac{\text{Net income before taxes}}{\text{Net sales}}$$

$$\text{After-tax profit margin} = \frac{\text{Net income}}{\text{Net sales}}$$

The before-tax profit margin is a more useful intermediate determinant of the return on assets than the after-tax profit margin, for purposes of assessing the efficiency with which assets are used.

The percentage of sales brought down to before-tax profit may be low (as for a food retailer), but if inventory turnover and capital investment turnover are high, then the rate of return on assets may still be large. Conversely, the before-tax margin may be relatively high (as for a public utility), but if inventory turnover and/or capital asset turnover are low, the return on assets may be low. These ratios are components of the return on assets, and must be interpreted in relation to asset turnovers. It is the return on capital committed that is important to an investor, not how that return is generated. Breaking the return on investment into its basic components, however, helps gain a better understanding of the firm's operating record and provides a better basis for forecasting.

Asset Turnover

Asset turnover is calculated by dividing the net sales by the total assets. There are numerous combinations of asset turnover and gross profit margin that will produce a given return on assets. An analyst should compare both the turnover ratios and the gross profit margins of a company to companies in the same industry. Such an analysis, especially when buttressed by information gained in the analysis of the economy, can reveal weaknesses as well as the potential strengths of a firm.

An analyst must go beyond a mere calculation of these ratios and a comparison to competitors. A weak margin suggests problems in controlling expenses for a firm. Vertical and horizontal analysis can help explore these problems. *Vertical analysis* is accomplished by dividing each expense item in the income statement of a given year by net sales. One would expect expenses to rise as sales rise. However, when a particular expense item rises at a faster rate than sales, it should be explored carefully. In *horizontal analysis*, each expense item of a given year is divided by that same expense item in the base year. This allows for the exploration of changes in the relative importance of expense items over time and the behavior of expense items as sales change.

The turnover of assets may fall sharply when a firm undertakes a major expansion. The large asset investment causes this, since there has not yet been adequate time for these assets to generate the anticipated growth in sales that motivated the expansion. One must, therefore, be careful to review capital expenditures when assessing asset turnover ratios.

Leased assets treated as operating leases are not recorded on the balance sheet and are not, therefore, a part of the total assets shown on the balance sheet. Still, leased assets do result in sales. A rising or relatively high turnover ratio could, therefore, be generated by a firm that increases the use of leasing to acquire assets. This would not indicate more efficient use of asset investment.

One of the best ways analysts can predict future downward earnings is through a careful analysis of accounts receivable and inventories. There are two signs that can indicate problems: a larger than average accounts receivable situation, and/or a bloated inventory. Either situation is a signal that the analyst should play the devil's advocate when assessing that particular company.

Accounts Receivable

The *accounts receivables turnover* can be determined by dividing the net credit sales by the average accounts receivable. That is,

$$\text{Accounts receivable turnover} = \frac{\text{Annual net credit sales}}{\text{Average accounts receivable}}$$

Here the average accounts receivable is equal to the average of the accounts receivable at the beginning of the year (i.e., the accounts receivable at the end of the previous fiscal year) and the accounts receivable at the end of the current fiscal year.

In practice, net sales typically is used as the numerator because information is not available as to the portion of sales that were on credit terms. This does tend to overstate the liquidity of receivables when cash sales are significant, as for a retailer.

The turnover may be converted into the number of days sales outstanding in receivables by dividing the accounts receivable turnover figure into 360. That is,

$$\text{Days sales in accts. receivable} = \frac{360 \text{ days}}{\text{Accounts receivable turnover}}$$

One would expect the accounts receivables turnover to be relatively in line with the firm's terms of sale. A high accounts receivables turnover could make a relatively low current ratio (discussed below) acceptable, from a liquidity standpoint, and lead to a higher return on assets. On the other hand, a high turnover could suggest inadequate inventory for meeting customers' demands and/or an overly tight credit policy that is causing the firm to miss potentially profitable sales.

Increases in days sales in accounts receivable can illustrate the granting of more liberal credit terms and/or difficulty in obtaining payment from customers. However, even more importantly, the analysis of sales and accounts receivable may provide a clue as to whether a company is merely shifting inventory from the corporate level to its customers because of a "hard sell" sales campaign or costly incentives. In such an instance, this type of sales may constitute "borrowing from the future." Within this context, it is important to note that in most instances, a sale is recorded by a company when the goods are shipped to the customer. Also, there is an added cost to the company in carrying an above-average amount of accounts receivable.

Inventories

Inventory turnover is computed by dividing the cost of goods sold by the average inventory for a year. That is:

$$\text{Inventory turnover} = \frac{\text{Cost of goods sold}}{\text{Average inventory}}$$

The analyst is interested in determining the physical turnover of the inventory, and needs a numerator (cost of goods sold) that is calculated on the same basis as the inventory. Price changes could distort this ratio, as an indicator of physical turnover, when net sales is used as a numerator.

A low ratio suggests the possibility that investment in inventory is too high for the sales capacity of the business. This will hurt future profitability, both because of the interest costs incurred by borrowing to support the inventory investment and the storage costs. On the other hand, a high ratio relative to the industry tends to suggest that inventories are too low. Sales might be lost by a firm because of inadequate selection for its customers.

The number of days' sales outstanding in inventory can be calculated by dividing the number of days in a year (360) by the inventory turnover ratio:

$$\text{Days to sell inventory} = \frac{360 \text{ days}}{\text{Inventory turnover}}$$

For example, if the inventory turnover ratio were 12, the number of days sales outstanding would be 30. This would mean that if the firm continued to sell at the same rate it has in the past, it would sell the entire inventory shown on the balance sheet in 30 days.

Why is inventory analysis so important? Obviously, higher trending inventories in relation to sales can lead to inventory markdowns, write-offs, etc. In addition, it is important to note that an excess of inventories has repeatedly proven to be a good indicator of future slowdown in production. Within this context, it is important to analyze the components of inventories. If the finished goods segment of inventories is rising much more rapidly than raw materials and/or work-in-process, it is likely that the company has an abundance of finished goods and will have to slow down production. Akin to accounts receivable, bulging inventories are costly to carry.

Profitability Analysis and Physical Data Ratios

Analysts frequently calculate physical data ratios and reduce them to a per share basis, to aid in studying profitability. These ratios are useful when calculated on the basis of specific characteristics of a given industry and used for comparing companies in that industry.

Physical Reserves

Reserves are of utmost importance to companies dependent on wasting assets for their operations (such as oil or timber companies). Reported reserves by major companies normally provide a conservative representation of such assets. The analyst should note the quality or grade of reserves as well as the quantity, with special attention to changes in grade from year to year. Changes from year to year indicate current extractive policy and possibly "high grading" (mining primarily the highest grade ores in the deposit) in any given year.

Reserves of oil and gas, normally stated in terms of millions of barrels and billions of cubic feet respectively, frequently are reported on a per share basis. The estimated value of reserves can be computed by multiplying the number of units in reserve by the going market price per unit. The value of reserves per share often is compared to current market price per share when looking for undervalued companies. This is not necessarily a valid indicator of value, however, since market prices for the physical resource can rise or fall sharply in the future (witness oil).

Capacity

Producers and processors of various materials normally have specific productive or fabricating capacities that may be expressed in physical terms. These data can be reduced to a per share or a per employee basis for comparison between companies. Capacity also can be related to order backlogs, both in units and dollars. Persistent excess capacity often is a symptom of decline for a firm.

Production Data

Production data in units can be related to capacity figures to assess whether or not excess capacity is present. This information should be compared to other firms in the industry. In companies concentrating principally on one type of product (e.g., crude oil, ingot steel, or copper), production data in units can be used to estimate selling prices, production costs, and profits per unit. Such data also help the analyst to determine the effects of changes in costs and selling prices, not the profit margins of the company.

Freight Volume and Other Specialized Ratios

Detailed information relative to volume, product composition, and geographical distribution of freight carried is valuable to the analyst in appraising the outlook for a transportation company such as a railroad, airline, trucking service, or barge line. Other examples of specialized physical ratios could be residential and commercial load for utilities, ton miles per dollar of debt for railroads, or the load factor for airlines. In the case of The Home Depot, Inc., information on the sales per average store and the sales per square foot should be analyzed.

SALES ANALYSIS

While some analysts have stressed growth in demand for a company's products, it is the growth in earnings power, not sales per se, that is the desired objective. This makes cost behavior important. Since cost economies are rarely repeated on a yearly basis, continued growth in profits is not likely unless sales are growing.

The aim of sales analysis is to project revenues for the next three to five years as a basis for generating cost and profit expectations. When studying historical revenue data the analyst should be concerned with the size, trend, composition, and underlying determinants of those revenue patterns.

For the purposes of developing future sales forecasts, the analyst could:

1. Calculate the compound growth rate in sales over a period of about ten years, to insure including the effects of the business cycle.
2. Calculate a standard deviation around the average of the above data to assess the stability of revenue patterns over time.
3. Observe the resistance of company sales to negative economic and other factors.
4. Assess the major factors underlying the sales pattern observed.

Analysts typically compare the sales patterns for a given company with those of its principal competitors and appropriate aggregate data (such as GDP data). Above average sales growth for a company usually is predicated on expected rapid growth of the industry in which the company operates. A company may, however, accomplish above average growth by gaining an increased share of total industry demand. Forecasting end-use demand for a company's products is therefore useful.

Trends and Common Size Statements

In a *common size statement*, all items are expressed as a percent of a base figure. Common size statements can be useful for purposes of analyzing trends and the changing relationship between financial statement items. For example, all items in each year's income statement could be presented as a percentage of net sales. This is shown for The Home Depot, Inc. in the last two columns of Exhibit 2. By reviewing several years of such statements, an analyst could observe changes in the relative importance of cost items and how cost items vary as sales change. In the case of the balance sheet, all items can be expressed as a percentage of total assets, as shown in the last two columns of Exhibit 2.

Horizontal analysis is also a useful tool. In horizontal analysis, each item in the income statement is expressed as an index number calculated by dividing a given year's number by the number of a base year.

Conglomerates and Sales Breakdowns

Analysts of diversified businesses face the problem of separating and understanding the impact that the different individual segments of the business have on the operational results of a firm. Opportunities for growth will vary among the different product lines, and this must be taken into account when forecasting sales and profitability. Analysts require information that is broken down to represent homogeneous groupings whose characteristics are similar in terms of growth potential, variability, and risk. Exhibit 4 shows the breakdown of the sales mix of The Home Depot by product category from fiscal years 1987 to 1991.

Exhibit 4: The Home Depot Sales Mix By Product Category: Fiscal Years 1987 to 1991

Product Category	1987	1988	1989	1990	1991
Plumbing, Heating & Electrical Supplies	29.2%	28.9%	29.0%	29.5%	28.9%
Building Materials, Lumber, Floor/Wall Covering	29.1	29.5	31.0	31.0	32.1
Hardware and Tools	13.1	12.7	12.2	12.1	12.1
Seasonal and Specialty Items	14.4	14.8	14.6	14.5	15.2
Paint and Furniture	14.2	14.1	13.2	12.9	11.7
Total	100.0%	100.0%	100.0%	100.0%	100.0%

FASB Statement No. 14 requires disclosure concerning information about operations in different industries, foreign operations, and major customers. Companies are required in their annual reports to offer breakdowns of significant segments in terms of revenues, operating profit, and identifiable assets. Also, the method of accounting for transfer pricing and cost allocations are to be disclosed. A segment is significant if sales, operating profit, or identifiable assets are 10% or more of the combined accounts for all of a company's industry segments.

While disclosure of information on business segments is helpful, an analyst must recognize the many judgments necessary for preparing such data, which limit its usefulness. Cost allocations are often arbitrary, and there are no generally accepted principles governing such allocations. Information on business segments must be treated as highly qualitative, and an analyst should not attribute undue accuracy to such data.

Industry Analysis

A firm's sales and profits typically are affected by economy-wide factors (e.g., interest rates and price level fluctuations), by factors specific to the product line or industry areas in which the firm operates, and by factors specific to the firm itself (e.g., quality of management and locational factors). Therefore, a part of the sales and earnings of a corporation is determined by industry forces.

Some writers, notably Julius Grodinsky,[13] drew a rough parallel between industry growth and the human life cycle. They point out that when new industries are born, there often is a rush by many companies to enter the field in this period of initial and rapid growth. This is followed by a shakeout period, which only a few survive, and then by a continuing period of strong growth, although the rate of growth is slower than in the initial period. Grodinsky described these first two periods as the pioneering stage and the expansion stage. Finally, industries are expected to stop growing, either living a relatively stable existence for an extended period of time or dying.

Grodinsky pointed out the great risk of selecting stocks in the pioneering stage, where little information about participants may be available. There is little or no past record to guide investors, or aid in preparing future projections.

[13] Julius Grodinsky, *Investments* (New York: The Ronald Press, 1953), Part II.

Exhibit 5: Do-It-Yourself Industry Leaders: 1986 and 1990

Company	Sales (in billions)		% Change
	1990	1991	
Lowe's Cos.	$2.5	$2.8	12.0%
Wickes Cos.	2.0	0.9	−55.0
Payless Cashways	1.5	2.2	46.7
Grossman's	1.0	0.8	−20.0
The Home Depot	1.0	3.8	280.0

Source: The Home Deport, Inc., Research Report by Christopher E. Vroom of Alex. Brown & Sons, Inc. dated September 5, 1991.

Michael Porter has suggested six basic factors that should be considered in projecting the sales of a firm:[14]

1. The threat of new entrants to the major markets served by the company.
2. The threat posed by substitute products or services.
3. The possible new entry of products by the company under analysis.
4. The rivalry among existing firms serving the markets important to the company, and the company's present and expected position in those markets.
5. The company's strategy for maintaining its leadership position in their market and their financial and other abilities to carry out these strategies.
6. The position in the life-cycle analysis approach of the major product lines of the company.

Once again, we return to The Home Depot, a company in the "Do-It-Yourself" home improvement industry. According to Christopher E. Vroom, an analyst in the Growth Retailers Group of Alex. Brown & Sons, this industry:

> is a large relatively stable and fast-growing component of residential construction accounting for over $100 billion in sales, or 24% of overall building activity (versus 16% in 1980). The industry has grown at a compound annual rate of 9% for the past ten years, driven largely by gains in the remodeling segment, which comprise roughly 70% of total sales.[15]

Vroom then goes on to highlight the favorable demographic and income shifts that "will drive sustained, strong growth in remodeling sales while the continued aging of the housing stock will likely spur growth in the repair business."

The five largest chains in the Do-It-Yourself industry account for only 12% of industry sales. Thus, this industry can be categorized as extremely fragmented. The five market leaders and their sales in 1986 and 1990 are shown in Exhibit 5.

[14] Michael E. Porter, *Competitive Strategy* (New York: The Free Press, 1980).
[15] Research Report on The Home Depot, Inc., September 5, 1991.

DEBT ANALYSIS

Our focus thus far in this chapter has been on been on net income and earnings per share. In this section, our focus is on the ability of a firm to meet its debt obligations. Traditionally, this has involved the calculation of various ratios that attempt to measure the company's short-term solvency, financial leverage, and debt burden. Once we have discussed these ratios and their limitations, we also discuss cash flow analysis.

Ratio Analysis

There are three sets of ratios that are used as indicators to assess the ability of a firm to satisfy its obligations: (1) short-term solvency ratios which assess the ability of the firm to meet debts maturing over the coming year, (2) capitalization (or financial leverage) ratios which assess the extent to which the firm relies on debt financing, and (3) coverage ratios which assess the ability of the firm to meet the fixed obligations brought about by debt financing.

Short-Term Solvency Ratios

Short-term solvency ratios are used to judge the adequacy of liquid assets for meeting short-term obligations as they come due. Firms go bankrupt, or get into financial difficulty, because they cannot pay obligations as they come due, not because they are not profitable. Therefore, an analyst should assure himself or herself that liquidity problems are not likely to appear.

    A complete analysis of the adequacy of working capital for meeting current liabilities as they come due and assessing management's efficiency in using working capital would require a thorough analysis of cash flows that will be discussed in the next section. Ratios, however, can in many instances provide a crude but useful assessment of working capital.

    The following four ratios should be calculated to assess the adequacy of working capital for a firm: (1) the current ratio, (2) the acid-test ratio, (3) the inventory turnover ratio, and (4) the receivables turnover ratio. We described the last two ratios earlier in this chapter. These two ratios indicate the approximate time needed to translate accounts receivables and inventory into cash, and as such, they are important for purposes of judging the adequacy of working capital. Below we discuss the first two ratios.

Current Ratio The *current ratio* is calculated by dividing current assets by current liabilities:

$$\text{Current ratio} = \frac{\text{Current assets}}{\text{Current liabilities}}$$

    The current ratio indicates the company's coverage of current liabilities by current assets. For example, if the ratio were 2:1, the firm could realize only half of the values stated in the balance sheet in liquidating current assets and still have adequate funds to pay all current liabilities. Exhibit 6 shows the calculation of the current ratio for The Home Depot, Inc. for 1991 and 1990. The balance sheet data are given in Exhibit 2.

A general standard for this ratio (such as 2:1) is not useful. Such a standard fails to recognize that an appropriate current ratio is a function of the nature of a company's business and would vary with differing operating cycles of different businesses.

As explained in the previous chapter, a current asset is one that is expected to be converted into cash in the ordinary operating cycle of a business. Inventory, therefore, is a current asset. In a tobacco or liquor company, inventory may be as much as 80% to 90% of current assets. However, for a liquor company that inventory may have to age four years or more before it can be converted into a salable asset. Such a company typically would require a much higher current ratio than average to have adequate liquidity to meet current liabilities maturing in one year. For a public utility company where there is no inventory or receivables collection problem, a current ratio of 1.1 or 1.2 to 1 has proved satisfactory. We suggest looking at industry averages, such as those produced by organizations like Dun & Bradstreet or Robert Morris Associates, rather than considering an overall standard. Industry averages have their faults, but are preferable to general standards that do not recognize operating differences among classes of companies.

Exhibit 6: Calculation of Financial Ratios for The Home Depot, Inc.: 1991 and 1990

Financial Measure	1991	1990
Current ratio:		
$\dfrac{\text{Current assets}}{\text{Current liabilities}}$	$\dfrac{\$713,574,000}{\$412,707,000} = 1.73$	$\dfrac{\$566,240,000}{\$292,389,000} = 1.94$
Acid-Test (Quick) Ratio:		
$\dfrac{\text{Current assets} - \text{Inventories*}}{\text{Current liabilities}}$	$\dfrac{\$204,552,000}{\$412,707,000} = 0.50$	$\dfrac{\$184,788,000}{\$292,389,000} = 0.63$
Long-Term Debt to Equity Ratio:		
$\dfrac{\text{Long-term debt**}}{\text{Shareholders' equity}}$	$\dfrac{\$543,394,000}{\$683,402,000} = 0.80$	$\dfrac{\$313,016,000}{\$512,129,000} = 0.61$
Total Debt to Equity Ratio:		
$\dfrac{\text{Current liabilities} + \text{Long-term debt}}{\text{Shareholders' equity}}$	$\dfrac{\$956,101,000}{\$683,402,000} = 1.40$	$\dfrac{\$605,405,000}{\$512,129,000} = 1.18$
Interest Coverage Ratio:		
$\dfrac{\text{Earnings before taxes} + \text{Interest charges paid}}{\text{Interest charges paid}}$	$\dfrac{\$265,635,000}{\$5,807,000} = 45.7$	$\dfrac{\$184,649,000}{\$2,634,000} = 70.1$

* Items classified as other current assets are ignored.
** Lease Obligations added to Long-Term Debt

The current ratio has a major weakness as an analytical tool. It ignores the composition of current assets, which may be as important as their relationship with current liabilities. Assume the components of the current ratio for some company are as shown below:

Current Assets		Current Liabilities	
Cash	$1,000	Accounts Payable	$5,000
Receivables	1,000	Bank Loans	2,000
Inventory	12,000		
Total	$14,000		$7,000

While this firm has a 2:1 current ratio, which might be more than the average in an industry, one could question its liquidity. The inventory has not been sold yet and appears high relative to the total of current assets. Therefore, current ratio analysis must be supplemented by other working capital ratios.

Acid Test (Quick) Ratio Since the problem in meeting current liabilities may rest on slowness or even inability to convert inventories into cash to meet current obligations, the *acid-test ratio* (also called the *quick ratio*) is recommended. This is the ratio of current assets minus inventories, accruals, and prepaid items to current liabilities; that is:

$$\text{Acid-test ratio} = \frac{\text{Current assets} - \text{Inventories} - \text{Accruals} - \text{Prepaid items}}{\text{Current liabilities}}$$

This ratio does assume that receivables are of good quality and will be converted into cash over the next year. Exhibit 6 shows this calculation for The Home Depot, Inc.

Capitalization Ratios

Analysts also calculate *capitalization ratios* to determine the extent to which the corporation is trading on its equity, and the resulting financial leverage. These ratios, also called *financial leverage ratios*, can be interpreted only in the context of the stability of industry and company earnings and cash flow. The assumption is that the greater the stability of industry and company earnings and cash flow, the more the company is able to accept the risk associated with financial leverage, and the higher the allowable ratio of debt to total capitalization (the total dollar amount of all long-term sources of funds in the balance sheet).

There are many variations to be found within the industry to calculate capitalization ratios. Two such ratios are shown below:

$$\text{Long-term debt to equity ratio} = \frac{\text{Long-term debt}}{\text{Shareholders' equity}}$$

$$\text{Total debt to equity ratio} = \frac{\text{Current liabilities} + \text{Long-term debt}}{\text{Shareholders' equity}}$$

For both ratios, the higher the ratio, the greater the financial leverage. The values used to measure debt in both ratios is the book value. It is useful to calculate shareholders' equity at market as well as at book value for the purpose of determining these ratios. A market calculation for common equity may indicate considerably more or less financial leverage than a book calculation.

Commercial rating companies and most Wall Street analysts rely heavily upon the long-term debt to equity ratio, and this is often provided in research reports sent out to clients. While this ratio can be useful, it should be noted that in recent years, given the uncertain interest rate environment, many corporations have taken to financing a good deal of their business with short-term debt. Indeed, an imaginative treasurer with a keen insight into money market activities can earn as much for a company as a plant manager, simply by switching debt from long-term to short, and vice versa, at the right time.

Other considerations in using the long-term debt to equity ratio involves leased assets. Many corporations rent buildings and equipment under long-term lease contracts. Required rental payments are contractual obligations similar to bond coupon and principal repayment obligations. However, assets acquired through leasing (i.e., those leases classified as operating leases) may not be capitalized and shown in the balance sheet. Two companies, therefore, might work with the same amount of fixed assets and produce the same profits before interest or rental payments, but the one leasing a high proportion of its productive equipment could show significantly lower financial leverage.

Exhibit 7 shows the two capitalization ratios for The Home Depot, Inc. In the calculation, capital lease are obligations that are added to long-term debt.

Exhibit 7: Analysis of Financial Flexibility
Kellogg Company and Subsidiaries ($000,000 omitted)

	1993
Basic Cash Flow*	$869.6
Less: Increase in adjusted working capital**	69.4
Operating Cash Flow	800.2
Less: Capital expenditures	449.7
Discretionary Cash Flow	350.5
Less: Dividends	305.2
Less: Asset sales and other investing activities	(89.5)
Cash Flow before Financing	134.8
Less: Net (increase) in long-term debt	(206.6)
Less: Net (increase) in notes payable	(176.7)
Less: Net purchase of company's common stock	545.2
Less: Miscellaneous	1.1
(Decrease) in Cash and Temporary Investments	($28.2)

* Includes net earnings, depreciation, and deferred income taxes, less items in net earnings not providing cash.
** Excludes cash and notes payable.
As prepared by Martin S. Fridson in *Financial Statement Analysis: A Practitioner's Guide* (New York: John Wiley & Sons, 1995), Exhibit 4-10, p. 113.

Coverage Tests

The earnings of a corporation are the basic source of cash flows. *Coverage ratios* are used to test the adequacy of cash flows generated through earnings for purposes of meeting debt and lease obligations.

Calculation of Earnings Available to Cover Interest and Fixed Charges

The calculation of an *interest coverage ratio* is simple: earnings available for paying the interest for a given year is divided by the annual interest expense. Interest expense is tax deductible and, therefore, all earnings before taxes are available for paying such charges. Also, the interest should be added back to earnings before taxes to determine the amount available to meet annual interest expenses. The ratio is:

$$\text{Interest coverage ratio} = \frac{\text{Earnings before taxes} + \text{Interest charges paid}}{\text{Interest charges paid}}$$

The interest coverage ratio for The Home Depot, Inc. for 1991 and 1990 is shown in Exhibit 6.

There are annual obligations other than interest payments that may have to be satisfied by a firm, the most important of which are lease payments. A more comprehensive coverage ratio that takes into account lease payments is the *fixed charge coverage ratio* which is computed as follows:

$$\text{Fixed charge coverage ratio}$$
$$= \frac{\text{Earnings before taxes} + \text{Interest charges paid}}{\text{Interest charges paid} + \text{Rental payment under long-term leases}}$$
$$+ \frac{\text{Lease payments under long-term leases}}{\text{Interest charges paid} + \text{Rental payment under long-term leases}}$$

Suggested standards for coverage ratios are based on experience and empirical studies relating the incidence of defaults over a number of years to such ratios. Different standards are needed for a highly cyclical company than for a stable company.

CASH FLOW ANALYSIS

Will the ratios just described be sufficient to help an analyst identify companies that may encounter financial difficulties? Consider the study by Largay and Stickney who analyzed the financial statements of W.T. Grant during the 1966-1974 period preceding its bankruptcy in 1975 and ultimate liquidation.[16] They noted that financial indicators such as profitability ratios, turnover ratios, and liquidity ratios showed some down trends, but provided no definite clues to the company's

---

[16] J.A. Largay III and C.P. Stickney, "Cash Flows, Ratio Analysis and the W.T. Grant Company Bankruptcy," *Financial Analysts Journal* (July-August 1980), pp. 51-54.

impending bankruptcy. A study of cash flows from operations,[17] however, revealed that company operations were causing an increasing drain on cash, rather than providing cash. This necessitated an increased use of external financing, the required interest payments on which exacerbated the cash flow drain. Cash flow analysis clearly was a valuable tool in this case since W.T. Grant had been running a negative cash flow from operations for years. Yet none of the traditional ratios discussed above take into account the cash flow from operations.

More recently, Dugan and Samson examined the use of operating cash flow as an early warning signal of a company's potential financial problems.[18] The subject of the study was Allied Products Corporation because for a decade this company exhibited a significant divergence between cash flow from operations and net income. For parts of the period, net income was positive while cash flow from operations was a large negative value. In contrast to W.T. Grant that went into bankruptcy, the auditor's report in the 1991 Annual Report of Allied Products Corporation did issue a going concern warning. Moreover, the stock traded in the range of $2 to $3 per share. There was then a turnaround of the company by 1995. In its 1995 annual report, net income increased dramatically from prior periods (to $34 million) and there was a positive cash flow from operations ($29 million). The stock traded in the $25 range by the Spring of 1996.[19] As with the W.T. Grant study, Dugan and Samson found that the economic realities of a firm are better reflected in its cash flow from operations.

Martin Fridson has demonstrated how the typical cash flow generation and uses of companies in different stages of their business life cycle (startup, emerging growth, established growth, mature industry, and declining industry) relate to their statement of cash flows.[20] In addition, he explains how the statement of cash flows allows the analyst to assess a firm's "financial flexibility." An analysis of this statement provides the analysts with the information needed to answer such questions as:

- How 'safe' is the company's dividend?
- Could the company fund its needs internally if external sources of capital suddenly become scarce or prohibitively expensive?
- Would the company be able to continue meeting its obligations if its business turned down sharply?[21]

---

[17] For the period investigated, a statement of changes of financial position (on a working capital basis) was required to be reported prior to 1988.

[18] Michael T. Dugan and William D. Samson, "Operating Cash Flow: Early Indicators of Financial Difficulty and Recovery," *Journal of Financial Statement Analysis* (Summer 1996), pp. 41-50.

[19] As noted for the W.T. Grant study by Largay and Stickney, cash flow from operations had to be constructed from the statement of changes in financial positions that companies were required to report prior to 1988.

[20] Chapter 4 in Martin S. Fridson, *Financial Statement Analysis: A Practitioner's Guide* (New York: John Wiley & Sons, 1995).

[21] Fridson, *Financial Statement Analysis*, p. 113.

To answer these questions, Fridson suggests reformatting the statement of cash flows as shown in Exhibit 7 for the 1993 Annual Report of Kellogg Company. From the basic cash flow, the nondiscretionary cash needs are subtracted. The resulting cash flow is referred to as "discretionary cash flow." The uses of cash deducted from the basic cash flow are deducted in the order from least to most discretionary. By restructuring the statement of cash flows in this way, the analyst can see how much flexibility the company has when it must make business decisions that may adversely impact the long-run financial health of the enterprise.

In the case of Kellogg, its discretionary cash flow in 1993 after satisfying working capital and capital expenditure requirements was $350.5 million. Even after maintaining a dividend payment of $305.2 million, its cash flow would be positive. Notice that asset sales and other investing activity were not needed to generate cash to meet the dividend payments.

The cash flow to capital expenditures ratio gives the analysts information about the financial flexibility of the company and is particularly useful for capital-intensive firms and utilities.[22] The larger the ratio, the greater the financial flexibility. The analyst, however, must carefully examine the reasons why this ratio may be changing over time and why it might be out of line with comparable firms in the industry. For example, a declining ratio can be interpreted in two ways. First, the firm may eventually have difficulty adding to capacity via capital expenditures without the need to borrow funds. The second interpretation is that the firm may have gone through a period of major capital expansion and therefore it will take time for revenues to be generated that will increase the cash flow from operations to bring the ratio to some normal long-run level.

SUMMARY

The earnings per share of a company is closely followed by participants in the stock market. It is calculated by dividing the earnings available to common stockholders by the weighted average number of common shares outstanding over the year for which the calculation takes place. Where there are dilutive securities, different earnings per share measures must be presented. For reporting periods ending on or before December 15, 1997, primary earnings per share and fully diluted earnings per share had to be reported. For periods ending after December 15, 1997, these two measures are replaced by basic earnings per share and diluted earnings per share.

In analyzing the quality of reported earnings per share, the analyst should consider in addition to the accounting policies, the treatment of nonoperating and nonrecurring items, and the manipulation of discretionary expenses. Also, when an analyst encounters differential disclosure (i.e., what the company says in one document is markedly different from what it says in another) caution should be exercised and the reasons for the differences should be investigated.

---

[22] Fridson, *Financial Statement Analysis*, p. 173.

Profitability ratios are utilized to explore the underlying causes of a change in earnings per share. Earnings must be related to total assets and stockholders' equity to be meaningful. The two basic determinants of earnings per share are the return on stockholders' equity and the book value per share. The two basic determinants of return on stockholders' equity are the return on total assets and the proportion of assets financed by owners as opposed to creditors. Return on total assets and the behavior of its components offer useful statistics for studying the operating efficiency of a firm. Two key ratios to look at in this area are those involving accounts receivable and inventories. Analysts frequently calculate physical data ratios, and reduce them to a per share basis, to aid in studying profitability.

Analysts must examine sales and cost structure to assess the future growth of earnings. Sales analysis typically involves comparing the sales patterns for a given company with those of its principal competitors and appropriate aggregate data. A firm's sales and profits typically are affected by economy-wide factors, by factors specific to the product line or industry areas in which the firm operates, and by factors specific to the firm itself.

Debt and cash flow analysis are used to evaluate the ability of a firm to satisfy its debt obligations. Ratios that are used include short-term solvency ratios, capitalization (or financial leverage) ratios, and coverage tests. Short-term solvency ratios measure the ability of a firm to meet obligations coming due within one year. Capitalization ratios indicate the degree to which the firm is financed by creditors. Coverage tests measure the ability of a firm to meet long-term obligations.

While these ratios are useful for analyzing the debt paying ability of an issuer, a better indication of this ability has been found to be is an analysis of the firm's cash flow. This information is obtained from the statement of cash flows which also can be used to provide information about a firm's financial flexibility.

Chapter 13

Security Analysis Using EVA®

James L. Grant, Ph.D.
Professor of Finance
Graduate School of Management
Simmons College

INTRODUCTION

The world of security analysis is undergoing a revolution of sorts with increased focus on "value-based" metrics that are designed to give shareholders their due. Chief among these measures of corporate financial success is a metric called *economic value added* (EVA). EVA and related value-based measures like *cash flow return on investment* (CFROI) are now making significant inroads into the realm of security analysis and equity portfolio management. These metrics are also paving the way for a "modern" school of equity fundamental analysis that departs from the traditional method, with its prior focus on accounting-based measures like earnings per share (EPS) and return on equity (ROE).[1]

Although competing measures exist, value-based metrics emphasize the importance of giving *shareholders* their due. The theory behind these measures of corporate financial success is quite simple and compelling: when investors contribute moneys to a firm, they expect to earn a return on those contributed funds which is commensurate with the risk. The firm's managers are thereby charged to invest in real assets (both physical and human) having a return on invested capital that exceeds the overall cost of capital. Wealth creating firms have positive residual profitability, while wealth wasters lose market value because their productive returns fall short of the overall cost of debt *and* equity capital. Indeed, wealth destroyers may lose market value even though their after-tax return on invested capital exceeds the cost of corporate debt financing.[2]

---

[1] EVA® is a registered trademark of Stern Stewart & Co. For an insightful discussion of their commercial economic profit measure along with many applications of how this metric can be used in a corporate finance setting, see G. Bennett Stewart III, *The Quest for Value* (New York: Harper Collins, 1991). CFROI is the investment and financial advisory product of Holt Value Associates, LP, and the Boston Consulting Group (BCG), respectively.

[2] For empirical evidence, see James L. Grant, *Foundations of Economic Value Added* (New Hope, PA: Frank J. Fabozzi Associates, 1997).

The objective of this chapter is to discuss value-based metrics and explain the issues that an equity analyst faces with implementing a value-based metric framework. Our focus will be on EVA.[3]

THE EVA MEASURE OF CORPORATE SUCCESS

Perhaps the best known value-based metric among today's corporate and investment players is a measure called EVA® — for Economic Value Added.[4] Hatched commercially in 1982 by Joel Stern and G. Bennett Stewart, this economic profit measure gained early acceptance among the corporate financial community because of its innovative way of looking at profitability *net* of the dollar weighted cost of debt *and* equity capital. Indeed, many firms — including corporate giants like AT&T and Coca-Cola — have used EVA to design incentive payment schemes that lead managers to make wealth-enhancing investment decisions in the interest of shareholders.

EVA is also gaining popularity in the investment community, as evidenced by the establishment in 1996 of CS First Boston's annual conference on "Economic Value Added." Spearheaded by renowned equity strategists like Abby Joseph Cohen and Stephen Einhorn, the U.S. Equity Research Group at Goldman Sachs now uses EVA to evaluate the performance potential of many sectors of the economy, while James Abate at BEA, a member of the Credit Suisse Asset Management Group, uses real economic profit concepts to actively manage investment portfolios from both a bottom-up and top-down perspective.[5]

The financial significance of using a value-based metric like EVA from a corporate valuation perspective is crystal clear. As explained (and demonstrated empirically), wealth-creating firms have positive EVA because their expected net after-tax operating profit exceeds the dollar weighted average cost of debt and equity capital.[6] On the other hand, wealth wasters lose market value *and* incur share price declines because their corporate profitability falls short of their overall capital costs. As mentioned before, this wealth loss can occur even though the firm's profitability is sufficiently high enough to cover its cost of debt financing. Moreover, it is shown how to select individual companies and industries by examining the quantitative relationship between the NPV-to-Capital and EVA-to-Capital ratios in the marketplace.

---

[3] For a more detailed discussion of these issues and the underlying theory, as well as CFROI, see Frank J. Fabozzi and James L. Grant, *Equity Management* (New Hope, PA: Frank J. Fabozzi Associates, 1998).

[4] EVA® is the registered trademark of Stern Stewart & Co. Their financial metric is a practitioner's tool for measuring the firm's economic profit or economic value added. Stewart-Stern refers to the present value equivalent of this profit measure as the firm's *market value added* (MVA).

[5] A growing number of investment firms now look at companies, industries and/or the macro-economy in an economic profit context. For examples, see Al Jackson, Michael J. Mauboussin, and Charles R. Wolf, "EVA Primer," *Equity-Research Americas* (CS First Boston: February 20, 1996); Steven G. Einhorn, Gabrielle Napolitano, and Abby Joseph Cohen, "EVA: A Primer," *U.S. Research* (Goldman Sachs, September 10, 1997); and, James A. Abate, "Select Economic Value Portfolios," *U.S. Equity Product Overview* (BEA Associates, January 1998).

[6] Grant, *Foundations of Economic Value Added*.

THE BASIC EVA FORMULATION

Central to the EVA (and therefore, NPV) calculation is the distinction between levered and unlevered firms.[7] A *levered* firm, like most real-world firms, is one that partly finances its growth with long-term debt. In contrast, equivalent business-risk *unlevered* firms are, in principle, 100% equity financed. This firm-type classification is helpful because EVA is calculated by subtracting the firm's dollar weighted average cost of debt *and* equity financing from its *unlevered* net operating profit after tax, UNOPAT.

$$EVA = UNOPAT - \$COC$$

UNOPAT is used in the EVA formulation for two reasons. First, emphasis on this unlevered term serves as a modern-day reminder that the firm largely receives its profitability from the desirability (or lack thereof) of its overall products and services. Second, since most firms have some form of debt outstanding, they receive a yearly interest tax subsidy — measured by the corporate tax rate times the firm's interest expense — that is already reflected in the dollar cost of capital (\$COC) calculation.

This latter distinction is important. An incorrect focus by corporate managers on the levered firm's net operating profit after taxes, LNOPAT, rather than its equivalent business risk profit measure, UNOPAT, would lead to an *upward* bias in the firm's reported economic value added. By avoiding the "double counting" of the firm's yearly debt-interest tax subsidy, the research analyst avoids imparting a *positive* bias in not only the firm's real corporate profitability but also its overall corporate valuation and underlying stock price.

In simple terms, the firm's unlevered net operating profit after tax, UNOPAT, can be expressed in terms of its tax-adjusted earnings before interest and taxes, EBIT, according to:[8]

$$UNOPAT = EBIT \times (1 - t)$$
$$= [S - CGS - SGA - D] \times (1 - t)$$

---

[7] The concept of levered and unlevered firms is central to the development of the Modigliani-Miller principles of corporation finance. These firm-type classifications were also used extensively by Eugene F. Fama and Merton H. Miller in their pioneering book, *The Theory of Finance* (New York: Holt, Rinehart, and Winston, 1972).

[8] A basic discussion of the EVA model is also provided by Thomas P. Jones, "The Economic Value Added Approach to Corporate Investment," in *Corporate Financial Decision Making and Equity Analysis* (Charlottesville, VA: AIMR, The Research Foundation of the ICFA, 1995).

Some of the major accounting adjustments that are necessary to estimate a firm's economic value added in practice are covered later in this chapter. For an extensive treatment of the EVA-based accounting adjustments, the reader is referred to Stewart, *The Quest for Value.*

where, in the first expression, EBIT $\times$ (1 - t) is the unlevered firm's net operating profit after tax. This profit term is a reflection of the firm's earnings before interest and taxes, EBIT, less its *unlevered* corporate taxes; namely, EBIT less t times EBIT. Likewise, the terms, S, CGS, and SGA in the UNOPAT specification refer to the firm's sales, cost of goods sold, and selling, general and administrative expenses, respectively. In principle, the depreciation term, D, should be a charge that reflects the *economic* obsolescence of the firm's assets.

In turn, the firm's *dollar* cost of capital, $COC, can be expressed as:

$$\$COC = [COC\%/100] \times TC$$

where %COC is its weighted-average percentage cost of debt *and* equity capital, while TC is the firm's total operating capital. The weighted capital cost percentage, %COC, is given by:

$$\%COC = \% \text{ After-tax Debt Cost} \times \text{Debt Weight} + \% \text{ Equity Cost} \times \text{Equity Weight}$$

Taken together, these financial developments show that the firm's "economic value added" for any given year can be expressed as:

$$\begin{aligned} EVA &= UNOPAT - \$COC \\ &= EBIT \times (1 - t) - COC \times TC \\ &= [S - CGS - SGA - D] \times (1 - t) - COC \times TC \end{aligned}$$

This expression shows that the firm's EVA is equal to its *unlevered* net operating profit after tax less the dollar cost of all capital employed in the firm. In the next section of this chapter, a simple income statement and balance sheet are used for a hypothetical firm named "OK-Beverage Company" to show how to measure a firm's "economic value added." The equity analyst who is already familiar with how to estimate a firm's economic profit in a basic setting may prefer to go to the section after that focusing on real-world EVA measurement challenges.

"OK-BEVERAGE COMPANY"

Let's use the basic financial statements for OK-Beverage Corporation (OK-B) to see how they can be interpreted in a traditional versus value-based context using EVA. Exhibits 1 and 2 show the income and balance sheets for OK-B at an established point in time.[9]

---

[9] As we will shortly see, OK-Beverage Company looks like a profitable company from a traditional (accounting) perspective. However, the value-based approach to measuring OK-B's corporate profitability shows that the beverage firm has *negative* economic value added. By present value extension, OK-B is a wealth *destroyer* in its status quo position.

Exhibit 1: Income Statement for OK-Beverage Corporation

	Status Quo Position
Sales	$130,000
CGS	90,000
SGA	23,000
Interest Expense	3,312
Pretax Profit	13,688
Taxes (at 40%)	5,475
Net Income	$8,213
Shares Outstanding	6,250
EPS	$1.31

Exhibit 2: Balance Sheet for OK-Beverage Corporation

Cash	$7,000		Accounts Payable	$8,000	
U.S. Govt. securities	8,000		Wages Payable	3,000	
Accounts Receivable	15,000		Tax Accruals	3,000	
Inventory	52,000		Current Liabilities		$14,000
Current Assets		$82,000	(non-interest bearing)		
Property	$4,000		Long-Term Debt (8% Coupon)		41,400
Plant	16,000				
Equipment	50,000		Common Stock at Par	625	
Fixed Assets		$70,000	(par value $0.10; 6,250		
			shares auth./outstanding)		
			Addit. Paid in Capital	14,000	
			Retained Earnings	81,975	
			Stockholders' Equity		$96,600
Total Assets		$152,000	Liab. and Stk. Equity		$152,000

Looking at OK-Beverage Corporation from a traditional accounting perspective, one sees that the firm appears to be a profitable beverage producer. Based on the income statement shown in Exhibit 1, the firm's management reports *positive* total and per share earnings, at $8,213 and $1.31, respectively. In addition, with stockholders' equity at $96,600 the company's return on equity (ROE) is positive, at 8.5% ($8,213/$96,600). From the traditional viewpoint, this ROE figure also results from multiplying OK-B's return on assets, 5.4%, by its equity-leverage multiplier (assets/equity) of 1.57.

A Look at OK-B's "Economic Profit"

To see if OK-Beverage Corporation is in fact a wealth creator having positive EVA, let's first calculate the firm's *unlevered* net operating profit after taxes.

Upon substituting the firm's sales, cost of goods sold, selling general, and administrative, and tax rate figures into the UNOPAT formula, one obtains:[10]

$$UNOPAT = [S - CGS - SGA] \times (1 - t)$$
$$= [\$130,000 - \$90,000 - \$23,000] \times (1 - 0.4) = \$10,200$$

Also, in order to calculate OK-B's projected *dollar* cost of capital, one needs to know something about (1) the after-tax cost of debt, (2) the estimated cost of equity capital, and (3) the "target" debt weight, *if any*, in the firm's capital structure, and (4) the amount of operating capital employed in the beverage business. With respect to the first requirement, OK-B's post-tax debt cost can be estimated according to:

$$After\text{-}tax\ Debt\ Cost = Pre\text{-}tax\ Debt\ Cost \times (1 - t)$$
$$= 0.08 \times (1 - 0.4) = 0.048\ or\ 4.8\%$$

where the pre-tax debt percentage, 8%, is taken as the firm's average coupon rate on the balance sheet. Of course, OK-B's pre-tax borrowing cost, at 8%, can also be obtained by dividing the firm's interest expense, $3,312, by the book value of the firm's long-term debt, at $41,400.

In turn, OK-B's cost of *equity* capital can be estimated according to the Capital Asset Pricing Model developed by William Sharpe, et al. With a risk-free interest rate (R_f) of 6.5%, a market risk premium (MRP) of 6%, and the firm's stock beta at 1.0, its Sharpe-based cost of equity becomes:[11]

$$CAPM = R_f + MRP \times Beta$$
$$= 0.065 + 0.06 \times 1.0 = 0.125\ or\ 12.5\%$$

Assuming that OK-B's "target debt-to-capital" ratio is, say, 30%, the firm's *percentage* cost of capital can be estimated according to:

$$\% COC = \% After\text{-}tax\ Debt\ Cost \times Debt\ Weight$$
$$+ \% Equity\ Cost \times Equity\ Weight$$
$$= 4.8\% \times (0.3) + 12.5\% \times (0.7) = 10.2\%$$

---

[10] For convenience, depreciation is assumed to be *zero* in the income statement shown in Exhibit 1.

[11] The "just right" way of calculating a firm's cost of equity capital has come under numerous empirical challenges in recent years — see, for example, Eugene F. Fama and Kenneth R. French, "The Cross Section of Expected Stock Returns," *Journal of Finance* (June 1992). However, it should be emphasized that the validity of the NPV (and therefore EVA) model does *not* require that security prices are set according to the single-factor CAPM.

Given that significant empirical challenges to CAPM exist, one might consider alternative approaches to estimating the cost of equity capital, including factor models and equity style (value/growth) approaches. Some alternative approaches to estimating the required return on equity capital are suggested at a later point in the text.

Exhibit 3: OK-Beverage's Operating and Financial Capital
(Aggregate Results)

Operating Capital:		Financing Capital:	
Net Working Capital			
Current Assets	$82,000		
Current Liabilities			
(non-interest bearing)	($14,000)		
	$68,000	Long-Term Debt	$41,400
Fixed Assets	$70,000	Stockholders' Equity	96,600
Totals:	$138,000		$138,000

Repackaging the Balance Sheet

With knowledge of OK-B's operating capital it would be possible to calculate the dollar-cost of capital, $COC, figure and then its underlying EVA. In this context, it is helpful to recognize that the firm's balance sheet can be "repackaged" in a way that shows the *equivalency* between the firm's operating and financial capital. Exhibit 3 illustrates this result.

The exhibit shows that OK-B's operating (and financing) capital is $138,000. The firm's overall dollar-cost of capital can be calculated by applying the percentage capital cost, 10.2%, to either the firm's physical operating capital or its equivalent financing capital. Whichever capital concept is chosen by the research analyst, OK-B's *dollar* cost of capital is $14,076:

$$\$COC = [COC\%/100] \times TC$$
$$= [10.2/100] \times \$138,000 = \$14,076$$

Most importantly, since OK-B's dollar-cost of financing is higher than its unlevered net after-tax operating profit, UNOPAT, the firm has *negative* projected EVA:

$$EVA = UNOPAT - \$COC$$
$$= \$10,200 - \$14,076 = -\$3,876$$

While OK-B *looks* like a profitable company from a traditional accounting perspective, the insight offered by EVA reveals that the firm is a wealth destroyer. This happens because the firm's operating profitability is not sufficient enough to cover the overall weighted average cost of debt *and* equity capital.

The Residual Return on Capital (RROC)

It should also be noted that OK-B has negative EVA because its underlying "*residual* (or *surplus*) return on capital" (RROC), is negative. This wealth wasting situation occurs when the firm's after-tax return on productive capital, ROC, falls short of the weighted average capital cost, COC. To illustrate this, simply define RROC as the firm's EVA-to-Capital ratio. At −2.8%, one sees that OK-B's adverse residual return on capital is caused by its negative economic value added:

$$RROC = EVA/Total\ Capital$$
$$= -\$3,876/\$138,000 = -0.028\ or\ -2.8\%$$

Likewise, since EVA can be expressed as OK-Beverage's initial capital, TC, times the residual return on capital, RROC, this same result is obtained by focusing on the *spread* between the firm's after-tax return on capital, ROC, and its weighted average cost of debt and equity capital, COC:

$$RROC = EVA/TC = [ROC - COC]$$
$$= [0.074 - 0.102] = -0.028 = -2.8\%$$

where ROC, at 7.4%, in the expression results by dividing UNOPAT, $10,200, by the firm's total capital, $138,000. The COC term (in decimal format) is the familiar capital cost percentage of 10.2%.

OK-B's Interest Tax Subsidy

When looking at the firm's profitability *net* of its capital costs, it is important to emphasize that its unlevered net operating profit after tax, UNOPAT, must be used in the *first* step of the EVA calculation. This consideration is important because the dollar cost of capital (step *two* in the EVA calculation) already reflects the interest tax subsidy received from the firm's outstanding debt obligations. By *double counting* the firm's interest tax subsidy, the analyst would not only overestimate the firm's real cash flows, but he would also — from a pricing perspective — impart a positive bias in the firm's market value and its outstanding shares.

To show the source of this cash flow bias, it is helpful to note that the *levered* firm's net operating profit after tax, LNOPAT, can be expressed in terms of the equivalent business-risk *unlevered* firm's operating profit *plus* the yearly interest tax subsidy. Looking at OK-Beverage Corporation in this levered (with corporate debt) and unlevered (without long-term debt) fashion yields:

$$LNOPAT = UNOPAT + t \times Interest$$
$$= \$10,200 + 0.4 \times \$3,312$$
$$= \$10,200 + \$1,325 = \$11,525$$

where, $t \times$ Interest (at $1,325), is the yearly interest tax subsidy that OK-Beverage receives as a levered firm, as opposed to a debt-free company. However, this *same* interest tax benefit is already reflected in the firm's overall capital cost through the reduced cost of corporate debt financing.

To show this, recall that OK-B's after tax cost of debt was previously expressed as:

$$\text{After-tax Debt Cost} = \text{Pre-tax Debt Cost} \times (1 - t)$$
$$= 0.08 \times (1 - 0.4) = 0.048 \text{ or } 4.8\%$$

In this formulation, the firm's pre-tax cost of debt, 8%, is reduced by 320 basis points due to the tax benefit that OK-B receives from deductibility of its corporate interest expense. Expressing this leverage-induced percentage reduction in the firm's dollar cost of capital yields the *same* yearly interest tax benefit that is already reflected in OK-B's levered cash flows.

$$\$\text{COC Tax Subsidy} = t \times [\text{Pre-tax Debt Cost}] \times \text{Debt}$$
$$= 0.4 \times [3,312/41,400] \times 41,400 = \$1,325$$

Therefore, to avoid the positive earnings bias, OK-B's EVA must be calculated by *first* estimating what its net operating profit after tax, UNOPAT, would be as an equivalent business-risk unlevered firm — namely, a "OK-B like" firm with no long-term debt — and *then* subtracting the overall dollar cost of debt and equity capital from this unlevered cash flow figure.

OK-B's EVA on a Pre-Tax Basis

If the equity analyst were inclined to calculate OK-B's EVA on a pretax basis, then the firm's unlevered net operating profit before taxes, at $17,000, would be used in conjunction with the *pre*-tax cost of capital.[12] The only real complication here is that the after-tax cost of equity capital needs to be "grossed up" by one *minus* the corporate tax rate to convert it to a pre-tax financing rate. To see this pre-tax EVA development, first note that OK-B's weighted average cost of capital on a *before* tax basis can be expressed as:

$$\text{Pre-tax COC} = \text{Debt Weight} \times \text{Pre-tax Debt Cost}$$
$$+ \text{Equity Weight} \times \text{Pre-tax Equity Cost}$$
$$= 0.3 \times 0.08 + 0.7 \times [0.125/(1 - 0.4)]$$
$$= 0.3 \times 0.08 + 0.7 \times [0.208] = 0.17 \text{ or } 17\%$$

where in this formulation, the firm's *pre-tax* cost of equity capital is 20.8%, and its pre-tax cost of capital is 17%.

---

[12] The pre-tax approach to estimating a firm's economic profit is helpful because the equity analyst focuses directly on the unlevered firm's operating profit without getting tangled up on tax issues arising from depreciation and related accounting complexities. However, tax considerations *do* arise when converting the after-tax cost of equity capital (CAPM or otherwise) to a pre-tax required rate of return — as shown in the illustration that follows.

From a real world perspective, it is interesting to note that Polaroid Corporation looks at EVA on a pre-tax basis when making strategic corporate decisions.

With this development, OK-B's *pre-tax* EVA is therefore:

$$\begin{aligned} \text{Pre-tax EVA} &= \text{Pre-tax Unlevered Net Operating Profit} - \text{Pre-tax \$COC} \\ &= \text{EBIT} - \text{Pretax COC} \times \text{TC} \\ &= \$17,000 - 0.17 \times \$138,000 \\ &= \$17,000 - \$23,460 = -\$6,460 \end{aligned}$$

Likewise, the firm's pre-tax EVA is also equal to its after-tax EVA "grossed up" by one *minus* the corporate tax rate:

$$\begin{aligned} \text{Pretax EVA} &= \frac{\text{After Tax EVA}}{1 - t} \\ &= \frac{-\$3,876}{1 - 0.4} = -\$6,460 \end{aligned}$$

Role of OK-B's Growth Opportunities

Given that OK-B has negative EVA, the firm has a clear need for a *positive* growth opportunity. In this context, let's suppose the firm's managers discover (finally!) that they can invest $20,000 in new technology that will increase the firm's sales each year by $40,000. Further suppose that OK-B's cost of goods sold and selling, general, and administrative expenses will rise by $25,000 and $5,000 per annum, respectively. With these assumptions, the firm's forecasted annual UNOPAT will go up by $6,000:

$$\begin{aligned} \Delta \text{UNOPAT} &= \Delta[S - CGS - SGA] \times (1 - t) \\ &= [\$40,000 - \$25,000 - \$5,000] \times (1 - 0.4) = \$6,000 \end{aligned}$$

Since the firm's operating capital rises by $20,000 to support the increased sales forecast, OK-B's estimated (annual) capital costs rise by $2,040:

$$\begin{aligned} \Delta \text{\$COC} &= \text{COC} \times \Delta \text{TC} \\ &= 0.102 \times \$20,000 = \$2,040 \end{aligned}$$

Taken together, the ΔUNOPAT and $\Delta$$COC figures reveal that OK-B's growth opportunity is a *desirable* real investment for the firm's shareholders. With these figures, OK-B's EVA rises by $3,960:

$$\begin{aligned} \Delta \text{EVA} &= \Delta \text{UNOPAT} - \Delta \text{\$COC} \\ &= \$6,000 - \$2,040 = \$3,960 \end{aligned}$$

As a result of OK-B's real growth opportunity, it is interesting to see that the firm has moved from a wealth-destroyer to a wealth-neutral position. Among other things, this implies that the firm's revised return on capital, 10.3% ($16,200/$158,000) is now close to the overall cost of capital, 10.2%. Likewise, in this wealth neutral situation, the firm's residual capital return, RROC, is nearly zero. With further growth opportunities, its seems that OK-B has the *potential* to become a wealth creator with (discounted) positive-average EVA. The absence of growth beyond wealth neutrality, however, may signal to investors that its beverage products are really *just* "OK."

EVA MEASUREMENT CHALLENGES

The OK-B illustration discussed above is helpful in showing how a value-based metric like EVA differs from a traditional measure of profit such as accounting net income. However, the basic example belies the complexity of the economic profit calculation in practice. This oversimplification is sometimes missed by real world EVA proponents as well. For instance, in a popular article in *Fortune*, the author states that "EVA is simply after-tax operating profit, a widely used measure, minus the total annual cost of capital." As with the OK-B example, this basic approach to calculating EVA is simple enough yet difficulties can arise when trying to implement the economic profit concept in practice.[13]

Specifically, Goldman Sachs U.S. Equity Research Group and David Young of INSEAD point out that there are some 160 accounting adjustments that can be made to a firm's accounting statements to convert them to a *value-based* format emphasizing cash operating profit and asset replacement cost considerations.[14] Many of the potential adjustments can have a material impact on the analyst's estimate of a company's after-tax return on capital through their *joint* impact on the firm's unlevered net operating profit after tax and the dollar-based capital estimate. Additionally, there are significant empirical anomalies and academic issues involved when estimating the firm's weighted average cost of debt *and* equity capital.

As we learned previously, the firm's after-tax return on capital is calculated by dividing its *unlevered* net operating profit after tax by the *economic* capital employed in the business. In practice, however, there are numerous accounting items that *jointly* impact the numerator and the denominator of the ROC ratio. These potential distortions arise from the accounting-versus-economic treatment of depreciation, intangibles (including research and development expenditures and goodwill arising from corporate acquisitions), deferred taxes, and inventory and other reserves. Such measurement issues are important because they impact the analyst's estimate of cash operating profit in the numerator of the ROC ratio (e.g., profit impact of accounting depreciation versus economic obsolescence) and the economic capital estimate used in the denominator (e.g., impact of net fixed assets on the balance sheet versus economic replacement cost of assets).[15]

---

[13] See Shawn Tully, "The Real Key to Creating Wealth," *Fortune* (September 20, 1993).

[14] See Einhorn, Napolitano, and Cohen, "EVA: A Primer," and S. David Young, "Economic Value Added," INSEAD (Fountainebleu, France: 1998).

[15] Goldman Sachs and Stern Stewart do not make any explicit cash adjustments to accounting depreciation on the income statement and (therefore) accumulated depreciation on the balance sheet. This approach to handling accounting depreciation seems at odds with the long established view that managers can manipulate earnings by the judicious use of accounting depreciation policies.

Exhibit 4: Calculation of NOPAT from Financial Statement Data

A. Bottom-up approach

Begin:
    Operating profit after depreciation and amortization

Add:
    Implied interest expense on operating leases
    Increase in LIFO reserve
    Goodwill amortization
    Increase in bad-debt reserve
    Increase in net capitalized research and development

Equals:
    Adjusted operating profit before taxes

Subtract:
    Cash operating taxes

Equals:
    NOPAT

B. Top-down approach

Begin:
    Sales

Add:
    Increase in LIFO reserve
    Implied interest expense on operating leases
    Other income

Subtract:
    Cost of goods sold
    Selling, general, and administrative expenses
    Depreciation

Equals:
    Adjusted operating profit before taxes

Subtract:
    Cash operating taxes

Equals:
    NOPAT

Note: Exhibit based on information in G. Bennett Stewart III, *The Quest for Value* (New York: Harper Collins, 1991).

ESTIMATING UNOPAT IN PRACTICE

The major EVA players — including CS First Boston and Goldman Sachs on the investment side, and Stern Stewart & Co. on the corporate advisory side — have narrowed the list of accounting adjustments to a firm's financial statements. In this context, Exhibit 4 shows Stern Stewart's "bottom up" and "top down" income statement approaches to calculating a firm's unlevered net operating profit after tax while Exhibit 5 shows how capital can be estimated in practice with some key balance sheet adjustments based on the equivalent "asset approach" and "financing sources of assets" approaches to measuring the firm's economic capital.[16]

---

[16] Numerous EVA-based accounting adjustments can be found in Stewart, *The Quest for Value*. The distinction between *levered* and *unlevered* firms in an economic profit context is emphasized by Grant, *Foundations of Economic Value Added*.

Exhibit 5: Calculation of Capital Using Accounting Financial Statements

A. Asset approach

Begin:

    Net operating assets

Add:

    LIFO reserve

    Net plant and equipment

    Other assets

    Goodwill

    Accumulated goodwill amortization

    Present value of operating leases

    Bad-debt reserve

    Capitalized research and development

    Cumulative write-offs of special items

Equals:

    Capital

B. Source of financing approach

Begin:

    Book value of common equity

Add equity equivalents:

    Preferred stock

    Minority interest

    Deferred income tax reserve

    LIFO reserve

    Accumulated goodwill amortization

Add debt and debt equivalents:

    Interest-bearing short-term debt

    Long-term debt

    Capitalized lease obligations

    Present value of noncapitalized leases

Equals:

    Capital

Note: Exhibit based on information in G. Bennett Stewart III, *The Quest for Value* (New York: Harper Collins, 1991).

The Stern Stewart Approach

In Stern Stewart's "bottom up" approach to estimating UNOPAT, the equity analyst begins with a firm's operating profit after depreciation and amortization. Accounting items that get added back to this figure include the increase in LIFO reserve, goodwill amortization, and the change in *net* capitalized research and development. Two other accounting figures that are shown in Exhibit 4 include the *implied* interest expense on operating leases as well as the increase in bad-debt reserve.

    The rise in LIFO reserve is added back to the firm's accounting-based operating profit to give the analyst a better gauge of the actual cost of inventory units used to manufacture the firm's product. In a period of rising prices (inflation), LIFO inventory cost understates corporate profit due to the higher cost of goods sold figure resulting from inventory costing (last in, first out) of newly produced product at near-to-current market prices. Coincidentally, current assets on the firm's balance sheet are understated due to an incorrect assumption about the replacement cost of inventory — namely, those units still in inventory having an assumed purchase cost based on the initial inventory units.

Also, the goodwill amortization on the income statement is added back to the operating profit because the companion accumulated figure on the firm's balance sheet — arising from patents, copyrights, internal software, and even corporate acquisitions (price paid for target firm in excess of underlying value of target's *physical* assets) — is viewed as a form of economic capital or asset investment. Since research and development are also viewed as capital investment, the value-based convention is to "capitalize" it on the balance sheet while slowly writing it off over an extended period of time (typically 40 years) on the income statement — rather than "expense" all R&D expenditures in the year incurred. With these adjustments, the analyst arrives at UNOPAT by subtracting "cash taxes" from the firm's estimated pretax cash operating profit. In practice, this means that the accrual-based "income tax expense" item on the income statement needs to be increased by (1) the interest tax subsidy on debt (as well as debt equivalents like leases), and (2) the tax on the firm's *non*-recurring income sources.

Exhibit 4 shows Stern Stewart's "top down" approach to estimating the firm's unlevered net operating profit after tax. As shown here, the analyst begins with sales (revenue), then subtracts the usual operating expenses such as cost of goods sold and selling, general, and administrative expenses. The LIFO reserve is added to the revenue figure, while accounting depreciation (in the Stern Stewart approach) is subtracted on the path to UNOPAT. Since the benefits of corporate debt financing (if any) are already reflected in the dollar cost of capital, $COC, the cash tax figure should be based on the marginal tax rate paid by the unlevered firm. A rigorous application of Stewart's approach to adjusting the firm's accounting operating profit to a cash operating profit figure for the EVA calculation is shown in an Association for Investment Management and Research (AIMR) publication by Pamela Peterson and David Peterson.[17]

Impact on Invested Capital

As Stewart points out, the amount of capital employed within a firm can be estimated by making adjustments to the left hand or right hand side of the firm's balance sheet. As revealed in Exhibit 5, it is possible to estimate the firm's operating capital using the "asset approach" or the equivalent "sources of financing

---

[17] Using the 1993 Annual Report for Hershey Foods Corporation, Peterson and Peterson provide a step-by-step instruction on how to calculate the firm's cash operating profit, dollar cost of capital, and economic value added (EVA). This practical guide can be found in Pamela P. Peterson and David R. Peterson, *Company Performance and Measures of Value Added* (Charlottesville, VA: The Research Foundation of the Institute of Chartered Financial Analysts, 1996).

approach." The asset approach begins with the "net (short-term) operating assets." This figure represents current assets less *non*-interest bearing current liabilities (accounts/taxes payables, and accrued expenses for examples). To this amount, Stewart adds familiar items like the LIFO reserve, net plant and equipment, and goodwill-related items. The capitalized value of research and development and cumulative write-offs from special items are also figured into their asset-based view of capital.

In the equivalent "sources of financing" approach, the firm's economic capital estimate is obtained by adding "equity equivalents" to the firm's book value of common equity, along with debt and "debt equivalents." Exhibit 5 shows that in the Stern Stewart model, equity equivalents consist of preferred stock, minority interest, deferred income tax reserve, LIFO reserve, and accumulated goodwill amortization. Likewise, debt and debt equivalents consist of interest bearing short-term liabilities, long-term debt, as well as capitalized lease obligations. With the income statement (Exhibit 4) and balance sheet (Exhibit 5) converted to a cash operating basis, an analyst is able to *jointly* estimate the firm's unlevered net operating profit after tax and the economic capital employed within the firm. As mentioned before, the firm's after-tax return on capital is calculated by dividing UNOPAT by total capital.

Overview of Goldman Sachs' Approach

Like Stern Stewart and others, Goldman Sachs has narrowed the field from 160 possible accounting adjustments down to a select number of accounting adjustments that can have a meaningful impact on the firm's assessed cash operating profit and its economic capital.[18] The key "equity equivalents" used by Goldman's U.S. Equity Research Group to measure the firm's economic capital (or equivalent financing thereof) are shown in the top portion of Exhibit 6. Based on the "sources of financing approach," they begin with stockholders equity on the firm's balance sheet and then "add back" (if any) the listed equity equivalents. On the income side, the increase in equity equivalents is added back to accounting net income as shown in the lower portion of Exhibit 6.

As shown in Exhibit 6, accounting-based items like deferred tax liabilities (and deferred assets resulting from *non*-recurring restructuring and environmental cleanup costs), minority interests, and LIFO reserves have balance sheet and income statement consequences that can impact the correct estimation of the firm's after-tax return on capital — through their *joint* impact on UNOPAT and economic capital. Also, the taxes used in measuring a company's post-tax capital returns should be a reflection of the cash taxes actually paid by the *unlevered* firm — as the interest tax subsidy (if any) is already reflected in the cost of capital calculation for the levered firm. On the tax issue, Goldman Sachs uses the *statutory* corporate tax rate rather than the firm's effective tax rate.

---

[18] See Einhorn, Napolitano, and Cohen, "EVA: A Primer."

Exhibit 6: Equity Equivalents Approach Used by Goldman Sachs U.S. Research Group

Derivation of Total Adjusted Capital Employed

Common Equity
+ Equity Equivalents*
+ Preferred Stock
+ Minority Interest
+ Long-Term Debt
+ Short-Term Debt
+ Current Portion of Long-Term Debt
= Total Capital Employed

Derivation of NOPAT

Net Income Available to Common
+ Increase in Equity Equivalents
+ Preferred Dividend
+ Minority Interest Provision
+ After-Tax Interest Expense
− ESOP Accrual
= NOPAT

* Accumulated amortization of intangibles, deferred taxes, cumulative non-recurring charges, LIFO reserves, and ESOP accruals.
Source: Steven G. Einhorn, Gabrielle Napolitano, and Abby Joseph Cohen, "EVA: A Primer," *U.S. Research* (Goldman Sachs, September 10, 1997).

Final Comments on UNOPAT Estimation in Practice

Hence, there are many accounting adjustments that an analyst can make when attempting to measure a firm's after-tax return on capital, ROC (measured by the UNOPAT/TC ratio). These ROC challenges are independent of the empirical and academic issues that arise when attempting to calculate the firm's cost of capital, COC (to be discussed shortly). Because the economic profit message can get muted as the number of accounting adjustments grows, it is important for equity analysts to find a practical balance between the number of UNOPAT and capital adjustments while still protecting the integrity of the EVA model. Conformity in the number of accounting adjustments also makes economic profit comparisons across firms and sectors more reliable.

In general, important items like research and development expenditures should be capitalized on the balance sheet and amortized on the income statement over a long period of time — rather than "expensed" in the current year. Also, goodwill which arises from corporate acquisitions (namely, the acquisition "premium" paid by acquirers) should be treated as economic capital. An inspection of Exhibits 4 through 6 reveals that the *major* adjustments to the accounting income statement and balance sheets made by U.S. Equity Research Group at Goldman Sachs as well as Stern Stewart & Co. are similar in scope and interpretation.

COST OF CAPITAL ESTIMATION CHALLENGES

Aside from any further accounting difficulties that may arise when calculating the firm's economic profit, there remains many challenging "cost of capital" issues that can impact the estimation of the EVA metric. These COC challenges have both theoretical and empirical foundations. In the former context, the standard approach — used by EVA players like CS First Boston, Goldman Sachs, and Stern Stewart — to calculate the cost of capital presumes that corporate debt financing is a "cheaper" source of financing in comparison with equity financing — thereby giving corporate managers an incentive to finance growth with debt versus equity.

Yet Merton Miller argues that even in a world of taxes with deductibility of debt interest expense, levered firms should be priced *as if* they were equivalent business-risk unlevered firms.[19] In his well-known "Debt and Taxes" model, the pre-tax rate of interest on taxable corporate bonds rises in the capital market to a level that offsets any perceived gains from corporate leverage at the firm level. As a result, Miller re-establishes the "capital structure irrelevance" predictions of the original MM (Miller-Modigliani) framework. These powerful principles of corporation finance suggest corporate debt policy has *no* meaningful impact on the value of the firm. In this view, the levered firm's weighted average cost of capital is the same as the capital cost estimate for the equivalent business-risk unlevered firm.

To illustrate the EVA-importance of Miller's arguments in a more direct way, consider the familiar expression of the relationship between the cost of capital for levered and unlevered firms. In this context, the levered firm's after-tax capital cost can be expressed in terms of (1) the after-tax cost of capital for the *equivalent* business-risk unlevered firm (UCOC), and (2) the expected tax benefit available to the company from the perceived debt-interest tax subsidy. In more formal terms, the levered firm's cost of capital (LCOC) can be represented as:

$$LCOC = UCOC \, [1 - t_e \times (D/C)]$$

where UCOC is the unlevered firm's cost of capital, t_e is the *effective* debt tax subsidy rate, and D/C is the firm's "optimal or target" debt-to-capital ratio.

In Miller's "Debt and Taxes" model, he argues that competition in the market for taxable and tax-exempt bonds dictates that the levered firm's cost of capital (LCOC) will be the same as the capital cost for the equivalent business risk unlevered firm, UCOC. This implies that the firm's weighted debt tax subsidy term, $t_e \times (D/C)$, in the cost of capital formulation must be *zero*. In effect, Miller's pioneering work throughout the years reveals that corporate debt policy *per se* has no impact whatsoever on the firm's after-tax cost of capital, and therefore, its overall market capitalization. In this sense, only real corporate investment opportunities (positive NPV projects) can have a material impact on shareholder wealth.

---

[19] See Merton H. Miller, "Debt and Taxes," *Journal of Finance* (May 1977).

Suffice it to say that the effective debt tax subsidy rate, t_e, that applies in the real world is considerably lower than the statutory corporate tax rate that managers and investors alike might use in the estimation of the firm's cost of capital. EVA estimates that are calculated in this simple way would of course be biased upward. This measurement error would result from the inherent downward bias in the levered firm's cost of capital due to the presumed debt-interest tax subsidy. Moreover, unless this seemingly favorable subsidy to the levered firm's cost of capital is noticed by investors, then the debt-induced EVA bias could lead to an overly optimistic assessment of the market value of the levered firm and its outstanding shares.[20]

Using the CAPM

An especially problematic cost of capital issue arises for the equity analyst in the context of estimating the required return on the firm's common stock. In principle, using CAPM to estimate the firm's anticipated cost of equity seems reasonable enough because this *single factor* model is an integral component of established financial theory. However, in recent years CAPM has been challenged by many empirical studies that question the validity of the one-factor expected return-risk predictions of the model.

Specifically, in this asset pricing framework, *beta* is considered to be the systematic (or relative) risk factor that drives the expected rate of return on the firm's outstanding common stock which is an estimate of the cost of equity capital. In this model, stocks of companies with high betas — due, perhaps, to volatile operating and/or leverage conditions — should offer relatively high expected returns, while stocks of firms with low betas should offer comparably lower anticipated returns. Over time, these positive expected return-risk anticipations should be revealed in *real-time* capital markets. However, recent empirical research does not seem to verify the predictions of the single-factor CAPM.[21]

CAPM Alternatives

Fortunately, there are alternative approaches to using CAPM when estimating a firm's cost of equity capital. In this context, James Abate at BEA Associates has developed a proprietary model that estimates a firm's required return on capital (largely, the expected return on equity capital) based on a model that incorporates (1) the market risk premium, (2) well-known fundamental factors including size and leverage considerations, and (3) the growth and stability in the firm's economic profit over time. Holding the first two equity risk considerations the same, firms that have demonstrated stability in their real economic profit growth will be

---

[20] The equity analyst should also be aware that even the unlevered firm's cost of capital (UCOC) is impacted by economywide changes in interest rates and the market-based business risk premium. This means that a firm's required return on capital (therefore EVA) can change *independently* of company specific happenings at the micro level. This macro economic concern is also voiced by Peterson and Peterson, *Company Performance and Measures of Value Added.*

[21] See, for example, Fama and French, "The Cross Section of Expected Stock Returns."

assigned a *lower* cost of capital score than firms that otherwise demonstrate substantial specific volatility in their economic profit.[22]

Exhibit 7 shows how the required return on invested capital (cost of capital) is estimated in the BEA model. As with CAPM, the firm's cost of equity is based on a market driven "base risk premium." To their estimate of the systematic market premium, BEA adds a "company specific" premium to arrive at the firm's overall cost of capital — based on established fundamental factors (size, etc.) and their proprietary scoring measure on the volatility of a company's economic profit. The lower the EVA-based volatility score, the lower the required return on invested capital (largely cost of equity capital). Other things the same, the higher the company specific risk score, the higher the BEA assessed cost of (equity) capital.

In addition, there are well-known factor-based equity models that can be used in lieu of the single-factor CAPM. In this context, the analyst might consider the benefits of using a multi-factor approach to estimating the firm's expected return on common stock, and (therefore) the required return on invested capital. Fundamental factor models (like BARRA) have been used to build forecasts of equity returns based on beta, size, earnings momentum, and book-to-price ratios — among other "common factors" that influence security return. Macro-factor models — such as Burmeister, Ibbotson, Roll, and Ross — have been used in practice to estimate the expected return on common stocks in the context of interest rate and economywide changes in corporate profits, among other macro-factors.[23]

Exhibit 7: Security Selection Analysis: Decomposition of Expected Return on (Equity) Capital

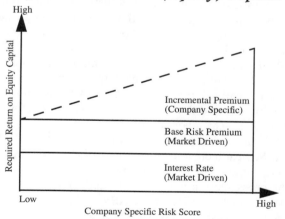

Source: James A. Abate, "Select Economic Value Portfolios," *U.S. Equity Product Overview* (BEA Associates, January 1998).

---

[22] See Abate, "Select Economic Value Portfolios."

[23] Fundamental and macroeconomic factor models are covered in most (quantitative-oriented) investment books. For one discussion of factor model theory *and* practice, see Fabozzi and Grant, *Equity Management*.

Exhibit 8: Goldman Sachs U.S. Research Group
Regression Analysis

A simple linear regression that correlates *changes* in EVA® to changes in share price for the S&P Industrials from 1978-1997E reflects an R^2 of about 27%. The regression line indicates statistical significance and can be expressed as*

$$\text{S\&P Industrials' Share Price} = \underset{(13.79)}{1.00} + \underset{(2.58)}{0.08\text{EVA}^{®}}; R^2 = 27.1\%$$

The R^2 is about 35% over the 1986-1997E period. The regression line can be expressed as

$$\text{S\&P Industrials' Share Price} = \underset{(9.92)}{1.07} + \underset{(2.34)}{0.11\text{EVA}^{®}}; R^2 = 35.4\%$$

* *t*-values reported in parenthesis.

Source: Steven G. Einhorn, Gabrielle Napolitano, and Abby Joseph Cohen, "EVA: A Primer," *U.S. Research* (Goldman Sachs, September 10, 1997).

THE EMPIRICAL EVIDENCE

There is a growing body of empirical research that shows that value-based metrics like EVA have a statistically significant impact on stock prices. For instance, at the economywide level, Goldman Sachs U.S. Research Group finds that about 27% of the movement in the S&P Industrials share price is explained by variations in EVA over the 1978 to 1997 (estimate) years.[24] Exhibit 8 shows that this percentage of price variation explained (R^2) for the market rises to 35% for the more recent decade covering 1986 to 1997E. This finding is also consistent with Grant's EVA findings, although he shows that the percentage of cross sectional NPV explained in the capital market by the economic profit measure is higher when the dependent and independent regression variables were adjusted by total capital.[25]

Although the percentage of variation in the economywide NPV over time (Goldman Sachs) and in the cross section of large U.S. firms (Grant) might seem low — because some 65% of fluctuations in the economywide NPV remain unexplained in the single-factor regressions — it is important to note that the findings mask some powerful economic profit happenings for wealth creators and destroyers. In this context, Exhibit 9 reports the NPV-to-Capital ratios versus the EVA-to-Capital ratios for selected deciles (100 firms) in the Performance 1000 Universe at year-end 1994 — as reported in the Grant study.

Exhibit 9 shows that 67% of the variation in the NPV-to-Capital ratios for the top 100 U.S. wealth creators at year-end 1994 is explained by *contemporaneous* movements in the EVA-to-Capital ratios. The percentage of NPV variation explained in the cross section is about 40% and 11% for fifth and sixth decile firms, respectively, while only 7% of the NPV variation is explained for the last 100 firms. In each decile, the "EVA betas" are statistically significant as the "*t*-values" exceed the significance benchmark of 2. As Grant points out, the low R^2 value between the NPV/Capital and EVA/Capital ratios in the last decile of the

---

[24] See Steven G. Einhorn, Gabrielle Napolitano, and Abby Joseph Cohen, "EVA® and Valuation of the S&P," *U.S. Research* (Goldman Sachs, January 8, 1998).

[25] See Grant, *Foundations of Economic Value Added.*

Performance 1000 may be due to the "clattering of conflicting financial sounds" and the "abundance of managerial noise" at these wealth destroying firms.

In general, the empirical research suggests that firms and investors have an incentive to discover those firms that will experience positive momentum in their real economic profit over time. Grant's empirical research also demonstrates that during the 1990 to 1994 period about 60% to 80% of movement in the relative NPV ratio of firms is explained by cross-sectional variations in relative economic profit for the top 50 wealth creators listed in the Performance Universe. A representative "scatter" of the NPV-to-Capital versus the EVA-to-Capital ratios for 50 wealth-creating firms is shown in Exhibit 10.[26]

COMPANY SELECTION USING EVA®

If the capital market is pricing efficient, then the firm's anticipated future EVA will be reflected in its current net present value (MVA in Stern Stewart terminology). This means that "growth stocks" will have high price relatives (price/earnings and price/book ratios) because they *should* have, while the so-called "value stocks" will have low price relatives because their poor EVA outlook leads to currently negative net present value. For value stocks, this adverse pricing circumstance happens because their anticipated return on capital falls short of the weighted average cost of debt *and* equity capital. Moreover, in such a rational world investors have little incentive to engage in active management activities as security prices "fully reflect" the EVA-generating opportunities of firms in the marketplace.[27]

Exhibit 9: Regression Statistics for Selected Deciles in Performance 1,000 Universe at Year-End 1994

NPV/Capital = Alpha + Beta × EVA/Capital

Decile Number	Intercept	EVA Beta*	Adjusted R^2
1	0.96	18.57	67.37%
	(7.25)	(14.26)	
5	1.14	11.72	39.74%
	(9.16)	(8.06)	
6	0.90	2.99	10.57
	(12.95)	(3.55)	
10	−0.12	0.46	7.47
	(−9.46)	(3.00)	

* *t*-values reported in parenthesis.

[26] Although value-based metrics like EVA have a significant impact on the firm's net present value they do *not* seem to have relative information content over traditional financial metrics. For rigorous studies that focus on the *relative* information content of value-based metrics, see Peterson and Peterson cited previously as well as Gary C. Biddle, Robert M. Bowen, and James S. Wallace, "Evidence on the Relative and Incremental Information Content of EVA®, Residual Income, Earnings, and Operating Cash Flow," (Working paper, University of Washington, 1996). On a positive note, it should be emphasized that value-based metrics (at the very least) are consistent with the principles of wealth maximization.

[27] For an extensive discussion on how to select companies and industries in an economic profit context, see Grant, *Foundations of Economic Value Added*.

Exhibit 10: NPV-to-Capital versus EVA-to-Capital Ratio:
50 Largest Wealth Creators in Performance Universe at
Year End 1994

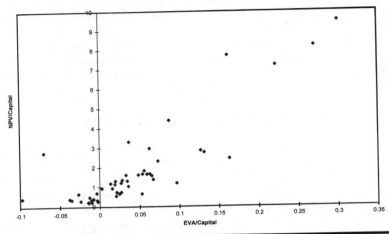

Suppose, however, that pockets of pricing inefficiency are present in the capital market. In this context, the active investor has an incentive to seek out those companies having attractive EVA potential given their current valuation. To operationalize this concept, the active investor could choose those securities — among a conventional universe of value and growth stocks — that offer the dual characteristics of (1) maximum EVA potential for their current relative valuation, and (2) minimum relative valuation for their projected level of economic value added. By selecting securities in this way, pro-active investors maximize the likelihood of active reward (positive EVA alpha) while minimizing the active risk of paying too much for the mispriced (debt and equity) shares of companies in the capital market.

SUMMARY

EVA and related value-based metrics are making significant inroads on how companies and even industries are being evaluated in a securities analysis context. The classical NPV model of corporation finance is the cornerstone of this new company-based approach to financial analysis. Aided by financial tools such as EVA and CFROI, wealth creating firms are identified by their fundamental ability to invest in real assets (both physical and human) having after-tax capital returns that exceed the required return on capital. Wealth destroyers on the other hand have negative residual capital returns because their post-tax capital returns fall short of the overall cost of capital. For wealth wasters, this adverse residual return on capital situation happens even though the firm's after-tax capital returns are sufficiently high enough to cover the cost of debt financing.

The economic approach to measuring corporate profit is different from the accounting approach in many important ways. Unlike traditional measures, such as EBITD, EBIT, and even net income, EVA — and similarly designed value-based metrics — attempts to estimate the firm's *economic income* by accounting for both the cost of debt *and* equity financing. The benefit of assessing corporate profits in this "top down" way is that managers are required to assess the feasibility of their capital investment decisions as if they were in fact share-holders. Projects having (discounted) positive economic profit should get funded because they enhance the firm's net present value, while negative-average EVA investments in real capital should be rejected as they ultimately destroy share-holder wealth.

This approach to measuring the firm's real corporate profitability can be used to actively select investment securities. Companies experiencing positive economic profit announcements should see noticeable increases in their stock price, as shareholders give a welcome response to the firm's positive growth opportunities. On the other hand, troubled firms with negative EVA outlooks are possibly sell or short-sell candidates as their adverse residual capital returns will eventually result in falling share price. As with other fundamental approaches to security analysis and equity portfolio management, the abnormal gains (if any) received from a value-based metrics strategy are limited by the degree of pricing efficiency in the capital market.

Chapter 14

Overview of Equity Style Management

Frank J. Fabozzi, Ph.D., CFA
Adjunct Professor of Finance
School of Management
Yale University

INTRODUCTION

In the early 1970s, several studies found that there were categories of stocks that had similar characteristics and performance patterns. Moreover, the returns of these stock categories performed differently than other categories of stocks. That is, the returns of stocks within a category were highly correlated and the returns between categories of stocks were relatively uncorrelated. The first such study was by James Farrell who called these categories of stocks "clusters."[1] He found that for stocks there were at least four such categories or clusters — growth, cyclical, stable, and energy. In the later half of the 1970s, there were studies that suggested even a simpler categorization by size (as measured by total capitalization) produced different performance patterns.

Practitioners began to view these categories or clusters of stocks with similar performance as a "style" of investing. Some managers, for example, held themselves out as "growth stock managers" and others as "cyclical stock managers." Using size as a basis for categorizing style, some managers became "large cap" investors while others were "small cap" investors. Moreover, there was a commonly held belief that a manager could shift "styles" to enhance performance return.

Today, the notion of an equity investment style is widely accepted in the investment community. The acceptance of equity style investing can also be seen from the proliferation of style indices published by several vendors and the introduction of futures and options contracts based on some of these style indices.

In this chapter, we will look at the practical aspects of style investing. First, we look at the popular style types and the difficulties of classifying stocks according to style. Second, we look at the empirical evidence on style management. Third, we discuss active style management and how it can be implemented.

---

[1] James L. Farrell, Jr. "Homogenous Stock Groupings: Implications for Portfolio Management," *Financial Analysts Journal* (May-June 1975), pp. 50-62.

TYPES OF EQUITY STYLES

Stocks can be classified by style in many ways. The most common is in terms of one or more measures of "growth" and "value." Within a growth and value style there is a sub-style based on some measure of size. The most plain vanilla classification of styles is as follows: (1) large value, (2) large growth, (3) small value, and (4) small growth.

The motivation for the value/growth style categories can be explained in terms of the most common measure for classifying stocks as growth or value — the price-to-book value per share (P/B) ratio.[2] Earnings growth will increase the book value per share. Assuming no change in the P/B ratio, a stock's price will increase if earnings grow. A manager who is growth oriented is concerned with earnings growth and seeks those stocks from a universe of stocks that have higher relative earnings growth. The growth manager's risks are that growth in earnings will not materialize and/or that the P/B ratio will decline.

For a value manager, concern is with the price component rather than with the future earnings growth. Stocks would be classified as value stocks within a universe of stocks if they are viewed as cheap in terms of their P/B ratio. By cheap it is meant that the P/B ratio is low relative to the universe of stocks. The expectation of the manager who follows a value style is that the P/B ratio will return to some normal level and thus even with book value per share constant, the price will rise. The risk is that the P/B ratio will not increase.

Each quarter the Mobius Group surveys institutional money managers and asks their style. In June 1996, there were 1,526 domestic equity money managers in the survey who responded that they follow an active strategy. Of these survey participants, 503 indicated that growth was an "accurate" or a "very accurate" description of their style. Moreover, these managers indicated that it was wrong to classify them as value managers. There were 460 managers of the 1,526 surveyed that responded that value was an "accurate" or a "very accurate" description of their style and that it would be wrong to classify them as growth managers.

Within the value and growth categories there are sub-styles. As mentioned above, one sub-style is based on size. The sub-styles discussed below are based on other classifications of the stocks selected.

Sub-Styles of Value Category

In the value category, there are three sub-styles: low price-to-earnings (P/E) ratio, contrarian, and yield.[3] The *low-P/E manager* concentrates on companies trading at

---

[2] Support for the use of this measure is provided in the following study: Eugene F. Fama and Kenneth R. French, "Common Risk Factors on Stocks and Bonds," *Journal of Financial Economics* (February 1993), pp. 3-56.

[3] Jon A. Christopherson and C. Nola Williams, "Equity Style: What it is and Why it Matters," Chapter 1 in T. Daniel Coggin, Frank J. Fabozzi, and Robert D. Arnott (eds.), *The Handbook of Equity Style Management: Second Edition* (New Hope, PA: Frank J. Fabozzi Associates, 1997).

low prices relative to their P/E ratio.[4] The P/E ratio can be defined as the current P/E, a normalized P/E, or a discounted future earnings. The *contrarian manager* looks at the book value of a company and focuses on those companies that are selling at low valuation relative to book value. The companies that fall into this category are typically depressed cyclical stocks or companies that have little or no current earnings or dividend yields. The expectation is that the stock is on a cyclical rebound or that the company's earnings will turn around. Both these occurrences are expected to lead to substantial price appreciation. The most conservative value managers are those that look at companies with above average dividend yields that are expected to be capable of increasing, or at least maintaining, those yields. This style is followed by a manager who is referred to as a *yield manager*.

Sub-Styles of Growth Category

Growth managers seek companies with above average growth prospects. In the growth manager style category, there tends to be two major sub-styles.[5] The first is a growth manager who focuses on high-quality companies with consistent growth. A manager who follows this sub-style is referred to as a *consistent growth manager*. The second growth sub-style is followed by an *earnings momentum growth manager*. In contrast to a growth manager, an earnings momentum growth manager prefers companies with more volatile, above-average growth. Such a manager seeks to buy companies in expectation of an acceleration of earnings.

Hybrid Styles: Value-Growth Managers

There are some managers who follow both a growth and value investing style but have a bias (or tilt) in favor of one of the styles. The bias is not sufficiently identifiable to categorize the manager as growth or value managers. Most managers who fall into this hybrid style are described as *growth at a price managers* or *growth at a reasonable price managers*. These managers look for companies that are forecasted to have above-average growth potential selling at a reasonable value.

As noted above, the Mobius Group surveys institutional money managers quarterly and asks them to classify their style. In the June 1996 survey, 503 indicated they were growth managers and 460 value managers. There were 252 managers who indicated that both value and growth styles were an "accurate" or "very accurate" description of their styles. Most of these managers probably fell into the category of growth at a price managers.

STYLE CLASSIFICATION SYSTEMS

Now that we have a general idea of the two main style categories, growth and value, and the further refinement by size, let's see how a manager goes about clas-

---

[4] For a discussion of an approach based on low price-earnings, see Gary G. Schlarbaum, "Value-Based Equity Strategies," Chapter 7 in *The Handbook of Equity Style Management*.
[5] Christopherson and Williams, "Equity Style."

sifying stocks that fall into the categories. We call the methodology for classifying stocks into style categories as a *style classification system*. Vendors of style indices have provided direction for developing a style classification system. However, managers will develop their own system.

Developing such a system is not a simple task. To see why, let's take a simple style classification system where we just categorize stocks into value and growth using one measure, the price-to-book value ratio. The lower the P/B ratio the more the stock looks like a value stock. The style classification system would then be as follows:

> *Step 1:* Select a universe of stocks.
> *Step 2:* Calculate the total market capitalization of all the stocks in the universe.
> *Step 3:* Calculate the P/B ratio for each stock in the universe.
> *Step 4:* Sort the stocks from the lowest P/B ratio to the highest P/B ratio.
> *Step 5:* Calculate the accumulated market capitalization starting from the lowest P/B ratio stock to the highest P/B ratio stock.
> *Step 6:* Select the lowest P/B stocks up to the point where one-half the total market capitalization computed in Step 2 is found.
> *Step 7:* Classify the stocks found in Step 6 as value stocks.
> *Step 8:* Classify the remaining stocks from the universe as growth stocks.

While this style classification system is simple, it has both theoretical and practical problems. First, from a theoretical point of view, in terms of the P/B ratio there is very little distinguishing the last stock on the list that is classified as value and the first stock on the list classified as growth. From a practical point of view, the transaction costs are higher for implementing a style using this classification system. The reason is that the classification is at a given point in time based on the prevailing P/B ratio and market capitalizations. At a future date, P/B ratios and market capitalizations will change, resulting in a different classification of some of the stocks. This is often the case for those stocks on the border between value and growth that could jump over to the other category. This is sometimes called "style jitter." As a result, the manager will have to rebalance the portfolio to sell off stocks that are not within the style classification sought.

Refinements to the Basic Style Classification System

There are two refinements that have been made to style classification systems in an attempt to overcome these two problems. First, more than one categorization variable has been used in a style classification system. Two types of categorization variables have been used: deterministic and expectational. Deterministic variables are those derived from historical data. These variables include dividend/price ratio (i.e., dividend yield), cash flow/price ratio (i.e., cash flow yield), return on equity, and earnings variability. Expectational variables are those based on expectations or forecasts. Examples are earnings growth estimates or variables which rely on some stock valuation model (such as a the dividend discount model or a factor model).

As examples of this refinement, consider the style classification system developed by one vendor of style indices, Frank Russell, and one developed by a broker/dealer, Salomon Brothers Inc. For the Frank Russell style indices, the universe of stocks (either 1,000 for the Russell 1000 index or 2,000 for the Russell 2000 index) were classified as part of their value index or growth index using two categorization variables. The two variables are the B/P ratio (a deterministic variable) and a long-term growth forecast (an expectational variable).[6] The latter variable is obtained from the Institutional Brokerage Estimates Survey (IBES). Salomon Brothers uses more than two variables. The variables included are P/B ratio, earnings growth, P/E ratio, dividend yields, and historical returns.[7]

When using several variables in the style classification system, a score is developed for each stock. The classification is then done as follows:

Step 1: Select a universe of stocks.

Step 2: Calculate the total market capitalization of all the stocks in the universe.

Step 3: Using the variables for classification, develop a score for each stock, with the highest score being value.

Step 4: Sort the stocks from the highest score to the lowest score.

Step 5: Calculate the capitalization-weighted median of the scores.

Step 6: Select the stocks with a score above the capitalization-weighted median found in Step 5 and classify them as value stocks.

Step 7: Classify the remaining stocks in the universe as growth stocks.

With this system, half of the market capitalization is in each group.

The second refinement has been to develop better procedures for making the cut between growth and value. This involves not classifying every stock into one category or the other. Instead, stocks may be classified into three groups: "pure value," "pure growth," and "middle-of-the-road" stocks. The three groups would be such that they each had one third of the total market capitalization. The two extreme groups, pure value and pure growth, are not likely to face any significant style jitter. The middle-of-the road stocks are assigned a probability of being value or growth. This style classification system is used by Frank Russell and Salomon Brothers Inc.

We will illustrate this approach using the Salomon Brothers model, called the *Growth/Value* (GV) *Model* for distinguishing between growth and value stocks.[8] The model uses a statistical technique called discriminant analysis to

---

[6] "Russell Equity Indices: Index Construction and Methodology," Frank Russell Company, July 8, 1994 and September 6, 1995.

[7] Sergio Bienstock and Eric H. Sorensen, "Segregating Growth from Value: It's Not Always Either/Or," Salomon Brothers Inc., Quantitative Equities Strategy, July 1992.

[8] Bienstock and Sorensen, "Segregating Growth from Value: It's Not Always Either/Or."

"discriminate" between growth and value stocks. Discriminant analysis gives a score, called the "discriminant score," and it is this score that is used to make the cut-off between growth and value. The bottom line output of the model is a ranking of a universe of stocks based on the probability that any particular stock will be a growth stock. This probability is called the "growth stock probability" and its complement, 1 minus the growth stock probability, is the "value stock probability." When the growth stock probability of a particular stock approaches 1, then it is concluded that that particular stock is a growth stock. Similarly, when the value stock probability of a particular stock approaches 1, then it is concluded that that particular stock is a value stock. Stocks that do not clearly fall into the growth or value categories are identified by the model based on these probabilities.

The product of the model is illustrated in Exhibit 1. The results of the GV model shown in the figure are the result of an application to the largest 3,000 capitalization stocks in 1991. The horizontal axis shows the discriminant score. The vertical axis shows the growth-stock probability. As the discriminant score increases, the growth-stock probability increases. The dots in Exhibit 1 are specific stocks from the 3,000 analyzed with the GV model. Because most of the stocks analyzed fall near the middle, it looks like a solid curve in that area. There are five vertical lines in the figure. These lines indicate the percentage of the 3,000 stocks that fall below the line. Specifically, moving from left to right, the first line represents 10%, the second 25%, the third 50%, the fourth 75%, and the last 90%. This means that 10% of the 3,000 stocks fell below the first line and 10% were above the last line. Salomon Brothers views stocks that fall below the 10% line as being unambiguously value stocks (because they have a low growth stock probability) and those that are above the 90% line as being unambiguously growth stocks (because they have a high growth stock probability). The stocks that fall in between are unassigned.

Thus far our focus has been on style classification in terms of value and growth. As we noted earlier, sub-style classifications are possible in terms of size. Within a value and growth classification, there can be a model determining large value and small value stocks, and large growth and small growth stocks. The variable most used for classification of size is a company's market capitalization. To determine large and small, the total market capitalization of all the stocks in the universe considered is first calculated. The cutoff between large and small is the stock that will give an equal market capitalization.

This simple classification based on size with value and growth has been refined by creators of style indices. For example, Wilshire Associates creates broad-based style indices. The broadest based index is the Wilshire 5000. Wilshire's approach to size was to limit the stocks to the largest 2,500 because it was felt that they better represent stocks held by institutional investors. This index is called the Wilshire Top 2500. Studies of the performance profile of the stocks in this index by Wilshire's Institutional Services/Equity Division found that there was different performance between the 700th and 800th stocks. Wilshire selected the 750th largest stock as the cut-off for the large category. This is the Wilshire Top 750 stocks. Stocks 751 to 2,500 are included in the Wilshire Next 1750.

Exhibit 1: Product of Salomon Brothers Growth-Value Model for Probability Ranking of 3,000 Largest Capitalization Stocks in 1991

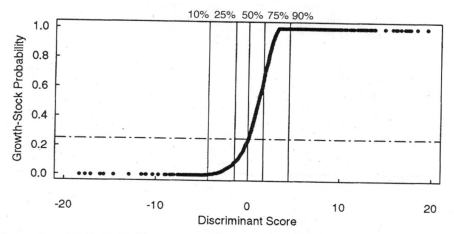

Source: Figure 2 in Sergio Bienstock and Eric H. Sorensen, "Segregating Growth from Value: It's Not Always Either/Or," Salomon Brothers Inc., Quantitative Equities Strategy, July 1992, p. 5.

RELATIVE PERFORMANCE OF VALUE AND GROWTH

Now that we understand the various style classification systems, we next look at the most important question associated with style management: is style management worth the effort and cost? To answer this question, we can look at the evidence on the relative performance of value and growth stocks.

Robert Arnott, David Leinweber, and Christopher Luck present evidence on this relative performance for the United States, Japan, United Kingdom, Canada, and Germany.[9] Using the simple measure of value and growth based on the P/B ratio, they calculated the growth of $1 invested in growth stocks and value stocks from January 1975 to June 1995. The results are reported in Exhibit 2. For the U.S. analysis, the universe of stocks included are those in the S&P 500. As can be seen from Exhibit 2 in every country, value outperformed growth based on the simple definition of growth and value. Exhibit 3 presents this superior performance over the entire time period in terms of the difference in the cumulative return between value stocks and growth stocks for the markets of the same five countries.

---

[9] David J. Leinweber, Robert D. Arnott, and Christopher G. Luck, "The Many Sides of Equity Style: Quantitative Management of Core, Value, and Growth Portfolios," Chapter 11 in *The Handbook of Equity Style Management*.

Exhibit 2: Growth of $1 Invested in Growth Stocks and Value Stocks Using Simple Price/Book Classification: January 1975 to June 1995

Country	Growth of $1 invested in			Portion of monthly returns where Growth exceeded Value
	Value Stocks	Growth Stocks	Best of Value-or-Growth	
U.S.	$23	$14	$42	45%
U.K.	42	24	82	44
Japan	37	10	89	39
Canada	12	5	31	39
Germany	14	9	30	45

Source: Exhibit 10 in David J. Leinweber, Robert D. Arnott, and Christopher G. Luck, "The Many Sides of Equity Style: Quantitative Management of Core, Value, and Growth Portfolios," Chapter 11 in T. Daniel Coggin, Frank J. Fabozzi, and Robert D. Arnott (eds.), *The Handbook of Equity Style Management: Second Edition* (New Hope, PA: Frank J. Fabozzi Associates, 1997), p. 188.

While the results are informative, they are based on raw returns. That is, they make no adjustment for differences in risk that might exist between growth and value stocks. A comprehensive analysis that addresses this issue was performed by Richard Roll.[10] He addressed the following three questions:

1. Are the observed differences in the performance between equity styles just statistical aberrations and therefore not likely to be repeated?
2. Are the observed differences in performance between equity styles simply a reflection of the compensation for the differences in the risks associated with each equity style?
3. Are the observed differences in performance between equity style truly an investment opportunity that can generate an enhanced return without incurring any additional exposure to loss?

To empirically address these questions, Roll used the following three categorization variables: (1) large or small size; (2) high or low earnings per share/price (E/P) ratio; and, (3) high or low book equity/market equity (B/M) ratio. A low relative P/E ratio is viewed as an indicator of value, therefore a high relative E/P ratio is a measure of value. A low relative P/B ratio is an indicator of value. It has the same meaning when expressed in terms of the B/M ratio (i.e., a low relative B/M ratio is an indicator of value); therefore a high relative B/M ratio is an indicator of value.

Only U.S. stocks were included in Roll's study. The universe of stocks included all listed NYSE and AMEX stocks available from the CRSP database. The period covered was April 1984 to March 1994. The number of stocks in the universe varied each month.

---

[10] Richard Roll, "Style Return Differentials: Illustrations, Risk Premiums, or Investment Opportunities," Chapter 5 in *The Handbook of Equity Style Management*.

Exhibit 3: Cumulative Returns of Value Minus Growth Stocks by Country: January 1975 to June 1997

A: U.S. S&P500 Value – Growth

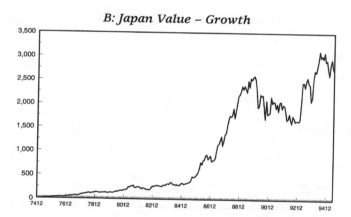

B: Japan Value – Growth

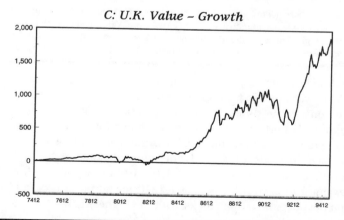

C: U.K. Value – Growth

Exhibit 3 (Continued)
D: Canada Value – Growth

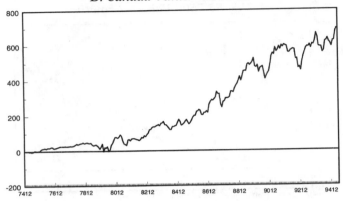

E: Germany Value – Growth

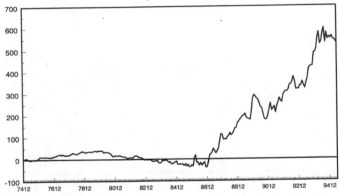

Source: Exhibit 5, 6, 7, 8, and 9 in David J. Leinweber, Robert D. Arnott, and Christopher G. Luck, "The Many Sides of Equity Style: Quantitative Management of Core, Value, and Growth Portfolios," Chapter 11 in T. Daniel Coggin, Frank J. Fabozzi, and Robert D. Arnott (eds.), *The Handbook of Equity Style Management: Second Edition* (New Hope, PA: Frank J. Fabozzi Associates, 1997), pp. 185- 187.

Each month the stocks in the universe were classified into one of eight portfolios. This was done as follows. The stocks were ranked separately from low to high based on a given style categorization variable. Then a stock was assigned to one of eight style portfolios as follows. Each portfolio was designated by three letters. Each letter represented the stock assignment within a style classification variable as either "low" denoted by "L" or "high" denoted by "H." The first letter for a portfolio indicated size, the second letter E/P ratio, and the third letter B/M ratio. For example, a portfolio designated LHL meant the stocks in this portfolio were the smallest capitalization stocks with the highest E/P ratio, and the lowest

B/M ratio. Each month the stocks in the style portfolio changed based on their classification according to the style categorization variable.

For each of the eight style portfolios, a value-weighted monthly total return was calculated. The total return included price change, dividends, and reinvestment of dividends. Exhibit 4 shows the growth of $1 invested in each style portfolio over the period and ranks the performance of the style portfolios. The best performing style portfolio was "LHH." This is a small capitalization portfolio that has a high E/P and a high B/M. This is clearly a value portfolio and the findings are therefore consistent with the results presented in Exhibit 2 of the superior performance of value stocks based on raw returns. The worst performing style portfolio was "LLL." The low E/P and low B/M indicate that this style portfolio is biased in the direction of growth. In terms of return performance, the best performing style portfolio outperformed the worst performing style portfolio by more than 15% annually.

Roll then statistically tested whether the monthly excess returns on the style portfolios (i.e., the difference between the return on a style portfolio and the risk-free rate) was significantly different. Using an elaborate statistical test, Roll found that they were statistically significant.

The results in Exhibit 4 (as well as those in Exhibit 2) are based on raw returns. No adjustment was made in the results reported to account for the risks associated with each portfolio style. Roll takes this into account by analyzing the risk-adjusted returns for the style portfolios. He used two risks models: the capital asset pricing model and a factor model. Roll does not find that accounting for risk can explain the difference in performance of the style portfolios. That is, he found that there were still differences in return performance after adjusting for risk. This suggests that equity style provided extra return without incurring additional risk.

Exhibit 4: Growth of $1 Invested and Performance of Style Portfolios from March 31, 1985 to March 31, 1994

Rank	Growth of $1	Style Size	Earnings/Price	Book/Market
1	$6.85	Low	High	High
2	5.34	High	High	High
3	5.15	Low	High	Low
S&P 500	3.96	—	—	—
4	3.49	High	High	Low
5	3.05	High	Low	Low
6	2.76	High	Low	High
7	2.02	Low	Low	High
8	1.64	Low	Low	Low

Source: Richard Roll, "Style Return Differentials: Illustrations, Risk Premiums, or Investment Opportunities," Chapter 5 in T. Daniel Coggin, Frank J. Fabozzi, and Robert D. Arnott (eds.), *The Handbook of Equity Style Management: Second Edition* (New Hope, PA: Frank J. Fabozzi Associates, 1997), p. 102.

Why Have Value Stocks Outperformed Growth Stocks?

There is considerable debate as to why it has been empirically observed that value stocks have outperformed growth stocks over extended periods. The results may merely be the result of data mining. There are other explanations that have been proffered.

The first explanation is that there are one or more risks that are not being recognized in the analysis.[11] If there are risks that are not identified, then it is possible that the premium realized by value stocks over growth stocks is a risk premium to compensate for such risks. While one can never be sure of capturing all the risks, the study by Roll described above uses the latest technology in asset pricing modeling and still finds differential performance. The second explanation is that there are systematic errors in forecasts that cause the difference in performance.[12]

A partial explanation for the difference in performance of growth and value stocks where the criteria for classification is the price-earnings ratio has been suggested by Scott Bauman and Robert Miller.[13] They looked at the earnings forecast and found that earnings were consistently underestimated for the lowest price-earnings stocks and consistently overestimated for the highest price-earnings stocks. The low price-earnings stocks are value stocks. An underestimate of future earnings means that such stocks will perform better than expected. In the case of growth stocks, which are the high price-earnings stocks, an overestimate of earnings will result in worse performance than expected. Why does this bias exist? Bauman and Miller argue that it is the result of too much reliance by analysts on recent past earnings trends in formulating forecasted earnings.

ACTIVE STYLE MANAGEMENT

The results of the studies by Arnott-Leinweber-Luck and Roll suggest that a value style outperforms a growth style. The outperformance of value over growth, however, did not occur for every time period studied. Even though the cumulative return differential favored value stocks, there were dips in the curves shown in Exhibit 5 (a) through (e). A dip means that there were periods where growth stocks outperformed value stocks. The last column in Exhibit 2 shows the percentage of months over the January 1975 to June 1995 period in which growth stocks outperformed value stocks.

The implication of this is that there are opportunities to switch styles based on expectations of what will be the best performing style. This portfolio strategy is called *active style management* or *tactical style management*. (Selecting one style

---

[11] Eugene F. Fama and Kenneth R. French, "The Cross-Section of Expected Returns," *Journal of Finance* (June 1992), pp. 427-465.

[12] This explanation has been suggested in the following studies: Josef Lakonishok, Andrei Shleifer, and Robert Vishny, "Contrarian Investment, Extrapolation, and Risk," *Journal of Finance* (December 1994), pp. 1541-1578; and, Robert A. Haugen, *The New Finance: The Case Against Efficient Markets* (Englewood Cliffs, NJ: Prentice Hall, 1995).

[13] W. Scott Bauman and Robert E. Miller, "Investment Styles, Stock Market Cycles, Investor Expectations, and Portfolio Performance," Chapter 8 in *The Handbook of Equity Style Management*.

and sticking with it is referred to as *passive style management*.)[14] The potential for enhanced performance by pursuing such a strategy can be seen by looking at what a style switching strategy would have done in terms of the growth of $1 if a manager could *perfectly predict* the better performing of the two styles each month and invested in that style. This is shown in the fourth column of Exhibit 2. For example, in the United States a perfect foresight style switching strategy would have generated a growth of $1 equal to $42 at the end of 20 years compared to $23 for value stocks.

Now we know that with perfect foresight a style switching strategy which ignores transaction costs would have produced a significantly enhanced return compared to a passive style management. The question is how to implement a real-world style switching strategy to enhance returns. To do so, it is necessary to accurately forecast returns to style. Moreover, any realistic style switching strategy must recognize the costs of trading large positions in one style into a large position of another style.

Implementing a Style Switching Strategy

Typically, the costs of implementation of style switching do not make it economic to pursue a style switching strategy over short time periods. There are more effective ways to implement a style switching strategy.[15] Rather than a style switching strategy from value to growth or growth to value, a policy of tilting a portfolio toward a style can be employed. For example, a style switching strategy means that at a given time either (1) 100% is allocated to a value portfolio and 0% to a growth portfolio or (2) 0% is allocated to a value portfolio and 100% to a growth portfolio. In a style tilting strategy, there is some allocation to each style, the percentage allocation based on the expected relative performance of the two styles. In addition to reducing transaction costs, style tilting reduces the size of the bet made on a style.

There are two additional ways to effectively implement an active style management strategy. First, as noted earlier, a probabilistic style classification system can be used so as to focus only on the strongest value stocks or growth stocks. This increases the probability that the manager is achieving the target style exposure and reduces transaction costs from stocks at the border crossing over. Second, a style switching or style tilting strategy should occur only based on longer-term forecasted better return performance of a style. The reason is that transaction costs associated with the frequent shifting of the portfolio between styles for short periods will more than likely eat up the potential enhanced return.

Transaction costs are critical in a strategy. Futures contracts provide a cost effective means for altering an exposure to an asset. Because of the increased interest in style investing, futures on style indices have been developed and are currently trading. Futures on style indices provide a means for reducing the transaction costs associated with active style management.[16]

---

[14] See Bruce I. Jacobs and Kenneth N. Levy, Chapter 1 of this book, for more on style and active equity management.

[15] Leinweber, Arnott, and Luck, "The Many Sides of Equity Style."

[16] See, Joanne M. Hill and Maria E. Tsu, "Value and Growth Index Derivatives," Chapter 19 in *The Handbook of Equity Style Management*.

SUMMARY

Studies suggest that there are categories of stocks that have had similar character-istics and performance patterns, and that the returns of these stock categories per-formed differently than other categories of stocks. Practitioners view these categories of stocks with similar performance as a "style" of investing. The notion of an equity investment style is widely accepted in the investment community. While stocks can be classified by style in many ways, the most common classifi-cation is in terms of "growth" and "value". The measure most commonly used to classify growth and value stocks is the price-to-book value per share.

Within a growth and value style there are sub-styles based on some mea-sure of size. The most plain vanilla classification of styles is as follows: (1) large value, (2) large growth, (3) small value, and (4) small growth. In the value category, there are three sub-styles: low price-to-earnings ratio, contrarian, and yield. In the growth manager style category, the two major sub-styles are consistent growth and earnings momentum growth. A common hybrid style is growth-at-a-price.

A style classification system is a methodology for classifying stocks into style categories. Developing such a system is not a simple task. A major concern in designing a style classification system is style jitter — the frequent jumping of stocks from one style category into the other. The two major refinements that have been made to style classification systems are (1) the use of more than one catego-rization variable and (2) development of better procedures for making the cut between growth and value stocks (probabilistic approach).

The empirical evidence appears to support the superior performance of value stocks over growth stocks, even after adjusting for risk factors. There is evi-dence that this superior performance is also the case in several non-U.S. equity markets. There are several major criticisms of these findings. First, the results may be due to data mining. Second, all risk factors may not be captured in the studies and therefore it is possible that the results reflect a risk premium required for investing in value stocks. The study by Roll, however, does not support this view. Finally, there may be systematic errors in forecasts that cause the difference in performance.

While the results of studies suggest that a value style has outperformed a growth style, the better performance did not occur for every period of time. This suggests that there are opportunities to switch styles based on expectations of what will be the best performing style. This is called active style management or tactical style management. The costs of implementation of style switching do not make it economic to pursue a short-term style switching strategy. More effective ways to implement a style switching strategy involve a policy of tilting a portfolio toward a style that is expected to perform best.

Chapter 15

Enhanced Equity Indexing

John S. Loftus, CFA
Executive Vice President
Pacific Investment Managment Company

INTRODUCTION

Enhanced indexing is, in a sense, an oxymoron. The essential task of indexing is to match the return of a benchmark index. Does enhanced indexing, then, imply doing a better job than regular indexing does of matching the index? Providers of enhanced indexing services will be quick to say, "No. It means beating the index." But that's the job of active managers. Elaborating, the enhanced indexer would say, "True, but enhanced indexing seeks to consistently outperform a benchmark index by a moderate amount, while closely controlling both tracking error and the risk of significant underperformance."

Given this definition, where does enhanced indexing belong? Active management seeks to outperform. Indexing seeks to match the index. If enhanced indexing is to outperform, it must involve active management techniques. If it is to closely track the targeted index, it must share with indexing certain techniques designed to control risk.

"Risk-controlled active management" would seem an apt phrase, synonymous with enhanced indexing but resolving the apparent oxymoron. That enhanced indexing has become the more popular phrase may reflect marketing imperatives more than any desire for linguistic precision. Whether the phrase is here to stay, however, will almost certainly be driven by the results. If enhanced indexing delivers consistent excess returns with close tracking and few disappointments, it is hard to imagine investors not preferring it to traditional forms of indexing or active management.

How enhanced indexing accomplishes its laudable objective varies across a spectrum of techniques. This chapter surveys the major methods of enhanced equity indexing. To help the reader distinguish between traditional active management and an enhanced index strategy, I develop a returns-based framework to motivate the distinction. I then divide the enhanced indexing world into two principal categories: stock-based strategies and synthetic strategies. After discussing the primary approaches in each category, the chapter closes with a discussion of how an investor may achieve optimal results by combining a synthetic strategy with a stock-based approach.

THE NATURE OF ENHANCED INDEXING

As noted above, enhanced indexing draws from active management techniques in order to generate excess returns, while controlling risk in part through methods common to indexing. In seeking to provide the best of both worlds, enhanced indexing does not deliver a free lunch. Excess returns stem from risk exposures, but providers of enhanced indexing tend to share a heightened emphasis on risk control as compared with traditional active management.

As an important illustration, one of the principal manifestations of risk control in enhanced indexing is the modest level of excess return both sought and delivered by the strategies. Simplistically, the "best" active manager could be thought of as the one who delivers the highest excess returns. Risk or tracking error is generally only a secondary consideration in traditional active management. In contrast, the "best" enhanced indexer would be the manager who optimizes the tradeoff between excess return and close tracking of the index.

While not universally valid, this qualitative distinction between active management and enhanced indexing leads to a potentially helpful quantitative means of separating active management from enhanced indexing. By focusing on returns or expected returns, it is possible for an investor to separate the two types of managers more easily than by focusing on the methods employed to achieve excess returns, as these methods often blur with those of active managers.

Returns-Based Tools

A returns-based distinction between active management and enhanced indexing relies on three tools: alpha, tracking error, and information ratio. These are defined in turn.

Alpha

Alpha is defined as risk-adjusted excess return over the benchmark, from the model:

$$\text{expected return} = \text{alpha} + \text{beta} \times (\text{index return})$$

For enhanced indexing, the simplified expressions,

$$\text{alpha} = \text{expected return} - \text{index return}$$

or

$$\text{alpha} = \text{expected excess return}$$

stem from the assumption that beta will be very close to one. This assumption is consistent with the intended design of most enhanced indexing strategies. A further simplifying assumption (and certainly a more heroic one) will allow alpha to be defined in terms of a manager's historical performance,

$$\text{alpha} = \text{historical excess return}$$

The usual disclaimers apply, of course. Nevertheless, a focus on *ex post* returns allows some inferences to be drawn based on observable rather than forecast returns.

Tracking Error

Tracking error measures the dispersion of excess returns and, therefore, the consistency of a manager's excess performance. Tracking error is sometimes confused with alpha, as in, "...the manager's negative tracking error was due to the decision to underweight energy stocks, the top-performing sector last year." In fact, tracking error is always a positive number, defined as follows:

tracking error = annualized standard deviation of monthly excess returns

Note that a manager does not necessarily have tracking error simply because of outperformance or underperformance. By the above definition, a manager who outperformed (or underperformed) by exactly 20 basis points every single month would have zero tracking error, despite a positive (negative) alpha.

Information Ratio

If alpha is taken to be a manager's mean historical excess return, then tracking error measures the standard deviation of the alpha. If one makes the assumption that managers' excess returns are normally distributed, then knowing the mean and the standard deviation of those excess returns allows statistical inferences to be drawn. The most common inference is the measure of confidence that a manager's historical alpha is not zero. In other words, if the manager demonstrates a positive excess return over time, what is the probability that the excess return did not arise simply by chance?

Defining the information ratio as,

$$\text{information ratio} = \frac{\text{alpha}}{\text{tracking error}}$$

we see that the information ratio is closely related to the *t*-statistic used to measure the statistical significance of a manager's alpha[1]

$$t = \frac{\text{alpha} \times \sqrt{T}}{\sigma}$$

where T is the number of independent observations and σ is the standard deviation.

Relating the information ratio to the *t*-statistic allows one to answer the question, "How confident am I that a given manager's historical results indicate an alpha that was achieved by skill rather than luck?" In other words, what is the confidence that the measured historical alpha is, statistically speaking, different

---

[1] Richard Grinold and Ronald Kahn, *Active Portfolio Management* (Chicago: Probus Publishing Company, 1995).

than zero. Let's assume we have measured a manager's annualized alpha and tracking error over a 5-year period and computed the information ratio. Exhibit 1 shows the degree of confidence (using a two-tail test) that historical alphas are non-zero for various information ratios. To be 95% confident that a manager's 5-year historical alpha was obtained by skill rather than luck, an information ratio of 1.25 is required.

Note that it would be inappropriate to say that the probability of future excess returns is given by the information ratio. Of course, hiring an active manager or an enhanced indexer implies a prediction that alpha will be positive. Otherwise, the correct choice would be a straight index fund. Having a high confidence that favorable historical performance was due to skill rather than luck would seem to be an appropriate precondition to making such a prediction, however.

A TAXONOMY OF EQUITY MANAGEMENT APPROACHES

Having defined the concepts of alpha, tracking error, and information ratio, I now propose a means of categorizing various equity management approaches using these measures. The following taxonomy is intended as a general guide for distinguishing between indexing, active management, and enhanced indexing. There are doubtless many equity managers whose results represent exceptions to these rules of thumb, but the rules are typical of the average results in each category, particularly with respect to large-capitalization portfolios for which the most appropriate benchmark, the S&P 500, has been the target of the lion's share of indexed assets.

Indexing

Indexing has an expected alpha of zero, and most successful managers of large index funds have exhibited historical tracking error of 0.2% (20 basis points) or lower. Thus, the information ratio of an index fund manager is essentially zero. In terms of the confidence measure discussed above, an information ratio of zero is not puzzling. Investors in index funds are not seeking positive alpha, so the lack of statistical confidence in a positive alpha (as implied by an information ratio of zero) is not troubling.

Exhibit 1: Confidence that Alphas are Non-Zero

Information Ratio	Confidence that alpha ≠ 0 (%)
0.25	39.4
0.33	49.8
0.50	67.3
0.75	83.1
1.00	91.1
1.25	95.1

Exhibit 2: Measures of Management Categories

	Indexing	Active Management	Enhanced Indexing
Expected Alpha	0%	2.0% or higher	0.5% to 2.0%
Tracking Error	0% to 0.2%	4% or higher	0.5% to 2.0%
Information Ratio	0	0.5 or lower	0.5 to 2.0

Exhibit 3: Factoring in the Length of Track Record

Information Ratio	Years to Achieve 95% Confidence in Significance of Alpha
0.25	64.0
0.33	38.0
0.50	18.0
0.75	9.5
1.00	6.5
1.25	5.0

Active Management

Classically, active managers have an expected annualized alpha of 2% (200 basis points) or higher. However, as the traditional focus within the active management community has been oriented more toward production of excess returns than toward controlling tracking error, it is common to find tracking error in excess of 4%. As a result, information ratios for active management have averaged 0.5 or less.

Enhanced Indexing

Enhanced indexing focuses on generating modest levels of alpha, generally 0.5% to 2.0% annualized. Enhanced index managers also strive for low tracking error. Most strategies marketed as enhanced indexing have exhibited historical tracking error of between 0.5% and 2.0% as well. Thus, the information ratios for offerings in the enhanced index category are often in the range of 0.5 to 2.0. Exhibit 2 summarizes these measures.

Recalling the statistical confidence analysis above, it is interesting to look at the typical information ratios of active management and enhanced indexing to perform a somewhat different analysis. Let's ask the question, "for a given information ratio, how many years long must the track record be to indicate at the 95% confidence level that the true alpha is not zero?" Exhibit 3 presents the results. Plan sponsors/consultants may wish to ask themselves how many managers they have hired/recommended based on five years of data whose information ratios require a significantly longer measurement horizon to attribute statistical significance to the alpha.

Of course, statistical significance of a manager's alpha is not the sole relevant criterion in a hiring decision. Economic significance of the alpha matters as well. Consider the manager who, using a very complex active-management or enhanced-indexing process, produces 10 basis points of alpha with 10 basis points of tracking error. This alpha is statistically significant at the 95% level after only

6.5 years of results. Relative to indexing, however, the plan sponsor may not find 10 basis points (gross of fees) of alpha to be worth the effort to understand and monitor the more complex process.

Alternatively, consider the very active manager who has produced 500 basis points of alpha in five years but with 1,500 basis points of tracking error. The manager's process is easy to understand and monitor. While one can only be about 50% confident that the true alpha of the process is nonzero, some plan sponsors might be willing to trade off lower statistical confidence for the chance of obtaining dramatic outperformance over the long run. Hopefully, however, the plan sponsor can endure the possibility of dramatic underperformance over shorter time horizons, as is implied by such high tracking error.

Information ratios then, while useful, are but one tool in assisting in a decision between indexing, active management, and enhanced indexing. The best choice for a given investor will be based on individual circumstances. An investor driven by a desire to reduce management fees and eliminate all uncertainty as to benchmark tracking will no doubt prefer traditional indexing. An investor focused primarily on maximizing return, who has confidence in his or her ability to identify successful managers, would most likely prefer traditional active management, although they should seek out long track records and the highest possible information ratios nevertheless. Enhanced indexing can represent a comfortable middle ground between these two emphases, bringing the potential for moderate but meaningful alpha with a greater degree of confidence and consistency.

Not surprisingly, investment management fees for enhanced indexing strategies tend to lie in between those of traditional active management and indexing. Perhaps driven by confidence in their own ability to generate consistent alpha, enhanced index managers commonly offer their services with performance-based fee options.

TYPES OF ENHANCED INDEXING STRATEGIES

Thus far, I've explained that enhanced indexing attempts to deliver moderate and consistent alpha with relatively low tracking error. In a qualitative sense, enhanced indexing differs from active management processes primarily in having moderate objectives for alpha and a significant emphasis on risk control. Successful enhanced indexing strategies produce relatively high information ratios that can greatly increase confidence in the statistical significance of the alpha and/or lower the required measurement period to gain such confidence.

The types of strategies marketed as enhanced index approaches can be divided into two broad groups: stock-based strategies and synthetic strategies. I'll characterize each group in turn, focusing on the sources of alpha, the different risk exposures taken to achieve the alpha, and the techniques involved in controlling tracking error.

Stock-Based Strategies

Stock-based enhanced indexing strategies are typically broadly diversified portfolios that rely on some form of stock selection process in an attempt to generate a moderate, consistent alpha. In common with traditional active management, for the strategy to be successful the manager must have some means of identifying stocks within the index that will either outperform or underperform the index. There will also generally be a risk control regimen that limits the degree of individual stock underweighting/overweighting as well as the degree of portfolio exposure to factor risks and industry/sector concentrations. A variety of approaches are pursued. These are discussed below.

Tilts

Probably the first stock-based strategies that could be characterized as enhanced indexing involved so-called *tilting techniques*. Starting with a pure index fund, a manager would obtain modest overweights in a direction favored by the client. Value, growth, and yield are among the more common tilts. Obviously, the expectation of alpha comes from the belief that value stocks, growth stocks, or high dividend-paying stocks outperform over time. (Note that yield tilts may be offered to or used by those with a motivation other than attempting to increase alpha.)

A plan sponsor opting for a value tilt strategy versus a traditional active manager with a clear value style believes in the outperformance of value stocks but either doesn't want to make a big bet in that direction or wants to minimize dependence on an active manager's stock selection process. The simplest value tilt would establish some price/earnings ratio threshold, overweight all stocks in the index below the threshold and underweight those above it. Risk control would depend on diversification (owning all stocks in the index to some degree) and limits on the underweights and overweights.

With the development in recent years of specific value and growth style benchmarks, style tilts have become less relevant as enhanced indexing strategies. Rather, the tilts have given way to passive style indexing as a way for plan sponsors to implement their style biases.

Portfolio Construction-Based Techniques

Another stock-based strategy that might qualify as an enhanced index would still own most or all of the stocks in the index but would combine them in a way that differs from the construction of the index itself. The simplest example might be equal weighting all stocks in a capitalization weighted index. Risk control again comes primarily from diversification although, depending on the index itself, a modified equal weighting strategy might be required to maintain tracking error below an acceptable threshold. As is the case with style tilts, equal weighted indices have been developed, and pure equal weighted index products have developed alongside, rendering this strategy more of a passive choice than an enhanced index approach.

Quantitative Strategies

A third form of stock-based enhanced indexing would attempt to use quantitative stock selection models in an effort to sort stocks into likely outperformers and underperformers, then weight the stocks accordingly. One or a combination of quantitative screens may be employed, including earnings growth, earnings surprise, earnings momentum, price momentum, foreign exposure, liquidity, etc, in addition to value/growth, yield, and capitalization. Risk controls would include diversification and limits on measured factor exposures in the portfolio, sector and industry weights, and other techniques.

Fundamental Strategies

A fourth stock-based method involves a manager forming opinions about the companies most likely to outperform or underperform based on fundamental research, then overweighting and underweighting stocks accordingly. Fundamental research, as opposed to quantitative techniques, focuses on the strengths of a company's underlying business (market share, proprietary technology, competitive position, trends in demand, quality of earnings, balance sheet strength, etc). Risk controls in addition to diversification might include limits on sector and industry weights, and possibly limits on exposures to quantitative factors as well.

Mathematical Strategies

As distinct from quantitative strategies, mathematical strategies focus on identifying patterns in the price of a stock, such as its trend persistence, volatility, mean reversion, etc., and basing overweighting and underweighting decisions on such mathematical properties. Some or all of the risk control techniques already listed can be applied to reduce tracking error.

Issues with Stock-Based Strategies

The success of any stock-based strategy is predicated on the belief that some form of active stock selection can add value. Proponents of the efficient market hypothesis may reject any such notion and prefer indexing. Yet the debate over the efficiency of the stock market continues. Some believe that small-cap stocks are less efficiently priced than large-cap stocks, raising the odds of success for stock-based enhanced index strategies against smaller capitalization indices. Whatever one's views are regarding market efficiency, in both large cap and small cap domains, the emphasis on risk control in these strategies can potentially improve confidence in success and lower the risk of dramatic underperformance.

Other important issues to consider in evaluating a stock-based strategy include:

- *Turnover/Transactions Costs* Too much of either can potentially swamp the alpha of an otherwise effective process.

- *Exploitation or Obsolescence* A successful model or an identified anomaly tends to attract both invested assets and imitators. Alphas can shrink through time as the model or anomaly becomes increasingly exploited.
- *Model Risk* Quantitative and mathematical models derived from analysis of historical factors, returns, and prices are always subject to the risk that the world can change.

Despite these concerns, a well-specified and managed stock-based strategy can fulfill the potential for alpha that enhanced indexing offers and can improve the consistency of results relative to traditional active management.

Synthetic Strategies

Synthetic enhanced indexing strategies make no attempt to select stocks within the index being tracked. Rather, they effectively obtain ownership of all the stocks in the index by means of futures, options, or stock index swaps. Some synthetic strategies rotate between these vehicles and a stock index itself, seeking to add value but at all times owning the index through the cheapest vehicle. Other synthetic strategies stay fully invested in a particular synthetic vehicle, focusing on managing the underlying cash reserves to generate a higher rate of return.

Within the field of synthetic strategies, there are three primary groups:

- Index arbitrage-related strategies
- Index futures plus enhanced cash management
- Volatility-based strategies

In the first two instances, the role of the futures or other synthetic investment vehicle is limited to completely capturing the price return of the underlying index. As such, the index futures become the primary risk control element in the strategy, completely eliminating any tracking error or risk of underperforming the index due to adverse results in stock selection. In the case of volatility-based strategies, stock index futures, options, or swaps can take on an additional role of altering overall market exposure in response to or anticipation of changes in overall stock market volatility and how that volatility is priced. I now describe the three synthetic categories in more detail.

Index Arbitrage-Related Strategies

Stock index arbitrage was perhaps the first enhanced index strategy employed. With the introduction of S&P 500 index futures in 1984, traders had an opportunity to observe two essentially equivalent assets, a basket containing the 500 stocks on the one hand and the futures on the other, trading simultaneously in different markets. Enhancements in the ability to trade all 500 physical stocks in the index in automated fashion created virtually riskless arbitrage opportunities. Any time the futures were trading at a price significantly different from their fair value (defined more fully below), a simultaneous order to buy/sell futures and sell/buy the 500 stocks generated a profit. During the first several years of S&P futures trading, index funds could employ this strategy and risklessly enhance their return by as much as 100 basis points annually.

Over time, the stock index arbitrage opportunity has become fully exploited. In S&P 500 stocks, the annualized excess returns available from arbitrage have shrunk to perhaps 20 basis points or less, and the ability to earn this excess return has gravitated for the most part to those able to execute the trades most efficiently, the primary dealers on Wall Street. As this trend has occurred, money managers offering index arbitrage as an enhanced index strategy have employed vehicles other than futures (including stock index swaps and index options structured as long call/short put combinations) in search of additional arbitrage opportunities. The trend towards increased pricing efficiency of these synthetic vehicles compared to fair value has continued, limiting the magnitude of alpha available from arbitrage-related strategies.

Index Futures Plus Enhanced Cash Management

An alternative to stock index arbitrage is to own futures (or swaps or long-call/short-put options combinations) as a permanent means of obtaining exposure to the underlying index. The use of futures, for example, as a more or less permanent means of obtaining equity exposure capitalizes on the prevalence of stock index arbitrage as the marginal price setting mechanism in the futures market.

The theory behind the approach is relatively straightforward. Because the price of the S&P futures contract is determined by arbitrage, for which the holding period is short and uncertain, a longer-term investor can expect to buy futures at fair value and invest his or her cash reserves at a higher rate of return which reflects his longer time horizon. So long as the risk exposures in the investment of the cash reserves are appropriately constrained, the potential alpha generated by the strategy can be obtained with relatively low tracking error.

To explain further, stock index futures and stocks are essentially equivalent ways of owning the S&P 500 index. One can pay cash today and own the 500 stocks that make up the S&P index. Alternately, one can own an equivalent value of futures on the S&P 500. A feature of the futures strategy is that an investor only has to post a small margin deposit (generally around 4% of the total contract value) in order to own the futures contract. To avoid leveraging the portfolio, the remaining 96% of the cash not needed for initial margin can be invested in short-duration securities which provide additional reserves to cover potential margin flows stemming from a decline in the value of the S&P futures.

The goal in the enhanced index strategy is to obtain a rate of return on the reserve assets which exceeds the implied interest rate in the S&P futures contract. To understand the concept of an implied interest rate, note that the investor in stocks receives dividends, while the investor in futures forgoes dividends but can earn interest on cash reserves. Thus, the fair value of futures (FV) is (simplistically):

FV = stock index price − dividend return + implied interest rate

As noted above, stock index arbitrage occurs whenever the actual price of futures deviates significantly from fair value, where the implied interest rate in the fair value calculation is the arbitrager's cost of capital. With the bulk of index arbitrage carried out by Wall Street dealers, their cost of capital (for which a reasonable proxy is short-term LIBOR) becomes the implied interest rate in the price of the futures contract. Thus, an investor who buys stock index futures at fair value and can invest reserves at a rate exceeding LIBOR should expect to outperform the underlying stock index with this strategy.

The strategies involved in generating above-LIBOR returns on the reserve assets are numerous, ranging from traditional fixed income techniques to other arbitrage trades and long/short strategies. Traditional fixed income strategies can exploit the term premium emanating from the prevailing upward slope of the short end of the yield curve as a structural advantage available to the investor with a longer time horizon.

The investor may also expect to earn a yield premium by attempting to use less liquid market sectors for that portion of the reserve portfolio which serves as a quasi-permanent layer of reserves after allowing for an appropriate liquidity pool to fund margin flows associated with a stock market decline. Risk control in the case of the more traditional fixed income techniques centers on limiting the duration or interest rate exposure as well as credit quality of the fixed income assets to a level consistent with low tracking error over time. Appropriate diversification of assets across issuers, security types, and fixed income market sectors is also important to risk control.

In the case of cash enhancement involving arbitrage trades and long/short strategies, an investor searches for pricing inefficiencies between, say, convertible bonds and the underlying stock, takes an offsetting position between the two, hedges out the economic risk differences, and awaits the anticipated convergence in price between the convertible and the stock. Long/short portfolios attempt to identify overpriced and underpriced securities in numerous markets and collectively outperform a risk-free rate with low total volatility. In these types of strategies it is important to limit potential tracking error by diversifying across a range of opportunities and employing stop loss limits in the event that the asset prices diverge rather than converge.

The common feature of futures plus enhanced cash strategies is that they offer the opportunity to "transfer" alpha from asset management arenas outside those represented by the indices being enhanced. This allows an investor who sees the assets in the index being enhanced as being efficiently priced to take advantage of perceived pricing inefficiencies or structural opportunities that may exist outside the index. If these enhancement opportunities show low total return volatility and low correlation to the index being enhanced, the alpha can be obtained at low total tracking error, resulting in a high information ratio.

Volatility-Based Strategies

Volatility-based strategies involve "owning" the market index through futures or options in a manner similar to the other synthetic strategies. However, an alpha is sought by making small alterations to the total market exposure based on realized or implied volatility in the underlying index.

These strategies may be based on various observations about stock price volatility that can be exploited in the context of a long holding period. For example, if a manager observes a tendency of stock prices to revert toward the mean after unusually volatile moves in one direction or the other, the manager may reduce market exposure to less than 100% after a volatile market rise, or increase market exposure above 100% after a violent market decline, then normalize the exposure back to 100% after prices exhibit the anticipated mean reversion.

Other volatility-based strategies entail the purchase or writing of put or call options against a fully invested portfolio to exploit perceived mispricing of the market volatility implied in options prices as opposed to actual or forecast market volatility. In both types of strategies, risk control centers on explicit limits on the extent to which market exposure will deviate from 100% at any given time, plus the implementation of stop loss strategies should the market make an unexpected move in the adverse direction. The potential alpha being captured by these strategies stems from a view that the market systematically prices volatility based on a horizon shorter than the investor's actual holding period for stocks. If so, the long-term investor may generally expect to profit by selling options to capture the higher implied volatility over time.

The key difference between volatility-based synthetic strategies and index arbitrage or futures plus enhanced cash is that the potential enhancement in volatility-based strategies comes from movements in the price of the underlying index. The enhancement from index arbitrage and futures plus enhanced cash strategies is independent of the movement of the market index.

Issues with Synthetic Strategies

The success of synthetic strategies is based on the view that individual stocks within the index are efficiently priced, but that pricing inefficiencies and structural factors exist outside the individual stocks. If these inefficiencies can be found and exploited, they can be "tacked on" to a market index such as the S&P 500 through the use of synthetic investment vehicles such as futures, options, or swaps. However, there are practical issues to be addressed in the use of such synthetic vehicles:

> • Futures may not at all times be priced at fair value, and some futures markets close their trading day at different times than the stocks in the underlying index. For example, the S&P 500 stocks close at 4:00 P.M. Eastern time, whereas the futures exchange continues trading until 4:15 P.M. While ultimately any tracking error which results from deviations from fair value

and non-simultaneous pricing tends to wash out over time,[2] the impact can be significant over short measurement periods.

- Futures must be "rolled" from one expiration month to the next in order to maintain market exposure over time. Any deviation between the actual price spread at which the roll occurs and the fair value of the spread will add to or subtract from performance.
- A manager wishing to avoid the risk of rolling futures quarterly at a price above fair value can employ a longer dated stock index swap. While this technique locks in the stock price exposure for a longer time period, swaps are generally less liquid and require management of a credit exposure to an individual swap counterparty. The larger futures exchanges are generally thought to involve counterparty exposure which is *de minimis*.

Despite the issues associated with synthetic vehicles, enhanced index strategies using such vehicles have proven effective in capturing index price exposure, eliminating the underperformance risk of individual stock selection, and opening up opportunities to add alpha to an index with low tracking error.

IMPLEMENTING AN ENHANCED INDEX PROGRAM

The preceding section analyzed the differences between stock-based and synthetic-enhanced indexing strategies. The major difference between the two is the reliance on versus the avoidance of stock selection as the means of enhancement. Plan sponsors and consultants who have employed or analyzed enhanced index strategies have frequently shown some preference for either stock-based approaches or synthetic approaches. Those who believe that the individual stocks are not efficiently priced or who find stock selection processes more readily understandable may prefer the stock-based approaches. Those who see individual stocks as efficiently priced but believe alpha can be found elsewhere are likely to favor the synthetic approaches.

This chapter closes with the view that a strong preference for one type of strategy versus another can be counterproductive. Indeed, there is value in the differences between the two major types of strategies. Because the sources of potential alpha in stock-based and synthetic strategies are so different, intuitively one may expect them to be uncorrelated. If so, then combining the two types of strategies in an enhanced index program will bring diversification benefits and provide superior results compared with using only one strategy or the other.

In what sense might a combination of a stock-based strategy and a synthetic strategy be superior? Consider the impact of the correlation of monthly excess returns between two distinct strategies that have similar alphas. If the

---

[2] The deviations from fair value exhibit a strong pattern of negative serial correlation, which is a statistician's fancy name for "noise."

excess returns are highly positively correlated, little diversification benefit results from a combination of the strategies. Total alpha and tracking error are about the same for the combination as they are for the individual pieces. If excess returns of two strategies were perfectly negatively correlated, then combining the strategies would bring about the ideal result of zero tracking error with the average of the two alphas. The information ratio would go to infinity! Unfortunately, the probability of finding two such strategies with perfect negative correlation of excess returns is quite low. If this result were easily attainable, one could hedge out the equity exposure and leverage the resulting alpha into a money machine.

Excess returns with near zero correlation, however, should be attainable from combining a stock-based and a synthetic manager. A combination of these two managers would preserve their average alphas, but the tracking error of the combination would be lower than that of the individual pieces, resulting in a higher information ratio for the combination. Again, intuition leads one to expect that the excess returns from, say a fundamental analysis stock-based strategy might have little correlation with those of a synthetic strategy whose alpha comes from fixed-income security selection.

Suppose, for example, that two such enhanced index managers generated monthly performance as indicated in the following exhibits. The managers produced consistent alphas and relatively low tracking errors individually, but their monthly excess returns had very low correlation. Exhibits 4 and 5 illustrate how monthly results from the two different enhanced index strategies with low correlation of excess returns interact in a combined portfolio.[3]

First, note from Exhibit 4 how the strategies exhibit a low, stable correlation of their excess returns. Next, in Exhibit 5, note the rolling 5-year alpha of the stock-based strategy, the synthetic strategy, and that of a 50-50 combination of the two. The alpha of the 50-50 combination is approximately the average of the two individual alphas. Now, in Exhibit 6, look at the tracking error of the two strategies separately and in combination. Note that the tracking error of the combination is not the average of the tracking errors of the individual strategies, but is instead significantly lower than that of either individual strategy. This is the benefit of diversification which stems from the low correlation of the alphas. As a result, the observed information ratio of a 50-50 combination of the strategies is higher than that for either strategy individually, as seen in Exhibit 7.

The analysis demonstrates how it might be possible to create powerful combinations of enhanced index strategies by combining different styles. If one starts with two strategies that have economically significant alphas, then combines them in such a way that the level of alpha is preserved but the information ratio increases, then the resulting gain in statistical significance should cause the combination to be preferred over either of the individual strategies.

---

[3] The monthly results presented in these exhibits bear a strong resemblance to actual quarterly results of two well-known enhanced index managers.

Exhibit 4: Rolling 5-Year Correlation of Excess Returns Between Synthetic Strategy and Stock-Based Strategy

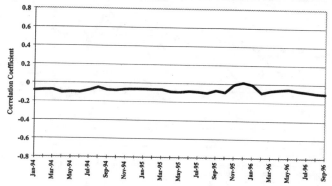

Exhibit 5: Rolling 5-Year Alpha

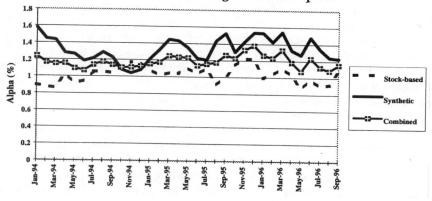

Exhibit 6: Rolling 5-Year Tracking Error

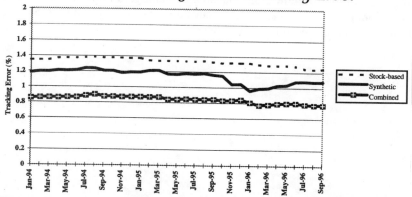

Exhibit 7: Rolling 5-Year Information Ratio

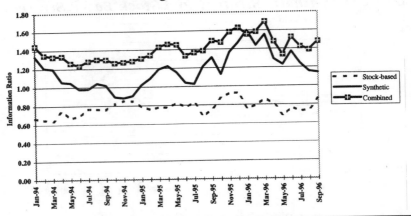

The analysis illustrates a point that even staunch proponents of active management may wish to consider. For years plan sponsors have been combining various active management styles (value, growth, large cap, small cap) effectively searching for the diversification of alphas (and absolute returns to an extent) that style mixes purportedly achieve. Against this backdrop, the same sponsors have had to cope with style drift as managers seek value outside their respective disciplines. As a result, plan sponsors may feel that the types of results illustrated in the exhibits above have proven elusive.

A well specified and executed enhanced index strategy may bring to the table more than just a higher information ratio than the average traditional active manager has achieved. In principle, at least, enhanced indexing should also attain a more stable adherence to a style or methodology as a result of the required emphasis on risk control. If true, it could be that, although enhanced indexing surely involves a degree of active management, as a discipline it may be better suited to obtaining efficient combinations of managers than has been the case with traditional active management. Enhanced indexing, while it may be an oxymoron for some, may be optimal for others.

Chapter 16

The Asian Growth Paradigm as an Investment Tool

Kara Tan Bhala
First Vice President and Senior Portfolio Manager
Merrill Lynch Asset Management

INTRODUCTION

This chapter constructs a model to explain the process of East Asian economic growth and, in particular, to identify and differentiate among the stages of this growth. In turn, the model is used to determine at each stage of growth the industries and companies that offer the best opportunities for a stock market investor.

THE ECONOMIC DEVELOPMENT CURVE

On their journey toward affluence, the Tigers and NIEs have followed, or are following, the same discernible path. It is a "road often traveled" that can be conceptualized in a model I call the *economic development curve*. The curve posits four phases through which a developing economy moves as its *per capita* income increases. These phases are the (1) agricultural stage, (2) low level industrial stage, (3) high level industrial stage, and (4) post industrial stage. Exhibit 1 represents the four stages on an S-curve. The horizontal axis represents time, while the vertical axis shows the *per capita* income. The S-curve starts off gently, steepens sharply, and then levels off again at the final stage. The S shape of the curve implies that growth in East Asia increases most rapidly during the second and third phases, which are the low and high level industrial stages.

The Agricultural Stage
Agriculture is the basic means by which an individual in a pre-industrialized society supports herself. She grows her own food, rears livestock, and sells or barters the surplus for other necessary goods. Humankind became industrialized more

---

The views in this chapter are those of the author alone and do not necessarily reflect the views of Merrill Lynch.

than 200 years ago with the invention of the steam engine in 1769. Before that, and for a large part of human history, every country's economy was mainly based on agricultural production. The level of technology and skills involved with agricultural production are low. Of course, productive efficiency and output in this sector can be enhanced greatly with increased mechanization, (i.e., by increasing capital inputs). Crop yields also can be significantly improved by the use of fertilizers, irrigation, and better hybrids of plants. However, value added in this sector is still relatively low compared to manufacturing. Although the processing of agricultural produce does increase its value added, there is a limit to this increase.

As the economic development curve suggests, most countries begin their economic lives as agricultural producers. A country can remain in the Agricultural Stage for an indefinite period of time. India is a case in point. It is one of the of oldest civilizations in the world — the Indus Valley Civilization was flourishing in 2000 B.C. Yet through all the subsequent centuries, India has remained a largely agricultural society. It is unlikely that India (or other agricultural economies) will achieve a high level of income *per capita* as long as it remains an agriculturally based economy. Conversely, a country can move out of the Agricultural Stage very quickly. In Korea during the early 1960s, agricultural products, which accounted for roughly 43% of total gross domestic product (GDP), were the biggest contributor to Korea's GDP. Twenty years later, agriculture comprised only about 6% of Korea's GDP. Thailand and Malaysia were largely agricultural economies in the 1970s. In China, Indonesia, India, and the Philippines, a large proportion of total output still comes from agriculture.

Exhibit 1: Economic Development Curve

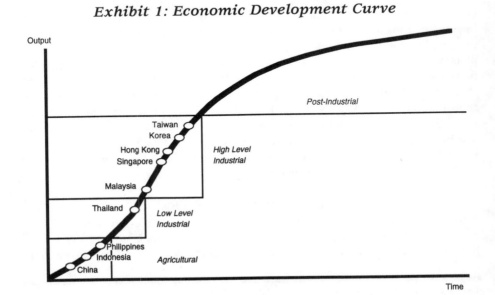

Thus, the paradigmatic East Asian country begins its economic life as an agrarian society. The bulk of the population is involved in agriculture, either directly as farmers or indirectly in the processing of agricultural produce. The level of technology is low, and its use is not widespread. During the agricultural stage, the economic development curve is almost flat as income *per capita* increases at a very slow rate.

The Low Level Industrial Stage

As the paradigmatic economy moves from the agricultural to the low (and high) level industrial stages, the S-curve steepens considerably. This transition implies that income *per capita* increases sharply in the industrial stages. In the low level industrial stage, production is centered on low value added goods such as shoes, textiles, and apparel. Output also increases because of increased use of labor, physical and human capital, and technology, and consequent increasing returns to scale. With respect to labor, employment begins to shift away from the low-wage agricultural sector to the relatively higher-wage manufacturing sector.

This shift is synonymous with a migration of population from rural to urban areas. Government policy encourages this shift. The paradigmatic East Asian government typically makes large investments in infrastructure at the low level industrial stage. With respect to technology, many of the manufacturing plants that are set up take the form of joint ventures with investors from mature industrial economies. Use of endogenous technology is more widespread in the low level industrial stage than in the agricultural stage, but equally important are the improvements in this technology as a result of exposure to exogenous technology. That is, through direct foreign investment and foreign joint venture partners, technology transfer from Japan, the United States, and Western Europe occurs. Not only do the foreigners inject financial capital into the economy, but they also show the locals new and better ways to manufacture.

However, the availability of technology is a necessary but not sufficient condition for the transition from the agricultural to low level industrial stage. The rate of investment must rise. In turn, increased investment "requires a radical shift in the society's effective attitude toward fundamental and applied science; toward the initiation of change in productive technique; toward the taking of risk; and toward the conditions and methods of work."[1] What causes a shift in attitude towards technology and risk-taking?

Nationalism provided the initial impetus in East Asia, especially in the case of the four Tigers. The countries survived the turmoil of World War II and various regional conflicts and insurgencies, and emerged victorious in the battle for independence from colonial rule with a sense of national bravado. A concomitant national desire to escape poverty fostered a desire to develop and adopt new technology and take entrepreneurial risks. Building a nation and challenging the mature industrial countries as political and economic powers meant economic

---

[1] W.W. Rostow, *The Stages of Economic Growth* (Cambridge, England: Cambridge University Press, 1971), p. 20.

growth and development, which meant industrialization. Typically, a single charismatic and visionary post-independence ruler, or an elite group of highly competent technocrats, set the country on its journey out of the agricultural stage. In other words, the change in attitude starts at the top.

Technology, investment, and attitudinal changes still are not the entire story. Top leaders facilitate the transition into the low level industrial stage through prudent policies. Classic examples of such policies in the paradigmatic East Asian country are preferential lending to emerging domestic industries and encouraging foreign investment through tax holidays and export credits. Korea, for instance, successfully used a preferential lending policy to encourage the development of *chaebols*, or conglomerates, which became the engines of economic growth that would propel Korea into the low and high level industrial stages. Loans subsidized by the government were given to certain industries such as shipbuilding, chemicals, and steel. High import tariffs were erected to make local goods more attractive to the Korean consumer. At bottom, the policies reflected a carefully crafted partnership between government and the anointed industrial sectors.

The High Level Industrial Stage

As the paradigmatic East Asian country moves into the high level industrial stage, several dynamic forces are at play. The pace of technological innovations and adoptions necessarily increases. High value added industries, that use sophisticated technology, begin to replace low value added industries. Industries in the electronic sector that produce microchips, semiconductors, and memory chips start to dominate manufacturing exports. A domestic car industry is likely to arise. Foreign capital flows into the local economy accelerate and spawn still more high value added industries.

Not surprisingly, the growth rate of output and income in this third stage increases sharply, just as it did in the second stage. However, there is an important potential constraint on these increases in both the low level and high level industrial stages: an educated, skilled workforce must be readily available. Workers are needed to operate machines and equipment of increasing complexity as new technologies — often English-language based — are engaged in the manufacturing process. Further, managers must be able to cope with new organizational and production systems. The paradigmatic Asian country has had the good fortune and foresight to invest heavily in human capital by educating the majority of children at least through high school. Quite rightly, more money was spent on giving lots of students a basic education than on giving a few elite students a tertiary education. The result was a literate workforce with basic arithmetic skills and even a rudimentary understanding of English.

The Post Industrial Stage

Ever greater demands are made on the skills and education of the workforce as the paradigmatic East Asian country journeys further on the economic development curve. In the fourth stage of development, knowledge and service-based industries tend to predominate. The types of industries in this stage match closely the ones that the Ministry of International Trade and Industry in Japan lists as the most rapidly growing industries in the 21st Century: microelectronics, biotechnology, new materials sciences, telecommunications, civilian aircraft manufacturing, machine tools and robots, and computer hardware and software.[2] The life blood of these industries is human capital.

Drucker writes that, "[b]y the year 2000 there will be no developed country where traditional workers making and moving goods account for more than one sixth or one eighth of the work force."[3] He writes of a knowledge economy where the means of production will not be capital nor labor, but it will be knowledge. In the low level and high level industrial stages, value is created through the optimum allocation of capital and labor to productive activity. In the post industrial stage, value will be created by productivity and innovation. The leading social groups, therefore, will be knowledge workers. In the post industrial stage, knowledge and sophisticated skills are the only source of domestic or global comparative advantage. While the United States has largely reached this stage of the economic development curve, East Asia is still some way from it.

EQUITY INVESTMENT IMPLICATIONS OF THE ECONOMIC DEVELOPMENT CURVE

There are unique features in each stage along the economic development curve, most notably relating to technology and human capital. In turn, these features should entice internationally minded stock market investors from mature industrial economies. After all, each stage boasts a different set of industries that provide attractive investment opportunities.

For example, an investor considering an East Asian country in the agricultural stage surely will prefer to buy shares in companies that produce or process primary goods. These companies are in the dominant industries. The companies will consist of agri-businesses (assuming that agriculture has developed into large businesses rather than remaining in small private holdings), and mining and other businesses associated with the extraction of natural resources. Likewise, the other three stages offer uniquely attractive investment opportunities, which are discussed below in greater detail.

Equity Investing During the Agricultural Stage

Not surprisingly, during the agricultural stage, a country's stock market is in its infancy in terms of development. There is a dearth of companies in which to invest, and their market capitalization tends to be small. In the 1970s, when Malaysia was in the agricultural stage, its economy was based on three main commodities: palm oil, rubber and tin. Palm oil, which is obtained from the fruit of the oil palm tree, is used

---

[2] Lester C. Thurow, *The Future of Capitalism: How Today's Economic Forces Shape Tomorrow's World* (New York, NY: William Morrow and Company Inc., 1996), p. 67.
[3] Peter F. Drucker, *Post-Capitalist Society* (New York, NY: Harper Business, 1994), p. 5.

mainly as a cooking oil. Rubber is used as a raw material in a variety of manufactured goods such as tires (the largest user of natural rubber). Although tin is not an agricultural product but one which is extracted from the ground, it is still a very basic industry with low added value. Malaysia's economy was extremely dependent on world prices of these commodities. Consequently, its business cycles were often reflective of the price cycles of these three major commodities. It was natural that the main source of employment was in those industries which were directly or indirectly related to the production and processing of these commodities. Exhibit 2 shows the significance of commodities as a percentage of Malaysia's exports in 1980. The proportion has fallen as Malaysia has moved into the high level industrial stage.

During the agricultural stage, the most profitable Malaysian equity investments were the shares of tin mining and plantation companies. Plantation companies were large agri-businesses engaged in growing palm oil, rubber, and cocoa. There were (and still are) several such companies listed on the Kuala Lumpur Stock Exchange. In the early 1980s, the major plantation companies had relatively large market capitalizations. Generally, they commanded high price to earnings ratios (PER). Indeed, the average PER for the industry was about 45. In part, the high PER was backed by large assets in the form of cultivated land. More importantly, the high PERs resulted from strong investor demand for the shares. In turn, this demand reflected the dearth of companies in the stock market that represented the agricultural sector. Investors were hungry for stocks that captured the gist of the agricultural stage.

To be sure, there were several tin mining companies in Malaysia engaged in the extraction of tin and other mineral ores. But, only a few such companies were listed on the stock exchange. Predictably, these companies were popular among investors. Their price earnings ratios tended to be lower than those of plantation company stocks, but higher than the average for the market.

Plantation and mining companies, together with their related industries, played an important role in the Malaysian economy during the agricultural stage and the subsequent transition to the low level industrial stage. These companies provided employment, and wages paid to workers flowed into the economy through consumption expenditure on low value added merchandise. Indeed, during the transition from an agricultural to an industrial economy, a country ought not to understate the important contribution of agriculture to the success of its modernization program. Stalin's Soviet Union and Mao's China did so, and the disastrous results are well known.

Exhibit 2: Malaysia's Products as a Percentage of Total Gross Exports (by value)

Commodity	1980 (%)	1996 (%)
Palm Oil	9.2	5.5
Rubber	16.3	2.2
Tin	9.2	0.3
Manufacturing	22.3	79.6

Source: ING Barings Securities

Agriculture plays three important roles in the transitional process from an agricultural to an industrial economy.[4] First, and most obviously, the agricultural sector must provide more food. There must be increased supplies of food from the rural area to feed expanding urban populations. Self-sufficiency in food keeps a country's import bill low, thus reducing pressure on the current account.

Second, the agricultural sector will be the main source of demand and revenue for the manufactured goods produced by the new industries. This is particularly true when a country is in the initial transition from the agricultural to low level industrial stage. If the majority of the population is still engaged in agricultural production, then this majority will be the main consumer base when a country first industrializes.

Third, during the transitional period agriculture must provide a substantial part of its surplus income to the industrial sector. There must be a recycling of savings from the agricultural sector into investments in the manufacturing sector. Most of the savings will be in bank deposits, which ought to find their way into loans to entrepreneurs setting up factories and businesses. Some of the savings may go into the stock market, if there is one, which will help finance the expansion of existing businesses. In other words, there must be a financial mechanism by which savings are translated into investments into the necessary sectors.

The Philippines is a salient example of an East Asian country that neglected its agricultural sector at great cost to overall economic development. Currently, the Philippines' economy is in transition from the agricultural to low level industrial stage. During the early 1990s, however, the government concentrated its efforts on increasing manufacturing investment and encouraging industrial growth. The country's policy makers learned the hard way about the importance of agriculture to its economy: the first role of this sector, providing food, was not satisfied. A shortage of rice at the end of 1995 forced the government to import large quantities of the grain in order to meet increasing demand. Unfortunately, the imports did not flow early enough to prevent a significant increase in inflation rates caused by rising food prices. Consequently, interest rates rose and remained high for a few calendar quarters. Only recently has the Philippines government identified agriculture as a key component in its development plans and started implementing policies to support the sector.

The importance of the agricultural sector as a source of demand and revenue for the industrial sector is illustrated by the fortunes of the largest brewery in the Philippines, San Miguel Corporation. The company's famous San Miguel beer has a 90% share of the Philippines beer market. But, the company's earnings are heavily dependent on the purchasing power of the rural population. Due to poor harvests, bad weather and low yields, 1995 was a relatively unproductive one for farmers. The drop in farm income had a negative impact on San Miguel's 1995 revenues. Net profits tumbled 28% in 1995 compared to the previous year. Clearly, the agricultural sector can have a large impact on the profits of manufacturing companies.

---

[4] Rostow, *The Stages of Economic Growth*, pp. 22-24.

Equity Investing During the Low Level Industrial Stage

During the low level industrial stage, the first industries likely to emerge are tex-tiles, shoes, garments, toys, simple electrical appliances, plastic products, and other goods which do not require a high level of sophisticated technology to pro-duce. These industries are relatively low on the value added scale, but are the ini-tial building blocks towards industrialization. The level of technology employed in the manufacture of the products is not high, and the manufacturing process contains a relatively large proportion of labor input. Companies in these indus-tries normally show strong earnings growth.

For example, in Thailand the shares of textile and shoe companies expe-rienced strong price appreciation during the initial stages of the country's indus-trialization. Companies such as Union Footwear and Bangkok Rubber were subcontractors for large sports shoes manufacturers like Nike and Reebok. Union Footwear and Bangkok Rubber produce shoes for Nike's and Reebok's exploding export markets. The Thai companies could produce shoes inexpensively because of low labor and plant costs. In addition, attractive tax incentives existed. During some periods, net profit margins of the Thai subcontractors were as high as 30%.

Similarly, when Hong Kong entered the low level industrial stage, the shares of textile companies such as Winsor Holdings and Novel Limited were in demand, due to their strong profit growth. As Hong Kong's economy matured and moved into the high level industrial stage, the profit growth of these companies became stagnant. As their own costs of production increased, Hong Kong textile manufacturers experienced competition from cheaper Asian producers. In an effort to boost its earnings, Winsor Holdings tried to move into property develop-ment. The property development division did turn out to be profitable. Unfortu-nately, the share price of the company continued to languish because investors were not impressed by the profits produced by the textile division.

The Philippines has just entered the low level industrial stage. Filipino companies with the highest earnings growth are those associated with the devel-opment of the country's infrastructure and the manufacture of consumer non-durables. An example of the latter is San Miguel Corporation, the Philippines largest beer maker. The company has seen impressive earnings growth until recently, for the reasons described above. Yet it is a good company to have at this stage of development of the Philippines because of a large, untapped, domestic market. Even though the San Miguel's earnings may be affected by the fortunes of the agricultural sector, the company will benefit as long as the country moves up the economic development curve. As the population becomes more affluent, per capita consumption of beer is very likely to increase.

Banks earnings also have been strong. These results come as no surprise. Indeed banks tend to be good investments during the low level and the high level industrial stages. During these two stages, banks benefit from the high level of loan demand from both corporates and individuals. Strong investments into manu-facturing normally translate into more bank loans to that sector. Individuals start to take out more mortgage loans as their incomes increase, because housing is now more affordable. As incomes grow, the population either buys new houses or trades up to better ones. Banks' profits are helped by fat margins. During the two industrial stages, banks tend to have little competition from foreign banks. The banks in many East Asian countries also tend to form oligopolies, which have some control over deposit and lending rates. However, banks are also most vulnerable in times of deep recession and financial distress. When there are widespread bankruptcies among its debtors, banks will normally experience rapidly rising non-performing loans. In addition, there is usually poor regulation and supervision of banks in some Asian countries, which is typical for emerging markets.

In the low level industrial stage, a country needs to develop its infrastructure, which is inadequate to support a modern industrial or post-industrial society. Building roads, railroads, port and container facilities, airports, and telecommunication links is usually initiated by the government. Financing these projects occurs through a mixture of private and public funds. For instance, road construction projects often are awarded to private companies, which are then given the right to collect tolls for a specified period of time.

Benpres Holdings typifies a company deeply involved with infrastructural development in the Philippines. It is a large conglomerate and has been awarded the Manila-Subic-Clark Tollway. This Tollway is a major road that will improve access to both Clark and Subic Bay. These two formerly renowned U.S. military bases have been converted to industrial parks. In other areas of the Philippines, Benpres is constructing two 440MW gas-fired power plants, developing a water distribution project, and installing over 300,000 phone lines. Thus, during the low level industrial stage of Philippine development, companies like Benpres are well situated to benefit from the high demand for new infrastructure.

With respect to infrastructural development, East Asian governments have been very conscious of the importance of social overhead capital. Resources, both private and public, have been channeled into infrastructural development. Obviously, a country's distribution system is of primary importance for the transport of raw materials and the delivery of finished goods. Building a network of roads, railways, and ports is therefore essential for industrialization to continue apace. Realizing the importance of this sector, countries such as China have opened up the development of their roads to private enterprises and joint ventures. Currently, Hong Kong companies such as New World Development and Cheung Kong Holdings are engaged in building roads in the major cities of China. Other companies have been given the right to develop ports in Shanghai. In Malaysia, the first highway which links the northern part of the country to the southern region was completed last year. The government awarded the project to a listed company, United Engineers Malaysia. The company is entitled to collect tolls on this highway for the next 20 years.

It is equally obvious that communication networks are necessary for an economy to function efficiently. Setting up a broad, encompassing telephone system, both land based and mobile, has been one of the top priorities of Asian governments. The Philippines government has put in place a sensible telecommunications plan to extend the availability of telephones in a country consisting of thousands of islands, at little cost to the central government. According to the plan, the country is divided into several regions. Each region's mobile phone service rights is awarded to a different vendor, or private enterprise. In return for the revenues from mobile services, the vendor must ensure that it builds a certain number of land lines in the region. In this way, each region of the country is assured of both mobile and land based telephone systems. The majority of the vendors are companies which are listed on the Manila stock exchange. They have been able to use retained earnings or equity issues to fund their expansion in telecommunications. Many of these telecommunication companies have also tied up with American and European partners in order to have access to their expertise and funds. For example, Benpres Holdings of the Philippines has Nynex as its partner in the development of a land based telephone system in Northern Manila.

Power generation is still another aspect of infrastructure vitally important in the journey up the economic development curve. As with the telecommunications and transportation sectors, electrical generation has been developed with a great deal of involvement by private enterprise. In Malaysia, Thailand, the Philippines, and China, many power stations are operated by private companies, which then sell the electricity to the national or regional grids. These companies are usually paid a certain rate of return by the main power distributor.

In general, therefore, Asian governments have been instrumental in the development of infrastructure in their countries. Some projects are funded by the government, with the help of international agencies such as the World Bank. More often, the projects are initiated by the government but are funded by the private sector.

Equity Investing During the High Level Industrial Stage

Currently, Malaysia has just entered the low to high level stage. In 1985-86, Malaysia suffered from a severe recession caused by a sharp decline in the prices of the three main export commodities: rubber, palm oil, and tin. The government correctly decided the country could no longer be held hostage by world commodity prices. The necessary ingredients to graduate from the agricultural stage and move into the low and high level industrial stages already existed. The missing piece was provided by the government: the right policy mix for the take-off. The government instituted very favorable tax policies for foreign investors, especially those engaged in export industries. For example, every company that manufactured goods for export was given a two year tax holiday. Onerous foreign ownership rules were relaxed, and foreigners were allowed to own more than 49% of a company. The government began a large infrastructural program of building roads, ports, and upgrading telecommunications.

The foreigners responded favorably, setting up manufacturing plants in the footwear, textiles, and apparel industries, and bringing in physical, human, and financial capital and new technology. By 1989, new industries involved in the manufacture of simple electrical appliances had emerged. Malaysia became the offshore manufacturing base for many Japanese companies. The appreciating yen made it necessary for companies such as Sony and Mitsubishi to find a cheaper place of production. It was, therefore, customary to find cassette players, stereos, and televisions bearing a Sony brand name but a "Made in Malaysia" country of origin label.

The Malaysian economy moved further up the industrialization curve as new manufacturing plants started producing chips, printed circuit boards, and semiconductors. Unemployment fell from 10% in 1986 to less than 5% in 1989. Population continued to migrate from rural areas to urban centers. Malaysia had moved rapidly through the low level industrial stage and entered the high level industrial stage.

In the new stage, company listings on the Kuala Lumpur Stock Exchange expanded in breadth and depth. That is, companies in new industries were listed, and companies already listed expanded into new businesses. No longer were the plantation companies the main attractions. Instead, companies involved in manufacturing and exports were much more profitable and had lower price earnings ratios. Their earnings growth was particularly striking because it started from low bases of comparison. Thus, investors flocked to stocks of companies producing air-conditioners, industrial gases, cars, and motorcycles. To be sure, Malaysia is still the world's biggest producer of palm oil. But, it is now also the second largest producer of air-conditioners. The dominant Malaysian air-conditioner manufacturer, OYL Industries, has become so successful that it has purchased an American air-conditioner maker called AAF McQuary. Through this acquisition, OYL hopes to improve its technology while extending its sales reach to the other Asian countries.

While Malaysia is still in the early phase of the high level industrial stage, Singapore, Taiwan, and Korea are well into the high level industrial stage. Korea and Taiwan have developed widely recognized name brands like Samsung and Acer and are trying to become globally competitive players. Many Korean and Taiwanese companies have set up offshore manufacturing facilities for the same reasons the Japanese moved offshore in the 1980s: to take advantage of cheaper manufacturing costs and to have a large presence in new markets. Independent research and development is carried out in these countries with the aim of developing innovations in design and technology. The products — computers, electronics, and machine tools — reflect sophisticated designs and technology.

For example, Samsung Electronics, a Korean chip manufacturer, is the largest producer of Dynamic Random Access Memory (DRAM) chips in the world. The company is in the forefront of research in this field and is expected to announce the production of a new larger memory chip. In the next few years, the East Asian countries in the High Level Industrial Stage must become highly competitive by developing proprietary new products and technology. In this age of rapid technological change and innovation, they cannot afford to sit still. There is enormous global pressure to increase productivity and continue moving up the technology ladder. Accordingly, Singapore, Taiwan, and Korea have no choice but to move from manufacturing to knowledge-based industries.

The Challenge of Getting into the Post Industrial Stage

In the post industrial stage of the economic development curve, the economic development model is one where the economy is dominated by service and knowledge industries. None of the East Asian economies is in this stage. The classic examples of service- and knowledge-based industries come from the financial sector: commercial banking, securities broking and underwriting, and portfolio management and investment. However, the classic examples are not limited to finance. The computer software industry, the entertainment industry (including movie and television production and distribution), and marketing and advertising are important knowledge and service industries.

To date, American firms dominate in all of these industries. There are precious few East Asian companies poised to challenge their position and, therefore, precious few opportunities for equity investments in these industries. Nevertheless, to remain globally competitive, East Asian countries eventually must move into service- and knowledge-based industries. Singapore, Taiwan, and Korea cannot hope to compete in the high level industrial stage with cheaper cost countries like Malaysia. Moreover, Singaporean, Taiwanese, and Korean youths aspire to high-wage, white collar professions, not the conventional "Third World" jobs their grandparents and parents held. As Lester Thurow writes, "[s]uccess or failure depends upon whether a country is making a successful transition to the man-made brainpower industries of the future..."[5]

Why is no East Asian country in the post industrial stage? One reason concerns factors of production. During the low and high level industrial stages, natural resources, labor and capital are important factors of comparative advantage for an industry. However, knowledge and skills stand as the source of comparative advantage at the top of the economic development curve. A country must have a deep pool of knowledge workers upon which its companies can draw. In other words, human capital becomes the key factor of production in the post industrial stage.

A second reason is an amalgam of political and educational culture. Absent significant immigration (which appears unlikely) it may take years of research and discovery to create a pool of knowledge workers. The pool is not created in a climate of rigidity, but rather in a free, open society. There must be well-funded universities and think tanks engaged not just in pure research, but also in the development of young minds that think critically about problems. The American political and educational experience is one of creativity, debate, and difference. East Asians are embarrassingly behind in these respects. Their schools foster rote learning, consensus, and conformity, which reflect either the (conveniently erroneous) Confucian values of many of their leaders, or the fear of these leaders of losing power. Consequently, the leaders themselves inhibit the creation of a pool of knowledge workers and the transition to the post industrial stage.

---

[5] Thurow, *The Future of Capitalism: How Today's Economic Forces Shape Tomorrow's World*, p.72.

Indeed, ironically a rigid political and educational culture in East Asia may exacerbate the gap between the U.S. and other mature economies, on the one hand, and the East Asian economies, on the other hand. Several East Asian countries, such as Taiwan and Korea, produce doctoral students, but the majority are educated in the United States and, if at all possible, choose to remain in the United States. In other words, East Asia's brain drain is America's brain gain. The result is that it will take even longer to create the necessary knowledge pool in East Asia.

THE 1997-1998 ASIAN FINANCIAL CRISIS AND ITS IMPLICATIONS FOR THE GROWTH MODEL

Currency Pegs

The 1997-1998 Asian financial crisis began with the devaluation of the Thai baht. That event had a domino effect on the rest of the Asian countries in that one by one, each nation saw its currency depreciating sharply over the course of a few months. Currency pegs were responsible for many of the strains and distortions evident in the economies of most Asian countries prior to the devaluations.

Declining Price Competitiveness

The weakness of the U.S. dollar for most of the 1980s and early 1990s has been extremely advantageous to the East Asian countries. These countries had linked their currencies to the dollar. The falling dollar allowed their exports to remain competitively priced in Japan and Europe, while the dollar link ensured that the price of exports to the United States would remain stable. This currency policy meant that East Asian central banks effectively surrendered monetary policy to the U.S. Federal Reserve Board, because interest rates had to be closely linked to maintain the currency peg. However, the effects of currency pegging began to turn against some East Asian countries.

Low interest rates associated with Fed policy during the past decade have resulted in high inflows of portfolio and direct investments in East Asia. Global liquidity was high and investors were seeking returns better than the returns from U.S. bonds. The liquidity flows have meant a high rate of growth of the money supply in several East Asian countries, which together with strong economic growth, fueled inflation. As it is difficult to raise rates without jeopardizing the currency peg, East Asian governments found it difficult to dampen inflationary pressures. Besides, raising interest rates while still keeping a peg actually adds to inflation because it results in large inflows of foreign money seeking higher returns. Over the past decade, high inflation rates have made Asian exports more expensive and therefore less competitive.

Large Current Account Deficits

Cheap capital through U.S. dollar borrowing and funds from foreign direct investors resulted in high rates of investments. This in turn led to large imports of capital goods, which caused some countries' current account deficits to increase to roughly 5% to 7% of GDP. As external demand faltered, their current account balance worsened further because the level of exports declined. A deteriorating current account balance put downward pressure on the currencies, therefore straining the link to the dollar. To make matters worse, when domestic demand declined, there was little scope for lowering interest rates to stimulate demand because lower rates would lead to an outflow of funds which had initially sought high rates of return. Instead of freeing liquidity, lowering rates would actually have led to a tightening of liquidity in the economy.

Large Debt Accumulation

Thailand's experience with a pegged baht illustrates this problems. During the past few years, Thai companies have been borrowing in U.S. dollars at U.S. rates, which are considerably lower than Thai rates. Foreigners have deposited large sums of money in the Thai banking system in order to take advantage of higher returns. The currency peg encourages this behavior because there is no perceived currency risk. The result was an accumulation of foreign debt, largely U.S. dollar denominated, by private Thai corporations in order to take advantage of the lower U.S. interest rates.

Misallocation of Resources

The cheap cost of capital led to a misallocation of resources. Much of the capital went into unproductive uses such as property development. This misallocation resulted from corporations basing their cost of capital on U.S. interest rates. Projects which were undertaken did not require a rate of return which was higher than the local cost of borrowing. Hence, a mispricing of the cost of capital resulted in a mistaken satisfaction with low rates of return.

These distortions to the economy outweigh the previous benefits of linking East Asian currencies to the U.S. dollar. The devaluation of South East Asian currencies which have taken place in the late summer of 1997 may be the impetus for governments to move to a more freely floating currency regime. The markets have sent the message to policy planners that distortions in the economy caused by currency pegs can no longer be tolerated. In the short term, there will be a period of painful readjustment as businesses and governments deal with the effects of devaluation. However, in the longer term, if the right policies such as flexible exchange rates, deregulation of the economy and financial reforms are pursued, then the devaluations may prove to be good for the economies of South East Asia.

The recommendation to move to a more flexible exchange rate policy is immediately relevant to Thailand and Malaysia, which have reached the stage in their economic development curve where they must move to higher value added industries. The loss of price competitiveness through currency appreciation must be countered by an increase in productivity. It is no longer sufficient to compete in the global market on price alone. Indeed, a few Asian countries, notably Singapore, have shed the policy of currency pegging. Singapore has allowed its currency to float more or less freely. This policy led to the appreciation of the Singapore dollar to the U.S. dollar over the past several years. However, through productivity increases, moving to higher value added industries and technological advancement, the country has been able to maintain its export competitiveness.

To be sure, Hong Kong is a special case. It has suffered the same problems as Thailand with its currency peg. However, the political situation involving Hong Kong's change in sovereignty adds a different dimension to resolving currency problems. For the foreseeable future, currency stability is more important to Hong Kong's economic vitality than correcting distortions associated with a pegged currency. It would, therefore, be wise to maintain the peg, at least until sustained political stability under Chinese rule is assured.

Implication of the Asian Financial Crisis for the Growth Model

Some of the distortions in the economies of East Asian countries are beginning to disappear as a consequence of the currency devaluations. The issue of declining competitiveness has been addressed by cheaper currencies in the region, which will make their exports more price competitive. However, this forced price competitiveness offers only temporary relief. In order to achieve global competitiveness, East Asian companies will have to be more productive, provide higher returns on capital than they have done so in the past, and move up the value added ladder. In the meantime, each country will be able to sell more of the goods which it predominantly produces at its particular stage of growth. Thailand (low level industrial stage) will sell its textiles, simple electrical appliances and plastic products; Malaysia will sell its electronic components; Korea its memory chips; and, Taiwan its computer peripherals. The best managed companies in these industries with the strongest balance sheets will survive the crisis. If they take advantage of the opportunities they may even enhance their positions through capturing more market share through organic growth and acquisitions.

Current account deficits also have been shrinking as capital investments and domestic demand have fallen steeply. However, the clearing of the large debt build-up will take some time as companies renegotiate and restructure their debt. Companies which are unable to do so will have to declare bankruptcy. Banks which have loans outstanding to many failing companies will most likely have to recapitalize. The problem of misallocation of resources is likely to be resolved over a period of time as companies adjust to the new cost of capital, not one based on U.S. interest rates but instead, more realistically, on domestic rates.

The new developments in Asia do not invalidate the conceptual model of growth for the region set forth in this chapter. Rather, these developments should be viewed as part of the process of the long-term economic development of Asian countries. Indeed, financial crises and instability sometimes punctuate rapid economic growth in developing countries. The structural changes that must take place, such as liberalization of the financial and trading systems, may temporarily slow or even stall a country's move up the economic development curve. But, if the necessary policy changes are made, then the country, with a strengthened financial system, should continue its upward ascent along the curve. The key question for Asia is whether governments will make the necessary policy changes with all deliberate speed.

THE ROADS AHEAD

Ironically, just as East Asia's economic rise is recognized as miraculous some commentators are now questioning East Asia's future. One economist suggests that East Asia's growth in the past few decades has been fueled by human and physical capital inputs rather than productivity growth.[6] This suggestion is responsible insofar as these countries started from an agricultural base and, therefore, required large inputs of human and financial capital to achieve industrialization. According to the economic development curve, it would have been extremely difficult for East Asian countries to move into the first stage of industrialization without capital inputs. At later stages of development, after factories are set up and operating, productivity growth is far more important than capital inputs. When countries have moved higher up the value added ladder, they must increase the marginal returns from capital.

Today many East Asian countries stand at a cross-road. Traveling down one road means continuing to produce low value added products, trying to retain price competitiveness by suppressing the local currency, and maintaining high tariff and non-tariff barriers to protect local industries. This road ends in stagnation. The other road entails greater competitiveness through innovation, higher productivity, continual upgrading of technology, and an education policy focussed on producing creative graduates. This road may cause short-term dislocation in some economic sectors. However, this road leads to long-term economic viability and global competitiveness. The second, more difficult, road must be taken if the Asian miracle is to continue.

---

[6] Paul Krugman, "The Myth of Asia's Miracle," *Foreign Affairs* (November/December 1994), pp. 62-78.

Chapter 17

Implementing Investment Strategies: The Art and Science of Investing

Wayne H. Wagner
President
Plexus Group

Mark Edwards
Director
Plexus Group

INTRODUCTION: THE IMPORTANCE OF THE IMPLEMENTATION PROCESS

"Success in investment management comes from picking good stocks. The rest is just plumbing." This quote from a well regarded money manager highlights one of the key reasons that active managers have failed to keep up with index funds over the past 10 years. Picking stocks is the Holy Grail, and the bulk of a manager's efforts and expenses goes to enhance their forecasting ability. To their credit, Plexus research suggests that active managers do pick stocks that outperform their respective market benchmarks over both a 6 week and a 52 week basis.[1] But, as the quote suggests, managers can become so attached to seeking winners that they become desensitized to the overall goal of maximizing returns.

Investment management can be viewed as a two part process: the information process and the implementation process. The *information process* is the core of stock selection, and is discussed at length throughout this book. The focus in this chapter is the implementation process, or executing investment ideas while preserving the underlying value. The combination of these actions — seeking valuable ideas and implementing them — is what we call the *investing* process. (See Exhibit 1.)

---

[1] W. Wagner, "Picking Good Stocks: Necessary, But Sufficient?" *Plexus Group Commentary #43* (January 1995) and "Decision Timeliness & Duration," *Plexus Group Commentary #46* (November 1995).

Exhibit 1: The Investing Process

Information Value	*less*	Implementation Cost	*equals*	Captured Value

The Vanguard S&P 500 fund has outperformed 80% of the active managers over the past decade.[2] But if managers are able to pick winning stocks, why are they losing? The bottom line is that there is more to the investing process than good stock selection. On average, the cost of getting ideas into portfolios exceeds the value of the research. Ironically, this does not have to be true. The problem is that implementation or trading costs have been understated and underestimated, leading to sub-par performance despite better than average ideas.

Industrial America has gone through a difficult process of self-examination that has led to dramatic improvements in productivity. The key to this process is TQM (Total Quality Management). The investment industry is now confronting the same issue. Managers need to look beyond the selection process to the implementation process — from invest*ment* to invest*ing*.

We will first discuss trading, the core of the implementation process. We will then look beyond trading to see how trading strategies fit within the manager's stock selection process.

WHY TRADING IS NOT LIKE PORTFOLIO MANAGEMENT

Equity trading is the action that results from portfolio management decisions. The portfolio manager's process is analytic and hypothetical; trading is in-the-trenches reality.

To the naive, trading can seem like a vending machine — an order to buy goes in, and a trade comes out. But vending machines purchases are expensive and inefficient compared to buying in bulk. To shift the analogy from the retail investor to the large institution, imagine trying to buy 10,000 cases of soda rather than one can. Even if the vending machine could supply that many sodas, the cost would be many times greater than buying wholesale. Similarly, trading strategies that work for the retail investor are inadequate to the task confronting institutional traders. Studies show that roughly two-thirds of institutional managers' orders are more than 50% of an average day's volume.[3] Executing these orders in a single trade can quickly overtax the market's liquidity. For these orders, a manufacturing process is a better analogy than a vending machine. Manufacturing liquidity means finding shares at a price that completes the trade at a price that preserves the value of the idea.

---

[2] Lipper Analytical Services. Ten-year comparison as of December 31, 1996. Comparisons include only managers with 10-year histories.

[3] M. Edwards and W. Wagner, "Best Execution," *Financial Analysts Journal* (January-February 1993).

Trading is fundamentally different from portfolio management in that selecting stocks does not require the cooperation of anyone else. The trader, however, needs somebody to trade with, and thus we move from a deductive exercise to a negotiation process. In a negotiation, one gives something in order to get something. In securities trading, one can trade for either liquidity or for information. Thus a trader is constantly concerned that value is received for value given. This is why large trades occur in successive pieces, each piece revealing only what is necessary to complete that step of the negotiation.

Trading can be thought of as the ongoing choice between trading now for a known price versus later for an unknown, and hopefully better, price. Effective trading requires a multi-step process:

1. Determine the motivation of the trade.
2. Assess market conditions and the liquidity of the stock.
3. Establish the initial trading strategy to assess supply and demand.
4. Probe for liquidity and information.
5. Adapt the strategy to changing market conditions.
6. Appraise the effectiveness when the trading is complete.

Trade Motivation

Jack Treynor[4] has identified three key trading motives: value, news/information, and cash flow. *Value* is represented by the familiar Graham and Dodd process, while information trading reflects the use of new information and changing expectations. *Cash flow* motivations arise from a desire to increase or decrease equity exposure, independent or even ignorant of the prospects for the stocks.

Information value is subject to rapid erosion, and information-based traders are always under pressure to complete trades before the information spreads across the market. This makes information traders time sensitive: their goal is to get the trades done quickly, even if this means paying up for liquidity.

In contrast, *value* trades are seldom timely. Value traders can use time to their advantage, stretching out the timeframe in an attempt to reduce the cost of trading. Value traders are more price sensitive than time sensitive.

Index traders and liquidity traders do not form opinions about the value of individual stocks. However, their buying and selling can exaggerate supply/demand imbalances.

Managers are quite consistent in their approach to investing. Their trade orders will reflect one of these styles for most — but not all — of their trading. The trader's job is to recognize which motivation applies to each trade, and to select a trading strategy that reflects the manager's here-and-now motivation.

---

[4] J. Treynor, "What Does it Take to Win the Trading Game?" *Financial Analysts Journal* (January-February 1981).

Assessing Market Conditions

The next step is to assess current market conditions to determine the expected cost of liquidity for the required size. An actively traded stock is like a supermarket with high turnover and low margins. But not all stocks trade in volume. The greater the desired percentage of the current trading volume, the greater the premium required to create liquidity. The liquidity cost must be added/subtracted from the decision price to determine the expected trading price.

In addition to how much stock typically trades, the trader also needs to consider how frequently the stock trades. Actively traded stocks require little broker intermediation, so there is little spread between the *bid* (the highest advertised buy price) and the *offer* (the lowest advertised selling price). As the frequency of trading drops, the broker is required to act as a middleman, carrying long and short inventories until buyers and sellers can be found. Holding stock creates a risk for the broker, resulting in higher spreads.

Diversity of opinion is another important characteristic of market condition. If everyone wants to sell and no one wants to buy, trading will be impossible. If buyers are now dominating the trading, buying will be difficult and costly, while selling will be easy and inexpensive. Trading tactics will be quite different depending on whether one is *supplying* or *demanding* liquidity.

The trader's first resource in assessing market conditions is the public information sources: ticker tape prints of recent trades and the display of bids and offers, either on the exchange or on the various proprietary trading and information networks.

This is not, however, the full story. All that can be seen here is that which someone else has chosen to reveal. Institutional traders frequently rely on block dealers to locate trading interest that has been quietly expressed but not publicly revealed.

Establish Initial Trading Strategy

At this point the buyside trader has two basic options: he can choose to buy stock directly from a broker (a principal trade), or slowly accumulate stock during the normal flow of the day (a working trade). Each approach carries some danger:

- The payment for immediate liquidity may exceed the value of the information motivating the trade.
- The patient trader risks share prices moving against him before the order is filled.

The art of trading is the balancing of these two risks, performed in the context of the manager's instructions and information.

Probing for Liquidity and Information

Trades occur only when a willing buyer meets a willing seller at a price acceptable to both. The seller may be a broker providing liquidity for a fee, or it may be a natural seller acting as though he believes the *opposite* of what the manager believes. Even though this negotiation may be conducted in private, the market is filled with prying eyes looking for a trading edge. Accumulating stock is a difficult activity to keep hidden in a closely watched market, and knowledge of unfilled trading interest is a most valuable commodity on Wall Street. Other traders try continuously to assess the potential size of the trade and the sagacity of the buyer, and will attempt to buy first and piggyback on likely future behavior. Seeking liquidity, therefore, creates additional risk — and potential cost.

Coaxing out a reluctant seller requires an elaborate give-and-take process to protect the value of the idea. Cagey traders will attempt to get as much information as possible while revealing as little as possible: What does she know that I don't? How big is her trading need? How much is she willing to pay? Everyone wants to be the last person to trade with a big contraparty — certainly not the first.

The buyer may start with *probing* trades to assess available liquidity and possible reactions. If liquidity is available, the buyer has time on his side. But probing may quickly give away the buyer's identity, so the buyer uses a broker to sniff out untapped sources of stock.

We learned in Economics 101 that price changes will attract more supply or demand. In the stock market, however, rising prices will not necessarily induce potential sellers to trade. Rather, rising prices may indicate previously unknown information that leads to a revised opinion, creating hoarding conditions that reduce the desire to sell.

Thus, while it may make sense to slowly trade a liquid stock motivated by a value decision, the same trade in an illiquid stock may trigger competition once other traders detect a short-term buying trend. In this case, the trader may be better served by using broker liquidity and letting the broker assume the time risk.

Adapting to Market Conditions

Every piece of information the trader receives has the potential to create a need for a mid-course correction in the trading strategy. When the assumptions underlying the initial strategy prove incorrect, the strategy must be changed — instantly. This implies that the trader needs a variety of skills to trade different stocks in different conditions — and the ability to switch quickly from one technique to another.

Assess Effectiveness

A critical component of TQM is an on-going process review. In the case of trading, what works when a firm is small may not work as the firm grows. Liquidity demands change, as does the tradable universe of stocks. In addition, the markets themselves are in constant state of change.

Every completed trade provides feedback to the trader, who in turn must constantly adapt to changing demands and changing market conditions. In a broader context, however, we can think of each trade as a manifestation of an ongoing process that involves the manager as well as the trader. The process itself is thus amenable to review and change in a wider context.

A FRAMEWORK FOR MEASURING IMPLEMENTATION

This section describes the process that Plexus clients use to assess the efficacy of their processes. By breaking down each step into definable and repeatable actions, the trader can see where actions add or lose value.

Trading costs are like an iceberg: the real danger comes from the portion that cannot be seen. Commissions are easily observed but represent only the tip of the iceberg. The remaining costs are far more significant, but because they cannot be easily observed, they have been too often ignored. Ignoring the real but hidden costs can compromise performance.

Andre Perold[5] developed a method to assess trading effectiveness in the context of the decisions being implemented. Simply stated, this *implementation shortfall*[6] approach compares the *information return* of the decision on a no-cost basis to the *realized return* on a fully-costed basis. For uncomplicated trades, this amounts to comparing the price at the time of the decision (strike price) with the average execution price. This puts the trading in context: what is the trader paying for liquidity, and does that payment square with the potential gain from executing the trade?

Further elaboration of the implementation shortfall approach allows a manager to disaggregate trading costs into components of commission, intraday impact, interday delay costs, and opportunity costs from abandoned trades. Furthermore, the computations can be made on subsets of the trading database to pinpoint whether problems are more prevalent in large trades, small cap trades, NASDAQ trades, etc.

Consider the following example:

What the ticker tape reveals:

• 30,000 NME bought @ $20.75.

What really happened:

• Manager wants to buy 50,000 shares of NME. The current price is $20.
• The trade desk parcels out an order to a broker to buy 40,000 NME. The price is $20.5.
• NME is bought at $20.75 plus a $.05 commission.
• Price jumps to $21.50, and the remainder of the order is canceled.
• 15 days later the price is $23.

---

[5] A. Perold, "The Implementation Shortfall: Paper versus Reality," *Journal of Portfolio Management* (Spring 1988).
[6] B. Collins and F. Fabozzi, "A Methodology for Measuring Transactions Costs," *Financial Analysts Journal* (March-April 1991).

An accurate assessment of the quality of trading requires knowledge of what really happened:

- What was the idea worth?
- How much did delay on the trade desk cost?
- What was the impact of the trade?
- How much was left on the table when the order was canceled?

Fortunately, modern paperless trading systems readily collect and organize data such as that above. The information provided shows (1) the portfolio manager's desires, (2) the strategies employed by the trade desk, and (3) the resulting executions. Thus we can observe the entire investing process and measure the parts.

THE COST COMPONENTS OF TRADING

Manager and trader actions can now be isolated and analyzed. We can define the actions and calculate the respective costs. When we observe a large number of trades, we can assess the costs within an organization. By gathering this data from many managers, we can assess the industry-wide components of the trading iceberg.

A *commission* is the explicit fee charged by the broker to handle and clear the trade. It is printed on the trade ticket, so it is readily available. In this example, the per share cost is $.05 — typical for an institutional trade.

Price impact is the price adjustment necessary to immediately purchase liquidity. We measure impact as the price difference between the time that the order is submitted to the broker and the actual trade. The broker received the order when the average price was $20.50, and the trade cost $20.75, resulting in a $0.25 per share impact.

Trader timing is the price move prior to contacting the broker. This can be thought of as the cost of seeking liquidity. We measure timing from the price when the order is submitted to the desk until it is released to the broker. The price was $20 when the order arrived on the desk, and the trader gave the order to the broker when the price was $20.50. Timing cost is $0.50 per share.

Opportunity cost is the cost of failing to complete the trade. What about the 20,000 shares that did not get traded? The idea generated a 15% return ($23/$20) over a 15-day period, but 40% of the order was never completed. On a dollar weighted basis, the manager "lost" 15% × 40%, or 6 percentage points of potential return. Good ideas are not always easy to come by, and it is as important to learn from what did not trade as it is to review what did trade.

THE ICEBERG OF TRADING COSTS

The example above simply illustrates what the costs are and how they are computed. Exhibit 2 represents nearly 700,000 trades by over 50 different management firms during the second half of 1996. This picture provides a realistic view of institutional trading costs.

Exhibit 2: The Iceberg of Trading Costs (in basis points)

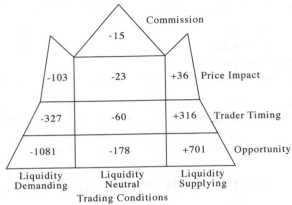

	Commission		
	-15		
-103	-23	+36	Price Impact
-327	-60	+316	Trader Timing
-1081	-178	+701	Opportunity
Liquidity Demanding	Liquidity Neutral	Liquidity Supplying	

Trading Conditions

Commissions

Commissions have been under steady pressure since they were deregulated in May 1975. Despite this pressure, commissions have been relatively stable for the services rendered. Full service brokers charge an average of 6¢, while smaller brokers that provide exchange floor access will charge 3-5¢. Automated trades executed via DOT (Direct Order Transmission to the floor) or the Proprietary Trading Systems (Instinet, ITG, AZX, and the Crossing Network) charge 1-3¢. An increasing proportion of trading executed through these lower cost alternatives results in combined rates dropping to 4.5¢.

Price Impact

The next level of the iceberg is shrouded in fog, leaving the viewer aware of its presence but uncertain about its size. Like fog, these costs expand and contract, reflecting changes in available liquidity.

Impact reflects both the dealer spread plus any price movement required to attract additional liquidity to complete the trade. Actively traded stocks will typically be quoted in one eighth increments. As the frequency of trading activity drops, the dealer spread typically rises.

The average impact is 23 bp, or 9¢ per share. Exhibit 3 shows that the most important factor affecting impact is whether or not the trade *supplies* liquidity to the market, *demands* liquidity from the market, or is liquidity *neutral*. A buy order placed into a market where prices are falling will supply liquidity to the market, and should capture a concession. While Exhibit 3 shows the difference between liquidity-demanding and liquidity-supplying orders, it also shows an interesting skew that reflects a high cost when demanding liquidity versus a modest gain for supplying liquidity. This is a typical pattern: traders are willing to supply liquidity for much smaller concessions than they end up paying when put on the other side of the trade. The brokers capture the difference, often described as "vigorish."

Exhibit 3: Impact and Spread

Liquidity Demanding	Liquidity Neutral	Liquidity Supplying
−103 bp	−23 bp	+36 bp

Exhibit 4: Trader Timing

Liquidity Demanding	Liquidity Neutral	Liquidity Supplying
−327 bp	−60 bp	+316 bp

Exhibit 5: Opportunity Cost

	Foregone Return	% Not Completed
Liquidity Demanding	−1081 bp	13%
Liquidity Neutral	−71 bp	11%
Liquidity Supplying	+701 bp	10%

Timing

The use of time as a trading tool for the buyside trader was previously discussed. By waiting for natural liquidity to appear at an acceptable price, the trader hopes to minimize direct price impact. This is why most large orders are broken up and worked in more easily digested pieces. Timing cost is the price change that occurs during this waiting period.

Timing is the counterpoint to impact. As time increases, impact should decrease. However, as time increases, so does the potential for adverse price moves. Because trading decisions usually reflect changes in publicly available information, short-term returns are likely to be positive. Consequently, delays to minimize impact leads to higher timing costs, as shown in Exhibit 4.

An information-sensitive trader who fails to find sufficient volume before prices move away will find the timing cost of delay to be very high. Conversely, a value-oriented trader providing liquidity may find that waiting leads to even greater gains than an immediate concession.

Opportunity

The final cost represents the base of the iceberg, never seen but possibly the most damaging to performance. This is the opportunity cost of uncompleted trades.

Money managers are like fishermen in their lament about the "one that got away." However, the manager's lament is legitimate: the most expensive trade is typically the one that never occurred. Exhibit 5 provides some insight into the average percentage of shares that are not completed by order type, as well as the 15-day opportunity effect.

There are two primary reasons for unexecuted orders. Either the trader cannot locate the shares to complete the trade, or the stock has moved out of the range that the manager is willing to pay. On a day to day basis, traders are quick to complete trades when the volume appears at an acceptable price — but as the timing costs show, they are not as willing to step up when a premium is required. Consequently, opportunity costs tend to be large. Exhibit 6 summarizes the definitions, computations, and cost experiences.

Conclusions about Trading Costs

Managing trading costs can be compared to squeezing a balloon: pushing in one side results in a distortion elsewhere. The commission, the most visible element of transactions costs, can be — and has been — driven down, but often at the cost of higher impact. Similarly, trade impact can be reduced by simply refusing to trade in high impact situations. In both cases, the trader diverts visible costs into less observable areas. This cannot be done without compromising investment performance. Thus the goal is to focus on total implementation costs, not simply trading costs.

This leads us to a functional definition of best execution: *best execution is that procedure most likely to capture the potential investment return.*

CASE STUDIES

In the remainder of this chapter we go beyond trading and explore the implications of different trading strategies within a manager's selection process. These are followed by some practical trading recommendations that we make to all desks.

Case Study #1: Momentum Manager Mismatched with Cautious Trader

Manager pattern: Manager reacts to news and price momentum to generate buying decisions. After the decision, the prices continue to appreciate. Selectivity is excellent: decisions appreciate 6% over the six weeks after decision.

Exhibit 6: Definitions, Computations, and Experienced Cost

Cost	Definition	Measurement	Experienced Costs
Commission	Explicit fee charged by a broker for services.	Provided for listed trades.	−4.5¢
Impact	Cost of immediate execution.	The difference between the average execution price and the price at the time the order is revealed to the broker.	−8¢
Timing	Cost of seeking liquidity.	Price change between the time the order goes to the trade desk and when it is released to the broker.	−23¢
Opportunity	Cost of failing to find liquidity.	15 day return for unexecuted shares.	−71¢
Total	Difference between costless and fully costed returns	Weighted sum of the above	−38¢

Exhibit 7: Comparison of Cost Components — Minimizing Impact: Case Study #1

	Timing	Impact	Comm.	Total	Benchmark*
Trading G/L	−175 bp	−3 bp	−12 bp	−190 bp	−115 bp

* Benchmark costs are determined by averaging the costs for similar trades executed in the previous six months by all manager in the database. Over 700,000 trades are used to derive the benchmark equations.

Exhibit 8: Comparison of Cost Components — Minimizing Total Costs: Case Study #1

	Timing	Impact	Comm.	Total	Benchmark
Trading G/L	−65 bp	−40 bp	−12 bp	−117 bp	−115 bp
Change	+106 bp	−27 bp	—	−73 bp	—

Trader pattern: Exhibit 7 shows the trader is sensitive to impact, and executes trades over several days. The table below reveals that although impact is low, timing costs run away as prices move while orders sit on the trade desk: when all costs are considered, the trader pays much more than other desks when faced with similar orders.

Recommendations: The trader's perspective focuses on creating zero impact with her trading. However, using a realistic cost benchmark of −115 bp rather than zero impact allows for more aggressive, and subsequently lower cost, trading.

Results: Within three quarters, timing costs had dropped to −65 bp while impact rose to −40 bp (Exhibit 8). Most importantly, total costs dropped from −190 bp to −117 bp. This case study perfectly illustrates the importance of controlling the total cost, instead of focusing on one component.

Case Study #2: Capturing an Insufficient Concession when Providing Liquidity

Manager pattern: Manager's buy decisions are deep value — almost contrarian. The more price drops relative to the fundamentals, the more likely this manager is to buy. Typical trade is very early, well in advance of the eventual price bottom.

Trader pattern: Exhibit 9 shows the trades are executed quickly, often at the best price of the day and at much better prices than the manager's decision price. However, there is no need to trade quickly given the repeating experience of subsequent weakness. Relative to other desks, this trader was providing a large concession to demanders of liquidity.

Exhibit 9: Comparison of Cost Components — Capturing Available Opportunities: Case Study #2

	Timing	Impact	Comm.	Total	Benchmark
Trading G/L	+35 bp	+11 bp	-14 bp	+35 bp	+90 bp

Exhibit 10: Comparison of Cost Components — Taking More Time to Probe: Case Study #2

	Timing	Impact	Comm.	Total	Benchmark
Trading G/L	+112 bp	+11 bp	−11 bp	+115 bp	+90 bp
Change	+77 bp	—	+3 bp	+80 bp	—

Exhibit 11: Comparison of Cost/Return Components — Low Cost, Low Return: Case Study #3

	Timing	Impact	Comm.	Total	Benchmark	Percent Traded	Net Returns Traded	Unex.
Trading G/L	-91 bp	+27 bp	-4 bp	-68 bp	-62 bp	48%	55 bp	655 bp

Recommendations: This case shows the opposite problem to the first case — fast trading in the face of weak returns. The trader should scale in gradually, letting the sellers come to him and making them pay for the privilege of liquidity. This is a case where probing trades to determine the level of buyer interest would be beneficial.

Results: Within three quarters, 95% completion was stretched out from 2 days to 5 days (see Exhibit 10). Timing gains rose to +112 bp while impact fell slightly. Total gains rose to +112 bp, slightly better than the benchmark.

Case Study #3: Over Reliance On Low Cost Brokers

Manager pattern: Manager used a quantitative model to generate lists of "alternate" trades. Model uses a timing overlay. Selectivity is good, with stocks rising 4% over six weeks.

Trader pattern: Trader believes strongly in using low cost proprietary trading systems to maintain anonymity and keep impact and commission costs to a minimum. (See Exhibit 11.) Trader takes pride in the low commission costs, avoiding the spread, and leaving no footprints in the market. Unfortunately, less than half the orders are completed, and there is evidence of strong adverse selection: stocks purchased appreciated 0.5%, while the untraded stocks went up 6.5%. The best model selections were left on the table. Performance suffers.

Exhibit 12: Comparison of Cost/Return Components — Higher Costs, Higher Return: Case Study #3

	Timing	Impact	Comm.	Total	Benchmark	Percent Traded	Net Returns Traded	Net Returns Unex.
Trading G/L	−51 bp	−10 bp	−6 bp	−67 bp	−62 bp	76%	110 bp	73 bp
Change	+40 bp	−37 bp	−2 bp	−1 bp	—	+28%	+55 bp	+582bp

Recommendations: The problem with over-reliance on crossing networks is that there is no guarantee of finding the desired liquidity through these routes. As a result, trading stretches out over many days while prices moved upward. The manager's good selection and timing ability dissipates.

Results: This trader learned that passive trading is but an arrow in a quiver, and effective trading requires the use of all tools to find and capture liquidity at an acceptable price. (See Exhibit 12.) Expanding broker use and monitoring incompletes at the end of each day leads to better prioritizing of the next day's trading. Within three quarters, completion rates rise to 76%, trading costs are flat, and realized returns rise to +110 bp despite weaker underlying decisions. More costly trading leads to better capture of investment ideas.

FOUR PRACTICAL TRADING RECOMMENDATIONS

In each of the case studies, the trader and the manager firmly believed they were doing a good job. The truth is that they were! The problem is not how they did their job, but how they *defined* their job, and how they defined their objective. By focusing on a part of the process, they missed the big picture. Once they were able to see and accept the wider viewpoint, the solutions were straightforward and improvement was rapid.

In closing, we would like to present four general recommendations that come from the practical experience of working with institutional trade desks.

Recommendation #1 — One Trading Strategy does Not Fit All Situations

Case Study #3 shows the problem of over reliance on passive trading. No matter how consistent a manager is, occasional trades will not fit the normal pattern and require special treatment. Not all orders should be traded with the same sense of urgency. Many managers sell stocks to fund new purchases, and sell decisions often contain less short term value than do buy models. As a result, the sells will often move up with the buys. An effective desk needs to offset trading costs generated by liquidity demanding trades with trading gains when providing liquidity. *Know why the manager wants to trade, and plan accordingly.*

Recommendation #2 — Prioritize and Make Contingency Plans

The worst tactic is to trade the minimal costs trades first, and wait to work orders with little available liquidity or with higher levels of competition. Instead, the desk needs to rank orders by urgency based on both motive (information-based trades are more urgent than value-based trades) and on current levels of supply and demand (an imbalance will often signal short-run information that may not be publicly available). *Do the hard trades first.* In addition, the desk needs to have a process alert when stocks move into higher urgency categories.

Recommendation #3 — Build Expected Costs into Portfolio Decision Making

Identifying potential buys and sells is a critical part of the money manager's job, and manager stock picks do add value. The problem is the number of decisions where costs exceed the return. As assets continue to grow, the problem is compounded. Knowing the expected exit cost of each holding can help the manager determine both the desired size and desirability of trading. Knowing the cost of acquiring new positions puts the value of the decision in proper context. *Strive to capture return, not minimize costs.*

Recommendation #4 — Rationalize Broker Use

One of the first lessons in business is to make vendors and customers dependent on you while not becoming dependent upon them. The same holds true for the trade desk. By concentrating business with a few brokers, the trader becomes important enough to the broker to make a difference. The trade desks with the best consistent results are those that concentrate brokerage, and make sure their brokers know what is expected of them. *Trust, but verify.*

Not all brokers are equal in skill. All brokers can take a simple trade to the floor of the exchange for simple market or limit order execution. Trades that require significant size relative to the trading volume require a broker who has the skill, inventory, and integrity to handle the order and protect the customer's interests. *Use the commission to buy the needed trading services.*

CONCLUSION

Remember the Dali painting "Lincoln in Dalivision?" At first glance your eye sees a seemingly random pattern of color. When you step back, you see the likeness that was there all along. To effectively evaluate an investing process, you need to look at each component in detail, then step back to understand how each piece fits together into the big picture.

Searching for alpha within the investment management shop may be the most overlooked obvious idea in investment management since risk measurement.

When managers widen their horizons beyond stock picking and analyze how their decisions thread into portfolios, they can capture risk-free, recurring returns. The secret to improving invest*ing* is to watch the handoffs and trade-offs.

Small improvements accumulate to make big differences in total performance. Since managers' track records are tightly bunched near the average, these improvements can raise a manager's ranking half a quartile or more. A good invest*ing* process is a crucial part of, and natural complement to, a good invest*ment* process.

Chapter 18

The Use of Derivatives in Managing Equity Portfolios

Roger G. Clarke, Ph.D.
Chairman
Analytic/TSA Global Asset Management

Harindra de Silva, Ph.D., CFA
Managing Director
Analytic/TSA Global Asset Management

Greg M. McMurran
Chief Investment Officer
Analytic/TSA Global Asset Management

INTRODUCTION

The growth of the derivatives markets in recent years has given the investment manager an important set of tools to use in managing the risk and return characteristics of equity portfolios. In this chapter we will discuss some of the common strategies available using three different derivatives contracts: index swaps, futures, and options. Each of these derivatives has their own special characteristics which make them useful for adjusting the payoff profile of the portfolio to reflect a manager's expectations or view of the market.

One of the main characteristics of derivatives contracts is that little, if any, up-front money is required to initiate the contract. This feature allows the manager to maintain the principal involved in the transaction in other securities while increasing or decreasing exposure to the market through the derivatives contract. This separation of market exposure from the need for immediate cash outlays is what makes hedging possible, for example. Market exposure generated by holding underlying securities can be hedged with a derivative without having to sell the underlying securities themselves.

A major difference between the types of derivative contracts is the shape of the payoff structure that results when the market moves. Both index swaps and futures contracts have linear payoff patterns. That is, the payoff is symmetric around current market levels. The payoff as the market goes up or down mirrors the movement of the market itself. As a result, swaps and futures are often referred to as *portfolio substitutes* since their effects can substitute for the market return on a well-diversified portfolio of stocks. However, options generate non-linear payoff patterns. Put options are more sensitive to down market moves while call options are more sensitive to up market moves. This asymmetry allows options to create special effects in managing the risk of a portfolio not available by using swaps or futures contracts. The choice of the optimal derivative strategy is naturally a function of the manager's objectives, risk preferences, and market view.

This chapter is organized as follows. We first outline the use of derivative strategies which have linear payoffs including swaps and futures. Call and put options, along with other combination strategies which have non-linear payoffs are reviewed in the next section. In the final section we discuss the typical framework used to price options and the limitations of using this approach to select an optimal derivative strategy. We illustrate a basic framework for selecting a particular strategy given a manager's risk and return expectations. Examples are provided for one of the more commonly used derivative strategies — the covered call strategy.

LINEAR PAYOFFS: SWAPS

The simplest index swap contract is structured between two parties where the counterparties agree to exchange the return between an equity index and a fixed interest rate (usually LIBOR) scaled by the principal or notional amount of the swap. We shall refer to the investor who pays the fixed rate and receives the market return as the swap buyer; the counterparty is the swap seller. The swap allows the investor buying the swap to gain exposure to the market without having to purchase the underlying equities themselves. The investor's funds can be left in cash reserves earning interest which is exchanged with the counter party who has agreed to pay the investor the return on the equity index.

This arrangement is illustrated in Exhibit 1. Investor A who has purchased the equity index swap receives the equity index return from Investor B while paying the agreed upon fixed rate. No principal is exchanged between the two parties, only the agreed upon return tied to the notional amount of the swap is exchanged. This allows the investors to achieve returns in one market without actually having to hold securities in that market. Swaps are usually negotiated, private-party transactions. Though the specific terms of a swap may vary, it is not unusual for the maturity or *tenor* of a swap to run for a year or more with returns being exchanged at quarterly intervals.

A simple way to look at the impact of using a swap to achieve equity market returns is illustrated in Exhibit 2. The purchaser of the swap holds the notional amount of the swap in cash which earns interest. When the return on the investor's cash reserve is combined with the return on the equity index less the payment of the promised fixed rate, the investor is left with the return on the equity index plus the difference in return earned on the underlying cash reserves less the fixed return paid to the counterparty. The purchaser of the swap has created a synthetic equity return on the investment without having to actually purchase equity securities.

The seller of the swap receives the fixed return and pays the return on the equity index. If the seller holds underlying stocks which mirror the return on the equity index, the net return to the seller will be the fixed rate received plus any difference in return between the actual return on the stocks and the return on the equity index. The seller of the swap has effectively created synthetic cash while the actual underlying portfolio is invested in equities as illustrated in Exhibit 3. This is part of the power of using derivatives to manage portfolios. Since derivative contracts do not require the exchange of principal, underlying assets may be held in one type of security but the net result may be the return on another type of security.

Exhibit 1: Equity Index Swap

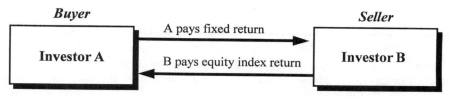
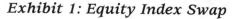

Exhibit 2: Return Equivalency from the Purchase of an Equity Index Swap

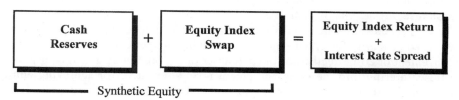

Exhibit 3: Return Equivalency from the Sale of an Equity Index Swap

Exhibit 4: Payoff of an Equity Index Swap as a Function of the Return on the Index

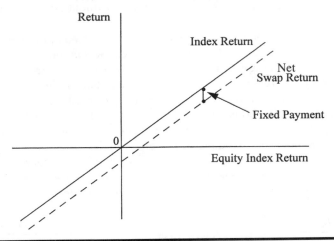

The return on the swap contract is referred to as being *linear* because it bears a straight line relationship to the return on the underlying equity index as shown in Exhibit 4. If the market goes up, the return on the swap contract will also go up. If the market goes down, the return on the swap contract also goes down. The difference between the index return and the swap return is the fixed rate the purchaser of the swap pays to the seller. When the swap return is added to the return the buyer earns on the underlying principal, the net result reflects the return on the equity index plus or minus the spread between what is earned on the cash reserve and what is paid to the seller.

Since swaps are usually entered into for an extended period of time, they are used primarily for either gaining or reducing market exposure. It may not be convenient or cost effective for the purchaser of a swap to buy actual equity securities. Entering into the swap agreement is an alternative for achieving equity exposure without the actual purchase of underlying equity securities. It has become popular in recent years to use swaps to create enhanced index funds. The investor may have a specific expertise in managing cash portfolios but no expertise in managing equity portfolios. If more can be earned on the cash portfolio than has to be paid to the seller of the swap, the investor ends up with an index-like return in the equity market but adds a spread generated by the difference in return between the actively managed cash portfolio and the fixed rate in the swap. This is sometimes referred to as *transporting alpha*. The alpha or differential return generated in one market can be converted to a differential return in another market.

Any type of equity index can be used in a swap as long as it is well defined and is agreed upon by both parties. It has become increasingly popular in recent years to use a swap on an international equity index. This saves the purchaser of the swap the difficulties of transacting in international markets and avoids directly paying for the accounting and custody fees. To the extent that the seller of the swap has potential economies of scale in assuming these costs and builds this reduced cost into the fixed return in the swap, the buyer of the swap may be able to generate international equity market returns at somewhat lower cost than purchasing the securities directly.

To illustrate an equity index swap transaction, suppose two investors agree to swap the return on the S&P 500 index in exchange for LIBOR plus 20 basis points on a $20 million notional value. The buyer of the swap pays the seller LIBOR plus 20 basis points in exchange for the total return on the S&P 500 index. If annualized LIBOR is 5.25% and the return on the S&P 500 index is 6.3% for the quarter, the buyer pays

$$\$20,000,000 \ (0.0545/4) = \$272,500$$

and the seller pays

$$\$20,000,000 \ (0.063) = \$1,260,000$$

In practice, the two amounts would usually be netted out against each other with the seller paying $987,500 to the buyer in this case.

Furthermore, suppose the buyer has invested $20 million in cash reserves earning an annualized rate of 5.85% for the quarter. The buyer of the swap has effectively earned a net return of

$$6.3\% + (5.85\% - 5.45\%)/4 = 6.40\%$$

or 10 basis points more than the index for the quarter. The extra 10 basis points comes from earning an annualized 40 basis points more per year than is required to be paid in the swap contract. If the seller of the swap has hedged the market obligation using a portfolio of stocks which has returned 6.5%, the seller's net return for the quarter will be

$$5.45\%/4 + (6.5\% - 6.3\%) = 1.56\%$$

or 6.25% at an annualized rate. The extra 100 basis points return over LIBOR with little market exposure is generated by receiving an extra 20 basis points from the fixed return in the swap plus an annualized differential return over the index of 80 basis points from the underlying equity portfolio.

LINEAR PAYOFFS: FUTURES

Futures contracts work much like swaps in their payoff pattern but there are some important institutional differences. One of the differences comes from the fact that futures contracts are traded on organized exchanges and are not negotiated directly between two counterparties. With a swap contract each counterparty is exposed to the credit risk of the other. With futures contracts the trading exchange and its members stand in the middle between two investors who have bought and sold futures contracts. The exchange plays the role of guarantor of the contract to ensure that all contract obligations are met. To help assure the financial integrity of the exchange and minimize the possibility that investors could build up losses beyond their ability to pay, investors initiating a position must deposit a performance bond with the exchange as *initial margin*. In addition, gains and losses are settled up on a daily basis between investors through the exchange (called *mark to market*) in contrast to swap contracts which are typically settled only quarterly. Finally, the interest rate which is fixed in the terms of a swap contract is embedded directly in the price of the futures contract so that it is not required to be independently specified up-front. The rate embedded in the futures contract is an implied market rate called the *implied repo rate* and matches the maturity of the contract in contrast to the fixed rate in the swap which usually resets each quarter when payments are exchanged

Exchange traded futures contracts typically carry a shorter term maturity than swap contracts. Maturities are usually staggered in three month segments with most of the liquidity found in the nearest maturity contract. There is often poor liquidity beyond the first two or three contracts. The shorter maturity of futures contracts allows them to be used with greater flexibility in managing equity portfolios, though like a swap, there are still only two things to do with a futures contract: buy it or sell it.

Applications of Buying Futures

The purchase of an equity index futures contract accomplishes the same thing as the purchase of an equity index swap. It adds equity exposure to the manager's portfolio. There are a variety of situations where a manager may want to add equity exposure. One of the most common is referred to as *cash equitization*. Equitizing cash through the purchase of futures contracts creates equity exposure synthetically without having to actually purchase underlying securities as illustrated in Exhibit 5. Many equity portfolios contain frictional amounts of cash that are difficult to keep fully invested. Dividends may be received from time to time or there may be new contributions that increase the cash in the portfolio. If the market moves up before these frictional amounts of cash can be invested in stocks, the portfolio performance will be exposed to *cash drag* and will not track the market as closely as it might. In a year when the market returns in excess of 25%, holding 5% cash would reduce portfolio performance by over 100 basis points. Since the market generally trends up over time, any frictional cash in the portfolio will tend to hurt performance.

Futures contracts might be purchased for more than just equitizing frictional amounts of cash. An entire portfolio could be left in cash reserves and futures contracts could be purchased to create a synthetic index fund. The combination of the cash reserve plus the futures contracts will behave as if a manager had purchased all of the stocks in the index. This creates tremendous liquidity in the portfolio. If funds are needed quickly, the futures contracts and the cash reserves are often easier to liquidate at lower cost than the underlying stocks. Furthermore, if the underlying cash reserve is actively managed to yield more than the implied repo rate in the futures contract, the index fund will have an enhanced return greater than the index itself. Futures contracts have been used to create enhanced index funds not only in the United States but in other countries that have actively traded equity index futures contracts. This achieves the same effect as purchasing a swap but with a shorter maturity.

Futures contracts are also useful in the trading process by helping manage the net market exposure of a portfolio as stocks are purchased or sold. It is not uncommon for slices of a portfolio to be traded involving multiple securities. These trades could be caused by the addition or withdrawal of funds in a portfolio or by a restructuring of positions internal to the portfolio. As long as the purchase or sale of securities leaves the portfolio temporarily overexposed or underexposed to the market while the trades are taking place, the portfolio manager can maintain market exposure until all of the security positions are in place by selling or buying the requisite number of futures contracts. The positions can then be closed out when they are no longer needed.

Applications of Selling Futures

The most common motivation for selling a futures contract in managing an equity portfolio is to temporarily hedge its market exposure. Like a swap, the sale of a futures contact against an underlying portfolio of stocks is equivalent to creating synthetic cash as illustrated in Exhibit 6. In essence, creating a hedged position is an attempt to counteract the market risk in the underlying securities and shift the risk to others willing to bear the risk. The risk can always be shifted by doing away with the underlying security position, but this may interfere with the nature of the investor's business or disrupt a continuing investment program. The futures market provides an alternative way to temporarily control or eliminate much of the risk in the underlying securities while continuing to hold the stocks.

Exhibit 5: Creating Synthetic Equity Exposure Using Index Futures Contracts

Exhibit 6: Creating Synthetic Cash Using Equity Index Futures Contracts: Hedging

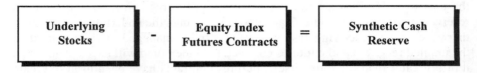

Exhibit 7: Return Profiles for Hedged Portfolios

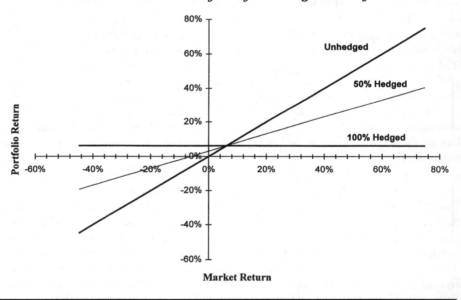

The impact of hedging can be seen by examining the effect of hedging on a portfolio's return profile and probability distribution. Exhibit 7 illustrates the return on the hedged portfolio relative to the return on the underlying market index. A partially hedged position reduces the slope of the return line, so that the hedged portfolio does not perform as well as the market when returns are high, but it also does not perform as poorly when returns are low. The greater the portion of the portfolio that is hedged, the less slope the line will have. A full hedge produces a flat line, indicating that the hedged portfolio will generate a fixed return no matter what the underlying market does. This fixed return should be equal to the riskless rate if the futures contract is fairly priced. The slope of the return line for an equity portfolio is often referred to as the portfolio's market sensitivity or beta. Hedging effectively reduces the market beta of the portfolio as it amounts to selling the equity exposure of the portfolio.

Exhibit 8: Return Distributions for Hedged Portfolios

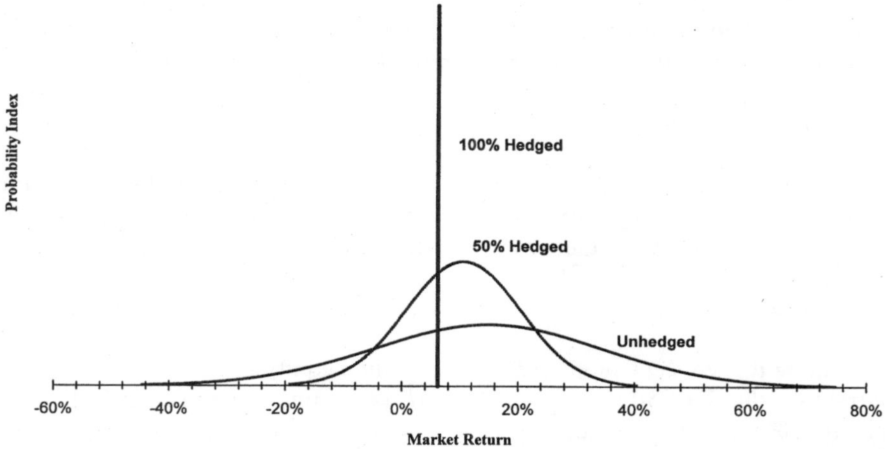

Exhibit 8 shows how the futures hedge changes the probability distribution of returns. If the return distribution for the market is symmetric with a wide dispersion, hedging the portfolio with futures gradually draws both tails of the distribution in toward the middle, and the mean return shrinks back toward the riskless rate. A full hedge draws both tails into one place and puts all of the probability mass at the riskless rate (the implied repo rate in the contract).

Hedging with futures will affect both tails equally. One of the main differences between options with their non-linear effects and futures is that options can affect one tail more dramatically than the other, so the distribution becomes quite skewed. Exhibit 9 illustrates the difference in the return distributions caused by a partial futures hedge versus a partial hedge created by using a put option. The put option hedge reduces the downside risk while leaving much of the upside potential. The use of options for hedging will be explained in more detail later.

Hedge Ratios Using Futures

A *hedge ratio* represents the amount of the futures used to construct a hedge relative to the amount of the underlying portfolio being hedged. In some cases there is a direct way to calculate the appropriate hedge ratio between futures and the portfolio. This technique can be used when the futures contract used for hedging is tied closely to the underlying portfolio being hedged as is the case when equity index futures are used to hedge a well diversified portfolio. Hedge ratios can be calculated easily because there is a direct link between the change in the value of the underlying portfolio and a change in the value of the associated futures contract.

To develop this idea, suppose an investor holds one unit of a portfolio containing securities S and wants to hedge it with a futures contract F. The change in the value of the combined position V as the portfolio value changes is

$$\Delta V = \Delta S + h\Delta F \qquad (1)$$

where h (the hedge ratio) represents the number of units of futures F used to hedge portfolio S. Solving for the hedge ratio directly from equation (1) gives

$$h = \frac{\Delta V - \Delta S}{\Delta F} \qquad (2)$$

For a complete hedge, or market neutral hedge ($\Delta V = 0$), the hedge ratio would be equal to the negative of the ratio of relative price changes between the portfolio being hedged and the futures contract. That is,

$$h = -\frac{\Delta S}{\Delta F} \qquad (3)$$

To illustrate this concept suppose S is a diversified equity portfolio, F is a futures contract on the S&P 500 Index, and $\Delta S/\Delta F$ is assumed to equal 0.95. That is, when the S&P 500 futures contract moves by $1, the underlying equity portfolio moves by only $0.95, indicating that the portfolio is slightly less volatile than the broad market represented by the S&P 500 Index. For a market neutral hedge, the hedge ratio is

$$h = -\frac{0.95}{1.00} = -0.95$$

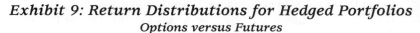

Exhibit 9: Return Distributions for Hedged Portfolios
Options versus Futures

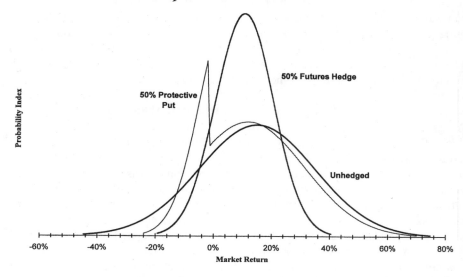

An investor would sell futures contracts worth 95% of the value of the equity portfolio to create the hedge. If the investor wanted only a partial hedge ($\Delta V = \frac{1}{3}\Delta S$, for example), the hedge ratio is

$$h = \frac{\frac{1}{3}\Delta S - \Delta S}{\Delta F} = \frac{-2}{3}\left(\frac{\Delta S}{\Delta F}\right) = -0.63$$

The investor would sell futures contracts worth only 63% of the value of the equity portfolio. With the hedge in place, the hedged portfolio would move only $\frac{1}{3}$ as much as the underlying portfolio.

Because the equity portfolio does not move one for one with the S&P 500 futures contract in the example, the investor does not want to use a hedge ratio of -1.0 to hedge the market risk in the underlying securities. A market-neutral hedge requires fewer futures contracts to be used because the underlying equity portfolio has only 95% of the movement of the futures contract.

The example above also shows what the hedge ratio must be if only a partial hedge is created to protect against the price movement in the underlying securities. If the combined hedged position is targeted to have $\frac{1}{3}$ of the movement of the underlying securities, a hedge ratio of -0.63 is needed. The investor would sell futures contracts worth only 63% of the value of the equity portfolio to create the partial hedge.

The arbitrage pricing relationship between the futures contract and the underlying market index links the two price changes together. This relationship can be used to calculate how the fair price of the futures contract will change as the price of the equity index changes. To see how this relationship can be used to estimate the hedge ratio directly, suppose that the price change of both the portfolio to be hedged and the futures contract are proportional to the change in the market index I in the following way:

$$\Delta S = \beta_S \Delta I, \text{ and } \Delta F = \beta_F \Delta I$$

where β_S and β_F represent the sensitivity to the index (market betas) of the portfolio being hedged and the futures contract, respectively.

Because portfolios and futures contracts are tied to the same underlying index, the hedge ratio is proportional to the ratio of their respective market betas. That is,

$$h = \frac{-\Delta S}{\Delta F} = -\frac{\beta_S}{\beta_F} \tag{4}$$

If the investor has an estimate of the market betas of the futures contract and the portfolio relative to the market index, the investor can calculate the appropriate hedge ratio directly.

For example, consider the calculation of the hedge ratio and the number of S&P 500 futures contracts required to hedge a $50 million equity portfolio with a beta of 1.05 relative to the S&P 500 Index. If the futures contract has a beta of 1.01 and the current level of the index is 900, the hedge ratio is

$$h = \frac{-1.05}{1.01} = -1.04$$

The contract size for the S&P 500 is 500 times the value of the S&P 500 Index, or \$450,000 (500 × 900), so the number of futures contracts required to be sold is

$$n = \frac{h(\text{Hedge value})}{\text{Contract size}} = \frac{-1.04(50,000,000)}{450,000} = -116 \text{ contracts}$$

Notice that the hedge ratio is slightly less than the beta of the portfolio. The short-term hedge ratio accounts for the slightly larger volatility in the index futures contract caused by its arbitrage pricing relationship. This additional volatility will shrink towards zero as the contract gets closer to maturity, reflecting a beta for the futures contract which converges to 1.0 at expiration. For longer term hedges with an investment horizon equal to the expiration date of the futures contract, a futures beta of 1.0 is typically used to calculate the hedge ratio.

NON-LINEAR PAYOFFS: OPTIONS

Simple options come in two forms: put options and call options. Unlike futures contracts and swaps, options require a small premium to be paid when purchased. Depending on the maturity of the option and the exercise price, the premium may range from less than 1% to more than 10% of the value of the underlying security or index. The payoff from an option at expiration depends on whether the security is above or below the level of the exercise or strike price. This lack of symmetry creates a non-linear payoff for the option at expiration. Put options have a non-zero payoff when the security price is less than the exercise price and call options pay off when the security price is greater than the exercise price. To see how options can be used in managing equity portfolios it is useful to review the payoff profile of put and call options.

Payoff Profiles for Options

Insight into the characteristics of options can be obtained by looking specifically at how options behave and what value they have at expiration. The matrix below is a simple technique for showing the value of option positions at expiration where S represents the value of the individual security or index and K represents the exercise price of the option:

	Payoff at Expiration	
	$S < K$	$S > K$
Call	0	$S - K$
Put	$K - S$	0
Security	S	S

At the expiration of the put or call option, its payoff depends on whether the security price is less than or more than the exercise price. The value of the underlying security is the same, S, whether it is below or above the option's exercise price. These payoffs form the basic building blocks for option strategy analysis.

Exhibit 10 illustrates the payoff pattern at expiration for a call option. On the horizontal axis is plotted the security price. The vertical axis measures the payoff at expiration. The trivial case representing the security's value is shown by the dashed line. For example, if the security ends with a value of K dollars, then the security will have a payoff of K dollars. The call option has a value of zero until the security price reaches the exercise price K, after which the call option increases one for one in price as the security price increases. The investor, however, must first purchase the option. So the net payoff from buying a call option is negative until the security price reaches the exercise price, and then it starts to rise (the dotted line). This line represents the payoff the investor receives net of the cost of the option. The investor breaks even with zero net profit at the point where the security price equals the exercise price plus the call option premium, C.

Note that the call option has a kinked or asymmetric payoff pattern. This feature distinguishes it from a futures contract. The future has a payoff pattern that is a straight line, as does the underlying security. This asymmetry in the option's payoff allows the option buyer to create specialized return patterns that are unavailable when using a futures contract.

Exhibit 11 illustrates the behavior of a put option. The put option has an intrinsic value of zero above the exercise price. Below there, it increases one for one as the security price declines. If an investor buys a put option, the net payoff of the option is the dotted line. The investor breaks even, with zero net profit, at the point where the security price equals the exercise price less the put option premium, P.

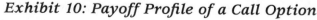

Exhibit 10: Payoff Profile of a Call Option

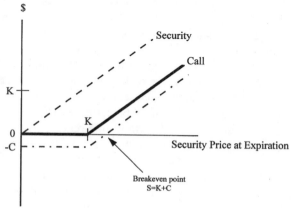

Exhibit 11: Payoff Profile of a Put Option

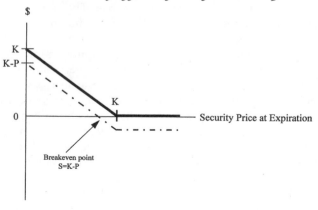

– · – · Net of option premiums

Selling Call Options: Exchanging Appreciation for Income

One of the most popular option strategies is known as a *covered call*. A covered call is constructed by holding the underlying security and selling a call option. The payoff matrix at expiration for this strategy is

	Covered Call Payoff at Expiration	
	$S < K$	$S > K$
Security	S	S
Short Call	0	$-(S - K)$
Total Payoff	S	K

The value of the security is S whether it finishes above or below the exercise price. The value of the call option is zero below the exercise price and $(S - K)$ above the exercise price. Since the call option has been sold by the investor, the payoff of the call option is owed and serves to reduce the total payoff below the value of the security itself. The total payoff of the covered call is found by adding up the value in each column. Below the exercise price, the portfolio is worth S dollars since the call has expired worthless. Above the exercise price, the portfolio is worth K dollars since the short call neutralizes the appreciation in the security above the exercise price.

The covered call strategy is shown graphically in Exhibit 12. The dashed line again represents the security value. The solid line represents the value of the security plus the payoff from the short call option. Below the exercise price the investor is left with the value of the security. Above the exercise price the security's appreciation is capped at the exercise price. In exchange for this limit on the security's appreciation, the investor receives the premium of the call option. The investor has traded the possibility of upside appreciation above the exercise price for income in the form of the option premium. The break-even point occurs when the security price is equal to the exercise price plus the call option premium. Below this point the covered call strategy gives a better payoff than holding the security by itself.

To demonstrate the result of a covered call strategy, consider an investor who holds a position in a stock worth $10 million. Assume that the current stock price is $100. The following example illustrates the effect of selling call options if the stock appreciates or depreciates 10% over the next six months.

	Stock Price	Underlying Portfolio Value	Portfolio Percentage Change
Current	$100	$10,000,000	
After six months	$110	$11,000,000	10.0
After six months	$90	$9,000,000	−10.0

Suppose the investor sells 100,000 6-month call options, each covering 100 shares with an exercise price of $105 to bring in premium income of $300,000. If the stock price declines by 10% to $90, the call options will expire worthless and the investor keeps the income from the sale of the call options giving a portfolio value of

$9,000,000 + $300,000 = $9,300,000

representing a decline of 7.0%. The value of the portfolio has declined by less than the 10% decline in the stock price because of the premium income received from the call options. If the stock price appreciates by 10%, the payoff of the call options owed by the investor will be

$100,000 (105 − 110) = −$500,000

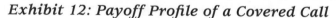

Exhibit 12: Payoff Profile of a Covered Call

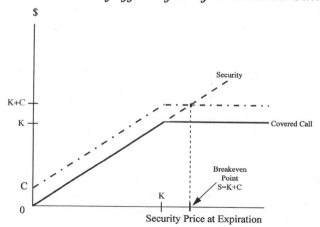

which when combined with the value of the stock and the premium income from the sale of the call options gives a portfolio value of

$$\$11,000,000 + \$300,000 - \$500,000 = \$10,800,000.$$

This represents a return of 8.0% on the value of the stocks in the portfolio compared to the stock price appreciation of 10.0%. The premium income from the call options has helped to offset the loss on the exercise of the options but the stock has appreciated beyond the break-even point so the net return on the portfolio is less than the appreciation in the stock itself.

Asymmetric Hedges: Protecting the Downside

The construction of an asymmetric hedge which responds to positive market returns differently than to negative market returns usually requires the use of an option. The most common strategies to hedge market exposure are (1) the protective put, (2) the protective put spread, and (3) the collar, range forward, or fence.

Protective Put

A *protective put* is constructed by holding the underlying security and buying a put option. The payoff matrix at expiration for this strategy is

Protective Put Payoff at Expiration		
	$S < K$	$S > K$
Security	S	S
Put	$K - S$	0
Total payoff	K	S

The value of the security is S whether it finishes above or below the exercise price. The value of the put option is $(K - S)$ below the option's exercise price and zero above the exercise price. The total value of the protective put is found by adding up the value in each column. Below the exercise price, the portfolio is worth K dollars at expiration. Above the exercise price, it is worth S.

This strategy is depicted graphically in Exhibit 13. The dashed line again represents the security value. The solid line represents the value of the security plus the put option. Below the exercise price, the put option compensates for the decline in the security price. Once the original cost of the put option is accounted for, the net payoff is represented by the dotted line. The break-even point occurs when the security price is equal to the exercise price less the cost of the put option. Below this point, the protective-put strategy gives a better payoff than holding just the security by itself.

The benefit of this strategy occurs below the break-even point. If the security price falls below this level, the portfolio is always worth more than the security itself. This protection is of great benefit if the market is going down. The market does not give this protection for free, however. Above the break-even point, the protected portfolio is always worth a little bit less than the security. The price paid for the option results in a slightly lower return on the upside. This strategy has sometimes taken on another name, portfolio insurance, because the put option protects the value if the security price falls while maintaining some market exposure if the price rises.

To illustrate the impact of put options to hedge equity exposure, consider the same investor who holds a stock position worth $10,000,000. Assume that the current stock price is $100 and can appreciate or depreciate by 10% over the next six months. Suppose also that the investor hedges the market risk by purchasing 100,000 6-month put options, each covering 100 shares with an exercise price of $100 at a cost of $600,000. If the stock price declines to $90, the payoff of the put options at expiration will be

$$\$100,000 \ (100 - 90) = \$1,000,000$$

The net value of the portfolio will be

$$\$9,000,000 + (\$1,000,000 - \$600,000) = \$9,400,000$$

representing a decline of 6%. The value of the portfolio has declined by less than the 10% decline in the stock price because of the net payoff of the options. The options will finish in the money and contribute some value to the portfolio. Without the option position, the unhedged value of the portfolio would have declined by the full 10%.

Exhibit 13: Payoff Profile of a Protective Put

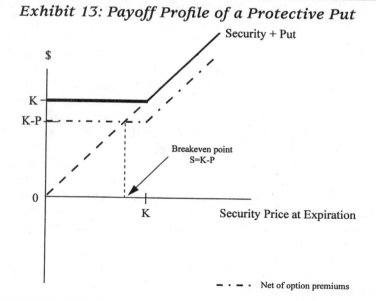

If the stock price increases to $110, the value of the put options at expiration will be zero giving a net value of the portfolio of

$$\$11,000,000 - \$600,000 = \$10,400,000$$

representing an increase of 4%. Due to the cost of the options, the hedged portfolio will underperform the unhedged portfolio which returns a full 10.0%.

Protective Put Spread

The *protective put spread* is constructed by purchasing a put option and selling a put option farther out of the money. The payoff matrix at expiration for this strategy is

Protective Put Spread Payoff at Expiration			
	$S < K_l$	$K_l < S < K_u$	$S > K_u$
Security	S	S	S
Put Purchased	$K_u - S$	$K_u - S$	0
Put Sold	$-(K_l - S)$	0	0
Total Payoff	$S + (K_u - K_l)$	K_u	S

The total payoff of the protective put spread is split into three pieces corresponding to whether the security price is below the lower exercise price (K_l), in between the two exercise prices, or above the higher exercise price (K_u). Below the exercise price the hedged portfolio is worth the value of the stock plus the difference between the higher exercise price and the lower exercise price. If the stock price falls in between the two exercise prices, the payoff is just equal to the higher exercise price. Finally, if the stock price is above both exercise prices, the payoff is equal to the stock price since both put options expire worthless.

The strategy is shown graphically in Exhibit 14. The dashed line represents the security value. The solid line represents the value of the security plus the payoff from the two put options. In between the two exercise prices, the put spread protects the value of the portfolio as before. Below the lower exercise price the portfolio is again exposed to the decline in the market price of the stock. Once the net cost of the put option spread has been accounted for, the net payoff is represented by the dotted line. The break-even point occurs when the security price is equal to the exercise price of the protective put less the net cost of the put option spread. The cost of the protective put option spread is less than that of the protective put by itself because of the premium brought in from the put option which has been sold. As a result the break-even point is higher. The stock has to decline less in order for the protective put spread to be better than leaving the security unhedged.

The previous example can be expanded to incorporate the put spread. Suppose that 100,000 put options with an exercise price of $90 were sold to bring in premium of $100,000 to help pay for the cost of the protective puts. Now the net cost of the option positions would be $500,000. If the stock price rises 10% to $110, the payoff of the hedged portfolio will be

Exhibit 14: Payoff Profile of a Protective Put Spread

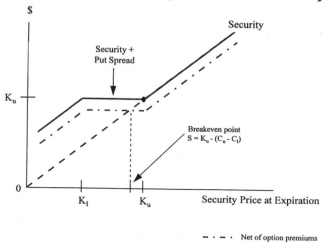

$11,000,000 - ($600,000 - $100,000) = $10,500,000

resulting in a portfolio return of 5%. If the price of the stock falls 10% to $90, the payoff of the hedged portfolio will be

$9,000,000 + $100,000 (100 - 90) - ($600,000 - $100,000) = $9,500,000

resulting in a portfolio return of −5% compared to the 10% decline in the stock and the 6% decline if only the protective put is used. The additional benefits resulting from the protective put spread come because the portfolio is not completely protected if the stock price falls below the lower exercise price. For example, a 20% decline in the stock price would result in a 15% decline using the protective put spread while resulting in only a 6% decline using the protective put by itself.

Collar (Range Forward or Fence)

The *collar, range forward, or fence* is constructed by selling a call option in addition to the purchase of a put option. The sale of the call again brings in cash which reduces the cost of purchasing the put option. The maturity of the call option is typically the same as that of the put, but has a higher exercise price. The sale of the call option eliminates the benefit of positive security returns above the level of the call's exercise price. If the exercise price of the call option is set close enough to that of the put, the cost of the put option can be offset entirely by the sale of the call option. This is typically referred to as a *zero cost collar.*

To accommodate the difference in exercise prices between the put and the call options, the payoff matrix must again be expanded. As a result, the payoff matrix for the collar is

Exhibit 15: Payoff Profile of a Collar

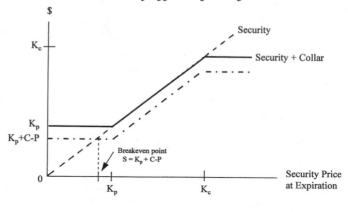

--- -- Net of option premiums

	Collar Payoff at Expiration		
	$S < K_p$	$K_p < S < K_c$	$S > K_c$
Security	S	S	S
Put	$K_p - S$	0	0
−Call	0	0	$-(S - K_c)$
Total payoff	K_p	S	K_c

K_p represents the put exercise price and K_c represents the exercise price of the call option. If the security is below the exercise price of the put at expiration, the payoff will be equal to the exercise price of the put. If the security is above the exercise price of the call option, the payoff will be equal to the exercise price of the call option. In between the two exercise prices the payoff will be equal to the underlying security price.

The payoff of the collar is shown graphically in Exhibit 15. The solid line represents the value of the security plus the payoff from the options. The dotted line represents the value of the strategy once the net cost of the options is considered. A zero cost collar would have no net option cost so the dotted line would converge to the solid line. The dashed line represents the value of holding the security unhedged. The benefit of this strategy occurs below the exercise price of the option similar to the protective put. The exact break-even point depends on the price of the call option sold to truncate some of the upside potential. This loss of upside potential beyond the break-even point of the short call position is the disadvantage of using the collar.

To continue the previous hedging example, suppose that call options are sold with an exercise price of $105 for $300,000 in addition to the purchase of put options with an exercise price of $100. If the stock price declines to $90, the put options will have value, but the call options will expire worthless. The net value of the portfolio will be

$$\$9,000,000 + \$100,000 \, (100 - 90) - (\$600,000 - \$300,000) = \$9,700,000$$

representing a decline of 3% compared to the stock price decline of 10%. The sale of the call option has helped offset the cost of the put option hedge which previously showed a decline of 6%.

On the other hand, if the stock price increases to $110, the put options will expire worthless and the value of the call option at expiration will detract from performance giving a portfolio value of

$$\$11,000,000 - \$100,000 \, (110 - 105) - (\$600,000 - \$300,000) = \$10,200,000$$

representing a net increase of only 2% compared to the 10% increase in the stock price.

Comparing the protective put strategy with the collar shows that the investor is better off using the collar if the stock price declines, but could be worse off if the stock price increases sufficiently beyond the exercise price of the call option. In the example here the loss on the value of the call option is more than the premium received when the option was sold so the investor has done slightly worse than the protective put strategy even though the stock price increased. In general, the collar or range forward works well as long as the market does not increase beyond the exercise price of the call option. If the market rallies much beyond that point, the investor will not participate in the upside market gains.

Buying Call Options: Creating Market Exposure

Two common option positions used to create market exposure are buying calls and buying call spreads. To add equity market exposure to a portfolio, the investor can buy call options on an equity index. If, for example, extra exposure to the U.S. equity market is desired, the investor can buy call options on the S&P 500. If the market appreciates, the option will increase in value. If the market declines, all the investor can lose is the cost of the option. The cost of the call option is the price the investor must pay to participate in the upside market potential while avoiding a loss in a declining market.

An alternative strategy would be to buy a call spread to create the market exposure. With a call spread, an investor buys calls with a lower exercise price than the call options sold. For example, if the market has only moderate upside potential, an investor might buy a call option with an exercise price at current market levels and sell a call option with a higher exercise price — at an exercise price above where the market is expected to be at expiration. Using a call spread, the investor participates in the market only up to a point, but at a reduced cost because the sale of the out-of-the-money call option offsets the cost of the long call option.

Exhibit 16: Payoff Profiles from Buying Calls and Call Spreads

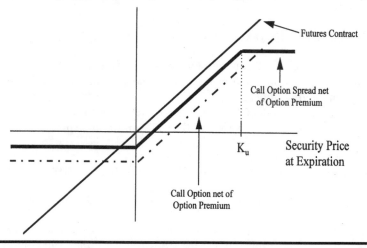

The payoff profiles at expiration for these two strategies, compared to buying a futures contract, are illustrated in Exhibit 16. If investors buy futures contracts, they will participate to the full extent of the market increase or decrease. If they buy a call option to create exposure, they participate if the market goes up, but if the market goes down, they will not suffer the full decline. The gap between the option and futures payoff on the upside represents the cost of the call option. If an investor's view about the market is positive, but not excessively bullish, the lower-cost call spread creates additional exposure but caps the market participation beyond a certain point.

Probability Distribution of Returns

In addition to using payoff diagrams to describe the effect of options, an investor can look at the probability distribution of returns for various strategies. Consider first the covered call strategy. Exhibit 17 shows the probability distribution of returns for an underlying security with and without the sale of call options. Note how the shape changes as an increasing proportion of call options are sold relative to the underlying security position. Selling call options draws the portfolio distribution back gradually on the right side and increases the chance that an investor will receive only moderate returns. Selling call options on 100% of the portfolio completely truncates the right-hand side of the probability distribution: the investor has a high probability of receiving moderate returns and no probability of receiving high returns. Most of the probability of receiving low returns is preserved, however.

Next consider the protective put strategy. Exhibit 18 shows the probability distribution of returns for an underlying security with and without the use of put options. Note how the shape changes as an increasing proportion of put options are purchased relative to the underlying security position. Purchasing put options draws the portfolio distribution back gradually on the left side and increases the chance that an investor will receive only moderate returns. Buying put options on 100% of the portfolio completely truncates the left-hand side of the probability distribution: The investor has a very high probability of receiving moderate returns and no probability of receiving low returns. Most of the probability of receiving high returns is preserved, however.

Exhibit 17: Return Distributions for Covered Calls

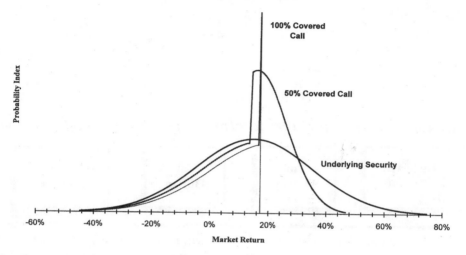

Exhibit 18: Return Distributions for Protective Puts

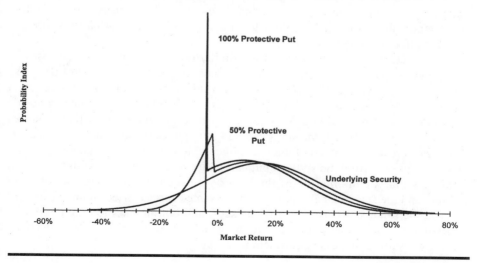

Exhibit 19: Return Distributions for Collars

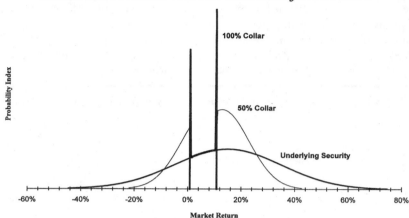

Exhibit 20: Creating a Synthetic Cash Reserve Using Options

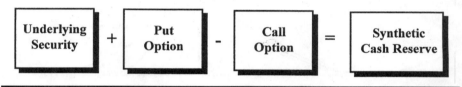

Exhibit 19 illustrates the effect of selling call options and buying put options simultaneously (a fence or collar). The combination causes quite a severe misshaping of the probability distribution in both tails. The distribution is no longer smooth and symmetric. The asymmetry of options allows an investor to shape and mold the probability distribution by truncating some parts and adding to others. Call options affect the right-hand tail most dramatically, while put options affect the left-hand tail.

Notice that the collar provides similar downside protection but loses its upside participation if the security return is positive beyond the level of the call's exercise price. Selling the call option with the same exercise price as the put option would protect against downside losses but would also eliminate any upside participation. This would make the hedge symmetric similar to selling a futures contract or swap. Indeed, the short call and long put position with the same exercise price creates a synthetic futures contract which produces a symmetric hedge. This can be seen from the stylized put/call parity relationship in Exhibit 20 which indicates that a combination of the underlying security, the purchase of a put option, and the sale of a call option with the same exercise price and maturity will behave the same as a cash reserve. The short call option and the long put option work to create a synthetic futures contract which offsets the risk in the underlying security resulting in a cash equivalent position.

Exhibit 21: Creating Synthetic Equity Exposure Using Options: Put/Call Parity

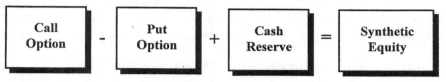

Exhibit 22: Creating a Synthetic Covered Call Strategy: The Collateralized Put

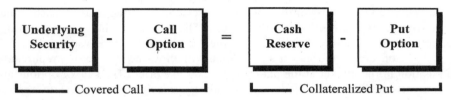

Exhibit 23: Creating a Synthetic Protective Put

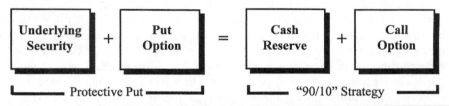

Rearranging the relationship to create a synthetic security instead of a synthetic cash reserve indicates that the combination of the cash reserve minus a put option plus a call option creates a market position as shown in Exhibit 21. In this case the long call option and the short put option work to create a synthetic futures position which adds market exposure to the cash reserve creating a synthetic security.

One last comment about the put/call parity relationship. Rearranging the components allows us to create the same payoff for the covered call and the protective put strategies in another way than previously described. The covered call strategy is normally constructed by purchasing the underlying security and selling a call option. An equivalent way to achieve the same payoff is to sell a put option and invest equivalent funds in an interest bearing cash reserve as shown in Exhibit 22. This alternative is sometimes referred to as a collateralized put and produces the same return profile as a covered call. In like manner, an equivalent way to create the same payoff as the protective put strategy is to purchase a call option and invest the remainder of the funds in an interest bearing cash reserve as illustrated in Exhibit 23.

This alternative is sometimes nicknamed the "90/10" strategy since roughly 90% of the investor's funds are held in a cash reserve with 10% used to purchase call options to give upside market participation. These configurations give equivalent payoffs because the arbitrage relationships between put and call options with the same maturities and exercise prices ensure that the payoff patterns will be preserved.

Automatic Changes in Market Exposure

Changes in market exposure can be triggered automatically as the market moves by selling options. The sale of a call option will truncate market participation above the option's exercise price. Selling some index call options against a long futures position or against exposure in the underlying stocks effectively pre-sells a portion of the exposure at the option's exercise price if the market reaches that level by the expiration date of the option. The receipt of the option premium effectively pays the investor for making the decision to sell in advance.

Conversely, the sale of a put option will allow the investor to prepurchase a position in the market at the put option's exercise price. The sale of options are frequently used in asset allocation and trading strategies to automatically reposition the portfolio if certain market levels are reached. Selling call options on 10% of the portfolio's exposure will automatically reduce the exposure by 10% if the market rallies up to the level of the call option's exercise price. Selling put options on 10% of the portfolio exposure will automatically increase the exposure by 10% if the market falls to the level of the put option's exercise price. At that point the investor can replace the option position by selling stocks for a gain and repurchasing the calls or by purchasing stocks at a discount and repurchasing the puts in order to make the shift permanent. The advantage is that the investor gets to keep the option premium for having made the decision in advance. The premium effectively increases the sale price of the appreciated stocks or reduces the purchase price of the depreciated stocks.

The purchase of additional market exposure by buying call options or the hedging of existing market exposure by buying put options can also be thought of as creating automatic changes in market exposure. The purchase of call options allows the investor to increase market exposure as the market rises while the purchase of put options allows the investor to decrease market exposure as the market falls. The options automatically adjust their levels of participation as the market reaches the options' exercise prices and go in the money. The non-linear payoff pattern of an option creates this automatic adjustment feature.

A VALUATION FRAMEWORK FOR SELECTING DERIVATIVE STRATEGIES

Since the advent of the listed equity option market in the United States in 1973, investors have used options both to reduce risk and enhance return. The majority of investors use options in combination with other securities — option covered-call writing strategies are an example of such a strategy, where options are sold on a portfolio of underlying stocks in order to generate incremental returns. In spite of the fact that options are used in such a fashion, there is no generally accepted framework to evaluate the impact the options have on the return of the overall portfolio. The most widely used option pricing models such as the model developed by Black and Scholes[1] or the model of Cox, Ross, and Rubinstein[2] are geared more to valuing options as opposed to computing the expected return from a combined stock and option position. These models do not help an investor in selecting an optimal choice of option or the optimal structure — i.e., how does an investor choose between the various covered call alternatives?

In this section we outline a framework which can be used to evaluate the combinations of stock and option positions. We do not cover the fundamentals of option pricing as there are a number of books that provide an introduction to this topic.[3] We do, however, briefly cover the assumptions underlying the Black-Scholes model in order to highlight the conditions under which actual option prices may significantly differ from their theoretical Black-Scholes prices. The primary focus of this section is to outline a valuation framework to be used in choosing the optimal trade-off between risk and return when deciding to invest in an option in combination with another security (such as a stock or bond). We focus on covered call or overwriting strategies in our examples, although the framework is applicable to any security and option combination.

The Problem with Black-Scholes

The typical investor has a specific view on the future outcome for an equity security in which he is considering making an investment. Option valuation models, however, take the current price of the stock as given and then price the security using the key assumption that it is possible to combine the option and the underlying security to form a risk-free security. This combination should in equilibrium earn the risk-free rate. These models, as we show using a simple example below, do not allow an investor to estimate the value or expected return from a particular option conditional on the investor's expected return distribution. In order to compute such an expected return it is necessary to compute the actuarial value of the option.

This actuarial value can then be used to compute the expected return from investing in a particular combination of stock and options. We illustrate this below using a simple example for a manager considering using a strategy of selling calls on stock he owns as a means of increasing the return on the portfolio.

---

[1] See F. Black and M. Scholes, "The Pricing of Options and Corporate Liabilities," *Journal of Political Economy* (May/June 1973), pp. 637-657 for the original derivation of this pricing model.

[2] This more general approach to option pricing was first presented in J. Cox, S. Ross, and M. Rubinstein, "Option Pricing: A Simplified Approach," *Journal of Financial Economics* (September 1979), pp. 279-263

[3] See for example R. Clarke, *Options and Futures: A Tutorial*, The Research Foundation of the Institute for Chartered Financial Analysts or J. Hull, *Options, Futures and Other Derivative Securities: 2nd ed.* (Englewood Cliffs, NJ: Prentice Hall, 1993).

Exhibit 24: Expected Stock Return

Current Value		Future Value	Probability	Future Price × Probability
		60	0.65	39
$50				
		40	0.35	14
Expected Value				$53
Return				6.00%

For example, consider a stock at $50 that can go up or down. This is shown graphically in Exhibit 24, where in a period of say one quarter the stock can move up to $60 or down to $40. Given this set of outcomes, how do we price a call option with an exercise price of $50. The Black-Scholes approach is to first create a riskless position — i.e., a position whose final value is independent of whether the stock price moves up or down. In this simple example, such a riskless position can be constructed by a buying one share of stock and selling two options. On expiration day, if the stock has appreciated to 60 the position will be worth the value of the stock less the value of the two call options (worth $20 at a price of $10 each) for a net position value of $40. Conversely, if the stock moves down, the two options expire worthless, so the net position is again worth $40. Given that this position is guaranteed to have a value of $40 at the end of the quarter, the current value of this position must be equal to $40 discounted at the risk-free rate. If we assume a risk-free rate of 5%, this amounts to $39.50. As the position is equivalent to buying the stock and selling two calls, both calls must be worth $10.50 — or $5.25 per option.

Notice that this does not require us to know the likelihood of outcomes to value options. The key observation in the Black-Scholes model and other risk neutral models is that information about the future outcomes is reflected in the price. From the perspective of a manager proposing to make an equity investment in a security about which he believes to have superior information, this valuation process is not very insightful.

One approach to overcoming this problem is to compute the actuarial return from investing in an option. Suppose in this case that the manager believes — based on his or her internal analysis — that the probability of the stock rising is 65% and the probability of the stock falling is 35% (the probabilities have to sum to one). Given the manager's analysis, the expected return from investing in the security as shown in Exhibit 24 is 6%. Using the Black-Scholes approach, if the manager observed the option selling at $6, he could sell the overpriced call option. However, selling the call would result in the expected return falling to 5.68%. (See Exhibit 25.)

The expected return is reduced because given the manager's expectations, the expected value of the call is $6.50. This is because there is a 65% probability that the option will be worth $10 and a 35% probability that it is worth zero. Note that this is more than the Black-Scholes value. This actuarial value is the criterion the manager should use in evaluating whether the option should be sold. Indeed, selling the option at a price less than the actuarial value will consistently reduce the expected return from the combined stock and option position *vis-à-vis* the stock position.

This does not imply that the Black-Scholes value is incorrect. However, it does highlight the notion that the Black-Scholes model is not useful when evaluating alternative option strategies given a view (in terms of expected return and risk) on a security. It also highlights the fact that an option's price being above that of the Black-Scholes does not assure that the seller should expect to gain from selling the option. The difference between the Black-Scholes value and the actual market price can only be earned if the seller of the option implements the complete Black-Scholes trade and re-balances the trade to maintain its risk neutrality until the expiration of the option. Transactions costs may often prevent such a strategy from being workable in the presence of limited liquidity and non-continuous markets or some of the other key assumptions underlying the Black-Scholes and other risk neutral models of option pricing as discussed below.

Why Observed Prices May Differ from Black-Scholes

The Black-Scholes model is one of the most widely used models to price securities. However there are key assumptions underlying the model which often result in observed option prices being different from their theoretical values. The factors which affect this usually arise from the violation of one or more of the economic assumptions underlying Black-Scholes. We discuss each of these briefly below.

Perfectly Liquid Markets

In order to construct the riskless hedge which underlies the Black-Scholes pricing model, we have to be able to buy or sell shares of the underlying stock and sell or buy a zero-coupon bond in the proportions required by the hedge. We must be able to trade at precisely the same price as we assumed in estimating the hedge parameters. In reality, when we actually make the purchase or sale, there is no guarantee that we will achieve our target price.

In addition, if the underlying stock is thinly traded the purchase or sale of shares will have a significant effect on the price. In such a case the cash flow of the purchase would not equal the amount required by the Black-Scholes formula.

Exhibit 25: Stock + Covered Call (at $6.00) Return

Current Value		Future Value	Probability	Future Price × Probability
$44		54	0.65	32.5
		40	0.35	14
Expected Value				$46.5
Return				5.68%

Constant Interest Rates

The risk-free rate of interest is not constant as assumed by the Black-Scholes formula. In other words, the costs built into the formula are not equal to the actual costs in carrying out the strategy. Whenever this happens it is no longer true that the total cost of constructing the hedge will be equal to the risk-free price.

Continuous Markets

The Black-Scholes hedging strategy works if the investor can continuously rebalance the hedge. This is seldom possible in the presence of transactions costs.

Geometric Brownian Motion

In computing the Black-Scholes hedge, it is necessary to assume that stock prices follow a geometric Brownian motion. In reality we observe serial correlation in stock prices and we also observe that the volatility of stock returns changes over time and often overreacts to new information. Stock returns also exhibit a tendency to "jump" — so Black-Scholes hedge positions will be susceptible to such jump risk.

Short Selling Assumption

The Black-Scholes hedge for an investor who is short call options consists of a bond sold short and a certain number of shares of the underlying security. The short position is used to finance the long position. If this money is not available, an opportunity cost (in terms of borrowing cost or foregone return) has to be incurred. In such a situation, the strategy will not be self financing.

Whenever one or more of these assumptions is violated, we would expect to see the implied volatility on an option being systematically greater than the expected actual volatility. Unless the assumptions are satisfied, however, it is not possible for an investor to attempt to capture the mispricing as he is unable to engage in the Black-Scholes riskless hedging strategy. The valuation approach identified here can then be used to identify the optimal option structure to exploit this mispricing without resorting to an active hedging strategy.

A Generalized Actuarial Model

In the example given above, we illustrated the concept of using an actuarial value approach. Here we outline a generalized approach under the usual assumption that stock returns follow a log normal distribution. We will use the following notation:

S_0 = initial stock price
C_0 = initial call price
W_0 = initial investment
D = dividends received over the time period of the option
S_f, C_f, W_f = values of the stock, call and investment on the expiry day of the option

$dS_f P_T(S_f/S_n)$ = probability density of stock price changing from S_0 to S_f in time T assuming log normal distribution

$$= \frac{dS_f}{S_f\sqrt{2\pi\sigma^2 T}}\exp\left(-\frac{\left(\ln\left(\frac{S_f}{S_0}\right)-\mu T\right)^2}{2\sigma^2 T}\right) \qquad (5)$$

T = time to expiration (T_{yr} = 1 year in same units)
σ^2 = variance of log of stock price return ($\ln(S_f/S_0)$)
μ = mean per unit time of stock log price return

Given this distribution, the expected return from an investment in the combination of stock and option is given by:

$$\int dS_f P_T(S_f/S_0)\ln\left(\frac{W_f(S_f)}{W_0}\right) \qquad (6)$$

For the covered call position:

$$W_0 = S_0 - C_0$$
$$W_f = S_f - \max[0, S_f - E] + D$$

The integral can be done numerically or approximated analytically. A similar approach handles any complex combination of stock, cash, and options, allowing an investor to identify the optimal security and option combinations. Note that using numerical techniques this same framework can be adapted to handle any arbitrary distribution. For example, the "fat tailed nature of stock price returns" can be taken into account. Transactions costs, including commissions and bid-ask spreads, are also easily incorporated into this valuation framework.

Examples of Actuarial Valuation

We illustrate the benefits of using the actuarial valuation approach to assess alternative covered call strategies — arguably one of the most popular option strategies. In this example, we assume that options on a $50 stock are priced at an implied volatility of 30% per annum. Given this assumption, call options with a maturity of one year on such a stock would take values similar to those shown in Exhibit 26. Our hypothetical investor forecasts the volatility on the stock to be 20% with an expected return of 12%. These forecasts can be derived using a variety of methods based on historical data, a factor model, or scenario forecasting. Obviously, given this volatility forecast, every option on the stock is overvalued because the implied volatility at 30% is greater than the forecast volatility of 20%. If the investor could trade the stock under the assumptions implicit under Black-Scholes, he could essentially engage in a continuous trading strategy to try and exploit the difference. However, for most investors this is not a feasible alternative — especially if the stock is not actively traded.

Exhibit 26: Call Option Prices

Strike Price	Call Price
40.00	13.19
42.50	11.42
45.00	9.80
47.50	8.35
50.00	7.06
52.50	5.93
55.00	4.95
57.50	4.11
60.00	3.40

Prices computed using Black Scholes model using a 30% annualized volatility, a risk-free rate of 5%, three months to maturity, and an underlying stock price of $50.

Exhibit 27: Gain from Alternative Stock Option Combinations
Expected Stock Return = 12% Standard Deviation = 20%

Strike Price	Stock + Covered Call Return (%)	Standard Deviation (%)	Negative Semi-Deviation (%)
40.00	7.8	3.6	2.4
42.50	9.3	4.6	2.9
45.00	10.3	6.3	3.8
47.50	11.4	7.2	3.8
50.00	12.6	8.8	4.3
52.50	13.8	10.2	4.4
55.00	14.6	12.4	5.4
57.50	15.0	13.7	5.5
60.00	15.3	14.8	5.5
Stock Only	12.0	20.0	7.5

The actuarial value approach described above, however, can be used to identify the preferred covered call position. Using equation (6), we compute in Exhibit 27 the expected return from the various covered call positions. Also computed is the standard deviation of the returns associated with each position, as well as the negative semi-deviation. Since selling the call "caps" the maximum return from the covered call position, this results in a non-symmetric distribution, and therefore standard deviation is not an appropriate measure of risk. To accurately capture the risk of loss, we compute the negative semi-deviation. This is a measure of downside risk. The data from Exhibit 27 demonstrate that the sale of an overpriced covered call should not necessarily be expected to generate incremental returns.

Selling of the calls with exercise prices of $52.5 or less actually decreases the expected return. However, it should be noted that the expected risk (assuming that negative semi-deviation is the appropriate risk measure for this investor) of each position is also lower. In contrast, the position with an exercise price of $60 has a higher expected return (15.3% versus 12%) and a lower downside risk (5.5% versus 8.5%) than simply investing in the stock.

Exhibit 28: Gain from Alternative Stock Option Combinations
Expected Stock Return = 12% Standard Deviation = 25%

Strike Price	Stock + Covered Call Return (%)	Standard Deviation (%)	Negative Semi-Deviation (%)
40.00	7.2	6.1	4.4
42.50	7.9	7.8	5.5
45.00	8.6	9.3	6.2
47.50	9.6	10.4	6.4
50.00	10.6	12.5	7.6
52.50	11.4	13.5	7.4
55.00	12.0	15.5	8.4
57.50	13.1	16.7	8.3
60.00	13.6	18.1	8.5
Stock Only	12.0	20.0	10.4

Exhibit 29: Gain from Alternative Stock Option Combinations
Expected Stock Return = 8% Standard Deviation = 20%

Strike Price	Stock + Covered Call Return (%)	Standard Deviation (%)	Negative Semi-Deviation (%)
40.00	7.6	4.8	3.3
42.50	8.6	5.4	3.3
45.00	9.5	7.2	4.3
47.50	10.4	8.7	4.9
50.00	10.9	10.6	5.6
52.50	11.5	12.2	6.1
55.00	12.1	13.7	6.6
57.50	12.1	15.2	6.8
60.00	12.4	16.6	7.3
Stock Only	8.0	20.0	10.4

Differing expectations for the volatility and return of the security will obviously generate differing expected returns from following this strategy. Using the same example as before, the expected return under the assumption that the investor forecasts volatility to be 25% per annum is recalculated — i.e., closer to the implied volatility of 30%. The resulting returns and risk measures are shown in Exhibit 28.

In this case it is only the sale of those call options with an exercise price greater than $55 that can be expected to generate incremental returns. Changes in the expected return for a stock can also have a dramatic impact on the expected return from entering into a covered call position. For example, suppose that the investor has an expected return forecast of 8% with a volatility forecast of 20%. The resulting expected returns from a covered call position are shown in Exhibit 29. With the exception of the option with the lowest exercise price, every covered call strategy has the potential to generate incremental returns and reduce risk. The magnitude of the value added is also substantially greater in this instance.

In addition to highlighting the use of the actuarial valuation process, the examples in this section also illustrate the importance of forecasting both the mean and standard deviation when attempting to exploit option market mispricing though the use of covered call writing option strategies. In each example presented here, the options were overvalued; however, it was only in the case when the return on the underlying security was low (8% per annum) that the choice of any of the call options would have added value. Without such forecasts with some demonstrated predictive power, it is doubtful that value can be added though a traditional covered call writing strategy considered here.

The implication of the examples presented above is that managers considering the use of option strategies to enhance the performance of their equity portfolios cannot simply rely on using a simple Black-Scholes or risk neutral valuation approach to attempt to add incremental returns to a portfolio. As the analysis in this chapter demonstrates, the observation that the implied volatility on an option is greater than the actual volatility is not a necessary condition to ensure that the sale of the option will generate incremental returns to a portfolio.

More generally, the valuation framework presented here can be utilized as a tool to identify optimal derivative strategies and test the implications of alternative return and volatility outcomes on expected returns. As outlined in this chapter, the potential for modifying the risk and return profile of a portfolio using derivatives is vast. Only by using such a formal valuation framework can managers systematically identify those strategies that efficiently exploit their risk and return forecasts of asset classes or individual securities.

Section III:

Fixed Income
Portfolio Management

Chapter 19

Fixed Income Analytics: Valuation and Risk Measurement

Frank J. Fabozzi, Ph.D., CFA
Adjunct Professor of Finance
School of Management
Yale University

INTRODUCTION

In this section of the book, fixed income portfolio management is covered. The purpose of this chapter is to explain the principles for valuing fixed income securities, the methodologies for valuing fixed income securities with embedded options (e.g., callable bonds, putable bonds, and mortgage-backed securities), and how to measure the interest rate risk of a security and a portfolio. Throughout this chapter and the chapters that follow, the terms fixed income security and bond are used interchangeably.

GENERAL PRINCIPLES OF VALUATION

Valuation is the process of determining the fair value of a financial asset. The fundamental principle of valuation is that the value of any financial asset is the present value of the expected cash flow. This principle applies regardless of the financial asset. In this section, we will explain the general principles of bond valuation.

Estimating Cash Flow

Cash flow is simply the cash that is expected to be received each period from an investment. In the case of a bond, it does not make any difference whether the cash flow is interest income or repayment of principal.

The cash flow for only a few types of bonds are simple to project. Noncallable Treasury securities have a known cash flow. In fact, for any fixed-rate bond in which neither the issuer nor the investor can alter the repayment of the principal before its contractual due date, the cash flow can easily be determined assuming that the issuer does not default. The difficulty in determining the cash flow for bonds arises under the following circumstances:

1. either the issuer or the investor has the option to change the contractual due date of the repayment of the principal;
2. the coupon payment is reset periodically based on some reference rate; or,
3. the investor has an option to convert the bond to common stock.

Many non-Treasury securities include a provision that grants either the issuer or the bondholder the right to change the scheduled date or dates when the principal repayment is due. Assuming that the issuer does not default, the investor knows that the principal amount will be repaid, but does not know when that principal will be received. Because of this, the cash flow is not known with certainty.

A key factor determining whether either the issuer of the bond or the investor would exercise an option is the level of interest rates in the future relative to the issue's coupon rate. Specifically, for a callable bond, if the prevailing market rate at which the issuer can refund an issue is sufficiently below the issue's coupon rate to justify the costs associated with refunding the issue, the issuer is likely to call the issue. Similarly, for a mortgage loan, if the prevailing refinancing rate available in the mortgage market is sufficiently below the loan's mortgage rate so that there will be savings by refinancing after considering the associated refinancing costs, then the homeowner has an incentive to refinance. For a putable bond, if the rate on comparable securities rises such that the value of the putable bond falls below the value at which it must be repurchased by the issuer, then the investor will put the issue.

What this means is that to properly estimate the cash flow of a bond it is necessary to incorporate into the analysis how interest rates can change in the future and how such changes affect the cash flow. As we will see in the next section, this is done in valuation models by introducing a parameter that reflects the expected volatility of interest rates.

Discounting the Cash Flow

Once the cash flow for a bond is estimated, the next step is to determine the appropriate interest rate to use to discount the cash flow. To determine the appropriate rate, the investor must address the following three questions:

1. What is the minimum interest rate the investor should require?
2. How much more than the minimum interest rate should the investor require?
3. Should the investor use the same interest rate for each estimated cash flow or a unique interest rate for each estimated cash flow?

The minimum interest rate that an investor should require is the yield available in the marketplace on a default-free cash flow. In the United States, this is the yield on a U.S. Treasury security. The premium over the yield on a Treasury security that the investor will require reflects the risks associated with realizing the estimated cash flow.

The traditional practice in valuation has been to discount every cash flow of a bond by the same interest rate (or discount rate). The fundamental flaw of this approach is that it views each security as the same package of cash flows. The proper way to view a bond is as a package of zero-coupon instruments. Each cash flow should be considered a zero-coupon instrument whose maturity value is the amount of the cash flow and whose maturity date is the date the cash flow will be received. The reason that this is the proper way is because it does not allow a market participant to realize an arbitrage profit. This will be made clearer later in this section.

To implement the contemporary approach it is necessary to determine the theoretical rate that the U.S. Treasury would have to pay to issue a zero-coupon instrument for each maturity. Another name used for the zero-coupon rate is the *spot rate*. As explained later, the spot rate can be estimated from the Treasury yield curve.

Spot Rates and their Role in Valuation

The key to the valuation of any security is the estimation of its cash flow and the discounting of each cash flow by an appropriate rate. The starting point for the determination of the appropriate rate is the theoretical spot rate on default-free securities. Since Treasury securities are viewed as default-free securities, the theoretical spot rates on these securities are the benchmark rates.

The Treasury Yield Curve

The graphical depiction of the relationship between the yield on Treasury securities of different maturities is known as the *yield curve*. The Treasury yield curve is typically constructed from on-the-run Treasury issues. Treasury bills are zero-coupon securities. Treasury notes and bonds are coupon securities. Consequently, the Treasury yield curve is a combination of zero-coupon securities and coupon securities.

In the valuation of securities what is needed is the rate on zero-coupon default-free securities or, equivalently, the rate on zero-coupon Treasury securities. However, there are no zero-coupon Treasury securities issued by the U.S. Department of the Treasury with a maturity greater than one year. Our goal is to construct a theoretical rate that the U.S. government would have to offer if it issued zero-coupon securities with a maturity greater than one year.

However, there are zero-coupon Treasury securities with a maturity greater than one year that are created by government dealer firms — stripped Treasury securities. It would seem logical that the observed yield on stripped Treasury securities could be used to construct an actual spot rate curve rather than go through the procedure we will describe. There are three problems with using the observed rates on stripped Treasury securities. First, the liquidity of the stripped Treasury market is not as great as that of the Treasury coupon market. Thus, the observed rates on stripped Treasury securities reflect a premium for liquidity. Second, there are maturity sectors of the stripped Treasury securities market that attract specific investors who may be willing to trade off yield in exchange for an attractive feature associated with that particular maturity sector, thereby distorting the term structure relationship. For example, certain foreign governments may grant investors preferential tax treatment on zero-coupon Treasuries. As a result, these foreign investors invest heavily in long-maturity stripped Treasury securities, driving down yields in that maturity sector. Finally, the tax treatment of stripped Treasury securities is different from that of Treasury coupon securities. Specifically, the accrued interest on stripped Treasury securities is taxed even though no cash is received by the investor. Thus they are negative cash flow securities to taxable entities, and, as a result, their yield reflects this tax disadvantage.

Constructing the Theoretical Spot Rate Curve for Treasuries A default-free theoretical spot rate curve can be constructed from the observed Treasury yield curve. There are several approaches that are used in practice. The approach that we describe below for creating a theoretical spot rate curve is called *bootstrapping*.[1]

To explain this approach, we use the price, annualized yield (yield to maturity), and maturity for the 20 hypothetical Treasury securities shown in Exhibit 1. Our focus is on the first four columns of the exhibit. Our goal is to explain how the values in the last two columns of the exhibit are derived.

Exhibit 1: Maturity and Yield to Maturity for 20 Hypothetical Treasury Securities

Period	Years	Yield to Maturity (%)	Price ($)	Spot Rate (%)
1	0.5	3.00	—	3.0000
2	1.0	3.30	—	3.3000
3	1.5	3.50	100.00	3.5053
4	2.0	3.90	100.00	3.9164
5	2.5	4.40	100.00	4.4376
6	3.0	4.70	100.00	4.7520
7	3.5	4.90	100.00	4.9622
8	4.0	5.00	100.00	5.0650
9	4.5	5.10	100.00	5.1701
10	5.0	5.20	100.00	5.2772
11	5.5	5.30	100.00	5.3864
12	6.0	5.40	100.00	5.4976
13	6.5	5.50	100.00	5.6108
14	7.0	5.55	100.00	5.6643
15	7.5	5.60	100.00	5.7193
16	8.0	5.65	100.00	5.7755
17	8.5	5.70	100.00	5.8331
18	9.0	5.80	100.00	5.9584
19	9.5	5.90	100.00	6.0863
20	10.0	6.00	100.00	6.2169

[1] For a discussion of these other approaches, see Chapter 2 in Frank J. Fabozzi, *Valuation of Fixed Income Securities and Derivatives: Third Edition* (New Hope, PA: Frank J. Fabozzi Associates, 1998).

Throughout the analysis and illustrations to come, it is important to remember that the basic principle is that the value of the Treasury coupon security should be equal to the value of the package of zero-coupon Treasury securities that duplicates the coupon bond's cash flow.

Consider the 6-month Treasury bill in Exhibit 1. Since a Treasury bill is a zero-coupon instrument, its annualized yield of 3.00% is equal to the spot rate. Similarly, for the 1-year Treasury, the cited yield of 3.30% is the 1-year spot rate. Given these two spot rates, we can compute the spot rate for a theoretical 1.5-year zero-coupon Treasury. The price of a theoretical 1.5-year Treasury should equal the present value of the three cash flows from the 1.5-year coupon Treasury, where the yield used for discounting is the spot rate corresponding to the cash flow. Since all the coupon bonds are selling at par, the yield to maturity for each bond is the coupon rate. Using $100 as par, the cash flow for the 1.5-year coupon Treasury is:

0.5 year	$0.035 \times \$100 \times 0.5 = \$1.75$
1.0 year	$0.035 \times \$100 \times 0.5 = \$1.75$
1.5 years	$0.035 \times \$100 \times 0.5 + \$100 = \$101.75$

The present value of the cash flow is then:

$$\frac{1.75}{(1+z_1)^1} + \frac{1.75}{(1+z_2)^2} + \frac{101.75}{(1+z_3)^3}$$

where

z_1 = one-half the annualized 6-month theoretical spot rate
z_2 = one-half the 1-year theoretical spot rate
z_3 = one-half the 1.5-year theoretical spot rate

Since the 6-month spot rate and 1-year spot rate are 3.00% and 3.30%, respectively, we know that z_1 is 0.0150 and z_2 is 0.0165.

We can compute the present value of the 1.5-year coupon Treasury security as:

$$\frac{1.75}{(1+z_1)^1} + \frac{1.75}{(1+z_2)^2} + \frac{101.75}{(1+z_3)^3} = \frac{1.75}{(1.015)^1} + \frac{1.75}{(1.0165)^2} + \frac{101.75}{(1+z_3)^3}$$

Since the price of the 1.5-year coupon Treasury security is par, the following relationship must hold:

$$\frac{1.75}{(1.015)^1} + \frac{1.75}{(1.0165)^2} + \frac{101.75}{(1+z_3)^3} = 100$$

Solving for the theoretical 1.5-year spot rate we would find z_3 is 1.75265%. Doubling this yield we obtain 3.5053%, which is the theoretical 1.5-year spot rate. That rate is the rate that the market would apply to a 1.5-year zero-coupon Treasury security if, in fact, such a security existed.

Given the theoretical 1.5-year spot rate, we can obtain the theoretical 2-year spot rate. The cash flow for the 2-year coupon Treasury in Exhibit 1 is:

0.5 year	$0.039 \times \$100 \times 0.5 = \$1.95$
1.0 year	$0.039 \times \$100 \times 0.5 = \$1.95$
1.5 years	$0.039 \times \$100 \times 0.5 = \$1.95$
2.0 years	$0.039 \times \$100 \times 0.5 + \$100 = \$101.95$

The present value of the cash flow is then:

$$\frac{1.95}{(1+z_1)^1} + \frac{1.95}{(1+z_2)^2} + \frac{1.95}{(1+z_3)^3} + \frac{101.95}{(1+z_4)^4}$$

where z_4 is one-half the 2-year theoretical spot rate. Since the 6-month spot rate, 1-year spot rate, and 1.5-year spot rate are 3.00%, 3.30%, and 3.5053%, respectively, then z_1 is 0.0150, z_2 is 0.0165, and z_3 is 0.0175265. Therefore, the present value of the 2-year coupon Treasury security is:

$$\frac{1.95}{(1.015)^1} + \frac{1.95}{(1.0165)^2} + \frac{1.95}{(1.0175265)^3} + \frac{101.95}{(1+z_4)^4}$$

Since the price of the 2-year coupon Treasury security is par, the following relationship must hold:

$$\frac{1.95}{(1.015)^1} + \frac{1.95}{(1.0165)^2} + \frac{1.95}{(1.0175265)^3} + \frac{101.95}{(1+z_4)^4} = 100$$

Solving for the theoretical 2-year spot rate we would find z_4 is 1.9582%. Doubling this yield, we obtain the theoretical 2-year spot rate of 3.9164%.

One can follow this approach sequentially to derive the theoretical 2.5-year spot rate from the calculated values of z_1, z_2, z_3, and z_4 (the 6-month, 1-year, 1.5-year, and 2-year rates), and the price and coupon of the bond with a maturity of 2.5 years. Further, one could derive theoretical spot rates for the remaining 15 semiannual rates. The spot rates thus obtained are shown in the next-to-the-last column of Exhibit 1. They represent the term structure of default-free spot rates for maturities up to ten years at the particular time to which the bond price quotations refer.

Applying the Spot Rates to Value a Treasury Coupon Security

To demonstrate how to use the spot rate curve, suppose that we want to price an 8% 10-year Treasury security. The price of this issue is the present value of the cash flow where each cash flow is discounted at the corresponding spot rate. This is illustrated in Exhibit 2. The theoretical price of this issue is $115.2619.

Exhibit 2: Determination of the Theoretical Price of an 8% 10-Year Treasury

Period	Years	Cash Flow ($)	Spot Rate (%)	Present Value ($)
1	0.5	4.00	3.0000	3.9409
2	1.0	4.00	3.3000	3.8712
3	1.5	4.00	3.5053	3.7968
4	2.0	4.00	3.9164	3.7014
5	2.5	4.00	4.4376	3.5843
6	3.0	4.00	4.7520	3.4743
7	3.5	4.00	4.9622	3.3694
8	4.0	4.00	5.0650	3.2747
9	4.5	4.00	5.1707	3.1791
10	5.0	4.00	5.2772	3.0828
11	5.5	4.00	5.3864	2.9861
12	6.0	4.00	5.4976	2.8889
13	6.5	4.00	5.6108	2.7916
14	7.0	4.00	5.6643	2.7055
15	7.5	4.00	5.7193	2.6205
16	8.0	4.00	5.7755	2.5365
17	8.5	4.00	5.8331	2.4536
18	9.0	4.00	5.9584	2.3581
19	9.5	4.00	6.0863	2.2631
20	10.0	104.00	6.2169	56.3828
			Total	115.2619

Why Treasuries Must be Valued Based on Spot Rates

The value of a Treasury security is determined by the spot rates, not the yield-to-maturity of a Treasury coupon security of the same maturity. We will use an illustration to demonstrate the economic forces that will assure that the actual market price of a Treasury coupon security will not depart significantly from its theoretical price.

To demonstrate this, consider the 8% 10-year Treasury security. Suppose that this Treasury security is priced based on the 6% yield to maturity of the 10-year maturity Treasury coupon security in Exhibit 1. Discounting each cash flow of the 8% 10-year Treasury security at 6% gives a present value of $114.88.

The question is, could this security trade at 114.88 in the market? Let's see what would happen if the 8% 10-year Treasury traded at $114.88. Suppose that a dealer firm buys this issue at $114.88 and strips it. By stripping it, we mean creating zero-coupon instruments. By stripping this issue, the dealer firm creates 20 zero-coupon instruments guaranteed by the U.S. Treasury.

How much can the 20 zero-coupon instruments be sold for by the dealer firm? Expressed equivalently, at what yield can each of the zero-coupon instruments be sold? The answer is in Exhibit 1. The yield at which each zero-coupon instrument can be sold is the spot rate shown in the next-to-the-last column. We can use Exhibit 2 to determine the proceeds that would be received per $100 of par value of the 8% 10-year issue stripped. The last column shows how much would be received for each coupon sold as a zero-coupon instrument. The total proceeds received from selling the zero-coupon Treasury securities created would be $115.2619 per $100 of par value of the Treasury issue purchased by the dealer. Since the dealer purchased the issue for $114.88, this would result in an arbitrage profit of $0.3819 per $100 of the 8% 10-year Treasury issue purchased.

To understand why the dealer has the opportunity to realize this arbitrage profit, look at the last column of Exhibit 2 which shows how much the dealer paid for each cash flow by buying the entire package of cash flows (i.e., by buying the issue). For example, consider the $4 coupon payment in four years. By buying the 10-year Treasury bond priced to yield 6%, the dealer effectively pays a price based on 6% (3% semiannual) for that coupon payment, or, equivalently, $3.1577. Under the assumptions of this illustration, however, investors were willing to accept a lower yield to maturity (the 4-year spot rate), 5.065% (2.5325% semiannual), to purchase a zero-coupon Treasury security with four years to maturity. Thus investors were willing to pay $3.2747. On this one coupon payment, the dealer realizes a profit equal to the difference between $3.2747 and $3.1577 (or $0.117). From all the cash flows, the total profit is $0.3819. In this instance, coupon stripping results in the sum of the parts being greater than the whole.

Suppose that, instead of the observed yield to maturity from Exhibit 1, the yields that investors want are the same as the theoretical spot rates that are shown in the exhibit. As can be seen in Exhibit 2, if we use these spot rates to discount the cash flows, the total proceeds from the sale of the zero-coupon Treasury securities would be equal to $115.2619, making coupon stripping uneconomic since the proceeds from stripping would be the same as the cost of purchasing the issue.

In our illustration of coupon stripping, the price of the Treasury security is less than its theoretical price. Suppose instead that the price of the Treasury coupon security is greater than its theoretical price. In this case, investors can create a portfolio of zero-coupon Treasury securities such that the cash flow of the portfolio replicates the cash flow of the mispriced Treasury coupon security. By doing so, the investor will realize a yield higher than the yield on the Treasury coupon security. For example, suppose that the market price of the 10-year Treasury coupon security we used in our illustration is $116. An investor could buy 20 outstanding zero-coupon stripped Treasury securities with a maturity value identical to the cash flow shown in the last column of Exhibit 2. The cost of purchasing this portfolio of stripped Treasury securities would be $115.2619. Thus, an investor is effectively purchasing a portfolio of stripped Treasury securities that has the same cash flow as an 8% 10-year Treasury coupon security at a cost of $115.2619 instead of $116.

It is the process of coupon stripping and reconstituting that will prevent the market price of Treasury securities from departing significantly from their theoretical price.

Yield Measures and their Limitations in Valuation

An investor who purchases a bond can expect to receive a dollar return from one or more of the following sources:

- the coupon interest payments made by the issuer,
- any capital gain (or capital loss — negative dollar return) when the bond matures, is called or is sold, and
- income from reinvestment of the coupon interest payments. This source of dollar return is referred to as *reinvestment income* or *interest on interest*.

Four yield measures are commonly cited by market participants — yield to maturity, yield to call, yield to worst, and cash flow yield. These yield measures are expressed as a percent return rather than a dollar return. However, the yield measure should consider each of the three potential sources of return cited above.

Yield to Maturity

The most popular measure of yield in the bond market is the *yield to maturity*. The yield to maturity is the interest rate that will make the present value of a bond's cash flow equal to its price plus accrued interest. The price plus accrued interest is called the *full price*.[2] To find the yield to maturity, we first determine the cash flow. Then we search by trial and error for the interest rate that will make the present value of the cash flow equal to the full price.[3]

To illustrate, consider a 7% 20-year bond selling for $67.91. The cash flow for this bond is (1) 40 6-month payments of $3.5 and (2) $100 40 6-month periods from now. The present value using various discount (interest) rates is:

Interest rate	3.5%	4.0%	4.5%	5.0%	5.5%	6.0%	6.5%
Present value	$100.00	$90.10	$81.60	$74.26	$67.91	$62.38	$57.56

When a 5.5% interest rate is used, the present value of the cash flow is equal to $67.91, which is the price of the bond. Hence, 5.5% is the semiannual yield to maturity.

The market convention adopted is to double the semiannual interest rate and call that interest rate the yield to maturity. Thus, the yield to maturity for the above bond is 11% (2 times 5.5%). The yield to maturity computed using this convention — doubling the semiannual yield — is called a *bond-equivalent yield*.

The following relationship between the price of a bond, coupon rate, and yield to maturity holds:

Bond selling at a	Relationship
par	coupon rate = yield to maturity
discount	coupon rate < yield to maturity
premium	coupon rate > yield to maturity

---

[2] The price without accrued interest is called the *clean price*.

[3] In the illustrations presented in this chapter, we assume that the next coupon payment will be six months from now so that the full price is just the clean price.

The yield to maturity considers not only the coupon income but any capital gain or loss that the investor will realize by *holding the bond to maturity*. The yield to maturity also considers the timing of the cash flow. It does consider reinvestment income; *however, it assumes that the coupon payments can be reinvested at an interest rate equal to the yield to maturity.* So, if the yield to maturity for a bond is 10%, for example, to earn that yield the coupon payments must be reinvested at an interest rate equal to 10%.

The investor will only realize the yield to maturity that is stated at the time of purchase if (1) the coupon payments can be reinvested at the yield to maturity and (2) if the bond is held to maturity. With respect to the first assumption, the risk that an investor faces is that future reinvestment rates will be less than the yield to maturity at the time the bond is purchased. This risk is referred to as *reinvestment risk*. If the bond is not held to maturity, the price of the bond may have to be sold for less than its purchase price, resulting in a return that is less than the yield to maturity. The risk that a bond will have to be sold at a loss is referred to as *interest rate risk*

There are two characteristics of a bond that determine the degree of reinvestment risk. First, for a given yield to maturity and a given coupon rate, the longer the maturity the more the bond's total dollar return is dependent on reinvestment income to realize the yield to maturity at the time of purchase. That is, the greater the reinvestment risk. The implication is that the yield to maturity measure for long-term coupon bonds tells little about the potential yield that an investor may realize if the bond is held to maturity. For long-term bonds, in high interest rate environments the reinvestment income component may be as high as 80% of the bond's potential total dollar return.

The second characteristic that determines the degree of reinvestment risk is the coupon rate. For a given maturity and a given yield to maturity, the higher the coupon rate, the more dependent the bond's total dollar return will be on the reinvestment of the coupon payments in order to produce the yield to maturity at the time of purchase. This means that holding maturity and yield to maturity constant, premium bonds will be more dependent on reinvestment income than bonds selling at par. In contrast, discount bonds will be less dependent on reinvestment income than bonds selling at par. For zero-coupons bonds, none of the bond's total dollar return is dependent on reinvestment income. So, a zero-coupon bond has no zero reinvestment risk if held to maturity.

A bond's price moves in the opposite direction of the change in interest rates. As interest rates rise (fall), the price of a bond will fall (rise). For an investor who plans to hold a bond to maturity and need not mark to market a position, the change in the bond's price prior to maturity is of no concern; however, for an investor who may have to sell the bond prior to the maturity date, an increase in interest rates subsequent to the time the bond was purchased will mean the realization of a capital loss. Not all bonds have the same degree of interest rate risk. In the last section of this chapter we shall explain the characteristics of a bond that determines its interest rate risk.

Yield to Call

When a bond is callable, the practice has been to calculate a yield to call as well as a yield to maturity. A callable bond may have a call schedule. The yield to call assumes that the issuer will call the bond at some assumed call date and the call price is then the call price specified in the call schedule. Typically, investors calculate a *yield to first call* and a *yield to first par call*.

The procedure for calculating the yield to call is the same as for any yield calculation: determine the interest rate that will make the present value of the expected cash flows equal to the price plus accrued interest. In the case of yield to first call, the expected cash flows are the coupon payments to the first call date and the call price. For the yield to first par call, the expected cash flows are the coupon payments to the first date at which the issuer can call the bond at par.

To illustrate the computation, consider a 7% 8-year bond with a maturity value of $100 selling for $106.36. Suppose that the first call date is three years from now and the call price is $103. The cash flows for this bond if it is called in three years are (1) 6 coupon payments of $3.50 every six months and (2) $103 in six 6-month periods from now. The process for finding the yield to first call is the same as for finding the yield to maturity. The present value for several semiannual interest rates is shown below:

Annual interest rate	Semi-annual rate	Present value of 6 payments of $3.5	Present value of $103 6 periods from now	Present value of cash flows
5.0%	2.5%	$16.27	91.83	108.10
5.2	2.6	16.21	91.30	107.51
5.4	2.7	16.16	90.77	106.93
5.6	2.8	16.12	90.24	106.36

Since a semiannual interest rate of 2.8% makes the present value of the cash flows equal to the price, 2.8% is the yield to first call. Therefore, the yield to first call on a bond equivalent basis is 5.6%.

Let's take a closer look at the yield to call as a measure of the potential return of a security. The yield to call does consider all three sources of potential return from owning a bond. However, as in the case of the yield to maturity, it assumes that each call flow can be reinvested at the yield to call until the assumed call date. As we just demonstrated, this assumption may be inappropriate. Moreover, the yield to call assumes that (1) the investor will hold the bond to the assumed call date and (2) the issuer will call the bond on that date.

These assumptions underlying the yield to call are often unrealistic. They do not take into account how an investor will reinvest the proceeds if the issue is called. For example, consider two 5-year bonds, M and N. Suppose that the yield to maturity for bond M, a 5-year noncallable bond, is 10% while for bond N the yield to call assuming the bond will be called in three years is 10.5%. Which bond is better for an investor with a 5-year investment horizon? It's not possible to tell from the yields cited. If the investor intends to hold the bond for five years and the issuer calls the bond after three years, the total dollars that will be available at the end of five years will depend on the interest rate that can be earned from investing funds from the call date to the end of the investment horizon.

Yield to Worst

A yield can be calculated for every possible call date. In addition, a yield to maturity can be calculated. The lowest of all these possible yields is called the *yield to worst*. For example, suppose that there are only four possible call dates for a callable bond and that a yield to call assuming each possible call date is 6%, 6.2%, 5.8% and 5.7%, and that the yield to maturity is 7.5%. Then the yield to worst is the minimum of these values, 5.7% in our example.

The yield to worst measure holds little meaning because of its underlying assumptions.

Cash Flow Yield

Mortgage-backed securities and asset-backed securities are backed by a pool of loans. The cash flows for these securities include principal repayment as well as interest. The complication that arises is that the individual borrowers whose loans make up the pool can prepay their loan in whole or in part prior to the scheduled repayment date. Because of prepayments, in order to project the cash flows it is necessary to make an assumption about the prepayment rate.

Given the cash flows based on the assumed prepayment rate, a yield can be calculated. The yield is the interest rate that will make the present value of the projected cash flows equal to the market price plus accrued interest. The yield calculated is commonly referred to as the *cash flow yield*.

Typically, the cash flows for mortgage-backed and asset-backed securities are monthly. Therefore the interest rate that will make the present value of the projected principal repayment and interest payments equal to the market price plus accrued interest is a monthly rate. The bond equivalent yield is found by calculating the effective 6-month interest rate and then doubling it. That is:

Cash flow yield on a bond-equivalent basis

$$= 2\,[(1 + \text{monthly yield})^6 - 1]$$

For example, if the monthly yield is 0.5%, then:

Cash flow yield on a bond-equivalent basis $= 2\,[(1.005)^6 - 1] = 6.08\%$

As we have noted, the yield to maturity has two shortcomings as a measure of a bond's potential return: (1) it is assumed that the coupon payments can be reinvested at a rate equal to the yield to maturity and (2) it is assumed that the bond is held to maturity. These shortcomings are equally present in application of the cash flow yield measure: (1) the projected cash flows are assumed to be reinvested at the cash flow yield and (2) the mortgage-backed or asset-backed security is assumed to be held until the final payout based on some prepayment assumption. The importance of reinvestment risk, the risk that the cash flow will be reinvested at a rate less than the cash flow yield, is particularly important for mortgage-backed and asset-backed securities since payments are typically monthly. Moreover, the cash flow yield is dependent on realization of the projected cash flows according to some prepayment rate. If actual prepayments differ significantly from the prepayment rate assumed, the cash flow yield will not be realized.

Price/Yield Relationship

If the yield the market requires on a bond increases, the price of the bond will decline. This is because by discounting each cash flow at a higher yield, the present value of the cash flow declines. If the yield on a bond decreases, the price of the bond will increase. Again, this is due to the use of a different yield to calculate the present value of the cash flow. A lower yield raises the present value of the cash flow and therefore the price.

In general, the price of a bond is inversely related to its yield. This is not true for all bonds. There are bonds whose price changes in the same direction as the change in yield. For example, there are mortgage derivative products that have this characteristic. The reason for this odd characteristic is that the cash flow for such securities is interest rate dependent. This means that the cash flow itself changes as interest rates change. Bonds that have this price/yield relationship are typically used for hedging fixed income products.

It is also important to note that the price/yield relationship just discussed is for an instantaneous change in yield. Over time, the price of a bond may change even if yields do not change. Specifically, a bond purchased at a discount to par will increase in price as it approaches maturity. The opposite is true for a bond purchased at a premium to par.

Yield Spread Measures

Traditional analysis of the yield premium for a non-Treasury bond involves calculating the difference between the bond's yield to maturity (or yield to call) and the yield to maturity of a comparable maturity Treasury coupon security. The latter is obtained from the Treasury yield curve. For example, consider the following 10-year bonds:

Issue	Coupon	Price	Yield to maturity
Treasury	6%	$100.00	6.00%
Non-Treasury	8%	$104.19	7.40%

The yield spread for these two bonds as traditionally computed is 140 basis points (7.4% minus 6%). We refer to this traditional yield spread as the *nominal spread*.

The drawbacks of the nominal spread are (1) for both bonds, the yield fails to take into consideration the term structure of the spot rates and (2) in the case of callable and/or putable bonds, expected interest rate volatility may alter the cash flow of the non-Treasury bond. Here, we focus only on the first problem: failure to consider the spot rate curve. We will deal with the second problem in the next section.

Zero-Volatility Spread

The *zero-volatility spread* is a measure of the spread that the investor would realize over the entire Treasury spot rate curve if (1) the bond is held to maturity and (2) the spot rates do not change. It is not a spread off one point on the Treasury yield curve, as is the nominal spread. The zero-volatility spread, also called the *static spread*, is calculated as the spread that will make the present value of the cash flow from the non-Treasury bond, when discounted at the Treasury spot rate plus the spread, equal to the non-Treasury bond's full price. A trial-and-error procedure is required to determine the zero-volatility spread.

To illustrate how this is done, let's use the non-Treasury bond in our previous illustration and the Treasury yield curve in Exhibit 1. The Treasury spot rates are reproduced in the fourth column of Exhibit 3. The third column in the exhibit is the cash flow for the 8% 10-year non-Treasury issue. The goal is to determine the spread that when added to all the Treasury spot rates that will produce a present value for the cash flow of the non-Treasury bond equal to its market price, $104.19.

Exhibit 3: Determination of the Zero-Volatility Spread for the 8%, 10-Year Non-Treasury Issue Selling at 104.19 to Yield 7.4%

Period	Years	Cash Flow ($)	Spot Rate (%)	Present Value		
				Spread 100 bp ($)	Spread 125 bp ($)	Spread 146 bp ($)
1	0.5	4.00	3.0000	3.9216	3.9168	3.9127
2	1.0	4.00	3.3000	3.8334	3.8240	3.8162
3	1.5	4.00	3.5053	3.7414	3.7277	3.7163
4	2.0	4.00	3.9164	3.6297	3.6121	3.5973
5	2.5	4.00	4.4376	3.4979	3.4767	3.4590
6	3.0	4.00	4.7520	3.3742	3.3497	3.3293
7	3.5	4.00	4.9622	3.2565	3.2290	3.2061
8	4.0	4.00	5.0650	3.1497	3.1193	3.0940
9	4.5	4.00	5.1701	3.430	3.0100	2.9826
10	5.0	4.00	5.2772	2.9366	2.9013	2.8719
11	5.5	4.00	5.3864	2.8307	2.7933	2.7622
12	6.0	4.00	5.4976	2.7255	2.6862	2.6537
13	6.5	4.00	5.6108	2.6210	2.5801	2.5463
14	7.0	4.00	5.6643	2.5279	2.4855	2.4504
15	7.5	4.00	5.7193	2.4367	2.3929	2.3568
16	8.0	4.00	5.7755	2.3472	2.3023	2.2652
17	8.5	4.00	5.8331	2.2596	2.2137	2.1758
18	9.0	4.00	5.9584	2.1612	2.1148	2.0766
19	9.5	4.00	6.0863	2.0642	2.0174	1.9790
20	10.0	104.00	6.2169	51.1833	49.9638	48.9630
			Total	107.5414	105.7165	104.2145

Suppose we select a spread of 100 basis points. To each Treasury spot rate shown in the fourth column 100 basis points is added. So, for example, the 5-year (period 10) spot rate is 6.2772% (5.2772% plus 1%). The spot rate plus 100 basis points is then used to calculate the present value of $107.5414. Because the present value is not equal to the non-Treasury issue's price ($104.19), the zero-volatility spread is not 100 basis points. If a spread of 125 basis points is tried, it can be seen from the next-to-the-last column of Exhibit 3 that the present value is $105.7165; again, because this is not equal to the non-Treasury issue's price, 125 basis points is not the zero-volatility spread. The last column of Exhibit 3 shows the present value when a 146 basis point spread is tried. The present value is equal to the non-Treasury issue's price. Therefore 146 basis points is the zero-volatility spread, compared to the nominal spread of 140 basis points.

Divergence Between Zero-Volatility Spread and Nominal Spread

Typically, for standard coupon paying bonds with a bullet maturity (i.e., a single payment of principal) the zero-volatility spread and the nominal spread will not differ significantly. In our example it is only 6 basis points (146 basis points versus 140 basis points).

For short-term bullet issues, there is little divergence. The main factor causing any difference is the shape of the yield curve. The steeper the yield curve, the greater the difference. The difference between the zero-volatility spread and the nominal spread is greater for issue's in which the principal is repaid over time rather than only at maturity. Thus the difference between the nominal spread and the zero-volatility spread will be considerably greater for sinking fund bonds, mortgage-backed securities, and asset-backed securities in a steep yield curve environment.

The Term Structure of Credit Spreads

The Treasury spot rates can be used to value any default-free security. As we illustrated earlier, failure of Treasury securities to be priced according to the Treasury spot rates creates the opportunity for arbitrage profits or enhanced returns. For a non-Treasury bond, the theoretical value is not as easy to determine. The value of a non-Treasury bond must reflect not only the spot rate for default-free bonds but also a risk premium to reflect default risk and any options embedded in the issue.

It has been common in practice for the spot rate used to discount the cash flow of a non-Treasury bond to be the Treasury spot rate plus a constant credit spread. For example, if the 6-month Treasury spot rate is 3%, and the 10-year Treasury spot rate is 6%, and a suitable credit spread is deemed to be 100 basis points, then a 4% spot rate is used to discount a 6-month cash flow of a non-Treasury bond and a 7% discount rate to discount a 10-year cash flow.

The drawback of this approach is that there is no reason to expect the credit spread to be the same regardless of when the cash flow is expected to be received. Instead, it might be expected that the credit spread increases with the maturity of the bond. That is, there is a term structure for credit spreads.

In practice, the difficulty in estimating a term structure for credit spreads is that unlike Treasury securities in which there is a wide-range of maturities from which to construct a Treasury spot rate curve, there are no issuers that offer a sufficiently wide range of non-Treasury zero-coupon securities to construct a zero-coupon spread curve. Robert Litterman and Thomas Iben describe a procedure to construct a generic zero-coupon spread curve for corporate bonds by credit rating and industry using data provided from a trading desk.[4]

Benchmark Spot Rate Curve

When the generic zero spreads for a given credit quality and in a given industry are added to the default-free spot rates, the resulting term structure is used to value bonds of issuers of the same credit quality in the industry sector. This term structure is referred to as the *benchmark spot rate curve* or *benchmark zero-coupon rate curve*.

For example, Exhibit 4 reproduces the default-free spot rate curve in Exhibit 1. Also shown in the exhibit is a hypothetical generic zero spread for AAA industrial bonds. The resulting benchmark spot rate curve is in the next-to-the-last column. It is this spot rate curve that is used to value a AAA industrial bond. This is done in Exhibit 4 for a hypothetical 8% 10-year AAA industrial bond. The theoretical price is $108.4615.

Zero-Volatility Spread

In the same way that a zero-volatility spread relative to a default-free spot rate curve can be calculated, a zero-volatility spread to any benchmark spot rate curve can be calculated. To illustrate, suppose that a hypothetical AAA industrial bond with a coupon rate of 8% and a 10-year maturity is trading at $105.5423. The zero-volatility spread relative to the AAA industrial term structure is the spread that must be added to that term structure that will make the present value of the cash flow equal to the market price. In our illustration, the zero-volatility spread relative to this benchmark is 40 basis points.

Thus, when a zero-volatility spread is cited, it must be cited relative to some benchmark spot rate curve. This is necessary because it indicates the credit and sector risks that are being considered when the zero-volatility spread is calculated.

VALUATION OF BONDS WITH EMBEDDED OPTIONS

In the previous section, our discussion of bond valuation has been limited to bonds in which neither the issuer nor the bondholder has the option to alter a bond's cash flows. Now we look at how to value bonds with embedded options.

---

[4] Robert Litterman and Thomas Iben, "Corporate Bond Valuation and the Term Structure of Credit Spreads," *Journal of Portfolio Management* (Spring 1991), pp. 52-64.

Exhibit 4: Calculation of Value of a Hypothetical AAA Industrial 8% 10-Year Bond Using Benchmark Spot Rate Curve

Period	Years	Cash Flow ($)	Treasury Spot Rate (%)	Zero-coupon Credit Spread	Benchmark Spot Rate (%)	Present Value ($)
1	0.5	4.00	3.0000	0.20	3.2000	3.9370
2	1.0	4.00	3.3000	0.20	3.5000	3.8636
3	1.5	4.00	3.5053	0.25	3.7553	3.7829
4	2.0	4.00	3.9164	0.30	4.2164	3.6797
5	2.5	4.00	4.4376	0.35	4.7876	3.5538
6	3.0	4.00	4.7520	0.35	5.1020	3.4389
7	3.5	4.00	4.9622	0.40	5.3622	3.3237
8	4.0	4.00	5.0650	0.45	5.5150	3.2177
9	4.5	4.00	5.1701	0.45	5.6201	3.1170
10	5.0	4.00	5.2772	0.50	5.7772	3.0088
11	5.5	4.00	5.3864	0.55	5.9364	2.8995
12	6.0	4.00	5.4976	0.60	6.0976	2.7896
13	6.5	4.00	5.6108	0.65	6.2608	2.6794
14	7.0	4.00	5.6643	0.70	6.3643	2.5799
15	7.5	4.00	5.7193	0.75	6.4693	2.4813
16	8.0	4.00	5.7755	0.80	6.5755	2.3838
17	8.5	4.00	5.8331	0.85	6.6831	2.2876
18	9.0	4.00	5.9584	0.90	6.8684	2.1801
19	9.5	4.00	6.0863	0.95	7.0363	2.0737
20	10.0	104.00	6.2169	1.00	7.2169	51.1833
					Total	108.4615

To develop an analytical framework for valuing a bond with embedded options, it is necessary to decompose a bond into its component parts. Consider, for example, the most common bond with an embedded option, a callable bond. A callable bond is a bond in which the bondholder has sold the issuer an option (more specifically, a call option) that allows the issuer to repurchase the contractual cash flows of the bond from the time of the bond's first call date until the maturity date.

Consider the following two bonds: (1) a callable bond with an 8% coupon, 20 years to maturity and callable in five years at 104 and (2) a 10-year 9% coupon bond callable immediately at par. For the first bond, the bondholder owns a 5-year noncallable bond and has sold a call option granting the issuer the right to call away from the bondholder 15 years of cash flows five years from now for a price of 104. The investor who owns the second bond has a 10-year noncallable bond and has sold a call option granting the issuer the right to immediately call the entire 10-year contractual cash flows, or any cash flows remaining at the time the issue is called, for 100.

Effectively, the owner of a callable bond is entering into two separate transactions. First, the investor buys a noncallable bond from the issuer for which he pays some price. Then, he sells the issuer a call option for which he receives the option price. Therefore, we can summarize the position of a callable bond-holder as follows:

long a callable bond = long a noncallable bond + sold a call option

In terms of value, the value of a callable bond is therefore equal to the value of the two components parts. That is,

value of a callable bond = value of a noncallable bond − value of a call option

The reason the call option's value is subtracted from the value of the noncallable bond is that when the bondholder sells a call option, he receives the option price. Actually, the position is more complicated than we just described. The issuer may be entitled to call the bond at the first call date and anytime thereafter, or at the first call date and any subsequent coupon anniversary date. Thus the investor has effectively sold an American-type call option to the issuer, but the call price may vary with the date the call option is exercised. This is because the call schedule for a bond may have a different call price depending on the call date. Moreover, the underlying bond for the call option is the remaining coupon payments that would have been made by the issuer had the bond not been called. For exposition purposes, it is easier to understand the principles associated with the investment characteristics of callable bonds by describing the investor's position as long a noncallable bond and short a call option.

The same logic applies to putable bonds. In the case of a putable bond, the bondholder has the right to sell the bond to the issuer at a designated price and time. A putable bond can be broken into two separate transactions. First, the investor buys a putable bond. Second, the investor buys a put option from the issuer that allows the investor to sell the bond to the issuer. Therefore, the position of a putable bondholder can be described as:

long a putable bond = long a nonputable bond + long a put option

In terms of value,

value of a putable bond = value of a nonputable bond + value of a put option

There are two main approaches to the valuation of bonds with embedded options: (1) the binomial lattice method, or simply, binomial method and (2) the Monte Carlo simulation method. There are two things that are common to both methods. First, each begins with an assumption as to the statistical process that is assumed to generate the term structure of interest rates. Second, each method is based on the principle that arbitrage profits cannot be generated. By this it is meant that the model will correctly price the on-the-run issues; or, equivalently, the model is calibrated to the market.

Before describing the two valuation methodologies, we discuss three important concepts: option-adjusted spread, option cost, and modeling risk.

Option-Adjusted Spread

A valuation model allows an investor to estimate the theoretical value of a security, which at this point would be sufficient to determine the fairness of the price of the security. That is, the investor can say that this bond is 1 point cheap or 2 points cheap, and so on. A valuation model need not stop here, however. Instead, it can convert the divergence between the price observed in the market for the security and the theoretical value derived from the model into a yield spread measure. This step is necessary since many market participants find it more convenient to think about yield spread than price differences.

The *option-adjusted spread* (OAS) was developed as a measure of the yield spread that can be used to convert dollar differences between value and price. Thus, basically, the OAS is used to reconcile value with market price. But what is it a "spread" over? As we shall see when we describe the two valuation methodologies, the OAS is a spread over the issuer's spot rate curve or benchmark. The spot rate curve itself is not a single curve, but a series of spot rate curves that allow for changes in rates.

The reason that the resulting spread is referred to as "option-adjusted" is because the cash flows of the security whose value we seek are adjusted to reflect any embedded options. In contrast, the zero-volatility spread does not consider how the cash flows will change when interest rates change in the future. That is, the zero-volatility spread assumes that interest rate volatility is zero. Consequently, the zero-volatility spread is also referred to as the *static spread*.

Option Cost

The implied cost of the option embedded in any security can be obtained by calculating the difference between the OAS at the assumed volatility of interest rates and the zero-volatility spread. That is,

Option cost = Zero-volatility spread − Option-adjusted spread

The reason that the option cost is measured in this way is as follows. In an environment of no interest rate changes, the investor would earn the zero-volatility spread. When future interest rates are uncertain, the spread is different because of the embedded option; the OAS reflects the spread after adjusting for this option. Therefore, the option cost is the difference between the spread that would be earned in a static interest rate environment (the zero-volatility spread, or equivalently, the static spread) and the spread after adjusting for the option (the OAS).

For callable bonds and mortgage passthrough securities, the option cost is positive. This is because the borrower's ability to alter the cash flow will result in an OAS that is less than the zero-volatility spread. In the case of a putable bond, the OAS is greater than the zero-volatility spread so that the option cost is negative. This occurs because of the investor's ability to alter the cash flow.

Exhibit 5: On-the-Run Yield Curve and Spot Rates for an Issuer

Maturity (Years)	Yield to Maturity (%)	Market Price ($)	Spot Rate (%)
1	3.5	100	3.5000
2	4.2	100	4.2147
3	4.7	100	4.7345
4	5.2	100	5.2707

In general, when the option cost is positive, this means that the investor has sold or is short an option. This is true for callable bonds and mortgage passthrough securities. A negative value for the option cost means that the investor has purchased or is long an option. A putable bond is an example of a security with a negative option cost. There are certain securities in the mortgage-backed securities market that also have an option cost that is negative.

While the option cost as described above is measured in basis points, it can be translated into a dollar price.

Modeling Risk

The user of any valuation model is exposed to modeling risk. This is the risk that the output of the model is incorrect because the assumptions upon which it is based are incorrect. Consequently, it is imperative that the results of a valuation model be stress-tested for modeling risk by altering the assumptions.

Binomial Method

The *binomial method* is a popular technique for valuing callable and putable bonds. To illustrate this, we start with the on-the-run yield curve for the particular issuer whose bonds we want to value. The starting point is the Treasury's on-the-run yield curve. To obtain a particular issuer's on-the-run yield curve, an appropriate credit spread is added to each on-the-run Treasury issue. The credit spread need not be constant for all maturities. For example, the credit spread may increase with maturity.

In our illustration, we use the hypothetical on-the-run issues for an issuer shown in Exhibit 5. Each bond is trading at par value (100) so the coupon rate is equal to the yield to maturity. We will simplify the illustration by assuming annual-pay bonds. Using the bootstrapping methodology explained in the previous section, the spot rates are those shown in the last column of Exhibit 5.

Binomial Interest Rate Tree[5]

Once we allow for embedded options, consideration must be given to interest rate volatility. This can be done by introducing a *binomial interest rate tree*. This tree

---

[5] The model described in this section was presented in Andrew J. Kalotay, George O. Williams, and Frank J. Fabozzi, "A Model for the Valuation of Bonds and Embedded Options," *Financial Analysts Journal* (May-June 1993), pp. 3546.

is nothing more than a graphical depiction of the 1-period or short rates over time based on some assumption about interest rate volatility. How this tree is constructed is illustrated below.

Exhibit 6 shows an example of a binomial interest rate tree. In this tree, each node (bold circle) represents a time period that is equal to one year from the node to its left. Each node is labeled with an N, representing node, and a subscript that indicates the path that the 1-year rate took to get to that node. L represents the lower of the two 1-year rates and H represents the higher of the two 1-year rates. For example, node NHH means to get to that node the following path for 1year rates occurred: the 1-year rate realized is the higher of the two rates in the first year and then the higher of the 1-year rates in the second year.[6]

Look first at the point denoted by just N in Exhibit 6. This is the root of the tree and is nothing more than the current 1-year spot rate, or equivalently the current 1-year rate, which we denote by r_0. What we have assumed in creating this tree is that the 1-year rate can take on two possible values the next period and the two rates have the same probability of occurring. One rate will be higher than the other. It is assumed that the 1-year rate can evolve over time based on a random process called a lognormal random walk with a certain volatility.

We use the following notation to describe the tree in the first year. Let

σ = assumed volatility of the 1-year rate

$r_{1,L}$ = the lower 1-year rate one year from now

$r_{1,H}$ = the higher 1-year rate one year from now

Exhibit 6: Four-Year Binomial Interest Rate Tree

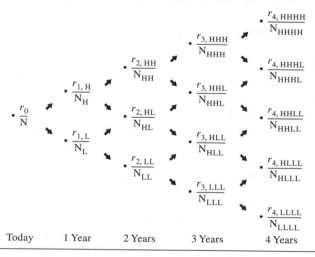

| Today | 1 Year | 2 Years | 3 Years | 4 Years |

[6] Note that N_{HL} is equivalent to N_{LH} in the second year and that in the third year N_{HHL} is equivalent to N_{HLH} and N_{LHH} and that N_{HLL} is equivalent to N_{LLH}. We have simply selected one label for a node rather than clutter up the figure with unnecessary information.

The relationship between $r_{1,L}$ and $r_{1,H}$ is as follows:

$$r_{1,H} = r_{1,L}(e^{2\sigma})$$

where e is the base of the natural logarithm 2.71828.

For example, suppose that $r_{1,L}$ is 4.4448% and σ is 10% per year, then:

$$r_{1,H} = 4.4448\%(e^{2 \times 0.10}) = 5.4289\%$$

In the second year, there are three possible values for the 1-year rate, which we will denote as follows:

$r_{2,LL}$ = 1-year rate in second year assuming the lower rate in the first year and the lower rate in the second year

$r_{2,HH}$ = 1-year rate in second year assuming the higher rate in the first year and the higher rate in the second year

$r_{2,HL}$ = 1-year rate in second year assuming the higher rate in the first year and the lower rate in the second year or equivalently the lower rate in the first year and the higher rate in the second year

The relationship between $r_{2,LL}$ and the other two 1-year rates is as follows:

$$r_{2,HH} = r_{2,LL}(e^{4\sigma}) \text{ and } r_{2,HL} = r_{2,LL}(e^{2\sigma})$$

So, for example, if $r_{2,LL}$ is 4.6958%, then assuming once again that σ is 10%, then

$$r_{2,HH} = 4.6958\%(e^{4 \times 0.10}) = 7.0053\% \text{ and } r_{2,HL} = 4.6958\%(e^{4 \times 0.10}) = 5.7354\%$$

In the third year there are four possible values for the 1-year rate, which are denoted as follows: $r_{3,HHH}$, $r_{3,HHL}$, $r_{3,HLL}$, and $r_{3,LLL}$, and whose first three values are related to the last as follows:

$$r_{3,HHH} = (e^{6\sigma}) r_{3,LLL}, r_{3,HHL} = (e^{4\sigma}) r_{3,LLL}, r_{3,HLL} = (e^{2\sigma}) r_{3,LLL}$$

Exhibit 6 shows the notation for a 4-year binomial interest rate tree. We can simplify the notation by letting r_t be the 1-year rate t years from now for the lower rate since all the other short rates t years from now depend on that rate. Exhibit 7 shows the interest rate tree using this simplified notation.

Before we go on to show how to use this binomial interest rate tree to value bonds, let's focus on two issues here. First, what does the volatility parameter σ represent? Second, how do we find the value of the bond at each node?

Volatility and the Standard Deviation It can be shown that the standard deviation of the 1-year rate is equal to $r_0\sigma$.[7] The standard deviation is a statistical measure of volatility. It is important to see that the process that we assumed gener-

---

[7] This can be seen by noting that $e^{2\sigma} \cong 1 + 2\sigma$. Then the standard deviation of the 1-period rate is

$$\frac{re^{2\sigma} - r}{2} \approx \frac{r + 2\sigma r - r}{2} = \sigma r$$

ates the binomial interest rate tree (or equivalently the short rates), implies that volatility is measured relative to the current level of rates. For example, if σ is 10% and the 1-year rate (r_0) is 4%, then the standard deviation of the 1-year rate is 4% × 10% = 0.4% or 40 basis points. However, if the current 1-year rate is 12%, the standard deviation of the 1-year rate would be 12% × 10% or 120 basis points.

Determining the Value at a Node To find the value of the bond at a node, we first calculate the bond's value at the two nodes to the right of the node we are interested in. For example, in Exhibit 7, suppose we want to determine the bond's value at node N_H. The bond's value at node N_{HH} and N_{HL} must be determined. Hold aside for now how we get these two values because as we will see, the process involves starting from the last year in the tree and working backwards to get the final solution we want, so these two values will be known.

Effectively what we are saying is that if we are at some node, then the value at that node will depend on the future cash flows. In turn, the future cash flows depend on (1) the bond's value one year from now and (2) the coupon payment one year from now. The latter is known. The former depends on whether the 1-year rate is the higher or lower rate. The bond's value depending on whether the rate is the higher or lower rate is reported at the two nodes to the right of the node that is the focus of our attention. So, the cash flow at a node will be either (1) the bond's value if the short rate is the higher rate plus the coupon payment, or (2) the bond's value if the short rate is the lower rate plus the coupon payment. For example, suppose that we are interested in the bond's value at N_H. The cash flow will be either the bond's value at N_{HH} plus the coupon payment, or the bond's value at N_{HL} plus the coupon payment.

Exhibit 7: Four-Year Binomial Interest Rate Tree with 1-Year Rates*

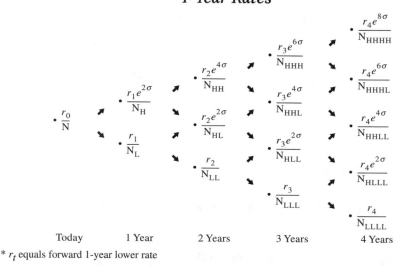

* r_t equals forward 1-year lower rate

Exhibit 8: Calculating a Value at a Node

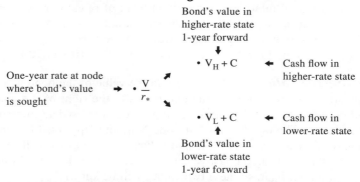

To get the bond's value at a node we follow the fundamental rule for valuation: the value is the present value of the expected cash flows. The appropriate discount rate to use is the 1-year rate at the node. Now there are two present values in this case: the present value if the 1-year rate is the higher rate and one if it is the lower rate. Since it is assumed that the probability of both outcomes is equal, an average of the two present values is computed. This is illustrated in Exhibit 8 for any node assuming that the 1-year rate is r^* at the node where the valuation is sought and letting:

V_H = the bond's value for the higher 1-year rate
V_L = the bond's value for the lower 1-year rate
C = coupon payment

Using our notation, the cash flow at a node is either:

$V_H + C$ for the higher 1-year rate or $V_L + C$ for the lower 1-year rate

The present value of these two cash flows using the 1-year rate at the node, r^*, is:

$$\frac{V_H + C}{(1 + r_*)} = \text{present value for the higher 1-year rate}$$

$$\frac{V_L + C}{(1 + r_*)} = \text{present value for the lower 1-year rate}$$

Then, the value of the bond at the node is found as follows:

$$\text{Value at a node} = \frac{1}{2}\left[\frac{V_H + C}{(1 + r_*)} + \frac{V_L + C}{(1 + r_*)}\right]$$

Constructing the Binomial Interest Rate Tree

To see how to construct the binomial interest rate tree, let's use the assumed on-the-run yields we used earlier. We will assume that volatility, σ, is 10% and construct a 2-year tree using the 2-year bond with a coupon rate of 4.2%.

Exhibit 9: The 1-Year Rates for Year 1 Using the 2-Year 4.2% On-the-Run Issue: First Trial

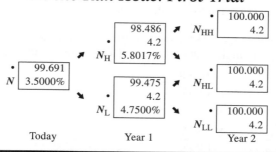

Today	Year 1	Year 2

Exhibit 9 shows a more detailed binomial interest rate Once with the cash flow shown at each node. We'll see how all the values reported in the exhibit are obtained. The root rate for the tree, r_0, is simply the current 1-year rate, 3.5%.

In the first year there are two possible 1-year rates, the higher rate and the lower rate. What we want to find is the two 1-year rates that will be consistent with the volatility assumption, the process that is assumed to generate the short rates, and the observed market value of the bond. There is no simple formula for this. It must be found by an iterative process (i.e., trial-and-error). The steps are described and illustrated below.

Step 1: Select a value for r_1. Recall that r_1 is the lower 1-year rate. In this first trial, we *arbitrarily* selected a value of 4.75%.

Step 2: Determine the corresponding value for the higher 1-year rate. As explained earlier, this rate is related to the lower 1-year rate as follows: $r_1 e^{2\sigma}$. Since r_1 is 4.75%, the higher 1-year rate is 5.8017% (= 4.75% $e^{2\times0.10}$). This value is reported in Exhibit 7 at node N_H

Step 3: Compute the bond value's one year from now. This value is determined as follows:

3a. Determine the bond's value two years from now. In our example, this is simple. Since we are using a 2-year bond, the bond's value is its maturity value ($100) plus its final coupon payment ($4.2). Thus, it is $104.2.

3b. Calculate the present value of the bond's value found in 3a for the higher rate in the second year. The appropriate discount rate is the higher 1year rate, 5.8017% in our example. The present value is $98.456 (= $104.2/ 1.058017). This is the value of V_H that we referred to earlier.

3c. Calculate the present value of the bond's value found in 3a for the lower rate. The discount rate assumed for the lower 1-year rate is 4.75%. The present value is $99.475 (= $104.2/1.0475) and is the value of V_L.

3d. Add the coupon to both V_H and V_L to get the cash flow at N_H and N_L, respectively. In our example we have $102.686 for the higher rate and $103.675 for the lower rate.

3e. Calculate the present value of the two values using the 1-year rate r^*. At this point in the valuation, r^* is the root rate, 3.50%. Therefore,

$$\frac{V_H + C}{1 + r_*} = \frac{\$102.686}{1.035} = \$99.213$$

$$\frac{V_L + C}{1 + r_*} = \frac{\$103.675}{1.035} = \$100.169$$

Step 4: Calculate the average present value of the two cash flows in Step 3. This is the value we referred to earlier as

$$\text{Value at a node} = \frac{1}{2}\left[\frac{V_H + C}{(1 + r_*)} + \frac{V_L + C}{(1 + r_*)}\right]$$

In our example, we have

$$\text{Value at a node} = \frac{1}{2}(\$99.213 + \$100.169) = \$99.691$$

Step 5: Compare the value in Step 4 to the bond's market value. If the two values are the same, then the r_1 used in this trial is the one we seek. This is the 1-year rate that would then be used in the binomial interest rate tree for the lower rate and to obtain the corresponding higher rate. If, instead, the value found in step 4 is not equal to the market value of the bond, this means that the value r_1 in this trial is not the 1-year rate that is consistent with (1) the volatility assumption, (2) the process assumed to generate the 1-year rate, and (3) the observed market value of the bond. In this case, the five steps are repeated with a different value for r_1.

When r_1 is 4.75%, a value of $99.691 results in Step 4 which is less than the observed market price of $100. Therefore, 4.75% is too large and the five steps must be repeated trying a lower rate for r_1.

Let's jump right to the correct rate for r_1 in this example and rework steps 1 through 5. This occurs when r_1 is 4.4448%. The corresponding binomial interest rate tree is shown in Exhibit 10.

Step 1: In this trial we select a value of 4.4448% for r_1, the lower 1-year rate.

Step 2: The corresponding value for the higher 1-year rate is 5.4289% (= 4.4448% $e^{2\times0.10}$).

Step 3: The bond's value one year from now is determined as follows:

Exhibit 10: The 1-Year Rates for Year 1 Using the 2-Year 4.2% On-the-Run Issue

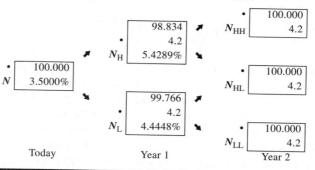

| | Today | Year 1 | Year 2 |

3a. The bond's value two years from now is $104.2, just as in the first trial.

3b. The present value of the bond's value found in *3a* for the higher 1-year rate, V_H, is $98.834 (= $104.2/1.054289$).

3c. The present value of the bond's value found in *3a* for the lower 1-year rate, V_L, is $99.766 (= $104.2/1.044448$).

3d. Adding the coupon to V_H and V_L, we get $103.034 as the cash flow for the higher rate and $103.966 as the cash flow for the lower rate.

3e. The present value of the two cash flows using the 1-year rate at the node to the left, 3.5%, gives

$$\frac{V_H + C}{1 + r_*} = \frac{\$103.034}{1.035} = \$99.550$$

$$\frac{V_L + C}{1 + r_*} = \frac{\$103.966}{1.035} = \$100.450$$

Step 4: The average present value is $100, which is the value at the node.

Step 5: Since the average present value is equal to the observed market price of $100, r_1 or $r_{1,L}$ is 4.4448% and $r_{1,H}$ is 5.4289%.

We can "grow" this tree for one more year by determining r_2. Now we will use the 3-year on-the-run issue, the 4.7% coupon bond, to get r_2. The same five steps are used in an iterative process to find the 1-year rates in the tree two years from now. Our objective is now to find the value of r_2 that will produce a bond value of $100 (since the 3-year on-the-run issue has a market price of $100) and is consistent with (1) a volatility assumption of 10%, (2) a current 1-year rate of 3.5%, and (3) the two rates one year from now of 4.4448% (the lower rate) and 5.4289% (the higher rate).

We explain how this is done using Exhibit 11. Let's look at how we get the information in the exhibit. The maturity value and coupon payment are shown in the boxes at the four nodes three years from now. Since the 3-year on-the-run issue has a maturity value of $100 and a coupon payment of $4.7, these values are the same in the box shown at each node. For the three nodes two years from now the coupon payment of $4.7 is shown. Unknown at these three nodes are (1) the three rates two years from now and (2) the value of the bond two years from now. For the two nodes one year from now, the coupon payment is known, as are the 1-year rates one year from now. These are the rates found earlier. The value of the bond, which depends on the bond values at the nodes to the right, are unknown at these two nodes. All of the unknown values are indicated by a question mark.

Exhibit 12 is the same as Exhibit 11 but complete with the values previously unknown. As can be seen from Exhibit 12, the value of r_2, or equivalency $r_{2,LL}$, which will produce the desired result is 4.6958%. We showed earlier that the corresponding rates $r_{2,HL}$ and $r_{2,HH}$ would be 5.7354% and 7.0053%, respectively. To verify chat these are the 1-year rates two years from now, work backwards from the four nodes at the right of the tree in Exhibit 12. For example, the value in the box at N_{HH} is found by taking the value of $104.7 at the two nodes to its right and discounting at 7.0053%. The value is $97.846. (Since it is the same value for both nodes to the right, it is also the average value.) Similarly, the value in the box at N_{HL} is found by discounting $104.70 by 5.7354% and at N_{LL} by discounting at 4.6958%. The same procedure used in Exhibits 7 and 8 is used to get the values at the other nodes.

Exhibit 11: Information for Deriving the 1-Year Rates for Year 2 Using the 3-Year 4.7% On-the-Run Issue

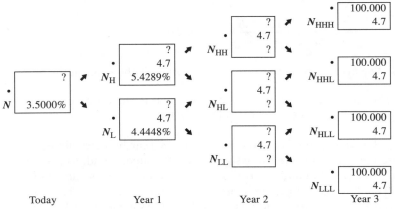

Exhibit 12: The 1-Year Rates for Year 2 Using the 3-Year 4.7% On-the-Run Issue

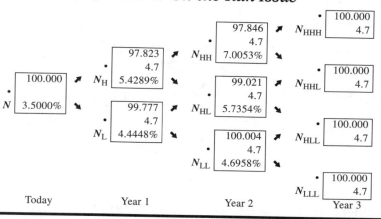

| Today | Year 1 | Year 2 | Year 3 |

Valuing an Option-Free Bond with the Tree

Now consider an option-free bond with three years remaining to maturity and a coupon rate of 6.5%. The value of this bond can be calculated by discounting the cash flow at the spot rates in Exhibit 5 as shown below:

$$\frac{\$6.5}{(1.035)^1} + \frac{\$6.5}{(1.042147)^2} + \frac{\$6.5}{(1.047345)^3} + \frac{\$100 + \$6.5}{(1.052707)^4} = \$104.643$$

An option-free bond that is valued using the binomial interest rate tree should have the same value as discounting by the spot rates.

Exhibit 13 shows the 1-year rates or binomial interest rate tree that can then be used to value any bond for this issuer with a maturity up to four years. To illustrate how to use the binomial interest rate tree, consider once again the 6.5% option-free bond with three years remaining to maturity. Also assume that the issuer's on-the-run yield curve is the one in Exhibit 5, hence the appropriate binomial interest rate tree is the one in Exhibit 13. Exhibit 14 shows the various values in the discounting process, and produces a bond value of $104.643.

This value is identical to the bond value found earlier when we discounted at the spot rates. This clearly demonstrates that the valuation model is consistent with the standard valuation model for an option-free bond.

Valuing a Callable Corporate Bond

Now we will demonstrate how the binomial interest rate tree can be applied to value a callable corporate bond. The valuation process proceeds in the same fashion as in the case of an option-free bond, but with one exception: when the call option may be exercised by the issuer, the bond value at a node must be changed to reflect the lesser of its values if it is not called (i.e., the value obtained by applying the recursive valuation formula described above) and the call price.

Exhibit 13: Binomial Interest Rate Tree for Valuing Up to a 4-Year Bond for Issuer (10% Volatility Assumed)

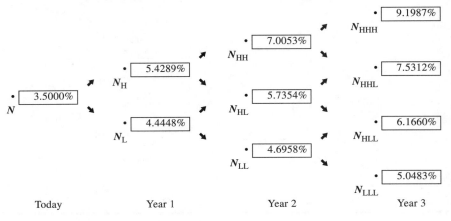

Exhibit 14: Valuing an Option-Free Corporate Bond with Four Years to Maturity and a Coupon Rate of 6.5% (10% Volatility Assumed)

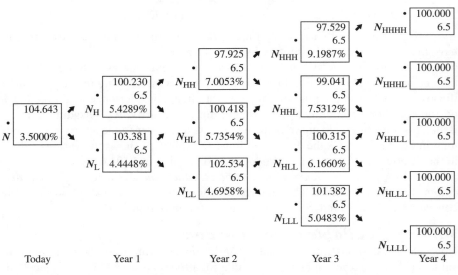

Exhibit 15: Valuing a Callable Corporate Bond with Four Years to Maturity, a Coupon Rate of 6.5%, and Callable in One Year at 100 (10% Volatility Assumed)

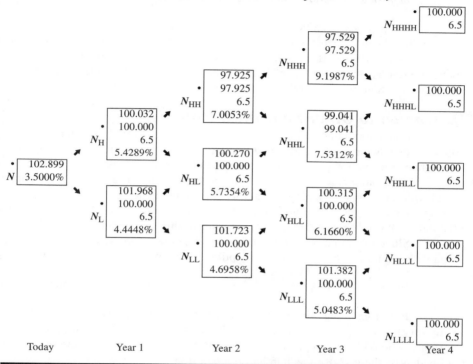

For example, consider a 6.5% corporate bond with four years remaining to maturity that is callable in one year at $100. Exhibit 15 shows two values at each node of the binomial interest rate tree. The discounting process explained above is used to calculate the first of the two values at each node. The second value is the value based on whether the issue will be called. For simplicity, let's assume that this issuer calls the issue if it exceeds the call price. Then, in Exhibit 15 at nodes N_L, N_H, N_{LL}, N_{HL}, N_{LLL}, and N_{HLL}. The values from the recursive valuation formula are $101.968, $100.032, $101.723, $100.270, $101.382, and $100.315. These values exceed the assumed call price ($100) and therefore the second value is $100 rather than the calculated value. It is the second value that is used in subsequent calculations. The root of the tree indicates that the value for this callable bond is $102.899.

The question that we have not addressed in our illustration, which is nonetheless important, is the circumstances under which the issuer will call the bond. A detailed explanation of the call rule is beyond the scope of this chapter. Basically, it involves determining when it would be economic for the issuer on an after-tax basis to call the issue.

Determining the Call Option Value The value of a callable bond is equal to the value of an option-free bond minus the value of the call option. This means that:

value of a call option = value of an option-free bond − value of a callable bond

We have just seen how the value of an option-free bond and the value of a callable bond can be determined. The difference between the two values is therefore the value of the call option. In our illustration, the value of the option-free bond is $104.643. If the call price is $100 in each year and the value of the callable bond is $102.899, the value of the call option is $1.744 (= $104.634 − $102.899).

Extension to Other Embedded Options

The bond valuation framework presented here can be used to analyze other embedded options such as put options, caps and floors on floating-rate notes, and the optional accelerated redemption granted to an issuer in fulfilling its sinking fund requirement.[8]

For example, let's consider a putable bond. Suppose that a 6.5% corporate bond with four years remaining to maturity is putable in one year at par ($100). Also assume that the appropriate binomial interest rate tree for this issuer is the one in Exhibit 13. It can be demonstrated that the value of this putable bond is $105.327.

Since the value of an option-free bond can be expressed as the value of a putable bond minus the value of a put option on that bond, this means that:

value of a put option = value of an option-free bond − value of a putable bond

In our example, since the value of the putable bond is $105.327 and the value of the corresponding option-free bond is $104.643, the value of the put option is −$0.684. The negative sign indicates the issuer has sold the option, or equivalently, the investor has purchased the option.

The framework can also be used to value a bond with multiple or interrelated embedded options. The bond values on each node are altered based on whether one of the options is exercised.

Volatility and the Theoretical Value

In our illustration, interest rate volatility was assumed to be 10%. The volatility assumption has an important impact on the theoretical value. More specifically, the higher the expected volatility, the higher the value of an option. The same is true for an option embedded in a bond. Correspondingly, this affects the value of the bond with an embedded option.

For example, for a callable bond, a higher interest rate volatility assumption means that the value of the call option increases and, since the value of the option-free bond is not affected, the value of the callable bond must be lower. For a putable bond, higher interest rate volatility means that its value will be higher.

---

[8] For examples, see Chapters 6 and 7 in Fabozzi, *Valuation of Fixed Income Securities and Derivatives.*

To illustrate this, suppose that a 20% volatility is assumed rather than 10%. The value of the hypothetical callable bond is $102.108 if volatility is assumed to be 20% compared to $102.899 if volatility is assumed to be 10%. The hypothetical putable bond at 20% volatility has a value of $106.010 compared to $105.327 at 10% volatility.

In the construction of the binomial interest rate, it was assumed that volatility is the same for each year. The methodology can be extended to incorporate a term structure of volatility.

Option-Adjusted Spread

Suppose the market price of the 3-year 6.5% callable bond is $102.218 and the theoretical value assuming 10% volatility is $102.899. This means that this bond is cheap by $0.681 according to the valuation model. Bond market participants prefer to think not in terms of a bond's price being cheap or expensive in dollar terms but rather in terms of a yield spread — a cheap bond trades at a higher yield spread and an expensive bond at a lower yield spread.

The OAS is the constant spread that when added to all the short-term rates on the binomial interest rate tree will make the theoretical value equal to the market price. In our illustration, if the market price is $102.218, the OAS would be the constant spread added to every rate in Exhibit 13 that will make the theoretical value equal to $102.218. The solution in this case would be 35 basis points. This can be verified in Exhibit 16 which shows the value of this issue by adding 35 basis points to each rate.

As with the value of a bond with an embedded option, the OAS will depend on the volatility assumption. For a given bond price, the higher the interest rate volatility assumed, the lower the OAS for a callable bond and the higher the OAS for a putable bond. For example, if volatility is 20% rather than 10%, it can be demonstrated that the OAS would be −11 basis points.

This illustration clearly demonstrates the importance of the volatility assumption. Assuming volatility of 10%, the OAS is 35 basis points. At 20% volatility, the OAS declines and, in this case, is negative and therefore overvalued.

Consequently, in comparing the OAS of dealer firms, it is critical to compare the volatility assumed. Moreover, it is important to inquire as to the benchmark on-the-run yield curve used in generating the binomial tree. Some dealers use the Treasury on-the-run issues. As a result, the OAS is capturing the credit spread. In contrast, some vendors and dealers use the issuer's on-the-run issue which embodies the issuer's credit risk. This is the approach used in our illustrations.

Monte Carlo Method

The second method for valuing bonds with embedded options is the Monte Carlo simulation, or simply Monte Carlo, method. The method involves simulating a sufficiently large number of potential interest rate paths in order to assess the value of a security along these different paths. This method is the most flexible of the two valuation methodologies for valuing interest rate sensitive instruments where the history of interest rates is important. Mortgage-backed securities (passthroughs, collateralized mortgage obligations, and stripped mortgage-backed securities) are commonly valued using this method.

Interest Rate History and Path-Dependent Cash Flows

For some fixed income securities and derivative instruments, the periodic cash flows are *path-dependent*. This means that the cash flow received in one period is determined not only by the current interest rate level, but also by the path that interest rates took to get to the current level.

In the case of mortgage passthrough securities (or simply, passthroughs), prepayments are path-dependent because this month's prepayment rate depends on whether there have been prior opportunities to refinance since the underlying mortgages were originated. Unlike passthroughs, the decision as to whether a corporate issuer will elect to refund an issue when the current rate is below the issue's coupon rate is not dependent on how rates evolved over time to the current level.

Exhibit 16: Demonstration that the Option-Adjusted Spread is 35 Basis Points for a 6.5% Callable Bond Selling at 102.218 (Assuming 10% Volatility

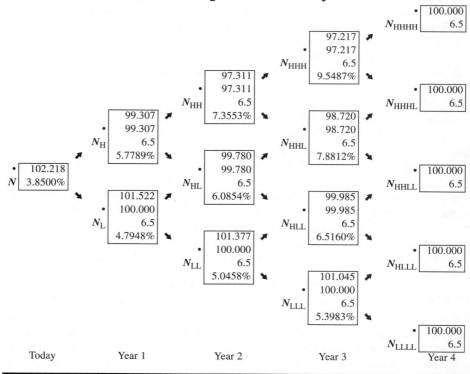

Moreover, in the case of adjustable-rate passthroughs (ARMs), prepayments are not only path-dependent but the periodic coupon rate depends on the history of the reference rate upon which the coupon rate is determined. This is because ARMs have periodic caps and floors as well as a lifetime cap and floor. For example, an ARM whose coupon rate resets annually could have the following restriction on the coupon rate: (1) the rate cannot change by more than 200 basis points each year and (2) the rate cannot be more than 500 basis points from the initial coupon rate.

Pools of passthroughs are used as collateral for the creation of collateralized mortgage obligations (CMOs). Consequently, for CMOs there are typically two sources of path dependency in a CMO tranche's cash flows. First, the collateral prepayments are path-dependent as discussed above. Second, the cash flow to be received in the current month by a CMO tranche depends on the outstanding balances of the other tranches in the deal. Thus, we need the history of prepayments to calculate these balances.

Valuing Mortgage-Backed Securities[9]

Conceptually, the valuation of passthroughs using the Monte Carlo method is simple. In practice, however, it is very complex. The simulation involves generating a set of cash flows based on simulated future mortgage refinancing rates, which in turn imply simulated prepayment rates.

Valuation modeling for CMOs is similar to valuation modeling for passthroughs, although the difficulties are amplified because the issuer has sliced and diced both the prepayment and interest rate risk into smaller pieces called tranches. The sensitivity of the passthroughs comprising the collateral to these two risks is not transmitted equally to every tranche. Some of the tranches wind up more sensitive to prepayment and interest rate risk than the collateral, while some of them are much less sensitive.

Using Simulation to Generate Interest Rate Paths and Cash Flows The
typical model that Wall Street firms and commercial vendors use to generate random interest rate paths takes as input today's term structure of interest rates and a volatility assumption. The term structure of interest rates is the theoretical spot rate (or zero coupon) curve implied by today's Treasury securities. The volatility assumption determines the dispersion of future interest rates in the simulation. The simulations should be normalized so that the average simulated price of a zero-coupon Treasury bond equals today's actual price.

Each model has its own model of the evolution of future interest rates and its own volatility assumptions. Typically, there are no significant differences in the interest rate models of dealer firms and vendors, although their volatility assumptions can be significantly different.

---

[9] Portions of the material in this section and the one to follow are adapted from Frank J. Fabozzi and Scott F. Richard, "Valuation of CMOs," Chapter 6 in Frank J. Fabozzi (ed.), *CMO Portfolio Management* (Summit, N.J.: Frank J. Fabozzi Associates, 1994).

Exhibit 17: Simulated Paths of 1-Month Future Interest Rates

Month	Interest Rate Path Number						
	1	2	3	...	n	...	N
1	$f_1(1)$	$f_1(2)$	$f_1(3)$	...	$f_1(n)$	...	$f_1(N)$
2	$f_2(1)$	$f_2(2)$	$f_2(3)$	...	$f_2(n)$	...	$f_2(N)$
3	$f_3(1)$	$f_3(2)$	$f_3(3)$	...	$f_3(n)$	...	$f_3(N)$
t	$f_t(1)$	$f_t(2)$	$f_t(3)$	...	$f_t(n)$	...	$f_t(N)$
358	$f_{358}(1)$	$f_{358}(2)$	$f_{358}(3)$	...	$f_{358}(n)$	...	$f_{358}(N)$
359	$f_{359}(1)$	$f_{359}(2)$	$f_{359}(3)$	...	$f_{359}(n)$	...	$f_{359}(N)$
360	$f_{360}(1)$	$f_{360}(2)$	$f_{360}(3)$	...	$f_{360}(n)$	...	$f_{360}(N)$

Notation:

$f_t(n)$ = one-month future interest rate for month t on path n

N = total number of interest rate paths

    The random paths of interest rates should be generated from an arbitrage-free model of the future term structure of interest rates. By arbitrage-free it is meant that the model replicates today's term structure of interest rates, an input of the model, and that for all future dates there is no possible arbitrage within the model. We will explain how this is done later.

    The simulation works by generating many scenarios of future interest rate paths. In each month of the scenario, a monthly interest rate and a mortgage refinancing rate are generated. The monthly interest rates are used to discount the projected cash flows in the scenario. The mortgage refinancing rate is needed to determine the cash flow because it represents the opportunity cost the mortgagor is facing at that time.

    If the refinancing rates are high relative to the mortgagor's original coupon rate (i.e., the rate on the mortgagor's loan), the mortgagor will have less incentive to refinance, or even a positive disincentive (i.e., the homeowner will avoid moving in order to avoid refinancing). If the refinancing rate is low relative to the mortgagor's original coupon rate, the mortgagor has an incentive to refinance.

    Prepayments are projected by feeding the refinancing rate and loan characteristics, such as age, into a prepayment model. Given the projected prepayments, the cash flow along an interest rate path can be determined.

    To make this more concrete, consider a newly issued mortgage passthrough security with a maturity of 360 months. Exhibit 17 shows N simulated interest rate path scenarios. Each scenario consists of a path of 360 simulated 1month future interest rates. Just how many paths should be generated is explained later. Exhibit 18 shows the paths of simulated mortgage refinancing rates corresponding to the scenarios shown in Exhibit 17. Assuming these mortgage refinancing rates, the cash flow for each scenario path is shown in Exhibit 19.

Calculating the Present Value for a Scenario Interest Rate Path Given

the cash flow on an interest rate path, its present value can be calculated. The discount rate for determining the present value is the simulated spot rate for each month on the interest rate path plus an appropriate spread. The spot rate on a path can be determined from the simulated future monthly rates. The relationship that holds between the simulated spot rate for month T on path n and the simulated future 1-month rates is:

$$z_T(n) = \{[1 + f_1(n)][1 + f_2(n)]...[1 + f_T(n)]\}^{1/T} - 1$$

where

$z_T(n)$ = simulated spot rate for month T on path n
$f_j(n)$ = simulated future 1-month rate for month j on path n

Consequently, the interest rate path for the simulated future 1-month rates can be converted to the interest rate path for the simulated monthly spot rates as shown in Exhibit 20.

Exhibit 18: Simulated Paths of Mortgage Refinancing Rates

Month	Interest Rate Path Number						
	1	2	3	...	n	...	N
1	$r_1(1)$	$r_1(2)$	$r_1(3)$	...	$r_1(n)$	...	$r_1(N)$
2	$r_2(1)$	$r_2(2)$	$r_2(3)$	...	$r_2(n)$	...	$r_2(N)$
3	$r_3(1)$	$r_3(2)$	$r_3(3)$	...	$r_3(n)$	...	$r_3(N)$
t	$r_t(1)$	$r_t(2)$	$r_t(3)$	...	$r_t(n)$	...	$r_t(N)$
358	$r_{358}(1)$	$r_{358}(2)$	$r_{358}(3)$	...	$r_{358}(n)$	...	$r_{358}(N)$
359	$r_{359}(1)$	$r_{359}(2)$	$r_{359}(3)$	...	$r_{359}(n)$	...	$r_{359}(N)$
360	$r_{360}(1)$	$r_{360}(2)$	$r_{360}(3)$	...	$r_{360}(n)$	...	$r_{360}(N)$

Notation:
$r_t(n)$ = mortgage refinancing rate for month t on path n
N = total number of interest rate paths

Exhibit 19: Simulated Cash Flow on Each of the Interest Rate Paths

Month	Interest Rate Path Number						
	1	2	3	...	n	...	N
1	$C_1(1)$	$C_1(2)$	$C_1(3)$	...	$C_1(n)$	...	$C_1(N)$
2	$C_2(1)$	$C_2(2)$	$C_2(3)$	...	$C_2(n)$	...	$C_2(N)$
3	$C_3(1)$	$C_3(2)$	$C_3(3)$	...	$C_3(n)$	...	$C_3(N)$
t	$C_t(1)$	$C_t(2)$	$C_t(3)$	...	$C_t(n)$	...	$C_t(N)$
358	$C_{358}(1)$	$C_{358}(2)$	$C_{358}(3)$	...	$C_{358}(n)$	...	$C_{358}(N)$
359	$C_{359}(1)$	$C_{359}(2)$	$C_{359}(3)$	...	$C_{359}(n)$	...	$C_{359}(N)$
360	$C_{360}(1)$	$C_{360}(2)$	$C_{360}(3)$	...	$C_{360}(n)$	...	$C_{360}(N)$

Notation:
$C_t(n)$ = cash flow for month t on path n
N = total number of interest rate paths

Exhibit 20: Simulated Paths of Monthly Spot Rates

Month	Interest Rate Path Number						
	1	2	3	...	n	...	N
1	$z_1(1)$	$z_1(2)$	$z_1(3)$	...	$z_1(n)$	...	$z_1(N)$
2	$z_2(1)$	$z_2(2)$	$z_2(3)$	...	$z_2(n)$	...	$z_2(N)$
3	$z_3(1)$	$z_3(2)$	$z_3(3)$	...	$z_3(n)$	...	$z_3(N)$
t	$z_t(1)$	$z_t(2)$	$z_t(3)$	...	$z_t(n)$	...	$z_t(N)$
358	$z_{358}(1)$	$z_{358}(2)$	$z_{358}(3)$	...	$z_{358}(n)$	...	$z_{358}(N)$
359	$z_{359}(1)$	$z_{359}(2)$	$z_{359}(3)$	...	$z_{359}(n)$	...	$z_{359}(N)$
360	$z_{360}(1)$	$z_{360}(2)$	$z_{360}(3)$	...	$z_{360}(n)$	...	$z_{360}(N)$

Notation:

$z_t(n)$ = spot rate for month t on path n
N = total number of interest rate paths

Therefore, the present value of the cash flow for month T on interest rate path n discounted at the simulated spot rate for month T plus some spread is:

$$PV[C_T(n)] = \frac{C_T(n)}{[1 + z_T(n) + K]^{1/T}}$$

where

$PV[CT(n)]$ = present value of cash flow for month T on path n
$C_T(n)$ = cash flow for month T on path n
$z_T(n)$ = spot rate for month T on path n
K = spread

The present value for path n is the sum of the present value of the cash flow for each month on path n. That is,

$$PV[Path(n)] = PV[C_1(n)] + PV[C_2(n)] +... + PV[C_{360}(n)]$$

where $PV[Path(n)]$ is the present value of interest rate path n.

Determining the Theoretical Value

The present value of a given interest rate path can be thought of as the theoretical value of a passthrough if that path was actually realized. The theoretical value of the passthrough can be determined by calculating the average of the theoretical value of all the interest rate paths. That is,

$$\text{Theoretical value} = \frac{PV[Path(1)] + PV[Path(2)] + ... + PV[Path(N)]}{N}$$

where N is the number of interest rate paths.

This procedure for valuing a passthrough is also followed for a CMO tranche. The cash flow for each month on each interest rate path is found according to the principal repayment and interest distribution rules of the deal. In order to do this, a CMO structuring model is needed. In any analysis of CMOs, one of the major stumbling blocks is getting a good CMO structuring model.

Option-Adjusted Spread

As explained in previous chapters, the option-adjusted spread is a measure of the yield spread that can be used to convert dollar differences between value and price. It represents a spread over the issuer's spot rate curve or benchmark.

In the Monte Carlo model, the OAS is the spread K that when added to all the spot rates on all interest rate paths will make the average present value of the paths equal to the observed market price (plus accrued interest). Mathematically, OAS is the spread that will satisfy the following condition:

$$\text{Market Price} = \frac{PV[\text{Path}(1)] + PV[\text{Path}(2)] + \ldots + PV[\text{Path}(N)]}{N}$$

where N is the number of interest rate paths.

Some Technical Issues

In the binomial method for valuing bonds, the interest rate tree is constructed so that it is arbitrage free. That is, if any on-the-run issue is valued, the value produced by the model is equal to the market price. This means that the tree is calibrated to the market. In contrast, in our discussion of the Monte Carlo method, there is no mechanism that we have described above that will assure the valuation model will produce a value for an on-the-run Treasury security (the benchmark in the case of agency mortgage-backed securities) equal to the market price. In practice, this is accomplished by adding a *drift term* to the short-term return generating process (Exhibit 17) so that the value produced by the Monte Carlo method for all on-the-run Treasury securities is their market price.[10] A technical explanation of this process is beyond the scope of this chapter.[11]

There is also another adjustment made to the interest rate paths. Restrictions on interest rate movements must be built into the model to prevent interest rates from reaching levels that are believed to be unreasonable (e.g., an interest rate of zero or an interest rate of 30%). This is done by incorporating *mean reversion* into the model. By this it is meant that at some point, the interest rate is forced toward some estimated average (mean) value.

The specification of the relationship between short-term rates and refinancing rates is necessary. Empirical evidence on the relationship is also necessary. More specifically, the correlation between the short-term and long-term rates must be estimated.

---

[10] This is equivalent to saying that the OAS produced by the model is zero.

[11] For an explanation of how this is done, see Lakhbir S. Hayre and Kenneth Lauterbach, "Stochastic Valuation of Debt Securities," in Frank J. Fabozzi (ed.), *Managing Institutional Assets* (New York: Harper & Row, 1990), pp. 321-364.

The number of interest rate paths determines how "good" the estimate is, not relative to the truth but relative to the valuation model used. The more paths, the more the theoretical value tends to settle down. It is a statistical sampling problem. Most Monte Carlo models employ some form of *variance reduction* to cut down on the number of sample paths necessary to get a good statistical sample. Variance reduction techniques allow us to obtain value estimates within a tick. By this we mean that if the model is used to generate more scenarios, value estimates from the model will not change by more than a tick. So, for example, if 1,024 paths are used to obtain the estimate value for a tranche, there is little more information to be had from the OAS model by generating more than that number of paths. (For some very sensitive CMO tranches, more paths may be needed to estimate value within one tick.)

Distribution of Path Present Values

The Monte Carlo simulation method is a commonly used management science tool in business. It is employed when the outcome of a business decision depends on the outcome of several random variables. The product of the simulation is the average value and the probability distribution of the possible outcomes.

Unfortunately, the use of Monte Carlo simulation to value fixed income securities has been limited to just the reporting of the average value, which is referred to as the theoretical value of the security. This means that all of the information about the distribution of the path present values is ignored. Yet, this information is quite valuable.

For example, consider a well protected planned amortization class (PAC) bond. The distribution of the present value for the paths should concentrated around the theoretical value. That is, the standard deviation should be small. In contrast, for a support tranche, the distribution of the present value for the paths could be wide, or equivalently, the standard deviation could be large.

Therefore, before using the theoretical value for a mortgage-backed security generated from the Monte Carlo method, a portfolio manager should ask for information about the distribution of the path's present values.

MEASURING INTEREST RATE RISK

In bond portfolio management, a key risk is interest rate risk. To effectively control a portfolio's exposure to interest rate risk, it is necessary to quantify this risk. In this chapter we explain how this is done. The most popular measure of interest rate risk is duration. We will explain this measure and demonstrate its limitations. In later chapters other interest rate risk measures are discussed.

Price Volatility Characteristics of Option-Free Bonds

A fundamental principle of an option-free bond (that is, a bond that does not have any embedded options) is that the price of the bond changes in the opposite direction from a change in the bond's yield.

Exhibit 21: Price/Yield Relationship for an Option-Free Bond

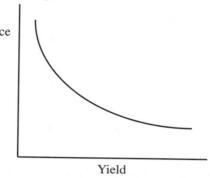

When the price/yield relationship for any option-free bond is graphed, it exhibits the shape shown in Exhibit 21. Notice that as the yield rises, the price of the option-free bond declines. However, this relationship is not linear (that is, it is not a straight line). The shape of the price/yield relationship for any option-free bond is referred to as convex. The price/yield relationship that we have discussed refers to an instantaneous change in yield.

Properties of Option-Free Bonds

The following four properties hold for an option-free bond.

Property 1: Although the prices of all option-free bonds move in the opposite direction from the change in yield, the percentage price change is not the same for all bonds.

Property 2: For small changes in yield, the percentage price change for a given bond is roughly the same, whether the yield increases or decreases.

Property 3: For large changes in yield, the percentage price change is not the same for an increase in yield as it is for a decrease in yield.

Property 4: For a given change in basis points, the percentage price increase is greater than the percentage price decrease.

The implication of Property 4 is that if an investor is long a bond, the price appreciation that will be realized if the yield decreases is greater than the capital loss that will be realized if the yield rises by the same number of basis points. For an investor who is short a bond, the reverse is true: the potential capital loss is greater than the potential capital gain if the yield changes by a given number of basis points.

An explanation for these four properties of bond price volatility lies in the convex shape of the price/yield relationship.

Characteristics of a Bond that Affect its Price Volatility

There are two characteristics of an option-free bond that determine its price volatility: coupon and term to maturity.

Characteristic 1: For a given term to maturity and initial yield, the lower the coupon rate the greater the price volatility of a bond.

Characteristic 2: For a given coupon rate and initial yield, the longer the term to maturity, the greater the price volatility.

An implication of the second characteristic is that investors who want to increase a portfolio's price volatility because they expect interest rates to fall, all other factors being constant, should hold bonds with long maturities in the portfolio. To reduce a portfolio's price volatility in anticipation of a rise in interest rates, bonds with shorter-term maturities should be held in the portfolio.

The Effects of Yield to Maturity

We cannot ignore the fact that credit considerations cause different bonds to trade at different yields, even if they have the same coupon and maturity. How, then, holding other factors constant, does the yield to maturity affect a bond's price volatility? As it turns out, the higher the yield to maturity that a bond trades at, the lower the price volatility.

To see this, we can compare a 6%, 20-year bond initially selling at a yield of 6%, and a 6%, 20-year bond initially selling at a yield of 10%. The former is initially at a price of 100, and the latter carries a price of 65.68. Now, if the yield on both bonds increase by 100 basis points, the first bond trades down by 10.68 points (10.68%). After the assumed increase in yield, the second bond will trade at a price of 59.88, for a price decline of only 5.80 points (or 8.83%). Thus, we see that the bond that trades at a lower yield is more volatile in both percentage price change and absolute price change, as long as the other bond characteristics are the same.

An implication of this is that, for a given change in yields, price volatility is lower when the yield level in the market is high, and price volatility is higher when the yield level is low.

Price Value of a Basis Point as a Measure of Interest Rate Risk

One measure of the dollar price sensitivity of a bond to interest rate changes is the *price value of a basis point* (PVBP). This measure, also referred to as the *dollar value of an 01* (D01), is the change in the price of a bond if the yield changes by 1 basis point. Typically, the price value of a basis point is expressed as the absolute value of the change in price; consequently, the greater the price value of a basis point, the greater the dollar price volatility. As we noted earlier, price changes are almost symmetric for small changes in yield. Thus, it does not make a great deal of difference whether we increase or decrease yields to calculate the price value of a basis point. In practice, an average of the change resulting from both an up and a down movement in yield is used.

We will illustrate the calculation of the price value of a basis point using the 9%, 20-year bond assuming this bond is selling to yield 6%. We know that:

yield at 6.00% = price of 134.6722
yield at 5.99% = price of 134.8159
yield at 6.01% = price of 134.5287

The PVBP per $100 of par value if the yield decreases by one basis point is 134.8159 − 134.6722 = 0.1437. This value is almost identical to the PVBP if the yield increases by one point 134.6722 − 134.5287 = 0.1435.

Some investors calculate the price value of more than one basis point.[12] The principle of calculating the price value of any number of basis points is the same. For example, the price value of 10 basis points is found by computing the difference between the initial price and the price if the yield changed by 10 basis points. Consider once again the 20-year, 9% bond trading to yield 9%, then:

yield at 6.00% = price of 134.6722
yield at 5.90% = price of 136.1193
yield at 6.10% = price of 133.2472

The price value of 10 basis points per $100 of par value if the yield decreases by 10 basis points is: 136.1193 − 134.6722 = 1.4471. The price value of 10 basis points per $100 of par value if the yield decreases by 10 basis points is: 134.6722 − 133.2472 = 1.4250. The price value of 10 basis is then the average of the two changes: (1.4471 + 1.4250)/2 = 1.4361.

Since the relationship is still nearly symmetric for a 10 basis point change in yield up or down, the price value of 10 basis points is approximately equal to 10 times the price value of one basis point. However, for larger changes in yield, there will be a difference between the price value of a basis point if the yield is increased or decreased, and the price change for a large number of basis points can no longer be approximated by the multiple times the price value of one basis point. Most investors who derive the price values of a basis point by calculating price changes for large movements in yields (such as 100 basis points), will average the PVBPs for an up move and a down move to get the PVBP of interest.

Duration as a Measure of Interest Rate Risk

The most obvious way to measure a bond's price sensitivity as a percentage of its current price to changes in interest rates is to change rates by a small number of basis points and calculate how its price will change.

---

[12] For example, in the municipal bond market it is common to calculate the price value of 5 basis points.

To do this, we introduce the following notation. Let

Δy = change in the yield of the bond (in decimal)
V_+ = the estimated value of the bond if the yield is increased by Δy
V_- = the estimated value of the bond if the yield is decreased by Δy
V_0 = initial price of the bond (per \$100 of par value)

There are two key points to keep in mind in the foregoing discussion. First, the change in yield referred to above is the same change in yield for all maturities. This assumption is commonly referred to as a parallel yield curve shift assumption. Thus, the foregoing discussion about the price sensitivity of a security to interest rate changes is limited to parallel shifts in the yield curve. Later in this chapter we will address the case where the yield curve shifts in a nonparallel manner.

Second, the notation refers to the estimated value of the bond. This value is obtained from a valuation model. Consequently, the resulting measure of the price sensitivity of a security to interest rates changes is only as good as the valuation model employed to obtain the estimated value of the bond.

Now let's focus on the measure of interest. We are interested in the percentage change in the price of a security when interest rates change. The percentage change in price per basis point change is found by dividing the percentage price change by the number of basis points (Δy times 100). That is:

$$\frac{V_- - V_0}{V_0(\Delta y)100}$$

Similarly, the percentage change in price per basis point change for an increase in yield (Δy times 100) is:

$$\frac{V_0 - V_+}{V_0(\Delta y)100}$$

As explained earlier, the percentage price change for an increase and decrease in interest rates will not be the same. Consequently, the average percentage price change per basis point change in yield can be calculated. This is done as follows:

$$\frac{1}{2}\left[\frac{V_- - V_0}{V_0(\Delta y)100} + \frac{V_0 - V_+}{V_0(\Delta y)100}\right]$$

or equivalently,

$$\frac{V_- - V_+}{2V_0(\Delta y)100}$$

The approximate percentage price change for a 100 basis point change in yield is found by multiplying the previous formula by 100. The name popularly used to refer to the approximate percentage price change is duration. Thus,

$$\text{Duration} = \frac{V_- - V_+}{2V_0(\Delta y)} \tag{1}$$

To illustrate this formula, consider the following option-free bond: a 9% coupon, 20-year bond trading to yield 6%. The initial price or value (V_0) is 134.6722. Suppose the yield is changed by 20 basis points. If the yield is decreased to 5.8%, the value of this bond (V_-) would be 137.5888. If the yield is increased to 6.2%, the value of this bond (V_+) would be 131.8439. Thus, Δy is 0.0020, V_+ is 131.8439, V_- is 137.5888, and V_0 is 134.6722. Substituting these values into the duration formula:

$$\text{Duration} = \frac{137.5888 - 131.8439}{2(134.6722)(0.002)} = 10.66$$

Interpreting Duration

The duration of a security can be interpreted as the approximate percentage change in the price for a 100 basis point parallel shift in the yield curve. Thus a bond with a duration of 4.8 will change by approximately 4.8% for a 100 basis point parallel shift in the yield curve. For a 50 basis point parallel shift in the yield curve, the bond's price will change by approximately 2.4%; for a 25 basis point parallel shift in the yield curve, 1.2%, etc.

A portfolio manager who anticipates a decline in interest rates will extend (i.e., increase) the portfolio's duration.[13] Suppose that the portfolio manager increases the present portfolio duration of 4 to 6. This means that for a 100 basis point change in interest rates, the portfolio will change by about 2% more than if the portfolio duration was left unchanged.

Dollar Duration

Duration is related to percentage price change. However, for two bonds with the same duration, the dollar price change will not be the same. For example, consider two bonds, W and X. Suppose that both bonds have a duration of 5, but that W is trading at par while X is trading at 90. A 100 basis point change for both bonds will change the price by approximately 5%. This means a price change of $5 (5% times $100) for W and a price change of $4.5 (5% times $90) for V.

The dollar price volatility of a bond can be measured by multiplying modified duration by the full dollar price and the number of basis points (in decimal form). That is:

Dollar price change = Modified duration × Dollar price × Yield change (in decimal)

The dollar price volatility for a 100 basis point change in yield is:

Dollar price change = Modified duration × Dollar price × 0.01

or equivalently,

Dollar price change = Modified duration × Dollar price/100

---

[13] How a portfolio's duration is calculated will be discussed below.

The dollar price change calculated using the above formula is called dollar duration. In some contexts, dollar duration refers to the price change for a 100 basis point change in yield. The dollar duration for any number of basis points can be computed by scaling the dollar price change accordingly. For example, for a 50 basis point change in yields, the dollar price change or dollar duration is:

Dollar price change = Modified duration × Dollar price/200

For a one basis point change in yield, the dollar price change will give the same result as the price value of a basis point.

The dollar duration for a 100 basis point change in yield for bonds W and Y is:

For bond W: Dollar duration = 5 × 100/100 = 5.0
For bond X: Dollar duration = 5 × 90/100 = 4.5

Modified Duration versus Effective Duration

A popular form of duration that is used by practitioners is *modified duration*. Modified duration is the approximate percentage change in a bond's price for a 100 basis point parallel shift in the yield curve assuming that the bond's cashflow does not change when the yield curve shifts. What this means is that in calculating the values of V_- and V_+ in equation (1), the same cash flow used to calculate V_0 is used. Therefore, the change in the bond's price when the yield curve is shifted by a small number of basis points is due solely to discounting at the new yield level.

The assumption that the cash flow will not change when the yield curve shifts in a parallel fashion makes sense for option-free bonds such as noncallable Treasury securities. This is because the payments made by the U.S. Department of the Treasury to holders of its obligations does not change when the yield curve changes. However, the same can not be said for callable and putable bonds and mortgage-backed securities. For these securities, a change in yield will alter the expected cash flow.

The price/yield relationship for callable bonds and mortgage passthrough securities is shown in Exhibit 22. As yields in the market decline, the likelihood that yields will decline further so that the issuer or homeowner will benefit from calling the bond increases. The exact yield level at which investors begin to view the issue likely to be called may not be known, but we do know that there is some level. In Exhibit 22, at yield levels below y*, the price/yield relationship for the callable bond departs from the price/yield relationship for the noncallable bond. If, for example, the market yield is such that a noncallable bond would be selling for 109, but since it is callable would be called at 104, investors would not pay 109. If they did and the bond is called, investors would receive 104 (the call price) for a bond they purchased for 109. Notice that for a range of yields below y*, there is price compression—that is, there is limited price appreciation as yields decline. The portion of the callable bond price/yield relationship below y* is said to be *negatively convex*.

Exhibit 22: Price/Yield Relationship for a Noncallable Bond and a Callable Bond

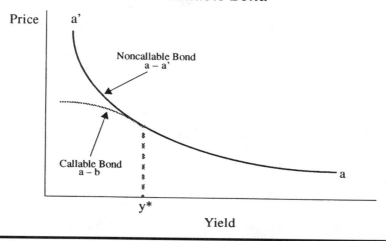

Negative convexity means that the price appreciation will be less than the price depreciation for a large change in yield of a given number of basis points. An option-free bond is said to exhibit *positive convexity*; that is, the price appreciation will be greater than the price depreciation for a large change in yield. The price changes resulting from bonds exhibiting positive convexity and negative convexity is summarized below:

Change in interest rates	Absolute value of percentage price change for:	
	Positive convexity	Negative convexity
−100 basis points	X%	less than Y%
+100 basis points	less than X%	Y%

The valuation models described in the previous section take into account how shifts in the yield curve will affect cash flow. Thus, when V_- and V_+ are the values produced from these valuation models, the resulting duration takes into account both the discounting at different interest rates and how the cash flow can change. When duration is calculated in this manner, it is referred to as effective duration or option-adjusted duration. Exhibit 23 summarizes the distinction between modified duration and effective duration.

The difference between modified duration and effective duration for bonds with an embedded option can be quite dramatic. For example, a callable corporate bond could have a modified duration of 7 but an effective duration of only 4. For certain collateralized mortgage obligations, the modified duration could be 7 and the effective duration 40! Thus, using modified duration as a measure of the price sensitivity of a security to a parallel shift in the yield curve would be misleading. The more appropriate measure for any bond with an embedded option is effective duration.

Exhibit 23: Modified Duration versus Effective Duration

Duration
Interpretation: Generic description of the sensitivity of a bond's price (as a percentage of initial price) to a parallel shift in the yield curve

Modified Duration	Effective Duration
Duration measure in which it is assumed that yield changes do not change the expected cash flow	Duration in which recognition is given to the fact that yield changes may change the expected cash flow

Calculating the Effective Duration Using the Binomial Model Earlier we explained the binomial model. The procedure for calculating the values to be substituted into the duration formula [equation (1)] using the binomial model is described below.

V_+ is determined as follows:

Step 1: Calculate the option-adjusted spread (OAS) for the issue.

Step 2: Shift the on-the-run yield curve up by a small number of basis points.

Step 3: Construct a binomial interest rate tree based on the new yield curve in Step 2.

Step 4: To each of the short rates in the binomial interest rate tree, add the OAS to obtain an "adjusted tree."

Step 5: Use the adjusted tree found in Step 4 to determine the value of the bond, which is V_+.

To determine the value of V_-, the same five steps are followed except that in Step 2, the on-the-run yield curve is shifted down by a small number of basis points.

To illustrate how V_+ and V_- are determined in order to calculate effective duration, we will use the same on-the-run yield curve that we used earlier in this chapter assuming a volatility of 10%. The 4-year callable bond with a coupon rate of 6.5% and callable at par selling at 102.218 will be used in this illustration. We showed that the OAS for this issue is 35 basis points.

While not shown here, if the yield curve is shifted down by 25 basis points and 35 basis points are added to each 1-year rate, the resulting value, V_-, is 101.676. The results are Δy is 0.0025, V_+ is 101.6760, V_- is 102.7650, and V_0 is 102.2180. Therefore,

$$\text{Effective duration} = \frac{102.765 - 101.676}{2(102.218)0.0025} = 2.1$$

Calculating the Effective Duration Using the Monte Carlo Simulation Model The same procedure is used to calculate the effective duration for a security valued using the Monte Carlo Simulation method. The short-term rates are used to value the cash flow on each interest rate path. To obtain the two values to substitute into the duration formula, the OAS is calculated first. The short-term rates are then shifted up a small number of basis points, obtaining new refinancing rates and cash flows. V_+ is then calculated by discounting the cash flow on an interest rate path using the new short-term rates plus the OAS. V_- is then calculated in the same manner by shifting the short-term rates down by a small number of basis points.

Macaulay Duration

It is worth comparing the modified duration formula presented above to that commonly found in the literature. It is common in the literature to find the following formula for modified duration:[14]

$$\frac{1}{(1 + \text{Yield}/k)}\left[\frac{1\text{PVCF}_1 + 2\text{PVCF}_2 + 3\text{PVCF}_3 + \dots + n\text{PVCF}_n}{k \times \text{Price}}\right] \qquad (2)$$

where

k	=	number of periods, or payments, per year (e.g., $k = 2$ for semiannual pay bonds and $k = 12$ for monthly pay bonds)
n	=	number of periods until maturity (i.e., number of years to maturity times k)
yield	=	yield to maturity of the bond
PVCF_t	=	present value of the cash flow in period t discounted at the yield to maturity

The expression in the bracket for the modified duration formula in equation (2) is a measure formulated in 1938 by an economist, Frederick Macaulay.[15] This measure is popularly referred to as *Macaulay duration*. Thus, modified duration is commonly expressed as:

$$\text{Modified duration} = \frac{\text{Macaulay duration}}{1 + \text{yield}/k}$$

The general formulation for duration as given by equation (1) provides a shortcut procedure for determining a bond's modified duration. Because it is easier to calculate the modified duration using the shortcut procedure, many vendors of analytical software will use equation (1) rather than equation (2) to reduce computation time. But, once again, it must be emphasized that modified duration is a flawed measure of a bond's price sensitivity to interest rate changes for a bond with an embedded option.

---

[14] More specifically, this is the formula for modified duration for a bond on a coupon anniversary date.

[15] Frederick Macaulay, *Some Theoretical Problems Suggested by the Movement of interest Rates, Bond Yields, and Stock Prices in the U.S. Since 1856* (New York: National Bureau of Economic Research, 1938).

Portfolio Duration

A portfolio's (effective) duration can be obtained by calculating the weighted average of the duration of the bonds in the portfolio. The weight is the proportion of the portfolio that a security comprises. Mathematically, a portfolio's duration can be calculated as follows:

$$W_1D_1 + W_2D_2 + W_3D_3 + \ldots + W_KD_K$$

where

W_i = market value of bond i/market value of the portfolio
D_i = effective duration of bond i
K = number of bonds in the portfolio

To illustrate this calculation, consider the following three-bond portfolio in which all three bonds are option free:

Bond	Par amount owned	Market value
10%, 5-year	$4 million	$4,000,000
8%, 15-year	5 million	4,231,375
14%, 30-year	1 million	1,378,586

In this illustration, it is assumed that the next coupon payment for each bond is six months from now. The market value for the portfolio is $9,609,961. Since each bond is option free, the modified duration can be used. The market price per $100 value of each bond, its yield to maturity, and its duration are given below:

Bond	Price ($)	Yield to Maturity (%)	Duration
10%, 5-year	100.0000	10	3.861
8%, 15-year	84.6275	10	8.047
14%, 30-year	137.8590	10	9.168

In this illustration, K is equal to 3 and:

w_1 = 4,000,000/9,609,961 = 0.416 D_1 = 3.861
w_2 = 4,231,375/9,609,961 = 0.440 D_2 = 8.047
w_3 = 1,378,586/9,609,961 = 0.144 D_3 = 9.168

The portfolio's duration is: 0.416 (3.861) + 0.440 (8.047) + 0.144 (9.168) = 6.47. A portfolio duration of 6.47 means that for a 100 basis change in the yield for all three bonds, the market value of the portfolio will change by approximately 6.47%. But keep in mind, the yield on all three bonds must change by 100 basis points for the duration measure to be useful. This is a critical assumption and its importance can not be overemphasized. We shall return to this point later in this chapter.

Similarly, the dollar duration of a portfolio can be obtained by taking calculating the weighted average of the dollar duration of the bonds in the portfolio.

Price Sensitivity to Non-Parallel Yield Curve Shifts

Both modified duration and effective duration assume that any change in interest rates is the result of a parallel shift in the yield curve. For some fixed-income securities, the price sensitivity to most nonparallel shifts will be very close to the estimated price sensitivity for a parallel shift in the yield curve. This is generally true for option-free bonds with a bullet maturity. However, for sinking-fund bonds and bonds with embedded options, particularly mortgage-backed securities, the price sensitivity to a nonparallel shift in the yield curve can be quite different from that estimated for a parallel shift.

Convexity Measure as a Second Order Approximation of Price Change

Notice that the duration measure indicates that regardless of whether the yield curve is shifted up or down, the approximate percentage price change is the same. However, this does not agree with the properties of a bond's price volatility described earlier in this chapter. Specifically, Property 2 states that for small changes in yield the percentage price change will be the same for an increase or decrease in yield. Property 3 states that for large changes in yield this is not true. This suggests that duration is only a good approximation of the percentage price change for a small change in yield.

To see this, consider once again the 9%, 20-year bond selling to yield 6% with a duration of 10.66. If yields increase instantaneously by 10 basis points (from 6% to 6.1%), then using duration the approximate percentage price change would be −1.066% (−10.66% divided by 10, remembering that duration is the percentage price change for a 100 basis point change in yield). The actual percentage price change is −1.07%. Similarly, if the yield decreases instantaneously by 10 basis points (from 6.00% to 5.90%), then the percentage change in price would be +1.066%. The actual percentage price change would be +1.07%. This example illustrates that for small changes in yield, duration does an excellent job of approximating the percentage price change.

Instead of a small change in yield, let's assume that yields increase by 200 basis points, from 6% to 8%. The approximate percentage change is −21.32% (−10.66% times 2). The actual percentage change in price is only −18.40%. Moreover, if the yield decreases by 200 basis points from 6% to 4%, the approximate percentage price change based on duration would be +21.32%, compared to an actual percentage price change of +25.04%. Thus, the approximation is not as good for a 200 basis point change in yield.

Duration is in fact a first approximation for a small parallel shift in the yield curve. The approximation can be improved by using a second approximation. This approximation is referred to as a bond's convexity.[16] The use of this term in the industry is unfortunate since the term convexity is also used to describe the shape or curvature of the price/yield relationship, as explained earlier. The convexity measure of a bond can be used to approximate the change in price that is not explained by duration.

Convexity Measure

The convexity measure of any bond can be approximated using the following formula:

$$\text{Convexity measure} = \frac{V_+ + V_- - 2V_0}{2V_0(\Delta y)^2} \tag{3}$$

where the notation is the same as used earlier for duration [equation (1)].

For our hypothetical 9%, 20-year bond selling to yield 6%, we know that for a 20-basis-point-change in yield Δy is 0.0020, V_+ is 131.8439, V_- is 137.5888, and V_0 is 134.6722. Substituting these values into the convexity measure formula,

$$\text{Convexity measure} = \frac{137.5888 + 131.8439 - 2(134.6722)}{2(134.6722)(0.002)^2} = 81.96$$

Percentage Price Change Adjustment for Convexity

Given the convexity measure, the approximate percentage change adjustment due to the bond's convexity (i.e., the percentage price change not explained by duration) is:

Convexity measure $\times (\Delta y)^2$

For example, for the 9% coupon bond maturing in 20 years, the convexity adjustment to the percentage price change if the yield increases from 6% to 8% is

$$81.96 \times (0.02)^2 = 0.0328 = 3.28\%$$

If the yield decreases from 6% to 4%, the convexity adjustment to the approximate price change would also be 3.28%.

The approximate percentage price change based on duration and the convexity adjustment is found by simply adding the two estimates. So, for example, if yields change from 6% to 8%, the estimated percentage price change would be:

Estimated change approximated by duration	=	−21.32%
Estimated adjustment for convexity	=	+3.28%
Total estimated percentage price change	=	−18.04%

The actual percentage price change is −18.40%.

For a decrease of 200 basis points, from 6% to 4%, the approximate percentage price change would be as follows:

---

[16] Mathematically, any function can be estimated by a series of approximations referred to as a Taylor series. Each approximation or term of the Taylor series is based on the corresponding derivative. For a bond, duration is the first approximation to price and is related to the first derivative of the bond's price. The convexity measure is the second approximation and related to the second derivative of the bond's price. It turns out that in general the first two approximations do a good job of estimating the bond's price so no additional derivatives are needed. The derivation is provided in Chapter 4 of Frank J. Fabozzi, *Bond Markets, Analysis, and Strategies* (Englewood Cliffs, N.J.: Prentice Hall, 1993).

Estimated change approximated by duration = + 21.32%
Estimated adjustment for convexity   =   + 3.28%
Total estimated percentage price change   = + 24.60%

The actual percentage price change is +25.04%. Thus, duration with the convexity adjustment do a good job of estimating the sensitivity of a bond's price change to large changes in yield.

Modified Convexity and Effective Convexity

The prices used in equation (3) to calculate convexity can be obtained by either assuming that when the yield curve shifts in a parallel way the expected cash flow does not change or it does change. In the former case, the resulting convexity is referred to as modified convexity.[17] Actually, in the industry, convexity is not qualified by the adjective modified. Thus, in practice the term convexity typically means the cash flow is assumed not to change when yields change. Effective convexity, in contrast, assumes that the cash flow does change when yields change. This is the same distinction made for duration.

As with duration, for bonds with embedded options there could be quite a difference between the calculated modified convexity and effective convexity. In fact, for all option-free bonds, either convexity measure will have a positive value. For callable bonds and mortgage-backed securities, the calculated effective convexity can be negative when the calculated modified convexity gives a positive value.

---

[17] The formula for modified convexity is

$$\frac{1(2)\text{PVCF}_1 + 2(3)\text{PVCF}_2 + 3(4)\text{PVCF}_3 + \ldots + n(n+1)\text{PVCF}_n}{(1 + \text{yield}/k)^2 k^2 \text{Price}}$$

Using this formula, the modified convexity for the 9%, 20-year bond selling to yield 6% is 82.04. While this number is slightly different from that obtained using equation (3), when we use this measure to obtain the approximate percentage price change due to convexity, the result will be the same.

Chapter 20

Quantitative Analysis of Fixed Income Portfolios Relative to Indices

Lev Dynkin
Senior Vice President
Lehman Brothers

Jay Hyman
Vice President
Lehman Brothers

INTRODUCTION

Over the past few years, we have seen a significant increase in the use of quantitative techniques for managing fixed income portfolios against standard or customized indices. Investor demand for these techniques has been driven by the combination of several factors. The progressive contraction of spreads has made it increasingly difficult for investors to achieve the desired levels of yield using assets in traditional indices, providing more incentive for extending into new asset classes. Index providers have responded with increased coverage of those new markets.[1] In addition, more investors began to express return objectives and risk constraints in terms of deviations from their benchmarks. Even for portfolios for which traditional market-weighted indices are inappropriate, investors such as insurance companies and central banks have sought market-based benchmarks for performance and risk measurement.

Quantitative techniques have been applied to almost every stage of the portfolio management process, from the initial establishment of investment policy through the analysis of achieved performance. The increasing use of benchmarks to express investment objectives and measure performance places demands on the

---

[1] For instance, the Lehman Brothers Family of Indices currently includes U.S. governments, corporates (investment-grade and high yield), MBS and ABS, Eurobonds (fixed and floating), global governments, global inflation-linked bonds, German local bonds, emerging markets, municipal bonds, and private placements. Plans for 1998 include a 144A Index and a Euro-Aggregate Index in anticipation of European Monetary Union.

set of analytical tools used by plan sponsors and portfolio managers to implement these techniques. To be effective, any quantitative analysis of a portfolio relative to an index requires that consistent pricing assumptions and models be applied to each security in both the portfolio and the benchmark.

The basic steps in quantitative portfolio management relative to an index can be categorized as follows:

- formulate an investment policy in terms of limits on allocations to asset classes, diversification and liquidity requirements, asset/liability constraints, or duration targets (if any)
- select a standard benchmark, or create a customized one if necessary
- profile a portfolio relative to its benchmark along multiple risk dimensions to identify intentional and unintentional exposures
- quantify risk exposures based on historical volatilities and correlations
- compare projected portfolio performance versus its benchmark under a set of scenarios
- establish a methodology for replicating the benchmark return in absence of a market view and creating proxy portfolios
- optimize the portfolio subject to constraints on deviation from the benchmark
- attribute achieved return to risk exposures taken

In this chapter, we provide a brief overview of models and techniques available for each step, with examples of corresponding strategies from our experience working with investors. Strategies discussed include the customization of benchmarks to liabilities, replication of benchmark returns using proxy portfolios or futures contracts, and maximization of expected return subject to risk constraints.

INVESTMENT POLICY AND BENCHMARKS

Every investment portfolio has its own set of objectives and constraints. These may stem from investor desires, legal requirements, or the need to balance assets and liabilities. These risk/return considerations are central both to the formulation of the investment policy, which specifies what securities may be purchased, and to the selection of the benchmark, which will serve as a performance yardstick.

The development of investment policy guidelines and benchmarks does not follow a set order. In many cases, the benchmark is selected first, and an investment policy is crafted to control the risk that a portfolio manager might take while trying to outperform the benchmark. Limits may be placed on the types and allocations of out-of-index securities that may be used, on concentrations in individual issues and issuers, and on the magnitude of allowed deviations from the benchmark. Such arrangements are commonly used by plan sponsors when enlisting external asset managers. In other cases, investment policy constraints are dictated by asset/liability issues, regulatory requirements or liquidity considerations. In these situations, which might occur within insurance companies, thrifts or central banks, it would be unfair to measure portfolio performance against an index which is not subject to these limitations. A custom benchmark must be designed to offer an objective point of reference for performance under the assigned constraints. Quantitative techniques can help guide the decision-making process in both cases.

The two basic methodologies for benchmark customization include narrowing the definition of an index to select a particular subset, or combining asset classes using weights that differ from market capitalizations. Examples of the first type of custom benchmark would be corporates excluding tobacco companies, or non-callable agencies. Examples of the second type would be a combination of 30% governments with 70% corporates (market capitalization in the Lehman Brothers Govt/Corp Index would give weights of 72% and 28%, respectively), or a combination of short and long Treasuries to achieve a given target duration.

Asset managers often rely on studies of the excess returns over duration-matched Treasuries that have been achieved historically by various spread sectors. Some investors have used these studies to map out risk/return tradeoffs across the fixed income landscape. Others have focused more sharply on the merits of extending existing investment guidelines to include a particular asset class.

For central banks, which typically use a duration target as a benchmark, analytical methods can help optimize the selection of the target duration and make dynamic adjustments. Analysis of historical Sharpe ratios (return per unit of risk) along a yield curve represents one possible approach to yield curve positioning.

Insurance companies typically divide their portfolios along product lines, with investment guidelines matched to the expected liability stream of each product. This creates demand for benchmarks tailored to liability cash flows while maintaining the advantages of using broad market-weighted indices. We have explored several analytical solutions to this problem. One approach is to construct an optimized portfolio from a universe of securities within the investment policy, which is constrained to match the liability cash flows as well as liquidity and diversification requirements. Another is to construct a term structure of spreads based on all securities in the investable universe, and combine it with a Treasury yield curve to obtain a yield curve reflective of the chosen asset mix. The liability cash flows can be modeled as a portfolio of hypothetical "zero-coupon bonds" which are marked to market by discounting along this curve. This portfolio can then be used as a benchmark to provide returns, durations, cash flow profiles, and other statistics for comparison with the actual portfolio.

MEASURING PORTFOLIO EXPOSURES VERSUS A BENCHMARK

An important first step in managing a portfolio relative to a benchmark is to analyze the composition of the benchmark in detail. In addition to aggregate statistics, such as average quality and duration, it is very important to know the allocations and exposures of the benchmark along all relevant risk dimensions. For example, a corporate benchmark might be profiled by sector, quality, and duration, and an MBS benchmark by product, coupon levels, and seasoning.

For a clear view of how a portfolio is positioned relative to its benchmark, we can profile the two along identical risk dimensions and compare their allocations, exposures, and returns within each cell. Segmenting by duration alone, for example, would highlight the yield curve exposures in a portfolio versus a benchmark. Segmenting by duration and sector would also show how those views were implemented (e.g., a yield curve barbell achieved by combining MBS at the short end with long corporates).

The amount of information a portfolio manager derives from such a profile depends on the proper selection of the risk dimensions and the quantities compared within each cell. For instance, both risk and return within a particular cell are functions of this cell's contribution to the overall portfolio or benchmark. Contribution is defined as the percentage allocated to a cell times the cell's average. (Contribution to duration equals percentage times duration, and is proportional to dollar duration.) To be sector-neutral to the benchmark, a portfolio should match contributions to spread duration within each sector cell. Information content can also be enhanced by including projected returns within each cell under various interest rate and credit spread scenarios. This provides one more measure of risk.

Heterogeneous risk axes might be particularly useful for certain portfolios. For example, a portfolio may be partitioned by sector and duration. The sector dimension could be sub-partitioned as follows: Treasury strips versus coupons, corporates by quality, and MBS by pricing tiers (premiums, current coupons, and discounts).

Return volatility for most fixed income portfolios is dominated by term structure risk. To control this risk at a basic level, portfolio duration and convexity are compared to those of the benchmark. However, this does not measure the full extent of yield curve risk. A multi-dimensional comparison of exposures along the yield curve could be very helpful in evaluating term structure risk and creating curve-neutral positions. One approach is to partition the portfolio and the benchmark into ranges of maturity, duration, or average life, and compare contributions to duration within each range. Another is to generate and compare cash flow profiles for the portfolio and index, aggregated to a common set of time intervals. For this purpose, cash flows must be represented on a discounted basis, as a percentage of total market value. Finally, the portfolio and benchmark could be compared by their sensitivities to representative changes in the yield curve: "key rate durations" are sensitivities to movements of a single point on the spot curve; "forward rate durations" — sensitivities to points on the forward curve; and "principal component durations" — sensitivities to historically likely shapes of yield curve movement. For a portfolio of bullet securities, the comparison of aggregated cash flows is equivalent to a comparison of key rate durations.

QUANTIFYING RISK: MULTI-FACTOR AND ASSET ALLOCATION MODELS

Portfolio managers must constantly monitor exposures versus the benchmark along many dimensions simultaneously. They may choose to express a market view by overweighing a particular part of the yield curve, sector, quality, or structure. However, they also need to be aware of any exposure that may develop unintentionally. Each difference between portfolio and benchmark composition provides the potential for return differences.

The comparison of allocations along each risk axis independently, as described above, has two shortcomings. First, it does not indicate which mismatches are likely to contribute the most to return deviations between the portfolio and benchmark. In fact, the greater mismatches are not necessarily those that carry the most risk. Second, it completely ignores any correlations that might exist between different risk axes.

There are two approaches to quantifying return deviation between the portfolio and benchmark. The first attempts to attribute most of the variance of an individual security return to a small set of systematic market influences or risk factors. In this method, known as *multi-factor risk analysis*, the sensitivities of the portfolio and benchmark to each of these risk factors are compared. The comparison of positions numbering thousands of bonds can thus be reduced to a comparison of a few risk exposures. However, common market risk factors combined do not always explain the full return variance of a security or an issuer. The unexplained part, known as non-systematic (or diversification) risk, can be quantified separately in this approach.

The second approach divides the market into a few asset classes and derives their return variances from historical observations, without addressing market causes for this variance. In this method, known as asset allocation, portfolio risk is calculated based on weight differentials relative to the benchmark within each asset class. When portfolios are represented only at the level of holdings of asset classes, there is no distinction between systematic and non-systematic risk.

Multi-factor risk models are based on historical time series studies of a set of risk factors such as changes in term structure, spreads, and volatility. The choice of a set of risk factors is particular to each implementation of such a model, and depends on the type of securities covered. The result of this analysis is a covariance matrix of risk factor volatilities and correlations. The model computes the sensitivities of each bond in a portfolio or an index to all risk factors and aggregates them to the universe level based on market weight. The difference between the resulting sensitivities is then multiplied by the covariance matrix to give the systematic risk. In addition, the differences in issuer concentrations of the portfolio and benchmark can be used to estimate the nonsystematic risk. The two are combined to produce the annualized total tracking error, the projected standard deviation of the difference between the portfolio and benchmark returns.

The asset allocation approach relies on historical time series of returns on different asset classes. A covariance matrix is formed directly from the return volatilities of each asset class and the correlations between them. A tracking error can be calculated based on differences between portfolio and benchmark allocations to these asset classes.

The asset allocation approach is often used to quantify risk in multi-currency portfolios. In this case, asset classes can be defined as maturity ranges within each currency. An asset allocation model could then compare portfolio holdings in long German bunds and short U.S. Treasuries to that of the benchmark, multiply the difference by the historical volatilities of each and the correlations between the two and compute the resulting tracking error. In some models, expected returns for each asset class are assumed to be equal to their historical means. In others, they may be projected based on user forecasts of yield curves and exchange rates. Optimization methods can then be used to calculate an efficient frontier of optimal allocations for different levels of risk tolerance.

The asset allocation approach works particularly well for assets with a low degree of correlation. For highly correlated assets, small changes in input expected returns can result in large changes in optimal allocations. In the multi-factor approach, the model can be designed such that the risk factors are not highly correlated with each other.

SCENARIO ANALYSIS

Another view of risk involves the comparison of projected portfolio and benchmark returns under a set of anticipated yield curve and spread scenarios. This approach can be used to project the distribution of possible performance outcomes, including expected returns, worst case returns, and variance of outperformance across multiple scenarios. The most commonly used scenarios are parallel shifts of the Treasury yield curve. However, it is important to consider other types of scenarios as well, such as non-parallel yield curve movements, changes in spread relationships, and changes in volatilities. The kind of exposures the portfolio has relative to the benchmark (curve exposure, sector, or optionality) determine which of these scenario types are most important to highlight potential risks.

Several workout mechanisms are used for horizon pricing of bonds for a changed yield curve: constant spread to the par curve, constant zero volatility (ZV) spread over the forward curve, or constant OAS over a lognormal tree of short rates. For MBS, workout modes might include constant ZV spread and constant OAS over a set of Monte Carlo interest rate paths. Common assumptions on the timing of a yield curve change include instantaneous change and linear phase-in over all or part of the horizon period. It is important for a portfolio manager to verify that all models used for scenario generation and horizon workout (e.g., term structure fitting, interest rate evolution, and volatility calibration) are consistent across all securities in the portfolio and the benchmark.

For portfolios with mixed currencies, scenario specifications include horizon yield curves in any of these currencies as well as horizon foreign exchange rates and costs of hedging. Implied hedging costs can also be derived from interest rate differentials between any two currencies. Investors are likely to have strong views for only a few of the large number of variables required to define a multi-currency scenario. Historical correlations can be used to allow investors to specify their views in partial form, leaving unspecified parameters to be derived from history.

REPLICATING BENCHMARK RETURNS: PROXY PORTFOLIOS

Investors often look for "index proxies" — portfolios with a small number of securities that deviate minimally from the returns of a target index. Proxies are of interest for two distinct purposes: for direct passive investment and for index analysis. Both passive portfolio managers and active managers with no particular view on the market in a given month might be interested in passive investment. Proxy portfolios represent a practical method of matching index returns while containing transaction costs. In addition, the large number of securities in an index can pose difficulties in the application of computationally intensive quantitative techniques. A portfolio can be analyzed against an index proxy of a few securities using methods that would be impractical to apply to an index of several thousand securities. As long as the proxy is carefully constructed to match the index along all relevant risk dimensions, this approach can be used to speed up many forms of analysis with just a small sacrifice in accuracy.

There are several techniques for creating index proxies and replicating index performance. Proxy portfolios can be built with the help of any of the three quantitative techniques described above: "cell-matching", tracking error minimization, and matching index scenario results. Replication of index returns can also be achieved using securities outside of indices, such as Treasury futures contracts. Another obvious way of getting index returns is entering into an index swap or buying an appropriately structured note.

In a simple "cell-matching" technique, a benchmark is profiled on an arbitrary grid, which reflects the risk dimensions along which a portfolio manager's allocation decisions are made. The index allocations to each cell are then matched by one or more liquid and representative securities. The duration (and convexity) of the benchmark within each cell can be used as targets when purchasing securities to fill out the cell. For MBS indices this produces proxy portfolios of 20-25 securities which track an index of 600 MBS generics to within 3 bp/month.[2] We have shown that such a technique can also be applied to replicate the

---

[2] A. Majidi, *Replicating the MBS Index Risk and Return Characteristics Using Proxy Portfolios*, Lehman Brothers, March 1997

term structure exposures of any fixed income index using Treasury futures.[3] This methodology tracks the Lehman Brothers Aggregate Index within 10.5 bp/month, and the Treasury Index to within 6.7 bp/month.

In the context of the multi-factor risk model, the systematic tracking error can be reduced by restructuring the portfolio so that its risk characteristics more closely match those of the index. The nonsystematic component can be reduced through diversification. The optimal path of reducing the tracking error is rarely obvious because each security contributes to many dimensions of risk. A constrained quadratic optimization could be used to solve for the best tracking portfolio with a given number of securities. Another very useful approach to reducing tracking error one step at a time is the "gradient descent" method, which guides portfolio managers through a sequence of optimal and practical transactions. This method ranks each security from the investable set and the portfolio by the sensitivity of tracking error to a change in its holding. From the ranked list of transactions leading to the largest reductions in tracking error, the portfolio manager is free to choose the most practical one. Minimization of tracking error proves to be particularly successful in creating indexed portfolios within the MBS passthrough market, in which the systematic risks (interest rates, volatility, and prepayment) dominate. For example, a proxy portfolio of seven MBS passthroughs constructed using the risk model was able to track the Lehman Brothers MBS index within 14 bp/year. Corporate proxy portfolios need more diversification due to a higher issuer-specific "event" risk.

An indexed portfolio could be optimized for a desired objective (e.g. liquidity) while being constrained in terms of deviation from its benchmark across a wide spectrum of scenarios. Ideally, those scenarios should cover all possible future states of risk parameters (yield curves, spreads, volatilities), which are consistent with current markets and historical volatilities. For interest rate scenarios a representative set can be generated by applying principal components of the yield curve evolution to the current curve at historical volatility levels. The optimal portfolio should have a return profile under each of those scenarios which is closely matched to the benchmark. In order for the scenario approach to give truly indexed portfolios, it is very important to consider changes in market risk along any relevant dimension.

PORTFOLIO OPTIMIZATION

The primary task in portfolio management is the determination of which securities to purchase into the portfolio. Credit analysis, relative value comparison, and market outlook all participate in the security selection process. Optimization techniques can help select securities out of specific pools of assets that best suit the

---

[3] L. Dynkin, J. Hyman, and W. Wu, *Replicating Index Returns with Treasury Futures,* Lehman Brothers, November 1997

stated objective. Examples of objectives include minimum risk relative to a benchmark (creation of an index proxy), maximum liquidity, minimum cost (dedication/immunization), or maximum yield. One very popular objective is maximum outperformance of the benchmark in the expected interest rate scenario, subject to constraints on underperformance in adverse scenarios, and a constraint on structural deviation from the benchmark. Transaction costs can be controlled either by reflecting them explicitly or by including a constraint on portfolio turnover. Diversification is also traditionally ensured by bounds on allocations to individual issuers and securities.

EXPLAINING ACHIEVED RETURNS

Regardless of the methods used to position the portfolio, the end result is the performance achieved relative to the benchmark. The identification of the source of any performance differences can help measure the effects of the various allocation decisions within the overall portfolio management process. In addition, careful analysis of return surprises can help point out unintended portfolio characteristics that should be corrected in the future. For these reasons, we have seen increased demand for quantitative analysis of past performance from all categories of investors.

Broadly, we can distinguish between two approaches to attribution of historical return. The first, which we call "return attribution," operates at the level of individual security returns. Similarly to a multi-factor risk model, this methodology seeks to attribute those returns to common market influences analogous to risk factors. The second approach, which we call "performance attribution", operates at the portfolio level. This approach seeks to analyze the return differences between the portfolio and the benchmark caused by differences in allocation to various risk dimensions. Performance attribution is thus closely related to the asset allocation methodology for modeling risk.

Another useful perspective on historical returns of different asset classes is given by a measure of "excess return" over duration-matched Treasuries. The objective here is to compare asset classes purely on the basis of spread performance, separating out any returns due to differences in yield curve exposures.

Return Attribution

Most return attribution models[4] explain returns by ascribing portions of each security's price return to such effects as the passage of time (coupon, accretion, rolldown), changes in the yield curve (shift, twist, butterfly), and changes in volatilities and spreads. Security level results can be aggregated to analyze the portfolio and benchmark separately, or to compare the two. Return subcomponents correspond to views commonly taken by portfolio managers. For example, if a

---

[4] See **Chapter XX** of this book for a detailed description of one return attribution model.

portfolio is barbelled to express a yield curve flattening view, the anticipated out-performance should come in the form of twist return.

Important considerations in selecting a return attribution model include intuitive clarity and computational accuracy. For instance, model definitions of yield curve movements could be based on changes in bellwether yields or on principal component analysis of historical yield curve movements. Evaluation of each return subcomponent could utilize beginning-of-month sensitivities to various effects or an OAS-based approach.

Performance Attribution

The performance attribution method, by contrast, explains *return differences* between a portfolio and its benchmark rather than the returns themselves. Instead of subdividing the total return of each security, it explains portfolio performance relative to the benchmark in terms of allocation differences between the two. The allocation dimensions are selected and prioritized to reflect the portfolio manager's decision process. For example, the primary decision could be yield curve positioning, with the secondary being the choice of credit sectors. The benchmark plays a central role in performance attribution, and thus the method can not be applied to a portfolio in isolation.

To attribute performance to portfolio management decisions, our model[5] attempts to answer two separate questions. First, had the portfolio earned within each market segment the exact same return as the index, how much would it differ in performance? This difference, due solely to the difference in the weights assigned to each segment, is attributed to the high-level allocation decision. Such attribution to allocation differences can be applied multiple times, by further partitioning each market segment along additional risk axes. Second, how much extra return was achieved due to differences in returns *within* each market segment? This portion of return may be attributed to security selection. For example, the model could start by evaluating the portfolio's positioning along the term structure in terms of allocation to duration ranges, and then further analyze the sector composition within each duration range. The outperformance of the portfolio versus its benchmark could then be explained in terms of curve positioning, sector allocation and security selection.

CONCLUSION

The rapid changes in fixed income markets pose a set of challenges to the analytical tools for setting or changing investment policy, and for designing, tracking, and outperforming benchmarks. First, they need to keep up with new security structures introduced into the marketplace in order to support analysis of complete portfolios. Second, the dynamic nature of many portfolios greatly compli-

---

[5] L. Dynkin, J. Hyman, and P. Vankudre, *The Lehman Brothers Performance Attribution Model*, 1998.

cates the attribution of historical return by introducing a changing basis for returns and an extra source of deviation from index performance.

Going forward, we see increasing investor demand for all aspects of quantitative portfolio management — benchmark customization, risk measurement, optimization of expected returns, and attribution of achieved returns. We expect continued growth in the use of indices by portfolio managers, accompanied by steady improvements to the models and systems required for comparison of portfolios to indices. While credit analysis, security selection, and market timing will always remain critical to the success of any portfolio management effort, quantitative portfolio analysis will play an increasing role in the decision-making process.

Chapter 21

A Return Attribution Model for Fixed Income Securities

Lev Dynkin
Senior Vice President
Lehman Brothers

Jay Hyman
Vice President
Lehman Brothers

Vadim Konstantinovsky
Vice President
Lehman Brothers

INTRODUCTION

The Lehman Brothers Family of Indices has always reported total returns and their components: price, coupon, paydown, and currency returns. This breakdown describes *how* each security contributes to the total return of a particular index or portfolio. Recently, we introduced a return attribution model that adds insight into *why* those returns have been realized.

The Lehman Brother's return attribution model is designed to help explain returns by ascribing portions of each security's price return to such effects as passage of time, yield curve movement, changes in volatility, and changes in spread. By aggregating these return components, a portfolio manager can better understand a portfolio's performance.

The return attribution model was designed to fulfill the two needs of intuitive clarity and computational accuracy. The need for clarity led us to define yield curve movements based on changes in bellwether yields; the need for accuracy led us to use a "full valuation" approach to return attribution. Rather than base the analysis on beginning-of-month sensitivities to various effects, the model calculates each component of return using a full option-adjusted spread (OAS) evaluation.

This chapter begins by defining the components of price return as they appear in the model. Then we test the model's historical accuracy and compare it with other methodologies. We then show how the Return Attribution Model can be used for portfolio management. In the last section, we discuss the numerical results of the model as published for major Lehman Brothers indices.

COMPONENTS OF PRICE RETURN

The Lehman Brothers' return attribution model itemizes the price return component of total return. The two largest sources of changes in prices for fixed income securities are the passage of time and changes in the Treasury yield curve. This chapter is concerned primarily with quantifying the effects of changes in the yield curve on price returns. Changes in volatility and spread provide additional sources of price return.

Price returns associated with the passage of time include accretion and rolldown returns. *Accretion returns* are due to the convergence of a bond's price to par as it approaches maturity. Typically, accretion return will be positive for discounts and negative for premiums, and over the long term accretion is the primary source of return for zero-coupon bonds. Accretion return is calculated by holding a bond's yield constant while moving the settlement date forward. For mortgage-backed securities (MBS), the calculation assumes a constant prepayment rate as well.

Rolldown return, the other type of price return associated with the passage of time, results from predictable changes in a bond's yield as time elapses, reflecting a change in the bond's placement along the yield curve. In a positively sloping yield curve environment (where longer maturities have higher yields), a bond's yield will fall as its maturity shortens, providing positive rolldown returns. When portions of the yield curve are negatively sloped, bonds may experience negative rolldown returns as their yields rise.

For bonds with embedded options, the time return includes the effect of option theta (i.e., erosion of the time value of the option as it nears expiration). For MBS, a constant yield curve assumption does not translate into constant prepayment rates under the Lehman Brothers' prepayment model. Because the model incorporates a lag of several months between refinancing incentive and prepayment activity, the rolldown return can be strongly influenced by an anticipated increase or decrease in prepayments following significant yield curve movements. As a result, negative rolldown returns are sometimes observed (even on a positively sloped yield curve) as MBS discounts lengthen or premiums shorten.

The largest source of price return for fixed income securities is the movement of the yield curve. The Lehman Brothers' return attribution model approximates actual changes in the yield curve using a combination of three curve movements: shift, twist, and butterfly. These curve movements are defined and quantified in the next section.

Components of price returns due to sources other than yield curve changes are volatility and spread returns. Volatility return is due to changes in market volatility and only affects securities with embedded optionality. An increase in volatility, for example, will increase the value of embedded options, giving rise to positive returns on securities that contain an implicit long option position (e.g., putable bonds) and negative returns on securities that contain an implicit short option position (e.g., callable bonds, mortgage passthroughs). Spread return is due to the widening or tightening of option-adjusted spreads versus the Treasury yield curve.

MODEL IMPLEMENTATION OF YIELD CURVE CHANGES

In a given month, the Lehman Brothers' return attribution model first identifies a set of changes in the marketplace and then divides each security's return into components due to each such change. The model defines the components of yield curve movement as intuitively as possible and strives to attribute accurately the returns realized due to each component.

In an effort to make the model as simple as possible, we based our representation of yield curve movement on changes of bellwether Treasury bond yields, which are directly observable in the marketplace, not on the output of computational procedures such as principal components analysis and linear regression analysis. The Lehman Brothers model decomposes the actual change in the Treasury yield curve in a given month into a combination of three basic shapes (shift, twist, and butterfly). Each of these components is a piecewise linear function, with prescribed values at 2-, 5-, 10-, and 30-years,[1] and a single parameter (s for shift, t for twist, and b for butterfly, see Exhibit 1) that specifies the magnitude of that component in a given month. The values of the parameters s, t, and b are based on observed changes in the yields of Treasury bellwether bonds, selected at the beginning of the month, as follows.

Shift returns are due to a parallel yield curve shift, the magnitude s of which we set equal to the average yield change of the 2-, 5-, 10-, and 30-year bellwethers (see Exhibit 1a). This type of change produces the same sign for all returns.

$$s = \frac{1}{4}(\Delta y_2 + \Delta y_5 + \Delta y_{10} + \Delta y_{30})$$

Twist returns are due to a yield curve flattening or steepening centered on the 5-year (see Exhibit 1b). We quantify these returns in a steepening move ($t>0$) as the 30-year yield moving up by $t/2$ while the 2-year moves down by the same amount; in a flattening move, the opposite occurs. The magnitude of twist t is determined by the change in the spread between 2- and 30-year bellwethers:

$$t = \Delta y_{30} - \Delta y_2$$

---

[1] The value at 10 years is always set halfway between the values at 5 and 30 years. See the section on model development and validation for a discussion of these assumptions.

Exhibit 1: Components of Yield Curve Movement
(a) Shift

(b) Twist

(c) Butterfly

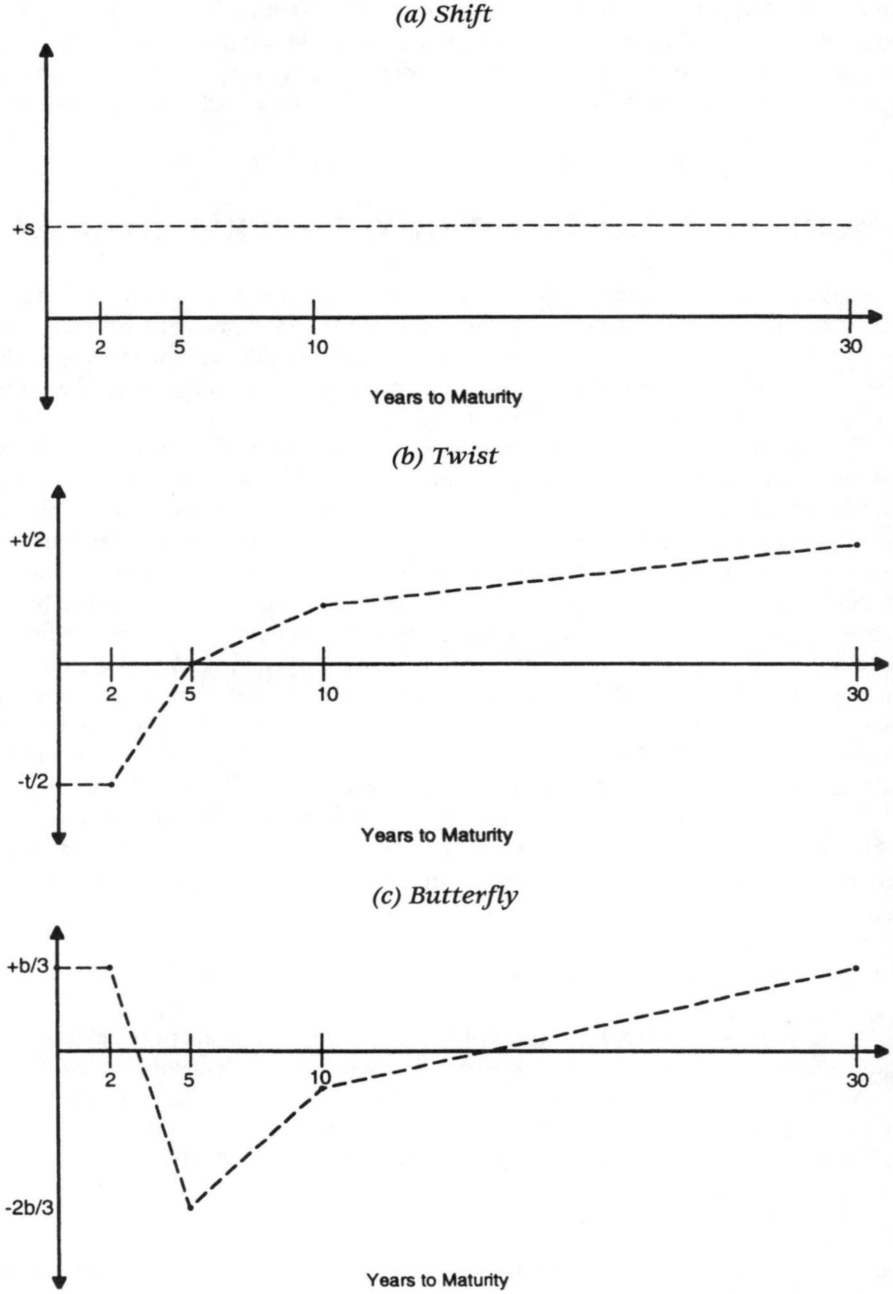

Exhibit 2: Illustration of Breakdown of Yield Curve Movement

a. Attribution of Changes in the Bellwether Curve between 1/1/96 and 2/1/96, in bp

Term	Beg.	End	Chg.	Shift	Twist	Bfly.	Shape
2 yr.	5.188%	4.934%	−25.3	−8.1	−16.1	1.7	−2.9
3	5.225	5.032	−19.3	−8.1	−10.7	0.0	-0.5
5	5.404	5.260	−14.4	−8.1	0.0	−3.4	−2.9
10	5.583	5.589	0.6	−8.1	8.0	−0.9	1.5
30	6.005	6.072	6.8	−8.1	16.1	1.7	−2.9

Shift: average of movements of 2-, 5-, 10-, and 30-year = -8.1 bp.
Twist: change in spread between 2- and 30-year = 32.1 bp steepening.
Butterfly: average of movements of 2- and 30-year minus movement of 5-year = 5.1 bp.

b. Beginning-of-month Bellwethers — Defining Yield Curve Movements

Term	Coupon	Maturity
2 yr.	5.375%	11/30/1997
3	5.500	11/15/1998
5	5.625	11/30/2000
10	5.875	11/15/2005
30	7.625	2/15/2025

c. Changes in Term Structure of Volatility

Term	1/1/96	2/1/96	Change
0 yr.	21.81%	21.87%	0.07%
2	20.85	20.90	0.05
5	19.18	19.19	0.02
7	18.20	18.18	−0.02
10	16.88	16.83	−0.05

Butterfly returns are those produced when the middle of the curve moves in the opposite direction from the wings (see Exhibit 1c). We define this as the 2- and 30-year yields moving up by the same amount $b/3$ while the 5-year yield moves down by double the same amount. The magnitude b of the butterfly effect is determined by the extent to which the 5-year bellwether moves differently from the average of the 2- and 30-year yields:

$$b = \frac{1}{2}(\Delta y_2 + \Delta y_{30}) - \Delta y_5$$

We define residual return, or *shape return*, as yield curve returns other than those explained by these three types of yield curve changes. Exhibit 2 shows the model's treatment of yield change for the month of January 1996.

OAS METHODOLOGY

One strength of the Lehman Brothers' model is the method used to attribute each security's return to its various components. The model constructs a sequence of stepwise changes by which the beginning of the month environment is transformed into the end of month environment, and reprices the bond at each of these steps using a full OAS-based valuation. Each component of price return is given by the difference in prices obtained by two successive valuations (see Exhibit 3).

Each row of Exhibit 3 represents a pricing relationship that relates the price of a bond to a particular set of assumptions. The first and last rows correspond to the actual prices of the bond at the beginning and end of the month; the intervening rows show the sequence of pricing calculations that incorporates progressively more of the effects of the month's events. For example, the third row of the table indicates that the bond is to be repriced for settlement at the end of the month, using the beginning of month yield curve, volatility, and OAS. The fourth row indicates that the beginning yield curve should be changed by the parallel shift and the bond repriced using the same OAS over this shifted curve. The difference between the prices calculated by these two operations (as a percentage of beginning price) is reported as the shift return. Each additional row moves one step closer to the end of month environment, and introduces an additional component of return. The right-most column of Exhibit 3 shows how the components of return are grouped into broader categories.

Exhibit 3: Calculation of Return Components by Successive Valuations

Pricing Operation	Settle Date	Yield	PSA	Yield Curve	Vola-tility	OAS	Return Component[a]	Broader Level Return Component[b]
Beginning Price	Beg	Beg	Beg	Beg	Beg	Beg		
Reprice including Accretion	End	Beg	Beg				Accretion	Time
Reprice including Rolldown	End			Beg	Beg	Beg	Rolldown	
Reprice with shifted yield curve	End			Beg + shift	Beg	Beg	Shift	
Reprice with shifted and twisted yield curve	End			Beg + shift + twist	Beg	Beg	Twist	Yield Curve
Reprice including shift, twist, and butterfly effects	End			Beg + shift + twist + butterfly	Beg	Beg	Butterfly	
Reprice with actual ending yield curve	End			End	Beg	Beg	Shape	
Reprice with ending volatility	End			End	End	Beg	Volatility	OAS Effect
Ending Price	End			End	End	End	Spread	

[a] Each return component in this column is computed as a difference in the current row price from the price in the row immediately above.

[b] Each return component in this column is a sum of two or more related return components from the previous column.

Exhibit 4: Return Attribution for a Callable Corporate Bond, January 1996: Alabama Power 6.850% of 8/1/02

Price Return due to:	
Accretion	−0.01
Rolldown	−0.03
Shift	0.24
Twist	0.13
Butterfly	0.04
Curve Shape	−0.01
Volatility	−0.06
Spread	−0.01
Price Return	0.29
Coupon Return	0.55
Paydown Return	0.00
Currency Return	0.00
Total Return	0.84
Breakdown by Type:	
Time (Accretion + Rolldown)	−0.04
Time + Coupon	0.50
Nonparallel Yield Change	0.16
Overall Yield Curve Change	0.41
OAS (Volatility + Spread)	−0.07

Government and corporate bonds are priced using the Lehman Brothers proprietary implementation of a tree-based lognormal pricing model. The full valuation pricing methodology, in which components of return are calculated by a sequence of OAS-to-price operations based on different yield curves, allows each component of return on a callable bond to be split into bullet and option components, by performing the same sequence of operations on both the callable bond and its bullet-to-maturity equivalent. An example of the return breakdown of a callable corporate bond is shown in Exhibit 4. The Alabama Power 6.85% of 2002 was priced for settlement on 1/1/96 at 101.712, for a yield to maturity of 6.525%. Repricing at this yield for settlement on 2/1/96, we obtain a price of 101.700, which would give a price return of −1 bp (the change in price is divided by the beginning price plus accrued: 101.712 + 2.854 = 104.566). We then reprice once more as of 2/1/96, using the beginning of month OAS of 21.6 bp, to obtain a price of 101.668, and calculate the rolldown return (101.668 − 101.700)/104.556 = −3 bp. A new lognormal tree is then created by applying a parallel shift of −8.1 bp (see Exhibit 2) to the beginning-of-month par curve, and the bond is repriced at the same OAS to give a price of 101.919, corresponding to 24 bp of return.

This operation is repeated for the twist and butterfly components: a steepening of 32.1 bp causes the price to change to 102.052, for 13 bp of return; the addition of the butterfly movement brings the price to 102.099, giving another 4 bp of return. At the next step, the lognormal tree is constructed using the actual yield curve as of 2/1/96, but still using the term structure of volatility as of 1/1/96, and the bond is repriced at 102.091, for a −1 bp return. Next the new term structure of volatility is put into play, and we reprice the bond using the lognormal tree fully calibrated to the market as of 2/1/96, but still using the beginning OAS. The resulting price of 102.032 gives a −6 bp return due to the change in volatility. Finally, the actual price of the security as of 2/1/96 is 102.020, which gives an OAS of 22.2 bp. This is interpreted as a −1 bp return due to change in spread.

Mortgage-backed securities are priced using a Monte Carlo approach and the Lehman Brothers' prepayment model. An example of the return breakdown of a mortgage passthrough is shown in Exhibit 5. The methodology is identical to the one for the callable corporate, except that as the yield curve is manipulated, we generate new sets of rate paths instead of lognormal trees.

The full valuation methodology employed by the Lehman Brothers' model holds a clear advantage over methods that rely on beginning of month sensitivities. For example, shift return could be calculated by multiplying the amount of shift by the beginning of period duration, and twist return by multiplying the measured twist by the beginning twist sensitivity. This approach, however, ignores the fact that changes in the yield curve can cause profound changes in the risk characteristics (e.g., duration, twist sensitivity) of all securities with interest rate-dependent cash flows, and can lead to significant errors in the reporting of return components.

Exhibit 5: Return Attribution for a Mortgage Passthrough, January 1996: 30-Year FNMA 8.0% (1993 origination)

Price Return due to:	
Accretion	0.02
Rolldown	−0.03
Shift	0.11
Twist	0.21
Butterfly	0.01
Curve Shape	0.03
Volatility	0.00
Spread	−0.31
Price Return	0.04
Coupon Return	0.63
Paydown Return	−0.03
Currency Return	0.00
Total Return	0.64
Breakdown by Type:	
Time (Accretion + Rolldown)	−0.01
Time + Coupon	0.62
Nonparallel Yield Change	0.25
Overall Yield Curve Change	0.36
OAS (Volatility + Spread)	−0.31

Exhibit 6: Explanatory Power of Different Definitions of Yield Curve Shift: 5/90-2/95

Shift Definition	R-squared
3-point shift	85.9%
4-point shift*	88.2
5-point shift	85.1

* Indicates the set of assumptions chosen for the Lehman Brothers' model.

MODEL DEVELOPMENT AND VALIDATION

The decomposition of yield curve movement in the Lehman Brothers' return attribution model was guided by statistical studies of the historical behavior of Treasury yield changes. Some of these studies were used to help decide on various details of model implementation, while others were used to help measure the accuracy of the completed model.

Yield Curve Shift

We investigated the definition of yield curve shift based on changes in bellwether bond yields using five years of monthly yield changes for off-the-run coupon Treasuries. Exhibit 6 summarizes the percentage of yield change explained by each of the three definitions of curve shift:

- 3-point shift (average yield change of 2-, 5-, and 30-year)
- 4-point shift (average yield change of 2-, 5-, 10-, and 30-year)
- 5-point shift (average yield change of 2-, 3-, 5-, 10-, and 30-year)

In measuring fit, we chose to weight the residual yield changes by duration, as a proxy for percentage of explained return. Based on these results, we selected the 4-point shift as superior to both the 3-point shift, which may use too sparse a representation of the curve, and the 5-point shift, which overrepresents the short end of the curve.

Yield Curve Twist and Butterfly

The magnitude of the twist in the yield curve is defined in the model by the change in the 2- to 30-year spread. Several choices were considered for the shape of the term dependence to be assumed for the twist.

- *Linear:* the twist is applied linearly between 2 and 30 years. This implies a pivot (no change from shifted curve) at 16 years.
- *2-piece linear, pivot at 5:* The 5-year point is assumed to be the pivot of the twist (experiences no twist). One wing of the twist is interpolated linearly from 2 to 5 years, and the second (opposite in sign) from 5 to 30.

Exhibit 7: Explanatory Power of Different Twist Shapes, *
5/90-2/95

Twist Definition	Cumulative Fit		
	Shift	Twist	Butterfly
Linear	88.2%	94.2%	94.5%
2-piece linear, pivot at 5	88.2	97.2	98.2
2-piece linear, pivot at 10	88.2	96.5	97.1
3-piece linear, pivot at 5**	88.2	97.3	98.3

* All use Lehman Brothers definitions of shift and butterfly.
** Indicates the set of assumptions chosen for the Lehman Brothers model.

- *2-piece linear, pivot at 10:* same as above, but with pivot at 10 years.
- *3-piece linear, pivot at 5:* the 5-year point is considered the pivot of the twist, but the 5-30 year twist is evenly split into two linear segments, 5-10 and 10-30, as shown in Exhibit 1b.

The definition of the 3-piece linear twist was motivated by a separate historical study, which showed that the yield change of the on-the-run 10-year is close to the average of the changes in the 5-year and the 30-year.[2]

We studied the explanatory power of these various twist shapes, using the same dataset and methodology as in our study of shift. Exhibit 7 shows the explanatory power added by each of the twist shapes when used in conjunction with the 4-point shift defined above. The two definitions in which the twist has its pivot at 5 years are clearly superior; we have chosen the 3-piece twist based on the improvement in explanatory power and the regression results described above.

The third component usually considered for yield curve decomposition and sometimes observed historically is the butterfly movement. This component results in a modest improvement in the explanatory power of the model, from 97.3% to 98.3%, but can be significant in certain periods.

Measuring Yield Change

Our definitions of shift, twist, and butterfly are based on the yield changes at specific points (2-, 5-, 10-, and 30-years) along the curve. These yield changes are defined in the model by a "beginning-of-month bellwether" method: we measure the month-to-month yield change of the beginning-of-month on-the-run Treasury securities of these maturities. We compared the explanatory power of this model with that of two alternative methods: a "rolling bellwether" method in which the yield change may be obtained by subtracting beginning and ending yields of two different bonds in auction months, and a theoretical par curve method in which the beginning and ending yields for the specified maturities are those of hypothetical par coupon Treasuries derived from an off-the-run spline model.

---

[2] Regression of Δy_{10} against Δy_5 and Δy_{30} indicates coefficients close to 0.5.

Exhibit 8: Effect of Different Techniques for Measuring Yield Change, 10/93-12/94

Measurement of Yield Change	Cumulative Fit		
	Shift	Twist	Butterfly
Beginning-of-month Bellwethers*	90.9%	98.1%	99.0%
Rolling Bellwethers	90.5	98.0	98.8
Off-the-run par curves	90.7	98.3	99.1

* Indicates the set of assumptions chosen for the Lehman Brothers model.

Exhibit 9: Evaluation of Model Accuracy, 5/90-2/95

Method of Yield Curve Decomposition	Cumulative Fit		
	Shift	Twist	Butterfly
Lehman Brothers Model*	88.2%	97.3%	98.3%
Principal Components Analysis	91.8	96.6	97.0

*Indicates the set of assumptions chosen for the Lehman Brothers model.

As shown in Exhibit 8, the beginning-of-month bellwether method used in the Lehman Brothers' model exhibits explanatory power roughly equivalent to that based on the par curve, and is more intuitive and accessible to market practitioners. It performs significantly better than the rolling bellwether assumption; the rolling bellwether assumption leads to large modeling errors in some auction months.

Comparison with Other Models

A frequently used method of decomposing yield curve movement is known as principal components analysis. In this method, a detailed analysis of historical yield curve movement is used to find the set of components that can be combined to approximate typical curve behavior. The three most significant components of such analysis tend to have shapes that can be roughly identified as shift, twist, and curvature, but are not explicitly defined as such. We applied this methodology to a monthly time series of changes in the par curve, where the monthly par curves were derived from a spline fitted to off-the-run Treasuries. For each month of data, these three components were then regressed to find the best fit with the set of changes in yields of all noncallable Treasuries. As shown in Exhibit 9, this analysis explained 97.0% of the changes in yield, while the Lehman Brothers' model explained 98.3%.[3]

Our analysis of historical data demonstrates that the power of the Lehman Brothers' model to capture the movement of the yield curve rivals that of more sophisticated approaches. The straightforward treatment of yield curve movement, which makes the model accessible and intuitive, does not incur any significant performance penalty.

---

[3] Theoretically, the regression of this set of components against actual yield changes should have explanatory power greater than that of any ad hoc breakdown. Indeed, when R-squared is computed based on equally weighted (rather than duration weighted) yield residuals, the principal components model slightly outperforms the Lehman Brothers' model, 97.4% to 97.1%.

Exhibit 10: Application of Return Attribution to Active Portfolio Management

Sample Outlook	Sample Strategy versus Benchmark	Measure of Outperformance
1 Unchanged yield curve, volatility and spreads	Buy high current yield.	Excess Coupon & Accretion Returns
2 ("no view").	Buy steepest part of curve.	Excess Rolldown Return
3 Upward parallel shift in curve.	Shorten duration.	Excess Shift Return
4 Yield curve to flatten.	Barbell portfolio versus benchmark.	Excess Twist Return
5 Implied volatility to decline.	Buy callables, derivatives, MBS.	Excess Volatility Return
6 Industrial spreads to tighten.	Overweight industrials.	Excess Spread Return

APPLICATIONS TO PORTFOLIO MANAGEMENT

A precise attribution of the returns of portfolios and benchmarks can be invaluable in assessing portfolio performance, in both active and passive management modes. In active portfolio management, a manager will typically attempt to enhance portfolio returns by executing a strategy corresponding to a particular view on the market, such as anticipation of a yield curve flattening or a systematic tightening of corporate spreads. To reflect this view, the portfolio will purposely be made structurally different from the benchmark in one or more ways. To assess the contribution of each such strategy to the overall outperformance (especially when multiple strategies are executed simultaneously), it is helpful to break returns into the appropriate components. These uses of return attribution are illustrated in Exhibit 10.

In passive portfolio management where the goal is to match benchmark performance, any significant deviations between portfolio and benchmark performance can be cause for concern. In such situations, a good understanding of the sources of these return differences can help identify structural differences that have given rise to an observed underperformance and suggest corrective action. Examples of this application of return attribution are given in Exhibit 11.

We can use the model to compare the return of the actively managed portfolio XYZ to that of its benchmark, the Lehman Brothers Intermediate Corporate Index, for the month of January 1996. The portfolio was duration-matched to the benchmark at the start of the month but was grossly mismatched in both sector composition and allocation along the yield curve. Exhibit 12 shows the returns achieved by the portfolio and benchmark, as attributed by the model. As would be expected for a duration-matched portfolio, the parallel shift component of the portfolio's return matches that of the benchmark. However, the portfolio underperforms by 22 bp of price return. The model shows that of this 22 bp, 4 bp is attributable to twist return and 14 bp to spread return.

Exhibit 11: Application of Return Attribution to Passive Portfolio Management

	Observed Return Deviation versus Benchmark	Implied Structural Difference
1	Different Coupon/Accretion Returns	Coupon distribution.
2	Different Rolldown Return	Allocation along yield curve.
3	Different Shift Return	Duration mismatch.
4	Different Twist Return	Cash flow distribution along yield curve.
5	Different Volatility Return	Exposure to callables, MBS.
6	Different Spread Return	Sector/quality distribution.
		Overexposure to individual issuers.

Exhibit 12: Return Attribution of Portfolio versus Index, January 1996

Portfolio: xyz.prt
Benchmark: icorp.q

	Portfolio	Benchmark	Difference
Price Return due to:			
Accretion	−0.09	−0.08	−0.01
Rolldown	0.02	0.00	0.01
Shift	0.34	0.34	0.00
Twist	−0.07	−0.02	−0.04
Butterfly	0.05	0.07	−0.02
Curve Shape	−0.10	−0.08	−0.02
Volatility	0.00	0.00	0.00
Spread	−0.02	0.12	−0.14
Price Return	0.13	0.35	−0.22
Coupon Return	0.6	0.58	0.02
Paydown Return	0.00	0.00	0.00
Currency Return	0.00	0.00	0.00
Total Return	0.73	0.93	−0.21
Breakdown by Type:			
Time (Accretion + Rolldown)	−0.07	−0.08	0.01
Time + Coupon	0.53	0.50	0.02
Nonparallel Yield Change	−0.12	−0.03	−0.09
Overall Yield Curve Change	0.23	0.32	−0.09
OAS (Volatility + Spread)	−0.02	0.11	−0.14
Implied Spread Change	0.01	−0.03	0.03

Exhibit 13: Market Structure Comparison of Portfolio versus Benchmark Twist Return, by Duration

Portfolio: xyz.prt
Benchmark: icorp.q
Pricing Date: 1/31/96

| | Modified Adjusted Duration (in years) | | | | | | |
Percent	0 - 2	2 - 3	3 - 4	4 - 5	5 - 6	6 +	Total
Portfolio	35.31	5.84	6.54	1.61	6.50	44.20	100.00
Benchamrk	14.99	11.01	17.81	14.65	20.84	20.70	100.00
Difference	20.32	−5.17	−11.27	−13.04	−14.34	23.50	0.00
Twist Return							
Portfolio	0.25	0.29	0.14	−0.06	−0.23	−0.37	−0.07
Benchamrk	0.22	0.27	0.15	−0.03	−0.16	−0.38	−0.03
Difference	0.03	0.02	−0.01	−0.03	−0.06	0.00	−0.04

January 1996 was characterized by an unusually large steepening of 32.1 bp and a modest parallel shift of −8.1 bp (see Exhibit 2). For many securities at the short and long ends of the yield curve, this steepening caused the twist return to dominate the shift return. (For the FNMA 30-year passthrough shown in Exhibit 5, with a duration of 1.5 years, the 21 bp twist return is almost double the 11 bp shift return.) The twist returns for this particular portfolio and benchmark are relatively small because their duration of 4.28 years is very near the assumed pivot point of our twist component at 5 years. This effect is illustrated in Exhibit 13. Both the portfolio and benchmark achieve small twist returns overall by averaging together positive twist returns for short durations with negative twist returns for longer durations. The 4 bp underperformance arises because the portfolio is strongly barbelled versus the index. It is overexposed by 35.31% versus 14.99% in the 0- to 2-year duration cell, underexposed throughout the 2- to 6-year duration cells, and overexposed to durations of 6 years and longer. This barbell position underperformed in the steepening environment; the negative twist returns in the longest cell outweighed the smaller positive twist returns in the shortest.

A similar analysis can explain the 14 bp underperformance in spread return. Exhibit 14 compares the sector and quality allocations of the portfolio and benchmark, along with the resulting spread returns. The portfolio is overweighted in industrials (75.10% versus 30.98%) and utilities (20.12% versus 13.01%), has no exposure to the financial or Yankee sectors, and has a 4.78% allocation to the MBS sector, which is not represented in the benchmark. Thus, the portfolio overemphasized the worst performing sector in the benchmark (industrials in the index earned 4 bp of spread return) while missing out on 18 bp of spread return in the finance sector and 12 bp in Yankees. However, this poor showing in sector allocation does not account for the full extent of the underperformance. Had the portfolio matched the benchmark performance within each sector, this allocation to industrials and finance would have given a spread return of about 5 bp (75.10%

× 4 + 20.12% × 10), while the portfolio's achieved spread return for these two sectors was only −0.3 bp (75.10% × −1 + 20.12% × 2). This underperformance is attributable to poor security choices in these sectors.

Exhibit 14: Market Structure Comparison of Portfolio versus Benchmark Spread Return, by Sector and Quality

Portfolio: xyz.prt
Benchmark: icorp.q
Pricing Date: 1/31/96   Percent and Spread Return

Quality			Sector					
			Indus.	Tele.-Utility	Finan.	Canadian-Supranat'l	MBS	Total
AAA	Percent	Portfolio	1.98	5.68	0.00	0.00	4.78	12.44
		Benchmark	0.67	0.49	0.62	2.47	0.00	4.25
		Difference	1.31	5.19	−0.62	−2.47	4.78	8.19
	Spread	Portfolio	−0.04	0.15	0.00	0.00	−0.41	−0.10
	Return	Benchmark	0.02	0.02	0.03	0.08	0.00	0.06
		Difference	−0.06	0.13	−0.03	−0.08	−0.41	−0.15
AA	Percent	Portfolio	11.78	5.88	0.00	0.00	0.00	17.65
		Benchmark	4.62	1.99	5.20	7.83	0.00	19.64
		Difference	7.16	3.89	−5.20	−7.83	0.00	−1.99
	Spread	Portfolio	0.05	−0.02	0.00	0.00	0.00	0.03
	Return	Benchmark	0.07	0.09	0.11	0.09	0.00	0.09
		Difference	−0.01	−0.11	−0.11	−0.09	0.00	−0.06
A	Percent	Portfolio	35.10	3.56	0.00	0.00	0.00	38.66
		Benchmark	14.36	5.63	25.32	7.98	0.00	53.28
		Difference	20.74	−2.06	−25.32	−7.98	0.00	−14.62
	Spread	Portfolio	0.07	0.13	0.00	0.00	0.00	0.08
	Return	Benchmark	0.06	0.10	0.18	0.13	0.00	0.13
		Difference	0.01	0.03	−0.18	−0.13	0.00	−0.05
BAA	Percent	Portfolio	26.25	5.00	0.00	0.00	0.00	31.24
		Benchmark	11.34	4.90	4.46	2.12	0.00	22.82
		Difference	14.91	0.10	−4.46	−2.12	0.00	8.42
	Spread	Portfolio	−0.15	−0.14	0.00	0.00	0.00	−0.15
	Return	Benchmark	0.02	0.11	0.28	0.27	0.00	0.11
		Difference	−0.17	−0.25	−0.28	−0.27	0.00	−0.26
Total	Percent	Portfolio	75.10	20.12	0.00	0.00	4.78	100.00
		Benchmark	30.98	13.01	35.61	20.40	0.00	100.00
		Difference	44.12	7.11	−35.61	−20.40	4.78	0.00
	Spread	Portfolio	−0.01	0.02	0.00	0.00	−0.41	−0.02
	Return	Benchmark	0.04	0.10	0.18	0.12	0.00	0.11
		Difference	−0.06	−0.07	−0.18	−0.12	−0.41	−0.14

A closer look at the performance within each cell reveals especially poor performance in BAA industrials, where the portfolio achieved a spread return of −15 bp versus +2 bp for the index, and in BAA utilities (−14 bp versus +11 bp). Exhibit 15 shows a security-level view of portfolio XYZ, with total return separated into three broad components: total time return (coupon, rolldown, and accretion), overall yield curve return, and spread return. Performance in the BAA utility sector was determined by the two bonds representing it in the portfolio — GTE Corp and Gulf States Utilities — which had spread returns of −12 bp and − 18 bp, respectively. The underperformance in BAA industrials was primarily due to the Northrop-Grumman issue, which widened from 81 bp to 141 bp in OAS after being placed on credit watch by Standard & Poor's and provided a huge − 373 bp of spread return.

The return breakdown used in Exhibit 15 handles zero-coupon bonds in a manner consistent with coupon-bearing securities. By grouping the accretion and rolldown components of price return together with coupon return as "total time return," the return of the Archer-Daniels-Midland zero coupon bond is seen on an equal footing with the other bonds in the portfolio. In a more traditional breakdown of total return into price return and coupon return, the entire return of the zero coupon bond is shown in the price return column, offering no additional insight.

Model Results for Published Indices

Attribution of returns on all individual securities in the Lehman Brothers Aggregate Index is performed monthly as part of index production and aggregated to index level for publication. The subcomponents of price return offer useful additional information on indices and benchmarks. Exhibit 16 shows the returns on some of the Lehman Brothers bond indices for our sample month, January 1996. Shift returns are positive for all indices while twist returns once again reflect that month's drastic steepening. The various intermediate indices, with a maturity range of 1-10 years, have relatively small twist returns since the 5-year pivot of the twist falls in the center of this range. Conversely, the long indices, containing maturities of 10 years and longer, experience large negative twist returns. Also apparent in the exhibit is the relative performance of the various spread sectors. Outperforming sectors for the month were long finance with a spread return of 45 bp and long Yankees with a spread return of 33 bp.

Time series analysis of the components of index returns can help characterize the risks inherent in different asset classes. Exhibit 17 shows the mean and standard deviation of each component of monthly return for several Lehman Brothers indices from January 1996 through November 1997. Differences between the various sectors are apparent in the non-yield curve components of return. The main source of mean return is coupon return. Both corporates and mortgages earn an average of 6 bp per month more coupon return than governments. This comes at the expense of higher variability in returns due to volatility and spread.

Exhibit 15: Security Level View of Portfolio XYZ

Issuer	Cpn. Rate (%)	Mty. Date	Par Value	Mod. Adj. Dur. (yrs.)	Quality Ending	OAS- Begin (bp)	OAS (bp)	Returns (%)			
								Total Time	Yld. Crv.	Total Sprd.	Total
AT&T Corp	7.000	5/15/05	1,200	6.77	AA3	39	39	0.53	-0.06	-0.02	0.46
American Home Products	7.900	2/15/05	1,200	6.38	A2	46	45	0.53	-0.01	0.07	0.59
Archer-daniels-midland	0.000	5/1/02	600	6.07	AA2	38	32	0.52	0.34	0.35	1.21
BP America Inc	8.875	12/1/97	600	1.67	AA3	29	29	0.46	0.43	0.01	0.89
Bellsouth Tele	6.500	6/15/05	1,200	6.95	AAA	32	30	0.52	-0.08	0.15	0.59
Black + Decker Mfg Co	7.500	4/1/03	300	5.43	BAA3	77	76	0.54	0.25	0.08	0.87
Boeing Co	6.350	6/15/03	300	5.80	A1	38	38	0.52	0.21	0.00	0.72
Coca - Cola Enterprises Inc.	6.500	11/15/97	700	1.65	A3	32	31	0.46	0.43	0.04	0.92
Conagra Inc	9.750	11/1/97	1,000	1.58	BAA1	43	43	0.47	0.41	0.01	0.88
Dupont E I De Nemours	8.650	12/1/97	500	1.67	AA3	29	29	0.46	0.43	0.01	0.89
Dupont E I De Nemours	8.125	3/15/04	300	5.90	AA3	40	43	0.52	0.12	-0.18	0.46
Eastman Chemical	6.375	1/15/04	700	6.16	A3	69	62	0.54	0.12	0.42	1.07
Ford Capital B.v.	9.125	5/1/98	400	2.00	A1	41	37	0.48	0.48	0.08	1.03
Ford Holdings, Inc	9.250	7/15/97	1,200	1.36	A1	34	33	0.44	0.34	0.03	0.82
GTE Corp	8.850	3/1/98	600	1.83	BAA1	74	80	0.50	0.46	-0.12	0.84
General Electric	7.875	9/15/98	400	2.30	AAA	23	24	0.47	0.51	-0.04	0.94
General Motors	9.625	12/1/00	400	3.88	A3	62	48	0.51	0.51	0.57	1.59
Gulf States Utilities	8.250	4/1/04	400	5.85	BAA3	122	125	0.59	0.12	-0.18	0.53
Intl Business Machines	6.375	11/1/97	1,000	1.62	A1	28	29	0.45	0.42	0.01	0.88
Lockheed Corporation	9.375	10/15/99	300	3.08	A3	42	47	0.49	0.53	-0.18	0.84
MCI Communications	7.500	8/20/04	700	6.18	A2	54	52	0.53	0.05	0.13	0.72
Mobil Oil Corp Esop	9.170	2/29/00	300	1.95	AA2	27	21	0.47	0.39	0.12	0.98
Nabisco	8.300	4/15/99	300	2.75	BAA2	78	72	0.52	0.53	0.15	1.19
Northrop Grumman	8.625	10/15/04	800	6.07	BAA3	81	141	0.56	0.05	-3.73	-3.12
Penney J C	6.375	9/15/00	300	3.88	A1	41	42	0.50	0.52	-0.06	0.96
Philip Morris Cos. Inc	9.000	5/15/98	200	2.04	A2	43	39	0.48	0.48	0.08	1.04
RJR Nabisco, Inc	8.750	8/15/05	1,100	6.22	BAA3	265	239	0.71	-0.02	1.72	2.41
TCI Comm Inc	8.000	8/1/05	1,200	6.70	BAA3	130	124	0.60	-0.05	0.37	0.92
Time Warner Ent	9.625	5/1/02	300	4.71	BAA3	100	101	0.56	0.38	-0.07	0.86
USX Corp	6.375	7/15/98	300	2.24	BAA3	73	69	0.50	0.50	0.10	1.10
WMX Technologies	6.375	12/1/03	500	6.06	A1	46	51	0.53	0.14	-0.31	0.36
Wal-Mart Stores, Inc	6.125	10/1/99	300	3.19	AA1	38	38	0.49	0.55	0.00	1.04
FNMA Convntnl Lg Tsy 30yr	8.000	8/1/22	500	1.47	AAA+	46	55	0.62	0.36	-0.31	0.64
GNMA I Single Family 30yr	9.000	11/1/20	500	1.34	AAA+	67	83	0.70	0.34	-0.50	0.43

Exhibit 16: Return Attribution for Some Lehman Brothers Indices, January 1996

	Accret	Rlldwn	Shift	Twist	Bfly	Shape	Volat	Spread	Price	Cpn	Paydwn	Total
Aggregate	−0.05	0.00	0.36	−0.17	0.01	−0.01	0.00	−0.03	0.11	0.57	−0.01	0.66
Government/Corporate	−0.08	0.00	0.42	−0.29	0.01	−0.01	0.00	0.02	0.07	0.55	0.00	0.62
Int. Gov/Corp	−0.09	0.01	0.26	0.09	0.04	−0.02	0.00	0.03	0.31	0.55	0.00	0.86
Long Gov/Corp	−0.03	−0.02	0.81	−1.23	−0.06	0.01	−0.01	−0.01	−0.53	0.57	0.00	0.03
Governments	−0.08	0.01	0.40	−0.27	0.00	0.01	0.00	0.00	0.07	0.54	0.00	0.61
Int. Governments	−0.09	0.01	0.24	0.12	0.03	−0.01	0.00	0.00	0.30	0.54	0.00	0.84
Long Governments	−0.04	0.00	0.88	−1.37	−0.07	0.04	0.00	−0.01	−0.58	0.55	0.00	−0.03
1-3 year Govt.	−0.09	0.01	0.13	0.24	−0.02	0.05	0.00	0.01	0.32	0.52	0.00	0.85
Treasuries	−0.09	0.01	0.41	−0.26	0.00	0.00	0.00	0.01	0.09	0.54	0.00	0.63
Int. Treasuries	−0.10	0.02	0.24	0.13	0.03	−0.01	0.00	0.00	0.32	0.54	0.00	0.86
Long Treasuries	−0.05	0.00	0.87	−1.35	−0.07	0.03	0.00	0.01	−0.55	0.56	0.00	0.00
20+ year Treasuries	−0.04	0.00	0.95	−1.57	−0.10	0.11	0.00	−0.01	−0.65	0.53	0.00	−0.12
Agencies	−0.03	−0.02	0.36	−0.30	−0.01	0.02	−0.01	−0.03	−0.03	0.53	0.00	0.50
Int. Agencies	−0.05	−0.02	0.18	0.09	0.02	−0.02	−0.01	0.01	0.21	0.54	0.00	0.75
Long Agencies	0.02	−0.03	0.91	−1.51	−0.11	0.14	−0.02	−0.17	−0.76	0.51	0.00	−0.26
Corporates	−0.06	−0.02	0.47	−0.37	0.04	−0.07	−0.01	0.07	0.06	0.59	0.00	0.65
Int. Corporates	−0.08	0.00	0.34	−0.02	0.07	−0.08	0.00	0.12	0.35	0.58	0.00	0.93
Long Corporates	−0.02	−0.05	0.68	−0.95	−0.03	−0.06	−0.02	0.00	−0.44	0.60	0.00	0.16
Industrials	−0.06	−0.01	0.49	−0.47	0.03	−0.06	0.00	−0.07	−0.16	0.60	0.00	0.45
Int. Industrials	−0.09	0.00	0.34	−0.02	0.07	−0.07	0.00	0.04	0.27	0.60	0.00	0.87
Long Industrials	−0.02	−0.03	0.67	−1.02	−0.03	−0.04	−0.01	−0.20	−0.69	0.61	0.00	−0.08
Utilities	−0.03	−0.04	0.50	−0.45	0.03	−0.07	−0.02	−0.01	−0.09	0.58	0.00	0.49
Int. Utilities	−0.05	0.00	0.35	−0.04	0.08	−0.09	0.00	0.10	0.34	0.56	0.00	0.90
Long Utilities	−0.01	−0.08	0.63	−0.76	−0.01	−0.06	−0.04	−0.10	−0.44	0.61	0.00	0.17
Finance	−0.07	0.00	0.38	−0.12	0.05	−0.08	0.00	0.22	0.38	0.58	0.00	0.96
Int. Finance	−0.08	0.00	0.32	0.01	0.06	−0.06	0.00	0.18	0.44	0.58	0.00	1.02
Long Finance	−0.01	−0.03	0.68	−0.84	0.00	−0.16	0.00	0.45	0.09	0.57	0.00	0.66
Yankees	−0.06	−0.02	0.52	−0.45	0.04	−0.07	0.00	0.20	0.15	0.59	0.00	0.73
Int. Yankees	−0.08	0.01	0.38	−0.08	0.08	−0.10	0.00	0.12	0.34	0.58	0.00	0.91
Long Yankees	−0.02	−0.09	0.77	−1.12	−0.05	−0.02	0.00	0.33	−0.19	0.61	0.00	0.41

Exhibit 17: Mean and Standard Deviation of Return Components for some Lehman Brothers Indices, January 1996 - November 1997

Return Component	Government		Corporate		Mortgage		Aggregate		Govt 1- to 3-yr		Treasury 20+ yr	
	Mean	Std. Dev.	Mean	Std. Dev.	Mean	Std. Dev.	Mean	Std. Dev.	Mean	Std. Dev.	Mean	Std. Dev.
Accretion	−0.03	0.02	−0.03	0.01	0.00	0.02	−0.02	0.02	−0.03	0.03	−0.01	0.02
Rolldown	0.02	0.02	0.02	0.03	−0.01	0.11	0.01	0.03	0.03	0.02	0.01	0.06
Shift	−0.08	1.22	−0.10	1.50	−0.05	0.97	−0.07	1.19	−0.03	0.41	−0.15	2.89
Twist	0.00	0.09	0.01	0.13	0.00	0.04	0.00	0.06	0.00	0.09	0.02	0.54
Butterfly	0.00	0.01	0.00	0.04	−0.01	0.04	0.00	0.02	0.00	0.02	0.02	0.11
Shape	0.02	0.07	0.03	0.08	0.01	0.06	0.02	0.07	−0.01	0.05	0.11	0.18
Volatility	0.00	0.00	0.00	0.00	0.02	0.11	0.01	0.04	0.00	0.00	0.00	0.00
Spread	0.00	0.03	−0.01	0.21	0.03	0.14	0.01	0.06	0.00	0.01	−0.01	0.03
Price	−0.07	1.23	−0.08	1.51	0.00	0.89	−0.05	1.17	−0.04	0.40	−0.02	2.84
Coupon	0.55	0.02	0.61	0.01	0.61	0.01	0.58	0.01	0.51	0.01	0.57	0.03
Paydown	0.00	0.00	0.00	0.00	−0.02	0.01	0.00	0.00	0.00	0.00	0.00	0.00
Total	0.48	1.24	0.53	1.52	0.59	0.89	0.52	1.17	0.47	0.41	0.55	2.84

As expected, the main source of return variance is shift return. For the Government and Corporate Indices, the standard deviation of shift return is slightly less than the standard deviation of price return. For the Mortgage Index, the standard deviation of shift return is 0.97%, significantly higher than the 0.89% for price return. This is explained in part by a strong negative correlation (−0.47) between shift return and volatility return for MBS.

It is apparent from Exhibit 17 that the shift component dominates the variance of index returns. To highlight this point, Exhibit 18 shows the percentage of variance of overall yield curve return that is explained by shift, and how this percentage increases as we incrementally add the effects of twist and butterfly return. For the Government, Corporate, Mortgage, and Aggregate Indices, over 99% is explained by shift alone. As noted above, these indices span a wide range of maturities centered roughly on the 5-year point, which is the pivot of our twist. Thus, even in January 1996, in which we saw an unusually large steepening of 32 bp, these indices had relatively small twist returns (Exhibit 16). For indices that are concentrated at either end of the curve, the shift return does not dominate the return variance to the same extent. The percentage of curve return variance explained by shift return is 92.63% for the Government 1-3 year Index and 95.46% for the Treasury 20+-Year Index. The twist return plays a more important role in explaining the behavior of these indices. Butterfly return has little impact on the Government, Corporate, and Mortgage Indices, but significantly improves the explanatory power of the model for the Government 1-3 Year Index.

How well has the model explained individual bond returns in practice? As noted above, the index results of Exhibits 16-18 are obtained by averaging over large numbers of bonds. As a result, variations in individual bond returns can cancel each other out. The results of Exhibit 18 are therefore not comparable to

Exhibits 6-9, in which we measured goodness of fit against historical returns of individual bonds. To obtain a comparable measure of fit, we need to analyze the components of individual bond returns. Exhibit 19 shows the percent of the variance of overall yield curve return explained by the model, using monthly returns on all bonds in the Lehman Brothers Treasury Index from January 1996 through November 1997. Over this short period, shift is seen to explain over 96% of the curve return variance, even at the individual bond level.

CONCLUSION

The Lehman Brothers' return attribution model offers several benefits. It breaks down portfolio and index returns into a practical set of components, which correspond to strategies commonly used by portfolio managers. It analyzes the movement of the yield curve based on changes in bellwether yields, in an intuitive, easily replicable manner. It uses full OAS-based valuation techniques, thus giving the most accurate treatment possible for securities with curve-dependent cash flows. The model has been shown to have superior explanatory power, both in validation testing against historical Treasury yield data and in practice. The model is used to attribute the returns of the domestic Lehman Brothers indices, the most popular domestic benchmarks. It provides managers of portfolios benchmarked against the Lehman Brothers indices with a powerful tool for performance measurement and analysis in the fixed income arena.

Exhibit 18: Model Results on Index Returns

Percentage of variance of overall yield curve return, January 1996 - November 1997, in %

Index	Cumulative Fit		
	Shift	Twist	Butterfly
Government	99.19	99.71	99.69
Corporate	99.01	99.74	99.74
Mortgage	99.49	99.56	99.61
Aggregate	99.47	99.72	99.68
Govt. 1-3 yr	92.63	97.42	98.47
Treas. 20+	95.46	99.33	99.61

Exhibit 19: Model Results on Individual Bond Returns

Cumulative fit of components of yield curve return, as percentage of variance of overall yield curve returns. Calculated from returns of individual bonds in Lehman Brothers Treasury Index, January 1996 - November 1997.

	Cumulative Fit
Shift	96.46%
Twist	99.10%
Butterfly	99.45%

Chapter 22

Credit Analysis for Corporate Bonds

Jane Tripp Howe, CFA
Vice President
Pacific Investment Management Company

INTRODUCTION

Traditionally, credit analysis for corporate bonds has focused almost exclusively on the default risk of the bond — the chance that the bondholder will not receive the scheduled interest payments and/or principal at maturity. This one-dimensional analysis concerned itself primarily with straight ratio analysis. This approach was deemed appropriate when interest rates were stable and investors purchased bonds with the purpose of holding them to maturity. In this scenario, fluctuations in the market value of the bonds due to interest rate changes were minimal, and fluctuations due to credit changes of the bond issuer were mitigated by the fact that the investor had no intention of selling the bond before maturity.

During the past two decades, however, the purpose of buying bonds has changed dramatically. Investors still purchase bonds for security and thereby forgo the higher expected return of other assets such as common stock. However, an increasing number of investors buy bonds to actively trade them with the purpose of making a profit due to changes in interest rates or in absolute or relative credit quality. The second dimension of corporate bond credit analysis addresses the latter purpose of buying a bond. What is the likelihood of a change in credit quality that will affect the price of the bond? This second dimension deals primarily with the ratios and profitability trends, such as return on equity, operating margins, and asset turnover, generally associated with common stock analysis.

In practice, both dimensions should be applied in corporate bond analysis. In a sense, both dimensions are addressing the same issue — default or credit risk. However, only by using both dimensions of credit analysis will the analyst address the dual purpose of bond holding: security of interest and principal payments and stability or improvement of credit risk during the life of the bond.

Historically, common stock and bond research areas have been viewed as separate. However, with the development of options theory, the two disciplines are beginning to be viewed as complementary. The value of the option is a direct

457

function of the company's aggregate equity valuation. As the market value of a company's stock increases, the value of the option increases. Conversely, as the market value of a company's stock declines, so does the value of the option. The practical implication of this theory for corporate bond analysis is that the perceptions of both markets should be compared before a final credit judgment is rendered. For the analyst who believes that there is a higher level of efficiency in the stock market than in the bond market, particular attention should be paid to the stock price of the company being analyzed.

Tracking stock prices can benefit the bond analyst in two major ways. First, tracking stock price movements is an efficient way of following a large portfolio of bonds. Second, following the stock price of one company may assist the analyst in following an issuer. For example, analysts should value a company's holdings in other companies to the extent possible. Once a company is public, this is fairly easy to accomplish as was the case of Associates and Ford Motor Company. In 1996, Ford Motor Company completed an initial public offering of 19.3% of Associates. Once the IPO was complete, analysts could easily value Ford's interest in Associates simply by looking up the price of Associates.

Significant price movements may indicate a change in credit quality and should be investigated. At the least, an explanation of major stock price movements either by themselves or relative to the stock prices of other companies should be sought with a call to management and a careful reading of related news stories. Sometimes a sharp run up in the price of a stock may indicate an acquisition. Acquisitions are often beneficial for the shareholders of the acquired company because of the premium paid for the stock. However, the effect of an acquisition on a bondholder varies from transaction to transaction. In a favorable scenario, the issuer of the bond is acquired by a higher rated entity. Such was the case in 1997 when AA rated Boeing Company acquired A– rated McDonnell Douglas Corporation. In an unfavorable scenario, the issuer of the bond is either acquired or merged with a lower rated entity and its ratings are lowered. Such was the case with the debt of BBB– rated Ohio Edison after it merged with Centerior Energy and its BB+ rated Cleveland Electric Illuminating and BB rated Toledo Edison.

Although there are numerous types of corporate bonds outstanding, three major issuing segments of bonds can be differentiated: industrials, utilities, and finance companies. This chapter will primarily address industrials in its general description of bond analysis, and then discuss the utility and finance issues.

INDUSTRY CONSIDERATIONS

The first step in analyzing a bond is to gain some familiarity with the industry. Only within the context of an industry is a company analysis valid. For example, a company growing at 15% annually may appear attractive. However, if the industry is growing at 50% annually, the company is competitively weak. Industry considerations can be numerous. However, an understanding of the following eight variables should give the general fixed income analyst a sufficient framework to properly interpret a company's prospects.

Several of these variables should be considered in a global context. For example, it is not sufficient to consider the competitive position of the automobile industry without considering the global overcapacity in the automobile industry. Over the past several years, the major automotive manufacturers have increased their international presence in terms of sales, manufacturing facilities, and platforms. These efforts are an attempt to capitalize on the growing secular demand for automobiles in Latin America, Southeast Asia, and India, and to take advantage of the lower wage rates in these areas. The globalization of the automotive industry has risks, however, because of currency fluctuations and political uncertainty. International competition is also an important factor in the paper industry. Although the U.S. industry has not increased capacity in many grades over the past several years, global supply has increased dramatically in Southeast Asia. As the Southeast Asian companies are the low cost producers of pulp and some lower grades of paper, any material oversupply and/or slowing in demand in the region could trigger more volatility in global paper prices as paper producers aggressively export to maintain production.

Economic Cyclicality

The economic cyclicality of an industry is the first variable an analyst should consider in reviewing an industry. Does the industry closely follow GNP growth, as does the retailing industry, or is it recession-resistant but slow-growing, like the electric utility industry? The growth in earnings per share (EPS) of a company should be measured against the growth trend of its industry. Major deviations from the industry trend should be the focus of further analysis. Some industries may be somewhat dependent on general economic growth but be more sensitive to demographic changes. The nursing home industry is a prime example of this type of sensitivity. With the significant aging of the U.S. population, the nursing home industry is projected to have above-average growth for the foreseeable future. Other industries, such as the banking industry, are sensitive to interest rates. When interest rates are rising, the earnings of banks with a high federal funds exposure underperform the market as their loan rates lag behind increases in the cost of money. Conversely, as interest rates fall, banking earnings outperform the market because the lag in interest change works in the banks' favor.

In general, however, the earnings of few industries perfectly correlate with one economic statistic. Not only are industries sensitive to many economic variables, but often various segments within a company or an industry move countercyclically, or at least with different lags in relation to the general economy. For example, the housing industry can be divided between new construction and remodeling and repair. New construction historically has led GNP growth, but repair and remodeling have exhibited less sensitivity to general trends. Therefore, in analyzing a company in the construction industry, the performance of each of its segments must be compared with the performance of the subindustry.

Growth Prospects

A second industry variable related to economic cyclicality is the growth prospects for an industry. Is the growth of the industry projected to increase and be maintained at a high level, such as in the nursing home industry, or is growth expected to decline, as in the domestic tobacco industry? Each growth scenario has implications for a company. In the case of a fast-growth industry, how much capacity is needed to meet demand, and how will this capacity be financed? In the case of slow-growth industries, is there a movement toward diversification and/or a consolidation within the industry, such as in the electric utility industry? A company operating within a fast growing industry often has a better potential for credit improvement than does a company whose industry's growth prospects are below average. However, barriers to entry and the sustainability of growth must be considered along with growth prospects for an industry. If an industry is growing rapidly, many new participants may enter the business, causing oversupply of product, declining margins, and possible bankruptcies.

Research and Development Expenses

The broad assessment of growth prospects is tempered by the third variable — the research and development expenditures required to maintain or expand market position. The technology field is growing at an above-average rate, and the companies in the industry should do correspondingly well. However, products with high-tech components can become dated and obsolete quickly. Therefore, although a company may be well situated in an industry, if it does not have the financial resources to maintain a technological lead or at least expend a sufficient amount of money to keep technologically current, its position is likely to deteriorate in the long run. In the short run, however, a company whose R&D expenditures are consistently below industry averages may produce above-average results because of expanded margins.

Evaluation of research and development is further complicated by the direction of technology. Successful companies must not only spend an adequate amount of resources on development, they must also be correct in their assessment of the direction of the industry. Deployment of significant amounts of capital may not prevent a decline in credit quality if the capital is misdirected. For example, computer companies that persisted in spending a high percentage of their capital expenditures on the mainframe component of their business suffered declines in credit quality as the mainframe business declined.

Competition

Competition is based on a variety of factors. These factors vary depending on the industry. Most competition is based on quality and price. However, competition is also derived from other sources, such as airlines operating in bankruptcy that are able to lower their costs by eliminating interest on debt and rejecting high-cost leases and thereby gain a cost advantage.

Increasingly, all forms of competition are waged on an international basis and are affected by fluctuations in relative currency values. Companies that fare well are those that compete successfully on a global basis and concentrate on the regions with the highest potential for growth. Consumers are largely indifferent to the country of origin of a product as long as the product is of high quality and reasonably priced.

Competition within an industry directly relates to the market structure of an industry and has implications for pricing flexibility. An unregulated monopoly is in an enviable position in that it can price its goods at a level that will maximize profits. Most industries encounter some free market forces and must price their goods in relation to the supply and demand for their goods as well as the price charged for similar goods. In an oligopoly, a pricing leader is not uncommon. Philip Morris, for example, performs this function for the tobacco industry. A concern arises when a small company is in an industry that is moving toward oligopoly. In this environment, the small company's costs of production may be higher than those of the industry leaders, and yet it may have to conform to the pricing of the industry leaders. In the extreme, a price war could force the smaller companies out of business. This situation has occurred in the building products industry. For the past two decades, as the building products industry has become increasingly concentrated, the leaders have gained market share at the expense of the small local firms. Many small local companies have either been acquired or gone out of business. These local firms have been at a dual disadvantage. They are in an industry whose structure is moving toward oligopoly, and yet their weak competitive position within the industry largely precludes pricing flexibility.

A concern also arises when there is overcapacity in the industry. Often, overcapacity is accompanied by price wars. This has periodically occurred in the airline industry. Generally, price wars result in an industrywide financial deterioration as battles for market share are accompanied by declining profits or losses.

Sources of Supply

The market structure of an industry and its competitive forces have a direct impact on the fifth industry variable — sources of supply of major production components. A company in the paper industry that has sufficient timber acreage to supply 100% of its pulp is preferable to a paper company that must buy all or a large percentage of its pulp.

The importance of self-sufficiency in pulp has increased over the past few years because of environmental restrictions related to the spotted owl and other endangered species. As a result of the spotted owl situation, over half of the timber provided by the federal forests in the Northwest was removed from the market. The removal caused pulp prices to skyrocket. As a result, companies with low self-sufficiency in the Northwest, such as Boise Cascade, have experienced significant losses in their paper segments. Affected companies were unable to pass along the increased costs because of the commodity nature of the business.

A company that is not self-sufficient in its factors of production but is sufficiently powerful in its industry to pass along increased costs is in an enviable position. RJR Nabisco is an example of the latter type of company. Although RJR Nabisco has major exposure to commodity prices for ingredients, its strong market position has historically enabled it to pass along increased costs of goods sold.

The ability to pass along increased costs has become increasingly difficult over the past several years as inflation has declined, global competition has increased, and customers have become highly resistant to price increases. Companies have reacted to these factors by cutting costs to maintain margins when their factors of production increase. Frequently these savings are generated by merging with other companies to generate economies of scale. In this environment, the small companies with little market power and few economies of scale are at a disadvantage.

Degree of Regulation

The sixth industry consideration is the degree of regulation. The electric utility industry is the classic example of regulation. Nearly all phases of a utility's operations have historically been regulated. However, the industry has a federal mandate to deregulate. Initially, it was thought that deregulation would proceed rapidly. However, the complexity of the process suggests that the deregulation of the electric utility industry will take longer than originally thought. This change in time frame was the result of change in perceptions. Originally, legislators focused on the fact that deregulation would result in lower aggregate rates. Next, legislators focused on the fact that the benefit of lower rates would be offset in large part by a loss of control over rates.

Currently, legislators are compromising. The states which have legislated deregulation have retained regulatory control over distribution and transmission and have required that generation be deregulated. This approach complicates the credit analysis. Prior to deregulation, the debt of an electric utility was generally the obligation of the entire entity. The process of deregulation suggests that some debt will be assigned to the less risky transmission and distribution entity while other debt will be assigned to the more risky generation entity.

The analyst should not be concerned with the existence or absence of regulation per se but rather with the direction of regulation and the effect it has on the profitability of the company. For the electric utility industry, the transition to deregulation will still be largely controlled by the regulatory authorities in a given state. In particular, regulatory commissions will have to deal with the treatment of stranded costs. Stranded costs include such items as generating plants whose cost/KW is above current market costs, and contracts with independent power producers to purchase power at above market prices. Although all electric utilities will transition to deregulation over the next decade, companies whose regulatory authorities assist in this effort will be better positioned than companies with unsupportive regulatory authorities.

The pace of deregulation has varied significantly from state to state. The states which have been the most active in deregulation, including Rhode Island, Massachusetts, and California, have generally traded full stranded cost recovery for immediate and substantial rate cuts which vary from 10% to 20%.

Other industries, such as the drug industry, also have a high, though less pervasive, degree of regulation. In the drug industry, however, the threat of increased regulation has been a negative factor in the industry for some time. This risk was heightened periodically with the Clinton administration's health care proposals. The anticipation of increased regulation leading to lower profits in the pharmaceutical industry has contributed periodically to a major sell-off in these securities.

Labor

The labor situation of an industry should also be analyzed. Is the industry heavily unionized? If so, what has been the historical occurrence of strikes? What level of flexibility does management have to reduce the labor force? When do the current contracts expire, and what is the likelihood of timely settlements? The labor situation is also important in nonunionized companies, particularly those whose labor situation is tight. What has been the turnover of professionals and management in the firm? What is the probability of a firm's employees, such as highly skilled engineers, being hired by competing firms?

The more labor intensive an industry, the more significance the labor situation assumes. This fact is evidenced by the domestic automobile industry, in which overcapacity and a high degree of unionization have contributed to high fixed costs and cyclical record operating losses.

Many think that the power of unions has weakened over the past decade as membership has declined. Unfortunately for managements negotiating contracts, this decline in power attributable to a decline in membership has been offset in part by the ability of unions to easily disrupt production because of "just-in-time" inventory management. Because corporations inventory small amounts of parts, a strike at a critical parts plant can halt production at an entire corporation in a short time.

Occasionally, analysts concentrate solely on the per hour wages of the labor force. Such an emphasis is misleading. An evaluation of the labor situation should concentrate on work rules because work rules are more important in the overall efficiency of an organization than the wage rates. This is an important factor in the profitability of some automobile supply companies. Although the employees of these companies are generally members of the UAW and receive UAW wages, their work rules are different and their efficiency is generally significantly better than that of captive supply companies.

Accounting

A final industry factor to be considered is accounting. Does the industry have special accounting practices, such as those in the insurance industry or the electric utility industry? If so, an analyst should become familiar with industry practices before proceeding with a company analysis. Also important is whether a company is liberal or conservative in applying the generally accepted accounting principles. The norm of an industry should be ascertained, and the analyst should analyze comparable figures.

Particular attention should be paid to companies which use an accounting system other than U.S. GAAP. Reported results should be reconciled with those which would have been reported under U.S. GAAP. In addition, changes in GAAP should be scrutinized. For example, most forms of GAAP require that debt issued in a currency other than the reporting currency should be adjusted to reflect any changes between the reporting currency and the currency in which the debt was issued. In this manner, a company in Southeast Asia which issued debt denominated in U.S. dollars but whose reporting currency devalued relative to the dollar would have to write up its U.S. dollar denominated debt to reflect the change. Such a write-up would increase the leverage of the firm. This was not the case for Indonesian companies because of the accounting change that was instituted on August 14, 1997. On that date, Indonesian regulators ruled that foreign exchange losses could be capitalized to the extent that the foreign denominated debt was used to acquire plant and equipment. In essence, the new accounting rule permits Indonesian companies to write-up both their fixed assets and their debt, thereby offsetting the increase in leverage that would be expected from a material devaluation.

Care should also be taken when dealing with historical data. Frequently, companies adjust prior years' results to adjust for discontinued operations and changes in accounting. These adjustments can mask unfavorable trends. For example, companies that regularly dispose of underperforming segments and then highlight the more profitable continuing operations may be trying to hide poor management. In order to fully appreciate all trends, both the unadjusted and the adjusted results should be analyzed.

FINANCIAL ANALYSIS

Having achieved an understanding of an industry, the analyst is ready to proceed with a financial analysis. The financial analysis should be conducted in three phases. The first phase consists of traditional ratio analysis for bonds. The second phase, generally associated with common stock research, consists of analyzing the components of a company's return on equity (ROE). The final phase considers such nonfinancial factors as management and foreign exposure, and includes an analysis of the indenture.

Traditional Ratio Analysis

There are numerous ratios that can be calculated in applying traditional ratio analysis to bonds. Of these, eight will be discussed in this section. Those selected are the ratios with the widest degree of applicability. In analyzing a particular industry, however, other ratios assume significance and should be considered. For example, in the electric utility industry, allowance for funds used in construction as a percent of net income as well as the total amount of stranded assets as a percentage of equity are important ratios that are inapplicable to the analysis of industrial or financial companies.

Pretax Interest Coverage

Generally, the first ratio calculated in credit analysis is pretax interest coverage. This ratio measures the number of times interest charges are covered on a pretax basis. Fixed-charge coverage is calculated by dividing pretax income plus interest charges by total interest charges. The higher the coverage figure, the safer the credit. If interest coverage is less than 1X, the company must borrow or use cash flow or the proceeds from the sale of assets to meet its interest payments.

Generally, published coverage figures are pretax as opposed to after-tax because interest payments are a pretax expense. Although the pretax interest coverage ratio is useful, its utility is a function of the company's other fixed obligations. For example, if a company has other significant fixed obligations, such as rents or leases, a more appropriate coverage figure would include these other fixed obligations. An example of this is the retail industry, in which companies typically have significant lease obligations. A calculation of simple pretax interest coverage would be misleading in this case because fixed obligations other than interest are significant.

The analyst should also be aware of any contingent liabilities such as a company's guaranteeing another company's debt. For example, there has been a dramatic increase in the insurance industry's guaranteeing of other company's debt. Today, this guaranteed debt exceeds the debt of the industry. Although the company being analyzed may never have to pay interest or principal on the guaranteed debt, the existence of the guarantee diminishes the quality of the pretax coverage. In addition, the quality of the guaranteed debt must be considered.

Once pretax interest coverage and fixed-charge coverage are calculated, it is necessary to analyze the ratios' absolute levels and the numbers relative to those of the industry. For example, pretax interest coverage for the transmission and distribution of an electric utility of 4.0 is consistent with a strong A rating, whereas the same coverage for an industrial company would indicate a lower rating.

Standard & Poor's 1994-1996 median ratios of pretax interest coverage ranges for the senior debt of industrial companies were as follows:

Rating Classification	Pretax Interest Coverage
AAA	16.05
AA	11.06
A	6.25
BBB	4.11

Leverage

A second important ratio is *leverage*, which can be defined in several ways. The most common definition is long-term debt as a percent of total capitalization. The higher the level of debt, the higher the percentage of operating income that must be used to meet fixed obligations. If a company is highly leveraged, the analyst should also look at its margin of safety. The margin of safety is defined as the percentage by which operating income could decline and still be sufficient to allow the company to meet its fixed obligations. Standard & Poor's 1994-1996 median ratios of leverage for the senior debt of industrial companies were as follows:

Rating Classification	Long-Term Debt/Capitalization
AAA	13.4
AA	21.9
A	32.7
BBB	43.4

The most common way to calculate leverage is to use the company's capitalization structure as stated in the most recent balance sheet. In addition to this measure, the analyst should calculate capitalization using a market approximation for the value of the common stock. When a company's common stock is selling significantly below book value, leverage will be understated by the traditional approach.

Occasionally, stockholders' equity can be negative, as was the case with FMC after it issued significant debt to repurchase its own stock in a leveraged recapitalization. Although FMC's equity was negative after the recapitalization, its stock market capitalization correctly indicated that the equity of FMC was valuable.

The degree of leverage and margin of safety varies dramatically among industries. Finance companies have traditionally been among the most highly leveraged companies, with debt to equity ratios of 10:1. Although such leverage is tolerated in the finance industry, an industrial company with similar leverage would have a more difficult time issuing debt.

In addition to considering the absolute and relative levels of leverage of a company, the analyst should evaluate the debt itself. How much of the debt has a fixed rate, and how much has a floating rate? A company with a high component of debt tied to the prime rate may find its margins being squeezed as interest rates rise if there is no compensating increase in the price of the firm's goods. Such a debt structure may be beneficial during certain phases of the interest-rate cycle, but it precludes a precise estimate of what interest charges for the year will be. In general, a company with a small percentage of floating-rate debt is preferable to a similarly leveraged company with a high percentage of floating-rate debt.

The maturity structure of the debt including bank loans should also be evaluated. What is the percentage of debt that is coming due within the next five years? As this debt is refinanced, how will the company's embedded cost of debt change? In this regard, the amount of original-issue discount (OID) debt should also be considered. High quality OIDs were first issued in sizable amounts in 1981, although lower quality OIDs have been issued for some time. This debt is issued with low or zero coupons and at substantial discounts to par. Each year, the issuing company expenses the interest payment as well as the amortization of the discount. At issuance, only the actual bond proceeds are listed as debt on the balance sheet. However, as this debt payable will increase annually, the analyst should consider the full face amount due at maturity when evaluating the maturity structure and refinancing plans of the company.

The existence of material operating leases can understate the leverage of a firm. Operating leases should be capitalized to give a true measure of leverage This approach is particularly enlightening in industries such as the airline industry, where leverage for the industry increases from approximately 60% to 80% when leases are considered.

A company's bank lines often comprise a significant portion of a company's total long-term debt. These lines should be closely analyzed in order to determine the flexibility afforded to the company. The lines should be evaluated in terms of undrawn capacity as well as security interests granted. In addition, the analyst should determine whether the line contains a Material Adverse Change (MAC) clause under which the line could be withdrawn. For example, a company that has drawn down its bank lines completely and is in jeopardy of activating its MAC clause may have trouble refinancing any debt.

Cash Flow

A third important ratio is cash flow as a percent of total debt. Cash flow is often defined as net income from continuing operations plus depreciation, depletion, amortization, and deferred taxes. In calculating cash flow for credit analysis, the analyst should also subtract noncash contributions from subsidiaries. In essence, the analyst should be concerned with cash from operations. Any extraordinary sources or uses of funds should be excluded when determining the overall trend of cash flow coverage. Cash dividends from subsidiaries should also be questioned in terms of their appropriateness (too high or too low relative to the subsidiary's earnings) and also in terms of the parent's control over the upstreaming of dividends. Is there a legal limit to the upstreamed dividends? If so, how close is the current level of dividends to the limit? Standard & Poor's 1994-1996 Median Ratios of Funds From Operations/Long-Term Debt for the senior debt of industrial companies were as follows:

Rating Classification	Funds from Operations/Total Debt
AAA	116.4
AA	72.3
A	47.5
BBB	34.7

Net Assets

A fourth significant ratio is net assets to total debt. In analyzing this facet of a bond's quality, consideration should be given to the liquidation value of the assets. Liquidation value will often differ dramatically from the value stated on the balance sheet. At one extreme, consider a nuclear generating plant that has had operating problems and has been closed down and has been removed from rate base as was the case with Northeast Utilities' Millstone Unit 1. This asset is probably overstated on the balance sheet, and the bondholder should take little comfort in reported asset protection. The issue of overstated values on the balance sheet of an electric utility will be increasingly highlighted as the electric utility industry deregulates and has to explicitly deal with stranded investments.

The extent to which nuclear assets are overvalued on the balance sheet will likely be more clear in 1998 as utilities continue to divest their generation assets. Although the first wave of generation sales involved non-nuclear assets, nuclear assets are also likely to be sold. On December 31, 1997, GPU announced that it was negotiating the sale of its Three Mile Island and Oyster Creek nuclear power plants. These units have book values of $600 million and $700 million, respectively. Although GPU would not publicly comment on the precise price targets, the company did state that it expected to receive less than book value for the units.

At the other extreme is the forest products company whose vast timber acreage is significantly understated on the balance sheet. In addition to the assets' market value, some consideration should also be given to the liquidity of the assets. A company with a high percentage of its assets in cash and marketable securities is in a much stronger asset position than a company whose primary assets are illiquid real estate.

The wave of takeovers, recapitalizations, and other restructurings has increased the importance of asset coverage protection. Unfortunately for some bondholders, mergers or takeovers may decimate their asset coverage by adding layers of debt to the corporate structure that is senior to their holdings. Bondholders may also be harmed by the spin-off of assets to stockholders as was the case with Ford Motor Company. Ford was downgraded as a result of its decision to distribute its 80.7% ownership stake in Associates. At the time of the announcement, Ford's ownership of Associates was worth approximately $17 billion. While the analyst may find it difficult to predict takeovers or restructurings, it is crucial to evaluate the degree of protection from takeovers and other restructurings that the bond indenture offers.

In extreme cases, the analyst must consider asset coverage in the case of bankruptcy. This is particularly important in the case of lease obligations because the debtor has the ability to reject leases in bankruptcy. In the case of lease rejections, the resulting asset protection may depend on a legal determination of whether the underlying lease is a true lease or a financing arrangement. Even if the lease if determined to be a true lease, the determination of asset protection is further complicated by a determination of whether the lease relates to nonresidential real property or to personal property. The difference in security (i.e., recovery in a bankruptcy) is significant. Damages under a lease of nonresidential real property are limited to three years of lease payments. Damages under a lease of personal property are all due under the lease.

Change of control covenants must be read carefully with particular attention to the definitions of change of control and whether the change of control has to be hostile in order to trigger the provisions.

In addition to the major variables discussed above, the analyst should also consider several other financial variables including intangibles, unfunded pension liabilities, the age and condition of the plant, and working capital adequacy.

Intangibles

Intangibles often represent a small portion of the asset side of a balance sheet. Occasionally, particularly with companies that have or have had an active acquisition program, intangibles can represent a significant portion of assets. In this case, the analyst should estimate the actual value of the intangibles and determine whether this value is in concert with a market valuation. A carrying value significantly higher than market value indicates a potential for a write-down of assets. The actual write-down may not occur until the company actually sells a subsidiary with which the intangibles are identified. However, the analyst should recognize the potential and adjust capitalization ratios accordingly.

Unfunded Pension Liabilities

Unfunded pension liabilities can also affect a credit decision. Although a fully funded pension is not necessary for a high credit assessment, a large unfunded pension liability that is 10% or more of net worth can be a negative. Of concern is the company whose unfunded pension liabilities are sufficiently high to interfere with corporate planning. For example, a steel company with high unfunded pension liabilities might delay or decide against closing an unprofitable plant because of the pension costs involved. The analyst should also be aware of a company's assumed rate of return on its pension funds and salary increase assumptions. The higher the assumed rate of return, the lower the contribution a company must make to its pension fund, given a set of actuarial assumptions. Occasionally, a company having difficulty with its earnings will raise its actuarial assumption and thereby lower its pension contribution and increase earnings. The impact on earnings can be dramatic. In other cases, companies have attempted to "raid" the excess funds in an overfunded retirement plan to enhance earnings.

In periods of declining interest rates, the analyst must also consider the discount rate companies use to discount their future obligations. Companies generally use the yield of AA corporate bonds as a discount factor. Companies that persist in using a higher rate may be understating their unfunded pension obligations dramatically. General Motors announced in May 1993 that the drop in long-term interest rates could result in a $5 billion increase in its unfunded pension obligations because of a potential drop in its discount rate.

Age and Condition of Plant

The age of a company's plant should also be estimated, if only to the extent that its age differs dramatically from industry standards. A heavy industrial company whose average plant age is well above that of its competitors is probably already paying for its aged plant through operating inefficiencies. In the longer term, however, the advanced age of the plant is an indication of future capital expenditures for a more modern plant. In addition, the underdepreciation of the plant significantly increases reported earnings.

The availability of information regarding the average age and condition of plants varies among companies. On one hand, airline carriers readily provide the average age of their fleet and the money each will save as they replace older aircraft with more fuel efficient aircraft that require fewer people in the cockpit. On the other hand, the average age of a plant compared with the industry average is not always available for some companies such as paper companies. Furthermore, management of older plants generally emphasize the capital improvements that have been made to the plants over the years which distort direct comparisons. In this case, it is helpful to carefully read several years of management's explanation of operating results which may be found in annual reports. Often this section will include reports of above average maintenance expense and machines which were out of service for a period of time for maintenance. Such comments indicate that the plants and machines may not be as efficient as initially portrayed.

The Financial Accounting Standards Board Statement Number 33 requires extensive supplementary information from most companies on the effect of changing prices. This information is generally unaudited, and there is still no consensus on the best presentation of such data. However, the supplementary information provision does give the analyst an indication of the magnitude of the effects of inflation on a given company. The effects differ dramatically from industry to industry. At one extreme are the high-technology and financial firms, where the effects are nominal. At the other extreme are the capital intensive industries, where the effects are major.

Working Capital

A final variable in assessing a company's financial strength concerns the strength and liquidity of its working capital. Working capital is defined as current assets less current liabilities. Working capital is considered a primary measure of a company's financial flexibility. Other such measures include the current ratio (current assets divided by current liabilities) and the acid test (cash, marketable securities, and receivables divided by current liabilities). The stronger the company's liquidity measures, the better it can weather a downturn in business and cash flow. In assessing this variable, the analyst should consider the normal working capital requirements of a company and industry. The components of working capital should also be analyzed. Although accounts receivable are considered to be liquid, an increase in the average days a receivable is outstanding may be an indication that a higher level of working capital is needed for the efficient running of the operation. In addition, companies frequently have account receivable financing. In this scenario, comparisons among companies in the same industry may be distorted.

The state of contraction or expansion should also be considered in evaluating working capital needs. Automobile manufacturers typically need increased working capital in years when automobile sales increase.

Analysis of the Components of Return on Equity

Once the above financial analysis is complete, the bond analyst traditionally examines the earnings progression of the company and its historical return on equity (ROE). This section of analysis often receives less emphasis than the traditional ratio analysis. It is equally important, however, and demands equal emphasis. An analysis of earnings growth and ROE is vital in determining credit quality because it gives the analyst necessary insights into the components of ROE and indications of the sources of future growth. Equity analysts devote a major portion of their time examining the components of ROE, and their work should be recognized as valuable resource material.

A basic approach to the examination of the components of return on equity breaks down this return into four principal components: pretax margins, asset turnover, leverage, and one minus the tax rate.[1] These four variables multiplied together equal net income/ stockholders' equity, or return on equity.

$$\left(\frac{\text{Nonoperating pretax income}}{\text{Sales}} + \frac{\text{Operating pretax income}}{\text{Sales}}\right)$$
$$\times \frac{\text{Sales}}{\text{Assets}} \times \frac{\text{Assets}}{\text{Equity}} \times (1 - \text{Tax rate}) = \text{Net Income Equity}$$

In analyzing these four components of ROE, the analyst should examine their progression for a minimum of five years and through at least one business cycle. The progression of each variable should be compared with the progression of the same variables for the industry, and deviations from industry standards should be further analyzed. For example, perhaps two companies have similar ROEs, but one company is employing a higher level of leverage to achieve its results, whereas the other company has a higher asset-turnover rate. As the degree of leverage is largely a management decision, the analyst should focus on asset turnover. Why have sales for the former company turned down? Is this downturn a result of a general slowdown in the industry, or is it that assets have been expanded rapidly and the company is in the process of absorbing these new assets? Conversely, a relatively high rise in asset- turnover rate may indicate a need for more capital. If this is the case, how will the company finance this growth, and what effect will the financing have on the firm's embedded cost of capital?

---

[1] Jerome B. Cohen, Edward D. Zinbarg, and Arthur Zeikel, *Investment Analysis and Portfolio Management* (Homewood, IL: Richard D. Irwin, 1977).

Exhibit 1: Adjusted Key Industrial Financial Ratios

Industrial long-term debt Three-year (1994-1996) medians	AAA	AA	A	BBB	BB	B
Pretax interest cov. (×)	16.05	11.06	6.26	4.11	2.27	1.18
EBITDA interest cov. (×)	20.3	14.94	8.51	6.03	3.63	2.27
Funds from operations/total debt (%)	116.4	72.3	47.5	34.7	18.4	10.9
Free operations/total debt (%)	76.8	30.5	18.8	8.4	2.4	1.2
Pretax return on perm. capital (%)	31.5	23.6	19.5	15.1	11.9	9.1
Operating income/sales (%)	24.0	19.2	16.1	15.4	15.1	12.6
Long-term debt/capital (%)	13.4	21.9	32.7	43.4	53.9	65.9
Total debt/capitalization incl. short-term debt (%)	23.6	29.7	38.7	46.8	55.8	68.9
Industrial long-term debt Three-year (1993-1995) medians	AAA	AA	A	BBB	BB	B
Pretax interest cov. (×)	13.5	9.67	5.76	3.94	2.14	1.17
EBITDA interest cov. (×)	17.08	12.8	8.18	6.0	3.49	2.16
Funds from operations/total debt (%)	98.2	69.1	45.5	33.3	17.7	12.8
Free operations/total debt (%)	60.0	26.8	20.9	7.2	1.4	(0.9)
Pretax return on perm. capital (%)	29.3	21.4	19.1	13.9	12.0	9.0
Operating income/sales (%)	22.6	17.8	15.7	13.5	13.5	12.3
Long-term debt/capital (%)	13.3	21.1	31.6	42.7	55.6	65.5
Total debt/capitalization incl. short-term debt (%)	25.9	33.6	39.7	47.8	59.4	69.5
Industrial long-term debt Three-year (1992-1994) medians	AAA	AA	A	BBB	BB	B
Pretax interest cov. (×)	17.99	9.74	5.35	2.91	2.09	1.01
EBITDA interest cov. (×)	22.63	12.82	8.0	4.82	3.5	1.9
Funds from operations/total debt (%)	97.5	68.5	43.8	29.9	17.1	9.9
Free operations/total debt (%)	51.0	29.7	20.2	6.2	3.1	1.1
Pretax return on perm. capital (%)	28.2	20.6	16.7	12.7	11.6	8.3
Operating income/sales (%)	22.0	17.7	15.2	13.2	13.6	11.6
Long-term debt/capital (%)	13.2	19.7	33.2	44.8	54.7	65.9
Total debt/capitalization incl. short-term debt (%)	25.4	32.4	39.7	49.5	60.1	73.4

EBITDA — Earnings before interest, taxes, depreciation, and amortization.
Source: *Standard & Poor's Credit Week*, September 3, 1997, p. 10.

The analyst should not expect similar components of ROE for all companies in a particular industry. Deviations from industry norms are often indications of management philosophy. For example, one company may emphasize asset turnover, and another company in the same industry may emphasize profit margin. As in any financial analysis, the trend of the components is as important as the absolute levels.

In order to give the analyst a general idea of the type of ratios expected by the major rating agencies for a particular rating classification, Standard & Poor's medians of key ratios for 1994-1996 by rating category are outlined in Exhibit 1. The analyst should use this table only in the most general applications, however, for three reasons. First, industry standards vary considerably. Second, financial ratios are only one part of an analysis. Third, major adjustments often need to be made to income statements and balance sheets to make them comparable with the financial statements of other companies.

The importance of adjusting financial statements to capture differences among firms was highlighted in November 1993 by S&P's introduction of "adjusted key industrial financial ratios." In calculating its adjusted ratios, S&P eliminates nonrecurring gains and losses. In addition, S&P includes operating leases in all of its calculations.

Analysts interested in financial ratios for specific industries should consult Standard & Poor's CreditStats Service. This service, introduced in October 1989, presents key financial ratios organized into 53 industry groups as well as ratio analysis by long-term rating category for utility companies.

Nonfinancial Factors

After the traditional bond analysis is completed, the analyst should consider some nonfinancial factors that might modify the evaluation of the company. Among these factors are the degree of foreign exposure and the quality of management. The amount of foreign exposure should be ascertainable from the annual report.

Sometimes, however, specific country exposure is less clear because the annual report often lists foreign exposure by broad geographic divisions. If there is concern that a major portion of revenue and income is derived from potentially unstable areas, the analyst should carefully consider the total revenue and income derived from the area and the assets committed. Further consideration should be given to available corporate alternatives should nationalization of assets occur. Additionally, the degree of currency exposure should be determined. If currency fluctuations are significant, has management hedged its exposure?

The internationalization of the bond markets and the ability of countries to issue debt in other countries highlights the importance of understanding the effect of currency risks. Many Mexican companies issued U.S. dollar denominated debt in the early 1990s. This issuance positively impacted the financials of these Mexican companies because of the generally lower interest rates available in the United States relative to Mexico. However, when the peso was significantly devalued in December 1994, the ability of some of these companies to meet their U.S. dollar denominated obligations was questioned. Of particular concern were the companies whose revenues were largely denominated in pesos but whose interest expense was denominated in U.S. dollars.

In a similar manner, many companies located in Southeast Asia issued U.S. dollar denominated debt in the 1990s and when the currencies of many of these issuers significantly devalued in the summer and fall of 1997, their ability to repay the debt was similarly questioned. Of particular concern is the ability of some companies to access U.S. dollars and the effect of the devaluations on the balance sheets.

The quality and depth of management is more difficult to evaluate. The best way to evaluate management is to spend time with management, if possible.

Earnings progress at the firm is a good indication of the quality of management. Negative aspects would include a firm founded and headed by one person who is approaching retirement and has made no plan for succession. Equally negative is the firm that has had numerous changes of management and philosophy. On the other hand, excessive stability is not always desirable. If one family or group of investors owns a controlling interest in a firm, they may be too conservative in reacting to changes in markets. Characteristics of a good management team include depth, a clear line of succession if the chief officers are nearing retirement, and a diversity of age within the management team.

INDENTURE PROVISIONS

An indenture is a legal document that defines the rights and obligations of the borrower and the lender with respect to a bond issue. An analysis of the indenture should be a part of a credit review in that the indenture provisions establish rules for several important spheres of operation for the borrower. These provisions, which can be viewed as safeguards for the lender, cover such areas as the limitation on the issuance of additional debt, sale and leasebacks, and sinking-fund provisions.

The indentures of bonds of the same industry are often similar in the areas they address. Correlation between the quality rating of the senior debt of a company and the stringency of indenture provisions is not perfect. For example, sometimes the debt test is more severe in A securities than in BBB securities. However, subordinated debt of one company will often have less restrictive provisions than will the senior debt of the same company. In addition, more restrictive provisions are generally found in private placement issues. In analyzing a company's indentures, the analyst should look for the standard industry provisions. Differences in these provisions (either more or less restrictive) should be examined more closely. In this regard, a more restrictive nature is not necessarily preferable if the provisions are so restrictive as to hinder the efficient operation of the company.

Bond indentures should be analyzed in conjunction with the covenants of bank lines. Frequently, bank lines can be more restrictive than bond indentures. The analyst should focus on the most restrictive covenants.

Outlined below are the provisions most commonly found in indentures. These provisions are categorized by industry because the basic provisions are fairly uniform within an industry. A general description of the indenture is found in a company's prospectus. However, notification is generally given that the indenture provisions are only summarized. A complete indenture may be obtained from the trustee who is listed in the prospectus.

Careful attention should be paid to the definitions in indentures as they vary from indenture to indenture. Frequently, the definitions of terms specify carveouts, or excluded items, that are material. For example, the definition of consolidated net assets may carve out or exclude changes resulting from unfunded pension liabilities.

Utility Indentures
Security

The security provision is generally the first provision in a utility indenture. This provision specifies the property upon which there is a mortgage lien. In addition, the ranking of the new debt relative to outstanding debt is specified. Generally, the new bonds rank equally with all other bonds outstanding under the mortgage. This ranking is necessary, but it has created difficulty for the issuing companies because some mortgage indentures were written more than 40 years ago. Specifically, because all bondholders must be kept equal, companies must often retain antiquated provisions in their indentures. Often these provisions hinder the efficient running of a company due to structural changes in the industry since the original writing of the indenture. Changes in these provisions can be made, but changes have occurred slowly because of the high percentage of bondholders who must approve a change and the time and expense required to locate the bondholders. Occasionally, a company may retire certain old issues in order to eliminate a covenant that has not been included in recent offerings.

The security provisions of first mortgage indentures must be carefully scrutinized because of the disaggregation in the industry. Particular attention must be paid to the release and substitution clause of the security provisions. In general, the release and substitution clause specifies the conditions under which collateral for the first mortgage bonds may either be released from the indenture or other collateral may be substituted. In the context of disaggregation, holders of first mortgage bonds must pay attention to the ability of a company to remove assets from under its mortgage indenture. Some companies require that removal of assets must be made at fair market value, while other indentures are silent on this point. Bondholders need to evaluate the degree to which they are protected from having valuable transmission and distribution assets released from the mortgage while retaining higher risk generation assets including overvalued nuclear assets. In addition, the ability of an issuer to effectively remove assets through the use of purchased money mortgages should be evaluated.

Issuance of Additional Bonds

The "Issuance of Additional Bonds" provision establishes the conditions under which the company may issue additional first mortgage bonds. Often this provision contains a debt test and/or an earnings test. The debt test generally limits the amount of bonds that may be issued under the mortgage to a certain percentage (often 60%) of net property or net property additions, the principal amount of retired bonds, and deposited cash. The earnings test, on the other hand, restricts the issuance of additional bonds under the mortgage unless earnings for a particular period cover interest payments at a specified level.

Although both of these tests may appear straightforward, the analyst must carefully study the definitions contained in the tests. For example, net property additions may be defined as plant that has operating licenses. This was a particular concern during the 1980s. During that time, there was a great deal of nuclear construction, but operating licenses were slow to be granted. As a result, there was a significant backlog of construction work in progress (CWIP) that had to be financed, but which was not operational for some time. This situation presented problems for companies whose indentures require net plant additions to be licensed and/or used and useful assets. In the extreme case, a company may find itself unable to issue bonds under the mortgage indenture.

In a similar circumstance, a company whose regulatory commission requires a substantial write-down related to nuclear construction may find itself unable to meet a debt test for several years if the write-down is taken in one quarter.

The potential for such write-downs has become more visible since the implementation of SFAS 90. SFAS 90 requires utilities to record a loss against income for any portion of an investment in an abandoned plant for which recovery has been disallowed. It further requires all costs disallowed for ratemaking purposes to be recognized as a loss against income as soon as the loss becomes probable with respect to disallowances of new plant costs resulting from a cap on expenditures. These losses may be reported by either restating financial statements for prior fiscal years or by recording the cumulative loss the year SFAS 90 is adopted.

The application of FAS 71 may similarly affect electric utilities. Continued use of FAS 71 requires that (1) rates be designed to recover specific costs of regulated service and (2) it is reasonable to assume that rates are set to continue to recover such costs. In the current environment of a transition to deregulation, utilities may be required to partially or totally write down assets that may not be recovered in rates. Such write-downs may affect these companies' ability to issue first mortgage bonds. In a similar manner, should regulators base interim stranded cost recovery on average prices in a region, as was suggested in February 1997 by the New Hampshire Public Utility Commission, the affected utilities would become ineligible for regulatory accounting and be required to book substantial write-offs.

Maintenance and Replacement Fund

The purpose of a maintenance and replacement fund (M&R) is to ensure that the mortgaged property is maintained in good operating condition. To this end, electric utility indentures generally require that a certain percentage of gross operating revenues, a percentage of aggregate bonded indebtedness, or a percentage of the utility's property account be paid to the trustee for the M&R fund. A major portion of the M&R requirement has historically been satisfied with normal maintenance expenditures. To the extent there is a remaining requirement, the company may contribute cash, the pledge of unbonded property additions, or bonds.

The rapid escalation of fuel costs during the 1970s greatly raised the required levels of many M&R funds that are tied to operating revenues. This situation precipitated a number of bond calls for M&R purposes. Bonds can still be called for this purpose, but investors are more cognizant of this risk and are less likely to pay a significant premium for bonds subject to such a call. Furthermore,

M&R requirements are slowly being changed toward formulas that exclude the large portion of operating income attributable to increases in fuel costs. Finally, a number of companies have indicated that they have no intention of using M&R requirements for calling bonds because of the original intent of the provision and also because of the disfavor such an action would generate among bondholders. However, the intent of companies in this regard would certainly be secondary if a call for M&R requirements were ordered by a commission.

Redemption Provisions

The redemption, or call, provision specifies during what period and at what prices a company may call its bonds. Redemption provisions vary. Refunding is an action by a company to replace outstanding bonds with another debt issue sold at a lower interest expense. (Refunding protection does not protect the bondholder from refunding bonds with equity or short-term debt.) The refunding protection is a safeguard for bondholders against their bonds being refunded at a disadvantageous time.

Declines in long-term interest rates have motivated corporate treasurers to investigate all methods of redeeming high-coupon debt. For example, some indentures allow bonds to be called in the event of municipalization or in the event that the majority of assets are sold to a government agency. An example of an aggressive interpretation of the redemption provision occurred in 1995 when Texas-New Mexico Power (TNP) announced that it was calling $29 million of its 11.25% first mortgage bonds at par with its proceeds from the sale of assets to Southwestern Public Service Company (SPS). The 11.25% bonds could not be called for property release purposes. However, the bonds could be called in the event "any municipal or governmental body exercises any right it may have to order the sale of all or any part of the Trustee Estate." TNP asserted that it sold its Texas Panhandle properties to SPS because eminent domain proceedings were threatened. Holders of the called bonds litigated that call and a settlement was reached which provided additional funds to the bondholders.

Sinking Fund

A sinking fund is an annual obligation of a company to pay the trustee an amount of cash sufficient to retire a given percentage of bonds. This requirement can often be met with actual bonds or with the pledge of property. In general, electric utilities have 1% sinking funds that commence at the end of the refunding period. However, there are several variations of the sinking fund provision with which the analyst (and bondholder) should be familiar because they could directly affect the probability of bonds being called for sinking fund purposes. Some companies have nonspecific, or funnel, sinkers. This type of sinker often entails a 1% or 1.5% sinking fund applicable to all outstanding bonds. The obligation can be met by the stated percentage of each issue outstanding, by cash, or by applying (or funneling) the whole requirement against one issue or several issues.

Other Provisions

In addition to the provisions discussed above, the indenture covers the events of default, modification of the mortgage, security, limitations on borrowings, priority, and the powers and obligations of the trustee. In general, these provisions are fairly standard. However, differences occur that should be evaluated.

Industrial Indentures

Many of the provisions of an industrial indenture are similar to those of a utility's indenture, although specific items may be changed. In general, there are five indenture provisions that have historically been significant in providing protection for the industrial bondholder.

Negative Pledge Clause

The negative pledge clause provides that the company cannot create or assume liens to the extent that more than a certain percentage of consolidated net tangible assets (CNTA) is so secured without giving the same security to the bondholders. This provision is important to the bondholders because their security in the specific assets of the company establishes an important protection for their investment. The specific percentage of CNTA that is exempted from this provision is referred to as exempted indebtedness, and the exclusion provides some flexibility to the company.

Limitation on Sale and Leaseback Transactions

The indenture provision limiting sale and leaseback parallels the protection offered by the negative pledge clause, except that it provides protection for the bondholder against the company selling and leasing back assets that provide security for the debtholder. In general, this provision requires that assets or cash equal to the property sold and leased back be applied to the retirement of the debt in question or used to acquire another property for the security of the bondholders.

Sale of Assets or Merger

The sale of assets or merger provision protects the bondholder in the event that substantially all of the assets of the company are sold or merged into another company. Under these circumstances, the provision generally states that the debt be retired or be assumed by the merged company. It should be noted that the merged company that assumes the debt may have a different credit rating.

Dividend Test

The dividend test provision establishes rules for the payment of dividends. Generally, it permits the company to pay dividends to the extent that they are no greater than pet income from the previous year plus the earnings of a year or two prior. Although this provision allows the company to continue to pay dividends when there is a business decline, it assures the bondholders that the corporation will not be drained by dividend payments.

The dividend or restricted payment test also establishes parameters for the payment of dividends from operating subsidiaries to the holding company. The degree to which payments are allowed varies widely. Clearly, if the issuer is the holding company, a bondholder would favor lenient restricted payment test because the holding company debt would benefit from the flexibility to upstream funds from the operating subsidiaries. On the other hand, if the issuer is the operating subsidiary, a bondholder would favor more stringent control over the ability of the holding company to upstream funds.

Debt Test

The debt test limits the amount of debt that may be issued by establishing a maximum debt/assets ratio. This provision is generally omitted from current public offerings. However, there are numerous indentures outstanding that include this provision. In addition, private placements often include a debt test. When present, the debt test generally sets a limit on the amount of debt that can be issued per dollar of total assets. This limitation is sometimes stated as a percentage. For example, a 50% debt/asset limit restricts debt to 50% of total assets.

Financial Indentures
Sinking-Fund and Refunding Provisions

Like industrial indentures, indentures for finance issues specify sinking fund and refunding provisions. In general, finance issues with a short maturity are noncallable, whereas longer issues provide 10-year call protection. Occasionally, an issue can be called early in the event of declining receivables. Sinking funds are not as common in finance issues as they are in industrial issues, although they are standard for some companies.

Dividend Test

Perhaps the most important indenture provision for a bondholder of a finance subsidiary is the dividend test. This test restricts the amount of dividends that can be upstreamed from a finance subsidiary to the parent and thereby protects the bondholder against a parent draining the subsidiary. This provision is common in finance indentures, but it is not universal.

Limitation on Liens

The limitation on liens provision restricts the degree to which a company can pledge its assets without giving the same protection to the bondholder. Generally, only a nominal amount may be pledged or otherwise liened without establishing equal protection for the bondholder.

Restriction on Debt Test

The debt test limits the amount of debt the company can issue. This provision generally is stated in terms of assets and liabilities, although an earnings test has occasionally been used.

UTILITIES

Historically, utilities have been regulated monopolies. These companies generally operate with a high degree of financial leverage and low fixed-charge coverage (relative to industrial companies). These financial parameters have been historically accepted by investors due to the regulation of the industry and the belief that there is minimal, if any, bankruptcy risk in those securities because of the essential services they provide. The changing structure of the electric utility industry brought about by significant investment in nuclear generating units and their inherent risk as well as the transition to deregulation has changed this belief. Initially, the faltering financial position of General Public Utilities precipitated by the Three Mile Island nuclear accident and the regulatory delays in making a decision regarding the units highlighted the default risk that exists in the industry. The defaults of several Washington Public Power Supply System issues, the restructuring of Tucson Electric Company, and the bankruptcies of Public Service Company of New Hampshire and E1 Paso Electric Company and the transition to deregulation have reemphasized the default risk. Most recently, the move to deregulation and disaggregation has spotlighted the risk.

The rating agencies have reacted to the changing fundamentals of the electric utility industry. In 1985, Standard & Poor's developed more conservative benchmarks for a given rating to reflect the increased risk in the industry. In 1993, S&P categorized the electric utilities into three groups to reflect their business risk profiles. More recently, in October 1997, S&P revised its analysis with respect to the first mortgage bonds. In its refinement, S&P placed more weight on the ultimate recovery of principal in the event of distress. The revision resulted in numerous one notch upgrades and several two notch upgrades for the first mortgage debt of electric utilities. These revisions were appropriate given the fact that first mortgage bonds may receive full recovery even in bankruptcy if they are fully collateralized as was the case with the mortgage bonds of Public Service Company of New Hampshire. Most recently, the rating agencies have addressed the differences between the transmission and distribution business and the generation business in terms of the business risk of each of these segments.

Segments within the Utility Industry

There are three major segments within the utility industry: electric companies, gas companies, and telephone companies. This chapter will deal primarily with the electric utilities.

Nonfinancial Factors

Although financial factors are important in analyzing any company, nonfinancial factors are particularly important in the electric utility industry and may alter a credit assessment. The six nonfinancial factors outlined below are of particular importance to the utility industry.

The importance of nonfinancial factors led S&P to revise its financial ratios for electric utilities to explicitly take these nonfinancial factors into consideration. Specifically, in October 1993, S&P divided the electric utility universe into three groups according to business risk profiles. These business profiles are: above average, average, and below average. Accordingly, the median financial parameters in the discussion of financial analysis later are segmented according to business risk as well as rating category. As disaggregation occurs in the electric utility industry, the financial parameters will be further segmented with the more risky generation operations requiring less leverage and higher interest coverage for a given rating than the less risky transmission and distribution operations.

Regulation is the most important variable in the electric utility industry because regulatory commissions largely determine how much profit an electric utility generates. All electric companies are regulated, most by the state or states in which they operate. If a company operates in more than one state, the analyst should weigh the evaluation of the regulatory atmosphere by revenues generated in each state.

The evaluation of regulatory commissions is a dynamic process. The composition of commissions changes because of retirements, appointments, and elections. The implications of personnel changes are not clear until decisions have been made. For example, it is not always the case that elected commissioners are pro-consumer and appointments by a conservative governor are pro-business. Several brokerage firms can assist in evaluations of commissions.

Most utilities are also subject to regulation by the Federal Energy Regulatory Commission (FERC). FERC regulates interstate operations and the sale of wholesale power. In addition, FERC approves mergers. Currently, FERC regulation is considered to be somewhat more favorable than that of the average state regulatory commission.

Utilities that are constructing or operating nuclear reactors are also subject to the regulation of the Nuclear Regulatory Commission (NRC). The NRC has broad regulatory and supervisory jurisdiction over the construction and operation of nuclear reactors. Importantly, the NRC approves licensing of nuclear reactors and must approve any transfer of a license.

Regulation by state commissions, FERC, and the NRC is most visible. However, regulation by Congressional action also has potential financial impact. For example, passage of acid rain legislation mandated the reduction of sulfur dioxide and nitrogen oxide emissions. In order to reduce these emissions, utilities can either install scrubbers or switch to low-sulfur coal. Either option is costly.

There is a potential for more federal regulation of electric utilities in the near term with respect to both deregulation and PUHCA (the Public Utility Holding Company Act.) If federal legislation is passed with respect to deregulation, it is unlikely to affect existing state initiatives. Rather, any federal legislation would likely extend the general attributes of existing state initiatives to states which have failed to deregulate. Many utilities would support the repeal of PUHCA in order to allow them more flexibility in mergers and acquisitions. PUHCA is likely to eventually be repealed because it has largely become antiquated. However, the timing of such a repeal is political.

Utilities may be affected by the decisions of state commissions even if the commissions are located in a different state. For example, California has imposed significant penalties on long-term purchases of coal-fired energy by publicly owned California utilities. Therefore, non-California utilities that have historically sold coal-fired energy to California may find their energy priced too high.

Regulation is best quantified by recent rate decisions and the trend of these decisions. Although a company being analyzed may not have had a recent rate case, the commission's decisions for other companies operating within the state may be used as a proxy. Regulatory commissions are either appointed or elected. In either case, the political atmosphere can have a dramatic effect on the trend of decisions.

The regulators determine numerous issues in a rate decision, although analysts often mistakenly focus only on the allowed rate of return on equity or the new rate levels. For example, a commission might rule that an electric utility must reduce rates by 10%. However, if the commission allows the electric utility to accelerate its depreciation, the negative effect on the cash flow of the company from the rate reduction may be largely offset. In addition, the commissions determine how much of construction work in progress (CWIP) is allowed into the rate base. A company may appear to have a favorable allowed ROE but be hurt by the fact that only a small portion of the company's capital is permitted to earn that return, and the CWIP earns nothing. Allowance of CWIP in the rate base was of critical importance during the 1980s because of the high construction budgets for nuclear generating plants and the length of time these plants are under construction. Some companies have had more than half of their capital in CWIP that is not permitted to earn a return.

The importance of whether CWIP is allowed in the rate base was highlighted by the financial distress and January 1988 bankruptcy filing of Public Service Company of New Hampshire (PSNH). PSNH's Seabrook Nuclear Unit I was virtually complete in 1986. However, licensing delays and New Hampshire's statutory prohibition of CWIP in the rate base were major contributing factors in the bankruptcy filing.

In addition, regulators have a high degree of control over the cash flow of a company through the allowance or disallowance of accounting practices and the speed with which decisions are made on cases.

The source of a company's energy is a second important variable. Currently, a company with a heavy nuclear exposure is viewed less favorably than a company with natural gas or coal units. Not only are nuclear assets subject to licensing procedures, but they will also require material decommissioning expenses. The energy source variable relates to a third variable — the growth and stability of the company's territory. Although above-average growth is viewed positively in an industrial company, it may be viewed negatively with respect to an electric utility. An electric utility with above-average growth may face construction earlier than its competitors. To the extent that CWIP is disallowed or only partially allowed in the company's rate base, the company is likely to have declining financial parameters until the unit is operational.

Slow growth is not necessarily positive if it places a utility in a position of excess capacity. The increase in cogeneration and the mergers executed in order to better match supply and demand can place a utility at risk. This could result if Utility A were selling power to Utility B. If the expiration of the contract coincides with Utility B's ability to purchase power for less and results in Utility B's nonrenewal of the contract, Utility A could be negatively affected unless it can sell the power to a third utility.

A fourth variable, whether or not a company is a subsidiary of a holding company, should also be considered. Holding company status permits nonutility subsidiaries, but these subsidiaries (even if successful) will not necessarily improve the overall credit quality of the company. This depends on the regulatory atmosphere. Furthermore, when there are several electric utility subsidiaries, the parent is more likely to give relatively large equity infusions to the relatively weak subsidiaries. The stronger subsidiary may have to support the other subsidiaries. Finally, holding companies should be analyzed in terms of consolidated debt. Although a particular subsidiary may have relatively strong financial parameters, off balance sheet financing may lower the overall assessment.

The current era of deregulation has contributed to a significant increase in international and nonutility investments. Companies which are active in this area emphasize the potential equity returns of these businesses. However, the analyst must carefully analyze the ability of the holding company to downstream funds to these operations and potentially reduce the overall credit quality of the entity.

A final nonfinancial factor is the rate structure of a utility. An electric utility with a comparatively low rate structure is generally in a stronger position politically than one with rates higher than national averages, and particularly one with rates higher than regional averages.

The competitive position of an electric utility is increasingly important as the industry deregulates. Those companies with high overall rates, and particularly those with high commercial rates, may find themselves losing customers as access to transmission and distribution lines increases.

In addition, those utilities with high stranded investments are vulnerable to competition. In the transition period to deregulation, many utilities have negotiated rates with their large industrial customers in order to retain them as customers. This negotiation is only a short-term solution if a utility's embedded costs are higher than those of utilities who have access to their service territory. At best, negotiated rates for industrial customers will buy time for utilities with high costs to lower their costs to make them more in line with the rates of their competitors.

Financial Analysis

There are four major financial ratios that should be considered in analyzing an electric utility: leverage, pretax interest coverage, cash flow/spending, and cash flow/capital. The ratios discussed below apply to electric utilities which still retain both their generation and transmission and distribution assets. However, as the process of deregulation accelerates, many companies in the electric utility industry will decide to either be in generation or in transmission and distribution business. As a result of these changes, traditional ratios will no longer be applicable to many electric utilities. After a utility has divested either its generation or transmission and distribution, the analyst will be required to use benchmark ratios that apply to either generation or transmission and distribution companies.

Leverage in the electric utility industry is high relative to industrial concerns. This degree of leverage is accepted by investors because of the historical stability of the industry. The expected ranges for AA, A, BBB, and BB companies are outlined below. No electric utility companies are currently rated AAA by Standard & Poor's.

Business Position	Total Debt/Total Capitalization (%)			
	AA	A	BBB	BB
Above average	47	52	59	65
Average	42	47	54	60
Below average	—	41	48	54

In calculating the debt leverage of an electric utility, long-term debt/ capitalization is standard. However, the amount of short-term debt should also be considered because this is generally variable-rate debt. A high proportion of short-term debt may also indicate the possibility of the near-term issuance of long-term bonds. In addition, several companies guarantee the debt of subsidiaries (regulated or nonregulated). The extent of these guarantees should be considered in calculating leverage. Subsidiary debt is likely to become an increasingly important factor over the next few years as utilities invest in international utility operations through subsidiaries.

Benchmark leverage figures for a given rating will differ materially from the above figures if a utility engaged solely in generation is being considered. In this case, leverage of 35% to 45% would be consistent with an "A" rating because of the higher level of risk involved. In a similar manner, higher leverage of 55% to 65% would be consistent with an "A" rating for a utility that is engaged exclusively in the less risky transmission and distribution business.

Fixed-charge coverage for the electric utilities is also low relative to coverage for industrial companies. Standard & Poor's expected ranges for coverage are as follows:

Business Position	Pretax Interest Coverage (×)			
	AA	A	BBB	BB
Above average	4.0×	3.25×	2.25×	1.75×
Average	4.5	4.0	3.0	2.0
Below average	—	5.0	4.0	2.75

These ranges are accepted by investors because of the historic stability of the industry. However, due to the changing fundamentals of the industry as discussed above, perhaps less emphasis should be placed on the exact coverage figures and more on the trend and quality of the coverage.

The utility industry is unique in that its earnings include an allowance for funds used during construction (AFUDC). AFUDC is an accounting treatment that allows utilities to recognize income (at a rate determined by individual regulatory commissions) on the amount of funds employed in construction. The percentage that AFUDC represents of total earnings varies significantly from almost zero to more than 70% of earnings. Obviously, the higher the percentage that AFUDC represents of net earnings, the lower the quality of earnings. This becomes evident when the cash flow of a utility is calculated. Often, the cash flow of a utility with substantial AFUDC is less than the dividend requirements of the company. In this instance, the company is returning the capital of the shareholders!

In calculating fixed-charge coverage, the analyst should calculate two sets of coverage figures — fixed-charge coverage including AFUDC and fixed-charge coverage excluding AFUDC, with the latter being more important.

A third important ratio is net cash flow/spending. This ratio should be approximated for three years (the typical electric company's construction forecast). The absolute level as well as the trend of this ratio give important insights into the trend of other financial parameters. An improving trend indicates that construction spending is probably moderating, whereas a low net cash flow/spending ratio may indicate inadequate rates being approved by the commissions and a heavy construction budget. Estimates for construction spending are published in the company's annual reports. Although these are subject to revision, the time involved in building a generator makes these forecasts reasonably reliable. In 1985, Standard & Poor's deemphasized this ratio primarily due to its volatility. Although it will still be considered, Standard & Poor's now emphasizes funds from operations/total debt as a preferable indicator of cash flow adequacy.

Over the past several years, less emphasis has been placed on the net cash flow/capital expenditures ratio because the majority of electric utilities have generated positive cash flow after capital expenditures. This positive cash flow has been the result of three factors. First, the aggregate electric utility industry has surplus energy and therefore new construction has been minimal. Second, interest rates have declined significantly and electric utilities have enjoyed lower interest expense as they have refinanced maturing debt at lower interest rates. Third, the electric utility industry has lowered its operating expenses in preparation for deregulation.

Standard & Poor's benchmarks for net cash flow/capital expenditures and for funds from operations/total debt are as follows:

Business Position	Net Cash Flow/Capital Expenditures %)			
	AA	A	BBB	BB
Above average	90%	70%	45%	30%
Average	110	85	60	40
Below average	—	10S	80	60

	Funds from Operations/Total Debt (%)			
Business Position	AA	A	BBB	BB
Above average	26%	19%	14%	11%
Average	32	25	19	13
Below average	—	34	29	20

In calculating cash flow, the standard definition outlined above should be followed. However, AETUDC should also be subtracted, and any cash flow from nonregulated subsidiaries should be segregated and analyzed within the total context of the company. Regulatory commissions take divergent views on nonutility subsidiaries. Some commissions do not regulate these subsidiaries at all, whereas other commissions give inadequate rate relief to an electric utility with a profitable nonutility subsidiary under the premise that the company should be looked at as a whole. In the extreme, the latter view has encouraged companies to sell or spin off some subsidiaries.

FINANCE COMPANIES

Finance companies are essentially financial intermediaries. Their function is to purchase funds from public and private sources and to lend them to consumers and other borrowers of funds. Finance companies earn revenue by maintaining a positive spread between what the funds cost and the interest rate charged to customers. The finance industry is highly fragmented in terms of type of lending and type of ownership. This section will briefly outline the major sectors in the industry and then discuss the principal ratios and other key variables used in the analysis of finance companies.

Segments within the Finance Industry

The finance industry can be segmented by type of business and ownership. Finance companies lend in numerous ways in order to accommodate the diverse financial needs of the economy. Five of the major lending categories are (1) sales finance, (2) commercial lending, (3) wholesale or dealer finance, (4) consumer lending, and (5) leasing. Most often, companies are engaged in several of these lines rather than one line exclusively. Sales finance is the purchase of third-party contracts that cover goods or services sold on a credit basis. In most cases, the sales finance company receives an interest in the goods or services sold. Commercial finance is also generally on a secured basis. However, in this type of financing, the security is most often the borrower's accounts receivable. In factoring, another type of commercial lending, the finance company actually purchases the receivables of the company and assumes the credit risk of the receivables.

Dealer or wholesaler finance is the lending of funds to finance inventory. This type of financing is secured by the financed inventory and is short-term in nature. Leasing, on the other hand, is intermediate to long-term lending — the lessor owns the equipment, finances the lessee's use of it, and generally retains the tax benefits related to the ownership.

Consumer lending has historically involved short-term, unsecured loans of relatively small amounts to individual borrowers. In part because of the more lenient bankruptcy rules and higher default rates on consumer loans, consumer finance companies have dramatically expanded the percentage of their loans for second mortgages. The lower rate charged to individuals for this type of loan is offset by the security and lower default risk of the loan.

There are numerous other types of lending in addition to those described above. Among these are real estate lending and export/import financing.

The ownership of a finance company can significantly affect evaluation of the company. In some instances, ownership is the most important variable in the analysis. There are three major types of ownership of finance companies: (1) captives, (2) wholly-owned, and (3) independents.

Captive finance companies, such as General Motors Acceptance Corporation, are owned by the parent corporation and are engaged solely or primarily in the financing of the parent's goods or services. Generally, maintenance agreements exist between the parent and the captive finance company under which the parent agrees to maintain one or more of the finance company's financial parameters, such as fixed-charge coverage, at a minimum level. Because of the overriding relationship between a parent and a captive finance subsidiary, the financial strength of the parent is an important variable in the analysis of the finance company. However, captive finance companies can have ratings either above or below those of the parent.

A wholly owned finance company, such as Associates Corporation of North America prior to its IPO, differs from a captive in two ways. First, it primarily finances the goods and services of companies other than the parent. Second, maintenance agreements between the parent and the subsidiary are generally not as formal. Frequently, there are indenture provisions that address the degree to which a parent can upstream dividends from a finance subsidiary. The purpose of these provisions is to prevent a relatively weak parent from draining a healthy finance subsidiary to the detriment of the subsidiary's bondholders.

Independent finance companies are either publicly owned or closely held. Because these entities have no parent, the analysis of this finance sector is strictly a function of the strengths of the company.

Financial Analysis

In analyzing finance companies, several groups of ratios and other variables should be considered. There is more of an interrelationship between these ratios and variables than for any other type of company. For example, a finance company with a high degree of leverage and low liquidity may be considered to be of high investment quality if it has a strong parent and maintenance agreements.

Variables should be viewed not in isolation but rather within the context of the whole finance company/parent company relationship.

Asset Quality

The most important variable in analyzing a finance company is asset quality. Unfortunately, there is no definitive way to measure asset quality. However, there are several variables which in the aggregate present a good indication of asset quality.

Diversification is one measure of portfolio quality. Is the portfolio diversified across different types of loans? If the company is concentrated in or deals exclusively in one lending type, is there geographic diversification? A company that deals exclusively in consumer loans in the economically sensitive Detroit area would not be as favorably viewed as a company with broad geographic diversification. Accounting quality is also an important factor in assessing portfolio quality. The security for the loans is also an important variable in portfolio quality. The stronger the underlying security, the higher the loan quality. The analyst should be primarily concerned with the level of loans compared with levels of similar companies and the risk involved in the type of lending. For example, the expected loan loss from direct unsecured consumer loans is higher than for consumer loans secured by second mortgages. However, the higher fees charged for the former type of loan should compensate the company for the higher risk.

Numerous ratios of asset quality such as loss reserves/net charge-offs, net losses/average receivables, and nonperforming loans/average receivables give good indications of asset quality. However, finance companies have a high level of discretion in terms of what they consider and report to be nonperforming loans and what loans they charge off. Therefore, unadjusted ratios are not comparable among companies. In addition, companies periodically change their charge-off policies. For example, in April 1990, ITT Financial Corporation liberalized its charge-off policy for consumer loans by changing to a modified recency basis from a present contractual basis. (Under a recency basis, delinquencies are measured from the date of last payment, regardless of payment history.) ITT reduced the implications of this change by eliminating "curing" activities under which the terms of the contractual loan are modified.

In spite of the drawbacks of the asset quality ratios, they are useful in indicating trends in quality and profitability. Of these ratios, loss reserves/net charge-offs is perhaps the most important ratio in that it indicates how much cushion a company has. A declining ratio indicates that the company may not be adding sufficient reserves to cover future charge-offs. Such a trend may lead to a future significant increase in the reserves and therefore a decrease in earnings as the increase is expensed. Net losses/average receivables and nonperforming loans/average receivables are other indicators of asset quality. An increasing ratio indicates a deterioration in quality. Declines may be exacerbated by an overall contraction or slow growth in the receivables. On the other hand, because of different accounting treatments, a stable net losses/average receivables ratio under deteriorating economic conditions may indicate a delay in loss recognition.

Consideration must also be given to the age of receivables. In recent years, some finance companies have dramatically increased their lending over a short period of time and reported material improvements in their overall financial parameters. These results have been misleading in some cases where the dramatic improvement has been quickly followed by increased losses as the portfolio ages.

Leverage

Leverage is a second important ratio used in finance company analysis. By the nature of the business, finance companies are typically and acceptably more highly leveraged than industrial companies. The leverage is necessary to earn a sufficient return on capital. However, the acceptable range of leverage is dependent on other factors such as parental support, portfolio quality, and type of business. The principal ratio to determine leverage is total debt to equity, although such variations as total liabilities to equity may also be used. In a diversified company with high portfolio quality, a leverage ratio of 5 to I is acceptable. On the other hand, a ratio of 10 to 1 is also acceptable for a captive with a strong parent and maintenance agreements. The analyst should always view the leverage of a finance company in comparison with similar companies.

Liquidity

The third important variable in finance company analysis is liquidity. Because of the capital structure of finance companies, the primary cause of bankruptcies in this industry is illiquidity. If for some reason a finance company is unable to raise funds in the public or private market, failure could quickly result. This inability to raise funds could result from internal factors, such as a deterioration in earnings or from external factors such as a major disruption in the credit markets or allegations of fraud. Whatever the cause, a company should have some liquidity cushion. The ultimate liquidity cushion, selling assets, is only a last resort because these sales could have long-term, detrimental effects on earnings. The traditional liquidity ratio is cash, cash equivalents, and receivables due within one year divided by short- term liabilities. The higher this ratio, the higher the margin of safety. Also to be considered are the liquidity of the receivables themselves and the existence of bank lines of credit to provide a company with short-term liquidity during a financial crisis. In general, the smaller and weaker companies should have a higher liquidity cushion than companies with strong parental backing who can rely on an interest-free loan from the parent in times of market stress.

Liquidity considerations were heightened with the implementation of the SEC's rule 2a-7 in June 1991. This rule limits to 5% of assets the amount of medium-grade securities that a money market fund can purchase. As a result, companies whose commercial paper was downgraded to medium-grade are excluded to a large extent from the commercial paper market. A company can avoid a liquidity crisis stemming from lack of access to the commercial paper market by retaining bank lines to back up their commercial paper. Westinghouse Credit was able to replace its commercial paper with bank financing in 1992, despite downgrades, because of the adequacy of its bank lines.

Asset Coverage

A fourth important variable in the analysis of finance companies that is related to the three variables discussed above is the asset coverage afforded the bondholder. In assessing asset protection, the analyst should consider the liquidation value of the loan portfolio.

A definitive assessment of the value of assets is difficult because of the flexibility finance companies have in terms of valuing assets. A finance company can value real estate assets on a number of bases. For example, a finance company that plans to liquidate its commercial real estate portfolio over twelve months in a depressed real estate environment will value its assets much lower than if it planned to systematically sell the same assets over a three- to five-year period. Westinghouse Credit's $2.6 billion write-off in the fourth quarter of 1992 demonstrates this difference.

Earnings Record

The fifth variable to be considered is the finance company's earnings record. The industry is fairly mature and is somewhat cyclical. The higher the annual EPS growth, the better. However, some cyclicality should be expected. In addition, the analyst should be aware of management's response to major changes in the business environment. The recent easing of personal bankruptcy rules and the fact that personal bankruptcy is becoming more socially acceptable have produced significantly higher loan losses in direct, unsecured consumer loans. Many companies have responded to this change by contracting their unsecured personal loans and expanding their portfolios invested in personal loans secured by second mortgages.

Management

The sixth variable to be considered is the finance company's management. This variable is difficult to assess. However, a company visit combined with an evaluation of business strategies and credit scoring methodologies will provide some insight into this variable.

Size

A final factor related to the finance company or subsidiary is size. In general, larger companies are viewed more positively than smaller companies. Size has important implications for market recognition in terms of selling securities and of diversification. A larger company is more easily able to diversify in terms of type and location of loan than is a smaller company, and thereby to lessen the risk of the portfolio.

In addition to an analysis of the financial strength of the company according to the above variables, the analyst must incorporate the net effect of any affiliation the finance company has with a parent. If this affiliation is strong, it may be the primary variable in the credit assessment. The affiliation between a parent company and a finance subsidiary is straightforward; it is captive, wholly-owned, or independent. However, the degree to which a parent will support a finance subsidiary is not as straightforward. Traditionally, the integral relationship between a parent and a captive finance subsidiary has indicated the highest level of potential support. However, it is becoming increasingly clear that a wholly-owned finance subsidiary can have just as strong an affiliation. For example, General Electric Credit Corporation (GECC) finances few or no products manufactured by its parent, General Electric Company. However, General Electric receives substantial tax benefits from its consolidation of tax returns with GECC. Additionally, General Electric has a substantial investment in its credit subsidiary. Therefore, although there are no formal maintenance agreements between General Electric and GECC, it can be assumed that General Electric would protect its investment in GECC if the finance subsidiary were to need assistance. In other instances, it may be that the affiliation and maintenance agreements are strong but that the parent itself is weak. In this case, the strong affiliation would be discounted to the extent that parent profitability is below industry standards.

In addition to affiliation, affiliate profitability, and maintenance agreements, the analyst should also examine any miscellaneous factors that could affect the credit standing of the finance company. Legislative initiatives should be considered to determine significant changes in the structure or profitability of the industry.

THE RATING AGENCIES AND BROKERAGE HOUSES

There is no substitute for the fundamental analysis generated by the fixed income analyst. The analyst has many sources of assistance, however. The major sources of assistance are the public rating agencies and brokerage houses that specialize in fixed income research.

Rating Agencies

Four rating agencies provide public ratings on debt issues: Standard & Poor's Corporation, Moody's Investors Service, Fitch IBCA, and Duff & Phelps.

Standard & Poor's (S&P) and Moody's are the most widely recognized and used of the services, although Duff & Phelps and Fitch IBCA are frequently cited. S&P and Moody's are approximately the same size, and each rates the debt securities of approximately 2,000 companies. If a company desires a rating on an issue, it must apply to the rating agency. The agency, in turn, charges a one-time fee. For this fee, the issue is reviewed periodically during the life of the issue, and at least one formal review is made annually.

All of the rating agencies designate debt quality by assigning a letter rating to an issue. Standard & Poor's ratings range from AAA to D, with AAA obligations having the highest quality investment characteristics and D obligations being in default. In a similar fashion, Moody's ratings extend from Aaa to C, and Fitch's from AAA to D. Duff & Phelps' ratings currently extend from AAA to CCC.

Public ratings are taken seriously by corporate managements because a downgrade or an upgrade by a major agency can cost or save a corporation thousands of dollars in interest payments over the life of an issue. In the event of downgrade below the BBB- or Baa3 level, the corporation may find its bonds ineligible for investment by many institutions and funds, by either legal or policy constraints. Corporations therefore strive to maintain at least an investment-grade rating (Baa3 or higher) and are mindful of the broad financial parameters that the agencies consider in deriving a rating.

Many factors promote the use of agency ratings by investors, brokers, and brokers. Among these strengths are the breadth of companies followed, the easy access to the ratings, and the almost universal acceptance of the ratings. On the other hand, the ratings are criticized for not responding quickly enough to changes in credit conditions and for being too broad in their classifications.

The slow response time of the agencies to changes in credit conditions is certainly a valid criticism. There are few instances in which the lag is significant in terms of a dramatic change, but the market generally anticipates rating changes. The rating agencies have become increasingly sensitive to this criticism and have been quicker to change a rating in light of changing financial parameters. On the other hand, the agencies recognize the financial impact of their ratings and their obligation to rate the long-term (as opposed to the short-term) prospects of companies. They therefore have a three- to five-year perspective and deliberately do not change a rating because of short-term fluctuations.

The rating agencies have responded to this criticism directly by establishing "Watch Lists" for companies which indicate which credit ratings are under surveillance for rating changes. The rating agencies have also expanded their evaluations of companies to indicate the credit trend of the ratings.

Investors who are concerned that the ratings are too broad in their classifications have several options among the brokerage-house services that offer more continuous ratings.

Brokerage-House Services

Numerous brokerage houses specialize in fixed income research. Generally, these services are available only to institutional buyers of bonds. The strength of the research stems from the in-depth coverage provided, the statistical techniques employed, and the fine gradations in rating. On the other hand, the universe of companies that these firms follow is necessarily smaller than that followed by the agencies.

In spite of the numerous services available, the market continues to demand more fixed income research. To partially satisfy this demand, many independent analysts are evaluating segments of the market previously not covered or inadequately covered.

CONCLUSION

This chapter has emphasized a basic method for analyzing corporate bonds. A format for analysis is essential. However, analysis of securities cannot be totally quantified, and the experienced analyst will develop a second sense about whether to delve into a particular aspect of a company's financial position or to take the financial statements at face value. All aspects of credit analysis, however, have become increasingly important as rapidly changing economic conditions and globalization change the credit quality of companies and industries.

Chapter 23

Term Structure Factor Models

Robert C. Kuberek
Vice President and Principal
Wilshire Associates Incorporated

INTRODUCTION

Quantitative models of risk provide portfolio managers with valuable tools in the construction and maintenance of investment portfolios that meet specific performance objectives. Fixed income portfolio management is especially amenable to quantitative risk modeling because so much structure is present in the pricing of fixed income securities and because the returns of investment grade fixed income securities are so highly correlated with one another. Factor models provide a particularly powerful technique for modeling fixed income portfolio risk. Moreover, because the main sources of risk (and correlation) in the returns of investment grade fixed income portfolios relate to the shape and position of the yield curve, *term structure* factor models represent the most important of these models.

The purpose of this chapter is to review some of the leading approaches to term structure factor modeling. However, to understand how term structure factor models work and how they fit into the risk management landscape it is useful first to define this important class of risk models and to put their development in historical perspective. This is the objective of the next section. Succeeding sections discuss the application of factor models to risk management, identify the major types of term structure factor models, describe leading examples of each type of term structure model, and discuss the advantages and disadvantages of each.

FACTOR MODELS DEFINED AND HISTORICAL BACKGROUND

Whether risk is measured in terms of standard deviation of return, standard deviation of tracking error relative to a benchmark, value-at risk or probability of underperforming some target, a useful first step in building a factor model is to develop a quantitative description of returns that relates returns meaningfully to other quantities and that has statistical moments that can be estimated easily and reliably. One of the simplest descriptions of return that meets these requirements is the market model for common stocks.[1] In this model, asset returns are generated by the process

---

[1] The market model follows from the assumption that stock returns are multi-variate normal. See Eugene F. Fama, *Foundations of Finance* (New York: Basic Books, 1976).

$$\tilde{R}_i = a_i + b_i \tilde{R}_m + \tilde{e}_i \tag{1}$$

where

R_i = the total return of asset i

R_m = the total return of the market portfolio

e_i = a random error term that is uncorrelated with the market return

and the tilde (~) denotes a random variable.

If it is further assumed that the residual error terms in equation (1) are uncorrelated *across* assets after taking out the influence of the single index return R_m, then this model is an example of a simple "factor" model where the single factor is the return of the market portfolio. It is also a *linear* factor model because it is linear in the factor return R_m. The particular description of the return-generating process in (1) is closely identified with the Capital Asset Pricing Model (CAPM) of William Sharpe[2] and John Lintner.[3]

Another well-known example of a linear factor model for risky assets underlies the Arbitrage Pricing Theory (the APT) of Stephen Ross.[4] This type of return model, which is very general, assumes that it is not possible to completely eliminate the correlations of residuals across assets with a single index. In this more general model, returns are generated by the following process:

$$\tilde{r}_i = a_i + b_{i1}\tilde{f}_1 + b_{i2}\tilde{f}_2 + \ldots + b_{ik}\tilde{f}_k + \tilde{e}_i \tag{2}$$

where

r_i = the excess return of asset i over the risk-free rate

f_j = the return to risk factor j

e_i = a mean-zero random residual error term that is uncorrelated with the factor returns and uncorrelated across assets

In the APT model, excess returns are generated by a linear process which is the sum of a risk premium a, a set of random factor effects bf, and a random, asset-specific residual. Examples of factors include index returns, unexpected changes in GNP, changes in corporate bond yield spreads, beta, and the ratio of earnings to price. It often simplifies matters further to assume that the factor returns and the residuals are normally distributed.

---

[2] William F. Sharpe, "Capital Asset Prices: A Theory of Market Equilibrium under Conditions of Risk," *Journal of Finance* (September 1964), pp. 425-442.

[3] John Lintner, "The Valuation of Risk Assets and the Selection of Risk Investments in Stock Portfolios and Capital Budgets," *Review of Economics and Statistics* (February 1965), pp. 13-37.

[4] Stephen A. Ross, "The Arbitrage Theory of Capital Asset Pricing," *Journal of Economic Theory* (December 1976), pp. 341-360.

USING FACTOR MODELS TO MEASURE RISK

The moments of a linear factor model are the means, variances and covariances of the factor returns, and the variances of the residuals (one for each asset).[5] The usefulness and power of factor models in risk management lie in the fact that once the values of the moments are determined together with the exposures of the risky assets to the factors, it becomes possible to compute portfolio risk using any one of a number of definitions.

For example, suppose that the k factors f in equation (2) have $k \times k$ covariance matrix Ψ. Furthermore, suppose that a particular portfolio holds n ($>k$) assets with the $n \times 1$ weight vector $\mathbf{x}$. The portfolio excess return can be written in matrix form as

$$\tilde{r}_p = x'a + x'\mathbf{B}\tilde{f} + x'\tilde{e} \tag{3}$$

where $\mathbf{B}$ is an $n \times k$ matrix of exposures in which the ith row consists of the b's in equation (2).

Equation (3) gives the portfolio return for a portfolio of assets whose returns are generated by equation (2). The first term in equation (3) is the average risk premium in the portfolio, which is a weighted average of the risk premiums of the individual holdings. The second term is the part of the return that is explained by the k common factors f, and the third term is the aggregate residual return, the unexpected return or noise in the portfolio return that is not explained by the risk factors.

The variance, or total risk, of the portfolio return then is

$$\text{var}(\tilde{r}_p) = x'\mathbf{B}\Psi\mathbf{B}'x + x'\mathbf{D}x \tag{4}$$

where $\mathbf{D}$ is an $n \times n$ diagonal matrix whose non-zero elements are the variances of the residuals in equation (2).[6] Decomposition of return variance in this way has important computational benefits. By reducing the size of the non-diagonal covariance matrix from $n \times n$ to $k \times k$, for example, portfolio optimization can be performed using significantly less cpu time and computer memory.[7]

---

[5] Factor models have moments and parameters. Moments are the means, variances and covariances of the factor returns. Parameters are used in defining and measuring the factors. For example, the *variance* of a factor is a moment, while the *weights* of the stocks in the index that represents the factor are parameters. The number of moments (means, variances and covariances) in a factor model is a function of the number of factors. The number of parameters in the model, on the other hand, depends on the specification of the model.

[6] The decomposition of return variance in this manner is traceable to William F. Sharpe, "A Simplified Model for Portfolio Analysis," *Management Science* (January 1963), pp. 277-293.

[7] In their original paper, which studied single and multiple index portfolios in portfolio selection, Kalman J. Cohen and Jerry A. Pogue ("An Empirical Evaluation of Alternative Portfolio Selection Models," *Journal of Business* 40 (1967), pp. 166-193), reported that a single optimization involving only 150 securities required 90 minutes of processing time on an IBM 7090 computer using the full $n \times n$ covariance matrix. While computers presumably have gotten faster in the years since Cohen and Pogue did their work, the relative advantage of equation (4) in computational time surely remains.

Equation (4) decomposes portfolio risk into two components. The first component represents the contribution to total risk from the exposures to the common risk factors while the second represents the contribution from residuals. The contributions to return variance can be separated in this way because of the assumption in equation (2) that the factor returns are uncorrelated with the residual returns. Moreover, the residual variance matrix $\mathbf{D}$ has the especially simple diagonal form because of the assumption in equation (2) that the residuals are uncorrelated *across* assets. An important feature of this measure of risk is that the second term, the residual variance, tends to shrink with the number of assets in the portfolio. Thus, portfolio managers can diversify away the residual risk in their portfolios but not the systematic, factor risk.

Furthermore, since equation (3) applies to any portfolio, including a benchmark portfolio, the variance of the tracking error of a portfolio relative to a benchmark can be written as

$$\text{var}(\tilde{r}_p - \tilde{r}_b) = [x_p - x_b]'\mathbf{B}\mathbf{\Psi}\mathbf{B}'[x_p - x_b] + [x_p - x_b]'\mathbf{D}[x_p - x_b] \qquad (5)$$

where the weighting vectors x are now subscripted to denote whether they relate to the portfolio or to the benchmark. The reader will notice that in equation (5) the variance of the tracking error goes to zero as the weight differences from the benchmark go to zero — if one holds the index, the tracking error variance is zero.

TYPES OF FACTOR MODELS

In terms of equation (2), factor models can be categorized according to how the factor exposures and factor returns are measured. In this regard, it is customary to classify factor models as macroeconomic, statistical or fundamental.

Macroeconomic Factor Models

In macroeconomic factor models, the factor returns in equation (2) represent unexpected changes in quantities that are observable. Quantities that are commonly employed as macroeconomic factors include the returns of specified indexes of common stocks, such as capital goods or materials and services indexes, as well as unexpected changes in measures of aggregate economic activity, such as industrial production, personal income or employment. Since the factor returns are directly observable, the moments of the factor model (the means, variances, and covariances of the factor returns) can be estimated directly from the *time series* of factor returns. Assets are differentiated by their exposures to these variables, which are the b's in equation (2). These exposures can be estimated by regressing time series of individual stock returns (or of portfolios of similar stocks) on the observed factor returns, using equation (2), with the stock returns as the dependent variable and the observed factor returns f as the independent variables. Examples of macroeconomic factor models include the single and multiple index models of Cohen and Pogue[8] and the APT model of Chen, Roll, and Ross.[9]

Macroeconomic factor models have the great advantage that because the factors are observable, they are easy to relate to the performance of individual stocks in an intuitive way. One can imagine (whether it is true or not), for example, that airline stocks would tend to do well in an economic upturn, while drug stocks might be relatively insensitive to general economic conditions. A disadvantage of this approach is that with only a small number of factors it may be difficult to eliminate correlation of residuals across assets. A second disadvantage of this type of factor model is that it may be difficult to measure either the exposures of the assets to the macroeconomic variables or the returns to these variables using data of arbitrary frequency. For example, one could identify a factor with the Federal Reserve's Industrial Production index, but this statistic is published only monthly, making it impossible to estimate and use the model in this form with daily returns data.

Statistical Factor Models

The second traditional type of factor model is the statistical model. In this type of model a statistical procedure, such as factor analysis or principal components analysis, is used both to identify the factors and to measure the factor returns. In principal components analysis, for example, a factor model is constructed using a multivariate time series of individual stock returns. The covariance (or correlation) matrix of stock returns is factored by identifying some small number of linear combinations (the principal components) of stock returns that account for most of the return variance in the sample. Thus the factor returns end up being linear combinations of individual stock returns and the factor exposures are the multiple regression coefficients of individual stock returns with these principal components.[10]

An advantage of this method relative to pure macroeconomic factor models is that one can remove as much of the correlation in residuals as one likes by including as many principal components as desired, all the way up to the number of stocks (or stock portfolios) in the original sample. A second advantage relative to macroeconomic factor models is that returns are the only inputs and thus frequency is not an issue: the model can be estimated with any frequency for which the individual stock returns are available.

A disadvantage of the statistical approach is that the factors are not observable in the sense that one cannot make measurements of the factor returns independently of the stock returns themselves and in the sense that the factors do not always correspond to quantities that can be related easily to stock returns.

---

[8] Cohen and Pogue, "An Empirical Evaluation of Alternative Portfolio Selection Models."

[9] Nai-Fu Chen, Richard Roll, and Stephen A. Ross, "Economic Forces and the Stock Market," *Journal of Business* (1986), pp. 383-404.

[10] For an early application of this approach, see Benjamin King, "Market and Industry Factors in Stock Price Behavior," *Journal of Business* 39 (1966), pp. 139-190.

A disadvantage of both the pure macroeconomic factor models (when the factor returns are observed and the exposures are estimated) and the statistical approaches is that the exposure of a given stock to a factor can, and probably does, change over time as the company's business mix and capital structure change. Because of their reliance on *time series* estimates of factor exposure, neither of these approaches handles this problem gracefully. A related disadvantage of both pure macroeconomic factor models and statistical factor models is that new securities are difficult to fit in a portfolio because there is no history with which to estimate the exposures.

Fundamental Factor Models

The fundamental approach combines some of the advantages of macroeconomic factor models and statistical factor models while avoiding certain of their difficulties.[11] The fundamental approach identifies the factors with a stock's exposures to a set of attributes, which can include the stock's beta, its ratio of earnings-to price (e/p), its economic sector (e.g., capital goods), and its industry classification (e.g., automotive). In this type of factor model the factor exposures are the exposures to the economic variables, the actual (or normalized) values of the fundamentals (e.g., the actual e/p ratio) and, in the case of a classification factor, simply a dummy variable that has a value of one if the stock falls into the category or zero otherwise. Factor returns are not observed directly but are inferred by regressing *cross-sections* of stock returns against their exposures to the set of factors.[12]

An important advantage of the fundamental approach relative to the macroeconomic and statistical approaches is that as the exposure of a stock to a given factor changes over time, these exposure changes can be tracked immediately so that measures of portfolio risk correctly reflect the current condition of the portfolio's underlying assets. By the same token it is easy to include new securities in a portfolio because no history is required to estimate their factor exposures.

TYPES OF TERM STRUCTURE FACTOR MODELS

The general framework of equation (2) can be applied to fixed income securities easily. However, for investment grade fixed income securities, the main sources of risk relate to the level and shape of the yield curve. Thus, the appropriate factor models are term structure factor models, where the factors in equation (2) are defined specifically to explain the returns of default free bonds, such as Treasuries or stripped Treasuries, and thus describe changes in yield curve level and shape.[13]

---

[11] Examples of this approach include, Eugene F. Fama and James MacBeth, "Risk, Return and Equilibrium: Empirical Tests," *Journal of Political Economy* (1973), pp. 607-636, and Eugene F. Fama and Kenneth R. French, "The Cross-Section of Expected Stock Returns," *Journal of Finance* (June 1992), pp. 427-465.

[12] In this case the beta, if it is included as a factor, is estimated or modeled using *a prior* time series.

[13] For non-Treasury securities additional factors can be important in determining portfolio risk. See, for example, Robert C. Kuberek, "Common Factors in Bond Portfolio Returns," Wilshire Associates Incorporated (1989).

An important feature of term structure factor models is that, because the factors mainly explain the risk of yield changes, in each model there is a characteristic yield curve shift associated with each factor. Still, as will be seen, each of the models described here bears a resemblance to one or another of the common stock models already described. Along these lines, term structure factor models can be classified in four types, as follows:

1. arbitrage models
2. principal components models
3. spot rate models
4. functional models

Term structure factor models that use equilibrium or arbitrage methods, especially Cox, Ingersoll, and Ross[14] and Richard[15] are analogous to macroeconomic factor models for common stocks. These models work by postulating dynamics for a set of observable state variables that are assumed to underlie interest rates and deriving (in the case of equilibrium models) or assuming (in the case of arbitrage models) some equilibrium condition for expected returns, then *deriving* the term structure.[16] Examples of state variables underlying these models include the short-term nominal interest rate, the short-term "real" rate of interest, the rate of inflation, and the unexpected component of the change in the Consumer Price Index. A unique feature of the equilibrium/arbitrage approach, relative to other types of term structure factor models, is that the equilibrium/arbitrage approach produces term structure factor models that are rigorously consistent with security valuation. In other words, these models provide both bond prices and dynamics.

Term structure factor models based on principal components or factor analysis, such as Gultekin and Rogalski[17] and Litterman and Scheinkman,[18] are

---

[14] John C. Cox, Jonathan E. Ingersoll, and Stephen A. Ross, "A Theory of the Term Structure of Interest Rates," Working Paper (August 1978) and John C. Cox, Jonathan E. Ingersoll, and Stephen A. Ross, "A Theory of the Term Structure of Interest Rates," *Econometrica* (1985), pp. 385-407.

[15] Scott F. Richard, "An Arbitrage Model of the Term Structure of Interest Rates," *Journal of Financial Economics* (1978), pp.33-57.

[16] In distinguishing the arbitrage approach from their own equilibrium approach, Cox, Ingersoll, and Ross write, "An alternative to the equilibrium approach taken here is based purely on arbitrage considerations. Here is a brief summary of this argument. Assume that all uncertainty is described by some set of state variables. If there are no pure arbitrage opportunities in the economy, then there exists a (not necessarily unique) set of state-space prices which support current contingent claim values... By assuming that the state variables follow an *exogenously* specified diffusion process, one obtains a valuation equation of the same general form as [CIR (1978) eq.] (25). However, the resulting equation contains *undetermined* coefficients which depend on both preferences and production opportunities and *can be identified only in a general equilibrium setting*" (italics supplied). Notwithstanding this criticism, however, as Richard and others have shown, arbitrage models are powerful, easy to develop, and, providing one is willing and has the means to solve them numerically, reasonably practical.

[17] N. Bulent Gultekin and Richard J. Rogalski, "Government Bond Returns, Measurement of Interest Rate Risk and the Arbitrage Pricing Theory," *Journal of Finance* (1985), pp. 43-61.

[18] Robert Litterman and José Scheinkman, "Common Factors Affecting Bond Returns," *Journal of Fixed Income* (June 1991), pp. 54-61.

analogous to the statistical factor models for common stocks described previously. In this type of model, factor analysis or principal components analysis is used to identify the factors underlying the returns of bonds of different maturities or, almost equivalently, to identify the factors underlying the movements of yields at different maturities. As with the common stock return models, the factor returns typically are linear combinations of the returns of zero-coupon bonds and the factor exposures are the multiple regression coefficients of individual bond returns with these principal components.

Two other approaches, spot rate models and polynomial models, bear some resemblance to fundamental models for common stocks in that the factors are most naturally identified with different measures of exposure. Spot rate models identify the term structure factors directly with the durations of zero-coupon bonds at specified points along the term structure. An important example of this type of model is J. P. Morgan's RiskMetrics™ model,[19] which identifies factors with the durations of zero coupon bonds at ten points along the yield curve, 3-months, 1-year, 2 years, 3-years, 5-years, 7-years, 10-years, 15-years, 20-years, and 30 years. Duration for coupon bonds can be calculated either directly from the cash flows, if the cash flows are well defined, using so-called cash-flow mapping techniques, or with the aid of a yield-curve-based valuation model (e.g., an option-adjusted-spread, or OAS, model), in the case of bonds with embedded options and payment contingencies.[20] The RiskMetrics™ model and approach are in wide use in a variety of risk management applications, but especially in applications focusing on value-at-risk.

Functional models, for example Kuberek[21] and Willner,[22] seek to represent yield curve risk using approximating functions that are based on, or related to, polynomials. These models fit smooth curves to actual yield curve movements, where the fitted shifts represent a composite of a basic set of yield curve shift components, reflecting, for example, change in yield curve level, change in slope, and change in curvature. Factors are identified with the durations of zero-coupon Treasuries with respect to these pre-specified shift components. Superficially, the basic yield curve shift components resemble principal components shifts, but are generated not by a historical data sample but by some underlying mathematical reasoning.

---

[19] For a comprehensive description of this approach, see "RiskMetrics — Technical Document," J.P. Morgan/Reuters, 1996.

[20] See, for example, Robert C. Kuberek and Prescott C. Cogswell, "On the Pricing of Interest Rate Contingent Claims in a Binomial Lattice," Wilshire Associates Incorporated (May 1990). These term-structure-based OAS models are prerequisite for measuring exposures to term-structure factors for any but the simplest fixed income securities. The general approach is to fit the model to the quoted price of a bond by iterating on a spread over the initial term structure, then numerically to compute the factor exposure by shifting the starting term structure and re-calculating the model value of the bond at the same spread.

[21] Robert C. Kuberek, "An Approximate Factor Model for U.S. Treasuries," *Proceedings of the Seminar on the Analysis of Security Prices* (November 1990), The University of Chicago Center for Research in Securities Prices, pp. 71-106.

[22] Ram Willner, "A New Tool for Portfolio Managers: Level, Slope and Curvature Durations," *Journal of Fixed Income* (June 1996), pp. 48-59.

In fact, as will be seen, all of the term structure factor models described here can be represented as a form of equation (2). Moreover, all of the term structure factor models described here share the property that the factor returns in the model represent the amounts and direction of each characteristic yield curve shift allowed in the model, and the exposures, the b's in equation (2), are the durations of the bonds with respect to these yield curve shifts. From this perspective, a useful way to distinguish the models is in the number of characteristic yield curve movements that each model implies and in the forms of these characteristic yield curve movements.

The remainder of this chapter will explore a leading example of each of the four term structure factor models described above. The examples that will be used are (1) for arbitrage models, the one-factor equilibrium term structure model of Cox, Ingersoll, and Ross; (2) for principal components models, Litterman and Scheinkman; (3) for spot rate models, J. P. Morgan's RiskMetrics™ model; and, (4) for functional models, Kuberek. To facilitate the comparison of the different models, each of the models is recast to describe yield curve risk at the same 12 points along the yield curve — 9 months, 1 year, 1.5 years, 2 years, 3 years, 4 years, 5 years, 7 years, 10 years, 15 years, 20 years, and 30 years.

ARBITRAGE MODELS

The Cox, Ingersoll, and Ross equilibrium term structure model (CIR) is developed fully within the context of a single-good production economy with stochastic production possibilities and uncertain technological change. However, the model can be developed using arbitrage arguments, providing that the specification of the equilibrium condition for expected bond returns is consistent with their general equilibrium formulation.[23]

Assume that there is one factor, which is represented by the short-term interest rate r. Further, assume that this rate evolves according to the process

$$dr = \kappa(\mu - r)dt + \sigma\sqrt{r}dz \tag{6}$$

where

μ = long-term average value of the short-term interest rate r
κ = rate of reversion of the short-term interest rate r toward its long-term average value
$\sigma r^{1/2}$ = standard deviation of unexpected changes in the short-term interest rate
dz = a standard Brownian motion

---

[23] The CIR model is constructed for an economy where money does not play a role and therefore the short-term interest rate in the model is a "real" rate. Nevertheless, by convention the one-factor CIR model is applied to the nominal term structure, where the short-term rate in the model is regarded as a nominal rate.

Equation (6) says that the change in the short-term interest rate r over the period dt is the sum of two components, a drift component, which represents the expected reversion of the short-term rate toward the mean, and a surprise term that reflects unexpected changes in interest rates. This description of interest rate dynamics has several important properties. These include mean reversion, volatility of interest rates that increases with the level of interest rates, and the fact that the future behavior of the interest rate depends only on it current value and not on the history of its movements.

If the price $P(r,T)$ of a zero-coupon bond paying \$1 in T years depends only on the short-term interest rate r and the maturity T, it follows from Ito's lemma[24] that the return over a period dt of a zero-coupon bond with maturity T is

$$\tilde{r}_T = \left\{ (P_r/P)k(\mu-r) + P_t/P + \frac{1}{2}(P_{rr}/P)\sigma^2 r - r \right\} dt + (P_r/P)\sigma\sqrt{r}dz \quad (7)$$

The first term on the right hand side of equation (7) is the expected excess return of the T-year maturity zero-coupon bond. It consists of four components. The first is that part of the return due to the expected movement of the short-term rate r toward its long-term average value μ. The second component is due to accretion toward par. The third component is that part of the expected return that is due to convexity. The fourth component is the current value of the short-term rate, subtracted to obtain the expected excess return.

The second term on the right hand side of equation (7) is the effect of the unexpected component of the change in the short-term interest rate.

If it is assumed that the expected excess return of the T-year zero-coupon bond in equilibrium is proportional to the bond's "duration" with respect to the short-term interest rate by a risk premium λr, that represents the price of interest rate risk per unit of duration, then equation (7) becomes

$$\tilde{r}_T = (P_r/P)\lambda r dt + (P_r/P)\sigma\sqrt{r}dz \quad (8)$$

Equation (8) says that the excess return on a zero coupon bond of maturity T is the sum of two components, a risk premium that is proportional to the product of the bond's duration with respect to r and the risk premium λr, and a surprise that is the product of the bond's duration and the unexpected change in the interest rate r.

Careful inspection of equation (8) shows that it has exactly the form of equation (2) where

$$a = (P_r/P)\lambda r dt \quad (9a)$$

and

---

[24] For a discussion of the application of Ito's lemma to the pricing of bonds, see S. Fischer, "The Demand for Index Bonds," *Journal of Political Economy* (1975), pp. 509-534.

$$b = (P_r/P) \tag{9b}$$

Under these conditions CIR provide a closed-form expression for the duration P_r/P of a zero-coupon bond maturity T. This is given by the following formula:

$$\frac{P_r(r, T)}{P} = -\frac{2(e^{\gamma T} - 1)}{(\gamma + k + \lambda)(e^{\gamma T} - 1) + 2\gamma} \tag{10}$$

where

$$\gamma = \sqrt{(\kappa + \lambda)^2 + 2\sigma^2}$$

The CIR model produces a single characteristic yield shift as illustrated in Exhibit 1. The shift, which resembles a twist at the short end of the curve, describes yield curve behavior when yield changes are perfectly correlated and when short-term yields tend to move more than long-term yields. This tendency for short-term interest rates to be more volatile than long rates is a result of the mean reversion in the short rate assumed for the model and described in equation (6). For example, suppose that the values of the parameters in equation (10) for this example are as follows: $\kappa = 0.1$, $\lambda = -0.04$ (a negative value corresponds to a positive term premium), and $\sigma = 0.03578$. These parameter values are consistent with a 10-year mean reversion time, a term premium of 20 basis points per year of duration, and an annual standard deviation of short-term interest rate changes of 80 basis points. Given these values for the parameters, if the short rate increases by 100 basis points, the 30-year zero-coupon rate will increase by only just over 20 basis points.

Exhibit 1: Characteristic Yield Shifts: CIR Model

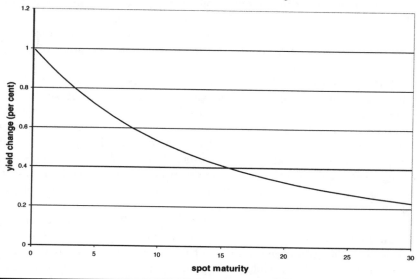

Exhibit 2: Bond Durations: CIR Model

Time to Maturity	b_1
0.75	−0.71
1.00	−0.93
1.50	−1.35
2.00	−1.74
3.00	−2.45
4.00	−3.05
5.00	−3.58
7.00	−4.43
10.00	−5.32
15.00	−6.16
20.00	−6.56
30.00	−6.84

As can be seen in Exhibit 2, for this combination of parameter values the CIR durations of zero-coupon bonds do not increase as rapidly as their ordinary durations, which are just the times-to-maturity of the bonds. This is a reflection of the tendency for long rates to rise by less than short rates, when short rates rise, and for long rates to fall by less than short rates, when short rates fall. Thus, CIR durations suggest that ordinary durations overstate the risk of long maturity bonds relative to short maturity bonds.

The CIR model has several advantages over other approaches. First, it is rigorously consistent with the valuation of fixed income securities. In other words, the model produces both prices and returns. A second advantage is that the model is defined continuously in maturity: exposures can be calculated for zero-coupon bonds of any maturity without recourse to approximation or interpolation. A third advantage, which has already been mentioned, is that the moments — the mean and variance of the (single) factor return — can be estimated directly by observing the time series of factor returns, in this case the time series of changes in the short-term interest rate.

A disadvantage of this model is that it allows only one type of yield curve shift and is thus very limited in the variety of actual yield curve behaviors that it can describe. This is not a shortcoming of the general approach, however. CIR also present a two-factor model, with uncertain short-term interest rates and uncertain inflation, within the context of their general equilibrium model, and Richard and others have proposed other two-factor and multi-factor models based on arbitrage arguments. However, for the variety of interest rate dynamics that have known solutions like equation (10), the models tend to have a large number of parameters and very complicated forms.

A second minor disadvantage of the one-factor CIR model as a factor model is evident from inspection of equation (8), namely, that the coefficients in the factor model depend on the level of interest rates. This dependence of the coefficients on the level of interest rates is plausible on the grounds that it is consistent with the presumption that interest rates tend to be more volatile when interest rate levels are higher. However, it means that this model cannot be implemented by regressing cross sections of bond returns on their durations, then averaging over time to obtain the moments, without first normalizing the exposures for the level of interest rates.

PRINCIPAL COMPONENTS MODELS

A second major category of term structure factor models is based on principal components analysis. In this approach, the returns of zero coupon bonds of different maturities are factor analyzed to extract a (hopefully small) set of characteristic yield curve shifts, defined at discreet maturities, that together explain a large proportion of the total variance of returns in the sample. The factors are thus the amounts and direction of each type of characteristic yield curve shift that combine to explain the returns of a cross-section of bond returns for a given performance period. Gultekin and Rogalski use this technique on coupon Treasuries, while Litterman and Scheinkman use the method to factor analyze the returns of Treasury implied zero-coupon bonds.[25] Because the use of implied zeros is more consistent with generalizations of equation (2) for any bond, the focus here will be on the approach of Litterman and Scheinkman (LS).

To illustrate the LS model, suppose that returns are available for implied zeros at twelve maturities, as follows: 9 months, 1 year, 1.5 years, 2 years, 3 years, 4 years, 5 years, 7 years, 10 years, 15 years, 20 years, and 30 years. With principal components one can specify any number of factors up to the number of securities in the data sample — in this case 12. Typically, a number is chosen such that most of the variance in the sample is explained by the factors selected. For the example here, the first three principal components typically explain more than 98% of the variance in the data sample, so three is chosen as the number of factors. The characteristic yield curve shifts that correspond to the first three yield curve factors are shown in Exhibit 3.

The first yield curve factor is the relatively flat curve near the top of Exhibit 3. This corresponds to a yield shift that is roughly, but not exactly, uniform. The second shift is a pivoting shift for which short rates fall and long rates rise. This shift is almost uniform for maturities greater than 15 years. The third shift is a change in curvature, with short rates rising, intermediate rates falling and long rates rising. Actual yield curve shifts are represented as composites of these three characteristic yield shifts. The principal components procedure works

---

[25] Implied zero-coupon bonds, or implied zeros, are hypothetical bonds that are priced using discount factors that are consistent with the discount factors that the market uses to price actual coupon Treasuries. While these bond prices cannot be observed directly, their existence is somewhat validated by the possibility of creating them synthetically by constructing hedge portfolio of coupon Treasuries. Also, a closely related security, the Treasury strip, does actually exist. The reason for using implied zeros in preference to actual Treasury strips to build a factor model is the availability of more history for backtesting: Treasury strips did not exist before the early 1980s, whereas Treasury prices are widely available back to 1974 and implied zero curves are available back even further.

in such a way that the factors are uncorrelated in the data sample that was used to generate them. This uncorrelatedness of the factors is a consequence of the property of principal components referred to as orthogonality.

The exposures or "durations" of the implied zeros with respect to each of these factors, the b's in equation (2) are shown in Exhibit 4. As with the analogous common stock models, factor returns are produced by the principal components procedure itself but, alternatively, can be estimated by regressing the returns of cross-sections of zero-coupon bonds on the durations implied by the characteristic yield shifts that are produced by the principal components analysis (Exhibit 4). The durations are scaled to the characteristic yield shifts themselves, so that, for example, one unit of return for the second factor corresponds to a yield shift of 0.38% at 30 years. Thus, to obtain the return of the 5-year zero coupon bond resulting from one half unit of return for the second factor, assuming the factor returns for the other factors are zero for a given period, it is only necessary to multiply the duration (−0.20) by the factor return (0.50) to get −0.10%. In practice, the realized factor returns will all be non-zero, but then the effects are computed in the same way for each factor and the results added together to get the total excess return predicted for that security, as in equation (2).[26]

Exhibit 3: Characteristic Yield Curve Shifts: Principal Components Model

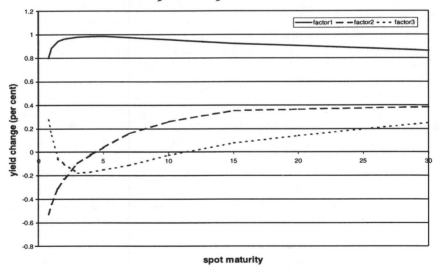

[26] The scaling of principal components models is pretty arbitrary. Thus, for example, the model here could have been scaled so that the characteristic yield shift of the second factor was 1.00% at 30 years instead of 0.38% (see Exhibit 2). In this case the duration of the 30-year bond with respect to the second factor would have had to have been scaled up accordingly. The content and explanatory power of the complete factor model would remain the same, however. In particular, the returns predicted for a bond, given its exposures and given the realized factor returns estimated for the performance period, would be identical.

Exhibit 4: Bond Durations: Principal Components Model

Time to Maturity	b_1	b_2	b_3
0.75	−0.60	0.40	−0.21
1.00	−0.88	0.44	−0.14
1.50	−1.41	0.46	0.08
2.00	−1.93	0.46	0.20
3.00	−2.93	0.29	0.53
4.00	−3.93	0.10	0.67
5.00	−4.92	-0.20	0.75
7.00	−6.83	−1.13	0.77
10.00	−9.56	−2.60	0.24
15.00	−13.84	−5.33	−1.17
20.00	−18.10	−7.35	−2.81
30.00	−25.89	−11.58	−7.51

An advantage of the principal components approach in term structure factor modeling is that the actual data provide guidance in defining the factors. A disadvantage of the principal components model, which is inherent in the approach, is the large number of parameters required. In the example here with three principal components, 36 parameters are required. These are the parameters required to describe the characteristic yield curve shift for each of the three factors at each of 12 maturities. A second disadvantage is that the exact definition of the factors, and therefore of the exposures, depends on the data sample used to extract the principal components. As experience is accumulated, the data change and the definition of the factors, and thus the durations of bonds, change.

A third disadvantage of this approach is that the model is not defined continuously on maturity. Thus, to calculate factor exposures for bonds with maturity or cash flow dates different from the maturities of the zeros used to define the factors, some interpolation of the characteristic yield curve shifts must be performed. The larger the number of maturities used to define the factors, the less interpolation is needed, but the more parameters are required. Of course, there is no guarantee that once the factors are defined, using a particular historical data sample, the factor returns still will be uncorrelated out of sample.

SPOT RATE MODELS

Spot rate models identify factors with the durations of zero-coupon bonds at each of a number of points along the yield curve. The factors thus can be interpreted as changes in the yields of these hypothetical zero-coupon bonds. Moreover, any number of yield curve points can be used to define the model, so the portfolio manager has wide latitude in defining the model to suit the specific application. Spot rate models have the least content in terms of economic assumptions and, correspondingly, the fewest parameters.

One of the leading examples of spot rate models is J. P. Morgan's Risk-Metrics™ model.[27] This model defines ten points along the yield curve and provides the variance-covariance matrix, the Ψ in equation (4), of spot rate changes for 13 countries including the United States. The RiskMetrics™ model is widely applied in measuring value-at-risk. The portfolio's "value-at-risk" is the largest *dollar* loss (or loss in terms of some other reference currency) that a portfolio will suffer "ordinarily." For example, if a portfolio will lose not more than $100, 95% of the time, then the value at-risk is said to be $100. Value-at-risk can be computed from equation (4), as follows:

$$\text{Value-at-Risk} = 1.65 \,(\text{Portfolio Value}) \, [\text{var}(r_p)]^{\frac{1}{2}}$$

As with all the term structure factor models described here, however, spot rate models can be estimated in at least two ways. The time series of factor returns can be estimated by measuring the yield changes at each yield curve point in the model, as with a macroeconomic factor model for common stocks. Alternatively, one may calculate the durations of the bonds with respect to the spot rate changes and regress bond returns cross-sectionally on these durations to create a time-series of factor returns. Typically, the second method is more direct because, by using this method, the yield curve itself does not need to be estimated.

Exhibit 5 shows the characteristic yield curve shifts for the first four spot rate factors in the 12-factor formulation. As the exhibit makes clear, the characteristic yield curve movements of spot rate models have a very extreme appearance. A yield change is either zero, off a given yield curve point, or 100 basis points, on the yield curve point. Yield changes are interpolated between adjacent points. In other words, if one of the bond's cash flows falls between the stipulated yield curve points, that cash flow has *some* duration with respect to both the adjacent points. Spot rate factors can be scaled, as in the example here, so that the duration of a zero-coupon bond to a given spot rate change is just equal to that bond's time to maturity.

Exhibit 6 shows durations for the first four factors in the 12-factor spot rate model. A feature of spot rate models is that because of the way the models are defined, the spot rate durations of a bond, if scaled this way, add up approximately to the ordinary duration of the bond.

A major advantage of spot rate models over principal components models is that fewer parameters are required. Where principal components models imply that spot rate changes at various maturities can combine only in the ways implied by the principal components, in spot rate models spot rate changes can combine in any way that is possible using the number of spot rates in the model. Like arbitrage models and unlike principal components models, the factors in spot rate models are not required to be orthogonal.

---

[27] For a discussion this approach as compared with the principal components approach, see Bennett W. Golub and Leo M. Tilman, "Measuring Yield Curve Risk Using Principal Components Analysis, Value at Risk and Key Rate Durations," *Journal of Portfolio Management* (Summer 1997), pp. 72 84.

Exhibit 5: Characteristic Yield Shifts: Spot Rate Model

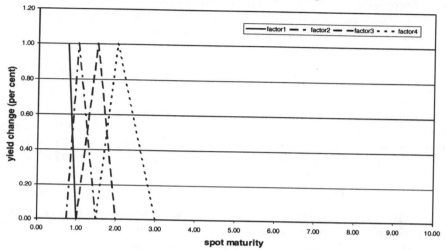

Exhibit 6: Bond Durations: Spot Rate Model

Time to Maturity	b_1	b_2	b_3	b_4
0.75	−0.75	0.00	0.00	0.00
1.00	0.00	−1.00	0.00	0.00
1.50	0.00	0.00	−1.50	0.00
2.00	0.00	0.00	0.00	−2.00
3.00	0.00	0.00	0.00	0.00
4.00	0.00	0.00	0.00	0.00
5.00	0.00	0.00	0.00	0.00
7.00	0.00	0.00	0.00	0.00
10.00	0.00	0.00	0.00	0.00
15.00	0.00	0.00	0.00	0.00
20.00	0.00	0.00	0.00	0.00
30.00	0.00	0.00	0.00	0.00

A disadvantage of the spot rate approach is the fact that the characteristic yield curve shifts in the spot rate model, as illustrated in Exhibit 3, do not correspond with yield curve movements that actually take place. Nor are the characteristic yield curve shifts defined continuously on maturity. Thus, as with principal components models, some interpolation of yield changes is required to apply the model to bonds with cash flows (or yield curve exposures) at times other than the points defined in the model.

A third disadvantage of spot rate models is the fact that a large number of factors are required to model yield curve risk accurately. To use an example, suppose that one wanted to reproduce with spot rate changes the characteristic yield curve movements of a principal components model as described in Exhibit 3. To accomplish this it would be necessary to combine 12 spot rate shifts in the appropriate proportions to recover the information in just one principal components shift. As a consequence, portfolio managers need to use a large number of durations to manage interest rate risk effectively using this approach.

FUNCTIONAL MODELS

Functional models combine the advantages of arbitrage models, continuity and consistency with equilibrium pricing, with the parsimony of principal components models. Functional models assume that zero-coupon yield changes are defined continuously in maturity, for example with a shift function $f(T)$:

$$f(T) = \Delta y(T) \tag{11}$$

where $\Delta y(T)$ is the change in the zero-coupon yield at maturity T. Then, a Taylor series or some other approximating function can be applied to the function $f(T)$, retaining the number of terms that are sufficient to describe actual yield curve movements adequately. Durations are computed from the approximating function directly. For example, the yield shift function $f(T)$ can be approximated by a Taylor series, as follows:

$$f(T) = c_0 + c_1 T + c_2 T^2 + \dots \tag{12}$$

The factors are identified with the resulting durations, which can be derived easily from equation (12).

Chambers, Carleton, and McEnally employ this idea to devolop risk measures for use in immunization and hedging, but do not explore the implications of this approach for developing term structure factor models.[28] Similarly, Nelson and Siegel use exponentials to fit yield levels at the short end of the yield curve, but do not extend their approach to the long end of the curve, except to test extrapolations of the model as fitted to Treasury bills, nor to the identification of a factor model.[29]

Kuberek uses the functionals that are proposed by Nelson and Siegel, to model the short-end of the forward rate curve, for the purpose of approximating the shift function given by equation (11) for zero-coupon yields. This three-factor model has the following form:

$$f(T) \approx c_0 + c_1 e^{-T/q} + c_2 (T/q) e^{1-T/q} \tag{13}$$

---

[28] D. R. Chambers, W. T. Carleton, and R. W. McEnally, "Immunizing Default free Bond Portfolios with a Duration Vector," *Journal of Financial and Quantitative Analysis* (1988), pp. 89-104. See also, D. R. Chambers and W. T. Carleton, "A More General Duration Approach," Unpublished Manuscript (1981).
[29] Charles R. Nelson and Andrew F. Siegel, "A Parsimonious Modeling of Yield Curves," *Journal of Business* (October 1987), pp. 473-489.

where q is a parameter.[30] The model given by equation (13) resembles equation (12) except that the second and third terms contain an exponential decay. This exponential form has the benefit that, in contrast to equation (12), changes in yield curve level and shape will not become unbounded in maturity.

With this formulation, the zero-coupon bond durations, the b's in equation (2), take the very simple form

$$b_{ij} = w_j(T_i)T_i \tag{14}$$

where

$$w_1 = -1$$
$$w_2 = -Te^{-T/q}$$
$$w_3 = -T^2/qe^{1-T/q}$$

and where the b_{ij} are the exposures of the ith zero-coupon bond to the jth factor.

Thus, the first factor in this three-factor model represents the effect of a precisely uniform change in the level of interest rates, the second factor represents the effect of a change in slope of the yield curve, and the third factor represents the effect of a change in curvature of the yield curve. Factor returns can be estimated by regressing cross-sections of zero-coupon bond returns on these durations.

Exhibit 7 shows these characteristic yield curve movements for the three-factor functional model in equation (13). In this exponential form the characteristic yield shifts represent changes in level (factor 1), slope (factor 2), and curvature (factor 3). The model is specified so that changes in slope affect short rates more than long rates. This is consistent with the behavior of the yield curve at certain times, where short rates are more volatile than long rates. To reproduce yield curve movements where long rates change by more than short rates, factors 1 and 2 can be combined. For example, an upward shift of one unit of factor 2 (100 basis points at the short end) combined with a downward shift of one unit of factor 1 (100 basis points uniformly) produces a flattening of 100 basis points at the long end, with short rates unchanged. Additional complexity in yield curve movements, including various combinations of change in slope and curvature, can be achieved by including factor 3.

The zero-coupon bond durations are given in Exhibit 8. As can be seen, the durations at various maturities with respect to the first factor are equivalent to the ordinary (effective) duration of the bonds. The durations with respect to the second factor, which represents a change in slope, increase in magnitude with maturity to seven years, then decrease. The third factor's durations increase in magnitude to 14 years, then decrease.

---

[30] The value of the single parameters q, which represents the location of the maximum in the third shift component and simultaneously determines the rate of decay in the second, can be chosen in any convenient way. Kuberek ("An Approximate Factor Model for U.S. Treasuries") uses the value of q that maximizes the ability of the three-factor model to describe a wide variety of yield curve shifts under diffuse priors.

Exhibit 7: Characteristic Yield Curve Shifts: Functional Model

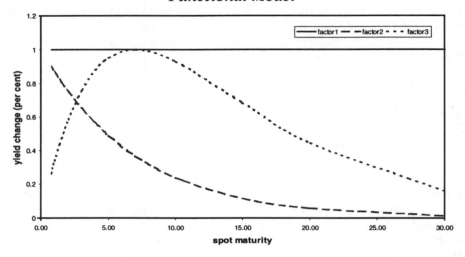

Exhibit 8: Bond Durations: Functional Model

Time to Maturity	b_1	b_2	b_3
0.75	−0.75	−0.67	−0.20
1.00	−1.00	−0.87	−0.34
1.50	−1.50	−1.21	−0.71
2.00	−2.00	−1.50	−1.17
3.00	−3.00	−1.95	−2.28
4.00	−4.00	−2.26	−3.51
5.00	−5.00	−2.45	−4.75
7.00	−7.00	−2.58	−7.00
10.00	−10.00	−2.40	−9.31
15.00	−15.00	−1.76	−10.25
20.00	−20.00	−1.15	−8.92
30.00	−30.00	−0.41	−4.81

The model described here, which is based on approximating functions, has several significant advantages. Most usefully, ordinary (effective) duration, as conventionally defined, is the first factor. Second, unlike the principal components models and spot rate models, the model is inherently consistent with rigorous equilibrium or arbitrage term structure models that imply yield changes that are continuous in maturity, including the CIR model already described. Third, it has only one parameter (and it has no more *moments* than any other three-factor model). Finally, the yield shifts implied by this model correspond with yield curve movements that portfolio managers can easily imagine occurring, namely, changes in level, slope, and curvature.

Because of the particularly simple form of equation (14), the durations of coupon bonds also have a very simple form, as follows:

$$b_j = \sum_h w_j(T_h)s_h T_h / \sum_h s_h \tag{15}$$

where s_h is the present value of the hth cash flow and where the w's are as given in equation (14). Equation (15) is simply the formula for ordinary duration, with an added weighting term $w(T)$. For the first factor, w has a value of unity for all maturities T equation (14), so the associated duration is simply the ordinary (effective) duration. More generally, bond durations in this model are calculated in the same way as ordinary (effective) duration, except that cash flows are weighted differently to reflect the differential exposure to various alternative yield curve shifts.

Like the arbitrage and spot rate models, the factors in functional models are not required to be orthogonal. However, if uncorrelatedness of factor returns is desired, the three factors in equation (14) can easily be rotated to have this property, for example, by estimating the factor returns and extracting the principal components.

CONCLUSION

Term structure factor models can be classified in one of four categories: arbitrage models, principal components models, spot rate models, and functional models. Examples of these reviewed here are the models of Cox, Ingersoll and Ross (arbitrage), Litterman and Scheinkman (principal components), J. P. Morgan's Risk-Metrics™ (spot rate), and Kuberek (functional). Each approach resembles, in some important way, one or another of the traditional types of factor models for common stocks, macroeconomic, statistical, and fundamental.

As with common stock models, the approaches to term structure factor models reviewed here differ primarily in the identification of the factors and in how the factor exposures and factor returns are measured. Arbitrage models assume some underlying set of state variables, then derive the term structure and its dynamics. Principal components models extract factor returns from the excess returns of zero-coupon bonds at specified maturities using statistical techniques. Spot rate models associate factors with yield changes at every point (of a specified set) along the yield curve, and functional models use pre-specified yield curve shifts to fit actual yield curve movements, where the shift components are motivated by equilibrium considerations.

At the extremes, the one-factor model of Cox, Ingersoll, and Ross is most rigorously consistent with equilibrium pricing, but is also the most restrictive in describing actual yield curve movements, while spot rate models are most descriptive, but have the most factors (and thus, the most durations) of any approach. Principal components and functional models find a middle ground, compromising between the structure and rigorousness of arbitrage models, with few factors, and the explanatory power of spot rate models, with many. Principal components models have the advantage that actual data guide in the identification of the factors, but suffer from the defect that the durations are sample dependent. Functional models have the advantage that the factors can be pre specified in a manner that is convenient to the portfolio manager, for example by defining the factors in such a way that ordinary duration, as conventionally defined, is the first factor.

An important common feature of the models reviewed here relates to the fact that each one associates factors with characteristic yield curve movements. Specifically, factor exposures can be estimated in these models by subjecting a bond to each of the characteristic yield shifts, using a term-structure-based valuation model, or OAS model, to see how much return results. Indeed, the application of term structure factor models crucially depends on the availability and usability of these ancillary valuation models.

The power and usefulness of term structure factor models lie in their application to risk management. Once the moments of the model are determined together with the exposures of the portfolio to each of the factors, it becomes possible to measure portfolio risk in any number of ways, including return variance, tracking error relative to a benchmark, and value-at-risk. By further assuming that the factor returns are normally distributed, it becomes possible to characterize the distribution of portfolio return fully, regardless of its composition.

Chapter 24

Measuring and Managing Interest-Rate Risk

Scott F. Richard, DBA
Partner
Miller Anderson & Sherrerd, LLP

Benjamin J. Gord
Vice President
Miller Anderson & Sherrerd, LLP

INTRODUCTION

How do we predict what will happen to the value of a client's fixed-income portfolio when interest rates change? This is one of the most important questions we have to answer in managing fixed-income assets. In this chapter we report on our research aimed at answering this question and explain how we use the results of this research in portfolio management.

If a client's portfolio contained only one bond, then the answer would be given, to a good approximation, by the bond's (modified) duration. The duration of the bond measures its percentage price change for a small change in the bond's yield. Suppose a portfolio contained only a 10-year-maturity Treasury note with a 6.5% coupon selling at par. Standard calculations indicate a duration of 7.3 years for this bond. Hence, if the 10-year note's yield rises 10 basis points, the bond's value, and the portfolio's value, will fall by approximately 73 basis points; conversely, if the 10-year note's yield declines 10 basis points, the value of the bond and the portfolio will rise by about 73 basis points.

In reality, portfolios are never so simple that they contain only one bond. The highly diversified portfolios that we manage typically contain more than 100 securities with a wide variety of maturities. Is duration a good measure of the relative interest-rate sensitivity of different portfolios? Consider another portfolio composed of 44.6% in cash, with a duration of zero years, and 55.4% in a 30-year Treasury bond with a 6.5% coupon, selling at par with a duration of 13.1 years. Standard calculations show that the portfolio has a duration of 7.3 years, which is the weighted average of zero years and 13.1 years. Usually portfolio managers

517

who use duration as a measure of interest-rate risk think of this barbell as having about the same interest-rate risk as the 10-year bullet we just discussed. But what does this duration figure mean? Presumably, it means that if yields rise by 10 basis points, the portfolio will decline in value by about 73 basis points. We must be more precise, however, about exactly what we mean by "if yields rise by 10 basis points" in order for 73 basis points to be the realized loss. In fact, both the 30-year and 10-year yields must change in the same direction and in the same amount for the price change of the bullet to equal the price change of the barbell. If both yields do not typically change in the same direction or by the same amount, then the change in the portfolio's value will be different, and duration will mismeasure the interest-rate risk of the portfolio.

Now let's extrapolate our reasoning to a portfolio containing many bonds with all maturities between cash and 30 years (or longer). Separating these bonds into their coupon and principal payments, we see that such portfolios commonly have cash flows at all points on the yield curve. Will the average duration[1] of all the bonds be an accurate measure of the portfolio's interest-rate risk? Extending our reasoning from the two bond portfolios, *we see that duration is an accurate measure of interest-rate risk for a portfolio only if all yields typically change in the same direction and by the same amount (i.e., if a typical yield-curve change is a parallel shift).*

We have now deduced that duration is an adequate measure of interest-rate risk only if parallel shifts typify changes in the yield curve. Luckily, this is an empirical issue that we test by examining yield-curve data.[2] If it is true, then we are done; if not, we must create a new measure of interest-rate risk that is consistent with the way yield curves actually reshape.

HOW DO YIELD CURVES CHANGE?

To answer this question, we examined yield data for zero-coupon Treasury bonds. We used zero-coupon bonds for two reasons. First, zero-coupon bonds are the building blocks for all coupon bonds, which can be separated into portfolios of zero-coupon bonds. Second, zero-coupon bonds give us a much richer set of bond durations to examine. The maturity of a zero-coupon bond is nearly equal to its duration, so that the duration range for zero-coupon bonds is one to 30 years. In contrast, coupon bonds have a duration range of about one to 13 years, the duration of a 30-year Treasury security.

---

[1] Actual Portfolios contain callable bonds such as mortgages and corporates. For callable bonds, when we refer to "duration," we mean the option-adjusted duration.

[2] There are solid theoretical foundations for thinking that parallel shifts are not likely. For example, if interest rates mean-revert, even very weakly, then long yields must be less volatile than short yields, which rules out a parallel shift. There is an increasing volume of empirical evidence from term-structure modeling and option pricing showing that interest rates mean-revert very slowly.

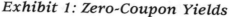

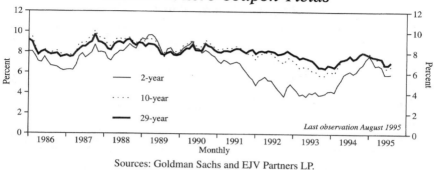

Exhibit 1: Zero-Coupon Yields

Last observation August 1995

Monthly

Sources: Goldman Sachs and EJV Partners LP.

Exhibit 1 shows monthly yield data for the 2-year, 10-year, and 29-year zero-coupon Treasury bond since 1986.[3] It appears that yields tend to change in the same direction across the yield curve, but not by the same amount. Just by looking at the data, it is difficult to identify a typical yield-curve shift, but it appears that short-term interest rates are more volatile than long-term interest rates (i.e., short-term yields have tended both to fall more and to rise more than long-term yields). In other words, the yield curve has tended to steepen during a rally and to flatten during a sell off.

Although Exhibit 1 is sufficient to confirm this general observation, we need to use statistical techniques to estimate typical yield-curve movements more precisely. In making this analysis, we examined beginning-of-month yields from October 1986 through August 1995 on zero-coupon bonds of constant maturities one through 29 years. Although these data represented 29 different yield series, the results — not surprisingly — did not suggest that there are 29 independent sources of change in the yield curve. Indeed, using principal-components analysis (discussed in the Appendix) we found that two types of systematic yield-curve reshapings explained almost 97% of the variation in interest rates. Remaining changes in yields at different maturities appear random.

We call the first type of systematic change a "yield-curve shift." This shift describes the movement in the yield curve that typically accompanies a general upward or downward movement of interest rates. Exhibits 2a and 2b show shifts for the yield curve of August 1, 1995. The yield-curve shift shown in Exhibit 2a corresponds to a bond-market decline and causes all yields to rise, but not by equal amounts; typically, short yields rise twice as much as very long yields. Exhibit 2b shows the yield-curve shift for the corresponding bond-market-rally scenario; again all yields fall, but not by equal amounts. Yield-curve shifts account for about 90% of the systematic variation in monthly yields over our sample. Each month the yield-curve shift will be slightly different because it depends on the level of yields and the shape of the yield curve.

---

[3] Our data for zero-coupon Treasury bonds begin in 1986 because that is when a 29-year-maturity noncallable zero-coupon bond was first available. We have replicated our study using coupon-bond data from 1952 through 1995 and have found nearly identical results.

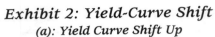

Exhibit 2: Yield-Curve Shift
(a): Yield Curve Shift Up

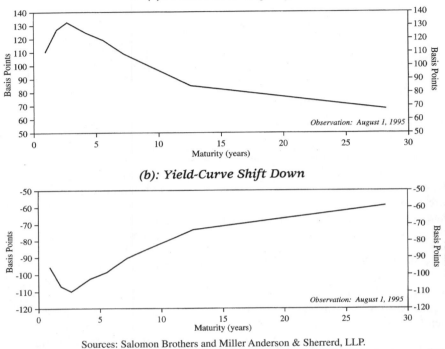

(b): Yield-Curve Shift Down

Sources: Salomon Brothers and Miller Anderson & Sherrerd, LLP.

Yield-curve shifts are not the whole story, though. There is a second systematic change, called a "yield-curve twist," as shown in Exhibits 3a and 3b for the yield curve of August 1, 1995. The yield-curve twist shown in Exhibit 3a causes yields under five years to rise and those over five years to fall. The opposite twist, shown in Exhibit 3b, causes short yields to fall and long yields to rise. Yield-curve twists account for approximately another 7% of the systematic variation in monthly yields. Yield-curve shifts and yield-curve twists are independent reshapings of the yield curve: knowledge of the direction and magnitude of a yield-curve shift is not helpful in predicting either the direction or magnitude of any simultaneous yield-curve twist.

Although yield-curve twists explain a smaller amount of systematic variation than yield-curve shifts, they are nevertheless quite important. The actual change in the yield curve during 1994 and the changes predicted by a yield-curve shift are shown in Exhibit 4. The predicted yield-curve shift shown in Exhibit 4 is calculated by observing the actual change in the yield of the 5-year zero-coupon bond and then using the statistical model to predict the change in the rest of the yield curve.[4] That is why the actual and the predicted changes exactly agree for a 5-year bond. The yield-curve shift captures most of what happened in 1994.

---

[4] Exhibit 4 shows the concentration of monthly changes for 1994.

Exhibit 3: Yield-Curve Twist
(a): Flattening Yield Curve

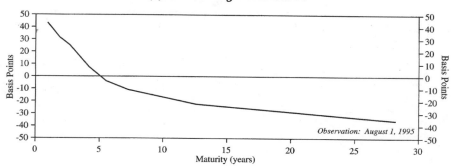

(b): Steepening Yield-Curve Twist

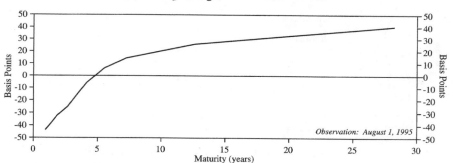

Sources: Salomon Brothers and Miller Anderson & Sherrerd, LLP.

Exhibit 4: Yield-Curve Shift in 1994

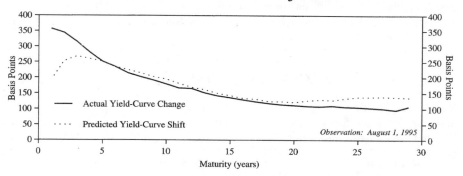

Sources: EJV Partners LP and Miller Anderson & Sherrerd, LLP.

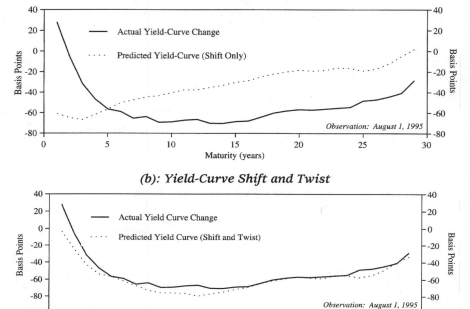

Exhibit 5: Yield Curve Changes in 1995
(a): Yield-Curve Shift

(b): Yield-Curve Shift and Twist

Sources: EJV Partners LP and Miller Anderson & Sherrerd, LLP.

For 1995, however, the yield-curve twist is vital in explaining changes in yields. Exhibit 5a shows the changes in actual yields from year-end 1994 to August 1, 1995, and the effect of a yield-curve shift. We can see that something besides a yield-curve shift has been important in 1995. In Exhibit 5b we added the appropriate yield-curve twist for 1995 to show that together the shift and twist capture the dynamics for the year.[5]

MANAGING INTEREST-RATE RISK

Recall that duration is a good measure of interest-rate risk only if a parallel shift is the predominant form of yield-curve change. Examining Exhibits 2a and 2b, we see that we can rule out a parallel shift as the usual yield-curve change. Rather,

---

[5] To calculate the effect of a yield-curve twist, we first observe the actual change in the yield of 5-year zero-coupon bonds and use the statistical model to predict a yield-curve shift. Next, we observe the part of the change in the yield of a 20-year zero-coupon bond that is not explained by the yield-curve shift and use the statistical model to predict the yield-curve twist. This is why the actual and the predicted changes exactly agree for both a 5-year bond and a 20-year bond.

we see that short yields usually move more than long yields; duration is therefore not an accurate measure of interest-rate risk for a diversified portfolio.

We have replaced duration with *interest-rate sensitivity* (IRS) as our standard measure of portfolio interest-rate risk. Duration measures a portfolio's percentage price change in response to a parallel shift in the yield curve. IRS measures a portfolio's percentage price change in response to a yield-curve shift. The unit of both measures is years. Exhibit 6 shows the relationship between duration and IRS as of August 1, 1995. IRS is measured relative to the yield change in a benchmark zero-coupon bond. We typically choose the 5-year zero-coupon bond as the benchmark because its interest-rate risk is closest to the inter-est-rate risk in the broad market indices, such as the Lehman Brothers Aggregate Index and the Salomon Brothers Broad Index. In constructing Exhibit 6, we used the 5-year zero-coupon bond as our benchmark security, so its duration and IRS are equal. The IRS of a lower-duration bond (e.g., the 2-year zero-coupon bond) is usually slightly higher than its duration, while a large-duration bond (e.g., the 25-year zero-coupon bond) has an IRS substantially lower than its duration.

The importance of using IRS instead of duration can be demonstrated by running an experiment that compares the performance of two portfolios, one man-aged with duration and one with IRS. Suppose a portfolio manager thought, in Sep-tember 1992, that long yields were too high and likely to decline and that the yield curve was too steep and likely to flatten.[6] Hence, the manager thought that the rewards for bearing interest-rate risk and yield-curve risk were unusually high. To profit from the view that the bond market would rally, the manager wanted a portfo-lio with longer duration than the index's, and to profit from the view that the yield curve would flatten, he wanted a barbell portfolio. The manager recommended a portfolio composed of cash and long-maturity zero-coupon Treasury bonds with 50% more interest-rate risk than that of the broad market index. The question he had to answer was how many long zero-coupon bonds to buy. The table below shows the calculations for constructing the portfolio using duration and IRS.

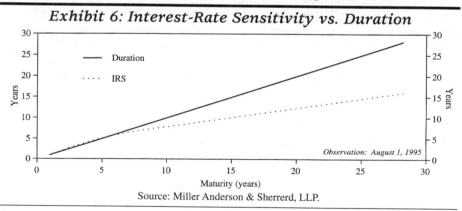

Exhibit 6: Interest-Rate Sensitivity vs. Duration

Maturity (years)

Source: Miller Anderson & Sherrerd, LLP.

---

[6] This is an unusual situation. Typically a downward yield-curve shift produces a steepening yield curve (i.e., yield curves typically steepen in a rally.)

	Duration Management	IRS Management
Index	4.5 years	4.6 years
Target	6.75 years	6.9 years
30-Year Zero-Coupon Treasury Bond	29.0 years	17.8 years
Fraction of Portfolio in Zero Coupons	23.3%	38.8%
Fraction of Portfolio in Cash	76.7%	61.2%

The subsequent bond-market rally would have resulted in some disappointment for an investor using duration, but not for someone using IRS. From September 30, 1992, to September 30, 1993, the yield curve rallied strongly and flattened as shown in Exhibit 7. Over this 12-month period, cash (1-month CDs) returned 3.3%, and 30-year zero-coupon Treasury bonds returned 56.0%. The portfolio constructed using duration returned 15.6%, which is only 30 basis points better than the 15.3% return on the equal-duration bullet portfolio composed of the 7-year zero-coupon Treasury bond. There was very little extra return from the equal-duration barbell portfolio over that of the bullet portfolio, despite a substantial flattening of the yield curve. In contrast, the portfolio constructed with use of IRS has a return of 23.7%, which is 840 basis points above that of the equivalent-IRS 7-year zero-coupon Treasury bond.

Since 1993, we have used IRS rather than duration as our primary measure of interest-rate risk. Over this period, the risk of our core portfolios relative to a broad market index differs significantly when calculated using the two risk measures. In Exhibit 8, we show the duration of our core fixed-income portfolios in comparison with that of the Salomon Brothers Broad Index.

If duration is used as a measure of interest-rate risk, it appears that we were longer than the index until March 1995, significantly so throughout most of 1993. However, in 1993, our portfolios were barbelled, using long-maturity zero-coupon Treasury bonds as part of the barbell, and the distinction between IRS and duration was vital, as can be seen in Exhibit 9. This exhibit compares the IRS of our core fixed-income portfolios with the IRS of the Salomon Brothers Broad Index.

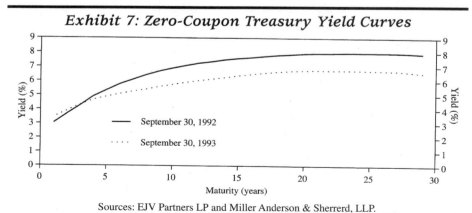

Exhibit 7: Zero-Coupon Treasury Yield Curves

——— September 30, 1992

····· September 30, 1993

Maturity (years)

Sources: EJV Partners LP and Miller Anderson & Sherrerd, LLP.

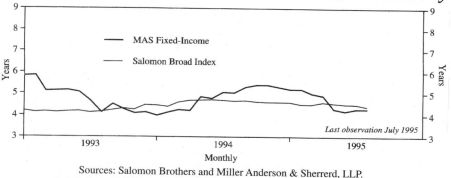

Exhibit 8: MAS Core Fixed-Income Duration

MAS Fixed-Income

Salomon Broad Index

Last observation July 1995

1993   1994   1995

Monthly

Sources: Salomon Brothers and Miller Anderson & Sherrerd, LLP.

Exhibit 9: MAS Core Fixed-Income Interest-Rate Sensitivity

MAS Fixed-Income

Salomon Broad Index

Last observation July 1995

1993   1994   1995

Monthly

Sources: Salomon Brothers and Miller Anderson & Sherrerd, LLP.

In our core portfolios, interest-rate risk as measured by IRS has varied much less than interest-rate risk as measured by duration. In fact, for 1993, 1994, and 1995, we have been alternately longer or shorter than the index rather than uniformly longer. The distinction between the two measures is important — not only as an internal tool for better managing assets, but also as a means of communicating our decisions to our clients. Solely on the basis of the duration of our core fixed-income portfolios, one would probably conclude that we have been bullish since the middle of 1993; on the basis of IRS, one can see that we have been alternately slightly bullish and slightly bearish.

Although IRS is a useful tool for portfolio management, its successful use requires a mixture of technical skill and judgment. Technically, using IRS requires a daily updating of our proprietary empirical model because IRS measures are sensitive to both the level of yields and the shape of the yield curve. Furthermore, the internal analytical models we use to evaluate callable securities, such as mortgages, are consistent with IRS in that the typical changes in the yield curve are very similar to empirical yield-curve shifts and yield-curve twists. This internal consistency is very important in managing a highly diversified portfolio of mortgage, corporate, and Treasury securities.

IRS is not a substitute for the critical judgments of our interest-rate team, which seeks to add value by deciding how much interest-rate risk and yield-curve risk we should bear. Our interest-rate team still must form a judgment about the likely direction of a yield-curve change. The team's view is then implemented with our IRS model rather than duration to ensure that our portfolios have the proper amount of interest-rate and yield-curve risk relative to their benchmark indices.

APPENDIX

In this appendix, we give a brief description of the statistical analysis through which we found the systematic yield-curve changes. The first step in our analysis is to adjust the data so that percent yield changes are of similar volatility over time.[7] This adjustment is required so that the data from periods of predictably high volatility do not swamp the statistical analysis. In Exhibit A-1, we have plotted the volatility of percent yield changes for 2-year, 10-year and 29-year zero-coupon bonds. We see that yield volatility generally declines with maturity. In other words, the volatility of zero-coupon yields typically falls as maturity lengthens.

We can also see from Exhibit A-1 that there is reason to believe that yield volatility is not constant over time. A comparison of Exhibit 1 and Exhibit A-1 suggests that yield volatility is related to yield levels. For example, for short-maturity zero-coupon bonds volatility tends to be high when rates are low and vice versa. Conversely, at long maturities we find the opposite effect: Volatility tends to be high when rates are high. The adjustment we make uses the beginning-of-month yield to help explain subsequent volatility. This adjustment is most important for shorter-maturity yields, especially those under five years. For example, Exhibit A-2 shows the effect of this adjustment on 2-year zero-coupon yield volatility. Having adjusted the data for changing volatility over time, we are now ready to perform our statistical analysis.

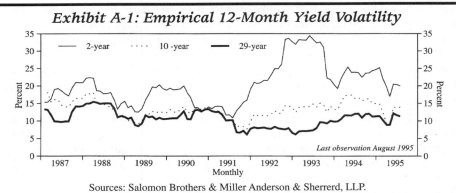

Exhibit A-1: Empirical 12-Month Yield Volatility

Sources: Salomon Brothers & Miller Anderson & Sherrerd, LLP.

[7] Technically, we use the changes in the natural logarithms of the yields.

Exhibit A-2: Two-Year Yield Volatility

Sources: Salomon Brothers & Miller Anderson & Sherrerd, LLP.

The question we want to answer is how the yield curve is ordinarily reshaped. We answer this question by using a statistical technique called principal-components analysis. Principal-components analysis allows us to identify and to simplify the joint movement (or covariation) of many data series. Our complete data series are the beginning-of-month yields from October 1986 through August 1995 on zero-coupon bonds of constant maturities one through 29 years. We performed principal-components analysis on the correlation matrix of the volatility-adjusted series of monthly yield-curve changes. As we reported in the text, we found two statistically significant principal components, which taken together explain 97% of the correlation in our monthly yield series. We also analyzed the covariance matrix of the volatility-adjusted series of monthly yield-curve changes, with very similar results.[8]

---

[8] The original study of systematic risks in the yield curve is Robert Litterman and José Scheinkman, "Common Factors Affecting Bond Returns," *Journal of Fixed Income* (June 1991). Our findings differ in two ways. First, they report that there are three systematic risks affecting yield-curve changes, while we found only two that are statistically significant. More important, their yield-curve shift is nearly a parallel shift. There are two reasons our results differ from theirs. First, we adjusted our data for the change in yield volatility associated with changes in yield levels. Second, we used more data from a longer time period. When we restrict our study to their time period (1984-1989) and do not adjust for yield levels, we closely replicate their results. As we mention in footnote 2, we have replicated our study using coupon-bond data from 1952 through 1995 with results nearly identical to our original ones. We conclude that the parallel yield shift found in data from 1984 through 1989 was an anomaly.

Chapter 25

Fixed Income Portfolio Investing: The Art of Decision Making

Chris P. Dialynas
Former Managing Director — Portfolio Management
Pacific Investment Management Company

Ellen Rachlin
Co-Head IBJI Agent Department
Aubrey G. Lanston & Co. Inc.

INTRODUCTION

Investing in today's worldwide open financial markets is a most complex task. The investor must develop a multitude of forecasts and utilize these forecasts in a variety of ways throughout the investment process. We will elaborate on the process and, occasionally, demonstrate the practical importance of some of the subtle subforecasts. We will show how inferences about a particular bond will effectively convey the important attributes of a forecast, as well as the clarity or confidence in the forecast. Ultimately, it is the quality of the macroeconomic analysis, integrated with the quantification of the asset universe that will yield a rewarding experience.

A bond portfolio manager's task is to predict the optimal combination of fixed income securities to hold in the portfolio that will allow him to outperform the market index and compare favorably in performance terms against his competitors. The bond portfolio manager selects, in his judgment, the optimal combination of securities from the pool of possible choices within his investment set, i.e., a mortgage fund manger will choose among various mortgage-backed securities and cash to hold in his portfolio. The bond portfolio manager must first assess the economy and the market environment. Based on this assessment, the portfolio manager then predicts levels of interest rates and determines the performance characteristics, in totality and in context, of his investment portfolio. The professional skills required of a bond portfolio manager are complex and challenging. The bond portfolio manager ultimately utilizes his skills to create a portfolio comprised of bonds representative of the set of interest rate forecasts in which he believes.

The main attributes of a bond portfolio include: (1) duration, (2) cash flow distribution on the yield curve, (3) convexity, (4) credit quality, and (5) non-dollar

The authors would like to thank John Brynjolfsson (PIMCO) and Stephen Hannah (IBJ International plc) for their technical and quantitative assistance.

bond and currency exposure. Each selected attribute is the result of multiple and complex evaluation techniques. And, the overall risk of the portfolio can be derived through a variety of nominalization techniques. Alternatively, a skilled practitioner should be able to examine a bond portfolio and derive the portfolio's embedded forecasts for: (1) interest rates, (2) volatility, (3) changes in yield curve shape, (4) inter-market spreads, and (5) intra-market spreads and relative currency values.

The creation of an interest rate forecast, which is the overall backdrop for the bond portfolio's construction, in and of itself requires a portfolio manager to call upon his knowledge of economics, politics, history, psychology, and statistics, in addition to other disciplines. A reliable interest rate forecast and an understanding of the differences between that forecast and the forecast of the market are critical to professional bond portfolio management. The portfolio manager must compare his interest rate forecast to the forward market prices and seek investment opportunities wherever his forecast deviates from market expectations. Therefore, it is insufficient to merely implement an externally developed forecast. The portfolio manager must have an in-depth knowledge of the assumptions inherent to the forecast, understand the subsector economic analysis, such as housing, auto sales, etc., and understand the marketplace for which he intends to apply his forecast.

It is a miscalculation to assume that a good economic forecast alone allows the portfolio manager to construct a high performing portfolio. Economic forecasts are merely an intermediate step in the portfolio manager's effort to devise an interest rate forecast. Economic forecasts are generally described in terms of real GDP, GDP deflators (inflation rates), unemployment rates and, occasionally, productivity changes. Wall Street economists provide important general conclusions to their economic forecasts such as near-term and long-term Fed funds rate and a 30-year Treasury rate that they believe are consistent with their overall economic forecasts. Additionally, Wall Street economists will provide the intermediate forecasts of forthcoming government economic statistics a week or two prior to release. While these projections may be valuable to traders, these projections are not of much value to the portfolio manager beyond their aggregate temporal validation or repudiation of portfolio manager's own forecast. The portfolio manager must thoroughly consider all important assumptions and components of his interest rate forecast, assigning a measure of confidence to his forecast. Moreover, he must consider for all possible outcomes and plan a strategy for the eventuality on the portfolio valuations, particularly should his critical assumptions prove incorrect.

This is illustrated in Exhibit 1. The exhibit shows the volume and the complexity of the information with which portfolio managers are bombarded. All this information must be considered for the construction of a high-performing bond portfolio. Within each graphic is a comment about the importance to a portfolio manager of the micro-elements of each macro-factor category. The micro-elements signal secular direction and potential macro-policy changes. The portfolio manager must decide whether the micro-element information is merely cyclical or whether it signals the beginning of a long-term trend. To do so, he must look for clues in the numbers and discern seminal changes well before they are upon him. The task seems utterly impossible. However, as decisions crystallize, the portfolio will take shape, reflecting those decisions.

Exhibit 1: The Open System: Global Policies and Free Market Prices

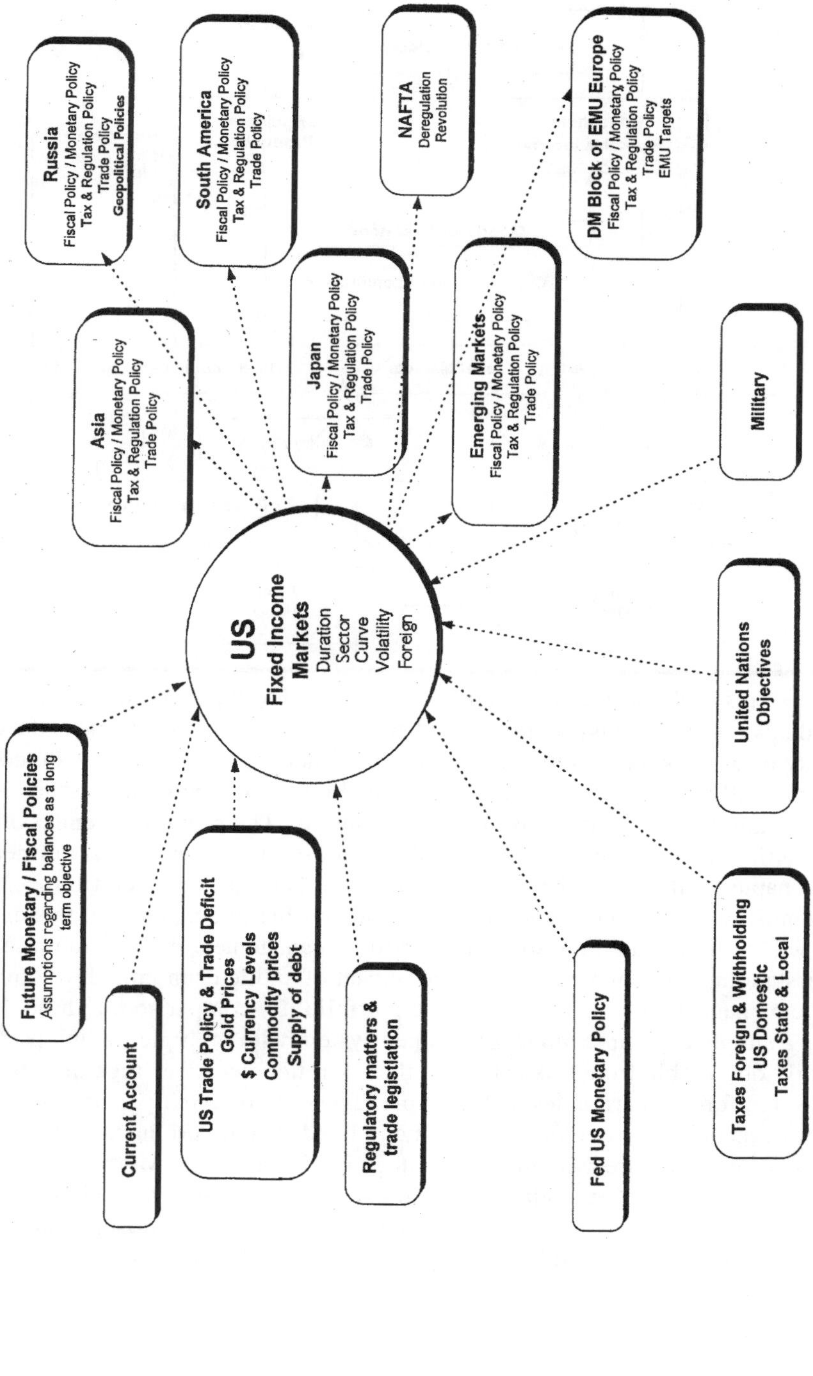

Russia
Fiscal Policy / Monetary Policy
Tax & Regulation Policy
Trade Policy
Geopolitical Policies

South America
Fiscal Policy / Monetary Policy
Tax & Regulation Policy
Trade Policy

NAFTA
Deregulation
Revolution

DM Block or EMU Europe
Fiscal Policy / Monetary Policy
Tax & Regulation Policy
Trade Policy
EMU Targets

Asia
Fiscal Policy / Monetary Policy
Tax & Regulation Policy
Trade Policy

Japan
Fiscal Policy / Monetary Policy
Tax & Regulation Policy
Trade Policy

Emerging Markets
Fiscal Policy / Monetary Policy
Tax & Regulation Policy
Trade Policy

US
Fixed Income Markets
Duration
Sector
Curve
Volatility
Foreign

Military

United Nations
Objectives

Future Monetary / Fiscal Policies
Assumptions regarding balances as a long term objective

Current Account

US Trade Policy & Trade Deficit
Gold Prices
$ Currency Levels
Commodity prices
Supply of debt

Regulatory matters & trade legislation

Fed US Monetary Policy

Taxes Foreign & Withholding
US Domestic
Taxes State & Local

Design: Marie Sacheli

Exhibit 2: Closed Economy: Macroeconomic Issues

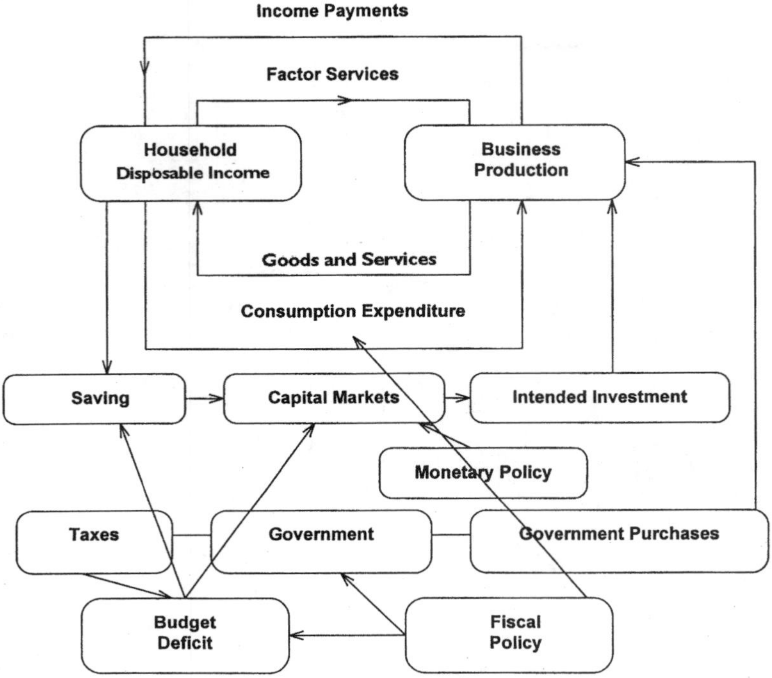

In simpler terms, although hardly simple, Exhibit 2 outlines some of the broad macroeconomic issues in a closed economy. The exhibit illustrates the complexity of the linkages among policy variables, markets, and economic outcomes. Exhibit 3 illustrates the complexities of monetary macroeconomic issues while only tangentially providing for an open economy. The graphics themselves are substantial and complex, let alone understanding the interrelations delineated. This chapter will present the practical transition that must be made from political economist to portfolio manager. For practical considerations, most of this discussion will be limited to domestic bond portfolio management in order to present an understanding and appreciation for the impact of subtle economic developments on the management of any fixed income portfolio. By comparison, Exhibit 4 provides a simple economic model of an open system with multiple trading partners. Readily observable from this exhibit is the point that decisions regarding foreign bonds and foreign currencies add multiple layers of complexity, particularly in a portfolio management context where many fixed income products (futures, forwards, swaps, etc.) are available for strategy implementation. Moreover, on some level, decisions must be made and constraints developed that relate international exposure to ultimate asset purpose. That important topic is philosophical as well as social and economic and is well beyond the scope of this chapter.

Exhibit 3: The Fed's "Big Six" Tools

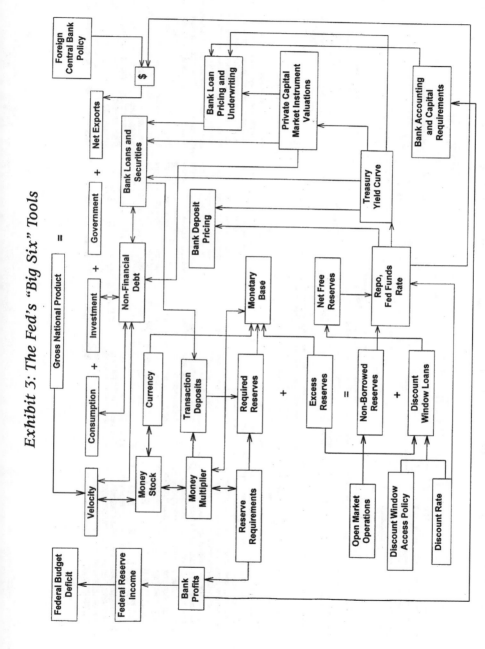

Exhibit 4: Global Bond Markets (Evaluating Impact of Global Monetary and Fiscal Policies

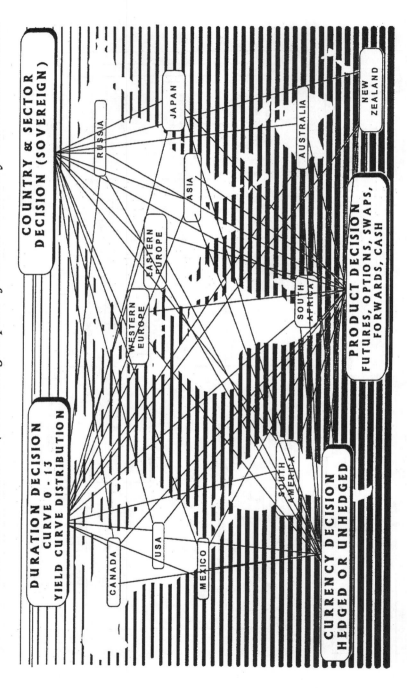

Design: Marie Sacheli

There are some practitioners who would argue that based upon the complexities of economic models and the volume of macro-information available, there is a strong case for technical analysis of the bond market. They argue that this information, and its potential unreliability, is noise and that all important information can be gleaned from security prices and patterns of prices. To technical practitioners, the prices themselves are the important clues to the future, so they apply technical analysis of market price levels of the various sectors of the market, from corporate spreads to foreign currencies, to structure a portfolio. We will not elaborate on this further other than to emphasize that the practice is prevalent and it is always useful to try to understand what other portfolio managers are doing and how their methods may impact the market.

THE CHALLENGE

The bond portfolio manager is generally posed with the challenge of outperforming a widely-recognized, well-defined bogey. He is provided with a clear set of investment guidelines from which his investment pool of securities is derived. The guidelines should allow for a set of investment choices that is at least as great as the pre-ordained composition of the bogey and, preferably, substantially greater. The performance measurement period should be well-defined and there should be a commitment to the manager for a meaningful period of time such that a set of strategies can be implemented and the intended results achieved. The challenge is thus defined.

PORTFOLIO PARAMETERS

Ultimately, the portfolio manager must make investment decisions. In practice, this means buying and selling bonds and bond surrogates to create a meaningful portfolio based on selected parameters. Among the most important parameters are the portfolio's duration, expected cash flow distribution (yield curve exposure), convexity, and sector allocation. These parameters may be unique or so interrelated that the purity of their meanings may become obscured. Nevertheless, the portfolio's definition is discerned by its parameters. (In the abstract, however, a meaningful portfolio could be achieved, perhaps more efficiently, by merely placing allocations among the various market indices.)

For example, the duration of a portfolio is the most potent source of forecast expression. Assuming a market-type bogey, extreme duration choices relative to the bogey represent expressions of the expectation for substantially higher or substantially lower interest rates. Implicit within an extreme duration-choice forecast is the expression of expectations for substantial volatility in interest rates.

Exhibit 5: Confidence Distributioins

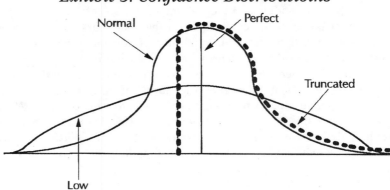

Low — Low Confidence
Normal — Moderate Confidence
Perfect, Truncated — High Confidence

FORECAST CONFIDENCE AND RELATIVE RISK

One of the most important assessments that a portfolio manager must make is the degree of confidence he has in each part of his forecast. Forecast conviction also plays an important role in model usage. Highly confident forecasts may enable the portfolio manager to alter the model or the output of the model to reflect a "biased" distribution of outcomes. In essence, the manager is affecting the quantitative outcome in a way that is consistent with the qualitative forecast. Of course, the objective "fair value" determination will be distorted. We previously elaborated upon the various forms of analysis that lead to the forecast. A strong conviction, high confidence forecast may result when the secular forecast is consistent with the cyclical forecast and both of those forecasts are consistent with the technical analysis. A weak conviction forecast may result when the conclusions the portfolio manager reaches are tentative, such as when a major institutional change has a reasonable probability of not only ocurring, but altering the investment lanscape, such as a close presidential election among extreme candidates. The forecast confidence is important because of its influence on the strength of the statement within the portfolio with respect to the portfolio parameters and character. Exhibit 5 illustrates the generalized statistical implication of forecast confidence.

A meticulous consideration of confidence levels may also help resolve potential portfolio contradictions. For example, a highly confident bullish interest rate forecast in conjunction with a low confidence yield curve steeping forecast will lead the portfolio manager to opt for high duration and essentially exclude yield curve considerations.

We will provide a few more examples to illustrate the role of forecast confidence in bond management. However, in the abstract, differences in forecast confidence translates into the following general portfolio management strategies:

(1) Low confidence – insure

(2) Moderate confidence – self-insure

(3) High confidence – employ leverage, sell insurance

Practically speaking, the low confidence forecast would be insured via the strategic purchase of put options or by selling or buying assets in the portfolio to reduce the risk of the portfolio by moving closer to the bogey. Each strategy will render a different set of expected payoffs. The moderate confidence forecast normally results in a self-insure strategy with bets consistent with the forecast. The high confidence forecast translates into making extreme, leveraged bets consistent with the manager's forecast. For example, in this latter case, the sale of put options on long bonds would reflect a highly confident forecast for lower yields on long bonds.

Examine a bond with the following characteristics: 30-year, non-callable, putable at par in five years to understand how it may be used in two cases: the high confident forecast and the weak confident forecast. In both instances, assume that the volatility embedded within the bond's put option is lower than the volatility of conventional put options in the market.

If a portfolio manager with a low-duration, 2.5-year assignment is highly confident that interest rates will drop, then he will seek ways to increase the portfolio sensitivity to his forecast without dramatically increasing the risk. He may decide to use the hypothetical put bond. The bond provides for the upside of a 30-year bond if he is correct and the downside of a 5-year bond if he is not correct. In effect, he is long a 5-year bond with a call option on a 25-year bond and therefore, has effectively increased his portfolio duration at the expense of yield, the alternative strategy.

Assume another portfolio manager holds a low confidence forecast for declining rates. He has a general market duration assignment. He decides to sacrifice yield to buy the insurance inherent in the put provision of the bond. He views his situation as being long a 30-year bond with the right to put the last 25 years back to the issuer. In this way he has decreased the "expected" cost to the portfolio of being wrong.

A much more powerful example of the importance of understanding forecast confidence to portfolio construction can be gleaned from an example involving the selection of foreign bonds. Let's assume two portfolio managers hold a very strong conviction that interest rates in Europe will decline. One of the managers believes European Monetary Union is a sure bet while the other manager believes there is no way that European Monetary Union will occur. These beliefs may be expressed in a portfolio as follows:

	High Confidence		Low Confidence	
	Integration	No Integration	Integration	No Integration
Bond Choice	Italian Government	German Government	German Government	German Government
Currency Choice	Lira	DM	DM	DM

REGULATORY CHANGES, DEMOGRAPHIC TRENDS AND INSTITUTIONAL BIAS

There are many important factors that are external to the economic system that may critically affect a bond portfolio's performance. These factors to varying degrees are difficult to anticipate. Topics such as demographics, mutual fund growth, and the multi-year plan for European integration are trending factors whose dynamics and influence may be discerned. However, sudden, meaningful changes — such as tax policy, pension plan allocation rules, investment guidelines, benefit payout rules, supply of bonds issued, types of bonds issued, Federal Reserve policy, and the implementation of credit controls among other issues — are more problematic to contemplate and incorporate. One step further are some abrupt aspects of life such as the outbreak of unanticipated wars or the formation of important economic cartels that are impossible to predict. All of these factors could induce dramatic changes in the following items: (1) direction of interest rates, (2) inter-market yield spreads, (3) shape of the yield curve, (4) volatility of the market and the pricing of expected volatility, (5) exchange rate values, (6) intra-country yield spread as well as other important financial valuations.

INFORMATION IN THE MARKETS

After considering big picture issues of regulations, demographics, and institutional trends, the portfolio manager then forms an opinion about the more cyclical aspects of current macroeconomic fiscal and monetary policies. The portfolio manager then examines the market for information. There are at least two types of information he will seek.

The first set, economic statistics, is readily available in a readable format. Some important economic indicators are contained in Exhibit 6. This information is used in a historical business-cycle context to examine the present state of the economy and to derive inferences regarding the future. Pieces of economic statistical data are used to validate or repudiate a particular forecast or portfolio theme.

Exhibit 6: Economic Indicators

Average Hourly Earnings	Factory Orders	Payroll Employment (Thous)
Capacity Utilization	Federal Reserve Beige Book	Personal Consumption
Chain-Weighted Deflator	Housing Starts (SAAR, Mils)	Personal Income
Consumer Confidence — Conf. Board	Industrial Production	PPI
Consumer Confidence — Univ. of Mich.	International Trade Balance (Bil $)	Productivity
Current Account Balance	Johnson Red Book Survey	Real GDP
CPI	Journal of Commerce Index	Retail Sales
CRB Index	Money Supply	S&P 500 Index
Durable Goods Orders	NAPM Diffusion Inddex (%)	Unemployment Rate (%)
Employment Cost Index	New Home Sales (SAAR, Thous)	Unit Labor Costs
Existing Home Sales (SAAR, Mils)	Nominal GDP, SAAR	

The second set of important information resides in the marketplace itself. This information is generally available in price form and its meaning or importance must be derived. Implied forward government rates which describe the inferences that may be derived from current prices are examples of this market information. The inferences result from inputting the market prices into complex computer valuation models (most of which are option pricing/contingent state models). For bond managers, the yield curve, money market rates and repo rates, public and OTC options markets, futures markets, forward markets, yield spread markets, currency markets, international bond markets, among others, are rich sources of information. Obviously, to the extent models differ or other subjective inputs to the model differ, the inferences will differ. Today, too many practitioners rely on institutional models provided by external vendors. The vendors are reputable, but the portfolio manager has little knowledge of the theoretical foundations of the models provided. If institutional models are employed, the portfolio manager must be familiar with the theoretical foundation of the model and cognizant of any biases produced by the model or its inputs.

The importance of inferential market information cannot be overemphasized. This information provides the basis for the performance expectation during a specified period or base case returns for bonds. Therefore it provides a benchmark from which the portfolio manager's forecast may be expressed. Consider the following scenario which is exaggerated for illustrative purposes.

Assume a portfolio manager is bearish on short-term interest rates. He expects a 25 basis point increase in Fed funds and his most bearish case is for a 75 basis point increase in Fed funds. He has a very strong conviction that interest rates will subsequently fall. He has a bogey reflective of 2-year Treasury notes. Based upon his forecast, he decides to reduce his duration by selling part of his 2-year securities position in the portfolio. Upon further reflection, he decides to consult with the market. He learns that the yield curve shape is reflective of a 150 basis point increase in short rates and the futures contracts for Fed funds has a similar increase priced in for short rates. Paradoxically, although his expectations for interest rates are bearish, compared to the market's expectations his expectations are actually bullish. He decides that selling may not be a good idea and reflects further about the possibility of actually buying.

Discrepancies in inferential information gleaned from different markets regarding the same variable can be very profitable. Sometimes these discrepancies provide a clue to a portfolio manager about a systematic mispricing in a particular market. Unfortunately, most frequently, the discrepant information is a clue that the models are misformulated and that some other variables, such as tax treatment, liquidity differences, or carry costs, are not being accounted for properly. Other times, the dynamics among the variables are not properly modeled or, perhaps, the dynamics inexplicably change over time. The point, of course, is that while market information is a rich input into evaluating bonds, the limitations of modeling reinforce the need for the portfolio manager to understand all parts of the process, including model development, and to think carefully about the meaning of the information considered. Uncertain truths are commonplace in the profession.

DURATION AND YIELD CURVE

The very extreme case of two assets, cash and 30-year Treasury bonds, provides an example of the clean, unambiguous meaning of duration. Over the short-term in this portfolio, the vast majority of return performance is determined by the change in long Treasury rates and the percentage of the portfolio allocated to the long Treasury. The yield history of 30-year Treasury bonds from 1985 through 1996 is indicative of the potential impact of good duration management on total return. There are numerous significant changes in yield direction within the context of a period of a very significant reduction in the yield of long-term Treasury bonds.

Ambiguities regarding intent and meaning increase with the number of investment choices. For example, merely adding a zero-coupon bond whose duration is similar to that of the long bond complicates the decision process. The zero-coupon bond, although similar in duration to the 30-year Treasury, has a unique set of performance characteristics: such as yield curve shape changes, volatility changes, as well as experiences duration decay with respect to time. It is unlikely, although possible, for a cross current of portfolio themes to prevail in this example. As the investment alternatives increase, the cross currents of decision making increase at a substantially greater rate, complicating the decision-making process. In Exhibit 7, the ambiguities of these choices and their impacts are noted by the double arrows ($\leftrightarrow$), indicating feedback effects. The exhibit attempts to include all of the possible investment choices available to the fixed income portfolio manager and to illustrate the volume of decisions that are constantly required to manage a portfolio.

Forward curves (future yield curves predicted by current interest rates) are rarely, if ever, realized. The management of yield curve shape changes by capitalizing on any disagreements is a portfolio manager's potent source of superior return. Historically, short-term interest rates have been more volatile than long-term interest rates. An implication of these differentials on historical volatility is that yield curve shapes are unstable. In fact, during the past 15 years there have been numerous large swings in the shape of the yield curve. Beyond, offering a rich arena of yield curve management, shape changes exert significant influences on inter-market bond spreads. It is easy to imagine a number of potentially conflicting strategies arising from a given forecast of particular interest rates during a particular period. It is through changes such as those associated with the yield curve coupled with a comprehensive understanding of the various classes of bonds that enable the construction of a portfolio consistent with a manager's forecasts and convictions. Exhibit 8 is a partial representation of sets of bonds and the influences that cause their prices to change, the logical investment strategy per bond type from a given economic and price environment.

Exhibit 7: Guide to Bond Portfolio Management

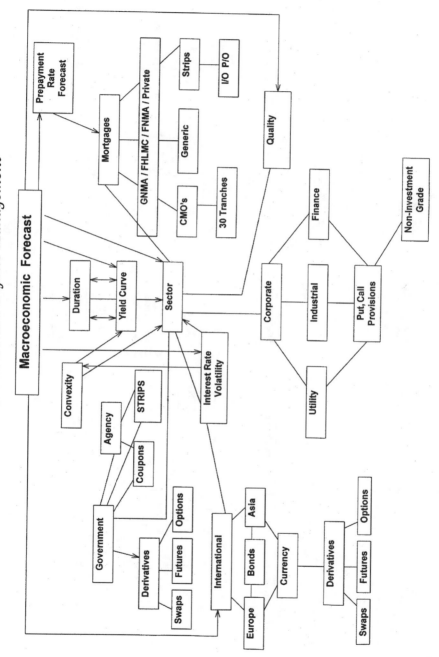

Exhibit 7 (Continued)

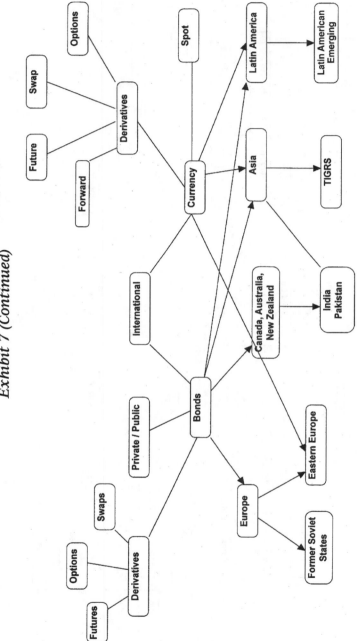

VOLATILITY

If a high degree of volatility is a natural implication of our interest rate forecast, then, the drift component specification and the assumptions for the correlation of volatility along the yield curve are important theoretical issues for quantitative analysis. (Inferences about volatility are difficult and model-dependent.) Practically speaking, however, a forecast for a substantial drop in rates implies change and change can be measured as a volatility factor. Once again, forecasted volatility may be derived from a model. The forecasted volatility expectation can then be compared to the market's pricing — that is the market's expectation for volatility. The decision to buy or sell volatility in the portfolio is the result of this comparison. Simply stated, if forecasted volatility exceeds (is less than) market volatility then the manager should employ strategies that buy (sell) volatility.

Volatility itself is an important characteristic that must be accounted for and traded by the portfolio manager in the following contexts. First is the option hedging of positions. As volatility increases, the value of a given option will increase. Therefore, the popular strategy of covered writes, where an investor shorts an option against an underlying cash position to gain extra income for the portfolio actually becomes a costly bet when volatility increases. The second context involves securities with embedded options. If the portfolio manager holds putable bonds as volatility increases, the value of the embedded option to put the bond to the issuer increases in value as volatility increases. If the portfolio manager is long a callable security, the issuer has the right to call the bond at a particular price. The value of this bond will decrease as volatility increases. The third context involves credit spread trading. As volatility increases, the price of "spread products" such as corporates or mortgages will decrease in value as the market will assign a greater value to more liquid securities. The last context involves trading implied volatility. A portfolio manager will assess the implied volatility in the market along the yield curve and may buy or sell different volatilities along the yield curve depending on his relative assessment of the market's valuation for these implied volatilities.

Interest rate volatility is usually the result of a reversal of a policy that has been maintained so long that adverse side effects develop. For example, initially, a generous monetary policy should reduce interest rates and promote growth but will ultimately hinder growth as factor prices increase. A reversal of monetary policy to a "tight" mode raises interest rates and slows economic growth. Dramatic changes in fiscal and tax policies also induce volatility into the bond market. The volatility characteristic of the portfolio is a very important decision. The expectation for a particular volatility factor is an input to the valuation of most bonds in the market. Forecasts for high volatility relative to the market normally imply that the embedded options in bonds, which investors are usually short, are of greater value thereby rendering the bonds less valuable. Mortgage securities and corporate bonds generally contain embedded options and are, as a class, substantially affected by volatility forecasts. In today's market, within all sectors, there are bonds that perform well for a particular volatility forecast. One word of warning, it is usually difficult to separate and differentiate between the liquidity influence and the quality influence on intermarket spread changes coincident with volatility changes.

Exhibit 8 provides a guide for strategy selection based on volatility, yield curve change, and economic forecasts. Details are provided for each sector of the bond market.

In addition to product-related volatility which has dominated our discussion so far, let's introduce financial volatility and the macroeconomic effects of prolonged periods of either high or low volatility. Then, let's consider how that may feed back into the portfolio manager's forecasts for interest rates. In general, sustained levels of high volatility will retard economic growth and sustained levels of low volatility will promote economic growth. This truth is the basis for the monetarist's advocacy of low stable money supply growth to achieve sustained, non-inflationary economic growth.

The portfolio manager must define interest rate volatility, specifying it as a function of both maturity and term. Generally, volatility is a declining function of both maturity and term. The natural implication of this proposition is that for a given portfolio duration, the portfolio's shorter securities are expected to be more volatile in a yield sense or more relative risk than its longer bonds. For substantiation of this point, the portfolio manager need only consider the over-the-counter market for options on Treasury securities to understand the market's pricing of yield curve volatilities.

The assignment or selection of volatility along the yield curve is an important decision for the bond manager. It not only affects the valuation of embedded and actual call options, but it affects the overall risk adjustments of the portfolio. Risk-adjusted durations, risk-adjusted convexities, and risk-adjusted portfolio yield are partially a function of volatility. Therefore, strategically, the portfolio manager may want to "buy" volatility on a particular part of the yield curve and "sell" it at another part to secure the desired risk-adjusted factors.

LIMITATIONS OF U.S. TREASURY ONLY BOND PORTFOLIOS

Assume a portfolio manager holds a high conviction that interest rates are going to drop across the entire yield curve. Furthermore, assume the manager believes that rates on the shorter end of the yield curve will decline substantially more than longer term interest rates. The implications of this forecast are (1) own a very high duration, (2) weight the duration to shorter term bonds as much as possible, and (3) avoid bonds that will be called away to the portfolio's detriment; i.e., bonds whose call-adjusted durations are short. A thorough evaluation of forward rates confirms that the manager is, in fact, more bullish and expects a greater steepening than the market.

Exhibit 8: Guide to Strategy Selection Based on Forecasts

Sector/ Forecast	High Volatility	Low Volatility	Lower Rates Steeper Yield Curve	Lower Rates Flatter Yield Curve	Higher Rates Steeper Yield Curve	Higher Rates Flatter Yield Curve
Corporates						
Growth	Lower Quality Non-Callable	Lower Quality Callable	Lower Quality Non-Callable	Lower Quality Non-Callable Putable	Lower Quality Callable	Lower Quality Putable Callable
Recession	Avoid	High Quality Callable	Avoid	Avoid	Avoid	Avoid
Mortgages						
Growth	Convex P.O. Discount Mtgs PACS	Premium PACS Non-Agency Pass-thru	Current Coupon PO Long Discount CMO	Current Coupon PO Long Z Tranches	Positively Convex IO Premium Pass-thrus	Avoid
Recession	Convex IO Discount Projects PACs	Negatively Convex Pass-thru Neg Convex IO	Current Coupon Pass-thru Intermediate PACs	Long PACs	Positively Convex IO Premium Pass-thrus	Positively Convex IO Premium Pass-thrus
Governments						
Growth	Barbell	Bullet	Long Bullet	Long Barbell	Cash	Cash
Recession	Barbell	Bullet	Long Bullet	Long Barbell	Cash	Cash
Foreign Bonds						
Growth	Industrialized Markets Low Duration (Avoid)	Emerging Markets Low Duration				
Recession	Industrialized Markets High Duration	Industrialized Nations High Duration				
Foreign Currency						
Growth	Emerging Markets	Emerging Markets				
Recession	Industrialized Markets	Industrialized Markets				

However, the manager will be bothered by the contradiction between the desire to be as short as possible on the yield curve to capitalize on the greater drop in short rates which will result from the yield curve steepening against the need to hold a high duration to capitalize on the drop in rates. It is understood that conventional short bonds are inherently of short duration. A seasoned portfolio manager initially reasons that absent leverage, the best that can be achieved is a portfolio of zero-coupon bonds at the targeted duration. This solution is less than satisfying. The manager considers other investment alternatives. Upon thinking about the implications of the forecast on other sectors of the bond market, the manager considers that corporate spreads will narrow as corporations re-liquefy, that prepayment rates on mortgages will increase as borrowers use the lower rates to re-finance existing mortgages and that, to the extent permitted, high coupon bonds will be called away. This is a forecast for which the manager has a high degree of confidence.

The integration of all of these ideas with the maximum of product considerations in conjunction with the high degree of certainty of the initial forecast leads the manager to a potent, more satisfying portfolio. The manager constructs a portfolio with a high concentration of principal-only mortgage strips (POs), whose underlying coupon is slightly above prevailing mortgage rates. The sole source of return for the PO is prepayments of the underlying mortgages. The PO is of a very high duration and very convex with respect to prepayment rates. It should be reasoned that the return on this long duration bond will be largely driven by the prepayment rates on mortgages. Because of the preponderance of adjustable-rate mortgages, this effect will be exaggerated by a dramatic reduction in short-term interest rates.

If the PO solution is not available and the portfolio manager is forced to choose between duration and yield curve, the normal solution would be a portfolio of zero-coupon bonds at the maximum duration as initially reasoned. In another anticipated scenario of abnormal large progressive shifts downward along the term structure, other portfolio combinations may be chosen. The choice is dictated by the magnitude of the drop in yield at any particular point of the curve, perhaps in combination with duration added from elsewhere — a hybrid barbelled portfolio. The final determination is driven by return calculations that must be adjusted by the degree of belief in each particular scenario.

In summary, absent a novel synthetic solution, if the portfolio manager is forced to choose between duration and yield curve, as previously suggested the normal solution would be a portfolio of zero-coupon bonds at the maximum duration. Furthermore, in an abnormal situation of large progressive shifts downward along the term structure, other portfolio combinations may be chosen, such as the hybrid barbell solution where duration is added from elsewhere on the yield curve. This choice will be dictated by the magnitude of the expected drop in yield at any particular point on the curve. The final determination is driven by return calculations that must be adjusted by the degree of belief in each particular scenario.

CORPORATE BONDS

The yield spread of a corporate bond relative to a government bond is negatively correlated to the growth of the economy. Greater economic growth in the economy generally provides greater profitability to corporations thereby reducing the probability of default. Therefore, yield spreads of corporate bonds over government bonds narrow as default risk diminishes. Exhibit 9 provides historical evidence of the cyclical influence on yield spreads. Cursory empirical evidence indicates that the inflection points of the yield spreads are related to turning points of bond yields.

A portfolio manager who can confidently identify the transition from recession to growth and vice versa can add substantially to portfolio performance. Not only will he accurately forecast the change in the direction of interest rates, but he will also add tremendous value with his sector choices. As Exhibit 8 suggests, low quality corporate bonds satisfy the confident high growth forecast. Holding government rates constant, the most potent returns would result from low quality, non-callable, long maturity corporates. Alternatively, corporate bonds should be sold entirely if an economic slowdown or recession is forecast.

The fact that corporate bond spreads are variable and that part of their variability is related to the quality of the credit (issuer's credit rating) has important yet subtly complex implications. For example, corporate bond spread variability implies that these bonds may be more volatile than government bonds. They may even perform asymmetrically with respect to the direction of volatility changes. That is to say, the price of the corporate bond will change by varying amounts, conditional on the direction of the change in the spread even though rates on government bonds do not change at all. (This is the simplest case to explore.) Asymmetrical changes in value occur in a typical callable corporate bond for two reasons: the embedded call features and the normal asymmetry associated with quality spread term structures.

We will use an example to better illustrate these issues. Assume we have an A rated corporate bond with a 30-year maturity and callable in five years at 105. The prevailing generic quality term spreads for similar structures are as follows: AAA — 0.50%, AA — 0.65%, A — 1.00%, BAA — 1.65%, BA — 2.75%. Exhibit 10 illustrates the asymmetry feature. It shows the possible performance result as the bond spread narrows. Because its duration shrinks, its price does not change significantly relative to the downgrade. If there is a downgrade and the call option goes "out of the money," the price change is quite large. The asymmetry is quite apparent. The portfolio manager must determine how much yield is required to compensate for this risk. He must first assign a particular volatility assumption to each issuer so that the proper yield premium can be determined. He may simply choose to assign a probability to both scenarios to assist in his decision process.

Exhibit 9: A Market Indicator of Interest Rate Direction
10-Year Treasury Note Yield

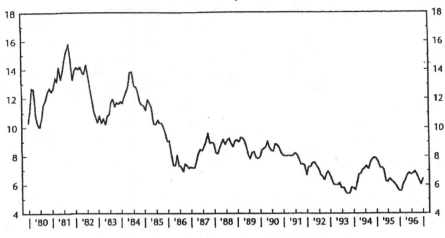

10-Year Treasury Note: BAA Ratio
3-Month Moving Average

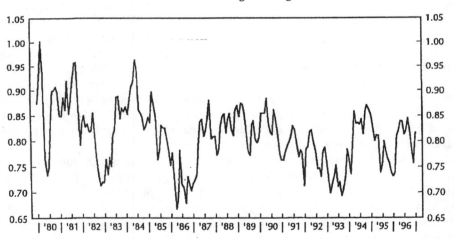

A narrowing of the ratio of yield spreads (i.e., a higher number) is indicative of an improving economy which is generally coincident with an increase in interest rates.

Exhibit 10: Credit Spreads and Price Asymmetry

Consider the following hypothetical "A" rated 7.25% bond maturing 3/15/27, callable 3/15/02 at 105*

Rating	Yield Spread (%)	YTM	YTC (%)	Price	Percent Change
AAA	0.50	N/A	6.75	106.39	6.39
AA	0.65	N/A	6.90	104.40	4.40
A	1.00	7.25	—	100.00	0
Baa	1.85	8.10	N/A	90.47	(9.53)
Ba	3.75	10.00	N/A	73.97	(26.03)

We observe credit improvements yield mediocre increases in price relative to the magnitude of the price declines associated with credit downgrades. The relatively small yield compression and the call date and call price combine to limit the price potential of a credit improvement.

* For simplicity, we assume a flat term structure at 6.25%, constant credit spreads along the term structure and a constant term structure volatility.

MORTGAGE-BACKED SECURITIES

The revolution in financial engineering in the 1980s made possible by the advancements in technology transformed the mortgage securities market. This revolution transformed a generic market of mortgage bonds whose values were derived from the mortgage coupons and expectations for prepayments into a market of securities whose characteristics could be altered to provide for any and all needs of the investor. Yet, the underlying assets of these "tailored securities" remained the same. Because the mortgage market is so diverse and complex, it is too difficult to provide a simple analytical framework to evaluate these engineered securities.

The simplest way to think about the mortgage market is to recognize that, in general, low interest rates and a steep yield curve benefit discount, low yielding mortgage bonds and hurt the value of high yielding, high coupon mortgage bonds. This is true because prepayment rates (refinancings) accelerate sharply in this environment. Prepayment rates are a critical variable in the analysis of most mortgage securities.

The steepening of the yield curve implies that cash flows generated by mortgage securities are discounted at lower rates and therefore, the value of the cash flows increase. If prepayment rates do not change assuming the steepening results from short rates dropping rather than long rates increasing, then virtually all mortgage securities benefit in performance terms.

The importance of the linkage between the interest rate forecast, the degree of confidence of the forecast, and the resultant investment strategy bears reiteration in context of mortgage securities. As Exhibit 8 suggests, there is a broad selection of mortgage strategies for all interest rate environments. As we demonstrated earlier, mortgage securities with inherent leverage, such as principal-only strips (POs), are ideally suited to extremely confident, extreme forecasts. On the other side of the coin, many mortgage securities, such as PAC bonds, were designed to provide stability of cash flows and expected maturity. These bonds inherently contain insurance. They are ideally suited for the weakly confident, weak forecast.

A useful thing about many mortgage securities is that their risk character can change substantially as market conditions change. For example, in a low interest rate environment, the duration of an interest-only strip (IO) whose underlying collateral consists of high coupon mortgages will be short and its value low. A strong, abrupt cyclical turn in interest rates will cause IO securities to perversely increase in both duration and value. As with the corporate market, the mortgage market is a rich universe for portfolio managers who are able to forecast changing interest rates. This allows them to hold those mortgages that benefit most from various interest rate changes. The prepayment function is a subset of the economic forecast as shown in Exhibit 7.

The knowledgeable portfolio manager is aware that the prepayment rate function is essentially an option embedded within the bond. The value of a bond whose price is very sensitive to changes in the prepayment function will also be sensitive to changes in volatility expectations. The importance of volatility estimates is crucial to the valuation of this sector. Besides the caps, collars, and other explicit options associated with many mortgage bonds, the state contingent character as a function of prepayment rates illustrated with the IO, highlights the importance of volatility expectations and the pricing process.

FOREIGN INVESTMENTS

The tasks confronting an international fixed income portfolio manager are increasingly complex. The world capital markets represent a huge and broadly distributed set of investment considerations and choices. Matters will be simplified at the outset, then a few layers of complexity will be added. Exhibit 4 is illustrative of how complex matters can become.

The value inherent to a bond is the enforceability of the bond contract. In a very real way, with substantial historical precedent, investments in bonds of foreign issuers are void of enforceability powers. Investments in foreign bonds are perhaps more akin to equity-type investments. In this regard their political default risk, as opposed to corporate default risk in equity investments, is extremely low but real. This risk should be considered in addition to the volatility risks implied by the options markets for foreign bonds and currencies and should be reflected in the portfolio risk adjustments.

A typical country consideration set for the international portfolio manager confines the investment choices to Canada, Europe, Asia, and Australia and New Zealand, although, of course, many other managers consider a complete set of emerging markets as well. A portfolio manager wishing to consider a more simplified country selection set representative of advanced capital markets may only consider Canada, Germany, and Japan. In any of the above instances, the analytical focus would continue to be on specific country macroeconomics (both cyclical and secular), but the political analysis would take on greater importance. Additionally, currency valuations are introduced.

There are three major components of risk and reward in international bonds: (1) yield, (2) change of interest rates, and (3) changes in currency values. Because the cash, futures, forward, options, and swap markets in the larger international capital markets are fairly well developed, market inferences about volatility expectations and forward break-even rates and prices for both currencies and bonds are easily discerned. Exhibit 11 provides examples of this information. Of course, the period represented is one of political stability. By contrast, the turbulent 1900-1945 period would, most likely, offer a substantially different result.

As mentioned above, the portfolio manager's analysis of government bonds in foreign countries is similar to that in the domestic market. However, the portfolio manager must now consider the currency risk as well. He must develop theoretical and technical models for currency analysis. The analysis must consider current accounts, trade accounts, monetary policy, fiscal policy, as well as, regulatory, institutional and tax policies and more. The bond decision ought to be considered as a currency-hedged one, i.e., the bond stripped of the currency exposure versus a currency non-hedged one. Investment choices then can be viewed more easily relative to the U.S. markets. More importantly, Exhibit 12 demonstrates the benefits of international diversification, i.e., moving beyond U.S. domestic security choices, even though the foreign currency exposures are hedged back into U.S. dollars. Empirically, considering just the 5-year period 1991-1996, superior returns were achieved by the G-5 portfolio hedged back to U.S. dollars. By increasing the "dollar" investment choices, the bond portfolio manager will increase his chances for higher returns. By adding currency exposure, the bond portfolio manager will further increase his chances for higher returns, but he will have also taken on greater risk or variance of returns via his exposure to a variety of foreign currency price fluctuations.

The task of international investing is complicated as the universe of investment alternatives increase. The universe can increase to include the emerging markets of Eastern Europe and Russia, Central and South America, Asia, and India and Pakistan. As Exhibit 12 illustrated, the investment universe is now almost unlimited, especially when bonds issued by private companies are introduced.

CURRENCY SELECTION

There are many theories about currency-value determination. The most popular fundamental ones are based on: (1) purchasing power parity (PPP), (2) trade balances, (3) real interest rate differentials, and (4) growth rates and growth prospects. None of these are very satisfying. Each has proved important but the importance of any one has varied over time. Therefore, technical analysis of the currency markets is quite prevalent.

Exhibit 11: International Fixed Income Investing

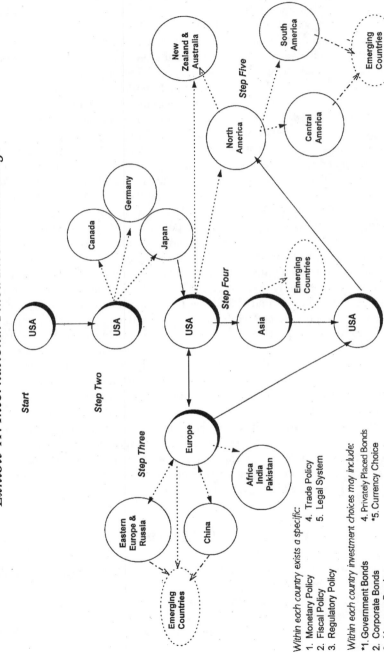

Within each country exists a specific:
1. Monetary Policy   4. Trade Policy
2. Fiscal Policy   5. Legal System
3. Regulatory Policy

Within each country investment choices may include:
*1. Government Bonds   4. Privately Placed Bonds
2. Corporate Bonds   *5. Currency Choice
3. Morgage Bonds

*Spot market, forward markets, option markets and in some cases, organinzed futures markets.

Design: Marie Sacheli

Exhibit 12: Diversification Analysis for Dollar-Based Accounts

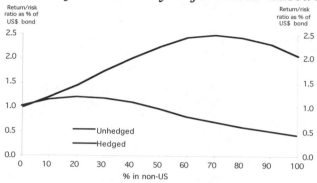

Total Returns Correlations — $, Unhedged, Latest 5 Years

	US	Jap	Ger	Fra	UK
US	1.00	0.13	0.30	0.31	0.32
Japan		1.00	0.57	0.48	0.21
Germany			1.00	0.91	0.56
France				1.00	0.63
UK					1.00

Total Returns Correlations —$, Hedged, Latest 5 Years

	US	Jap	Ger	Fra	UK
US	1.00	0.28	0.39	0.28	0.33
Japan		1.00	0.43	0.10	0.17
Germany			1.00	0.74	0.69
France				1.00	0.68
UK					1.00

Market Statistics for 5-Year Bonds
(January 1992-December 1996, Monthly Data)

	US	Japan	Germany	France	UK
Local Currency					
Average Monthly Return (%)	0.5	0.7	0.8	0.8	0.8
Variance (%)	1.7	1.7	1.0	1.5	2.8
Return/Risk Ratio	0.3	0.4	0.8	0.5	0.3
Unhedged					
Average Monthly Return (%)	0.5	0.7	0.7	0.7	0.7
Variance (%)	1.7	11.8	8.4	6.6	6.7
Return/Risk Ratio	0.3	0.1	0.1	0.1	0.1
Fully Hedged					
Average Monthly Return (%)	0.5	0.8	0.6	0.6	0.6
Variance (%)	1.7	1.7	1.0	1.5	2.7
Return/Risk Ratio	0.3	0.5	0.6	0.4	0.2
Spot FX Rate					
Average Monthly Return (%)		-0.1	0.1	0.0	-0.1
Variance (%)		9.6	9.2	8.8	9.6
Return/Risk Ratio		0.0	0.0	0.0	0.0

Source: Steven Hannah, Chief Economist IBJ International

The portfolio manager must decide upon the relative weights of each of the factors, in conjunction with technical analysis since, most often, the signals will be mixed. For example, PPP may be positive for the currency while the trade balance is negative. The portfolio manager must also consider the influence of cartels, such as European Monetary Union efforts and government intervention in the currency markets. A simplified analysis is provided below:

	PPP	Growth Rate	Balance of Trade	Real Interest Rate Differential
Correlation with currency valuation	+	+	+	+

The yen/dollar forward values are derived from the prevailing interest rate term structure differentials between the two markets. For example, the approximate 5% difference between the 1-year rate in the U.S. and the 1-year rate in Japan, yields an approximate 5% drop in currency values. However, we know that forward currency values are affected by other variables as well. So, we can express our conviction that the interest rate term structure differentials are not fully incorporating the influence of those other variables by being long or short the forward currency exchange rates.

The following hypothetical example may help illustrate the point. Assume our secular forecast for the United States is dominated by demographic influences. The predominant aspect of this forecast is an aging of the baby boom generation and, as implied, the transformation from consumers to savers. Therefore, we conclude that the demand for exports will decline and the savings rate will increase. Both of these phenomena imply an improved current account balance. Moreover, we believe that the demographics in Japan are such that savings will decline substantially and a secular deterioration in the Japanese current account will result. Because of this secular forecast we adopt a "strong dollar" forecast. We know that the interest differentials imply a weak dollar. We bet against the market's pricing by buying dollars forward five years and selling yen forward at an exchange rate of 90.635 dollars per yen. This is a 22% discount to the prevailing spot exchange rate of 116.15. The purchase of options on 5-year forward dollar/yen is the weaker form of expression of the secular strong dollar forecast.

CONCLUSION

The portfolio manager has a significant role to play in benefiting a client who elects to invest in the fixed income market. The market consensus, as reflected in current prices on a forward basis, can be an incorrect predictor of future rates. A skillful portfolio manager will be able to assess all the germane bits of market information accessible to him and apply his knowledge in the form of market bets that express his disagreement with current forward prices. That is to say, in order to achieve effective results and reach responsible investment decisions the portfolio manager must be diligent in gathering information and be able to process that information in an independent fashion. After he has gone through this process, he must create a portfolio that reflects his beliefs in a cost and risk effective way in the context of current market prices of his investment set.

The basic factors that the fixed income portfolio manager must examine include: economic, political, historic, psychological, monetary and fiscal policies, products available, transaction costs, the impact on other investors of market movements, regulatory issues, and the competitive advantages of other competing portfolio managers. Once the portfolio manager has gathered all this information, he must decide on a short- and long-term interest rate forecast and the expected time frame for his investment decisions to perform as well as alternative strategies should market conditions alter his initial assumptions. Then the portfolio manager must create a portfolio considering all the possible securities within his "bogey" set of investment possibilities, deciding on duration and how to achieve the duration goal, cash flows and distribution of securities on the yield curve, convexity, credit quality, hedged international exposure, and non-dollar or currency exposure. In doing so, the fixed income portfolio manager, armed with his interest rate forecast, is faced with the eternal trade-off between returns or percentage total returns against risk or the variance of the percentage of total returns regardless of his set of investment or "bogey" alternatives. The process of fixed income portfolio management is, therefore, always an exercise in constrained optimization.

Chapter 26

Managing Indexed and Enhanced Indexed Bond Portfolios

Kenneth E. Volpert, CFA
Principal and Senior Portfolio Manager
The Vanguard Group, Inc.

OVERVIEW OF DOMESTIC BOND MANAGEMENT

Domestic bond management can be likened to a sailing regatta. The index is the lead boat, since it does not have expenses and transaction costs to contend with, and all managers (including index fund managers) are the other boats, trying to make up the distance and pass the index boat. Strategies that may be used to make up the difference and pass the lead boat comprise a wide spectrum of styles and approaches. Exhibit 1 displays the major elements of these approaches.

Pure Bond Index Matching

Pure bond indexing is the lowest risk (and lowest expected return) approach to bond management versus a specific benchmark. This approach essentially guarantees that returns will lag behind the index boat by the cost difference (expenses plus transaction costs). Pure bond index matching attempts to fully replicate the index by owning all the bonds in the index in the same percentage as the index. Hence, this approach is also called the *full replication approach.* In the bond market, however, such an approach is very difficult to accomplish and very costly to implement. Many bonds in the index were issued years ago, and are consequently illiquid. Many bonds were also issued when interest rates were significantly different from current rates. Today's holders may be unwilling to incur a gain or loss by selling their bonds to an index fund.

The author wishes to acknowledge the professional and personal contribution of Irwin E. Jones, who retired from the business in 1996. Irwin introduced the author to the bond indexing business in 1986. Irwin's highest integrity, his inquisitive nature, his professional mentoring role, and his personal friendship have deeply affected the author. Thank you Irwin!

Exhibit 1: Bond Management Risk Spectrum

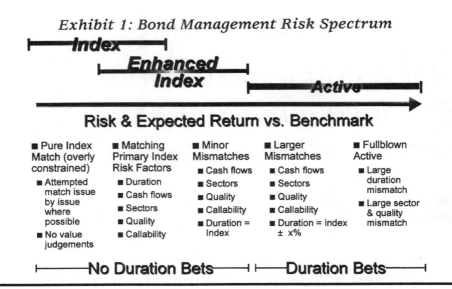

Risk & Expected Return vs. Benchmark

| ■ Pure Index Match (overly constrained) ■ Attempted match issue by issue where possible ■ No value judgements | ■ Matching Primary Index Risk Factors ■ Duration ■ Cash flows ■ Sectors ■ Quality ■ Callability | ■ Minor Mismatches ■ Cash flows ■ Sectors ■ Quality ■ Callability ■ Duration = Index | ■ Larger Mismatches ■ Cash flows ■ Sectors ■ Quality ■ Callability ■ Duration = Index ± x% | ■ Fullblown Active ■ Large duration mismatch ■ Large sector & quality mismatch |

├─────No Duration Bets─────┤ ├────Duration Bets────┤

On September 30, 1996, the Lehman Brothers Aggregate Bond Index contained 169 Treasury issues, 1,144 federal agency issues, 3,507 corporate issues, 106 asset-backed issues, and 611 broadly categorized mortgage issues (essentially hundreds of thousands of mortgage pools). Full replication is feasible (although not desirable for reasons to be mentioned later) in the Treasury market, but cannot be reasonably implemented in the agency, mortgage or corporate markets. Thousands of the agency and corporate issues are locked away in long-term bond portfolios and could only be purchased from these investors by paying extremely high prices. For this reason, full replication of a broad bond index (including corporates and mortgages) is very inefficient, if not impossible.

Enhanced Indexing/Matching Primary Risk Factors

The *enhanced bond indexing/matching primary risk factors approach* involves investing in a large sample of bonds such that the portfolio risk factors match the index risk factors. The result is a portfolio that, when fully implemented, will have higher average monthly tracking differences (standard deviation of tracking differences) than the full replication (i.e., pure index matching) approach, but it can be implemented and maintained at much lower cost resulting in net investment performance that is much closer to the index. Returning to the regatta analogy, the portfolio boat stays on the same "tack" as the index boat, but "trims its sails" to run a little more efficiently. Staying on the same "tack" means that the sails are set to take the portfolio boat in the same direction as the index boat, thereby being exposed to the same winds and elements. "Trimming the sails" means that the little details of the sail position and sail shape are performed better and executed more efficiently than on the index boat. The risk factors that need to be matched are duration, cash flow distribution, sector, quality, and call exposure (more on this later). This approach is considered a form of enhanced indexing because the return is enhanced (more on this later) relative to the full replication indexing approach.

Enhanced Indexing/Minor Risk Factor Mismatches

The *enhanced bond indexing/minor risk factor mismatches approach* allows for minor mismatches in the risk factors (except duration) to tilt the portfolio in favor of particular areas of relative value (sector, quality, term structure, call risk, etc.). Because the mismatches (and impact on tracking) are very small, this is still considered enhanced indexing. These additional enhancements are essentially "sail trimming" strategies designed to make up additional distance versus the index boat, while staying on the same tack, and being exposed to the same elements.

Active Management/Larger Risk Factor Mismatches

The active management/larger risk factor mismatches approach is a conservative approach to active management. The manager will make larger mismatches in the risk factors to attempt to add greater value. This approach may also make small duration bets. In most cases, the management fee and transaction costs are significantly higher than for pure or enhanced indexing, yet the net investment return is usually lower. The addition of these additional costs is the reason why a typical index portfolio often outperforms the average active manager in performance universes. Since this strategy has higher costs (higher expenses and transaction costs), the manager will moderately "change tack" to seek greater winds elsewhere, resulting in increased manager risk (i.e., greater risk of deviating from the "market" return and structure).

Active Management/Full-Blown Active

The *active management/full-blown active approach* is an aggressive active style where large duration and sector bets are made, and where significant value-added (or lost) relative to an index can be experienced. Above-average performance consistency is difficult to find in this group of managers, so investors who choose this management style need to look deeper than just at recent performance to discern the good from the bad. This approach may significantly change the "course" relative to the index boat and may risk significant tracking and portfolio structure variations from the index boat in the hope of adding much greater return.

WHY INDEX BOND PORTFOLIOS?

There are several reasons for indexing: broad diversification, competitive performance, low cost, consistent relative performance, market performance predictability, time-tested, and redirection of focus on asset allocation. Each reason is discussed below.

Broad Diversification

Broad bond index portfolios provide excellent diversification. The Lehman Brothers Aggregate Bond Index, which is designed to capture the entire U.S. investment-grade bond market, has over 5,500 issues and more than $4.5 trillion in market value as of September 30, 1996. A large bond index portfolio designed to replicate this Index may have 500 or more issues, resulting in significant issuer diversification benefits. Most active portfolios have much heavier specific issuer concentrations, resulting in significant exposure to issuer event (credit) risk.

In addition, an index portfolio designed to match the Lehman Brothers Aggregate Bond Index will have exposure to not only Treasury and agency sectors, but also to mortgages, industrials, electric and telephone utilities, finance, dollar-denominated foreign, and asset-backed sectors. Such a portfolio will also have broad exposure to the yield curve with holdings from one year to over 30 years to maturity. These sources of diversification result in a portfolio with lower risk for a given level of return than is available from less diversified portfolios.

Competitive Performance

Since index portfolios have lower management fees and lower transaction costs (resulting from significantly lower portfolio turnover), it is not surprising that they usually outperform the average active portfolio in most universes. After all, a broad index is by design a representation of the whole pie of investment alternatives. Therefore, the sum of all active managers should equal the index in composition. Also, the sum of the investment performance of all active managers (grossed up for the higher management fees and transaction costs) should also equal the index in performance. In the mutual fund market, where the bond index expense ratio advantage is about 0.8% per year, the largest bond index portfolio (managed against the Lehman Brothers Aggregate Bond Index) outperformed over 85% of its Lipper Group over 1, 3, and 5 years ending 12/31/95. In the large institutional market, where the expense advantage of indexing is lower, index portfolios outperformed 60% to 75% of actively managed portfolios over the same period (depending on the universe chosen).

Low Cost

The primary reason for competitive performance of index funds is lower cost. This lower cost takes two forms: (1) lower management fees and (2) lower transaction costs associated with lower portfolio turnover rates. This lower cost advantage is durable and predictable — year after year. Don Phillips, President of Morningstar, summarizes the impact of higher costs: "if you pay the executive at Sara Lee more, it doesn't make the cheesecake less good. But with mutual funds (investment management), it comes directly out of the batter." Indeed it does!

Consistent Relative Performance

Exhibit 2 shows the performance for the largest bond index mutual fund against its Lipper universe (Intermediate Government) for calendar years starting in 1989.

In fairness, this portfolio has approximately 30% in corporates (the other 70% is U.S. Treasury and agency securities, and agency mortgage-backed securities), so a comparison against a government universe is not entirely appropriate. The only year where the portfolio outperformed less than 50% of the universe was 1990 (42%). For all the other years the portfolio outperformed between 65% to 88% of the competition in its maturity and quality category. The primary reason for this consistent outperformance is the significantly lower expenses and transaction costs incurred by the portfolio.

Market Performance Predictability

A properly managed broad bond index portfolio can be assured of performing in line with the market as a whole. Therefore, regardless of the direction the market takes, the investor can be assured of the performance of a diversified broad index (the "market").

Time Tested

Bond index portfolios have been successfully managed since the early 1980s — through rising and falling interest rate cycles as well as through increasing and declining credit spread cycles. Through all these market changes, bond indexing has proven to provide a more than competitive return with low to moderate risk.

Redirects Focus to Most Important Decision — Asset Allocation

Perhaps the most significant reason to index bonds is that it enables investors to concentrate on the more important asset allocation decision. Very often, limited decision-making time and effort is wasted on the hope of adding 20-40 basis points on the bond portion of a portfolio, when existing misallocation of assets to stocks or international investments are resulting in hundreds of basis points of underperformance for the entire portfolio. Indexing helps facilitate more effective use of limited decision-making resources available to most investors.

Exhibit 2: Annual Performance Consistency Analysis
Index Portfolio versus Lipper Intermediate Government

	Index Portfolio Return (%)	Lipper Rank	Total in Lipper Group	Percent Outperformed (%)
1989	13.65	4	25	84
1990	8.65	15	26	42
1991	15.25	5	24	79
1992	7.14	4	32	88
1993	9.68	12	50	76
1994	-2.66	27	77	65
1995	18.18	13	98	87
1996 (Oct.)	2.67	37	124	71

Exhibit 3: Lehman Brothers Aggregate Bond Index Composition (As of 9/30/96)

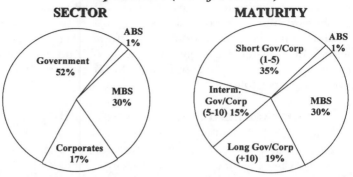

WHICH INDEX SHOULD BE USED?

A bond index is defined by a set of rules (characteristics) that are then applied to all issues in the marketplace. The rules include maturity, size, sector, and quality characteristics. The issues that fit the rules are then combined, as if in a portfolio, with each issue's weight determined by its relative market value outstanding.

For indexing, the broader the Index (for a given level of risk) the better the benchmark. The broadest U.S. bond index is the Lehman Brothers Aggregate Bond Index (essentially identical to the Salomon Broad Investment Grade Index and the Merrill Lynch Domestic Master Index). At September 30, 1996, the Lehman Brothers Aggregate Bond Index had more than 5,500 issues representing a market value of over $4.5 trillion. Exhibit 3 shows that the composition of the Aggregate Bond Index as of September 30, 1996 was 45% Treasury bonds, 7% agency bonds, 19% corporate and asset-backed bonds, and 29% mortgage-backed securities. The option-adjusted duration (a duration number that reflects the possibility of bonds being called by the issuer) was 4.7 years, with an average maturity of 8.7 years, making it the broadest domestic intermediate index available. Sub-indices of the Lehman Brothers Aggregate Bond Index can be created that result in different risk/return profiles. For example, a corporate-only index can be replicated for those who do not want as much quality as exists in the Lehman Brothers Aggregate Bond Index; or a 1-5 year government/corporate Index can be created, for those who would rather have a short duration portfolio.

Market Value Risk

Generally, the longer the maturity of the bond portfolio, the higher its yield, assuming a "normally" sloped yield curve. The total return on a bond is made up of the coupon (or income) component and the principal (or price change) component. Since the yield curve (which impacts the principal component of total return) is highly unlikely to remain unchanged, the longer bond portfolio will not necessarily have a higher total return. Exhibit 4 shows the 1-year total return of different maturity securities (short: 3 years; intermediate: 7 years; and, long: 20 years) in both high-rate and low-rate environments, assuming yields rise or fall 1%. Clearly, as the maturity or duration of the portfolio lengthens, the greater the market value risk. In addition, the lower the yield environment, the greater the market value risk, especially for the intermediate-term and long-term portfolios. This is the result of the portfolio having a longer duration (greater duration risk) in the low-rate environment, in which the portfolio's lower yield provides less of a cushion to offset principal losses. Therefore, for investors who are risk averse in terms of their principal, the short-term or intermediate-term index as a benchmark may be more appropriate than the long index.

Income Risk

Many investors invest for income, spending only the income distributed by an investment without dipping into principal. Foundations and retirees invest for a stable and hopefully growing income stream that they can depend on for current and future consumption. Exhibit 5 shows the income stream (distributed mutual fund income) from a $10,000 investment in a short (3-year), intermediate (7-year), and long (20-year) mutual fund over the last 15 years, assuming equivalent growth rates for the portfolios. It's obvious that if stability and durability of income are the primary concerns, than the long portfolio is the least risky and the short portfolio is the most risky.

Liability Framework Risk

Pension funds and financial institutions invest to finance future liabilities. Long-term liabilities (like active retired lives liabilities) require investments in long-term assets to minimize risk, resulting in both a portfolio and a liability stream that is equally sensitive to interest-rate changes. A portfolio that invests in short bonds may look less risky on an absolute return basis, but it is actually much riskier (because of its mismatch with long liabilities) when the portfolio market value is compared to the present value of the pension liability (the difference is the surplus or deficit). The "surplus" risk will be minimized on a fully funded plan against small changes in market rates when the duration of the portfolio is matched (or immunized) to the duration of the liability.

Exhibit 4: Market Value Risk

High Interest Rate Environment				1 Year Return (Income + Price Return	
Coupon	Maturity	Price	Duration	Rates Rise 1%	Rates Fall 1%
12	3 year	100	2.5	9.6	14.5
12	7 year	100	4.6	7.5	16.8
12	20 year	100	7.5	4.9	20.0

Low Interest Rate Environment				1 Year Return (Income + Price Return)	
Coupon	Maturity	Price	Duration	Rates Rise 1%	Rates Fall 1%
6	3 year	100	2.7	3.3	8.8
6	7 year	100	5.6	0.5	11.8
6	20 year	100	11.6	−4.7	18.6

Exhibit 5: Income Risk

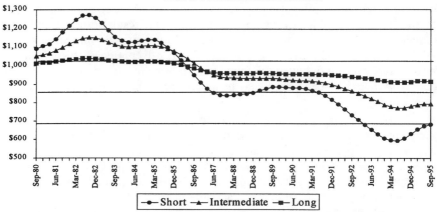

Dividend Volatility Analysis
Assumes Initial $10,000 Investment
With No Dividend Reinvestment

Exhibit 6: Bond Market Risk Summary

NAV Type	Market Value Risk	Income or Liability Risk	Average Maturity	Current Duration	Portfolios
Stable Dollar NAV	Lowest	Highest	30-90 Days	0.1	Money Market Portfolios
Variable NAV	Low	High	2-4 Years	2.5	Short-Term Portfolios
	Medium	Medium	7-10 Years	5.0	Intermediate-Term Portfolios
	High	Low	15-25 Years	10.0	Long-Term Portfolios

Exhibit 6 contains a summary comparison showing that the investment with the lowest market value risk has the highest income or liability risk. Likewise, the investment with the highest market value risk has the lowest income or liability risk. Clearly, the risk framework chosen depends on whether the investment objective is principal preservation or income durability.

PRIMARY BOND INDEXING RISK FACTORS

Effective bond indexing does not require full replication, nor is it desired. What is required is matching the primary risk factors of the benchmark index in a credit diversified portfolio. Exhibit 7 lists the primary risk factors that apply to the government, corporate, and mortgage sectors, accompanied by an explanation of these primary risk factors.

Exhibit 7: Primary Bond Index Matching Factors

	Government	Corporate	MBS
Modified Adjusted Duration	X	X	
Present Value of Cash Flows	X	X	
Percent in Sector and Quality		X	
Duration Contribution of Sector		X	
Duration Contribution of Credit Quality		X	
Sector/Coupon/Maturity Cell Weights		X	X
Issuer Exposure Control		X	

Modified Adjusted Duration

The modified adjusted duration (or option-adjusted modified duration) is a simple single measure of interest rate risk of the portfolio. It's a great place to start, but is entirely too rough of a measure to adequately track an index. The portfolio duration will give the manager a rough approximation of the price change observed if interest rates rise or fall (in a parallel fashion) immediately by 1%. If rates rise by 1%, a 5-year duration portfolio will experience an approximate 5% decline in value ((+1% yield change) × (5-year portfolio duration) × (−1)). If the yield curve does not move in a parallel fashion, then the duration is of limited value. For obvious reasons, it is important to match the duration of the portfolio to the duration of the benchmark index.

Present Value Distribution of Cash Flows

A more accurate way to capture yield curve risk is by matching the cash flow distribution of the index. Yield curve changes are composed of parallel shifts, curve twists (e.g., short rates down, intermediate rates unchanged, long rates up), and curve butterfly (e.g., short and long rates down, intermediate rates up) movements. By decomposing the index (and portfolio) into a stream of future payments and discounting each payment to the present value and summing these values, one calculates the index (and portfolio) market value. By matching the percent of the portfolio's present value that comes due at certain intervals in time (each vertex) with that of the benchmark index, the portfolio will be largely protected from tracking error (versus the benchmark) associated with yield curve changes. Since the portfolio duration is equal to the benchmark index duration (duration is the sum of all vertices (Exhibit 8), of the percent of present value multiplied by the vertex (time)), this method will guard against parallel changes in yield. Since all points in time (vertices) are closely matched in percent, any local term structure movements (non-parallel changes) will not affect tracking (these yield change risks are essentially immunized). For callable securities, the cash flows need to be distributed to the vertices in accordance with the probability of call. A 10-year bond that is highly likely to be called in three years should have cash flows that are primarily allocated to the 3-year vertex.

Exhibit 8: Cash Flow Distribution Analysis

Time	Percent of Value	Duration Contribution	Percent of Duration
0	3.1	0.00	0.0
0.5	6.6	0.03	0.7
1	8.5	0.09	1.8
1.5	10.1	0.15	3.2
2	13.1	0.26	5.6
3	13.1	0.39	8.4
4	10.2	0.41	8.6
5	7.4	0.37	7.9
6	5.2	0.31	6.6
7	4.5	0.32	6.8
8	3.7	0.29	6.2
9	3.4	0.30	6.4
10	2.7	0.27	5.7
12	2.4	0.29	6.1
15	2.2	0.33	7.0
20	2.3	0.45	9.7
25	1.0	0.24	5.1
30	0.6	0.18	3.8
40	0.0	0.01	0.3
Total	100.0	4.70	100.0

Percent in Sector and Quality

The yield of the index is largely replicated by matching the percentage weight in the various sectors and qualities, assuming that all maturity categories are fully accounted for by the replicating portfolio. Exhibit 9 shows the Lehman Brothers Aggregate Bond Index weights in the various sectors and qualities as of 9/30/96.

Duration Contribution of Sector

The best way (without excessively constraining the process) to protect a portfolio from tracking differences associated with changes in sector spreads (industry risk) is to match the amount of the index duration (Exhibit 9) that comes from the various sectors. If this can be accomplished, a given change in sector spreads will have an equal impact on the portfolio and the index.

Duration Contribution of Quality

Similarly, the most effective way to protect a portfolio from tracking differences related to changes in quality spreads (leverage/economic risk) is to match the amount of the index duration that comes from the various quality categories. This is particularly important in the lower-rated categories, which are characterized by larger spread changes.

Sector/Coupon/Maturity Cell Weights

The call exposure of an index is a difficult factor to replicate. The convexity value (convexity measures how a bond's duration changes as yield levels change) alone is inadequate since it measures expected changes in duration over a small change in yield levels. In addition, the change in convexity can be very different as yield levels change. Managers who attempt only to match the index convexity value often find themselves having to buy or sell highly illiquid callable securities to stay matched and, in the process, generate excessive transaction costs. A better method of matching the call exposure is to match the sector, coupon, and maturity weights of the callable sectors. By matching these weights, the convexity of the index should be matched. In addition, as rates change, the changes in call exposure (convexity) of the portfolio will be matched to the index, requiring little or no rebalancing.

In the mortgage market, call (prepayment) risk is very significant. The volatility in the option-adjusted duration of the Lehman Brothers Mortgage Index, which measures the extent of the call exposure of the mortgage market, is shown in Exhibit 10. Also shown in the exhibit is the Mortgage Bankers Refinancing Index (inverted), which measures the extent of mortgage refinancing occurring in the market. Clearly, the greater the refinancing activity, the shorter the index duration due to the greater likelihood that the higher coupons (issues priced above par) will be refinanced with lower coupon securities. For this reason, matching the coupon distribution of the mortgage index is critical. The best risk management is accomplished by matching the index weights in a multi-dimensional matrix of the maturity (balloon, 15-year, 30-year), sector (FNMA, FGLMC, GNMA), coupon (50 basis point increments), and seasoning (new, moderate, and seasoned). This level of detail is easily accomplished in a large portfolio (more than $1 billion in assets), but more difficult to accomplish in smaller portfolios.

Exhibit 9: Sector and Quality Distribution Analysis

Sector	Percent of PV	Duration	Duration Contribution	Percent of Duration
Treasury	45.2	4.76	2.15	45.8
Agency	6.5	4.75	0.31	6.6
Industrial	6.1	6.28	0.38	8.2
Telephone	1.1	6.75	0.08	1.6
Electric/Gas	1.9	5.81	0.11	2.3
Finance	4.7	4.56	0.22	4.6
Canadian	1.1	6.55	0.07	1.6
Sovereign	0.9	5.34	0.05	1.0
Foreign Corporate	1.5	6.18	0.09	1.9
Supranational	0.3	6.12	0.02	0.4
GNMA	8.5	4.11	0.35	7.4
FNMA	9.9	3.95	0.39	8.3
FHLMC	1.3	4.02	0.45	9.6
Asset-Backed	1.0	2.90	0.03	0.6
Total	100.0	4.70	4.70	100.0
Quality				
AAA	83.2	4.49	3.73	79.5
AA	3.3	5.42	0.18	3.8
A	9.4	5.81	0.55	11.6
BAA	4.2	5.84	0.24	5.2
Total	100.0	4.70	4.70	100.0

Exhibit 10: Mortgage Call Exposure Analysis

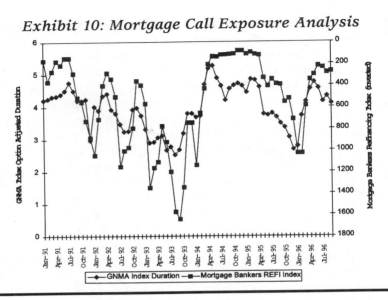

Issuer Exposure

If the major risk factors described above are matched, but with too few issues, there remains significant risk that can still be diversified away. "Event" risk, a risk widely watched in the late 1980s, when there was significant corporate leveraging taking place (LBOs), is the final primary risk factor that needs to be measured and controlled. Issuer exposure, like sector and quality, needs to be measured in more than percentage terms only, versus the index benchmark. Setting percent of market value limits without regard to issuer duration risk and issuer index weights is not adequate. Immediately after a negative credit event, the spread widens. Therefore, the best measure of the issuer event risk impact on a portfolio is the impact on portfolio market value of that spread widening. This can be measured by calculating how much of the portfolio duration ("duration contribution") comes from the holdings in each issuer. This calculation should also be figured for the index. The basis point impact on tracking of a spread-widening event will be the spread change (of the issuer) multiplied by the difference in duration contribution (portfolio − index) multiplied by (−1).

Exhibit 11 contains an example of this analysis. Issuer XXX Corp has an equal percent weight to the Index, but its duration contribution is 0.16 greater. If an event occurred that would widen XXX Corp spreads by 100 basis points, the portfolio would suffer an unfavorable tracking difference of 16 basis points versus the index (100 basis point spread change × 0.16 duration contribution overweight × −1). If the same 100 basis points widening were to occur to XYZ Corp bonds, the tracking difference would be a favorable 8 basis points (100 basis point spread change × −0.08 duration contribution underweight × −1), even though the percent weight is matched to the index. For effective index fund management, duration contribution exposure limits (versus the index) need to be set at the issuer level.

Exhibit 11: Issuer Exposure Comparison — Percent of Market Value versus Duration Contribution

	Portfolio		
	Percent of Market Value	Duration	Duration Contribution
XXX Corp	4	8	0.32
ZZZ Corp	4	4	0.16
XYZ Corp	4	2	0.08

	Index			Portfolio-Index	
	Percent of Market Value	Duration	Duration Contribution	Percent Difference	Contribution Difference
XXX Corp	4	4	0.16	0	0.16
ZZZ Corp	4	4	0.16	0	0.00
XYZ Corp	4	4	0.16	0	−0.08

BOND INDEX ENHANCEMENTS

Details, Details, Details

As in sailing, speed (returns versus the benchmark) comes from paying close attention to the details, not simply from "watching the wind" (interest rates). Portfolio managers can "trim" their portfolio sails to more efficiently compete in the investment management race. The trimming strategies include: (1) lower costs, (2) issue selection, (3) yield curve positioning, (4) sector and quality positioning, and (5) call exposure positioning.

Why Enhancements are Necessary

Since the index does not incur expenses or transaction costs, enhancements are necessary just to provide a net return equal to the index. A primary source of return shortfalls besides expenses is the transaction costs associated with portfolio growth.

Exhibit 12 shows the transaction costs and resulting tracking error associated with single contribution growth versus multiple contribution growth. In the example, the single contribution portfolio had tracking error of 18 basis points associated with investing net cash flow. In the multiple contribution portfolio the tracking error is a significantly higher 41 basis points, even though the dollar cost of transaction costs is the same ($450,000). Therefore, portfolios with high growth rates will suffer additional negative tracking error, making enhancements necessary simply to stay equal to a no-growth or slow-growth portfolio.

Exhibit 13 shows in graphical form the cumulative adverse tracking impact resulting from portfolio growth for Treasury, government/corporate, and corporate portfolios. The greater the growth rate and/or the less liquid the market, the greater the adverse impact on tracking error.

Exhibit 12: Why Enhancements are Necessary
Analysis of the Tracking Impact of Growth
Single Contribution versus Multiple Contributions

	Portfolio Market Value	Contributions	Trans. Cost ($ at 18bp)	New Portfolio Value	Tracking Error from Trans Cost (bp)	Cumulative Tracking Error from Trans Cost (bp)
Single Contribution	$ —	$250,000,000	$450,000	$249,550,000	18.0	18.0
Multiple Contributions	$ —	$50,000,000	$90,000	$49,910,000	18.0	18.0
	$49,910,000	$50,000,000	$90,000	$99,820,000	9.0	27.0
	$99,820,000	$50,000,000	$90,000	$149,730,000	6.0	33.1
	$149,730,000	$50,000,000	$90,000	$199,640,000	4.5	37.6
	$199,640,000	$50,000,000	$90,000	$249,550,000	3.6	41.2
		$250,000,000	$450,000			

Exhibit 13: Why Enhancements are Necessary
Return Impact of Transaction Costs Over 1 Year

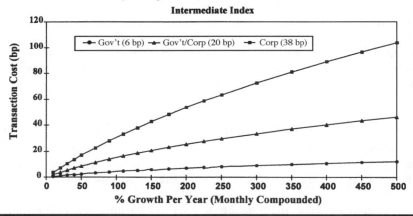

Lower Cost Enhancements

One of the simplest but most overlooked forms of enhancements is to keep costs down. Costs that impact portfolio performance are expenses/management fees and transaction costs.

Enhanced indexers work hard to add an incremental 10 to 30 basis points per year to portfolio returns, yet in the mutual fund arena, the average bond fund expense ratio is 80 basis points greater than the lowest index portfolio expense ratio. As a result, returns of such funds are significantly lower. Even in the indexing arena, expenses vary by large margins. Simply shopping around for the index fund with the lowest expenses, provided the net return is competitive with other index funds, is a simple way to enhance returns. For a plan sponsor with outside index managers, having the existing manager and one or two other reputable indexers re-bid the business every few years will make sure the expenses are as low as possible.

The other major cost factor is transaction costs. Since bond index funds have low annual turnover (about 40%) versus active portfolios (generally over 100%), transaction costs are significantly lower for index portfolios. In addition, the development of a competitive trading process will further reduce the transaction cost impact. It's obvious when seeking bids to include many brokers in the bidding process. For rapidly growing portfolios, where most of the transactions are offerings, an effective competitive trading process is essential. Since there is no central exchange for corporate bonds, an efficient system of evaluating real-time offerings of target issuers from many different brokers to compare relative value, will yield significant transaction cost savings, hence further enhancing the returns.

Issue Selection Enhancements

For U.S. Treasury securities, the primary tool for selecting cheap bonds is comparing actual bond prices to the theoretical "fitted" price. The theoretical curve is derived that will minimize the pricing errors of all Treasury issues in the market, subject to various curve-smoothing rules. Each actual bond's yield is then compared to the bond's "fitted" yield (calculated using the theoretical curve). Bonds yielding more than the "fitted" yield are cheap, and those yielding less are rich. Another useful supplement is an analysis of the recent history of the bond yield versus the fitted yield. This analysis will indicate whether a cheap bond has been getting cheaper or richer.

Corporate issue selection enhancements come primarily from staying clear of deteriorating credits, and owning (generally overweighted versus the index) improving credits. The greater the quality of the credit opinion (based on the quality and timeliness of the credit analyst), the larger can be the maximum issuer exposure limit. (This is discussed later in this chapter.)

Yield Curve Enhancements

Various maturities along the term structure are consistently overvalued or undervalued. For example, the 30-year Treasury region tends to be consistently overvalued, resulting in an inverted yield curve from 25 to 30 years. Likewise, the high-coupon callable bonds maturing in 2009-2012 tend to be consistently undervalued. Strategies that overweight the undervalued maturities and underweight the overvalued maturities, while keeping the same general term structure exposure, will tend to outperform the index. This analysis is similar to looking for the maturities that have the more favorable "roll down" characteristics — meaning that the near-term passage of time may result in the bond rolling down the yield curve and, therefore, it will trade at a lower yield resulting in potential price appreciation. Cheap parts of the curve tend to have favorable "roll down," while rich parts of the curve (e.g., 30-year area) tend to have little or no "roll down" opportunities.

Exhibit 14: Lehman 1-5 year Corporate Index versus Lehman 1-5 year Treasury Index

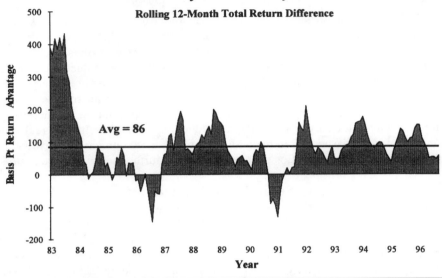

Sector/Quality Enhancements

Sector and quality enhancements take two primary forms: (1) ongoing yield tilt toward short duration corporates and (2) periodic minor over or underweighting of sectors or qualities.

The ongoing yield tilt enhancement (also called "corporate substitution") strategy recognizes that the best yield spread per unit of duration risk is available in short-term corporates (under 5 years). A strategy that underweights 1-5 year government bonds and overweights 1-5 year corporates will increase the yield of the portfolio with a less than commensurate increase in risk. Exhibit 14 shows the rolling 12-month return differential of the Lehman Brothers 1-5 Year Corporate Index versus the Lehman Brothers 1-5 Year Treasury Index.

The persistent return enhancement is obvious for all periods except the brief spread widening periods of 1986-87 and 1990-91. The primary reason the strategy is effective is that the yield advantage of short corporates requires a significant corporate spread widening move over a 1-year period for short corporates to perform as poorly as short Treasuries. Exhibit 15 shows the spread increases that would be required to break-even with equal risk Treasury securities over a 1-year holding period for corporates of varying maturities and spreads levels. With the passage of time, the duration of corporate bonds shorten, and the yield spread over comparable Treasury securities generally narrows (positive credit curve spread). These two risk reducing and return enhancing forces, when combined with the yield spread advantage, provide compelling reasons to overweight short corporates. Even at narrow spreads, significant protection is available in maturities under five years. A 2-year corporate with a yield spread of 20 basis points, can widen by 32 basis points versus a comparable Treasury security over the next year before it performs as poorly as the comparable Treasury security. Clearly, as the maturities increase, the spread widening protection decreases.

The risks involved in the strategy are recessionary spread widening risk and issuer default risk. The recessionary spread widening risk tends to be short lived and quickly overcome by the increased yield advantage of the strategy. The issuer default risk can be minimized by broad issuer diversification (50 or more issuers) and by credit analyst oversight.

The periodic over- or underweighting of sectors and qualities is a scaled back version of active "sector rotation." The primary way this can be implemented on a cost effective basis is to allow new cash flow (net new portfolio growth) to facilitate the mismatching. For example, if spreads are narrow going into the fourth quarter and the manager expects some widening, new money may be invested primarily in Treasury securities, resulting in a gradual reduction in the corporate exposure versus the index. Once the corporate spread widening materializes, Treasury securities (with low transaction costs) can be sold and corporates overweighted. Expected first quarter asset growth will eventually bring the corporate weighting back in line with the Index. A strategy of outright selling of corporates to buy Treasury securities is always difficult to justify because of the higher corporate transaction costs involved, in addition to the yield "penalty" associated with Treasury securities.

Call Exposure Enhancements

The option-adjusted duration of a callable bond is the average of what the model duration is, if rates rise and fall marginally. These durations (under rising and falling rates) can be quite different for bonds that are trading at a price where the bond changes from trading to maturity, to trading to call (or visa versa). The result is a situation where the actual performance of a bond could be significantly different than would be expected given its beginning of period option-adjusted duration.

Exhibit 15: Breakeven Spread Widening Analysis — Corporates versus Treasuries

Maturity	Wide Spreads	Breakeven additional Widening	Moderate Spreads	Breakeven additional Widening	Narrow Spreads	Breakeven additional Widening
2 year	60	75	40	53	20	32
3 year	70	48	50	37	30	26
5 year	80	29	60	23	40	17
10 year	100	19	75	14	55	11
30 year	130	12	100	9	75	7

Generally, the greater the expected yield change, the greater the desire to have more call protection. With regard to near-term yield changes: (1) for premium callable bonds (bonds trading to call), the empirical duration (observed price sensitivity) tends to be less than the option-adjusted duration, resulting in underperformance during declining rates and (2) for discount callable bonds (bonds trading to maturity), the empirical duration tends to be greater than the option-adjusted duration, resulting in underperformance in rising rates. Any large deviations from the index exposure to call risk should recognize the potential significant tracking implications and the market directionality of the bet.

MEASURING SUCCESS

Common sense dictates that "you can't manage what you can't measure." Managers know this to be true, yet so often find themselves without the tools necessary to measure the extent of their bets and the value added or lost from those bets. Measuring the extent of the bets was covered earlier in this chapter. This section will discuss how to measure whether any value has been added and from what bets.

Outperform Adjusted Index Returns

Returning to the sailing theme, how is the portfolio sailboat doing versus the index sailboat? Is the portfolio making any ground against the index? To evaluate relative performance, the portfolio returns need to be adjusted for each of the following: (1) pricing, (2) transaction costs of growth and rebalancing, and (3) expenses. Pricing is a critical factor that needs to be considered, especially in enhanced indexing where deviations versus the index are small and pricing errors can hide valuable information. If a Lehman Brothers Index is the benchmark, then the portfolio needs to be re-priced with Lehman Brothers prices. Small differences in either the time of pricing or the pricing matrix, may result in large differences (among pricing services) in periodic returns over short measurement periods. Over longer periods, these pricing differences will average zero, but for value-added measurement purposes, periodic pricing accuracy is critical.

Since the index does not have transaction costs associated with asset growth, principal reinvestment, or income reinvestment, accurate adjustments need to be made to portfolio returns to account for these differences. A simple way to account for this is to maintain a trading log with implied transaction costs as a percent of total portfolio assets. The periodic summation of these implied costs will provide a good estimate of tracking error drag associated with growth and income reinvestment.

Finally, an adjustment for expenses is required. As was discussed earlier, keeping low expenses is a simple way to enhance returns. Nevertheless, portfolio returns should be "grossed up" by these expenses to put the portfolio on equal footing with the index for measurement purposes.

Exhibit 16: Consistent Positive Tracking

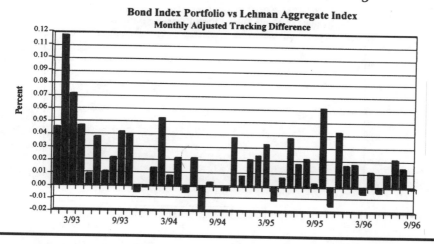

Exhibit 16 shows the monthly *adjusted* tracking of the largest bond index (enhanced) mutual fund. This portfolio is managed against the Lehman Brothers Aggregate Bond Index. If the sources of enhancements are multiple and of a controlled nature, it's expected that the average tracking difference would be small and usually positive. As shown, the monthly tracking differences are small (between +12 basis points and -2 basis points) and mostly positive. Exhibit 17 shows a rolling 12-month summation of the monthly *adjusted* tracking differences. An enhanced indexing strategy that has good risk management and diversified enhancements should be able to consistently perform above the index. Falling below the index return over 12 months most likely would be the result of either not matching the index risk properly, or, of the enhancement strategies not be adequately diversified.

Low and Stable Monthly Tracking Differences

The other measure of success, from an indexing standpoint, is how closely the portfolio is exposed to the same risk factors of the index. This can be measured by evaluating the rolling 12-month standard deviation of *adjusted* tracking differences of the portfolio versus the index. Exhibit 18 is an example from the same bond index mutual fund managed against the Lehman Brothers Aggregate Bond Index. If a portfolio is properly exposed to the index risk factors, the standard deviation will be low and stable, as shown.

Detailed Performance Attribution

To accurately measure the success of risk factor management and the enhancement strategies, the manager needs excellent performance attribution tools. The performance attribution analysis should be able to attribute tracking error to term structure factors, sector bets, quality bets, and issue selection across sectors and qualities.

Exhibit 17: Consistent Positive Tracking

Bond Index Portfolio vs Lehman Aggregate Index
Trailing 12-Month Total Adjusted Tracking Difference

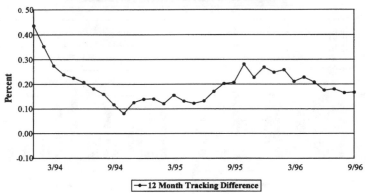

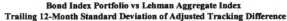

Exhibit 18: Consistently Low Tracking Error

Bond Index Portfolio vs Lehman Aggregate Index
Trailing 12-Month Standard Deviation of Adjusted Tracking Difference

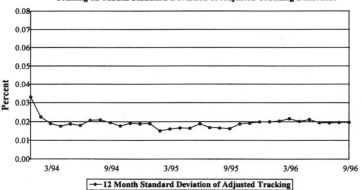

The term structure attribution should be analyzed at the portfolio level versus the index. The sector and quality attribution (allocation and issue selection) should be analyzed at the sector and sub-sector levels (detailed sector and maturity categories) with the ability to drill down to issue level detail. Issue performance should be risk adjusted (versus Treasury equivalent returns) with sub-sector, sector, and portfolio returns rolled up from the security level. This level of attribution will provide the manager with the tools to measure with precision the risk matching and return enhancing strategies, with the result being "winning the race" against the index and against most managers.

Chapter 27

Global Corporate Bond Portfolio Management

Jack Malvey, CFA
Managing Director
Lehman Brothers

INTRODUCTION

The corporate bond market is the most fascinating subset of the global capital markets. Beyond the abstractions of rating symbols, media reports of new issues each day, and portfolio performance measurement, thousands of organizations with different credit "stories" sell debt to finance their expansion. These organizations range from Canadian provinces, development banks such as the Asian Development Bank, sovereigns like Italy, Poland, and Malaysia to corporations in North America, Europe, and Asia; their credit quality spans from impeccable to defaulted. These borrowers use dozens of different types of debt instruments (first mortgage bonds, debentures, equipment trust certificates, subordinated debentures, medium-term notes, floating-rate notes, private placements, preferred stock) in multiple currencies (dollars, yen, Euros, marks, Swiss francs, pounds) at any maturity ranging from one year to even a thousand years. Sometimes, these debt structures carry embedded options, which may allow for full or partial redemption prior to maturity at either the option of the borrower or the investor. Sometimes, the coupon payment floats with short-term interest rates or resets to a higher rate after a fixed interval or a rating change.

Investors are rewarded for the assumption of credit risk. Except near and during recessions, corporate bonds usually outperform U.S. Treasury securities. Since the inception of the Lehman Indices in 1973, investment-grade corporates (9.82%) have outperformed U.S. Treasuries (9.36%) by 46 bp per year on average through 1997.

Each day, hundreds of corporate bond portfolio managers face thousands of choices in the primary (new issue) and secondary markets. These portfolio managers consist of individuals in the pursuit of high yields, commercial banks arbitraging the difference between the higher yields on floating-rate notes and their lower cost of funding, mutual funds attempting to maximize both yield and total return, insurers and state pension funds seeking to fund their projected long-term liabilities, "pure" total-return maximizers competing against each other on a monthly, quarterly, and annual basis to satisfy their clients or risk their loss, and

577

hedge funds staking out leveraged long positions in credits with short-term spread contraction potential and short positions in credits likely to widen sharply. These investment choices are partially driven by the existing security population of the corporate market (sector, issuer, structure, and currency) and partially by the psychology of the portfolio managers (overall risk tolerance, shortfall risk aversion, and internal politics of the investment-management institution).

Borrowers and investors intersect mainly through dealers. Each day, a few dozen corporate bond dealers convey information about secondary positions and new issue offerings from any of the thousands of corporate borrowers to the hundreds of corporate bond portfolio managers. Through their investment banking and syndicate operations, dealers also advise issuers on when and how to sell new debt. Through their fixed-income research, sales, and trading arms, dealers relay investment recommendations to portfolio managers.

The task of global corporate bond portfolio management is to process all of this rapidly-changing information about the corporate bond market (issuers, issues, dealers, and competing managers) and to construct the portfolio with the best return for a given risk tolerance. This discipline combines the excitement and qualitative tools of equity analysis with the quantitative precision of fixed-income analysis. This chapter provides a brief guide to methodologies which may help portfolio managers meet this formidable challenge.

CORPORATE RELATIVE-VALUE ANALYSIS

Should U.S. investors add Eurobonds of non-U.S. issuers? Should London portfolio managers buy fixed-rate U.S. industrial paper and swap into floating-rate notes? Should U.S. insurers buy perpetual floaters issued by British banks and swap back into fixed-rate corporates? When should investors fade the corporate sector and increase allocation to governments, pursue the "strategic upgrade trade" (sell Baa/BBBs and add higher-rated A corporate debt), rotate from industrials into Yankees, and deploy a credit derivative (i.e., short the high-yield index) to hedge their portfolios? To respond to such questions, investors need to begin with an analytical framework (relative-value analysis) and to develop a strategic outlook for the global corporate market.

Economists have long debated the concept and measurement of "value." But fixed-income practitioners, perhaps because of the daily pragmatism enforced by the markets, have developed a consensus about the definition of value. In the bond market, "relative value" refers to the ranking of fixed-income investments by sectors, structures, issuers, and issues in terms of their expected performance during some future interval.

For the day trader, relative value may carry a maximum horizon of a few minutes. For a large insurer, relative value may have a multi-year horizon. Accordingly, "relative-value analysis" refers to the methodologies used to generate such rankings of expected returns.

Within the global corporate market, "classic" relative-value analysis is a dialectical process combining the best of top-down and bottom-up approaches. This method picks the sectors with the most potential upside, populates these favored sectors with the best representative issuers, and selects the structures of the designated issuers at the curve points that match the investor's outlook for the benchmark curve.

For many corporate investors, the use of classic relative-value analysis has been sufficient to ensure a measure of portfolio success. Although sector, issuer, and structural analyses remain the core of superior relative-value analysis, the increased availability of information and technology have transformed the analytical process into a complex discipline. To assist their endeavors, corporate portfolio managers in the 1990s have far more data than ever on the total returns of sectors, issuers, and structures, quantity and composition of new-issue flows, distribution of product demand by investor classes, aggregate credit-quality movements, multiple sources of credit analyses on individual issuers, and spreads.

RELATIVE VALUE METHODOLOGIES

In this section, the main methodologies for corporate relative-value maximization are reviewed.

Total Return Analysis

Corporate relative-value analysis begins with a detailed dissection of past returns and a projection of expected returns. Capital markets have regular rhythms. For instance, the economic cycle is the major determinant of overall corporate spreads. During recessions, the escalation of default risk widens spreads (which are risk premiums over underlying, presumably default-free government securities). Conversely, economic prosperity reduces bankruptcies and tightens corporate spreads.

Thanks to the development of corporate indices (effectively databases of prices, spreads, issuer, and structure composition), analyses of monthly, annual, and multi-year total returns have uncovered numerous patterns (i.e., seasonality, election-cycle effects, and auction effects) in the global corporate market. Admittedly, these patterns do not always reoccur. But an awareness and understanding of these total-return patterns are essential to optimizing portfolio performance.

Total return analysis also justifies portfolio objectives and constraints. After years of admonitions by various academics, market analysts, and consultants, total return data have been used to justify the relaxation of credit-quality constraints for many U.S. corporate portfolios during the 1990s.

Primary Market Analysis

Supply is often a misunderstood variable in the tactical relative-value calculus. Prospective new supply induces many traders, analysts, and investors to advocate a defensive stance toward the overall corporate market as well as toward individual sectors and issuers. Yet the premise, "supply will hurt spreads" is more cliche than fact. In the first quarters of 1991, 1992, 1993, and the first two months of 1996, origination surges were associated with market spread contraction and strong relative returns for corporates. In contrast, the sharp supply decline during the first quarter of 1994 was accompanied by spread expansion and a major decline in both relative and absolute returns for corporates.

In the investment-grade corporate market, heavy supply often helps spreads/returns as the new primary valuations validate and enhance secondary valuations. When primary origination declines sharply, secondary traders lose reinforcement from the primary market and tend to raise their bid spreads. Counter to intuition and cliche, relative corporate returns often perform best during periods of heavy supply.

Given their immediate focus on the deals of the day and week, portfolio managers often overlook market-structure dynamics in making portfolio decisions. Because the pace of change in market structure is gradual, market dynamics have less effect on short-term tactical investment decision-making than on long-term strategy.

The composition of the global corporate bond market has shifted markedly during the 1980s and 1990s. Medium-term note (MTN) origination has come to dominate the front end of the corporate curve. Rule 144A bonds (quasi-private placement bonds) have captured a growing share of Yankee, high yield, and emerging-market debt. Structured notes and index swaps have heralded the introduction of derivative instruments into the mainstream of the corporate market. The high-yield corporate sector has become just another asset class after having been stress-tested in 1989-1990. Global origination has become a more popular technique for agencies, supranationals, sovereigns, Canadians, and some large corporate borrowers.

Although the growth of derivatives and high-yield instruments stands out during the past decade, the globalization of the corporate market has been the most profound development. The rapid growth of the Eurobond market since 1975 and the emergence of the Dragon bond market (dollar offerings initially made only in Asia) in the early 1990s have led to the proliferation of truly transnational corporate portfolios. From a broad viewpoint, the rapid development of the emerging-debt market may be seen as a subset of this globalization process.

Partially offsetting this proliferation of issuers, the global corporate market has become structurally more homogeneous (intermediate bullets) during the past decade for three reasons. First, there has been a continued shift away from utility issuers, who had preferred long-dated maturities to fund long-term capital assets. Second, new origination was less costly at the front of very steep yield curves. Third, the emergence and tremendous growth of the swap market made intermediate origination more convenient.

The trend toward bullet securities does not pertain to the high-yield market, where callables remain the structure of choice. With the hope of credit-quality improvement, many issuers expect to refinance prior to maturity at lower rates.

There are three strategic portfolio implications for this structural evolution. First, scarcity value must be considered in corporate relative-value analysis. The dominance of bullet structures translates into scarcity value for structures with embedded call and put features. This aspect is not captured by option-valuation models.

Second, long-dated maturities will decline as a percentage of outstanding corporate debt. This shift will lower the effective duration of all outstanding corporate debt and reduce aggregate sensitivity to interest-rate risk. For asset/liability managers with long horizons, this shift of the maturity distribution suggests a rise in the value of long corporates and helps to explain the warm reception afforded to most new Century offerings (100-year maturities).

Third, the use of corporate derivatives will escalate rapidly. The maturation of corporate bond derivatives, whether on a stand-alone basis or embedded in structured notes, will give rise to new strategies for investors and issuers.

Liquidity and Trading Analysis

Short-term and long-term liquidity influence portfolio management decisions. Citing lower expected liquidity, some investors are reluctant to purchase equipment trust certificates, Rule 144A's, private placements, MTNs, and non-local corporate issuers. Other investors gladly exchange a potential liquidity disadvantage for incremental yield. For investment-grade issuers, these liquidity concerns often are exaggerated.

During the past decade, secondary trading has boomed from an accumulation of factors: the great refunding blitz of the early 1990s; the resulting multiplier effect of record origination as most new issues were sold partially on swap against existing issues; the market volatility triggered by the 1990-1991 recession; a variety of secular sector swings (such as buying U.S. bank debt in the early 1990s and coping with the "Asian Contagion" of 1997-1998); the effects of the descent of the yield curve as investors sought call protection in bullets, some defense against the yield curve in put structures in 1994, and short-term yield maximization in high-coupon callables in 1992-1993; the cyclical steepening of the U.S. yield curve in the early 1990s, which facilitated the expansion of dealer inventories to take advantage of the "positive carry trade" and the flattening of the U.S. yield curve in 1997, which induced some dealers to stock lower inventory; the entrants of new dealers into the corporate bond market, especially from the ranks of commercial banks; the conversion of some total-return managers to an equity-style approach; and the conversion of some insurers to a total-return style approach.

Secondary Trade Rationales

Capital-market and issuer expectations constantly change. Recession may arrive sooner rather than later. The yield curve may have steepened instead of flattened. The auto and paper cycles may be moving down from their peaks. An industrial may have announced a large debt-financed acquisition, earning an immediate ratings rebuke from the agencies. A major bank may plan to repurchase 20% of its outstanding common stock, great for shareholders but leading to higher financial leverage for debtholders. In response to daily information flows, portfolio managers amend their portfolios. To understand trading flows and the real dynamics of the corporate market, investors should consider the most common rationales to trade and to not trade. There are dozens of rationales to execute secondary trades in the pursuit of portfolio optimization. Several of the most popular are discussed below.

Yield/Spread Pickup Trades

These trades represent the most common secondary transactions across all sectors of the global corporate market. Based on our observation, 60% of all secondary swaps reflect investor intentions to add additional yield within the duration and credit-quality constraints of a portfolio. If 5-year, A3/A− GMAC paper trades at 60 bp, 10 bp behind 5-year, A1/A+ Ford Motor Credit at 50 bp, then some investors will deem the rating differential irrelevant and swap into GMAC for a spread gain of 10 bp per annum. This "yield-first psychology" mirrors the institutional yield needs of long-term asset/liability managers, commercial banks, and mutual funds. Despite the passage of two decades, this investor bias toward yield maximization also may be a methodological relic left over from the era prior to the introduction and market acceptance of total-return indices in the mid-1970s. There is empirical support for the effectiveness "yield-first psychology." Baa corporates (10.74%) outperformed A-rated securities (9.80%) by 94 bp from 1973 through 1997 according to Lehman indices. But this tactic is not without risk. As measured by the standard deviation of total return, Baa returns (11.74%) have been considerably more volatile than A's (10.48%). In general, yield/spread maximization works reasonably during periods of economic growth.

Credit-Upside Trades

Credit-upside trades are closely related to yield/spread maximization transactions. In the illustration of the GMAC and Ford Motor Credit trade described above, some investors may swap based on their view of potential credit-quality improvement for GMAC. Credit-upside trades are particularly popular in the crossover sector (securities with ratings between Ba2/BB to Baa3/BBB- by either rating agency). From the early 1990s through the mid-1990s, such notable issuers as Chrysler, McDonnell Douglas, and Transco Energy regained investment-grade status and produced exceptional relative returns for holders.

Credit-Defense Trades

Credit-defense trades become more popular with the gathering of economic storm clouds. Secular sector transformations often generate uncertainties and induce defensive repositioning by investors. In anticipation of greater competition, some investors reduced their portfolio exposures in the mid-1990s to sectors like electric utilities and telecommunication firms. And as some Asian currencies and equities swooned in mid-1997, some portfolio managers cut their allocation to the Asian debt market. Unfortunately because of yield-maximization needs and a general reluctance to realize losses by some institutions (i.e., insurers), many investors tend to react more slowly to credit-defense propositions. Ironically once a credit sours sufficiently to invoke the wrath of the rating agencies, internal portfolio guidelines often dictate security liquidation immediately after the loss of single-A or investment-grade status. This is usually the worst possible time to sell a security and maximizes the harm incurred by the portfolio.

New-Issue Swaps

New-issue swaps contribute to secondary turnover. Because of perceived superior liquidity, many portfolio managers prefer to rotate their portfolios gradually into more current, on-the-run issues. This disposition, reinforced by the usually superior market behavior of newer issues in the U.S. Treasury market, has become a self-fulfilling prophecy for some issues. In addition, some portfolio managers buy certain new issues to generate sufficient commissions to pay vendors through soft dollars. Rarely, an underwriter may insist on cash-only purchases for "hot" transactions. As a result of these practices, investors usually pay for their new-issue purchases through some combination of cash and swap of an existing security in their portfolio.

Sector-Rotation Trades

Sector-rotation trades, within corporates and among fixed-income asset classes, have become more popular during the 1990s but do not rival the activity in the equity market. As soon as the Fed launched its preemptive strike against inflation in February 1994, some investors exchanged fixed-rate corporates for floating-rate corporates. In 1995, the specter of U.S. economic weakness prompted some investors in high-yield corporates to rotate from consumer-cyclical sectors like autos and retailing into consumer non-cyclical sectors like food, beverage, and healthcare. The anticipation of slower U.S. economic growth in 1998 induced a defensive tilt by some asset managers away from other cyclical groups like paper and energy.

Curve-Adjustment Trades

Curve-adjustment trades are undertaken to reposition overall portfolio duration. For most corporate investors, their portfolio duration resides within a range from 20% below to 20% above the index duration. If corporate investors could have predicted yield curve movements perfectly in 1994 and 1995, then they would have lowered their portfolio duration at the beginning of 1994 and extended their duration in late 1994. Although most fixed-income investors prefer to reconfigure the duration of their aggregate portfolios in the more-liquid Treasury market, strategic portfolio duration tilts also can be implemented in the corporate market.

Structure Trades

These trade also gain appeal with movements in volatility and the shape of the yield curve. As shown during the second quarter of 1995, the rapid descent of the yield curve contributed to underperformance of callable structures. With curve stabilization during the third quarter of 1995, investors were more willing to trade into an extra 35 bp of spread for high-quality callables compared to bullets of similar quality and less put off by the possible cost of negative convexity. The sharp downward rotation of the U.S. yield curve during the second half of 1997 also contributed to poor relative performance by put structures. The yield sacrifice for protection against higher interest rates instead constrained total return as rates fell.

Cash Flow Reinvestment

Cash flow reinvestment needs force investors into the secondary market on a regular basis. Some cash flows arrive during interludes in the primary market. And sometimes, the composition of recent primary supply may not be compatible with portfolio objectives.

Bias for Activity

Bias for activity affects both passive (indexers) and active managers as well as dealers. Referring to the overall capital markets, the late Fisher Black perfectly characterized some of this activity as "noise trading." Dealers closely monitor the aging of their security inventories. Stale positions, usually on the books for more than 90 days, justifiably are viewed with suspicion by risk managers. Ancient holdings may be worth less than their marks, otherwise they would have been purchased by investors. Accordingly, all corporate traders seek to limit their stale positions. At the same time in their quest for portfolio optimization, indexers are rebalancing their portfolios to conform with the ever shifting composition of indices and active managers are surfing among primary and secondary flows for the slightest glimmer of incremental value. The sum total of dealer activity, indexer realignments to cut tracking error, and active managers searching for valuation nuances breeds a natural bias for activity in the global corporate market.

Trading Constraints

Market analysts should also understand the main rationales for not trading.

Portfolio Constraints

Collectively, these inhibitions are the single biggest contributor to the persistence of market inefficiency across the global corporate market. Many U.S. state pensions cannot purchase corporate securities with ratings below A3/A- and Rule 144A's under administrative and legislative guidelines. Some pension funds also have limitations on MTNs and non-U.S. corporations. Regulators have limited the exposure of U.S. insurers to high-yield corporates. At the same, many European investors are restricted to issues, rated at least single-A and sometimes Aa, manufactured originally in annual-pay Eurobond form. Globally, many commercial banks must operate exclusively in the floating-rate realm; all fixed-rate securities, unless swapped, are out of bounds.

"Story" Disagreement

Traders, salespersons, sell-side analysts and strategists, and buy-side colleagues have dozens of potential trade rationales that will supposedly benefit portfolio performance. The proponents of the secondary trade may have a legitimate point, but the portfolio manager may be unwilling to accept the "shortfall" risk if the investment recommendation does not pan out. For example in early 1998, analysts and investors alike were about equally divided on short-term prospects for better valuations of Asian sovereign debt. Asia enthusiasts had little chance to persuade pessimists to buy Asian debt.

Buy-and-Hold

Although many long-term asset/liability managers claim to have become more total-return focused in the 1990s, accounting constraints (cannot sell positions at a loss compared to book cost or take too extravagant a gain compared to book cost) limit the ability of these investors to transact. Effectively, these investors remain traditional "buy-and-hold" investors.

Administrative Burdens

Marketing, compliance, and accounting demands have soared during the 1990s. Many asset management firms spend almost 50% of their schedule on these administrative chores. In turn, some investors are burdened with multiple functions: analysis; portfolio management; and marketing. In particular, portfolio managers with heavy marketing obligations to existing and potential clients may be limited in their capability to react to short-term valuation anomalies in the corporate bond market.

Seasonality

Secondary trading slows at month ends, more so at quarter ends, and the most at the conclusion of calendar years. Dealers often prefer to reduce balance sheets at year-end. And portfolio managers take time to mark their portfolios, prepare reports for their clients, and chart strategy for the next period. During these intervals, some of the most compelling secondary offerings can languish.

Spread Analysis

By custom, some segments of the high yield and Eurobond markets still prefer to measure value by bond price or bond yield rather than spread. But for the rest of the global corporate market, nominal spreads (the yield difference between corporate and government bonds of similar maturities) have become the basic units of both price and relative-value analysis. Starting in Europe during the early 1990s and gaining momentum during the late 1990s, swap spreads have emerged as the common denominator to measure relative value across fixed- and floating-rate note structures. During the next decade, the U.S. investment-grade and high-yield markets eventually may switch to swap spreads to be consistent with Europe.

Unlike the mortgage-backed securities market, the corporate market has not adopted and is not likely to adopt option-adjusted spreads or zero-volatility spreads as measures of price/value for two reasons. First, almost all Eurobonds and MTNs as well as a growing percentage of public investment-grade corporate debt are bullet securities that do not feature embedded options. Second, the standard one-factor binomial models of the 1990s do not account for credit-spread volatility.

Investors should develop a rigorous understanding of the strengths and weaknesses of spread tools. The most common technique for analyzing spreads among individual securities and across industry sectors is mean-reversion analysis. Buy this *cheap* sector or issuer because the spread used to be much tighter. Sell this *rich* sector or issuer because the spread used to be much wider.

Mean-reversion analysis can be instructive as well as misleading. The mean is highly dependent on the interval selected. And there is no market consensus on the appropriate interval.

Quality-spread analysis examines the spread differentials between low and high-quality credits. "Percent yield spread" analysis (the ratio of corporate yields to government yields for securities of similar duration) is another popular technical tool with some investors. This methodology has serious drawbacks that undermine its usefulness. Percent yield spread is more a derivative than an explanatory or predictive variable.

Structure Analysis

Leaving aside credit, issue structure analysis and structural allocation decisions usually hinge on yield curve and volatility forecasts as well as interpretation of option-valuation model outputs (see the discussion below). In the short run, these factors largely will influence structural performance. But investors should also take into account long-run market dynamics.

Specifically, callable structures have become a rare species in the investment-grade corporate bond market. Thanks to an almost continuous positively-sloped yield curve during the 1990s, the curve's decline to approximately three-decade lows in 1993, late 1997, and early 1998, the composition of the public U.S. corporate bond market has been converging toward its intermediate-bullet Eurobond cousin. Bullets climbed from 24% of Lehman's investment-grade index at the start of 1990 to 75% at year-end 1997. Over the same interval, callables declined at an astounding rate from 72% to a 20% index share. Sinking-fund structures, once the structural mainstay of natural-gas pipelines and many industrial sectors, are on the "structural endangered species list" with a drop from 32% of the public bond market in 1990 to only 1% in 1997. Despite a flurry of origination in 1994 and early 1995, put market share also has fallen from 5% in 1990 to

4% in 1997. Pure corporate zero's are in danger of extinction with a fall from 4% market share in 1990 to negligible in 1997.

Bullets

Front-end bullets (1-5 year maturities) have great appeal to the growing cadre of barbellers (use corporates at the front of the curve and Treasuries in longer maturities) and asset swappers (non-U.S. institutions who convert short bullets into floating-rate products). Intermediate corporates (5-12 maturities), especially in the 10-year neighborhood, have become the most popular segment of the U.S. investment-grade and high-yield corporate markets. Fifteen-year maturities are comparatively rare and have been favored by banks who occasionally uncover arbitrages in the asset-swap market. Because 15-year structures take five years to roll down a positively-sloped yield curve, these structures hold less appeal for many investors.

In contrast, 20-year structures are favored by many investors. Spreads for these structures are benched off the 30-year Treasury. With a positively-sloped yield curve, the 20-year structure provides higher yield than a 10-year or 15-year security and less vulnerability (lower duration) than a 30-year security.

The 30-year maturity is the most popular form of long-dated security in the global market. But in 1992, 1993, late 1995, and 1997 there was a minor rush to issue 50-year (half-Centuries) and 100-year (Centuries) securities. These longer-dated securities provide investors with extra positive convexity for only a modest increase in modified-adjusted duration.

Callables

Typically after a 5-year or 10-year wait, these structures are callable at the option of the issuer at any time. Call prices usually are set at a premium above par (par + the initial coupon) and decline linearly on an annual basis to par 5-10 years prior to final scheduled maturity. The ability to refinance debt in a potentially lower-interest rate environment is extremely valuable to issuers. Conversely, the risk of earlier-than-expected retirement of an above-current market coupon is bothersome to investors. To place callables, issuers pay investors an annual spread premium (about 30 bp to 40 bp for high-quality issuers) for being short the call option. This call premium varies through time. During 1993, some high-quality issuers sold new 30-year callable structures at market-clearing spread premiums of only about 20 bp over a bullet to the same maturity. In 1994, callable spread premiums rose with rates. By the second quarter of 1995, callable spread premiums for some high-quality issuers like DuPont, Wal-Mart, and Wisconsin Power & Light had risen to 40 bp to 45 bp over a bullet to the same maturity.

Sinking Funds

This structure allows an issuer to execute a series of partial call (annually or semi-annually) prior to maturity. There is also usually a provision to retire an additional portion of the issue on the sinking fund date, typically ranging from 1 to 2 times the mandatory sinking fund obligation.

Putables

Put structures are simpler than callables. Unlike American-option callables (allow call at any time at the designated call price after expiration of the noncallable/ nonredemption period), puts typically feature a single one-time, one-date put option (European option). Less frequently, put bonds offer a second or third put option. With falling rates, issuers have shied away from new put structures during the 1990s. Rather than run the risk of refunding the put bond in five years or ten years at a higher cost, many issuers would prefer to pay an extra 10 bp to 20 bp for the privilege of issuing a longer-term liability. Put structures provide investors with a partial defense against sharp increases in interest rates.

Corporate Curve Analysis

The rapid development of credit derivatives in the mid-1990s has inspired a groundswell of academic interest in the development of more rigorous techniques to analyze the term structure of corporate spread curves. In particular, the corporate market has a fascination with the slope of issuer credit curves between 10-year and 30-year maturities. Like the underlying Treasury benchmark curve, corporate spread curves change shape over the course of economic cycles. Typically, spread curves steepen when the bond market becomes more wary of interest rate and general credit risk.

Credit Analysis: Cornerstone of Corporate Portfolio Analysis

Superior credit analysis has been and will remain the most important determinant of the relative performance of corporate bond portfolios. For too many years, investors and dealers have had to relearn the hard way that credit analysis has no easy shortcuts or model magic. Specifically, variables like interest-rate volatility and binomial processes imported from option-valuation techniques are not especially helpful in ranking the expected performance of a pool of individual credits like British Gas, Commonwealth Edison, Pohang Iron & Steel, and Tenneco.

Credit analysis is both non-glamorous and arduous for many top-down portfolio managers and strategists, who focus primarily on macro variables. Genuine credit analysis encompasses actually studying issuers' financial statements, interviewing issuers' management, evaluating industry issues, reading indentures and charters, and developing an awareness of (not necessarily concurrence with) the views of the rating agencies about various industries and issuers.

Unfortunately, the advantages of such analytical rigor may clash with the rapid expansion of the universe of global bond credits. At the beginning of 1998, there were approximately 4,000 different credits in the dollar-denominated corporate bond market. With continued privatization of state enterprises, new entrants to the high-yield club, and the rapid growth of the developing markets, the global roster of issuers could reach 5,000 by 2000.

Asset Allocation/Sector Rotation

Sector rotation strategies have long been popular with equity investors. In the corporate bond market, "macro" sector rotation strategies also have a long history. During the past two decades, there have been major shifts in investor sentiment toward the four major sectors: utilities (wariness of nuclear exposure in the early-to-mid 1980s); financial institutions (concern about asset quality in the late 1980s and early 1990s); industrials (event risk in the late 1980s and recession vulnerability during 1990-1992), and Yankees (periodic wariness about the implications of sovereignty for Quebec, political risk for sovereigns, and the "Asian Contagion" of 1997-1998).

In contrast, "micro" sector rotation strategies have a briefer history in the corporate bond market. A detailed, unbundling of the four main corporate sectors into their prime subcomponents (i.e., breaking financial institutions down into banks, brokerage, finance companies, insurance, REITs) was not available from the firms providing corporate indices until 1993. Beginning in the mid-1990s, "micro" sector rotation strategies have become much more influential as portfolio managers gain a greater understanding of the relationships among intra-corporate sectors.

CONCLUSION

The evolution of the global corporate asset class will accelerate over the next decade. Although destined to become more structurally homogeneous with intermediate bullets as the instrument of choice, this asset class will become more heterogeneous in terms of credit quality (more lower-quality credits) and geography (more European and emerging-market corporates). Over the same interval, the eventual arrival of real-time corporate indices as well as improved analytics will lead to a proliferation in the use of credit derivatives to enhance risk-adjusted returns.

Chapter 28

International Bond Portfolio Management

Christopher B. Steward, CFA
Senior Vice President
Putnam Investments

J. Hank Lynch, CFA
Vice President
BankBoston

INTRODUCTION

Management of an international bond portfolio poses more varied challenges than management of a domestic bond portfolio. Differing time zones, local market structures, settlement and custodial issues, and currency management all complicate the fundamental decisions facing every fixed income manager in determining how the portfolio should be positioned with respect to duration, sector, and yield curve.

The following fundamental steps in the investment process apply to domestic and international investing alike:

1. setting investment objectives
2. establishing investment guidelines
3. developing portfolio strategy
4. constructing the portfolio
5. monitoring risk and evaluating performance

The added complexities of cross-border investing magnify the importance of a well defined, disciplined, investment process. The chapter is organized to address each of these challenges in turn.

To provide a broad overview of the many aspects of international fixed income investing within the scope of one chapter implies that many topics do not receive the depth of discussion that they deserve. The topic of currency management alone has provided material enough for many books and articles. Wherever possible, footnotes are provided referencing additional sources that offer a more detailed discussion of each topic.

INVESTMENT OBJECTIVES

Most investors are attracted to global bonds as an asset class because of their historically higher returns than U.S. bonds. Others are drawn to global bonds because of their diversification value in reducing overall portfolio risk. The investor's rationale for investing in international bonds is central to developing appropriate return objectives and risk tolerances for a portfolio. Broadly speaking, investor objectives can be divided into four categories: total return, diversification or risk reduction, current income, and asset/liability matching. Each of these investment objectives has implications for the management of an international bond portfolio and should be reflected in the investment guidelines. At a minimum, investment guidelines should include return objectives, risk tolerances, benchmark selection, and an appropriate time horizon for judging performance.

Return objectives are often expressed in terms of the benchmark return, e.g., benchmark return plus 100 basis points after management fees. The investment objectives will indicate not only the most appropriate benchmark, but also the most suitable management style. Investors who are primarily concerned with diversification may wish to place tight limits on the size of positions taken away from the benchmark to ensure that the diversification benefit is not weakened. A total-return oriented investor might be far less concerned with how the portfolio composition differs from the benchmark, but may be more critical of shortfalls in performance.

Investment guidelines should be flexible enough to allow the portfolio manager sufficient latitude for active management while keeping the portfolio close enough to the benchmark to ensure that the portfolio remains diversified. The guidelines should address allowable investments including, the countries in the investment universe, minimum credit ratings, and the use of derivatives such as futures, options and structured notes. The time horizon over which investment performance is to be measured is also important. A short-term time horizon, such as a calendar quarter, may encourage more short-term trading which could diminish the natural diversification benefit from international bonds as an asset class. Investors who emphasize the risk reduction, or diversification aspect of international bond investing should have a longer time horizon of perhaps two to three years. As differences between economic cycles can be prolonged, this would provide enough time for a full economic cycle to play out and the diversification benefit to take effect be realized.

Benchmark Selection

Benchmark selection for an international bond portfolio has many ramifications and should therefore be done carefully. As is the case when choosing an international equity benchmark index, the choice of a pure capitalization (market value) weighted index may create a benchmark that exposes the investor to a disproportionate share in the Japanese market relative to the investor's liabilities or diversification preferences. While international equity indices chosen for benchmarks are most often quoted in the investor's local currency (i.e., unhedged), international bond benchmarks may be hedged, unhedged, or partially hedged depending on the investors objectives.[1] The choice of a hedged, unhedged, or hybrid benchmark will likely alter the risk and return profile of the resulting investment portfolio and should thus be done with careful consideration of the primary rationale for investing in international bonds.

Benchmarks can be selected from one, or a combination, of the many existing bond indices: global, international (ex-U.S.), currency-hedged, G7 only, 1-3 year, 3-5 year, 7-10 year, emerging markets, Brady bonds, etc., or a custom index can be created. The most frequently used benchmarks are the J.P. Morgan Global Government Bond Index, or the Salomon Brothers World Government Bond Index, although many other investment houses such as Merrill Lynch, Lehman Brothers, Goldman Sachs, and UBS offer full index services as well. The benchmark often provides both the return objective and the measure of portfolio risk.

Benchmark Currency Position

Currency management is a matter of much debate in the academic literature.[2] The natural currency exposures incurred through international investing require portfolio managers to adopt either an active or passive approach to currency management. Many managers are attracted to active currency management because of the large gains that can be attained through correctly anticipating currency movements. Some international fixed income portfolio managers, however, prefer not to actively manage currency exposures. This may reflect doubts about their own ability to add value through active currency management, or a belief that no one can forecast currency movements with any degree of reliability. The former often hire outside currency overlay managers to manage the residual currency risk determined by the bond allocation, the latter often run fully hedged or unhedged portfolios as a matter of policy. Both approaches, in our opinion, are sub-optimal[3] as compared to an integrated approach that determines bond and currency allocations simultaneously. Although many international fixed income portfolio managers place greater emphasis on bond market allocations while managing currency exposure as a residual, the same fundamental economic factors which influence bond prices also impact currency levels. The integrated approach to determining bond and currency allocations explored later in this chapter illustrates how a more explicit accounting of the risk and expected return due to currency can result in superior investment performance.

---

[1] Indices are expressed in local currency, U.S. dollars (unhedged), and hedged U.S. dollars. However the local currency index, which expresses market returns in each of the 16 or so currencies in the index, is not investable but is provided as a reference for comparing bond market vs. currency performance.

[2] For an excellent overview of currency management practices, including a detailed review of historical data, see Roger G. Clarke and Mark P. Kritzman *Currency Management: Concepts and Practices*, (Charlottesville, VA: The Research Foundation of the Institute of Chartered Financial Analysts, 1996).

[3] See Philippe Jorion, "Mean/Variance Analysis of Currency Overlays," *Financial Analysts Journal* (May/June 1994), pp. 48-56. Jorion argues that currency overlays, although they can add value, are inferior to an integrated approach to currency management.

Exhibit 1: Returns and Standard Deviation of Returns of the Salomon Non-U.S. Government Bond Index and Lehman Aggregate Index (Monthly Data, Unhedged, and Hedged Basis)

	1985-96	1985-88	1989-92	1993-96	1989-96
Annualized Total Return					
Unhedged Index	14.45%	25.15%	7.91%	11.00%	9.45%
Hedged Index	8.75	10.23	6.60	9.45	8.02
50% Hedged	11.26	16.93	7.00	10.09	8.53
U.S. Aggregate Index	10.10	11.76	11.66	6.94	9.28
Standard Deviation of Returns					
Unhedged Index	10.97%	13.34%	11.21%	6.89%	9.31%
Hedged Index	3.77	4.23	3.39	3.56	3.50
50% Hedged	6.65	8.28	6.57	4.17	5.52
U.S. Aggregate Index	4.86	5.90	4.12	4.24	4.22
Sharpe Ratio					
Unhedged Index	0.77	1.37	0.12	0.93	0.42
Hedged Index	0.73	0.80	0.00	1.37	0.70
50% Hedged	0.79	1.22	0.60	1.33	0.54
U.S. Aggregate Index	0.84	0.84	1.23	0.56	0.87

Most of the academic research on currency hedging for U.S. dollar-based investors suggests that a partially hedged benchmark offers superior risk-adjusted returns as compared with either a fully hedged or unhedged benchmark.[4] This research has led some to recommend a 50% hedged benchmark for either a passively managed currency strategy, or as a good initial hedged position for an active currency manager. In addition to selecting an appropriate benchmark, a suitable currency hedge position, or benchmark hedge ratio, needs to be determined. For example, a U.S. dollar-based fixed income investor whose primary goal is risk reduction might adopt a hedged or mostly hedged benchmark as the diversification benefit has historically been greater from hedged international bonds. Despite a higher correlation with the U.S. bond market than unhedged international bonds, hedged international bonds offer better risk reduction due to a lower standard deviation of return than even the U.S. market. In addition, this lesser volatility of hedged international bonds results in more predictable returns. Conversely, an investor who has a total return objective, and a greater risk tolerance, would be more likely to adopt an unhedged, or mostly unhedged benchmark and allow more latitude for active currency management.

International bonds have historically provided higher returns than U.S. bonds. As seen in Exhibit 1, over the 12 years through 1996, the Salomon Non-U.S. Government Bond Index has outperformed the Lehman Aggregate Bond Index by an average of 435 basis points per annum. When looked at on a hedged basis, however, the non-U.S. index lagged the U.S. performance by 135 basis

---

[4] See Gary L. Gastineau, "The Currency Hedging Decision: A Search for Synthesis in Asset Allocation," *Financial Analysts Journal* (May-June 1995), pp. 8-17 for a broad overview of the currency hedging debate.

points. The standard deviation of returns for the non-U.S. unhedged index is substantially higher than the standard deviation of U.S. returns. However, the standard deviation of returns for the hedged index is lower than the standard deviation of U.S. returns during all periods. Using Sharpe ratios to compare returns on a risk-adjusted basis,[5] both the hedged and unhedged non-U.S. index underperformed the U.S. over the 12-year period. However, the results for each of the three 4-year periods are too variable to draw a firm conclusion about which provides the better risk-adjusted return.

Although the unhedged non-U.S. bond index often provided higher returns than the hedged index, the nearly 15 percentage points in annualized outperformance of the unhedged over the hedged index from 1985 through 1988 was extremely unusual. This was due to the dollar's rapid decline from its 1984 peak. If instead only the eight years from 1989 through 1996 are analyzed, the picture changes dramatically with the unhedged index outperforming the hedged index by 143 basis points. The Sharpe ratios for this period are 0.42 for the unhedged index and 0.70 for the hedged index, compared with 0.87 for the Lehman Aggregate index. According to the data in Exhibit 1 the argument for international bonds as an asset class for U.S dollar-based investors hardly seems compelling. However, it is the correlations of different asset classes that provide the diversification benefit, and when international bonds are included as a component of a U.S. dollar-based fixed income portfolio, the analysis provides dramatically different results.

Exhibit 2 shows that when the same analysis used in Exhibit 1 is applied to a portfolio composed of a 30% allocation to international bonds, the risk-adjusted returns improve substantially. Over the 12-year period, the portfolio with an allocation to unhedged bonds provided 130 basis points of added return over a domestic-only portfolio while slightly lowering overall portfolio volatility. Although the portfolio including hedged international bonds returned 41 basis points less than the domestic-only portfolio, its Sharpe ratio was higher than the domestic-only portfolio because its standard deviation was 25% lower than that of the domestic-only portfolio. In fact, the domestic-only portfolio had the highest standard deviation of any of the four portfolios, giving it the lowest Sharpe ratio.

As shown above, returns from currency have been highly variable depending on the time period chosen. The academic literature, and the data in Exhibits 1 and 2, support adopting a partially hedged currency benchmark. A benchmark currency position should be established in accordance with careful consideration for risk tolerances and return objectives.

Returns of those portfolios with a 30% international bond allocation over the 1989 to 1996 period are lower than the full 12-year performance figures, but the risk-adjusted performance of each of these portfolios remains higher than the

---

[5] The Sharpe ratio measures returns in excess of the risk-free rate, per unit of standard deviation. The formula is $(R_p - RFR)/\sigma_p$ where R_p is the return on the portfolio, RFR is the risk-free rate, and σ_p is the portfolio standard deviation. The U.S. Treasury bill component of the Salomon Brothers World Money Market Performance Index was used as the risk-free rate.

domestic-only portfolio. The return on the portfolio including a 30% allocation to unhedged international bonds of 9.33 was five basis points higher than the domestic-only portfolio, and its standard deviation of 4.12% was ten basis points lower than the domestic-only portfolio, giving it a Sharpe ratio of 0.91 compared to the domestic portfolio's 0.87. The Sharpe ratios for the other two portfolios that include hedged and 50% hedged international bonds are even higher at 1.04 and 1.01 respectively.

Risk Limits

Many investment guidelines will include explicit risk limits on bond and currency positions as well as duration and credit risk. Exposure limits can be either expressed as absolute percentages, or portfolio weights relative to the benchmark. Expressing limits in terms of trading blocs, which exhibit a high degree of correlation, allows the portfolio manager more scope for shifting exposures without adding significantly to overall portfolio risk. Bond markets can be divided into five trading blocs: the *dollar bloc* (the U.S., Canada, Australia, and New Zealand), *core Europe* (Germany, France, Holland, and Belgium), *peripheral Europe* (Italy, Spain, the U.K., Denmark, Sweden, Finland, and Portugal), Japan, and the *emerging markets*. These dividing lines, however, are somewhat subjective. For example, the U.K. often trades more closely with dollar bloc than European markets, and many might place Denmark with the core European countries. Limits on investment in countries outside the benchmark should also be specified at the outset. Despite the pitfalls of using duration to measure interest rate risk across countries, risk limits on duration are nonetheless useful and should be established.

Exhibit 2: Returns and Standard Deviation of Returns of a Portfolio with 30% International Bonds and 70% Domestic Bonds (Monthly Data)

	1985-96	1985-88	1989-92	1993-96	1989-96
Annualized Total Return					
Unhedged Index	11.40%	15.78%	10.54%	8.16%	9.33%
Hedged Index	9.69	11.30	10.14	7.70	8.90
50% Hedged	10.45	13.31	10.26	7.89	9.05
U.S. Aggregate Index	10.10	11.76	11.66	6.94	9.28
Standard Deviation of Returns					
Unhedged Index	4.79	5.82	4.51	3.63	4.12
Hedged Index	3.64	4.38	3.10	3.20	3.18
50% Hedged	4.00	4.89	3.56	3.25	3.44
U.S. Aggregate Index	4.86	5.90	4.12	4.24	4.22
Sharpe Ratio					
Unhedged Index	1.13	1.54	0.87	0.43	0.91
Hedged Index	1.02	1.02	1.14	0.98	1.04
50% Hedged	1.11	1.33	1.03	1.02	1.01
U.S. Aggregate Index	0.84	0.84	1.23	0.56	0.87

Exhibit 3: Examples of Bond and Currency Risk Limits for an International Bond Portfolio

Bond Exposures

Currency Bloc	Benchmark	Minimum	Maximum
Yen	32%	15%	45%
U.S.	0%	0%	15%
Dollar Bloc	6%	0%	18%
Core Europe	47%	30%	65%
Peripheral Europe	16%	0%	35%
Other Markets	0%	0%	15%
Total Duration as a % of Index	100%	80%	120%

Currency Exposures

Currency Bloc	Benchmark	Minimum	Maximum
Yen	32%	10%	40%
U.S.	0%	20%	95%
Dollar Bloc	6%	0%	20%
Core Europe	47%	15%	55%
Peripheral Europe	16%	0%	25%
Other Markets	0%	0%	10%
Total Foreign Currency Exposure	100%	5%	80%

The risk limits in Exhibit 3 might be appropriate for a moderately risk averse investor. Note that in Exhibit 3 the range of allowable exposures is wider for bond exposures than currency exposures and that the minimum U.S. dollar exposure is 20%.

Credit risk limits, usually a minimum average credit weighting from the two major credit rating agencies, and limits on the absolute amount of low or non-investment grade credits, should also be included. Apart from default risk, the illiquidity of lower rated securities poses another type of credit risk as international fixed income portfolio managers tend to shift funds in and out of markets frequently. Due to the lack of a liquid corporate bond market in most countries, and the relative illiquidity of Eurobonds compared to domestic government bond markets, most credit risk in international bond portfolios is concentrated in U.S. and emerging market bonds.

Derivatives

Investment guidelines should specify the permitted use of derivatives in the portfolio. Although derivatives are required to hedge currency exposures, they are a useful, but not necessary, tool for duration management. Guidelines will usually place limitations on the leverage[6] that can be obtained through use of derivatives, for example by requiring cash to be set aside equal to the notional amount of a

---

[6] Implicit in most derivatives, both fixed income and currency derivatives, is an exposure to shifts in short-term interest rates.

long futures position, or by prohibiting the writing of uncovered put or call options. Structured notes, which combine derivatives, such as swaps and options, with a certificate of deposit or medium-term note to create a specific exposure to interest rates or currencies, should be subject to the same limitations on leverage. Many structured notes were engineered to have risks commensurate with, or less than, plain vanilla bonds. The separation of coupon and principal payments in most structures notes gives them a similar appearance to fixed income securities. However, structured notes, like the derivatives of which they are composed, can also be highly levered. The risk to capital incorporated in some of these securities, if poorly understood, can result in substantial losses. Thus, the use of structured notes need not be prohibited, but guidelines for their use should contain criteria consistent with those applied to the derivatives of which they are composed.

Custodian Banks

Other housekeeping issues include setting up an account with a global custodian bank, usually a large international bank with branches or correspondent banks in each of the countries in which the portfolio will invest.[7] Although the ultimate responsibility for all aspects of the investment process rests with the portfolio manager, the custodian bank will be responsible for the settlement and delivery of any securities and foreign exchange transactions, collection of coupon income, and maintenance of cash balances. The custodian bank will also provide portfolio and trading reports, although the portfolio manager should have internal portfolio account systems for a variety of reasons including identification of trading errors and risk management.

PORTFOLIO STRATEGY

Once the investment guidelines have been established, the portfolio manager needs to develop a portfolio strategy appropriate to the investor's objectives and risk tolerances. Just as in many other areas of investment management, portfolio managers often subscribe to different management styles, or investment disciplines. As the performance of most portfolio managers is judged against the benchmark return, they are constantly seeking opportunities to outperform the benchmark. There are a number of means by which portfolio managers can add to returns, however, the bulk of excess returns relative to the benchmark come from broad bond market and currency allocation decisions. A disciplined investment approach, based upon fundamental economic factors and market indicators of value, can facilitate the market and currency selection process. Because of the historically high volatility of currency returns, the approach to currency management should be of primary concern.

---

[7] See Robert Binney "Implementation Issues: Global Custody," pp. 78-83, from *Global Portfolio Management* (Charlottesville, VA: AIMR, 1996).

Styles of International Bond Portfolio Management

The image that many people have of international bond managers is that of a jet fighter pilot: well seasoned, cool under fire, and ready to pit his nerve and skill against the market. However, the metaphor that best describes the international bond manager is not that of the fighter pilot, but the captain of a 747. Rather than "pushing the envelope" of his machine's performance, the jumbo jet pilot relies more on checklists and management of computer flight and navigation systems than piloting skill. The modern jetliner is an extremely complicated piece of machinery that requires a depth of experience and skill in managing the wealth of resources available on the flight deck. The pilot, in addition to drawing from his own years of experience, relies on other inputs as well; some from other members of the crew, and some from talking to controllers and meteorologists on the ground. Like managing a portfolio, piloting a jetliner involves managing risks, and a safe arrival is better achieved by avoiding dangerous situations than by deft manipulation of the controls in an emergency.

The complexity of the international fixed income markets is more akin to the complexity of the U.S. equity market than the U.S. bond market. First, the global fixed income portfolio manager must operate in the U.S. bond market *plus* 10 to 20 other markets, each with their own market dynamics. Second, changes in interest rates generally affect all sectors of the U.S. bond market in the same way (with the exception of mortgage-backed securities), although the magnitude of the changes may vary. Like the equity market, where it is not unusual to have some industries or market sectors move in opposite directions, international bond markets may also move in different directions depending upon economic conditions and investor risk tolerances.

Equity managers use a variety of investment disciplines, such as value, growth, or small capitalization, to try to create some sense of order out of the chaos of the market. Equity investors also use a variety of indicators, such as price-to-earnings ratios, earnings momentum, and technical analysis, to help identify attractive opportunities. As different as each of these approaches are, they are all designed to provide superior market returns. International bond managers also utilize one or more different management styles. These can be divided into four general categories:

- *The Experienced Trader.* These managers use experience and intuition to identify market opportunities. They tend to be active traders, trying to anticipate the next market shift by international fixed income and hedge fund managers. The basis for these trades is derived from estimates of competitors' positions and risk tolerances bolstered by observation of market price movements and flow information obtained from brokerage houses. The experienced trader is often a contrarian, looking to profit from situations where many investors may be forced to stop themselves out of losing positions.
- *The Fundamentalist.* This management style rests upon a belief that bonds and currencies trade according to the economic cycle, and that the cycle is forecastable. These managers rely mostly upon economic analysis and forecasts in selecting bond markets and currencies. These managers tend to

have less portfolio turnover as the economic fundamentals have little impact on short-term price movements.

- *The Black Box.* The quantitative manager believes that computer models can identify market relationships that human beings cannot. These models can rely exclusively on economic data, price data, or some combination of the two. Quantitative managers believe that use of computer models can create a more disciplined investment approach which, either because of other managers' emotional attachment to positions, their lack of trading disciplines, or their inability to process more than a few variables simultaneously, will provide superior investment results.
- *The Chartist.* Some investors may rely primarily on technical analysis to determine which assets to buy or sell. Chartists will look at daily, weekly, and monthly charts to try to ascertain the strength of market trends, or to identify potential turning points in markets. Trend following approaches, such as moving averages and stochastics aim to allow the portfolio manager to exploit market momentum. Counter-trend approaches, such as relative strength indices and oscillators try to identify when recent price trends are likely to reverse.

Very few international bond portfolio managers rely on only one of these management styles, but instead use some combination of each. Investment managers that rely on forecasts of the economic cycle to drive their investment process will from time to time take positions contrary to their medium-term strategy to take advantage of temporary under or overvaluation of markets identified by technical analysis, or estimates of market positions. Even "quant shops" that rely heavily on computer models for driving investment decisions will sometimes look to other management styles to add incremental returns. Regardless of the manager's investment style, investment decisions must be consistent with the investor's return objectives and risk tolerances, and within the investment guidelines.

International bond portfolio managers would do well to emulate equity investors in maintaining a disciplined approach to buy and sell decisions. This would require each allocation away from the benchmark to have a specified price target (or more often yield spread or exchange rate level), and stated underlying rationale. As long as the investment rationale that supported the initial decision remained unchanged, the position would be held, or potentially increased if the market moves in the opposite direction. Each trade should be designed with consideration for the relevant bond yield or exchange rate's behavior through time. For example, an exchange rate that exhibits a tendency to trend will require a different buy and sell discipline than an asset that is mean reverting.[8]

---

[8] For example, if the widening of a yield spread to an all-time wide level causes a portfolio position to suffer losses, the temptation may be to increase the size of the position. This would be rational if the spread has historically shown mean reverting patterns and is expected to continue to do so. Then profits could be made as the spread converges towards its mean. If, however, the yield spread tended to follow long-term tightening and widening trends then a discipline applying stop-loss limits would be more appropriate.

Exhibit 4: U.S. Bonds and Non-U.S. World Index versus Best and Worst Performing Markets

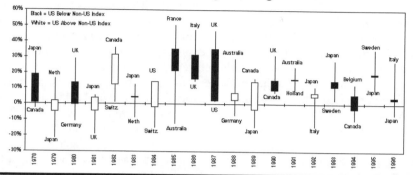

Sources of Excess Return

The baseline for any international bond portfolio is the benchmark. However, in order to earn returns in excess of the benchmark, after management fees, the portfolio manager must find ways to augment returns. These excess returns can be generated through a combination of five broad strategies: bond market selection, currency selection, duration management/yield curve plays, sector/credit/security selection, and, if permitted, investing in markets outside the benchmark. Each of these strategies can add to returns, however, currency and bond market selections generally provide the lion's share of returns.

Bond Market Selection

Incremental returns from overweighting the best performing bond markets can be extremely large. Annual local currency return differentials between the best and worst performing bond markets ranged from 7% to 39%, with an average difference of 17 percentage points according to the 18 years of annual return data from the Salomon Brothers World Government Bond and Bond Performance Indices which include only developed markets.[9] When currency movements are added, the return differentials nearly double. As shown in Exhibit 4, in U.S. dollar terms, the smallest range between the best and worst performing market was 14% and the widest was 65% with an average differential of 31 percentage points. Thus, international bond portfolio managers can significantly enhance returns by overweighting the better performing bond markets, and currencies, in the index.[10]

[9] The Salomon World Government Bond Index began in December of 1984, and presently contains 15 markets. The Salomon Bond Performance Index began in 1978 and was discontinued in 1995. The Bond Performance Index contained 10 markets, and included Euro and Foreign issues as well as Government bonds. Exhibit 4 uses the Bond Performance Index from 1978 through 1984, and the World Government Bond Index thereafter.

[10] As of this writing, it appears likely that at least several countries will adopt the Euro as a common currency when European Monetary Union is scheduled to commence in January 1999. Although the impact of this event is a matter of some debate, the bond markets in the countries which have adopted the single currency will trade much more closely than before.

Currency Selection

Regardless of the initial portfolio hedge ratio, most guidelines will allow for some active management of currency exposures. The attraction of active currency management is strong because the potential gains are so large. However, as the volatility of currency returns is generally higher than that of bond market returns, the incremental returns gained from currency exposures must be evaluated relative to the additional risk incurred. For an active currency management strategy to consistently provide superior risk-adjusted performance, a currency forecasting method is required that can predict future spot rates better than forward foreign exchange rates. As shown later, forward foreign exchange rates are not forecasts of future spot foreign exchange rates, but are determined by short interest rate differentials.

Academic studies have shown that several strategies have been successful in generating consistent profits through active currency management. The fact that forward foreign exchange rates are poor predictors of future spot exchange rates is well known. Historically, discount currencies (i.e., those with higher interest rates than the base currency) have depreciated less than the amount implied by the forward rates, providing superior returns from holding unhedged positions in currencies with higher interest rates. Overweighting of currencies with high real interest rates versus those with lower real interest rates has also been shown to provide incremental returns.[11] In addition, currency movements are not a random walk, but exhibit serial correlation, or a tendency to trend.[12] Thus, simple technical trading rules, such as the crossover of a short and long moving average, can provide opportunities for incremental currency returns.[13] These findings, demonstrating that excess currency returns can be generated consistently, provide a powerful incentive for active currency management.

Duration Management

Although closely aligned with the bond market selection decision, duration management can also enhance returns. Bullet versus barbell strategies in a curve steepening or flattening environment can enhance yield and total return. In addition to these strategies that are also available to domestic portfolio managers, the international fixed income portfolio manager has the option of shifting duration between markets while leaving the portfolio's overall duration unchanged. Likewise, duration-neutral positions across markets can be achieved by targeting preferred sectors of the yield curve.[14]

---

[11] See Gastineau, "The Currency Hedging Decision," pp 13-14.

[12] One suggestion as to why currency markets trend is that central banks attempt to smooth foreign exchange rate movements through intervention. Thus, because central bank participation in the foreign exchange market is not motivated by profit, their actions keep the market from being truly efficient. See Robert D. Arnott and Tan K. Pham, "Tactical Currency Allocation," *Financial Analysts Journal*, (May/June 1993) pp. 47-52.

[13] See Richard M. Levich and Lee R. Thomas, "The Merits of Active Currency Risk Management: Evidence from International Bond Portfolios," *Financial Analysts Journal*, (September/October 1993) pp. 63-70.

[14] As discussed later, a duration-neutral position to the benchmark would mean having the same contribution to duration from each country as the benchmark. Contribution to duration, measured as the weight times duration of a given market can be achieved with a large market weight of short duration bonds or a small market weight of long duration bonds.

Duration management, however, is more difficult in international bond investing as very few foreign bond markets have liquid bond issues with an original maturity longer than 10 years. Most foreign bond markets also lack the broad range of instruments, such as strips and repos, that allow for low-cost, active management of duration. Recent progress on these fronts is being made in the U.K., Italy, and Germany. Interest rate futures, available in most markets, offer a very liquid and low cost vehicle for changing duration or market exposure quickly. The interest rate swaps market is generally very liquid across international bond markets; however, counterparty credit, technical, and operational barriers limit effective participation in this market to large institutional investors.

Sector Selection

Investing in non-government bonds can also enhance returns as most indices include only government bonds. However, options are more limited as government and government-guaranteed issues account for 62% of all bond issues outstanding[15] compared with 12.7% for the corporate bonds. If the U.S. is excluded, where corporate bonds account for one third of all U.S. dollar-denominated bonds outstanding, the figure drops to only 4.2%. Corporate bonds account for less than 15% of the market capitalization in all other bond markets — except for a 26% share in the Netherlands. In several large countries, such as Germany and Italy, non-financial corporate bonds are virtually nonexistent. This scarcity of corporate bond markets outside the U.S. is due to a policy of discouraging the raising of capital through bond issuance in favor of bank financing and equity issuance in many countries. Other instruments are also available in selected markets including Eurobonds, mortgage bonds, and inflation indexed bonds.

Investing in Markets Outside the Index

If allowed by portfolio guidelines, allocating assets to markets outside the index can significantly enhance returns without dramatically altering the risk profile of the portfolio. For example, Finland was one of the best performing bond markets during 1995, but, because of its small size, was not included in the Salomon Brothers World Government Bond Index (WGBI) until June 1996. Similarly, New Zealand's very attractive U.S. dollar return of 18% during 1996 would have ranked it as the fourth best performing market in the WGBI. For those investors with a higher risk tolerance, exposure to emerging markets can significantly add to returns. For example, a portfolio composed of 80% exposure to the Salomon Non-U.S. Government Bond Index and 20% exposure to the Salomon Brady Bond Index from 1991 through 1996 would have added 186 basis points to the return of the international index and *reduced* the standard deviation of returns by 13%.

---

[15] Data from Salomon Brothers, "How Big is the World Bond Market? — 1996 Update," (August 1996).

Exhibit 5: G7 Industrial Production and Change in Bond Yields

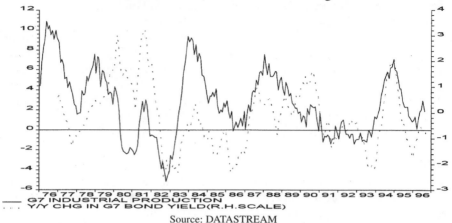

G7 INDUSTRIAL PRODUCTION
Y/Y CHG IN G7 BOND YIELD(R.H.SCALE)

Source: DATASTREAM

A Fundamental-Based Approach to Investing

The portfolio strategy is often composed of both a medium term *strategic* allocation, and a shorter term *tactical* allocation. The strategic allocation is composed
of positions designed to take advantage of longer term economic trends designed
to be held for one to three months, or longer. The tactical allocation generally
relies on technical analysis or flow information to identify shifts in market prices
that are likely to occur within a few days to several weeks. Tactical allocations are
often contrarian in nature, driven by expectations of a reversal in a recent price
trends; however, tactical allocations can also be momentum following, especially
if a breakout of a technical range appears likely. The strategic allocation can be
compared to the course set by a sailing ship. The tactical allocation may result in
substantial divergence from the course setting at times, much as a ship must tack
when sailing into the wind. The trick, however, is to be able to identify when
changing conditions warrant a change in the set course, or only a small detour.

The strategic decision of which bond markets and currencies to overweight usually begins with an outlook for the economic cycle and bond and currency forecasts in each of the markets to be considered for investment. As shown in
Exhibit 5, the long-run economic cycle is closely correlated with changes in bond
yields, and trends in both the economic cycle and bond yields tend to persist for a
year or longer. The millions of dollars spent each year by money management
firms, banks, and brokerage houses in forecasting economic trends is testimony to
the potential returns that can be achieved by correctly forecasting economic
growth, especially turning points in the economic cycle. Forecasting interest rates,
however, is extremely difficult and the academic literature generally holds that
interest rate forecasts are unable to generate consistent risk-adjusted excess returns.
This is partly because market prices can deviate substantially over the short term

from the level consistent with the economic fundamentals which only impact bond and currency prices over the medium to long term. Also, the volatile nature of certain economic data series may result in an exaggerated market reaction to an individual data release that may be at odds with the actual trend in the economy. These deviations may persist for several months until either the initial figure is revised, or several subsequent data releases reveal the error in the initial interpretation.

The creation of an independent economic outlook can be useful in several ways. It can help identify when market interpretations of the economic data are too extreme, or add value through correctly anticipating economic shifts not reflected in the market consensus. Also, as it is often not absolute changes in interest rates, but changes in interest rates relative to other markets that determines the margin of performance in international fixed income investing, an independent economic outlook does not require accurate growth forecasts for each individual market, but only economic growth differentials to be able to add value. Whether the portfolio will invest in U.S. bonds or not, the large influence of the U.S. dollar and the Treasury market on foreign markets underlines the importance of an independent outlook on the U.S. economy.

Thus, the economic outlook forms the foundation for the *strategic* allocation for bonds and currencies. The economic outlook should also include an indication of the relative conviction regarding the economic view for each country to assist in ranking the relative attractiveness of markets. However, even though economic fundamentals in a particular country may be extremely bond supportive, bond prices may be too high to make it an attractive investment. Likewise, bonds are sometimes excessively cheap in countries with poor economic fundamentals thus providing an attractive investment opportunity. Thus, the economic outlook must be compared with either consensus economic forecasts, or some measure of market value to identify attractive investment opportunities. In addition, the volatilities and correlations of the various bond and currency markets should be used to assess the incremental impact of any position on overall portfolio risk compared with its expected return.

The strategic allocation decision of which markets to over or underweight relative to the benchmark is thus a complex interaction of expected returns derived from assessments of economic trends, technical and value factors, and risk factors, estimated from historical volatilities and cross-market correlations. Each set of variables is defined and explored below, beginning with the fundamental factors used to create the economic outlook.

Fundamental Economic Factors

The seven main categories of fundamental economic influences are: cyclicals, inflation, monetary policy, fiscal policy, debt, the balance of payments, and politics. Each factor needs to be evaluated against market expectations to determine its likely impact on bond and currency prices. For example, a drop in inflation in a country such as Germany which has a history of low inflation may have a much lesser impact on bond prices than a drop in Italian inflation.

Cyclicals

As shown above, bond and currency valuations are heavily influenced by the economic cycle. A strong economy raises fears of higher inflation which erodes the value of fixed income securities and the purchasing power of the currency. In assessing the potential inflationary impact of stronger growth, analysts examine both the pace and composition of growth. One measure of inflationary pressures caused by economic growth, used by both academics and market participants, is the output gap. The output gap is a measure of the difference between present growth rates and the long-term potential growth rate of the economy. The economy's potential growth rate can be estimated using either a long-run historical average growth rate or a projection based on such factors as estimated growth in the labor force and productivity growth rates. If an economy is growing below its potential growth rate, it has excess labor and manufacturing capacity that should act as a constraint on wage and price increases. Conversely, if the economy is growing above its potential growth rate, bottlenecks should soon appear prompting business to bid up wages and the cost of raw materials to meet demand, and eventually pass these increased costs onto consumers.

The composition of growth also has a direct bearing on the potential for fueling inflation. Growth that is driven by capital investment rather than consumer demand is less likely to be inflationary (unless investment spending results in a competition for raw materials that drives up producer price inflation.) Likewise, strong export growth, is less likely to be inflationary, unless it is driven by a currency depreciation that raises the cost of imported goods. Thus, the outlook for economic growth and its composition will have a strong impact on inflation expectations.

Inflation

Inflation expectations have a direct impact on financial asset prices. As the future purchasing power parity of a country's currency is eroded by higher inflation, this prompts investors to demand a higher return for their savings (which represents deferred consumption) as they come to believe that their money will purchase less in the future. In its impact on the financial markets, it is the direction and magnitude of changes in the inflation rate *relative to market expectations* that counts. Bonds may rally on an increase in the rate of inflation which falls below market expectations while unanticipated increases in inflation usually cause bond yields to rise reflecting an increase in the inflation risk premium. The required rate of return demanded by the market may also change over time as risk appetites change. The required rate of return has become more uniform across markets as capital controls and other barriers to cross-border investment have been removed. The role that real yields play in market valuation is explored below.

A change in the rate of inflation can have a very different impact on currencies over the short and long run. Over the short run, an unexpected rise in inflation may lead to currency strength as the market anticipates a hike in managed interest rates to combat the inflation pressure. Over the long run, if the higher inflation persists, the erosion of purchasing power due to higher inflation leads to a depreciation of the currency relative to lower inflation countries. The Exhibit 6 shows that there has been a strong correlation between the change in exchange rates relative to the dollar since the demise of fixed exchange rates in the early 1970s, and changes in the price level. For example, the price level in Australia grew more than six times from 1972 levels, about half again as much as the nearly fourfold increase in U.S. prices. Thus, the U.S. dollar now buys about 50% more Australian dollars than it did 25 years ago. The currencies of Japan, Germany, Switzerland, and the Netherlands, whose price levels grew only 60% to 80% as much as in the U.S., all appreciated significantly against the U.S. dollar, which could purchase only one third to one half as much of these currencies as in 1972.

Monetary Policy

Central Banks throughout the developed world place great importance on price stability. In recent years, nearly all central banks have accepted price stability as their primary goal. Central banks in eight countries (Australia, Britain, Canada, Finland, Italy, New Zealand, Spain, and Sweden) have adopted, at least temporary, explicit inflation targets. An additional four (France, Germany, Switzerland, and Denmark) have medium term inflation objectives. Some central banks, such as the Bank of England, the Bank of Canada, and Sweden's Riksbank, also publish regular reports on the inflationary outlook. Other central banks (such as the Bank of Canada with its Monetary Conditions Index) also take explicit account of the impact of exchange rate movements in assessing the overall tightness of monetary policy.

Exhibit 6: U.S. $ versus Foreign Currencies and Change in Price Level 1972-1996

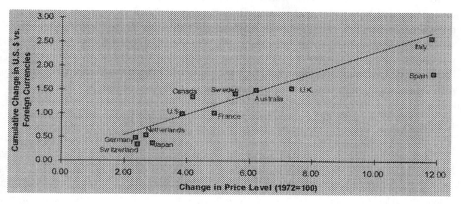

Source: OECD

Exhibit 7: Budget Deficit and 1994 10-Year Yield Change

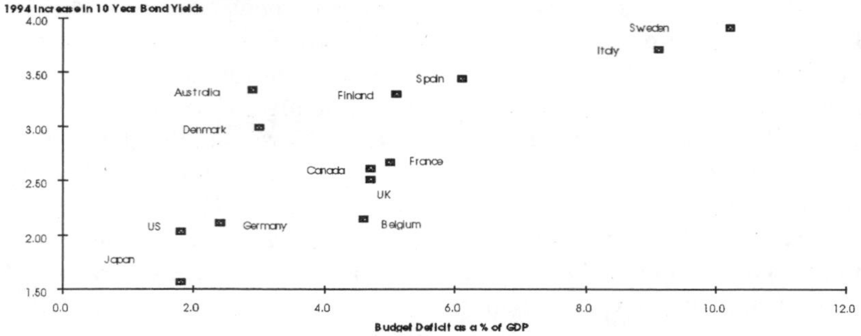

Source: OECD

Monetary policy is effective in allowing central banks to control short term interest rates but has only an indirect influence on bond yields. Nevertheless, short interest rate movements, especially changes in the direction of monetary policy, do have a significant impact on rates across the yield curve. Changes in short term interest rates have a direct impact on currencies as they impact both the returns to investors and hedge costs. Because the gains from effectively forecasting changes in official rates can be substantial, many in the financial markets devote resources to examining the personalities and decision making process at the Federal Reserve and other central banks. Some also use models to predict the direction of monetary policy, such as the Taylor Rule,[16] which utilizes the output gap, and a stated or implied inflation target, to measure the relative monetary policy stance.

Fiscal Policy

Although fiscal policy is more long term in nature, it can have a significant impact on financial asset prices, especially when fiscal policy is in the process of being tightened or loosened. A higher fiscal deficit will result in higher rates through the "crowding out" of private borrowers and increased demand for capital. The greater a country's dependence upon the capital market for funding, the more its long term interest rates will tend to fluctuate over the business cycle. The Exhibit 7 shows the increase in 10 year bond yields during 1994, a severe bear market for global bonds, plotted against deficit to GDP. Clearly, fiscal policy can have a large influence on bond prices, especially during a period when investors are becoming more risk averse.

Debt

The national debt is simply the accumulation of past deficits. Debt levels are normally analyzed in relation to GDP both for ease of comparison internationally, and because economic growth facilitates the servicing of debt. Debt service costs

[16] John B. Taylor, *Discretion versus Policy Rules in Practice*, Policy Paper No. 327 (Stanford, CA: The Center for Economic Policy and Research at Stanford University, 1992).

are a function of the size of the debt and the average interest rate paid on that debt. Countries such as Italy where nearly two thirds of their government bonds are either floating rate or less than one year in maturity, find that their debt service costs can fluctuate substantially from year to year with interest rate changes. If a country's debt levels rise to the point where investors are reluctant to hold its bonds, then it could fall into a debt trap. As investors demand a higher risk premium for holding the highly indebted country's bonds, interest rates on new debt issues are driven up adding further to debt service costs, until credit concerns prompt the market to halt lending altogether and default or debt restructuring becomes inevitable.[17] However, debt levels can have an impact on bond prices well before reaching levels where the debt trap becomes a concern.

In addition to the size of the debt, the amount held by foreigners is also important. Some countries, such as New Zealand issue little in other currencies, yet have more than half of their government bonds held by foreign investors. Canada and the U.S. have approximately one quarter of their government bonds held offshore. Interest rates in countries that depend on foreign capital to finance local spending, usually because local savings have already been tapped, can be particularly sensitive to changes in foreigner's willingness to lend. For emerging market countries the debt to exports ratio is commonly used as a measure of the country's ability to generate foreign exchange to service its foreign currency debt.

The Balance of Payments

Capital flows have a much greater impact on international markets than on U.S. asset prices as the sizes of foreign capital markets are smaller, and the dependence of their economies on foreign trade is often much larger than in the United States. Shifts in the balance of trade, however, often take years to work their way through the economy. These shifts may be obscured by noise in the data or other factors such as the "J-curve" effect. The impact of a shift in the balance of payments on financial asset prices, although long term in nature, can still offer opportunities for investment outperformance by identifying longer term secular shifts that will affect the long term growth potential of a country and the underlying demand and supply situation for its currency represented by its current account position.

For example, much of the strengthening of the U.S. dollar against the yen during 1996 can be attributed to a steep drop in the size of the U.S./Japanese bilateral trade deficit as shown in Exhibit 8. The U.S. dollar/Japanese yen exchange rate is heavily influenced by the cumulative current account deficit of the U.S. with Japan. The current account, which measures the flows of goods from one country to another, is offset by the capital account. The capital account represents the investment of the trade surplus in either direct investment (the building of physical plant), or portfolio investment (the purchase of debt or equity securities). Hence, the cumulative current account represents the transfer of wealth from one country to another.

---

[17] For a more complete discussion of the dynamics of the debt trap see *OECD Economic Outlook*, No. 58, (Paris: OECD, 1995), pp. 19-23.

Exhibit 8: Yen/Dollar Exchange Rate and Bilateral Trade Balance

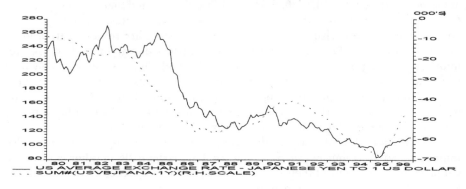

US AVERAGE EXCHANGE RATE - JAPANESE YEN TO 1 US DOLLAR
SUM#(USVBJPANA.1Y)(R.H.SCALE)

Source: DATASTREAM

Politics

While they may be the most difficult of the factors to quantify, there is no denying that, at times, political events can have a profound impact on financial asset prices. Elections, changes of government, parliamentary votes, and political scandals all have the power to move bond and currency prices. Perhaps the best illustration of the impact of a political event on the financial markets is the case of European Monetary Union, or EMU. Although EMU has far-reaching economic consequences, the entire undertaking is essentially political, including deciding which countries will be allowed to participate and when the switch from national currencies to a single currency will take place. In financial markets, unforeseen political events more often have the consequence of precipitating drops in asset prices, thus monitoring of the political environment and events can be instrumental in controlling portfolio risk.

Value and Technical Indicators

Identification of trends in economic fundamentals can help identify attractive investment opportunities in markets, but without some yardstick with which to measure value, we are like Archimedes with his lever but with no fulcrum on which to rest it. The determination of relative value is highly subjective. Most investors have preferred measures for assessing market over or undervalution, however, even the most respected market strategists often get it wrong. Some more objective measures of value, including real yields, technical analysis, and market sentiment surveys are explored below.

Real Yields

A real yield is the inflation-adjusted rate of return demanded by the market for holding long-term fixed income securities whose value can be quickly eroded by sustained increases in inflation. Real yields are impacted by supply and demand for capital as well as inflation expectations. Real yields are nominal bond yields minus *expected* inflation, however, expected inflation is often difficult to quantify. A few countries, such as the U.K., Canada, and Australia, and, as of January 1997, the U.S., have inflation-indexed bonds that pay a real rate of interest above the inflation rate. These bonds not only provide investors with protection against a surge in inflation but also offer a means of gauging investor inflation expectations.[18] Surveys often include inflation expectations, but these have a relatively short history .

Nominal bond yields deflated by *current* inflation, although not a precise measure of the market's real interest rate premium, are easily measurable and can still provide some useful insight into bond valuation. Real yields can be compared across markets or against their long run averages, such as 5 or 10 years, in each market. As shown in Exhibit 9, a strong correlation exists between nominal 10 year bond yields and the average inflation rate over the last 10 years. This relationship tends to be stable over time despite changes in the absolute level of yields. This suggests that the market has a long memory and will need to be convinced of a fundamental change in a country's inflation prospects before reducing the inflation risk premium on its debt. Thus the early recognition of such a change creates the potential for substantial profit.

Exhibit 9: Nominal 10-Year Bond Yields and 10-Year Average Inflation

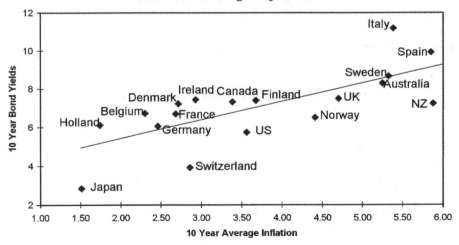

---

[18] Nominal yield to maturity is composed of a real yield and an inflation expectations component (Yield to Maturity = Real Yield to Maturity + Expected Inflation to Maturity). In these markets the nominal government bond yield and the real yield offered by inflation-indexed debt of the same maturity can be used to calculate the expected inflation rate to the maturity, sometimes called the breakeven inflation rate.

Technicals

Technical analysis can be as simple as drawing a trend line on a chart or as complicated as calculating the target of the third impluse wave of an Elliott wave analysis. In addition to bonds and currencies, technical analysis is applied to everything from stocks, to gold, to pork bellies. What all technical analysis has in common, is that it tries to predict future prices solely from examining past price movements. Most technical analysis models fall into one of two camps: trend following and counter trend. The former try to identify trends that should persist for some period of time, and the latter attempt to predict when a recent trend is likely to change. Trend following models include: simple or exponential moving averages, stochastics, and MACDs. Counter trend technical models include: relative strength indices and oscillators.

Market Sentiment

Market sentiment can be used as a contra-indicator of value as a heavy overweight of a particular market implies that fewer managers are likely to add to that market, and more managers, at least eventually, are likely to sell. Several surveys of investor sentiment are available including a quarterly Merrill Lynch survey of money managers, and a monthly Lehman Brothers survey, among others. Historic trends, as well as the overall levels should be taken into account when assessing market sentiment. For example, an indication that the market is underweight Japanese bonds might lead some to conclude that they are due for a rally, when historically, international fixed income managers have consistently underweighted the Japanese market, in part due to its low nominal yields. Sentiment surveys, however, do not tell the whole story as buying and selling by domestic investors, who are often not included in sentiment surveys, can also move markets.

PORTFOLIO CONSTRUCTION

Translating the strategic outlook into a portfolio allocation requires a framework for assessing expected returns against incremental portfolio risk. The following discussion on sources of return illustrates how returns can be separated into three components: excess returns on bonds, excess returns on currencies, and the risk-free rate. This methodology can assist in identifying where market prices are most out of line with the strategic outlook and whether bond market exposures should be hedged or left unhedged. However, the potential for higher returns is often associated with greater risk, and reference to market correlations can help estimate the incremental risk posed to the portfolio by any change in allocation. A brief discussion of other tools for portfolio construction, such as breakeven analysis and forward curves, closes this section.

Components of Return

The total return of an unhedged international bond portfolio for a U.S. dollar based investor can be expressed in the following equation:[19]

$$R_\$ \approx \sum w_i(r_i + \varepsilon_{\$, i}) \tag{1}$$

where

$R_\$$ = total portfolio return in U.S. dollars
r_i = bond market return for country i in local currency
$\varepsilon_{\$,i}$ = percentage change of the dollar exchange rate with country i
w_i = weight of the bonds of country i in the overall portfolio

Thus, the expected return on the portfolio is a function of the expected returns on the bonds and currencies in each market and their weights in the portfolio. However, in order to fully comprehend the impact of currency exposures on returns, the mechanics of currency hedging must first be understood.

Mechanics of Currency Hedging

Hedge costs are driven by short-term interest rate differentials. The covered interest rate parity theorem, associated with Keynes and Fisher, states that the forward foreign exchange rate for a fixed period must be equal to the interest rate differential between the two countries, otherwise riskless arbitrage would occur to bring the two back into equilibrium.[20] The formula is:

$$F = S_0\left(\frac{1 + c_d}{1 + c_f}\right) \tag{2}$$

where F is the forward foreign exchange rate, S_0 is the spot foreign exchange rate, and c_d and c_f are the domestic and foreign cash returns, or short-term (risk-free) interest rates, which match the maturity of the forward contract. By rearranging equation (2), the forward discount or premium f (or the percentage change of the forward rate from the spot exchange rate), becomes approximately the differential between the risk-free rates.[21]

$$f = F - S_0 \approx c_d - c_f \tag{3}$$

---

[19] The structure of this discussion is taken from Brian D. Singer and Denis S. Karnosky, *The General Framework for Global Investment Management and Performance Attribution* (Charlottesville, VA: The Research Foundation of the Institute of Chartered Financial Analysts, 1994). An abridged version also appeared in *The Journal of Portfolio Management* (Winter 1995), pp. 84-92. The relationship in equation (1) is approximate because bond market and currency returns of a foreign investment is more accurately expressed as the compounded gain of the two components: $(1 + r_i) \times (1 + \varepsilon_{\$,i}) - 1$.

[20] Uncovered interest rate parity would hold if the forward rates were an unbiased indicator of future foreign exchange rates, which was shown to be false in the portfolio strategy section. For an excellent introduction to currency terminology and the calculation of forward exchange rates see Chapter 1 of Clarke and Kritzman, *Currency Management: Concepts and Practices*.

The forward rate can also be expressed in "points" or the difference between the forward and spot rate, $F - S_0$. When interest rates are lower in the foreign country (i.e., the forward points are positive), the forward foreign exchange rate trades at a premium. That is, for the return on cash deposits to be equal in both currencies, the lower interest rate currency must appreciate to the forward foreign exchange rate. For example, as German rates are presently lower than U.S. rates, the forward points are positive for the U.S. dollar against the German mark. Thus, if cash returns are to be the same in both currencies, the percent appreciation of the German mark against the U.S. dollar would have to be exactly equal to the forward premium.

The Currency Hedge Decision

If the possibility of hedging using currency forwards is allowed, the portfolio return of equation (1) changes. The currency term would be left unhedged if the percentage return from currency is expected to be greater than the forward discount or premium, $\varepsilon_{\$i} > f_{\$,i}$, or hedged with forwards if the expected currency return is expected to be less than the forward discount or premium $\varepsilon_{\$i} < f_{\$,i}$. Thus the equation for a hedged portfolio becomes:

$$HR_\$ = \sum w_i(r_i + f_{\$,i}) \tag{4}$$

As equation (3) showed, the forward premium or discount is effectively equal to the short-term interest rate differential; thus, $f_{\$,i} = c_\$ - c_i$. By substituting this identity for the forward hedge, the equations for individual country unhedged and hedged returns become:

$$R_{\$i} = r_i + \varepsilon_{\$,i} \qquad \text{(unhedged return)} \tag{5}$$

$$HR_{\$i} = r_i + f_{\$,i} = r_i + (c_\$ - c_i) \qquad \text{(hedged return)} \tag{6}$$

where $R_{\$i}$ is the unhedged returns from country i for a U.S. dollar-based investor and $HR_{\$i}$ is the hedged return. There remain, however, two further options: cross hedging and proxy hedging. Cross hedging replaces the currency exposure to country i with currency exposure in country j, ($\varepsilon_{\$,j}$), through a cross forward rate, ($f_{j,i}$). Proxy hedging keeps the currency exposure in country i, but creates a hedge by establishing a short position in country j's currency ($-\varepsilon_{\$,j}$). These strategies would normally be considered only where the currencies of country i and j are highly correlated, and the hedge costs in country j, are lower than in country i.

---

[21] Equation (2) assumes that exchange rates are quoted in "direct terms," i.e., the U.S. dollar value of one foreign currency unit, though quote conventions vary by market. Futures and options on currencies traded on the Chicago Mercantile Exchange are all quoted in direct terms; however, over-the-counter forward contracts use market convention, most of which are in indirect terms (foreign currency units per U.S. dollar). Using indirect terms, the forward discount or premium in equation (3) becomes $f = c_f - c_d$. To avoid the complexities of compounding, the time period is assumed to be one year.

$$CR_{\$i} = r_i + (f_{j,i} + \varepsilon_{\$,j}) \qquad \text{(cross-hedged return)} \qquad (7)$$

$$PR_{\$i} = r_i + \varepsilon_{\$,i} + (f_{\$,j} - \varepsilon_{\$,j}) \qquad \text{(proxy-hedged return)} \qquad (8)$$

By substituting short term interest rate differentials for the forward returns and rearranging equations (5), (6), (7), and (8), it becomes apparent that the difference in return among the three strategies is entirely due to short term interest rates and currency exposure. The bond component of returns thus becomes the bond return minus the domestic short term interest rate, rather than the full measure of return.

$$R_{\$i} = (r_i - c_i) + (c_i + \varepsilon_{\$,i}) \qquad \text{(unhedged return)} \qquad (9)$$

$$HR_{\$i} = (r_i - c_i) + c_\$ \qquad \text{(hedged return)} \qquad (10)$$

$$CR_{\$i} = (r_i - c_i) + (c_j + \varepsilon_{\$,j}) \qquad \text{(cross-hedged return)} \qquad (11)$$

$$PR_{\$i} = (r_i - c_i) + (c_i + \varepsilon_{\$,i}) + [(c_\$ - c_j) - \varepsilon_{\$,j}] \quad \text{(proxy-hedged return)} \qquad (12)$$

Equations (9), (10), (11), and (12) show how integral the short-term interest rate differential is to the currency hedge decision. Hence, the short-rate differential should be attributed to the currency decision, and bond market returns should be calculated minus the domestic short-term interest rate. This can be made explicit by adding and subtracting the U.S. cash rate from each of the four equations above. This allows the forward premium ($f_{\$,i} = c_\$ - c_i$) to be inserted into the currency term creating three distinct components of return: the risk free rate ($c_\$$), the excess bond return ($r_i - c_i$), and the excess currency return, either hedged, unhedged, cross-hedged, or proxy hedged.

$$R_{\$i} = c_\$ + (r_i - c_i) + (\varepsilon_{\$,i} - f_{\$,i}) \qquad \text{(unhedged return)} \qquad (13)$$

$$HR_{\$i} = c_\$ + (r_i - c_i) \qquad \text{(hedged return)} \qquad (14)$$

$$CR_{\$i} = c_\$ + (r_i - c_i) + (\varepsilon_{\$,j} - f_{\$,j}) \qquad \text{(cross-hedged return)} \qquad (15)$$

$$PR_{\$i} = c_\$ + (r_i - c_i) + [(\varepsilon_{\$,i} - \varepsilon_{\$,j}) - f_{j,i}] \qquad \text{(proxy-hedged return)} \qquad (16)$$

Thus, the excess currency return becomes the currency return in excess of the forward premium (or discount). It can be seen that the bond decision is purely a matter of selecting the markets which offer the best expected excess return and that the bond and currency allocation decisions are entirely independent. This method of analyzing sources of return in effect treats bond and currency returns as if they were synthetic futures or forward positions. Equations (13) through (16) could be applied to a purely leveraged investor, such as a hedge fund, by simply omitting the risk free rate term. Cash investors with limited ability to take currency exposures independently of bond positions may find equations (9) through (12) more useful where the risk free rate is treated as an integral part of the currency hedge decision.

This methodology of attributing cash returns to the currency decision, and the excess return over cash to bonds, has implications for how allocation decisions are made. The returns of higher yielding markets, or those with inverted yield curves, will look somewhat less attractive when analyzed net of the cash interest rate. For example, at the beginning of 1996, Italian 10-year bond yields were 10.70% and 1-year Italian interest rates were 10.10%, thus the running yield that could be attributed to bond performance was only 60 basis points. In order to gain the additional 10.10% in running yield, the position would have to be run unhedged. One-year interest rates in the U.S. were 6% resulting in 410 basis point differential with Italy. Thus, it would have cost a U.S. dollar-based investor 4.1% to hedge exposure to the Italian lira over 12 months using currency forwards. In other words, hedging the Italian lira exposure in essence would have substituted the U.S. cash yield (or risk-free rate) of 6% for the Italian cash yield of 10.10%. Thus, if the Italian lira depreciated by less than the 4.1% against the U.S. dollar implied by the forward rate over 1996, the unhedged lira position would have added value over a hedged position.

In actuality, the Italian lira appreciated by 4.3% against the dollar during 1996, and the Italian bond component of the Salomon Brothers World Government Bond Index returned 27.2% in U.S. dollar terms. Thus, it might seem that 4.3% of the return from holding unhedged Italian bonds should be attributed to currency gain, and 22.9% to bond returns. However, following the methodology laid out in equations (13) and (14), the 4.1% Italian/U.S. 1-year interest rate differential should be added to the currency component of return because it was the decision not to hedge that allowed the manager to earn that full measure of return. The Italian 1-year interest rate should then also be subtracted from the Salomon Index's Italian bond market return of 21.9% in local currency terms. Thus, less than half of the gain from holding unhedged Italian bonds, 8.4%, came from excess currency returns, and 11.8% came from excess bond returns. The hedged return would have been only 17.8%, calculated from the Italian bond excess return of 11.8% plus the U.S. 1-year cash return of 6%.[22]

Market Correlations

Two factors that aid in assessing the incremental risk of changes to a portfolio are the volatility of returns and the correlation (or covariance) of returns with the portfolio as a whole. Normally when a decision is made to overweight a market, a less attractive market will be identified to be reduced by the same amount. Otherwise the trading costs associated with keeping all other markets in the same relative proportion to each other would be excessively high.[23] Thus, two risks, rather

---

[22] Due to compounding of the bond and currency returns, the sum of the currency and local bond market return figures is 1% less than the U.S. dollar-based total return figure (i.e., 4.3% currency gain × 21.9% local currency bond return = 1%). The Salomon U.S. dollar-hedged index return for Italian lira bonds, based on a rolling 1-month hedge, was 17.5%.

[23] In other words, if a particular market is selected for a 1% overweighting relative to the benchmark, it is often too costly to reduce all other markets by an equal fraction of that 1% to raise the money for the new purchase.

than one, need to be evaluated: the portfolio risk incurred from the overweight position, and that from the underweight position. A more rigorous approach involves an estimate of the impact on total portfolio risk from each hypothetical change in allocation. A model that utilizes the variance/covariance matrix of portfolio assets can be used to explicitly calculate the incremental impact on portfolio volatility (value at risk and similar models are examined in the final section). Nonetheless, a reasonable estimate of the impact on portfolio risk can be obtained by taking account of the historical volatility and correlations of the two markets to each other through the use of a correlation matrix like the one in Exhibit 10.

Market correlations for both bonds and currencies within trading blocs are much higher than across trading blocs. For example, correlations for the core European bond markets of Belgium, France and the Netherlands with Germany are an extremely high 89%, 80%, and 93%, respectively. Currency correlations among these four markets are all close to 100%. Bond market correlations with Germany for the peripheral European markets of Italy, Spain, Sweden, and Denmark are not quite as high, but still significant, ranging from 46% to 64%. Correlations of peripheral European currencies with the German mark range from 83% to 99%. At the same time, standard deviation of return in European bond and currency markets are fairly similar. Thus, shifting exposure from one of these markets to another to take advantage of tactical trading opportunities should have a minimal impact on a portfolio's overall risk or variance profile, especially within the core European markets.

As seen in Exhibits 11 and 12, 10 year bond yield correlations among the G3 (the U.S., Germany, and Japan) are highly variable, sometimes hovering near zero or even showing negative correlation. However, within trading blocs correlations tend to be much more stable, generally staying above 75% for the past several years, and only dropping below 60% during periods of great stress, such as the breakup of the Exchange Rate Mechanism in 1992 and 1993. This allows portfolio managers to actively over or underweight countries within a trading bloc while only modestly altering a portfolio's risk profile. Although the correlation of bond yields within trading blocs may be high, differences in magnitude of yield changes between markets offer significant opportunities for profit.

Forward Rates and Breakeven Analysis

In the previous section, various methods of evaluating value were explored. Before these can be translated into a market allocation, the strategic outlook needs to be compared with that which is already priced into the market. This can be accomplished by either converting the economic outlook into point forecasts for bond and currency levels, or looking at the forward rates implied by current market conditions and comparing them with the economic outlook. Bond and currency breakeven rates, those which make two investments produce identical total returns, are usually calculated versus the benchmark market (e.g., against German bunds for all European markets) over a specific time horizon. A large yield spread between two markets implies a larger "cushion" (the required spread widening to equate total returns in both markets, or the breakeven rate) the longer the investment time horizon.

Exhibit 10: Bond and Currency Correlation Matrix

	AUD	BEF	CAD	DEM	DKK	ESP	FRF	GBP	ITL	JPY	NLG	SEK	AUD Bond	BEF Bond	CAD Bond	DEM Bond	DKK Bond	ESP Bond	FRF Bond	GBP Bond	ITL Bond	JPY Bond	NLG Bond	SEK Bond	USD Bond
AUD	1.00																								
BEF	0.10	1.00																							
CAD	0.06	-0.32	1.00																						
DEM	0.12	0.99	-0.33	1.00																					
DKK	0.14	0.99	-0.33	0.99	1.00																				
ESP	0.14	0.98	-0.34	0.98	0.98	1.00																			
FRF	0.04	0.97	-0.34	0.97	0.97	0.96	1.00																		
GBP	0.43	0.37	0.00	0.39	0.41	0.36	0.31	1.00																	
ITL	0.30	0.84	-0.34	0.84	0.85	0.85	0.84	0.48	1.00																
JPY	-0.25	0.45	-0.20	0.45	0.43	0.45	0.42	-0.09	0.25	1.00															
NLG	0.11	0.99	-0.34	1.00	0.99	0.98	0.97	0.38	0.84	0.45	1.00														
SEK	0.20	0.82	-0.26	0.83	0.84	0.84	0.83	0.33	0.77	0.28	0.83	1.00													
AUD Bond	-0.20	-0.18	-0.03	-0.16	-0.15	-0.14	-0.18	-0.11	-0.17	0.08	-0.17	-0.06	1.00												
BEF Bond	0.22	-0.56	0.22	-0.54	-0.52	-0.53	-0.56	-0.04	-0.39	-0.29	-0.54	-0.37	0.09	1.00											
CAD Bond	0.16	-0.27	0.59	-0.27	-0.26	-0.30	-0.30	0.20	-0.21	-0.33	-0.28	-0.11	-0.04	0.46	1.00										
DEM Bond	0.20	-0.53	0.35	-0.50	-0.50	-0.50	-0.55	0.00	-0.39	-0.27	-0.51	-0.36	0.03	0.89	0.58	1.00									
DKK Bond	-0.04	-0.62	0.19	-0.60	-0.59	-0.56	-0.62	-0.27	-0.53	-0.20	-0.60	-0.40	0.29	0.70	0.17	0.64	1.00								
ESP Bond	0.06	-0.50	0.27	-0.51	-0.49	-0.47	-0.47	-0.09	-0.37	-0.29	-0.51	-0.30	0.08	0.66	0.35	0.62	0.49	1.00							
FRF Bond	0.08	-0.65	0.30	-0.63	-0.63	-0.60	-0.64	-0.18	-0.54	-0.26	-0.63	-0.46	0.21	0.82	0.37	0.80	0.82	0.62	1.00						
GBP Bond	0.28	-0.28	0.13	-0.29	-0.28	-0.26	-0.31	-0.01	-0.15	-0.37	-0.29	-0.09	0.04	0.64	0.50	0.63	0.34	0.59	0.53	1.00					
ITL Bond	0.10	-0.45	0.11	-0.44	-0.43	-0.37	-0.42	-0.18	-0.32	-0.13	-0.45	-0.25	0.33	0.62	0.18	0.55	0.58	0.65	0.62	0.47	1.00				
JPY Bond	0.13	-0.25	-0.13	-0.22	-0.21	-0.22	-0.22	0.07	-0.17	-0.30	-0.22	-0.19	0.26	0.33	0.06	0.24	0.32	0.04	0.32	0.14	0.30	1.00			
NLG Bond	0.21	-0.56	0.28	-0.55	-0.54	-0.53	-0.58	-0.08	-0.41	-0.36	-0.56	-0.36	0.06	0.92	0.52	0.93	0.69	0.66	0.81	0.67	0.60	0.29	1.00		
SEK Bond	0.00	-0.56	0.18	-0.56	-0.55	-0.54	-0.55	-0.16	-0.47	-0.33	-0.56	-0.36	0.03	0.51	0.17	0.46	0.65	0.55	0.64	0.33	0.48	0.19	0.55	1.00	
USD Bond	0.16	-0.22	0.31	-0.21	-0.21	-0.21	-0.21	-0.03	-0.14	-0.20	-0.22	-0.12	-0.13	0.52	0.71	0.59	0.16	0.43	0.39	0.54	0.36	0.02	0.55	0.10	1.00

Source: JP Morgan Riskmetrics as of 12/19/96. Bond markets are estimated using 5-year government zero-coupon bond equivalents in each market.

Exhibit 11: G3 10-Year Bond Yield Correlations

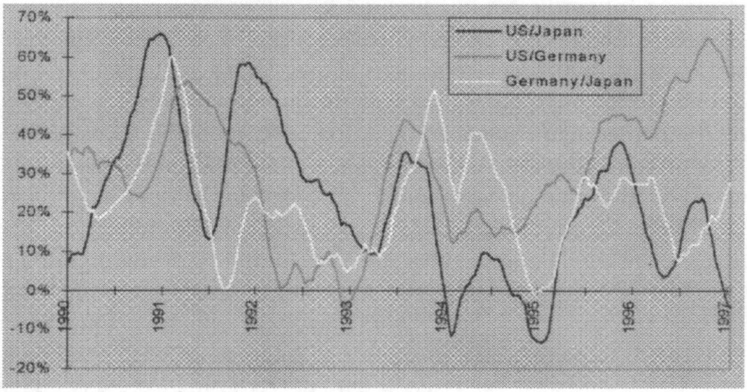

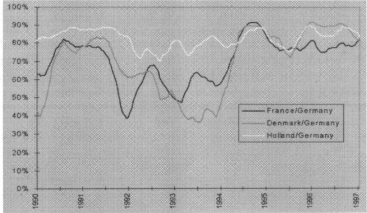

Rolling 6-month correlations of weekly data (smoothed).

Exhibit 12: Correlation of Core Eropean 10-Year Bond Yields

Rolling 6-month correlations of weekly data (smoothed).

Comparisons of forward interest rates can be instrumental in identifying where differences between the strategic outlook and market prices may present investment opportunities. Forward interest rates, which use the shape of the yield curve to calculate implied future bond yields, allow a quick comparison of what is required in terms of yield shifts for bonds in each market to provide a return equal to the risk free rate (a zero excess return). This would correspond to a bond excess return of zero in equations (9) through (16), or $(r_i - c_i) = 0$. Forward interest rates represent a breakeven rate, not across markets necessarily, but within markets. The strategic bond allocation can then be derived by increasing exposure to markets where the expected return of bonds over the cash rate is most positive, that is where the expected bond yield is furthest below the forward yield. Forward rate calculators are also available on systems such as Bloomberg as can be seen in the graph of German forward rates in Exhibit 13.

The forward foreign exchange rate represents a breakeven rate between hedged and unhedged currency returns as shown above in the analysis on components of return. In terms of equations (11) through (14), currency excess return is zero when the percentage change in the currency equals the forward premium or discount. As forward foreign exchange rates are determined by short term interest rate differentials, they can be estimated from Eurodeposit rates as in equations (2) and (3), or obtained from market data services such as Bloomberg and Reuters.

Breakeven analysis provides another tool for estimating relative value between markets. Because the prices of benchmark bonds are influenced by coupon effects and changes in the benchmark, many international fixed income traders and portfolio managers find it easier to keep pace with changes in yield relationships than price changes in each market. Exhibit 14 displays page MEUR from Reuters' market information service which provides 10-year conventional yields and yield spreads to both the U.S. and Germany expressed on an annual-pay basis.[24] A constant spread between markets when yield levels are shifting, however, may result in a variation in returns as differing maturities and coupons of benchmark bonds result in a wide spread of interest rate sensitivity across markets. For example, of the benchmark 10-year bonds listed in Exhibit 13, the modified duration ranges from a low of 6.13 in Spain to 8.56 in Japan where yields are less than half that of the next lowest yielding market. Thus, market duration must be taken into account in determining breakeven spread movements.

Exhibit 13: Forward Yield Curve Analysis

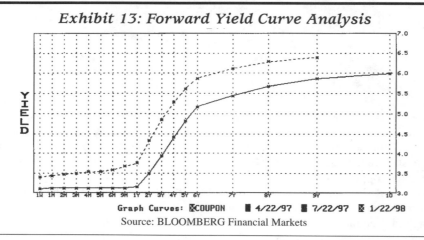

Graph Curves: ⊠COUPON ■ 4/22/97 ■ 7/22/97 ⊠ 1/22/98

Source: BLOOMBERG Financial Markets

---

[24] U.S. bonds, and most other dollar bloc bonds, pay coupons semiannually, whereas in Japan, and the European markets (except for the U.K.) bonds pay interest annually. This difference in market convention understates the yield of dollar bloc bonds when compared to Japanese or European bonds, so when calculating the yield spread, semiannual yields are converted to annual yields using the formula:

Annual yield = $(1 + \text{Semiannual yield}/2)^2 - 1$

Exhibit 14: 10-Year Benchmark Bond Yield Spreads

0000 1154 COUNTRY	JP MORGAN		BENCHMARKS ISSUE		PRICE	CNV YLD	JP MORGAN O/UST	MEUR O/GER
1154	US	6.50	15-10-06	T	98.95-99	6.64		
1154	JAPAN	2.90	20-12-06	JGB	102.28-28	2.61	-410	-326
1154	GERMANY	6.00	04-01-07	BUND	100.60-66	5.91	-84	
1154	FRANCE	5.50	25-04-07	OAT	97.04-18	5.88	-87	-3
1154	UK	7.50	07-12-06	GILT	99.02-02	7.64	+103	+187
1154	ECU	7.00	25-04-06	ECU	105.61-71	6.17	-58	+26
1154	ITALY	8.75	01-07-06	BTP	108.73-93	7.57	+82	+166
1154	SPAIN	8.80	30-04-06	BONO	112.99-14	6.84	+9	+93
1151	BELGIUM	6.25	28-03-07	OLO	101.53-63	6.03	-72	+12
1151	HOLLAND	6.00	15-01-06	DSL	101.71-79	5.75	-101	-17
1151	SWEDEN	6.50	25-10-06	SGB	98.22-42	6.74	-2	+82
1154	DENMARK	8.00	15-03-06	DGB	109.52-62	6.57	-18	+82

For example, calculation of the breakeven yield spread of Italy to Germany over a 3-month time horizon, requires an analysis of the price changes in both bond markets, as well as the difference in yield earned over the period. The spread differential of 166 basis points equates to 41 basis points of additional income over a three month period. The modified duration of the Italian 10-year benchmark bond of 6.21 implies that this yield "cushion" provided by the higher yield of Italian bonds over German bunds translates to less than 7 basis points of spread widening over a 3-month period (6.21 times − 0.07 is approximately equal to 41 basis points). This is not much of a cushion given that 7 basis points is far less than the average weekly volatility of Italian bond yields. The breakeven spreads of Spain and Sweden to Germany even tighter at 4 and 3 basis points. Thus, the anticipated direction of bond market movements is of paramount importance in the portfolio allocation decision.

Security Selection

Once the bond market allocation decisions have been made and the optimal duration and yield curve profile selected for each market, this overall portfolio structure needs to be constructed through the purchase or sale of individual securities. Many international bond investors prefer to trade only benchmark issues as they offer more liquidity than other bonds of a similar maturity. This can sometimes lead to a "hump" in the yield curve as investors prefer a certain issue or maturity sector. The same phenomenon can result from a squeeze of certain issues in the repo market, or short-term demand imbalances for bonds deliverable into short bond futures positions. As mentioned earlier, few foreign markets have a developed corporate bond market, however, other instruments are available such as mortgage bonds, Eurobonds, and inflation-indexed bonds.

Taxation issues also need to be taken into account when selecting individual bonds for purchase. For example, several markets have tax systems that encourage investors to hold lower coupon bonds, hence certain bonds will tend to trade rich or cheap to the curve depending on their coupon. In markets that impose withholding taxes on coupon payments, international fixed income portfolio managers often minimize their tax liability by replacing a bond that is near its coupon date with another bond of similar maturity. Market anomalies can also arise from differing tax treatment within markets. For example, Italian Eurobond issued before 1988 are exempt of withholding tax for Italian investors, hence they tend to trade at a lower yield than similar maturity bonds issued after 1988.

MEASURING RISK AND EVALUATING PERFORMANCE

Once the portfolio has been created, it must be monitored to assess how changing market conditions affect the portfolio's performance and risk profile; hence, a system for tracking portfolio positions and measuring returns is needed. One of the most basic portfolio monitoring tools is the *position report*, which breaks down the interest rate and currency risk market by market. More technically demanding is a portfolio variance approach such as value-at-risk, which estimates potential losses based upon statistical analysis of historical volatilities and correlations. The value-at-risk approach can also be translated into a *tracking error report* that evaluates portfolio risks against the benchmark. These risk models can be used together with performance attribution to assist the portfolio manager in identifying the strengths or weaknesses of his portfolio strategy.

Portfolio Profile

A portfolio profile is usually designed to monitor exposures to the two major sour of risk in international bond portfolios: currency risk and interest rate risk. T market-by-market breakdowns are also useful in estimating how positions will a portfolio performance versus the benchmark. A sample portfolio profile versu Salomon Brothers Non-U.S. Government Bond Index is provided in Exhibit 1. profile shows the percentage allocation to bonds and currencies for each cou well as the duration, relative to the index. A breakdown by duration cell of ea market allocation is provided to highlight any yield curve positions. (The breakdown by duration cell for the index, which has been excluded for sim presentation, would be extremely helpful in identifying where yield curve ns differ from the index.) Finally, the portfolio profile provides a measure of tion weighted exposure (from equation (17)), and currency exposure net of hed rela-tive to the index. Summary exposure figures for each of these categories, broken down by trading bloc, are provided at the bottom of the report.

The measure of portfolio interest rate risk in each individual market is a combination of its weight in the portfolio and its duration relative to the duration of the index for that country. For example, the U.K.'s contribution to duration is neutral to the index (i.e., a relative weight of zero percent) despite the higher percentage allocation to U.K. due to the portfolio's shorter U.K. duration. The larger-than-index market weighting in the U.K. is unhedged as indicated by the equivalence of the market weight and the currency exposure, 11.9%, and represents a nearly 4% portfolio overweight position in pound sterling relative to the index.

Exhibit 15: Sample Portfolio Profile
Portfolio Profile versus Salomon Non-U.S. Government Bond Index

Market	Market Weight (%)		Average Duration (Yrs)		Currency Exposure (%)	Portfolio MV% by Duration Cell					Relative Weights (%)	
	Index	Portfolio	Index	Portfolio	Portfolio	0-2	2-4	4-6	6-9	9+	Duration	Currency
Austria	1.3		4.1								-1.1	-1.3
Australia	1.5		4.3								-1.3	-1.5
Belgium	3.9	3.0	4.8	6.0	3.0				3.0		-0.2	-0.9
Canada	4.6	4.6	5.2	11.7	4.6					4.6	6.1	0.0
Switzerland	0.7		5.2								-0.7	-0.7
Germany	14.9	18.0	4.2	6.6	15.0				18.0		11.4	0.1
Denmark	2.6	8.0	4.3	6.0	8.0				8.0		7.5	5.4
Spain	3.7		3.8								-2.9	-3.7
Finland	0.7		4.3								-0.6	-0.7
France	11.4	5.0	5.1	2.7	5.0		5.0				-9.1	-6.4
U.K.	8.1	11.9	5.9	4.0	11.9			11.9			0.0	3.8
Italy	9.5	15.0	3.3	2.	15.0	15.0					-0.4	5.5
Japan	29.1	30.0	5.7	3.4	24.0		30.0				-13.2	-5.1
Netherlands	5.2	2.0	5.0	3.2	2.0		2.0				-4.0	-3.2
Sweden	2.6	2.5	4.2	2.9	2.5		2.5				-0.8	-0.1
Other												
Total	100.0	100.0	4.9	4.4	91.0	15.0	39.5	11.9	29.0	4.6	-9.5	-9.0

Currency Bloc	Index	Portfolio	Index	Portfolio	Portfolio	0-2	2-4	4-6	6-9	9+	Duration	Currency
Japan	29.1	30.0	3.3	2.0	24.0		30.0				-0.4	5.5
Dollar Bloc	6.1	4.6	5.0	11.7	4.6					4.6	4.7	-1.5
Core Euro	38.1	28.0	4.7	5.6	25.0				29.0		3.0	-3.2
Periph Euro	26.7	37.4	4.4	3.5	37.4	15.0	9.5	11.9			-16.8	-9.7
Other												
Total	100.0	100.0	4.2	4.0	91.0	15.0	39.5	11.9	29.0	4.6	-9.5	-9.0

The summary figures in the bottom right hand corner of the portfolio profile suggest that the sample portfolio's greatest bond market underweight is in peripheral Europe. The 16.8% underweight position there is larger than the sum of the overweight positions in the dollar bloc and core Europe, leaving the portfolio 9.5% underweight duration, or 90.5% of the 4.9 year benchmark duration or 4.4 years. In currencies also, the largest deviation from the benchmark is in peripheral Europe where exposures are 9.7% underweight the index. The overweighting in the yen, and underweighting in core Europe and dollar bloc are largely offsetting in this framework. The overall portfolio is 9% underweight currency exposure, or 9% hedged relative to the unhedged benchmark.

As helpful as they are in quantifying risk within individual markets, the traditional risk measures of duration and percent currency exposure have significant shortcomings when aggregated as a measure of portfolio risk. These shortcomings are explored in more detail below, along with some complimentary approaches to risk measurement that can be instrumental in addressing them.

Contribution to Duration

Many international fixed income portfolio managers measure their bond market exposures in terms of the simple percentage allocation to each particular market. However, a better measure of exposure to any individual bond market is one that combines the percentage of portfolio assets allocated to that market with the duration of that exposure. As seen in equation (17), contribution to overall portfolio duration for each market is the weighted duration in that market multiplied by the percentage weight of that market in the portfolio where D is the duration and w percentage weight of market i in the overall portfolio. Thus, the sum of the contribution to duration of each market will equal the portfolio's overall duration. The duration weighted exposure is calculated by dividing the contribution to duration in each market by the total benchmark duration, D_B as shown in equation (18). The duration weighted exposure figure can then be compared directly with the benchmark composition, providing a more useful gauge of market risk than percent allocation. The sum of the weighted duration figures may add up to more or less than 100%.

Contribution to Duration: $CD_i = D_i \times w_i$ (17)

Duration Weighted Exposure: $WD_i = CD_i/D_B$ (18)

Duration can be a helpful measure when comparing a portfolio's allocation relative to the index, however, its inability to capture the effect of non-parallel shifts in rates is compounded by further shortcomings when used as a measure of interest rate risk in a global setting. Portfolio interest rate exposure will not be equal to a simple sum of the duration weighted exposures from equation (18) in each market as interest rate movements in different countries are not perfectly correlated. Also the differing volatility across markets means that the contribution-to-duration from a given market is not entirely comparable to that of another market. The use of volatility-adjusted duration[25] is one means of addressing this impracticality. An additional compromise would be to compare volatility-adjusted contribution-to-duration only between the highly correlated markets within each trading bloc. Thus, a portfolio could have the same modified duration as the benchmark but show a different sensitivity to global bond market moves as a result of different weightings in especially low or high volatility markets or in markets with low correlation to other markets.

The shortcomings of duration as a measure of interest rate risk internationally can be reduced by accounting for differing volatilities and correlations across markets. This requires either a manual interpolation of portfolio risk from a volatility and correlation matrix or use of a risk measure that incorporates these relationships. One example would be a market risk measure that captures the relative volatility of markets and yield curve sectors as well as the correlation to the "market," which could be defined as a hedged, or unhedged, global or international bond index. One approach, suggested by Goldman Sachs & Co., is to make use of beta measures similar to those found in the capital asset pricing model.[26] A portfolio with a weighted average market risk of 1.12, for example, would be 12% more sensitive to bond price changes than the international bond index. This approach could be extended to currencies as well.

Currency Exposures

Portfolio currency exposures, examined separately from the bond exposures, suffer from some of the same shortcomings as duration as an overall risk measure. A simple aggregation of currency exposures across a portfolio ignores the sometimes substantial differences in currency volatilities across markets. For example, from 1987 to 1996 a U.S dollar-based investor would have experienced three times more volatility from movements in the value of the yen than in the Canadian dollar. Thus, offsetting short or long currency positions relative to the benchmark in the yen with the opposite positions in either the dollar bloc or core Europe could lead to a misunderstanding of the portfolio's true exposure to currency risk.

Direct comparison of currency and interest rate risk measures poses another difficulty. For example, a 5% duration-weighted position in a bond market and a 5% currency exposure can represent significantly different risks to the overall portfolio. Again, measures incorporating volatility and correlation measures allow these different sources of risk to be evaluated on an equal footing. The next section discusses the virtues of a value-at-risk approach that also incorporates volatility and correlation of interest rate and currency risk.

---

[25] For example, if interest rates were twice as volatile in Italy than in Germany, a factor of 2 could be applied to bond holdings in Italy when comparing them to the German bond holdings.

[26] Beta can be estimated by either regressing historical returns of the given market sector versus the market as a whole, or by using the following formula: Beta = Cov (R_i, R_m)/Var (R_m) where R_i and R_m represent the historical returns of the market sector and the entire market, respectively.

Derivatives

Because of their inherent leverage, futures and options can significantly change the risk profile of the portfolio with a minimal cash outlay. Hence, they present special difficulties in calculating their impact on the portfolio. Treatment of futures contracts are relatively straightforward. For currencies, the notional amount of the currency position in either futures or forwards, can be added and subtracted from the relevant currency pair. For bonds, the duration impact of a futures position in any country can be estimated by multiplying the duration of the cheapest-to-deliver bond for that contract by the notional amount of bonds represented by the contract. In any futures contract there is also a small short-term interest rate effect that is also to be considered. Options can be treated in a similar fashion, once a delta for the option is calculated. However, it must be kept in mind that option payouts are inherently asymmetric whereas the framework discussed so far assumes that returns are linear.

Tracking Error and Value at Risk

Each portfolio allocation decision should be evaluated on the basis of the expected return enhancement of the trade versus its impact on portfolio volatility, both in absolute terms and relative to the benchmark. Volatility is often expressed in standard deviations of returns, i.e., movements either up or down. On the assumption that most international bond investors are concerned about limiting downside volatility (i.e., losses) more than upside volatility, the value-at-risk concept, popularized by JP Morgan, serves as a constructive framework.[27] The value-at-risk approach uses historical volatility and correlations across bond and currency markets to arrive at an estimate of the likely loss, expressed either in dollars or as a percent of the portfolio, only in the case of an extreme shift in market prices against portfolio positions. For example a value-at-risk figure calculated with a 95% confidence interval (or a 1.65 standard deviation downward move in market prices) would estimate the magnitude of the loss that should be exceeded no more than 5% of the time.

Value-at-risk measures are especially useful for estimating the risks of assets with non-normally distributed returns, such as bond and currency options. Thus, a model that can capture the differences between the risks of a long (or purchased) option position which has a limited downside, and a short (or written) option position which has open-ended downside risk, will serve as an important risk management tool.

---

[27] The value-at-risk concept, known in prior academic papers as semi-variance or lower partial moment, is simply a transformation of the more traditionally used standard deviation measure of volatility, but expressed as a measure of downside risk only. Traditional mean-variance optimization will produce similar results when using either portfolio value-at-risk or volatility as the constraint if portfolio returns are assumed to be normally distributed. For a more detailed discussion, see JP Morgan Riskmetrics Technical Document, and W.V. Harlow, "Asset Allocation in a Downside-Risk Framework," *Financial Analysts Journal* (September-October 1991).

Exhibit 16: Tracking Error Report

Market	Portfolio Profile Summary Relative Weights		Contribution to Tracking Error (bp)		Contribution to Tracking Error (%)		Marginal Tracking Error (bp)	
	Bond (%)	Currency (%)	Bond	Currency	Bond	Currency	Bond	Currency
Austria	−1.1	−1.3	−0.2	10.8	0	7	0.0	−7.6
Australia	−1.3	−1.5	1.0	-2.4	1	−2	−1.0	1.5
Belgium	−0.2	−0.9	0.7	7.9	0	5	3.6	−7.6
Canada	6.1	0.0	27.2	0.5	17	0	7.1	2.6
Switzerland	−0.7	−0.7	0.1	6.8	0	4	0.7	−10.1
Germany	11.4	0.1	50.3	0.1	32	0	3.7	−7.6
Denmark	7.5	5.4	22.1	−43.2	14	−27	2.9	−6.9
Spain	−2.9	−3.7	−11.8	27.4	−8	17	4.2	−7.3
Finland	−0.6	−0.7	0.0	4.3	0	3	0.0	−6.2
France	−9.1	−6.4	−17.2	43.5	−11	28	2.1	−7.6
U.K.	0.0	3.8	−4.6	3.9	−3	2	3.0	1.2
Italy	−0.4	5.5	−3.4	−20.5	−2	−13	2.8	−4.1
Japan	−13.2	−5.1	6.6	28.3	4	18	−0.1	−5.8
Netherlands	−4.0	−3.2	−14.8	39.3	−9	25	−2.4	−7.8
Sweden	−0.8	−0.1	−0.4	−5.0	0	−3	2.7	−4.3
Other	0.0	0.0			0	0	2.8	0.0
Japan	−13.2	−5.1	6.6	28.3	4	18		
Dollar Bloc	4.7	−1.5	28.1	−1.9	18	−1		
Core Europe	3.7	−3.3	36.6	69.1	23	44		
Peripheral Europe	−4.7	0.9	−15.6	6.1	−10	4		
Other								
Total	−9.5	−9.0	55.7	101.5	35	65		

Total Portfolio Diversified Tracking Error	Fully Diversified	Non-Diversified
	157.3	1267

Although portfolio tracking error has traditionally been defined as the historical variance of portfolio returns about the benchmark, it can be extremely useful in the portfolio management process when used as an estimate of future deviation from the index, or more specifically as the relative value at risk. The total value at risk of the sample portfolio in Exhibit 16 is 590 basis points at the 95% confidence level, while tracking error equals 157 basis points. In other words, the portfolio should, at worst, lose 5.90% in value in any year, or underperform the benchmark by 157 basis points, with 95% confidence. Which measure deserves more emphasis depends on the portfolio objectives and risk constraints. For example, an income-oriented investor with little tolerance for losses could set a portfolio constraint on value-at-risk equal to the expected income earned over a given time horizon. This could provide some assurance, with 95% confidence for example, that portfolio total return will remain positive. An investor more concerned with diversification, however, might find tracking error a more suitable risk measure as it better identifies large deviations from the benchmark which could alter the portfolio's correlation to other asset classes.

The value-at-risk framework may uncover risks to the portfolio not fully apparent in traditional measures while providing the portfolio manager a common yardstick to evaluate the risks of bond market and currency positions.

In Exhibit 16, the sample portfolio is shown to have 101.5 basis points of tracking error (65% of the total) due to currency positions away from the benchmark and 55.7 basis points (35% of the total) due to bond market positions. A manager could use these measures to ensure that the magnitude of risks taken relative to the benchmark are consistent with the level of conviction and the investment style relied upon to outperform. Presumably, this manager is comfortable taking a larger currency position than bond market position. The underweight bond and currency position in France, summarized in the left-hand column, is a net contributor to tracking error. However, the bond market position actually has the effect of reducing tracking error by 17.2 basis points. The 9.1% duration underweight in France constitutes a large allocation away from the benchmark, however, it offsets portfolio overweight in other core European bond markets; markets to which French bonds are highly correlated. The same could be said for the UK, Italy and Spain as the correlation between peripheral and core European bond markets is a high 0.76 (see Exhibit 18). As shown in the far right column of Exhibit 16, marginal tracking error (the portfolio impact from a 1% shift in assets) from a 1% shift into French government bonds results in an increase of 2.1 basis points in portfolio tracking error. Thus, the existing underweight in French bonds is a risk-reducing position and adding back French bond market exposure will increase tracking error. Almost all readings in the far right hand column are negative suggesting that adding foreign currency exposure will reduce tracking error to the benchmark. This is consistent with the estimated 65% of tracking error coming from currency positions, most of which are underweight or hedged back into U.S. dollars.

The Value at Risk report in Exhibit 17 provides a summary of the sources of absolute risk. For example, the profile summary at left shows that the portfolio has twice as much of its market value exposed to Japanese yen as it does British pound sterling. However, after adjusting for volatility and correlation differences the contribution to portfolio value at risk from the yen position is 30% more than that for sterling, 104.0 versus 79.9 basis points. Interestingly, the bond market contributions to risk total only 4% of total risk. This results from the low volatility estimates of bond market risks and negative correlation to currency risk that are input into the model. As can be seen in the right hand column of Exhibit 17, shifting 1% of portfolio assets to either Dutch or Swedish bond markets reduces portfolio value at risk by 1.9 and 1.0 basis points respectively.

A manager looking to maximize expected excess return per unit of risk would be able to compare return expectations to the contribution to value at risk or tracking error. A certain threshold of return per unit of risk may be required to meet a portfolio target. Model outputs in this context allow managers to weigh the risks against return potential for various portfolio assets and, using the marginal value at risk and tracking error numbers, have a reasonable estimate of how potential portfolio trades will impact, portfolio risk, both relative to the benchmark and on an absolute basis. Traditional mean-variance optimization, where portfolios exhibiting the most attractive Sharpe ratios are identified on the so-called efficient frontier between expected excess return over cash and volatility, can offer some insights about portfolio risk not captured by the framework presented above. However, the flexibility and detail offered by the careful break-down of portfolio risk above can offer significant advantages to managers seeking to better understand the sources of risk and fine-tune portfolios.

Exhibit 17: Value at Risk Report

Market	Portfolio Profile Summary		Contribution to Value at Risk (bp)		Contribution to Value at Risk (%)		Marginal Value at Risk (bp)	
	Contribution to Duration	Currency Weight (%)	Bond	Currency	Bond	Currency	Bond	Currency
Austria	—	0	0.0	0.0	0	0	0.0	8.7
Australia	—	0	0.0	0.0	0	0	0.0	3.8
Belgium	0.18	3	0.1	25.0	0	4	0.0	8.5
Canada	0.54	5	11.5	−2.7	2	0	1.4	−0.6
Switzerland	—	0	0.0	0.0	0	0	0.6	9.6
Germany	1.18	15	4.7	128.6	1	22	0.2	8.7
Denmark	0.48	8	−4.8	72.9	−1	12	−0.7	8.3
Spain	—	0	0.0	0.0	0	0	−0.5	8.2
Finland	—	0	0.0	0.0	0	0	0.0	7.0
France	0.14	5	−1.3	38.4	0	7	−0.7	7.8
U.K.	0.48	12	8.8	79.9	1	14	0.8	6.7
Italy	0.30	15	02	96.8	0	16	−0.2	6.6
Japan	1.01	24	7.9	104.0	1	18	0.0	4.3
Netherlands	0.06	2	0.0	0.0	0	0	−1.9	8.8
Sweden	0.07	3	−2.9	22.9	0	4	−1.0	6.0
Other	—	0					0.5	0.0
Japan	1.01	24	7.9	104.0	1	18		
Dollar Bloc	0.54	5	11.6	−2.7	2	0		
Core Euro	2.52	45	7.5	344.8	1	58		
Peripheral Europe	0.37	18	−2.7	119.7	0	20		
Other								
Total	4.44	91	24.2	565.8	4	96		

Total Portfolio Diversified Tracking Error	Fully Diversified	Non-Diversified
	590.0	1505

Exhibit 18: Bond Market and Currency Correlation by Currency Bloc

	Core Europe	Peripheral Europe	Japan	Dollar Bloc	Core Eur. Currency	Peripheral Currency	Japanese Yen	Dollar Bloc Currency
Core Europe	1.00							
Peripheral Europe	0.76	1.00						
Japan	0.40	0.19	1.00					
Dollar Bloc	0.65	0.44	0.43	1.00				
Core Eur. Currency	−0.39	−0.57	0.12	−0.18	1.00			
Peripheral Currency	−0.40	−0.16	−0.17	−0.28	0.51	1.00		
Japanese Yen	−0.19	−0.48	0.07	−0.14	0.64	0.24	1.00	
Dollar Bloc Currency	−0.08	0.04	0.09	0.17	−0.13	0.04	−0.26	1.00

The value-at-risk approach to calculating tracking error, however, is not a perfect measure of portfolio risk. For one thing, portfolio variance measures such as value-at-risk assume that market relationships do not change, which can be misleading. For example, it has been shown that correlations tend to rise during periods of above-average volatility which suggests that value at risk models will tend to underestimate risk during periods of extreme volatility.[28] Thus, many practitioners advocate the use of worst-day or disaster scenario measures to supplement the use of value-at-risk measures. Another approach compares the diversified value-at-risk measure (the traditional portfolio variance approach) with the non-diversified measure (which assumes no correlation among assets), as the ratio of diversified to non-diversified risk can be used as a proxy for the correlation risk inherent in the diversified risk measure.

Performance Attribution

A performance attribution analysis can assist in the portfolio management process by identifying the source of returns (and losses) versus the benchmark. The breakdown of components of return in equations (9) through (16) above provides a good foundation for a rigorous performance attribution analysis will analyze returns in terms of bond market weight, duration, yield curve position, and currency weight, both market by market and for the portfolio as a whole.[29] Performance attribution systems, however, are extremely data intensive, requiring daily updates of index returns and portfolio returns and allocation, including a separate accounting of each transaction. The performance report in Exhibit 19 offers a simplified version of attribution in that it identifies the sources of return from bond and currency allocations in each market. A majority of the returns in excess of the benchmark in the sample portfolio came from bond market allocations, while currency allocations added only marginally to the portfolio's excess return. In addition to identifying the sources of return, the performance attribution analysis can be combined with other risk reports to estimate the additional risk incurred to generate those returns. For example, the source of excess returns over the benchmark can be compared with the sources of risk identified by the tracking error report to assess the performance of the portfolio strategy on a risk-adjusted basis. Such an analysis can contribute to future returns by helping allocate resources toward areas that have added to returns, and identify areas that have tended to detract from performance.

---

[28] See Bruno Solnik, Cyril Boucrelle, and Yann Le Fur, "International Market Correlation and Volatility," *Financial Analysts Journal* (September/October 1996), pp. 17-34.
[29] See Karnosky and Singer, op.cit.

Exhibit 19: Performance Attribution

Nov-95	Relative Duration Weight	Hedged Bond Market Return Salomon Index Return	Contrib. to Index Return	Portfolio Return	Contrib to Port Return	Relative Return	Currency Return Relative Currency Rate	Currency Return	Relative Return	Total Outperf
Other	0.0	0.00	0.00	0.98	0.00	0.00	0.0	0.00	0.00	0.00
Cash	0.0	0.42	0.00	0.00	0.00	0.00	0.0	0.00	0.00	0.00
Japan	-6.1	0.56	0.16	0.55	0.14	-0.03	-5.4	-0.05	-0.03	-0.06
Germany	1.3	1.85	0.27	1.74	0.35	0.08	9.9	-1.56	-0.14	-0.07
France	-1.9	1.98	0.23	2.43	0.15	-0.07	-7.1	-2.21	0.15	0.08
U.K.	0.7	2.22	0.18	1.92	0.18	-0.01	0.6	3.18	-0.02	-0.02
Belgium	-3.7	1.85	0.07	0.00	0.00	-0.07	-3.9	-1.55	0.06	-0.01
Denmark	2.1	1.67	0.04	1.99	0.11	0.07	-3.9	-1.55	0.06	-0.01
Netherlands	-5.1	1.81	0.09	0.0	0.00	-0.09	-5.1	-1.68	0.09	-0.01
Austria	-1.1	1.56	0.02	0.0	0.00	-0.02	-1.4	-1.56	0.02	0.00
ECU	-0.6	1.41					-0.7			0.00
Italy	-1.1	2.82	0.27	1.56	0.25	-0.03	-0.4	0.09	-0.01	-0.03
Spain	0.3	3.55	0.13	3.44	0.14	0.00	0.3	-1.55	-0.01	0.00
Sweden	1.4	2.45	0.06	2.62	0.08	0.01	0.3	-2.24	0.01	0.01
Norway	4.2	1.19	0.00	1.46	0.04	0.04	3.5	-1.26	-0.04	-0.01
Canada	0.1	2.60	0.12	2.89	0.12	0.00	0.0	-0.48	0.00	0.0
Australia	2.3	1.30	0.02	1.50	0.04	0.02	-0.6	2.71	0.01	0.03
Totals	-2.6	Local	1.68	Local	1.84	0.16			0.02	0.18
		Ccy	-0.54	Ccy	-0.52					
		Total	1.15	Total	1.32					
Summaries										
U.S.	0.0		0.0		0.17	0.17	4.9		-0.02	0.15
Japan	-6.1		0.16		0.14	-0.03	-5.4		-0.03	-0.06
Europe-Core	-8.4		0.91		0.79	-0.13	-3.9		0.11	-0.02
Europe-Other	4.8		0.47		0.46	-0.01	3.7		-0.02	-0.03
Dollar Bloc	7.2		0.14		0.26	0.12	1.5		0.02	0.15

* Interest Rate Derivatives Value Added (incorporated above)

Short German Bund Call Options   0.16

Long Call Options Italian BTPs   0.10

Exhibit 20: Expected Returns French/German Swap

	France	Germany	Cross Hedge
Expected Bond Market Return			
Expected Bond Return (A)	3.5%	3.0%	
c_i = Domestic Cash Rate (B)	−3.0%	−3.0%	
Bond Excess Return (C = A − B)	0.5%	0.0%	
Expected Currency Return			
$\varepsilon_{\$i}$ = Expected Currency Appreciation	2.3%	2.5%	2.5%
c_i = Domestic Cash Rate (B)	3.0%	3.0%	3.0%
Unhedged Currency Return (E = B + D)	5.3%	5.5%	5.5%
$c_\$$ = Hedged Return (F or U.S. Interest Rate)	5.5%	5.5%	
$\varepsilon_{\$i} + c_i - c_\$$ = Excess Currency Return (G = E − F)	−0.2%	0.0%	
Unhedged Expected Return (C + E)	5.8%	5.5%	
Hedged Expected Return (C + F)	6.0%	5.5%	

CONCLUSION: AN INTEGRATED INVESTMENT PROCESS

The objective of this chapter was to provide a broad overview of the issues facing international fixed income portfolio managers at each step of the portfolio management process. This process involves a continuous cycle of evaluating risks and returns, implementing portfolio strategy, and monitoring market movements and portfolio performance. The complexities of the international arena increase the value of a disciplined approach to investing, of which the fundamental-based approach outlined in this chapter is but one variation.

Exhibit 20 attempts to tie the themes of the portfolio construction and risk management sections together by showing how a portfolio manager might turn a market view into a portfolio allocation. The outlook is for the French bond market to outperform Germany's bond market, but for the French franc to provide a lower return than the German mark. The bond and currency return forecasts may have been generated by a fundamental economic approach, such as the one outlined in this chapter, or from one of the other management styles. The expected return from any allocation should be evaluated against the incremental risk it is likely to add to the portfolio.

An example comparing explicit return forecasts for 5-year duration bonds in the French and German government bond markets (i.e., duration neutral) is provided in Exhibit 19. Total returns are expressed as the sum of the excess bond market return plus the excess return due to currency, consistent with the approach explained in equations (13), (14), (15), and (16), which are restated below.

$$R_{\$i} = c_\$ + (r_i - c_i) + (\varepsilon_{\$,i} - f_{\$,i}) \qquad \text{(unhedged return)}$$

$$HR_{\$i} = c_\$ + (r_i - c_i) \qquad \text{(hedged return)}$$

$$CR_{\$i} = c_\$ + (r_i - c_i) + (\varepsilon_{\$,i} - f_{\$,i}) \qquad \text{(cross-hedged return)}$$

$$PR_{\$i} = c_\$ + (r_i - c_i) + [(\varepsilon_{\$,i} - \varepsilon_{\$,j}) - f_{j,i}] \quad \text{(proxy-hedged return)}$$

For example, the expected excess return from bonds $(r_i - c_i)$ of 0.5% in France, equal to the expected return on bonds (3.5%) less that on French cash (3.0%), is the same regardless of whether the currency is hedged, unhedged, or cross hedged. The currency hedge decision is based upon whether the expected currency appreciation is greater than the interest rate differential $\varepsilon_{\$,i} > (c_\$ - c_i)$ or less than the interest rate differential $\varepsilon_{\$,i} < (c_\$ - c_i)$ Thus, as the expected return on French francs of 2.3% is less than the interest rate differential of 2.5% over the 1-year horizon (5.5% in the U.S. − 3.0% in France), the position would offer a higher return when hedged back into U.S. dollars. Stated another way, the expected excess currency return component to a U.S. dollar-based investor from an unhedged holding of French bonds is −0.2%.

Cross hedging allows portfolio managers to create a currency exposure which can vary substantially from the underlying bond market exposure. A cross hedge replaces one foreign currency exposure with another that usually has a higher expected return. Using the currency (or far right hand) components of equations (8) and (10), a cross hedge will be attractive when $(c_j + \varepsilon_{\$,j}) > (c_i + \varepsilon_{\$,i})$; or the cash rate plus expected return in the cross currency is greater than the cash rate plus expected return in the exposure currency. Of course, if the U.S. dollar cash rate is greater than either of these two terms, a hedged, or proxy hedged, position is preferable to either foreign currency exposure. In terms of the present example, the expected excess currency return from the additional French franc exposure is a negative 20 basis points. Hence this currency exposure would probably be hedged back into the dollar. A cross hedge into German marks could also be used, however, the expected excess currency retrun from holding German marks is zero.

The next step is to estimate the incremental risk to the portfolio associated with the transaction. Exhibit 21 provides several risk measures for evaluating the proposed swap from Germany into France on overall portfolio risk. The historical volatilities of the bond and currency movements in each market can provide a rough approximation of incremental risk from the portfolio allocation (the volatility of a hedged bond market return would be approximately the same as the volatility of the local bond market return). The similar bond and currency volatilities in France and Germany,[30] and the high correlation between the markets, suggests that a shift of market exposure from one market to the other would be relatively risk neutral. However, some of the tools developed in the risk management discussion allow for a much more accurate estimation of risk. The two columns entitled marginal tracking error and marginal value at risk from Exhibits 16

---

[30] The variance formula treats the bond and currency components as separate assets in calculating the expected volatility for any country using the following equation: $\sigma_i^2 = \sigma_x^2 + h_y^2 \sigma_y^2 + 2 h_y \text{Cov}_{xy}$, where subscript i represents a country, x represents bonds, y represents the currency and h represents the percent currency exposure (i.e., $1 - h$ = the hedge ratio), and Cov_{xy} is the covariance between the bonds and currencies.

and 17 provide estimates of the incremental addition to risk that would result from a 1% shift of the portfolio's market value into any individual bond market or currency. For example, on the basis of the figures from the Total column of Exhibit 21, the swap from German to French bonds reduces both value at risk and tracking error by 1.6 basis points. Risk can also be evaluated on a hedged basis, using the data in the bond market column. The risk reduction figures in this case are very similar on either a hedged or unhedged basis. However, the 50 basis points of incremental expected return from a hedged swap from Germany into France is greater than the 30 basis points of expected return on an unhedged basis. One possible conclusion from this example is that the expected return enhancement per unit of excess tracking error is most attractive when the swap is done on a hedged basis. If the differences between value at risk and tracking error were greater, a portfolio managed more for capital preservation might place more weight upon the value at risk measure perhaps leading to a different conclusion.

As the prior example shows, the implementation of portfolio strategy can clearly be a highly involved process of evaluating the risk and reward trade-off between different portfolio investment alternatives. However, the simplified example above did not address other types of decisions confronted by international fixed income portfolio managers including ongoing management of currency hedges, yield curve strategies, and using options to take views on the direction of actual or implied volatilities. In addition to conveying the complexities presented by international fixed income investing, hopefully this chapter has been able to convey some of the excitement that comes from meeting the challenges of investing in a dynamic global market.

Exhibit 21: Risk Analysis French/German Swap

	Bond Market	Currency	Total
Volatility			
France	6.7%	13.7%	4.8%
Germany	7.4%	14.2%	5.1%
Marginal Value at Risk			
France	−0.7	7.8	7.1
Germany	0.2	8.7	8.9
Marginal Tracking Error			
France	2.1	−7.6	−5.5
Germany	3.7	−7.6	−3.9
Net Impact on Portfolio – Germany into France			
Value at Risk	−0.9	−0.9	−1.8
Tracking Error	−1.6	0.0	−1.6

Correlations			
French to German Bonds:	0.80	French Bonds to French Francs:	−0.64
Francs to German marks:	0.97	German Bonds to German marks:	−0.50

Marginal Value at Risk and Tracking Error (from Exhibits 16 and 17) are estimates of the change, in basis points, to portfolio Value at Risk and Tracking Error for a 1% addition of the relevant bond of currency exposure to the portfolio profiled in Exhibit 15.

Chapter 29

Emerging Fixed Income and Local Currency: An Investment Management View

Luis R. Luis, Ph. D.
Managing Director
Scudder, Stevens & Clark

INTRODUCTION

Investment managers had an early and important role in the development of emerging markets fixed income as an asset class following the developing country debt crisis of the 1980s. Investment companies were created to take advantage of opportunities for excess return from investing in emerging bonds and defaulted bank loans to developing countries. Some of these initial investment vehicles were established as offshore entities, beginning in 1989, to facilitate access to the market by global retail investors who often resided in emerging countries themselves.[1] Thereafter, investment companies registered in the United States provided diversified emerging market portfolios for investors in developed countries. These dedicated funds generally aimed at providing high income with substantial potential for capital appreciation.

A second stage in the development of investment management involved the use of emerging market instruments as part of broader portfolios, often global and international bond portfolios. Emerging bonds also found their way to accounts and investment vehicles focused on U.S. bond markets. At the same time, dedicated accounts were established for institutional clients, mainly in the United States, and more recently in Europe, Japan, and other developed areas.

A third stage, evolving alongside deepening capital markets in emerging countries, is the management of local currency fixed income. The initial development of emerging fixed income was centered primarily in bonds and defaulted bank loans largely denominated in dollars and, to a lesser extent, other currencies of industrial countries. Although some use was made of instruments issued in the

---

[1] The first offshore vehicle to invest in emerging bonds is generally acknowledged to be the Sovereign High Yield Investment Company registered in Curacao, Netherlands Antilles, in 1989. This investment company was designed to invest primarily in bearer bonds issued by governments in emerging countries.

currencies of emerging markets, these were complementary rather than central to the asset class. They mostly comprised Treasury bills and other money market securities of a handful of countries, most prominently Mexico and other Latin American nations.

Investment managers face multiple challenges in seeking value while managing risk in the asset class. Value is derived from analysis of credit quality, market risk, and pricing relationships within the asset class and in relation to established bond markets. Information gaps played a major role in the early evolution of the asset class. Long lags in the availability of data, large voids in the data, and, most importantly, partial understanding of economic and political variables determining sovereign credit quality created opportunities to add value while presenting substantial risks. Value is enhanced and risk reduced in direct relation to analysis, information, and investment discipline.

As countries and other emerging issuers have strived to improve the flow and transparency of information following the 1994 Mexican peso crisis, the limiting factor is analysis of variables that determine credit quality and vulnerability to random events or shocks, not the lack of basic data and qualitative information.

As the marginal issuers in global capital markets, emerging countries are highly exposed, as may be expected, to shifting financial patterns and liquidity effects derived from core bond markets. As analysis improves and average credit quality rises, these effects are likely to diminish in size but will not be eliminated. Because relationships are not easily predictable, portfolio shifts within the asset class and in relation to other investments will characterize this market in the foreseeable future. This means that investment managers, possibly more than in other fixed income classes, are expected to design and manage portfolios in ways that take advantage of these shifts.

INVESTMENT OBJECTIVES

Investment managers view emerging markets as capable of satisfying a broad set of objectives. In general, portfolios and investment vehicles are classified into two main categories: those primarily seeking high income and those principally aiming at obtaining total return. Because price appreciation is most often a secondary objective and sometimes the primary goal, emerging markets fixed income is sometimes viewed as a "quasi-equity" asset class in contrast with traditional investment-grade fixed income investments. A third type of investor views emerging markets as primarily a means to diversify global or domestic fixed income portfolios.

Emerging market bonds are expected to provide high yield, certainly compared to investment-grade securities and even when placed against speculative grade corporate bonds. Most emerging countries are rated below investment grade. In mid-1997, emerging markets sovereign bonds had an average credit quality approximately equivalent to a BB/Ba as rated by the major agencies. Moreover, emerging bonds denominated in dollars have historically traded at wider spreads to benchmark U.S. Treasury bonds than other bonds of similar credit rating. For example, at the end of May 1997 emerging market bonds yielded approximately 417 basis points (bps) (net of collateral) and 294 bps (collateral included) over similar maturity U.S. Treasuries while similarly BB-rated U.S. high yield bonds yielded 185 bps.[2]

Spread curves for emerging market bonds in relation to U.S. Treasury bonds are upward sloping with the slope increasing in proportion to duration. This relationship holds for both normal Eurobonds and non-collateralized Brady bonds, as well as for Brady bonds which have collateralized principal and partial interest payments. In this case, market price reflects the view of the major rating agencies that collateral does not significantly improve the credit quality of the bond. This apparent paradox, captured by market pricing as well as rating agency views (even when the percentage of present value composed of high grade U.S. Treasury collateral increases as average maturity declines) provides a source of excess return for investors.

Many investment vehicles seek to generate *steady* as well as high *current* income from a portfolio of emerging bonds. Portfolios can be designed to optimize current income at the expense of other objectives such as price appreciation or stability of net asset value. As emerging market bonds comprise a wide variety of fixed- and floating-rate securities, portfolio management strategies can be found that help optimize or stabilize current income throughout the interest rate cycle. Utilization of interest rate swaps or other derivatives can contribute substantially to achieving income objectives. As an illustration, during the period of low short-term interest rates from 1992-1993, swapping floating-rate Brady cash flows to fixed rates added over 200 bps in current yield.

Investment vehicles can also be designed to generate steady *dividends* composed of current income, realized capital gains, and, depending upon accounting conventions, accretion of discount. Exhibit 1 shows the historical cumulative dividends and total return in U.S. dollars per share of the Sovereign High Yield Investment Company. The main investment objective of this fund is to provide high income with a secondary objective of capital appreciation. A steady dollar dividend has been maintained for long periods since the inception of the fund.

Investment vehicles aiming at total return are managed differently from those that primarily seek high income. Among the many differences in management and orientation, vehicles seeking total return will often consider a wider set of potential investments, particularly highly discounted bonds and loans or high spread duration bonds. Collateralized Brady bonds are also favored for strategies involving higher interest duration as the U.S. Treasury zero-coupon bonds backing the principal value of the bonds supplies additional interest duration.

---

[2] These are the approximate yields of the Emerging Markets Bond Index (EMBI) of J. P. Morgan (sovereign yield and blended yield) and of the Lehman Brothers BB index (long) of U.S. high yield bonds.

Exhibit 1: SHYIC Returns

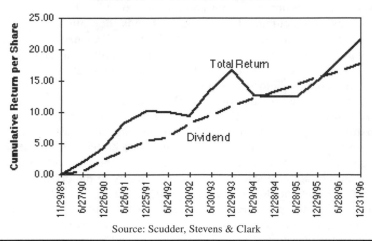

Source: Scudder, Stevens & Clark

A wide range of risk profiles is consistent with a total return orientation. Although discounts from par value — and the potential for above average price appreciation — are larger for issuers of lower credit quality, there are ample opportunities to invest in highly discounted securities of issuers with improving credit. Success in recent years in rapidly and effectively turning around countries involved in acute financial instability — Argentina, Brazil, Peru, and Poland, to name a few — provides evidence that even in cases of fragile credit quality framed in unstable macroeconomic conditions, successful turnaround can be produced within short periods of time. The record also shows that most of these major turnaround cases have led to sustained improvements in creditworthiness, breaking the cycle of stop-go progress that characterized major developing economies for most of the post-1945 years of the decade.

A number of portfolio management styles and techniques can be used to reach a total return objective. These range from long-term, research based portfolios which seek capital appreciation based on steady or improving fundamental conditions to trading-oriented vehicles which aim to take advantage of country- or issuer-specific events, U.S. bond market trends, or the global liquidity cycle. The deepening of emerging bond markets is providing increased liquidity, reducing the transaction costs of trading-oriented strategies. After the Mexican crisis at the end of 1994, a trend towards lower price volatilities lowered the cost of hedging and entering into derivative strategies which can enhance total return. Growing demand for hedging products will tend to lower transaction costs for derivatives as the markets mature.

Aggressive total return portfolios, as can be anticipated, are highly susceptible to conditions outside of the emerging markets, both of a fundamental nature and liquidity related. Brady bonds and long duration emerging Eurobonds are much more sensitive to fluctuations in the U.S. Treasury yield curve than implied by interest duration, spread duration, and other parameters that measure price sensitivity to yield or spread changes. While this sensitivity will tend to decline as discounts to par recede, markets mature, and the quality of information and analysis improves, emerging dollar bonds are likely to remain more exposed to shifts in Treasury bonds than other asset classes. Liquidity effects are another important consideration, particularly for portfolios that aim at boosting total return by employing a wide variety of trading strategies.

This pattern of sensitivity does not apply to local currency instruments, which have short duration and are segmented from global capital markets. Although the incipient development of local yield curves provides for only partial evidence, it appears that long duration bonds issued in local currencies have also reduced sensitivity to events in major global markets as compared to dollar pay issues. The segmentation of local fixed income markets from global markets results from the use of flexible exchange rates, restrictions or taxes on capital flows, and the lack of effective arbitrage between the local and international markets.

A third investment objective is asset diversification within a comprehensive investment program. It is not a distinct objective. Rather, it is achieved jointly with the other two objectives. Brady bonds and long-dated Eurobonds are sensitive to conditions in the U.S. bond market. Hence, these instruments are often not considered to provide much risk diversification for U.S. or dollar-based global bond investors. It is possible, however, to construct emerging bond portfolios which offer much greater potential for diversification by weighting more heavily emerging regions less associated with the U.S. bond market. Bonds of Asian, Central European, and Middle Eastern issuers historically have a lower correlation with the U.S. bond market than Latin American bonds. The latter account for about 80% of the mid-1997 capitalization of Brady and emerging Eurobonds.

Total return correlations of local currency markets with the U.S. and other developed country bond markets in recent years are generally not statistically different from zero at a high level of significance and as such can provide diversification advantages for U.S. and global bond investors. The substitution or addition of local currency instruments to U.S. or global portfolios can significantly reduce portfolio volatility and, sometimes, potentially increase returns. These results apply to local currency portfolios of short duration. The diversification benefits of local currencies are also enhanced because of the low correlation among the local currency markets themselves which helps explain the low volatility of local currency portfolios.

Asset diversification can be managed tactically or strategically to enhance returns during perceived favorable conditions in U.S. or global bond markets. Alternatively, diversification can be a primary defensive tool, for example by increasing the allocation to local currency investments. It too can help achieve interest duration objectives in diversified global portfolios.

ANALYTICAL ISSUES

The central principle behind a fundamental approach to emerging bond investments is that value, consistency, and risk control can be enhanced by systematic analysis. In a largely speculative asset class such as emerging markets fixed income, return optimization requires particular emphasis on risk control as the basis for portfolio construction and management. Analysis is needed as the centerpiece in gauging risks, determining relative value, and establishing potential arbitrage opportunities.

Although there are a number of ways to integrate analysis into the investment process, tilting research attention and resources towards particular aspects of the asset class, a fundamental approach, at a minimum, involves the following: sovereign risk, corporate credit, security analysis, market sensitivity, and for local currencies, currency or exchange rate risk.

Sovereign Risk

Sovereign risk encompasses several dimensions of risk. In its more general form, it measures transfer risk, sometimes denoted as *convertibility risk*. This is the probability that a government will not make foreign exchange available to meet foreign currency obligations. As such, sovereign credit quality will depend on the ability of the government to obtain foreign exchange and its willingness to maintain unimpeded flows of international capital to public and private borrowers.

The probability of default is a parameter that can be estimated either explicitly or implicitly. Ordinarily, however, the evaluation of sovereign risk involves more subtle differentiation among sovereign credits than just estimating a probability of default. Such probability tends to approach zero for periods of one year or less for investment-grade credits, but increases non-linearly as credits decline in quality below the investment-grade frontier. Nonetheless, markets are very sensitive to gradations in the perception of sovereign risk trends. Experience also indicates that markets tend to discount swiftly perceived improving trends in creditworthiness.

A key element for investment managers is the anticipation of changes in sovereign credit quality. A method to determine such changes is very useful as a guide to potential value and pricing of specific sovereign issues. This can be approached in a number of ways. The most desirable method is a thorough evaluation of macro, financial, and policy variables which will determine the government's ability and willingness to supply foreign exchange to entities operating within the country. Alternative approaches, which can be used as consistency checks, involve the use of quantitative models, indicators of creditworthiness, and check lists.

Among the key determinants of sovereign credit quality, to be assessed by thorough analysis, quantitative estimation, or other methods, are the following: the structure of the government's debt and debt service (external and internal), its international asset position, the fiscal position of the government, prospects for domestic output and demand, and a projection of dollar cash flows for the country derived from international trade and investment. The quality of economic policies in place, which can be quantified by indicators such as the status of International Monetary Fund programs, are also an important determinant. It is far more difficult to analyze and quantify institutional and political stability. Nonetheless, it is apparent that both markets and rating agencies devote considerable importance to this element which often helps to explain discrepancies in rating from that implied by more objective criteria.

Econometric analysis suggests that the structure of external debt is the central element involved in ratings of emerging markets by the major agencies. That this is the case should not be a surprise. After all, the probability of continuing to service external obligations will vary inversely with the burden of the debt. This is also the most readily quantifiable indicator of creditworthiness. It can be represented in simple form by the ratio of external debt to exports of goods and services. Other alternative ratios are also calculated, for example, the ratio of external debt to GDP. Likewise debt service ratios are often used to measure the current burden of servicing external debt.

Statistical analysis of sovereign debt ratings of the two major rating agencies, Moody's and Standard and Poor's, suggests that a small set of debt and economic indicators fits well the variation of ratings from a sample of 23 of the most important emerging countries. The results of two regressions, shown in Exhibit 2, indicate that the ratio of external debt to total exports, the ratio of total interest payments to exports, the trend growth of real GDP (average of the last three years) and the level of inflation for the last year account for 82% of the variance of Moody's ratings and 75% of the variance of ratings from Standard and Poor's. These results do not imply that the rating process used by the agencies is based solely or even primarily on these commonly used indicators. The standard errors of 0.39 rating and 0.53 rating, respectively, indicate that these equations are approximations of the process. Likewise, having 11 of 23 ratings split between the two agencies point out the important judgmental elements involved in the rating process. A statistical difference between the agencies appears to be that Standard and Poor's assigns somewhat greater weight to macroeconomic stability and growth than does Moody's as can be seen in the larger coefficients for trend growth and inflation in the regressions.

Exhibit 2: Determinants of Sovereign Credit Ratings*

	Constant	Debt/Exports	Interest/Exports	Trend Growth	CPI Inflation	
Moody's	4.58	0.008	−0.027	−0.072	0.0084	R2 = 0.82
(t ratio)	19.2	2.85	−0.58	−2.88	2.2	s.e.= 0.39
Standard & Poor's	4.51	0.009	−0.049	−0.077	0.016	R2 = 0.75
(t ratio)	13.95	2.33	−0.79	−2.29	3.13	s.e. = 0.53

* Estimated from data in the Institute of International Finance, *Near Term Prospects for Emerging Market Economies* (Washington, D.C., April 1997). Ratings are those in effect as of June 1, 1997. For purposes of estimation, ratings were converted to a numerical equivalent where BBB/Baa is equal to 5.00 and BB/Ba equals 6.00 and so forth.

An evaluation of the mix of economic policies used by the government to attain financial and price stability and to help foster investment, growth, and financial deepening is essential in determining whether a country is on its way to achieving sustainable economic growth. Largely because of the diffusion of policy know-how and evidence that market-led policies instill confidence on investors and consumers, the quality of policies followed by developing countries has improved greatly in the 15 years since the debt crisis of 1982, the debacle which deeply set back development prospects for many middle-income countries. The lesson of the 1990s is that markets are rapid to acknowledge the benefits of stabilization based on a sound fiscal, monetary, and deregulatory policy mix. Likewise, selling state assets can rapidly provide signals to markets of a change in direction and an increase in the potential for solid fiscal policies.

A checklist can be a useful device to gauge the quality of the institutional and political environment in a country. The checklist may include factors such as the likelihood of a smooth transition of power, the stability of governing coalitions, and the chances for continuity of policies. Absent high political instability, which can lead to sharp reversal of policies, shifting coalition governments, and other nonviolent signs of political change are not necessarily a huge negative in the evaluation of credit quality. It is when policies are affected negatively by either peaceful or violent political change that potential for a major reversal in credit trends exists.

Corporate Credit

Debt securities of emerging country corporations provide a means to enhance returns in emerging debt, high yield, or other fixed income portfolios. Credit research is essential in determining proper valuation and the identification of investment opportunities. Corporate credits can also be a source of diversification as a complement or an alternative to sovereign credits. On the other hand, corporate credits can be very sensitive to movements in sovereign credit quality in the country of corporate residence. It follows that corporate credits do not always provide much diversification to emerging debt portfolios.

Evaluation of corporate risk in emerging markets presents formidable challenges. Rapidly evolving operating environments, accounting and legal systems, and rapid shifts in financial variables compound uncertainty in assessing credit risk for corporations. Management quality is arguably even more of a determining variable in developing countries than in industrial ones. Because of these factors, financial outcomes for emerging country companies are often subject to greater error than is the case in developed economies.

The operating environment for companies in developing countries is deeply affected, almost by definition, by rapid structural change arising out of institutional development, liberalization of markets, the creation and transformation of regulatory systems, and the opening to competition from foreign companies. It is also characterized by greater cyclical variation in demand and output than in developed countries.

Accounting standards are shifting rapidly in many emerging countries and are converging gradually to U.S. GAAP. Some countries such as Chile and Argentina now use accounting standards which are close to those of the United States and other developed countries. The issuance of American Depository Receipts and international bonds by many emerging country corporations also forces these companies to restate their financial statements in harmony with either U.S. or commonly accepted international standards. Privatization is another force pressing for updating accounting standards as widening interest in state companies by potential strategic or portfolio investors requires a thorough restatement of financial data. The pace of change is strongest among many larger Latin American and East Asian companies which are now accessing the international capital market. Central European, South Asian, and African companies lag in these efforts.

There is a debate regarding the relative evaluation of corporate and sovereign credits. Traditionally, the sovereign ceiling, or the credit rating given to the government, has set a limit on the rating of corporations residing and largely operating in that country. In some cases, however, market prices signaled that investors viewed corporations as a better credit. For example, some Argentine corporate credits traded for substantial periods of time with spreads through sovereign bonds of comparable duration or maturity. Recently some credit agencies, among them Standard and Poor's and Fitch, have indicated conditions under which corporate credits could be subject to a higher hard currency credit rating than the sovereign.[3]

Historical price behavior gives some support to the view that corporate bonds may be more susceptible to systemic shocks than sovereign bonds. A shock is an unexpected shift in a financial or real variable that substantially alters the probabilities given by investors and consumers to normal economic outcomes. A sudden devaluation of the currency or a large drop in the price of a key commodity, such as copper for Chile or oil for Nigeria, can generate shocks. After the devaluation of the Mexican peso in December 1994, spreads of Eurobonds issued by Mexican and other Latin American companies widened significantly over comparable maturity sovereigns. In this case, the currency devaluation in one of the most prominent emerging debtors provided a systemic shock to the market which deeply hit corporate credits. A systemic shock affects a set of international investors and markets as opposed to a country-specific shock which disrupts only investors in a given country and its securities.

Banks and other financial companies in emerging countries are especially sensitive to the stress generated by structural change and to the dislocations provided by shocks. The combination of rapid credit growth, often prevalent in

---

[3] This refers mainly to "dollarized economies" where there is little or no difference between credit quality measured in local currency or in dollars. The limiting case of a dollarized economy is one where the dollar is legal and sole legal tender, such as Panama. Countries with a currency pegged to the dollar through a "currency board" system or other mechanism that maintains full backing of the monetary base by dollar reserves or equivalent assets can be considered dollarized. For a company operating in a fully dollarized economy, transfer risk approaches zero.

emerging economies during price stabilization and deregulation of the financial sector, and inadequate risk management and other controls at lending institutions, leads to a deterioration of loan portfolios. Shocks can exacerbate the situation by causing rapid downward shifts in economic activity or an increase in key prices and interest rates. Banking difficulties are common throughout the developing world and, paradoxically, in the more rapidly developing countries. Analyzing financial credits is one of the most challenging aspects of corporate credit evaluation in emerging markets.

Bonds issued by companies facing steady demand through the economic cycle and capable of reacting rapidly to shocks offer less risk and at times present opportunities for yield and yield-compression significantly over the sovereign. This is the case of some electric utilities and companies in the food processing sector. Transformation of energy pricing and regulation in emerging countries to systems based on fuel and capacity costs or, alternatively, on marginal cost pricing, such as in Argentina and Chile, are reducing uncertainty in evaluating company cash flows while increasing the likelihood that adequate interest coverage ratios can be maintained.

Investing in debt securities of all but the largest listed companies in emerging markets requires specialized credit work and wide access to local data and company management. Locally traded debt securities as well as private placements offer ample opportunities for excess return. However, this is a market segment which remains terra incognita for most investors located outside of the domestic market. The comments above regarding credit analysis, which pertain largely to the better capitalized corporations, are even more applicable to this much larger set of companies where the problems of risk evaluation are compounded by local operating environments, regulatory questions, and limitations of data and institutional understanding.

Security Analysis

Sovereign and corporate credit analysis provide essential inputs for security evaluation, country selection, and portfolio management. Additional evaluation is necessary to proceed with security selection in the investment process. Much like other debt securities, emerging bonds can be analyzed in terms of parameters determining yield and return, price sensitivity, and properties of the yield curve. The analytical issues are similar to those encountered in the evaluation of other debt securities. Analytical questions of special relevance for emerging market bonds concern collateral and unusual coupon structures in many Brady bonds, the abundance of floating-rate issues, and embedded options.

Collateral associated with Brady bonds requires calculation of stripped yields and spreads or, as alternatively called, sovereign yields and spreads, apart from the usual yield-to-maturity calculations. A stripped yield is derived from the cash flows net of collateral. This is straightforward when only the principal is collateralized, typically by a matching U.S. Treasury zero. It becomes more complex as two, or sometimes three, coupons are also collateralized. Such coupon collateralization can be evaluated by using alternative methodologies which incorporate the probability of default per coupon period.

Spread duration measures the sensitivity of price to changes in sovereign yield, as contrasted to ordinary yield-to-maturity (YTM) or "blended yield." This calculation is necessary for all Brady bonds except fixed-rate, non-collateralized bullets, where ordinary YTM calculations produce identical results. Spread duration is a central parameter in Brady bond evaluation and portfolio construction and management. It provides a measure of the sensitivity of total return of Brady bonds to changes in sovereign spreads over comparable U.S. Treasury bonds or other base yields.

Floating-rate bonds of intermediate and long-maturities were issued by the 15 countries that completed Brady debt restructurings in the 1989-1996 period.[4] Floating-rate syndicated loans of several countries, among them Russia and Morocco, trade actively in international markets. Several countries issued floating-rate Bradys and Eurobonds of varying maturities as part of their financing programs. These floaters have low or negative modified interest duration. Because of the discounts on most of these floating-rate bonds, interest duration provides a weak measure of the sensitivity of these bonds to shifts in the U.S. Treasury curve as well as to the sensitivity of the bonds to shifts in credit spreads. It is therefore essential to evaluate sovereign spread duration for these floaters as part of relative value, total return, and other portfolio summary statistics.

Call options to the issuer are embedded in most Brady bonds and in some sovereign Eurobonds. Corporate bonds are also issued in callable form. As long as call options on Brady bonds were deeply out-of-the-money, their value was safely ignored by investors. Brady bonds traded at deep discounts immediately after their issuance upon exchange of restructured loans. As Brady prices approach levels where the call options offer significant value, option-adjusted-spread (OAS) calculations become necessary as a means of establishing precise valuation, helping portfolio construction, and trading. OAS evaluation methodologies for Brady bonds are not yet standard and tend to produce substantial differences. This partly follows from Brady bonds' complex structures with one or two types of collateral and discrete coupon patterns. Furthermore, the probability distribution of Brady prices appears to differ appreciably from the lognormal distribution utilized widely to price options.

Market Sensitivity

Emerging market bond prices show, as a rule, high sensitivity to random events and to the impact of changes in international markets. For example, emerging bonds show more responsiveness to shifts in the U.S. yield curve than indicated by intrinsic measures of price sensitivity such as interest and spread duration. That this is so should not be a big surprise. Partly, it can be explained by the prevailing discount in most emerging bonds or other measures of risk premium.

---

[4] These countries are Albania, Argentina, Brazil, Bulgaria, Costa Rica, Dominican Republic, Ecuador, Jordan, Mexico, Panama, Peru, The Philippines, Poland, Uruguay, and Venezuela.

Exhibit 3: Sensitivity to Changes in U.S. Yield Curve (December 1990 to April 1996)

	Sensitivity	Interest Duration (years)
EMBI	−11.9	5.4
Fixed Rate Bonds	−15.0	10.7
Floaters	−8.7	0.4

Source: Calculated from J.P. Morgan's Emerging Markets Bond Index.

Brady bonds are highly sensitive to conditions in U.S. markets. Sensitivity of the Emerging Markets Bond Index of J.P. Morgan, which is composed mostly of Brady bonds, to changes in the U.S. yield curve in the period December 1990 to March 1996 is −11.9. This means that a change in U.S. rates on average produces a percentage change about −12 times larger in the EMBI index. This was calculated by regression of the EMBI on a U.S. yield curve (3 months to 30 years) weighted to produce interest duration equal to that of the EMBI plus a variable for emerging market shocks (such as the Real Plan in Brazil and the Mexican peso shock of December 1994).

Fixed-rate Bradys show a sensitivity of −15 compared, for example, to interest duration of 10.7 years. The data also show clearly that Brady floating-rate bonds are also very sensitive to shifts in U.S. interest rates. While the interest duration of floating Bradys (April 1996) is only 0.4 years, they show a statistical sensitivity of −8.7. Markets overshoot when U.S. rates fall as credit risk is perceived to decrease. Conversely, markets react negatively to rising interest rates partly because credit risk is negatively impacted. Vanishing liquidity, in turn, compounds these effects. This applies to both fixed- and floating-rate Bradys. Consequently, in periods of weakness in U.S. markets, Brady bonds will tend to overreact. Market sensitivity of Brady bonds to the U.S. yield curve may be presumed to fall as discounts recede.

There is an additional explanation for the sensitivity to the U.S. market. Emerging countries are the marginal issuers in international debt markets and they — and the holders of their debt securities — will be among the first to be affected or benefited by changing patterns of international capital flows. As risk is perceived to decrease, either because of changes in fundamental trend or improved information and analysis, sensitivity may tend to decline.

Can market sensitivity be measured in any systematic and reliable way? Usual calculations, including those implied by the capital asset pricing model, such as betas, or other statistical relationships, similar to those in Exhibit 3, are typically not very stable. Likewise, there are reservations about usual measures of variability, such as the standard deviation, since total return of individual emerging debt securities may show deviations from normality.

The heightened volatility of emerging debt securities appears to be related to the size of the risk premium. It may also be argued that often this risk premium may be larger than is implied by the excess volatility of emerging debt securities. While this is debatable, the risk premium is a potential source of excess returns and arbitrage opportunities.

Options on emerging bonds suggest as well that there is a premium paid for excess volatility, apart from premia caused by other factors such as liquidity and shortcomings in option modeling. Implied volatilities exceeded actual volatilities for the main Brady bonds in the two years to mid-June 1997. This is probably derived from a period of declining long-term volatility in the market. Nonetheless, the additional risk premia has probably hindered the use of hedging strategies.

Currency or Exchange Rate Risk

Investment in emerging debt securities issued and payable in local currencies presents separate analytical issues in addition to the topics covered above. The central issue presented by these local currency investments is the evaluation of currency risk. This is the risk of devaluation of the currency in terms of dollars. In most instances, devaluation risk could be narrowed further as the risk of a real devaluation of the exchange rate, or a devaluation in excess of the inflation differential with the United States. Measuring the risk of real devaluation enables comparisons among currencies of exchange rate risk.

Investing in local currency securities can provide excess returns over those of securities of similar duration in developed markets. Part of this return arises from prevailing local yields which in real terms are higher than required by underlying credit and currency risks. This could be the result of the need to maintain high positive real interest rates during financial stabilization and disinflation or derived from rigid expectations of policy or market behavior.

Evaluating the probability of a real devaluation enables the quantification and cross country comparison of currency risk. In most emerging countries, this requires the evaluation of the exchange rate regime and the policy rule followed. Most emerging currencies are managed according to preset rules, i.e., by pegging to the dollar or a basket of hard currencies, by keeping the currency within limits of a peg, or following a crawling peg. Quantification of the expected devaluation then involves evaluation of the policy rule and the ability of the central bank to follow it. Since most emerging currencies are managed against some central peg, as a rule they are more predictable and less volatile than developed currencies. In the 12 months to the end of May 1997, for example, the exchange rates of the deutsche mark and yen to the dollar were more volatile than the rates against the U.S. dollar of 15 of the more widely traded emerging currencies.

INVESTMENT PROCESS AND PORTFOLIO CONSTRUCTION

Portfolio construction and management are designed to reach the investment objectives within the risk tolerance indicated in the investment guidelines or prospectus. Alternative approaches to portfolio construction are determined by the investment process established to manage the portfolio. The investment process integrates all the elements needed to achieve investment objectives.

Investment Process

Emerging debt securities are generally in the lower segment of the credit quality spectrum. Investing in emerging debt consequently requires an especially rigorous process of country, security, and asset allocation as a means to control risk and provide for consistency of returns. It also requires comprehensive knowledge of trading conditions to provide for efficient timing of entry, exit, and hedging decisions.

While conceivably a variety of investment processes may produce superior and consistent performance, all of them require close integration of research and analysis on the one hand, and portfolio management and trading on the other. Likewise, a variety of investment styles will produce a number of investment processes, for example, very active, arbitrage-oriented portfolios or longer-term, value-oriented approaches.

Independent of the characteristics of the investment process, analytical support for the process involves a top-down component, centered on fundamental sovereign, sector, and market analysis and a bottom-up component that incorporates security, corporate, or sub-national analysis. This is then integrated with the timing decision, which requires a sharp understanding of trading conditions for specific securities.

Some investment processes emphasize security selection and the bottom-up aspect of the process. This may be akin to traditional corporate high yield investments. However, in emerging markets, companies operate within a wide variety of macroeconomic and institutional environments. So it is not easy to succeed with a pure bottom-up approach to the investment process, and a foundation of macro analysis is required to provide for differentiation across countries and interpretation of national and global events. Inasmuch as emerging markets become more integrated into the international economy through lifting of barriers to trade and capital, national operating conditions could become somewhat less important. The central premise in a bottom-up approach is security valuation.

A second type of process emphasizes the top-down component and the identification of potential gains from credit improvement or pricing divergence derived from analysis of fundamental country and macro trends. Just as the first approach requires integration with macro analysis, the top-down orientation must involve security analysis as an essential input in the determination of value. This said, since the majority of emerging countries are issuers of a few or even only one liquid security, country and security analysis often converge to the establishment of relative value in terms of individual securities.

In practice, disciplined investment processes involve both a top-down and a bottom-up component. The differentiation comes from the relative importance of each approach and the time dimension of investment decisions. Trading-oriented approaches may emphasize flow analysis, event appraisal, and global market effects, for instance, as the force driving investment decisions. These approaches can be viewed as complementary where they make most sense in managing global emerging market portfolios. For specialized portfolios, they can be considered stand-alone processes, for example, in managing country funds, where the investment process will largely be driven by security analysis.

Portfolio Construction

Construction of emerging market portfolios follows the same principles as other fixed income portfolios. Conceptually, this involves estimating, over the investment horizon, total return and its components for each security in the investable universe as well as estimation of risk characteristics. Research inputs are necessary in the estimation of total return. Risk characteristics could formally be projected from historical data on price and spread movements or from appropriate matrices of correlation coefficients. In practice, however, experience quickly teaches that such calculations have wide confidence intervals and are not stable enough to be interpreted without a great amount of care and sophistication. Quantitative analysis of risk and return and the use of optimization techniques can provide a rough and useful guide to the return and risk parameters for a portfolio.

One approach to portfolio construction involves having core and trading positions within the portfolio. Core positions will be driven by fundamental value to be realized within an intermediate investment horizon, say, three to six months, which in the dynamics of emerging countries can contain a sizable number of fundamental events. Core positions are adjusted as fundamental views change. They are changed in response to price action to realize price targets or implement a stop loss. Positions can also be altered as risk patterns change, for example, because of major deviations in volatility or security correlations. Nonetheless, the idea behind the core is that it should represent long-term views of credit direction, value, and relationship to the U.S. and other more developed bond markets.

Maintaining a core position requires much portfolio discipline and reliable inputs from analysis and research. By reason of the rapid change in emerging nations and the young stage of their financial institutions, governance, and markets, investors are continuously exposed to a substantial flow of information denoting the evidence of change and the resistance to and costs of change. Inevitably, this will be mixed news, often suggesting signals of some impending catastrophe. Exposed to this information flow and accompanying events, it helps to understand why turnover ratios in emerging debt portfolios are high.

A good example of the virtues of having core portfolios is provided by the massive correction and spectacular recovery that followed the devaluation of the Mexican peso in December 1994. The veritable collapse of the Brady bond market after the devaluation was followed with a sharp turnaround. Liquidity effects, including deleverage, rather than any sharp deterioration of fundamentals explained the market reaction, as well as the rapid recovery of prices. Sustaining core positions through this massive upheaval was no mean task, but it paid in terms of ultimately benefiting with the rapid recovery in prices. This would have required strong conviction derived from competent analysis. Instead, most investors tried timing the turning points in such rapid recovery, and a few succeeded.

Trading positions aim to take advantage of mispricing, event anticipation, and other elements which can give rise to temporary deviations from fundamental value. To be effective and to maintain overall control of risk, trading positions should be separate from the core. Of course, in a limiting case, the entire portfolio can be viewed as a collection of trades, subject to constant adjustment. This may work well, but strict accounting of trading and hedging costs must be made to ascertain the merits of the strategy.

Buy-and-hold portfolios are the other limiting case, when there is no adjustment of positions other than resulting from a change in core views. This could be derived from long-term fundamental views, or, in another limiting case, because the portfolio may be entirely passive, tracking a given benchmark. The latter are not used very widely, and it is not difficult to show that emerging market benchmarks are unlikely to be optimal from return or risk characteristics. Buy-and-hold portfolios may have limited room for flexibility when they are designed to match, directly or synthetically, certain desired characteristics such as maturity, duration, or current income. Specific purpose investment structures composed of emerging debt securities often fit well in the portfolios of insurance companies, banks, and other financial institutions.

Ordinarily, portfolio adjustments are made continuously as a result of changes in pricing or trading opportunities, and, less frequently, following the appreciation of shifts in fundamental value. Adjustments are also made when the portfolio profile no longer is within desired characteristics of spread and interest duration, currency exposure, or risk.

In a smoothly working investment process, initiative for portfolio changes may come from traders and portfolio managers, who are close to the price action, or from analysts who gauge credit or macro trends. In cases when fundamental variables drive adjustments, analysts can become involved in the process, even as origination may come from the portfolio management team. In practice, rapid events challenge the portfolio management process, as communication lags, for example, can lead to incomplete integration of the investment process and decisions which do not fully use the potential of the investment management team.

Failure to perform consistently up to expectations is usually the consequence of a failure in appraisal of fundamentals and not of errors in market timing. Of course, gauging the probability and impact of powerful positive or negative events adds value. It does and can provide for a large measure of success in managing emerging debt portfolios. Market and event related decisions, such as the timing of Brady buyback announcements, which have been made by several of the most prominent issuers of Brady bonds (Mexico, Argentina and Brazil), can be gauged by analysis of government finances and cash flows but equally require a keen understanding of capital market conditions.

One of the crucial aspects of managing emerging portfolios is the need to appraise the impact upon emerging borrowers of variables outside the investable universe, that is, financial and economic changes and expectations in advanced countries. This calls for an investment process integrated closely with fundamental and market analysis of U.S. and international bond markets. The flow of causality is almost exclusively from developed to emerging markets. Defensive or hedging strategies as well as strategies to take advantage of patterns in benchmark markets are a key part of the portfolio management process.

CONTROLLING RISK

Risk management is an essential ingredient in emerging markets fixed income. Risk management can be viewed in several ways, depending on the dimension of risk. In emerging markets, limiting credit risk, sovereign and corporate, is a central aim of the investment process and of portfolio management.

Risk control also involves mitigating market risk. This often involves reducing price or total return volatility. Investors will have widely differing levels of tolerance for volatility, depending on their ultimate aim. For an equity investor who views emerging debt as an equity alternative, maintaining low or moderate portfolio volatility may not be important or even highly desirable. On the other hand, a fixed income investor who aims at seeking excess return over U.S. bonds but maintaining volatility within some upper bound of the U.S. bond market will want to have a different portfolio profile than an equity-oriented investor.

Risk could also be viewed asymmetrically, for example, reducing downside risk. This can also be approached in a number of ways. The selected strategy to reduce downside risk will vary with the prospectus or guideline restrictions. At one end, it may require capping downside price movement by purchasing put options. Or, it may involve selling call options, matching assets and liabilities, or simply lowering interest duration. The cost of reducing downside risk will be gauged in the context of overall investment objectives and may not always be by itself a determining variable.

Another potential area for risk control would be to reduce the risk of underperformance versus a established benchmark or appropriate index. This can be thought of as aiming to keep tracking error within bounds from a benchmark. Tracking error is the standard deviation of the difference in performance (usually total return) between a portfolio and the benchmark. A portfolio guideline or constraint may be to maintain tracking error within ±2% of total return for a given benchmark or reference index. Since emerging market portfolios can have high volatility, there could be a sizable cost in potential return for keeping tracking error low, for example, at less than 1%. Limiting tracking error is probably best viewed as an exercise in performance management rather than risk management as it merely focuses on a narrow aspect of the risk dimension.

Comprehensive risk management can also be viewed from a value-at-risk perspective. This would involve ascertaining the potential loss resulting at a given level of confidence from a change in some variable. It could measure, for instance, the impact of a change in the price of the 10-year U.S. Treasury note on emerging Eurobonds in the portfolio at a 95% level of confidence.

Managing Credit Risk

Management of credit risk requires making sound judgments on sovereign and corporate credits. Fiduciary responsibilities usually require that investment managers make independent evaluation of credit risk and do not rely on the judgment of credit rating agencies, brokers, or other intermediaries. Credit agency ratings are an important guide to credit quality and have great bearing on security pricing and price movements. In many cases, investment guidelines impose a constraint based on agency credit ratings. This means that agency ratings have to be taken as a central reference point for investment managers, who, nonetheless, will have to form their own opinions regarding the quality of the credit.

Managing sovereign risk requires continuing assessment of factors that may imply or signal a deterioration of risk. Such monitoring can be done by research analysts or even by portfolio managers. Dependence on market information, made available by third parties such as banks, brokers, consultants, and the press does not relieve investment managers of their responsibilities versus clients.

The following steps are recommended as part of a continuing credit review process: (1) weekly, or at least monthly, review of all credits in a portfolio; (2) assessment of the impact on capacity to service debt of major changes in operating capability, government policies, external factors, or other exogenous changes; (3) analysis of interrelations among credits focusing on material impact that changes in one credit may have on other credits; (4) mitigation of elements that can lower the probability of serious impact upon the credit; and, (5) use of a value-at-risk or similar approach to quantify overall sensitivity to changes in key variables.

While quantitative techniques and management systems will enhance capabilities, management of credit risk involves a continuing assessment of fundamental variables that affect valuation. A review of technical, flow, or statistical associations that may affect market prices is very useful but not the central aspect. That is, managing credit risk involves making fundamental judgments about intrinsic risk that can potentially be expressed in fundamental value.

Managing Market Risk

Investors in emerging debt usually concern themselves with two types of market risk — volatility and pricing risk. The first is associated with variation of total return or prices as measured by traditional statistical measures such as the standard deviation or the standard error of estimate. In this section we will direct our comments mainly to the management of volatility and not to pricing risk.

Pricing risk is often a consequence of the lack of liquidity in issues with thin secondary markets. While a concern in portfolios that seek value and diversification by investing in minor sovereign and, especially, corporate issues, pricing risk is generally low in all the major Brady bonds and large sovereign issues. One obvious way to reduce pricing risk is to confine investments to major liquid issues.

Emerging debt is usually viewed as one of the most volatile fixed income asset classes. This is generally the case for long duration emerging bonds, particularly Brady bonds and long Eurobonds. On the other hand, as discussed in the next section, portfolios of local currency investments exhibit low volatility when properly diversified.

In the two years since the Mexican peso crisis, the volatility of Bradys and liquid Eurobonds declined steadily as indicated in Exhibit 4. By June 1997, the volatility of the Emerging Brady Bond Index Plus produced by J.P. Morgan (EMBI+), the most widely used benchmark, reached a little over 8% (26 week annualized volatility) from levels of around 25% at the beginning of 1995. Lower volatility is reflected in pricing of options on Brady bonds.

Investors assign variable degrees of importance to volatility. For some investors it is of secondary importance in the context of attaining investment objectives and no restrictions are desired to limit volatility beneath a given threshold. For others high volatility may be undesirable or must be kept within bounds to match liabilities, complement other assets, or to keep within a range of the benchmark.

The following approaches to managing volatility can be used in emerging debt portfolios: portfolio diversification, asset allocation, and sell disciplines. Option strategies are a fourth alternative, which can be used tactically or as an integral part of core portfolios.

Portfolio Diversification

One of the virtues of portfolio diversification is that it can dampen market risk as well as provide a mechanism for managing other types of risk (sovereign, credit, currency, event) over a set of securities. The capability of diversification to dampen market risk is a function of the interaction of price and return among emerging debt securities and with securities in other asset classes.

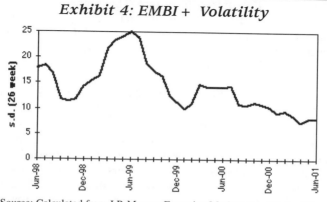

Exhibit 4: EMBI+ Volatility

Source: Calculated from J.P. Morgan Emerging Markets Bond Index Plus.

Correlations and other statistical measures of association show that Brady bonds and Eurobonds are closely correlated. In addition, as mentioned before, volatility is not necessarily dampened in close proportion to the bonds' duration and other intrinsic properties. This means than when considering portfolios consisting mainly of Bradys and Eurobonds, there is only reduced scope for limiting low volatility by diversification within this asset class.

Other alternatives, such as strategies which imply use of options and other derivatives, can reduce volatility but their cost is generally high. This limits derivatives-based techniques to tactical and trading strategies, where they can add the most value. Ordinarily they do not provide an efficient approach to capping downside risk to the entire portfolio. As a comprehensive approach, extensive use of put options, covered calls, and other protective techniques is too costly for all but the most defensive strategies. Derivatives have an important role, when allowed by investment guidelines, in tactical positioning of portfolios or as a means of attaining implicit leverage. The growth of emerging debt derivatives trading in over-the-counter markets and in exchanges offers smooth execution and much more efficient pricing than was possible in the early stages of the evolution of the asset class.

One possible diversification strategy, blending Bradys and emerging Eurobonds on one side and local currency emerging debt on the other can often provide desirable risk-return characteristics and a substantial reduction in portfolio volatility.

Asset Allocation

Brady bonds and emerging market Eurobonds have lower correlation with other fixed income and equity securities than among themselves, providing for the possibility of constructing portfolios that will meet a wide range of desired objectives. The correlation matrix in Exhibit 5 illustrates correlations for 1993-1997 among the main emerging market debt indices — the EMBI and EMBI+ — and other fixed income and equity indices. In particular, it shows that whereas the EMBI+ and EMBI have moderate correlation with the U.S. bond and equity markets (Lehman G/C and S&P 500), correlation with global bonds (G. Govt) is essentially not statistically different from zero. This suggests that emerging bonds can be a useful complement to global and international bond portfolios. It implies also that adding global bonds to emerging market portfolios could be an efficient strategy in terms of risk-return trade-off for many investors who do not wish to have full exposure to emerging market risk.

Sell Disciplines

Emerging markets debt management requires strict sell disciplines in portfolios and trading strategies. There are several reasons for this emphasis on sell disciplines. Emerging countries are in the process of solidifying policies, institutions, and regulations aiming at providing a constructive environment for long-term investments and market development. But, unfortunately, setbacks and failures occur frequently, sometimes in difficult to predict conditions. This calls for continuing evaluation of positions and the taking of swift action to reduce, alter, or eliminate positions from the portfolio.

Exhibit 5: Emerging Markets Correlation Matrix
(Monthly data — December 1993 to March 1997)

Index*	Annualized Volatility	EMBI+	EMBI	ELMI	ELMI-EW	S&P 500	Lehm G/C	G. Govt.	MS EAFE
EMBI+	17.81	1							
EMBI	17.75	0.98	1						
ELMI	7.62	0.54	0.50	1					
ELMI-EW	3.74	0.42	0.34	0.82	1				
S&P 500	10.22	0.48	0.52	0.13	0.07	1			
Lehm G/C	4.89	0.45	0.47	0.02	0.07	0.60	1		
G. Govt.	5.14	0.03	-0.01	0.04	0.32	0.27	0.52	1	
MS EAFE	10.85	0.20	0.20	0.15	0.05	0.45	0.12	0.36	1

Source: Calculated on the basis of index data from J.P.Morgan, Lehman Brothers, and Morgan Stanley Capital International.

*Indices are as follows:
   EMBI+: J.P. Morgan Emerging Market Bond Index Plus
   EMBI: J.P. Morgan Emerging Market Bond Index
   ELMI: J.P. Morgan Emerging Local Markets Index
   ELMI - EW: Adjusted Equal-Weighted ELMI
   S&P 500: Standard and Poor's 500 Stock Index
   Lehm G/C: Lehman Brothers Government/Corporate Index
   G. Govt: J.P. Morgan Global Government Index
   MS EAFE: Morgan Stanley Capital International, Europe, Australia and the Far East Index

The high sensitivity of emerging bonds to conditions in global fixed income markets also calls for strict sell disciplines as a defensive posture when faced with potential setbacks in the U.S. bond market or, for many Asian issuers, in Japanese money or bond markets. Alternative management techniques can be used to complement sell disciplines such as careful management of interest and spread duration. As explained above, however, duration strategies do not always work well in emerging debt securities.

Trading-oriented investment processes likewise need to be based firmly on precise sell disciplines. This is, of course, critical in leveraged portfolios or those which employ short positions. Even in portfolios where leverage on short positions are not allowed by prospectus or investment guidelines, tactical positions must be controlled and gains taken or losses curtailed as price action surpasses set limits.

Derivatives can substitute for sell actions and can frequently be a superior alternative. As pricing efficiency increases, options can be employed at lower cost to cushion portfolios from adverse price movements. The fall in price volatility in Brady and Eurobonds in the two years to mid-1997 supports arguments that volatility is priced reasonably low compared to the historical trend in the market. The contrary argument is that implied volatilities remain higher than historical volatilities for most Brady bonds as of mid-1997.

LOCAL CURRENCY MARKETS

Local currency markets are the fastest growing component of the emerging debt asset class, driven by the explosive development of capital markets in developing nations. Three factors argue for an even more rapid development of liquid markets for local debt securities: (1) the deregulation of local capital markets; (2) the revolution in pension and savings systems in developing countries; and, (3) the swift advances in price and financial stability by nearly all large emerging nations.

Local debt markets are now the largest part of the emerging debt asset class. Money markets instruments and local bonds in 75 emerging countries by the end of 1996 exceeded $850 billion, according to estimates derived from International Monetary Fund, World Bank, and national data. By contrast, the market value of Brady bonds and other Eurobonds issued in international markets by governments and corporations in the same countries is estimated at $230 billion. Some $370 billion of local markets securities are located in Asia, $250 billion in Latin America, $90 billion in Africa south of the Sahara, and the rest in Central and Eastern Europe and the Middle East. These numbers exclude many government and corporate bond issues and commercial paper of lesser liquidity.

The bulk of liquid local assets are money market instruments, mainly government securities. Commercial paper is usually placed privately. A handful of countries have developed liquid bond markets, most importantly Argentina, South Africa, and, to a lesser extent, Chile and the Czech Republic. Government bills and notes are traded extensively in most countries, mainly in the interbank market but also in other active secondary markets. Clearing and custody are often sophisticated with book entry at the central bank or other central depository a common practice.

Local instruments are rarely traded offshore in direct form. However, liquid forward markets for local currencies are rapidly developing in major emerging countries and others that do not have strict capital controls. Offshore markets are also found in lesser currencies. By mid-1997, forwards and offshore notes were available in some 30 emerging currencies, most with reasonable liquidity. Banks are also active in designing offshore structures to capture the properties of local money market instruments when trading may be hindered by local operational practices such as lack of proper custody or certain types of exchange controls. These services are gradually becoming more competitive as international banks set up operations in new countries and local banks begin to enter the business through their offshore subsidiaries.

Exhibit 6 provides a sample of monthly money market returns in dollar terms comprising the ten emerging countries in J.P. Morgan's Emerging Local Markets Index (ELMI). The exhibit shows an average correlation of 0.11 from inception of the index in December 1993 to October 1996. Most coefficients in the exhibit are not statistically significant or negative among pairs of countries. Even among countries in some regions, the correlations are low. For example, the average correlation among the four Southeast Asian countries in the matrix is only 0.09.

Exhibit 6: Local Currency Correlation Matrix
(Monthly data — December 1993 to October 1996)

	Argen	Czech	Indon	Malay	Mexico	Philip	Poland	S.Afri	Thaild	Turkey
Argentina	1									
Czech Republic	−0.279	1								
Indonesia	0.200	−0.260	1							
Malaysia	0.239	0.240	−0.032	1						
Mexico	0.218	−0.219	0.384	0.145	1					
Philippines	0.218	−0.119	0.135	0.191	0.196	1				
Poland	0.098	0.564	0.030	0.183	−0.216	−0.086	1			
South Africa	−0.161	0.208	0.160	−0.204	−0.178	0.019	0.346	1		
Thailand	0.026	0.637	−0.046	0.375	0.106	−0.089	0.583	0.019	1	
Turkey	0.239	0.134	0.183	0.198	0.084	0.152	0.049	−0.023	0.154	1

* Based on portfolio of 90-day money market securities at market exchange rates.
Source: SS&C on the basis of data from J.P. Morgan.

Low correlations could well increase over time as currencies within a region may move together given an external shock or a change in external variables. Likewise, a successful speculative attack on one currency may well encourage speculators and investors to attack a neighboring currency or pull out massively from the currency. Recent evidence suggests that there may be links between attacks on currencies in separate regions, such as pressure on the Philippine peso following the Mexican peso 1994 devaluation and spillover effects from the Thai baht to neighboring currencies and the Czech koruny. Increased cooperation in Southeast Asia and other regions to share foreign assets and reserves should help reduce systemic currency risks. In effect, the Mexican peso devaluation of December 1994 had little impact on other Latin American currencies. Its impact was largely concentrated on bond and equity markets. Only Argentina experienced a sustained increase in money market rates resulting from the Mexico crisis.

As shown in Exhibit 5, the Emerging Markets Correlation Matrix in the previous section, ELMI had a correlation of 0.02 with the U.S. bond market as expressed by the Lehman Brothers Government/Corporate Index. The correlation with J.P. Morgan's Global Government Index was 0.04 and 0.15 with the EAFE index of Morgan Stanley Capital International. The correlation with the Emerging Markets Bond Index of J.P. Morgan was 0.50, reflecting the ELMI's nearly 25% average weight in Mexican pesos in most of the sample period of December 1993 to March 1997.

Greater diversification can reduce the volatility of local currency investments. This is shown by the use of an equally-weighted ELMI index or ELMI-EW, which could be considered as a potential alternative benchmark. This involves giving a 10% weight to each of the ten components of the standard J.P. Morgan index. Calculations were performed using a monthly sample for the period from the end of 1993 to March 31, 1997. As can be expected, this significantly improves the performance of the index in terms of portfolio volatility and lowers the correlation with the EMBI and EMBI+ index. Annualized monthly volatility of total return of the ELMI benchmark during the period was 7.62% as against 3.74% for the ELMI-EW. Correlation of the ELMI-EW with the EMBI was 0.34 compared with 0.50 for the ELMI. Comparisons with the EMBI+ are 0.54 and 0.42.

Aggressive investors may want to look at high yielding local currency investments such as those provided by countries in earlier stages of stabilization and reform than other emerging countries. In these cases also, diversification of local currency portfolios will help lower volatility as interest rates and currencies are determined principally by domestic factors and events.

The next stage in the development of local currency markets is the formation of full yield curves. In nearly all emerging countries, bonds with an average life longer than two years issued by governments and corporations are held to maturity by local banks, insurance companies, pension funds, and wealthy individuals. Thus there is no liquid secondary market. In some countries, there is limited liquidity of corporate and municipal bonds which can trade at the main security exchanges. Only in Argentina and South Africa is there extensive secondary trading of sovereign and corporate bonds issued in Argentine pesos and rands with ample participation by local and foreign investors. With the improvement in credit quality and the growth of financial savings in many emerging countries, issuance in local currency is likely to be transformed in coming years. Corporate and municipal issuers look at the local securities markets as a largely untapped and natural source of financing which could provide an alternative to bank financing as a source of long-term funds.

Chapter 30

Hedging Corporate Securities with Treasury and Derivative Instruments

Shrikant Ramamurthy
Senior Vice President
Fixed-Income Research
Prudential Securities Incorporated

INTRODUCTION

The corporate bond market has grown significantly in the 1990s, with total debt outstanding rising from $1.4 trillion in 1990 to $2.1 trillion at the end of September 1997.[1] The variety of fixed-rate products that are issued by corporations has also expanded to include not only bullet bonds, but also amortizing and option-embedded bonds. With this type of growth and product diversity in the market, corporate bond portfolios and dealer inventories of corporate products have also increased significantly.

Since corporate securities, like other fixed income securities, exhibit price volatility on a daily basis, hedging price volatility has become more important in this expanding market. The price of a corporate bond is affected by many factors, including movements in interest rates, changing credit spreads, and changing values of any embedded options. Hedging strategies offer a mechanism to minimize the price volatility of corporate securities to many of these factors. Hedging strategies are of importance to many market participants, such as underwriters and dealers whose goal is to provide liquidity, portfolio managers who are trying to either shorten duration or protect positions from potential losses, and corporate treasurers who want to lock in rates prior to refinancing or issuing new debt.

This chapter provides an introduction to hedging corporate securities, both bullet and option-embedded securities, using Treasury securities, futures contracts

---

[1] Outstanding debt statistics are from the Bond Market Association.

and/or interest rate swaps.[2] Each of these hedging instruments provides an alternative mechanism to hedge the price risk of a corporate bond and each has its own distinct advantages and disadvantages in terms of cost and suitability. Treasury securities are generally the most common hedge instruments but, as we shall see, futures and swaps may be more appropriate instruments for many hedging applications.

The starting point of this chapter is a discussion of the mechanics and goals of a hedging strategy. Hedging strategies are then developed using the dollar-value-of-a-basis-point (DVBP) approach. The DVBP approach is applied using Treasuries and other derivative instruments. Examples of constructing and evaluating hedge strategies for bullet bonds and option-embedded corporate bonds are included. As will be demonstrated, DVBP-based hedging strategies are flexible and applicable to many different types of securities; however, ultimately, any hedging strategy has its limits in providing absolute price protection.

THE MECHANICS OF HEDGING

The goal of any hedging strategy is to minimize price volatility. Corporate bond prices are generally affected by movements in interest rates, changes in credit risk, changes in the price of credit risk, optionality, financing costs, supply, liquidity, event risk, perception of future growth, inflation, earnings, etc. Since movements in interest rates are the primary source of price volatility, this chapter will deal primarily with hedging interest rate risk. We will also discuss spread risk and techniques to mitigate the credit risk inherent in corporate securities. Many corporate securities contain embedded call or put options, or optional sinking fund provisions. These embedded options, in any form, affect pricing, and we will discuss how these risks can be mitigated.

A successful hedging strategy for a specific bond position or portfolio has several components that can be broken down as follows:

- identify the sources of price volatility
- determine the amount of price volatility that is acceptable
- find the appropriate hedge instrument
- determine the optimal position in the hedge instrument
- analyze the cost and effectiveness of the hedge strategy

---

[2] For more information on the basics of hedging fixed-income securities, see Shrikant Ramamurthy, "The Basics of Cash Market Hedging," Chapter 10 in Frank J. Fabozzi (ed.), *Perspectives on Interest Rate Risk Management for Money Managers and Traders* (New Hope, PA: Frank J. Fabozzi Associates, 1998). For more information on hedging with interest rate swaps, see Shrikant Ramamurthy, "Hedging Fixed-Income Securities with Interest-Rate Swaps," Chapter 11 in *Perspectives on Interest Rate Risk Management for Money Managers and Traders*. For more information on hedging in the asset/liability context, see Anand K. Bhattacharya, Edward Fitzgerald, and Shrikant Ramamurthy, "Risk Management in an Asset/Liability Framework," Chapter 8 in Frank J. Fabozzi and Atsuo Konishi (eds.), *The Handbook of Asset/Liability Management*, (Chicago, IL: Probus Publishing, 1996).

Identifying the Sources of Price Risk

The first step in hedging a security is determining the factors that contribute to its price fluctuations. Typically for corporate securities, changes in interest rates and credit spreads are the primary factors that affect prices. For example, a short-term corporate bond's price changes as short-term interest rates change, or as perceptions of the issuer's credit quality changes. On a long-term corporate bond, prices change as long-term rates change or as long-term corporate credit spreads change.

For an option-embedded corporate bond, interest rates affect not only the bond component of the security, but also the option component. For example, a callable bond can be decomposed into a bullet bond position with the same maturity and a short position in a call option. That is,

$$\text{Callable Bond} = \text{Bullet Bond (to Maturity date)} - \text{Call option} \tag{1}$$

A put bond can be decomposed into a bullet bond of the same maturity and a long put option position on the underlying bullet bond. That is,

$$\text{Put Bond} = \text{Bullet Bond (to Maturity date)} + \text{Put option} \tag{2}$$

For option-embedded bonds, interest rates affect both the value of the bullet bond and the option. For a callable bond, as rates rise, the value of the bullet bond falls; however, the value of the option also falls, dampening the decrease in the value of the callable bond. Similarly, when rates decline, the increase in the value of a callable bond is dampened by an increase in the value of the embedded call option. For put bonds, as rates rise, the value of the bullet bond falls; however, the value of the put option increases, which dampens the decrease in the value of the put bond. When hedging option-embedded corporate securities, the effects of interest rate movements on optionality need to be explicitly accounted. For option-embedded bonds, the shape of the yield curve and movements in volatility also affect the value of the embedded option.

Once the sources of price risk have been identified, the next step is to determine the amount of price protection that is required from a hedge strategy. A perfect hedge will theoretically (but never practically) eliminate all price risk and, in effect, lock in the future price of a security under any scenario. Of course, in this circumstance, any price appreciation potential is also eliminated. The elimination of all risk eliminates all the potential return as well. The goal of a hedge strategy may instead be to eliminate some, but not all, price uncertainty in order to achieve some incremental return. A hedge alters the risk/return profile of a portfolio and, by adjusting the amount invested in the hedge instrument, an appropriate risk/return profile can be derived and maintained.

Determining the Appropriate Hedge Position

Once the sources of price risk and the amount of risk to be hedged have been determined, the next steps are to find appropriate hedge instruments and to determine the appropriate investment in the hedge instruments. The appropriate position in the hedge instrument is a function of the dollar-value-of-a-basis-point (DVBP) of both the security to be hedged and the hedge instrument.

The DVBP of a security is the security's price change for a 1 basis point change in interest rates. In other words, DVBP expresses a security's dollar sensitivity to interest rates. For a bullet bond with no embedded options, DVBP is a function of the duration and price of the security, and is given by,

$$\text{DVBP} = \frac{\text{Par amount} \times (\text{Price} + \text{Accrued}) \times \text{Modified duration}}{1,000,000} \qquad (3)$$

Since the price movement for a bond is different for an increase or a decrease in interest rates due to the bond's convexity, the DVBP is effectively an average price change for a 1 basis point change in interest rates. Exhibit 1 shows the DVBP calculation for a $1 million position in a non-callable bond, in this case a 10-year corporate bond issued by Citicorp.

The implicit assumption in equation (3) is that the modified duration of a security accurately describes a security's percentage price change for a 1% change in interest rates and that interest rate movements and yield movements on the corporate security are simultaneous and identical. This typically is not true for option-embedded bonds and for bonds priced off two benchmark securities. For option-embedded bonds, the modified duration does not describe the price movement of the security as interest rates change. Also, movements in option-embedded bond yields are not identical to movements in interest rates. Generally, for a callable bond, yield movements are smaller than interest rate movements. If rates move 10 basis points, yields on callable bonds will move less than 10 basis points because of the changing value of the call option. Also, for a corporate bond priced off two benchmarks, say the average of the 5- and 10-year Treasury notes, the corporate bond's yield will change by only half a basis point for every basis point move in the 10-year Treasury.

Exhibit 1: DVBP Computation for $1 Million Par Amount of 10-Year Citicorp Notes

Issuer	Coupon (%)	Maturity (Yrs.)	Price ($)	Accrued ($)	Yield (%)	Spread (BPs)	Mod. Dur.
Citicorp	7.20	6/15/07	104.882	0.34	6.50	+75	6.837

$$\text{DVBP} = \frac{\text{Dollar par amount} \times (\text{Price} + \text{Accrued}) \times \text{Modified Duration}}{1,000,000}$$

$$= \frac{1,000,000 \times (104.882 + 0.34) \times 6.837}{1,000,000}$$

$$= \$719.40$$

* Price information as of 12/29/97.

Exhibit 2: DVBP Computation for $1 Million Par Amount of 10-Year Callable FNMA Notes

Issuer	Coupon (%)	Maturity (Yrs.)	Call Date (Yrs.)	Price ($)	Yield (%)	Spread (BPs)	OAS (BPs)
FNMA	6.65	1/19/07	1/19/00	99.78	6.68	+93	25

Constant-OAS Prices			
Yield Curve Shift	Price	Yield (%)	Spread (BPs)
Up 25 BPs	98.595	6.85	+85
Down 25 BPS	100.916	6.52	+102

$$\text{DVBP} = \frac{\text{Dollar par amount} \times \text{Change in Constant-OAS Price}}{\text{Yield-Curve Shift} \times 100}$$

$$= \frac{1,000,000 \times (100.916 - 98.595)}{50 \times 100}$$

$$= \$464.20$$

* Price information as of 12/20/97. Note: OASs computed at 14% volatility.

For option-embedded bonds and for any bond in general, including bullet bonds, the DVBP of a security is a function of the explicit price movements of the security to changes in interest rates. In its general form, DVBP can be defined as,

$$\text{DVBP} = \frac{\text{Dollar par amount} \times (\text{Change in constant-OAS price})}{\text{Yield curve shift in bps} \times 100} \tag{4}$$

In the above formulation, the DVBP explicitly accounts for the change in the value of a security due to the changing values of any embedded options. The price changes in equation (4) must be determined either from a theoretical model or empirically. Generally, when a model is used to generate prices under different rate scenarios, a constant-OAS pricing assumption is used, although any assumption can be used. For example, callable premiums currently trade at wider OASs than callable discounts. This market reality can be readily accounted for in the DVBP computation by using the appropriate OASs in computing the respective scenario prices.

Typically, the DVBP for option-embedded bonds is computed assuming parallel interest rate shifts occurring in increments of 10 to 25 basis points. Exhibit 2 shows the computation of the DVBP of a 10-year FNMA issue that is callable after three years. Notice in the example that, as interest rates move 25 basis points, the yield on the FNMA callable changes by less than 25 basis points.

The Hedge Ratio

Once the DVBP of the security to be hedged has been determined, the next step is to find an appropriate hedge instrument and to determine the appropriate position in the hedge instrument. The hedge ratio describes the appropriate position in a hedge instrument and is a function of the DVBP of both the security being hedged and the hedge instrument. The position in the hedge instrument is determined such that the change in the market value of the hedge instrument is equal to the change in the market value of the position being hedged for a given change in rates. A hedge is implemented by taking an opposite position in the hedge instrument. Mathematically the hedge ratio is given by,

$$\text{Hedge ratio} = \frac{\text{DVBP of security to be hedged}}{\text{DVBP of hedge instrument}} \tag{5}$$

Typically the hedge ratio is computed using the DVBP for a $1 million par amount of the underlying security. If many units of a security are to be hedged, multiplying the hedge ratio by the number of units to be hedged will determine the position needed in the hedge instrument.

CHOOSING A HEDGE INSTRUMENT

For hedging corporate securities, many different types of hedge instruments can be utilized, including cash market securities, like Treasury notes, and other instruments, like futures contracts and interest rate swaps. In the following sections we discuss the hedging implications of using these instruments.

Cash Market Securities

The most common instruments used for hedging in the cash market are Treasury securities. Since most corporate securities are priced off Treasury securities, using similar Treasuries as hedge instruments provides ideal protection against interest rate risk. Also, Treasury securities have no credit risk and are extremely liquid. From a hedge implementation standpoint, using Treasuries is fairly simple. The DVBP of a bullet Treasury is given by equation (3) and the hedge ratio is given by equation (5).

There can be disadvantages to using Treasuries as hedge instruments. First, many corporate bonds are priced off on-the-run Treasury securities that may be on "special." For example, the 10-year Treasury note currently is on special. When a security is on special, it is in short supply and is expensive to borrow in the repo markets. As a result, the financing income that can be earned from a short position is greatly reduced, which increases the cost of hedging.

Another disadvantage is that Treasury securities are on-balance-sheet items, unlike futures contracts and swaps, which, for some market participants, may have capital structure implications. A third negative with using Treasury securities to hedge is that they only provide protection against interest rate risk and no protection against spread risk. In spite of these limitations, Treasuries are the most common hedge instruments, especially for hedging individual positions.

Futures Instruments

Treasury futures contracts are available on 2-, 5-, and 10-year notes, as well as on the long bond. These contracts are actively traded and are widely used for hedging. The contracts are based on hypothetical 8% coupon bearing instruments maturing in 2, 5, 10, and 20 years. The bond, 10- and 5-year note contracts are the most liquid futures contracts.

Treasury futures contracts contain several timing and delivery options that complicates scenario pricing and DVBP computations. Treasury futures contracts require physical delivery at maturity. The seller has the right to deliver any one of many securities during a designated time period. As a result, a Treasury futures contract will track the one cash security that is cheapest to deliver (CTD) against the contract. As rates change, however, the CTD security also may change. Generally, low duration issues tend to be CTD when rates are low and high duration issues tend to be CTD when rates are high. A futures contract tends to lose duration in a rallying market and gain duration in a bear market, making the contract a negatively convex security.

The DVBP of a futures contract needs to be computed using a model that explicitly accounts for the changing values of the options embedded in the futures contract. As a quick and simple approximation, the DVBP of the CTD security (after adjusting for the conversion factor) is sometimes used to represent the DVBP of a futures contract. This approximation is more appropriate when the CTD security is unlikely to change, even for large moves in rates, as is currently the case for the 10- and 30-year futures contracts.

Hedging with futures has several advantages/disadvantages relative to hedging with cash instruments. One advantage is that, because a futures contract typically tracks an off-the-run Treasury issue,[3] the sometimes prohibitive cost of shorting on-the-run Treasuries that are on special is reduced. Furthermore, a futures contract enables a hedger to participate in the off-the-run market, using a more liquid instrument than off-the-run Treasuries. This is especially useful when hedging corporates that are priced to off-the-run Treasuries.

The major disadvantage of using a futures contract versus a Treasury security is basis risk. Basis risk, in the context of hedging with futures, refers to the scenario in which movements in futures prices do not correspond to movements in cash prices. A futures contract's price movements are largely related to price movements in the Treasury security that is the cheapest to deliver into the futures contract. Typically, the CTD security is not an on-the-run Treasury security. Thus, when hedging a security that is priced to an on-the-run Treasury with a futures contract, there is risk that movements in futures prices will not fully hedge price movements in the security that is being hedged. Currently, the CTD issue for the 10-year futures contract is the Treasury 7.875% coupon of 11/04, a 7-year security. To the extent that 7- and 10-year Treasury rates do not move in unison, hedging a 10-year corporate bond with 10-year futures contracts will be less effective.

Generally speaking, futures contracts are used in hedging bond portfolios rather than individual positions. Futures are most useful when exposure to a cer-

---

[3] At the time of this writing, the CTD security on the March 1998 bond contract is the Treasury 11.25s of 2/15 and the CTD on the 10-year futures contract is the 7.875s of 11/04.

tain part of the curve, and not specifically to a particular Treasury, is required. Futures are used to hedge individual positions when liquidity is required, or if there are balance sheet or cost considerations associated with using Treasuries.

Interest Rate Swaps

To understand how interest rate swaps can be used as hedge instruments, it is useful to characterize swaps in an alternative fashion. An interest rate swap is a contractual agreement between two parties to exchange fixed and floating cash flows periodically. In a generic interest rate swap, one party agrees to pay a floating interest rate (typically based off LIBOR), while the counterparty agrees to pay a fixed rate of interest for a specified period of time, where the interest cash flows are computed off some notional amount.

The exchange of fixed and floating cash flows in a swap is equivalent to the cash flows from a long position in a fixed-rate bond, and a short position in a floating-rate bond. As a result, a swap can alternatively be viewed as a long position in a fixed-rate bond that is 100% financed at short-term interest rates, like term repurchase (repo) rates or LIBOR rates. The coupon cash flows on this portfolio replicate the cash flows on the swap, and the par amount that is received at maturity from the fixed-rate bond repays the borrowing used to finance the purchase of the fixed-rate bond. Essentially, a swap in the hedging context can be viewed as a financed fixed-rate bond.

Swaps are priced on a spread basis relative to Treasuries like most corporate securities. As a result, swaps can serve as an alternate hedging instrument to Treasury securities and futures contracts. Interest rate swaps have many advantages over Treasuries. First, interest rate swaps are off the balance sheet. Second, when an off-the-run maturity needs to be hedged, or when the hedge instrument is a Treasury security that is on special, a swap can be a less expensive hedging instrument. Swaps can be structured for any maturity, and are not constrained by any supply issues. Currently there are over $5 trillion in notional amount of U.S. dollar swaps outstanding. Third, since swaps are priced off Treasury securities, swaps provide the same protection from interest rate risk as Treasury securities. In addition, to the extent that swap spreads (the spreads between swap rates and similar maturity Treasuries) are correlated with corporate spreads, interest rate swaps will provide additional price protection over Treasuries.

Interest rate swaps have advantages over interest rate futures contracts in the context of hedging fixed income securities. Swaps are available for any maturity; however, exchange-traded futures contracts[4] have limited maturities. Also, hedging with futures contracts, as discussed earlier, exposes the hedged portfolio to basis risk.

The disadvantage of using swaps as hedge instruments is lack of liquidity. Bid/offer spreads in the swap market can amount to a few basis points in yield and

---

[4] Our discussion on futures is limited to the 2-year, 5-year, 10-year and bond futures contracts and do not include Eurodollar futures contracts. Eurodollar futures are a proxy for interest rate swaps and can be used to synthetically create swap positions.

swaps are not readily tradeable instruments. Usually, an interest rate swap agreement cannot be traded to another party without the prior approval of the original counterparty to the swap. As a result, swaps at times are not traded and are instead liquidated at their market value when a party to the swap wants to cancel the swap arrangement.

In general, interest rate swaps are useful in managing the overall interest rate risk of a portfolio and are less useful in managing the interest rate risk of an individual position. Also, swap spreads are correlated with generic corporate bond spreads but not with specific corporate credit spreads. Thus, swaps will be more effective in providing a hedge against portfolio credit risk.

The mechanics of hedging with swaps are similar to that of using any other instrument, except care must be taken in computing and understanding the DVBP of a swap. The DVBP of a swap can be shown to be equal to,[5]

$$\text{DVBP (Swap)} = \text{DVBP (Fixed-rate bond)} - \text{DVBP (Floating-rate bond)} \quad (6)$$

In general, the DVBP of a swap is approximately equal to the DVBP of a fixed-rate bond with maturity spanning from the next reset date to the maturity date of the swap. The DVBP of a 5-year swap is similar to the DVBP of a 4.75-year fixed-rate bond; the DVBP of a 2.25-year swap is similar to the DVBP of a 2-year fixed-rate bond.

Although the DVBP of a swap is similar to that of a slightly shorter fixed-rate bond, it will change differently over time than the DVBP of a fixed-rate bond. This is very important to note in the hedging context. The DVBP of a swap just prior to a reset date will be identical to the DVBP of a fixed-rate bond because the DVBP of the floater at this time is zero. However, just after the reset date, the floater will have a DVBP that is similar to the DVBP of a fixed-rate bond that matures on the next reset date. As a result, the DVBP on a swap will immediately decline by the DVBP of the floater just after the reset date. Between reset periods, the DVBP of the swap will not change much as both the DVBP of the fixed-rate bond and that of the floater will decline in similar fashion. This is very different from the DVBP of a fixed-rate bond, which declines steadily over time.

Exhibit 3 graphically displays over time the DVBP for a 2-year swap and a fixed-rate bond. The DVBP of the fixed-rate bond declines as a function of time, while the DVBP of the swap declines in a jump fashion around the quarterly reset date of the floating rate on the swap. The DVBP of the swap between reset dates is relatively stable and actually increases incrementally as the next reset date approaches. This is because the DVBP of a floating-rate note declines slightly faster than the DVBP of a fixed-rate note during these time periods.[6]

---

[5] For more information on the pricing and interest rate sensitivity of interest rate swaps, see David Audley, Richard Chin, and Shrikant Ramamurthy, "The Interest-Rate Swap Market: Valuation, Applications and Perspectives," *Fixed- Income Research*, Prudential Securities Incorporated, April 1994.

[6] The modified duration and DVBP of a bond is a concave monotonic function of maturity (i.e., the duration and DVBP increase at a decreasing rate as a function of maturity). As a result, the DVBP of a floating-rate bond, which behaves essentially like a short dated fixed-rate bond, decreases faster over time than the DVBP of a long dated fixed-rate bond.

Exhibit 3: DVBP of a 2-Year Swap and Fixed-Rate Bond over Time

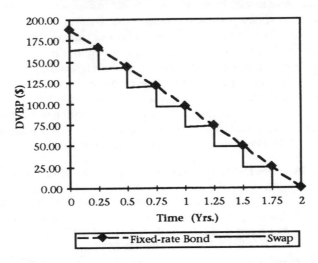

HEDGING APPLICATIONS

In this section, we apply the hedging concepts discussed herein to hedge a bullet corporate security and a callable corporate security. Treasuries, futures contracts, and swaps are each used as hedge instruments, although, only one of these instruments will be most appropriate in an actual application.

Bullet-Bond Hedge

Exhibit 4 displays a hedge for the Citicorp 7.20s of 6/07. For a long $10 million position in Citicorp notes, either $9.67 million in Treasury notes or $10.11 million in swaps need to be shorted as a hedge. If futures contracts are used, the hedge would utilize 123 10-year futures contracts, where each futures contract requires the delivery of $100,000 par amount of eligible Treasury notes. These hedge ratios are a function of the respective DVBPs of the individual instruments, and equation (5).

As can be seen from Exhibit 4, all three hedge instruments provide protection against interest rate risk. If rates move 50 basis points, the unhedged Citicorp notes can gain or lose more than $350,000. If the Citicorp position is hedged with Treasuries or swaps, the price variation of the portfolio is minimized to under $1,100 in a 50 basis point range for rates. If futures are used, the hedged position actually gains $1,000 to $2,000 in scenarios where rates rise or fall by 50 basis points.

Exhibit 4: Hedging a Corporate Bullet Bond

Objective: Hedge $10 million of Citicorp 7.20s of 6/07.

Issuer	Coupon (%)	Maturity	Price ($)	Yield (%)	Spread (BPs)	DVBP ($)	Hedge Ratio
Citicorp	7.20	6/15/07	104.882	6.50	+75	719.40	—
Hedge Instruments							
10-Yr. Treasuries	6.125	8/15/07	102-22+	5.75	—	743.70	0.967
10-Yr. Futures	—	3/20/98	112-05	—	—	58.60	12.300
10-Yr. Swap	—	1/02/08	0.00	—	+48	711.60	1.011

	Change in Portfolio Value	
	Rates Decrease 50 BPs	Rates Increase 50 BPs
Unhedged Portfolio	367,500	−352,200
Hedge w/ Treasuries	340	−907
Hedge w/ Futures	960	2,040
Hedge w/ Swaps	−807	−1,079

* Price information as of 12/29/97.

While the hedges in Exhibit 4 clearly limit price movements in the Citicorp hedged position, none of the hedges are "perfect" hedges. This is so for several reasons. First, the hedge ratios that are used have been rounded and are not exact. Second, the prices on 10-year Treasuries and futures have been rounded to the nearest 64th to reflect trading convention. A third reason that the hedges are not perfect is because of the effect that convexity has on DVBP.

A non-callable bond's price will change more for a given decrease in interest rates than for the same magnitude increase in rates due to its positive convexity. Since the DVBP of a bond is computed using the average price change for a 1 basis point change in interest rates, the hedge ratio will never be the exact ratio needed (although it will be very close) for a given realization of interest rate change. If there is a strong opinion about the general direction of future interest rate movements, then the hedge ratio could be adjusted appropriately for the given directionality in interest rates, and a more efficient hedge could be constructed. Generally, however, for modest interest rate movements, this convexity effect is not large.

The futures based hedge in Exhibit 4 is the best hedge for two reasons. Generally, because a futures contract provides the seller the right to deliver any one of several bonds into the contract, a futures contract has negatively convex price characteristics; that is, futures tend to lose duration in market rallies and gain duration when interest rates rise. This is an advantage in the hedging context where futures contracts are sold as hedge instruments. A second reason that futures contracts look attractive in hedging the Citicorp notes is because the analysis of the hedge does not account for any basis risk. If the 7- to 10-year part of the Treasury yield curve steepened or flattened, the futures hedge in Exhibit 4 would be far less successful in hedging interest rate risk than the other instruments.

Spread Risk

One important assumption that has been made in the hedging analysis thus far is that credit spreads remain constant. This may not be the case. The pricing spread associated with any security can change as interest rates change or as the perceived credit risk of the issuer changes. Other event-related risk can also affect the pricing spread. A good case in point is the sell-off in the corporate market due to the turmoil in Asia in late 1997/earlier 1998.

Yield spread risk that is due to event risk is difficult to hedge. However, general sector risks may be hedged to an extent if they are properly anticipated. Upcoming problems in particular sectors can sometimes be anticipated by examining trends in the economy or interest rates, or by anticipating the effects of upcoming changes in regulations, political structure, etc. In these scenarios, and in situations in which portfolio managers wish to maintain holdings in corporate securities, the effect of widening spreads may be mitigated by buying put options on a sector index, by shorting a basket of stocks in the sector or by taking a position in any portfolio that will be similarly affected by such changes. These positions would be in addition to any positions used to hedge interest rate risk.

Yield spread risk due to changing interest rates may be mitigated if there is a known correlation between the direction and magnitude of interest rate moves and spread changes. If spreads widen when the market rallies and spreads tighten when the market sells off, then the price volatility associated with these spread changes can be reduced by shorting fewer Treasury securities than the number given by the hedge ratio.

Among all the interest rate hedge instruments available, interest rate swaps probably provide the best protection against spread risk. Generally, swap spreads move in the same direction as corporate spreads, although the degree and timing of movements are not always symmetric. To the extent that a corporate portfolio's spread is positively correlated with swap spreads, swaps will provide protection against spread risk and be more effective hedging instruments than futures or Treasury notes.

In general, the effects of yield spread changes can be accommodated into a hedging strategy. However, in the short run, pricing spreads are generally not volatile, and the risks that yield spreads will change dramatically may not be an overriding factor in the hedging context.

Hedging Option-Embedded Bonds

Option-embedded bonds, such as callable bonds or put bonds, can be hedged using basically the same approach as that for bullet bonds. Since yield spreads on option-embedded bonds change as interest rates change due to the changing value of the embedded option, the DVBP on an option-embedded bond needs to explicitly account for these changes. A constant-OAS approach to determining the DVBP for an option-embedded bond is one approach that explicitly accounts for the changing value of any embedded options. A non-constant OAS assumption can also be utilized in computing DVBP if such an assumption better reflects the expected trading characteristics of a security.

Exhibit 5 displays a hedge for FNMA 6.65s of 1/07 that are callable from 1/00. The DVBP of the FNMA callable is $464.20 per $1 million par amount, and the DVBP is the average price change for a 1 basis point change in interest rates. For $10 million FNMA callables, a hedge can be constructed by either shorting $6.24 million 10-year Treasuries or by shorting $6.52 million notional amount of 10-year swaps. If futures contracts are used, 79 contracts are required. Notice that for the FNMA callable, each of the hedge ratios are much smaller than the hedge ratios used for hedging the Citicorp bullet bonds in the earlier example. Callable bonds have lower durations than similar maturity bullet bonds because of the embedded short call option position, which results in callable bonds having less price sensitivity and smaller hedge ratios than bullet bonds.

If the FNMA callable is not hedged, the position can vary in value substantially for a 50 basis point move in rates. If rates rise by 50 basis points, the position will decline in value by $352,000. If rates decline by 50 basis points, it will gain in value by $221,600. If the position is hedged using either Treasury notes, futures contracts or swaps, the variation in portfolio value for a 50 basis point move in rates is reduced to approximately $15,000. The best performing hedge instrument is the futures contract, again because of the small amount of negative convexity in the futures contract. The futures contract, like the FNMA callable, loses duration in a rallying market and gains duration when rates rise, which provides for a more effective hedge. The futures contract does not provide a perfect hedge because the FNMA callable is more negatively convex than the 10-year futures contract.

Exhibit 5: Hedging an Agency Callable Bond

Objective: Hedge $10 million of FNMA 6.65s of 1/07.

Issuer	Coupon (%)	Maturity	Call Date	Price ($)	Yield (%)	Spread (BPs)	DVBP ($)	Hedge Ratio
FNMA	6.65	1/19/07	1/19/00	99.78	6.68	+93	464.20	—
Hedge Instruments								
10-Yr. Treasuries	6.125	8/15/07	—	102-22+	5.75	—	743.70	0.624
10-Yr. Futures	—	3/20/98	—	112-05	—	—	58.60	7.900
10-Yr. Swap	—	1/02/98	—	0.00	—	+48	711.60	0.652

	Change in Portfolio Value	
	Rates Decrease 50 BPs	Rates Increase 50 BPs
Unhedged Portfolio	221,600	−352,200
Hedge w/ Treasuries	−15,325	−14,612
Hedge w/ Futures	−13,820	−13,780
Hedge w/ Swaps	−15,924	−14,860

* Prices as of 12/29/97.

Hedging Considerations for Option-Embedded Notes

In general, for any option-embedded security, including corporate callable notes, the hedge ratio will change as interest rates change. For example, as the market rallies and continues to rally, callable spreads will continue widening and the hedge ratio for a callable note will decline. If rates rise, then the hedge ratio will increase.

The hedge ratio using Treasury notes, swaps or even futures contracts at current levels, is not static because callable notes are negatively convex instruments, while Treasuries and swaps are positively convex instruments and futures are less negatively convex instruments.[7] As rates rally, Treasury prices rise at a faster rate than callable bond prices and the position in the hedge instrument consequently needs to be reduced. For example, if rates rally 25 basis points, the hedge needs to reduced by buying back some of the short position in the hedging instrument. If this adjustment is not made, then the hedge will not provide absolute price protection and, in fact, may over- or under-hedge a position. The hedges in Exhibit 5 are not perfect hedges because the hedges were constructed for 25 basis point movements in rates, but were evaluated assuming that rates moved by 50 basis points without any adjustment to the hedge positions.

An alternative way to hedge option-embedded notes is to use bullets like Treasuries or swaps to hedge just the bullet component and to use options to hedge the option component. This type of hedge will not need to be monitored as frequently and the hedge ratio will be less volatile as like securities are being hedged with like securities. An alternative to this approach is to use callable swaps. A callable swap is a swap in which one party has the right to terminate the swap prior to maturity. Since a callable swap has an embedded long position in a call position, this may be a more natural and efficient way to hedge a callable security that has a short position in a call option. However, for hedging an option-embedded security for short time horizons like a week or a month, the use of options or callable swaps in a hedging strategy can be expensive given the reduced liquidity in these markets. Typically, individual option-embedded bonds are hedged using just Treasuries or futures, with the hedge ratio adjusted periodically for interest rate movements.

A second consideration in the hedging analysis presented here is the assumption of constant OAS in determining the DVBP and associated hedge ratio. The use of a constant OAS assumption in this chapter was made more for simplicity. OASs are not constant in the marketplace and may change as rates change. For example, in the federal agency debt market, OASs for similar-duration premiums are much wider than for discounts. This market dynamic can be explicitly accounted for in the DVBP approach by using different OASs to compute the scenario prices in equation (5). Also, the use of an empirical hedge ratio, where historical data are used to compute a hedge ratio, would implicitly account for

---

[7] At current levels, the optionality in most financial futures contracts is limited.

changing OASs in different environments.[8] However, to the extent that history may not be a gauge for the future trading characteristics of a security, an empirical hedge ratio may be less useful.

Another consideration to keep in mind is that any option-embedded bond's price is dependent on factors other than just credit risk and changes in the yield of the pricing instrument. These factors include the shape of the curve and volatility. As volatility increases, callable spreads widen and put bond spreads tighten to reflect the higher cost of the embedded option.[9] The hedging analysis presented in this chapter does not hedge this volatility risk. Effectively, the hedging example for the FNMA callable maintains a short position in volatility. If volatility rises in our example, the callable bond's price will decline with no change in the value of the hedge instruments. If volatility risk is of concern, the use of options is necessary in any hedging strategy. If changes in volatility can be anticipated as interest rates move, then this can be accounted for by under or over utilizing a hedge. In this type of application, the DVBP of a security would be computed using scenario-based volatility levels to compute scenario prices.

The shape of the curve is also an important determinant of callable spreads. The hedge ratios described in this chapter are based on parallel interest rate movements and do not account for the effects of a change in the shape of curve. Generally, as the curve flattens, callable spreads widen, and if the curve steepens callable spreads tighten.[10] For example, spreads on a 10-year maturity bond callable after three years (10/NC-3Y) will widen if 3-year yields rise and 10-year yields remain unchanged. Ten-year hedging instruments will not provide any price protection when 10/NC-3Y prices fall in this environment.

To hedge yield curve risk for option-embedded securities, it is best to use multiple hedge instruments from all the parts of the curve that affect the pricing of the security being hedged. In the case of the 10/NC-3Y, both 3-year and 10-year instruments would be appropriate. The hedge ratio relative to the 3-year part of the curve can be computed by using a DVBP for the 10/NC-3Y that is computed by assuming that only Treasury yields three years and in change, while the rest of the yield curve remains unchanged. Similarly, the hedge ratio relative to the 10-year part of the curve can be computed by using the DVBP of the 10/NC-3Y that is computed by assuming that Treasury yields three years and in do not change, while yields on the longer end of the curve change. This type of strategy

---

[8] As an alternative to model determined hedge ratios (also known as theoretical hedge ratios), hedge ratios can also be empirically determined. Empirical hedge ratios are typically determined by regressing recent price changes on the security to be hedged on price changes of the hedging instruments.

[9] Callable spreads can widen 3 to 8 basis points for a 100 basis point increase in volatility. For more information on the effects of the volatility on callable spreads, see Shrikant Ramamurthy, "Federal Agency Debt," *Spread Talk*, Fixed-Income Research, Prudential Securities Incorporated, February 21, 1997.

[10] Callable spreads can widen two to five basis points for every ten basis points of curve flattening. For more information on the effects of the shape of the curve on callable spreads, see Shrikant Ramamurthy, "Federal Agency Debt," *Spread Talk*, Fixed-Income Research, Prudential Securities Incorporated, March 21, 1997.

would provide hedge exposure to multiple parts of the curve and would be effective for both parallel and non-parallel yield curve shifts.

Typically, for individual bond positions, yield curve risk is generally not accounted for in a hedging strategy. Instead, the pricing benchmark is used as a hedging instrument and the hedge ratio is adjusted to account for a particular view on the future shape of the yield curve. As in the case of hedging spread, OAS or volatility risk, this is more art than science. In the final analysis, the DVBP that is used to compute a hedge ratio needs to reflect the anticipated price behavior of a security (incorporating any views on spreads, curve, and volatility) and, to that extent, should reflect both theory and market reality. These combined approaches should work together to produce a more effective hedge.

SUMMARY

Hedging price volatility is a very important function in the fixed income marketplace. This chapter has provided an introduction to hedging corporate bullet and callable securities using Treasury notes, futures contracts, and interest rate swaps. The basic procedure for constructing a hedge starts by correctly identifying the sources of price risk including the effects of interest rates, the curve, volatility, and spread movements. A hedge is constructed by taking an opposite position in a hedge instrument with similar price sensitivity to the security to be hedged.

The appropriate position in the hedge instrument is a function of the DVBP of both the security being hedged and the hedge instrument. The DVBP of any security is effectively an average price change for a 1 basis point change in rates and should incorporate any spread/OAS changes that are anticipated in different rate environments. In the context of the above framework, DVBP is a very flexible tool and also can incorporate other factors that may be important in the hedge strategy. Once a hedge is constructed and implemented, it needs to be monitored over time. The DVBP of a security, the hedge vehicle, and the hedge ratio will change over time and as interest rates change. An effective hedge strategy should reflect this dynamic behavior to the highest extent possible and may need to be adjusted periodically.

Among the hedge instruments generally used in hedging applications, Treasuries are the most common for obvious reasons. Treasury notes are very liquid and, since most corporate notes are benchmarked off Treasury notes, Treasuries provide the best price protection against interest rate risk. Futures contracts are also desirable hedge instruments because they are very liquid and are off-balance-sheet instruments. In addition, the negative convexity embedded in a futures contract has positive implications in the hedging context. The biggest negative in using futures contracts for hedging corporate securities is the exposure to basis risk, which reflects the risk that price movements in the futures position may not reflect price movements in the underlying security that is being hedged. This typically happens when the curve steepens or flattens.

Interest rate swaps are also off-balance-sheet instruments and, given their customized nature, offer tremendous flexibility as hedge instruments. To the extent that swap spreads are correlated with corporate spreads, swaps often can reduce spread risk in addition to hedging interest rate risk. When Treasuries are on special, swaps and futures have the added advantage of being cheaper hedge instruments. The disadvantage to using swaps is that they are less liquid than Treasuries or futures. Therefore, swaps may be more appropriate for longer-term hedging applications. Also, given that swap spreads are correlated to generic corporate spreads and not to individual credit spreads, swaps are more appropriate for hedging corporate portfolios rather than individual positions.

Chapter 31

Index Total Return Swaps and Their Fixed Income Portfolio Management Applications

Mary Rooney
Derivatives Strategist
Merrill Lynch

INTRODUCTION

Index total return swaps (index swaps) have greatly expanded the arena of fixed-income investment and risk management. An additional tool for increasing the flexibility of fixed-income asset allocation, index swaps enable investors to engage in broad market investment strategies, as well as to take leveraged views on a specific sector of the market. Index swaps have evolved in the fixed-income marketplace because they are needed. Fixed-income investors are faced with growing exposures to classes of fixed-income products whose price volatilities cannot be fully explained by interest rate risk. As a result, fixed-income market participants increasingly need the ability to hedge spread risk.

In this chapter, we introduce the index swap product as well as some of its many applications. Generally, index swaps enable fixed-income investors to:

- lock-in market returns
- sell a market short
- hedge underlying portfolios
- gain or reduce leverage on a specific sector of the market
- engage in tactical asset allocation
- manage tax-related event risk
- lower capital charges associated with holding certain types of credit sensitive assets in portfolios

While relatively new to the fixed-income market, equity-market participants are well acquainted with the use of market indices and the practice of indexation. The seminal work on portfolio optimization in the early 1970s laid the groundwork for the development of these types of financial instruments, most notably the S&P 500 futures contract. Investment strategies employed using index instruments have long been acceptable in equities because of their low transaction costs, minimal maintenance requirements, and high degree of flexibility. Index vehicles are also the natural hedging tools of systematic risk. Fixed-income investors can replicate the index strategies common in the equity market with index swaps.

Index vehicles also afford a new set of applications—distinct from equities—as fixed-income asset classes can be disaggregated into a handful of easily identifiable sectors (governments, investment grade corporates, mortgages, high yield, emerging markets, and non-dollar governments). This characteristic of the market sets the stage for several types of portfolio applications that can be implemented with index swaps. In the classic efficient frontier framework, the ability to short a specific part of the fixed-income market means that index swaps can be employed to attain superior returns. This is of particular interest in fixed-income investing, as asset allocation decisions among sectors are broadly determined by four variables: interest rates, credit, volatility, and currencies.

Finally, it is important to understand why, compared to equities, index vehicles are emerging so belatedly. The absence of exchange-traded futures market derivatives, the over-the-counter effect of lower price transparency, and the lack of a well established and uniform benchmark have together hindered the development of fixed-income index products. Most recently, these impediments have been diminishing as the over-the counter derivative market has matured, bond pricing has become more homogeneous, and established standards or benchmarks of market performance have been well tested. Thus, with the heightened need for hedging and diversification tools, the backdrop for fixed-income index vehicles is now firmly in place.

THE INDICES AND INDEX REPLICATION

As the underlying "assets" of an index swap trade, the fixed-income indices are the first step in understanding how index swaps can be used. In Exhibit 1, we show the major markets on which index swaps are available.[1] In addition to the broad market aggregates, index swaps can be customized for specific maturity and duration needs. Similarly, in credit sensitive sectors, the swaps can be broken down by credit quality, ranging from triple-A to single-B.

When considering index swaps, it is important to note the differences between the various indices and their underlying cash markets. Depending on the investor's objectives and investment parameters, a swap in one index may add unique value to the investment process, while another index may not prove particularly useful. Generally, however, there are several common benefits of receiving the total return of an index to gain or alter sector exposure. First, an index swap allows for

---

[1] Descriptions, analytics, and historical information for these indices can be accessed on Bloomberg. For example, type J0A0 <index> <go> to access the High Yield market aggregate.

immediate diversification to a specific sector at a relatively low cost. A second advantage of index swaps is operational; receiving the total return on the index obviates the need for portfolio rebalancing. Third, investors can use index swaps to gradually gain exposure to new markets. Lastly, since index swaps are off-balance-sheet, they usually will have different regulatory and accounting treatments than will cash bonds.

Below, we highlight some important distinctions between major market indices:

- *High yield.* Among the key benefits of receiving the total return of the high-yield index stems from a high level of diversification of credit risk. This can have rating agency and balance-sheet implications. For insurance companies, for example, the swap will be rated as a swap agreement, not NAIC 3, as would an actual noninvestment-grade bond. Since it can be expensive to leverage in the cash market, because of liquidity and haircuts, hedge funds may find that an index swap provides an efficient way to get exposure to the high yield market.
- *Mortgages.* Mortgages tend to require more operational and back-office infrastructure than other markets. Also, receiving the mortgage aggregate offers investors a return that is structurally well diversified.
- *Corporates and Treasuries.* In sectors where spreads are narrow or relative performance is mainly dependent on portfolio structure versus the index, market-neutral investors can use indices to cheaply replicate the index structure. For example, a corporate investor could receive the total return of the corporate aggregate to achieve diversification and invest in fewer bonds, but in credits in which it has high levels of confidence.
- *Emerging markets.* Investors can gain exposure to emerging markets without having to deal with some of the structural attributes of Brady bonds. As in the high-yield market, the NAIC rating of the swap will not be as low as the individual bonds that comprise the index.
- *Global governments.* This market is operationally intensive in that it requires both bond and currency transactions. Not only are these transactions subject to different settlement periods, but cash bonds can have different forms of clearing and delivery, depending on the country.

Exhibit 1: Total Return Swaps on Major Market Sector Indices

Market	Bloomberg Ticker	Market	Bloomberg Ticker
Domestic Aggregate	DOAO	High Yield	JOAO
U.S. Government	GOAO	BB, B subsectors	
Government, ex-Agency	GOQO		
Mortgage	MOAO	Global Government (J.P. Morgan)	JPMGGLTR
U.S. Corporate	COAO	Emerging Markets (J.P.Morgan)	JPMOEMBI
AAA, AA, A, BBB subsectors			
Maturity subsectors			

Unless noted, index source is Merrill Lynch.

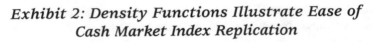

Exhibit 2: Density Functions Illustrate Ease of Cash Market Index Replication

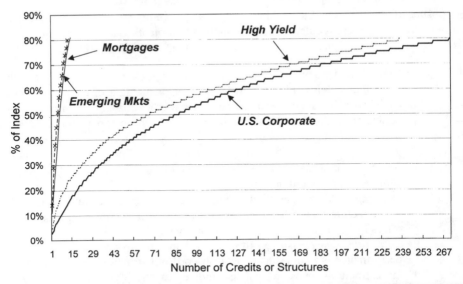

In Exhibit 2, we compare the ability to replicate four fixed-income market sectors. The density functions shown in the exhibit reveal how many individual credits or structures are required to attain 80% of the market value of the index. For example, an investor would have to purchase 270 out of a total of 829 credits to attain 80% of the market value of the investment grade corporate index. In contrast, for the mortgage index, an investor only needs to buy 12 types of collateral (denoted by coupon, dwarfs/30-years, and GNMA/non-GNMA — Fannie or Gold's) to get exposure to 80% of the market. The ease at which an index can be replicated in the cash market is also a very important consideration when hedging using index swaps. Like any hedge, a short position in an index swap is subject to basis risk. When hedging, the ability to access the basis risk as well as the ability to replicate at least a good portion of the risk of an index needs to be carefully examined.

In general, it is easier to replicate noncredit markets than credit markets. As the density functions show, credit sensitive markets require a larger number of bonds to insure replication. Since the covariance between many credits in an index is high, replication can be achieved with fewer credits than the density functions suggest. Nevertheless, the index is less vulnerable to default events than a replicated portfolio. While noncredit markets are easier to replicate, they usually have higher operational and back office cost. Managing their structural complexity can be resource intensive and they generally require more frequent rebalancing.

Exhibit 3: Index Swaps Cash Flows

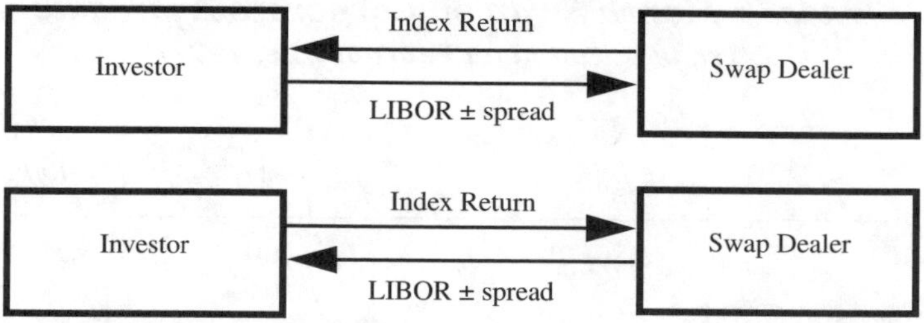

INDEX SWAP BASICS

An index swap is simply a variant of a conventional swap. Compared to the more ubiquitous equity index futures, index swaps on debt indices are over-the-counter agreements, where two counterparties exchange the total return of an index for LIBOR plus or minus a spread. The swap does not entail a principal payment. The terms of the swap can range from three months to several years. In this discussion, we will focus on swaps with tenors of one year or less. The analysis of longer-dated swaps is somewhat more complex and such swaps are usually designed for very specific investor needs.

In Exhibit 3, we have shown the basic payments exchanged in an index swap transaction. An investor who receives the index is long the index return and short LIBOR (upper diagram), while an investor who pays the index return is short the index return and long LIBOR (lower diagram). As one can see from the diagrams, an index swap is very similar to a fixed-rate swap. Just like a fixed-rate swap, an index swap can be thought of as a leveraged position in a synthetic asset whose funding is referenced versus LIBOR. Rather than a hypothetical fixed-rate bond, the underlying "asset" of an index swap is the universe of bonds that comprise an index. There are two other important differences:

> *Quote convention:* While interest-rate swaps trade at a spread to the Treasury curve and fund at LIBOR flat, index swaps trade "index flat" and fund at a spread to LIBOR.
>
> *Coupon payment convention:* In a fixed rate swap, the fixed-rate coupon is locked in upon initiation of the swap. In comparison, an index swap is a floating-rate for floating-rate swap; the coupon payments of *both* sides of an index swap float. The LIBOR rate will set in the beginning of each reset date, whereas the index payment will be equal the percentage change in the index value over the coupon period. This payment will reflect all the cash flow of the index (price change, coupon income, and reinvestment income). Both cash flows are in terms of the swap's notional value.

Exhibit 4: Periodic Cash Flows, 9-Month Swap: Trade- 9-Month Swap on Corporate Aggregate
(Trade initiated on February 28, 1997)

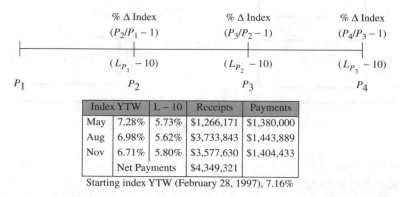

Index YTW	L – 10	Receipts	Payments
May	7.28%	5.73%	$1,266,171	$1,380,000
Aug	6.98%	5.62%	$3,733,843	$1,443,889
Nov	6.71%	5.80%	$3,577,630	$1,404,433
	Net Payments		$4,349,321	

Starting index YTW (February 28, 1997), 7.16%

Note: All cash flows multiplied by the notional of the swap ($100 million in this example).

In Exhibit 4, we show the cash flows of a 9-month total return swap on the Corporate market aggregate (C0A0) that resets and pays quarterly. *When an index swap is initiated, both the starting index value and the starting LIBOR payment are set.* In this example, the investor is long the index and funding the swap at $L - 10$. At each reset date and payment date, the index receiver will receive the percentage change in the index value from the prior reset date and pay $L - 10$ bps. Assuming the swap was executed at the end of February 1997, the starting value of the index was 850.91. Each quarter, its value changed by 1.3%, 3.7%, and 3.6%, respectively. The swap earned $4.35 million on a $100 million notional. While the quarterly LIBOR payments were relatively stable over the life of the swap, the index receipts obviously varied by the changes in the index value attributed to both the spread and interest rate duration inherent in the index.

SWAP PRICING

An index swap quote is denoted as a spread to LIBOR. Analytically, like an S&P 500 index futures contract, an index total return swap can be viewed as a forward on the underlying index. Unlike a futures contract, the swap is quoted on a financing basis, rather than a price basis. On either basis, forward pricing reflects the cost of borrowing or lending the "index" over the life of the agreement. Since the index coupon cash flows are paid out in the swap, whereas S&P futures dividends are not traded, the index swap quote simplifies to the repo or reverse repo rate observed for the underlying cash bonds. This is because the fair value spread of an index swap reflects the cost of hedging the swap in the cash market, as referenced to LIBOR.[2] Thus, index swap pricing is expected to be arbitrage free.

In actuality, the pricing of the swap is not perfectly arbitrage free. This should not be a surprise, considering that even the pricing of well developed, highly liquid index vehicles, while constrained by no arbitrage conditions, is not completely arbitrage free. Like equity index futures, arbitrage free pricing is defined by upper and lower bounds that are a function of several factors, such as:

- liquidity or transaction costs in both the cash and repo markets
- supply and demand conditions for the underlying cash markets
- leverage factors and collateral requirements for the market's cash instruments
- dealer positions

The swap quotes do change over time, just as supply and demand conditions in the respective markets change. These technicals also affect where a position can be financed versus LIBOR.

Cash Market Liquidity

To illustrate how cash market liquidity affects the swap quote, consider a trade where the investor enters into a swap to receive the index. The counterparty is now short the index and must hedge exposure by purchasing (borrowing) the index forward. The hedge must include enough cash bonds to sufficiently replicate the index. This position will be financed at an "all in" financing rate that includes the costs of financing all the bonds that comprise the hedge. When the swap expires, the hedge will be unwound and the counterparty will sell back the bonds. Conceptually, the swap provider must pay the bid/ask spread of these bonds; hence, when the bid/ask in the cash market changes, it is likely that the pricing of the index swap will too.

---

[2] Arbitrage free pricing is determined by cash market hedge. Consider the hedge of a counterparty that is paying (short) the index. (Cash flows are denoted in dollars.)

$$\text{Profit} = 0 = [-P_S - P_S\text{Repo} + \text{Coupon}] + [P_F - \text{Coupon}]$$

where

P_F = forward price or value of index
P_S = spot price or value of index

Rearranging:

$P_F = (P_S + P_S\text{Repo})$
Let: $P_F = P_S(1 + \text{Swap rate})$
$P_F = P_S + P_S(\text{Swap rate}) = P_S + P_S(\text{Repo})$
$P_S(\text{Swap rate}) = P_S(\text{Repo})$
Swap rate = Repo
Therefore: $(L - x) = \text{Repo}$

Exhibit 5: Cross Market Comparisons

Market	Index Replication*	Liquidity		Rebalancing	Admin. Costs	Leverage Haircut
		Cash Market	Repo Market			
Domestic Aggregate	2	Med	Med	Med	Med	4%
U.S. Government	1	High	High/Med	Med	Low	2%
Mortgage	1	High	High/Med	Med	Med	2%
U.S. Corporate	2	Med	Low	Med	Low	20%
High Yield	3	Med/Low	Low	Low	Low	20%
Global Government	1	High/Med	Med/Low	Med	High	NA
Emerging Market	1	Med/Low	High/Med	Low	Low	10%

* Expected ease at which index can be replicated in the cash market, with 1 having the highest ease of replication.

Financing Market Liquidity

The characteristics of the underlyer's repo market play a large role in the bid/ask of an index swap spread. In the repo market, the magnitude of the bid/ask spread itself is dynamic. For example, in periods when demand to borrow a specific security is high, the issue will trade at a very low repo rate, but liquidity in the repo market will diminish and the repo bid/ask will widen. Liquidity declines because, in most instances, market participants all want to borrow the cash security at the same time for the same reason: to hedge some type of market risk. The financing market for Treasuries provides a benchmark for the liquidity in the repo market; on average, the bid/ask in this market is 15 bps, but if there is a serious short in a specific issue the spread can trade as wide as 100 bps. In a spread sector, the swap hedge will most likely entail a Treasury position, used to hedge part of the interest rate exposure in the swap. Obviously, not all bonds in a specific market trade expensive in the repo market when market conditions are such that several types of market participants want to short sell securities. Since the index swap counterparty will need to construct a hedge sufficient to replicate the market, however, it will be subject to the changes in the average repo market bid/ask spreads of the sector.

Leverage Factors

The quote and bid/ask of an index swap also embeds differences between borrowing and lending haircuts for individual securities.[3] Markets with higher collateral requirements generally have wider bid/ask index swap spreads. In credit sensitive markets like high yield and corporates, a long position must be collateralized by 120%, a 20% haircut. Conversely, if an investor wanted to establish a short position (lend dollars and borrow securities) in the same market, the dealer counterparty would overcollateralize the trade by 2%. In Exhibit 5, we have summarized the haircut requirements in the financing markets across sectors.

---

[3] Haircuts are, of course, very counterparty specific. This discussion assumes market conventions.

Dealer Positions

One of the benefits of an index swap is that the dealer's pricing advantage in the financing markets is passed along to the counterparty. Another benefit is that if a dealer has a position in a particular swap, pricing will reflect the fact that the dealer can run a matched book. At times, this means investors can use index swaps to more cheaply implement contrarian strategies. Lastly, note that the global government swap pricing is more intricate than straight repo because the swap is quoted in *dollar* LIBOR terms. Thus, currency will partly determine pricing.

INDEX SWAP APPLICATIONS

In this section we present some of the many ways that investors can use index swaps. Below, we show how swaps can be used in portfolio management, hedging and asset allocation (index overlay).

Enhanced Index Strategies

In the preceding section, we discussed the basic mechanics of an index trade. Being a swap, the trade does not involve principal and is a leveraged transaction. Most investors have principal to invest and do not desire leverage. Moreover, an investor may or may not desire exposures associated with a "straight" index swap position. For a long (short) index position, an investor has three exposures:

- long the duration of the index (short the duration of the index)
- long convexity, except mortgages (short convexity, except mortgages)
- long the yield curve versus LIBOR (short the yield curve versus LIBOR)

To an investor that wants to earn index returns, all but the latter exposure is probably desirable. If the yield curve flattened dramatically, it could become increasingly costly to fund the index position.

The most straightforward way to eliminate both the leverage and curve exposure of the swap is to buy an asset-backed floater that has a maturity equal to the tenor of the swap. In Exhibit 6, we illustrate this strategy assuming a 1-year asset-backed floater trades at L + 5 and an investor has $100 million of funds to allocate to a market trading at L − 10 on an index swap basis. Since the LIBOR payments net out, the resulting cash flow is the index return plus 15 bps.

This example shows one way investors can use index swaps to beat the market. As of this writing, with the purchase of an asset-backed floater, all index swaps converted to Index plus a spread. The reason for this is that the implicit collateralized borrowing rate of the index swap is less than the rate that one can lend money to an asset-backed issuer. The net swap cash flows of an index and asset-backed position provide a measure of relative value in the asset swap. For example, in early November, a time when sentiment about all spread sectors was negative, the AAA rated sector of the corporate market swapped to Index plus 25 bps. For market neutral investors, this swap was very cheap considering that the spread of the index was T + 55 bps at the time. Note that lower-rated sectors may swap to Index minus a spread because the collateralized borrowing rates may be above LIBOR, commensurate with the higher price volatility of the indices underlying cash bonds. Lastly, rather than using ABS floaters, a more active enhanced index strategy is to invest in short duration floating-rate assets such as ARMs or home equity loans.

Hedging Sector Spread Risk

One of the most important applications of index swaps is hedging. Investors can use index swaps to hedge exposure to markets that have incomplete hedging vehicles. Index swaps can be used to hedge an anticipated adverse sector shock, thus obviating the need to: (1) liquidate assets at times when liquidity may be poor, and (2) experience tax events. For leveraged investors, short index positions can be used to hedge the market risk versus a specific credit, subsector, or security that is expected to earn above market returns.

For example, consider a leveraged investor who owns a portfolio of BBB-rated intermediate, privately placed securities. The portfolio of 5- to 7-year securities has an average spread of T + 175 and is being financed at L + 50. In the absence of an index swap hedge, the investor, who expects the spreads of this portfolio to tighten, would hedge interest rate exposure by shorting Treasuries or Treasury futures that match the duration of the portfolio. Assuming the Treasury short is L – 25, the net carry of the position will be 100 bps. If the trader wanted to hedge both the interest rate risk and spread risk of the sector, however, he could pay the 5- to 7-year part of the BBB-rated index (C3A4) and receive L – 40 (see Exhibit 7). The position now has zero carry since the hedger pays 85 bps in spread and receives 15 bps less in repo. However, over a 3-month period, portfolio spreads would only need to outperform the market by 5 bps, *rather than tighten*, to be profitable. Five basis points is the amount required to monetize the 100 bps of carry earned in the unhedged portfolio.

Exhibit 6: Enhanced Index Strategies Using Asset-Backed Securities

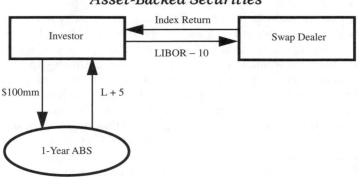

Exhibit 7: Hedging a BBB-Rated 5- to 7-Year Bond Portfolio

Let: Index = T + Spread = T + 85

	Receipts	Payments
Bond Portfolio	T + 175	L + 50
Index Swap	L - 40	T + 85
Net Carry	0 bps	

Like any hedge, the index swap hedge is subject to basis risk. The ability to gauge and manage this basis risk obviously varies across markets and it is critical to assess the nature of this risk when constructing a hedge. For example, since we care about hedging spread risk, we want to be sure that if we think market spreads have moved in a particular direction, it is reflected in the relative price performance of the index swap to the Treasury. One way to test how tracking has worked over time is to calculate an imputed excess return to the Treasury hedge and compare this to the actual performance of the Treasury hedge.

This entails five steps:

1. construct a Treasury "benchmark," using a blend of securities, that matches the duration of the index
2. calculate the difference in the yield of the index and the Treasury[4]
3. with the monthly "spread" of the index, calculate the monthly spread change
4. compute an "imputed" excess return over Treasury which is the sector's monthly spread income plus the price change due to spread volatility, or:

   monthly imputed excess return = (spread/12) − (duration × Δspread)

5. compare to *actual* excess return over comparable Treasury return

Returning to the BBB-rated trade, we analyzed the tracking since early 1996. In constructing the Treasury hedge, we used a duration weighted blend of the active 5- and 10-year Treasury, for which we have historical yield, duration, and return data. Alternatively, we could have used a basket of Treasuries. Since we did not have a sufficient effective duration and yield history for the index, we use yield to worst measures. These measures compare well to the effective measures for periods of overlapping data.

In Exhibit 8, we have presented the difference between actual and imputed excess return for 1996 and 1997. Over the period, the tracking errors failed statistical tests for autocorrelation, and more importantly, the R^2 is 0.80. Thus, 80% of the variation of the index's actual excess return (to Treasury) can be explained by the imputed index spread changes we calculated from the yield and duration to worst data. We think this is an acceptable hedge ratio considering that we have not "fine tuned" the hedge to account for optionality of the basket and that within the index, the unweighted average spread may not always reflect that spread curves may be flattening or steepening.

---

[4] We recommend using the pricing convention of the given market— either effective yield (OAS) or yield to worst.

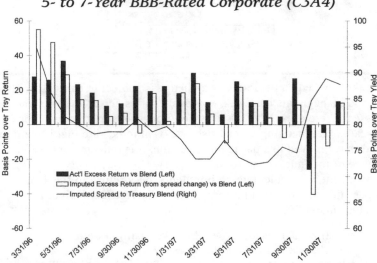

**Exhibit 8: Tracking the Basis Risk on a Hedge:
5- to 7-Year BBB-Rated Corporate (C3A4)**

If an index has a high degree of structural complexity (callables, putables, sinkers, and century bonds), the hedge should be designed to reflect this attribute. If the optionality of the index is high, the hedge may need to be managed more actively. Concerning index structure, the more difficult it is to replicate an index's structure, the more work required to hedge. For this reason, we recommend that investors use the index swap that most closely matches the rating and maturity subsectors of the portfolio that is being hedged. This strategy is most relevant for investment grade portfolios, where most of the variance in returns is due to changes in interest rates.

For mortgage portfolios, in contrast, the hedge may be designed to explicitly capture the structural difference between the mortgage portfolio and the mortgage index. For example, if an investor is expects market rates to fall and prepayments to rise faster than the pace priced into the market, they may want to pay the mortgage index, and invest in low coupon passthroughs.

In the preceding example, part of our tracking error can be attributed to the fact that we did not account for the fact that the index included callable bonds. About 13% of the index is callable. Over 2% of the bonds in the index had effective durations below two years. This simply means that the index contains high coupon, callable bonds. Since we structured our hedge using duration-to-worst, our hedge was slightly short the effective or OAS duration measure. Conversely, had we used the modified duration of the index, the hedge would have been too long.

Asset Allocation

A third application of index swaps is strategic asset allocation. Two examples are managing cash flows and fixed-income sector overlay. Equitizing cash enables portfolio managers to control exposure to a specific market in a timely low-cost manner. Once the exposure is established, managers can select the desired cash bonds and unwind the swap position. Similarly, index overlay strategies can be used to manage changes in sector allocation at the "macro" level. This can be particularly valuable for money managers with sizable market exposures where the sale of cash assets could affect market pricing and attract undesired publicity. Another benefit of overlay strategies is that they allow investors to opportunistically exploit changes in perceived value across fixed-income sectors that are short-term in nature.

The basic concept of an overlay is to use a derivative security to strategically alter a portfolio's exposure either to an asset class or between asset classes. For example, consider a scenario where an investor has a market-weighted allocation to mortgages and is concerned that the market is underestimating prepayment risk. Rather than liquidate cash holdings, the investor can reduce the allocation by paying the Mortgage index via an index swap for three months. The asset allocation will be to sell mortgages and buy Treasuries.

In Exhibit 9, we present an example of one way this trade could be structured. Before implementing the overlay, the portfolio has $100 million of mortgages. To reduce the exposure to 80% of the market, the investor will sell 2% of the holdings to raise cash to help fund what would be the equivalent of a change in variation margin on the swap trade. He would then short $18 million notional on the mortgage index swap and either receive the Government index through a swap or buy Treasuries outright and finance in the repo market.

If the overlay is implemented with the Government index, the strategy would obviously not be duration neutral since the Government index is currently more than one year longer than the mortgage index. From a top-down perspective, however, the strategic decision to underweight the mortgage market and overweight the Treasury market implicitly involves a duration decision since the attribution of the Treasury allocation will most likely be measured against the longer Treasury index. If the trade is implemented on a duration neutral basis, we recommend that the Treasury side of the overlay be delta hedged with cash Treasuries. Given the current duration of the mortgage index, we would use 5-year notes. We think this is an attractive maturity since a long position in the security finances in the overnight market at around $L - 100$. Moreover, the mortgage market is sufficiently short that several market participants are using 5-year Treasuries to hedge at least a fraction of mortgage longs. This means that if uncertainty about the sector increases, the 5-year could become an extremely good financing trade.

REGULATORY CONSIDERATIONS

Compared to the underlying cash assets, an index swap can significantly alter the capital requirements of various levels of market risk. From a regulatory point of view, index swaps can be a more efficient way to reduce exposure to certain types of markets.

Exhibit 9: Structuring an Index Overlay to Reduce Mortgage Exposure

	Overlaid Assets	Index Swap Account	Overlaid Portfolio Exposures
Mortgage Exposure:			
Overlaid mortgages	$98	$0	$98
Mortgage index swap exposure	$0	−$18	−$18
Net mortgage	$98	−$18	$80
Treasury Exposure:			
Treasury index swap exposure	$0	$20	$20
Net Treasury	$0	$20	$20
Cash Exposure (cash equivalent)	$0	$0	$0
Overlay portfolio value	$95	$5	$100

Figures in millions of dollars.

Exhibit 10: Risk Based Capital Charges, by Rating

Category	S&P	Charge
1	AAA to A	0.3%
2	BBB	1.0%
3	BB	4.0%
4	B	9.0%
5	CCC	20.0%
6	In/near default	30.0%

Note: Risk based capital charges for life and health companies only. Factors are different for property and casualty companies.

Insurance Company Investors

The National Association of Insurance Commissioners (NAIC) controls the statutory accounting for insurance companies, and thereby determines the Risk Based Capital (RBC) factors for the assets held by insurance companies. These factors are based on the historical default and delinquency data. Rating agency credit ratings generally map to, as well as provide a cap on, NAIC designations. The Standard and Poor's ratings shown in Exhibit 10 are indicative of appropriate NAIC designations. As one would expect, the capital reserves required against a given asset will be significantly greater for noninvestment grade assets than for investment grade assets.

Since index swaps are off-balance-sheet items, they do not fall under the statutory accounting guidelines of the NAIC. For swaps, the risk based capital charge is based on the credit quality of the counterparty (measured as a factor) and the remaining term of the swap. Currently, under the Model Investment Law (MIL) the capital charge associated with an index swap would fall under the "prudent person" test. (Note that in this regard, the mandates of the MIL are superseded by Statutory Accounting.) Through asset adequacy analysis, an actuary would determine a voluntary capital reserve. Thus, an index with a low credit rating, such as the single-B or the emerging markets index, would generally be more capital efficient than owning a portfolio of cash bonds.

Exhibit 11: RBC Breakevens to Treasuries*

Category	Annuity Comp. (bps)	Life Comp. (bps)
1	9	4
2	30	14
3	120	56
4	270	126
5	600	280
6	900	421

* The derivation of company-specific breakevens will vary.

This is one of the indirect economic benefits associated with an index swap. To give the capital charge differences more meaning, we can analyze "break-even" spreads to Treasuries. The break-even is the minimum spread over the Treasury required to monetize the higher capital charge associated with holding an asset that has credit risk. Lower-rated credits have higher breakeven spreads (see Exhibit 11). Consider an example of representative insurance companies: on a risk-based cost of capital basis, the corporate spread of a double-B credit must be at least 120 bps for an annuity company purchaser and approximately 56 bps for a life insurance company purchaser to have comparable relative value to a Treasury. Hence, on a capital adjusted basis, a total return swap for either emerging markets or high yield is several basis points cheaper than a portfolio of a similarly rated cash asset. Naturally, the extent to which the reduction in RBC affects the break-even spread of the asset will differ across institutions, depending on several factors, particularly overall asset/liability mix. For example, if an insurance company has excess risk-based capital, the economic benefit will be lower.

Looking forward, the NAIC has undertaken what has become a 5-year initiative to adopt standards for synthetic assets. There is a chance that the NAIC initiative is drawn out for a sixth year. However, should standards be adopted for the reserve factors for index swaps, specific guidelines would be enacted no sooner than early 1998. Under the NAIC's operating procedures, the earliest new regulations could be implemented would be 1999. Since the tenors of most index swaps range from three months to a year, any event risk stemming from a regulatory change would be negligible.

Bank Investors

For banks, the minimum amount of capital required to be held against an asset increases proportionally with the risk weighting of that asset. The Bank for International Settlements (BIS) sets the general guidelines for the minimum level of capital that banks of member countries should maintain. Individual assets are assigned risk weightings ranging from 0% to 100%. The concept of risk-weighted assets is an attempt to measure the level of credit risk inherent in the assets held by a bank. Though the BIS sets the guidelines, banks usually use more comprehensive measures to determine suitable reserves that are based on the expected market volatility of the asset.

Index swaps can be used to alter the reserves held against bank loans and credit portfolios. If a short index position in a credit index lowers the overall volatility of the credit portfolio, for example, the net position could receive a lower market risk weighting. A long position in the index of a credit market will usually have a different market risk factor than a portfolio of bonds of the same credit quality. For instance, on a high yield index swap, principal is not at risk, as it would be for a portfolio of high yield cash bonds. An adverse event for the swap would occur if the counterparty defaulted on a swap that was "in the money" with respect to the other counterparty.

CONCLUSION

Index swaps provide fixed-income investors with a new tool. The contribution of index swaps to the fixed-income marketplace is unique— there is no cash market substitute. Moreover, at times, index swaps can offer good relative value to cash market instruments. The index swap applications presented in this chapter serve as an introduction and are by no means exhaustive, but should illustrate the use of index swaps and suggest other applications.

Section IV:

Performance Measurement and Evaluation

Chapter 32

Stock Portfolio Attribution Analysis

Frank J. Jones, Ph.D.
Chief Investment Officer
Guardian Life Insurance

Ronald N. Kahn, Ph.D.
Director of Research
BARRA

INTRODUCTION

Attribution analysis, to be succinct, means assigning an overall effect to multivarious causes of some observation or outcome. Thus, attribution analysis could apply to social behavior, the weather, portfolio returns or even sports. To use the latter example, after a college football game on Saturday afternoon, the coaching staff either engages in the agony of defeat or the thrill of victory for a few hours, and on the next day begins the difficult job of game evaluation. On Sunday, they watch the all-important game films to attribute the "W" or the "L" (win or loss) to its component factors. The factors addressed include, even in victory, who did not play well and, even in loss, who did play well. The taxonomy in Exhibit 1 provides a superficial structure of the evaluations which must be made based on the game films.

In this context, the authors believe that football represents a better analogy for the attribution analysis of a stock portfolio than most other sports, for example basketball. In football, there are 11 closely packed players on the field for a team and a good attribution analysis may not be feasible until the game films are watched and evaluated position by position. On the other hand, in basketball there are only five typically widely dispersed players on the court and subsequent analysis may not be necessary for a position-by-position evaluation. Thus, stock portfolio attribution analysis seems more like football than basketball in this regard.

To conduct an attribution analysis, depending on the context, a model of human behavior, meteorology, portfolio returns, or team play must be specified and utilized. In this chapter, attribution analysis is applied to stock portfolio returns. For this purpose, a model of stock market returns is necessary.

Exhibit 1: Football Game Evaluation

Coaching	Offense	Defense	Special Teams	Referees

Offense	Line
	• Run
	• Pass
		Line
		• Against Run
		• Against Run
			Kickoff
			• Kicking
			  – On side
			• Receiving
			  – On side	

Defense	Tight Ends/H. Backs
	• Run
	• Pass
	  – Patterns
	  – Hands/Fumbles
		Line Backers
		• Against Run
		• Against Pass
			Punt Game
			• Punts
			• Return	

Special Teams	Wide Receivers • Patterns Hands • Blocking	Backs (Defensive Backs/Safeties) • Against Run • Against Pass	Extra Points Field Goals	
Clock Management	Running Backs • Running – Hands/Fumbles • Receiving • Blocking All-Penalties	All-Penalties	All-Penalties	

STOCK PORTFOLIO MODELS — FACTOR ANALYSIS

Asset portfolio return models are typically linear models wherein the dependent variable is the portfolio return, or alternatively the portfolio return minus a benchmark return, often called the *active return*. The independent variables, called *factors*, are typically market variables, such as the return on the overall stock market; the return on large cap versus small cap stocks; the return on value versus growth stocks, etc., although macroeconomic variables are also used, as indicated below.

The coefficients of the independent variables, typically called *factor sensitivities* or *exposures* or *factor loadings*, are asset or portfolio characteristics.

In general, a factor model for a managed stock portfolio return, *MP*, can be formulated as follows:

$$R_{MP} = B_{MP}(1)F(1) + B_{MP}(2)F(2) + \ldots + B_{MP}(N)F(N) + E \qquad (1)$$

where

$F(i)$ = the i th factor of the managed portfolio (*MP*)

$B_{MP}(i)$ = the i th coefficient (factor-sensitivity, exposure or factor loading)
R_{MP} = the return on the managed portfolio
E = the residual or error term

This model is called an "*N-factor model*." In this context, it is called a *return generating process*.

Applying the same model to the portfolio's benchmark or standard portfolio, S, provides the following:

$$R_S = B_S(1)F(1) + B_S(2)F(2) + ... + B_S(N)F(N) + E \qquad (2)$$

where

$B_S(i)$ = the i th coefficient for the benchmark portfolio

Subtracting equation (2) from equation (1) provides:

$$R_{MP} - R_S = [B_{MP}(1) - B_S(1)]F(1) + [B_{MP}(2) - B_S(2)]F(2) + ... \\ + [B_{MP}(N) - B_S(N)]F(N) \qquad (3)$$

In this case, $R_{MP} - R_S$ is called the Active Return. Equation (3) is the basis for performance attribution analysis. Obviously, to conduct an attribution analysis, the returns on the managed portfolio and the standard portfolio must be calculated (called *performance measurement*) and the factors must be known. Knowing the $F(i)$, R_{MP} and R_S, the $B_{MP}(i)$ and $B_S(i)$ can be estimated and, as a result, the difference in the return on the managed portfolio and the return on the benchmark can be attributed to the various risk factors. This exercise is called *attribution analysis*.

Note that the factors for the managed portfolio and the benchmark are the same, but that the factor coefficients are different due to the differences in the composition of the managed portfolio and the benchmark. This methodology is the foundation for attribution analysis, which is attributing the difference in the returns of the two portfolios to the various factors due to their differences in portfolio compositions.

In the next chapter, an attribution analysis based on a factor model analysis for bonds is provided. A succinct summary of a bond portfolio return factor model is provided in Exhibit 2. There is a longer and more controversial tradition of factor analysis for common stock returns than for bond returns.

Exhibit 2: Bond Portfolio Return Factor Model

Coefficient (Factor Sensitivity)	Factor (Market Variable)
Duration	Yield Change (Parallel)
Duration Buckets	Yield Curve Change
Sector Composition	Sector Returns
Security Selection (in Sectors)	Rich/Cheap Security Behavior

THE USE OF ATTRIBUTION ANALYSIS

In football, the coach could use attribution analysis to determine whether to trade the offensive right guard and give a better contract to the defensive left end, or vice versa. In stock portfolio return analysis, attribution analysis can be used for the following:

- Mutual fund executives selecting, promoting, and demoting portfolio managers.
- Plan sponsors selecting, or terminating asset mangers.
- Money management executives evaluating portfolio managers.
- Individuals selecting mutual funds.
- Portfolio managers developing/fine tuning investment strategies.

STOCK MARKET RETURN FACTOR MODELS

The original "factor model" of the stock market was CAPM (the Capital Asset Pricing Model) which was a single factor model. In CAPM, the factor is the excess stock market return (the stock market return minus the risk-free rate), where the factor sensitivity β, called "beta," is the volatility of the stock portfolio relative to the overall stock market return, typically measured by the S&P500. This one-factor model is specified as:

$$R_P - R_{RF} = \alpha + \beta (R_M - R_{RF}) + E$$

where

R_P = the return on the stock portfolio
R_M = the return on the overall stock market
R_{RF} = the risk-free return (typically the 90-day Treasury bill yield)
E = the error term

and α and β are the coefficients which are empirically determined from the other measured variables.

Fama and French have expanded the one-factor CAPM model to three factors, adding to the market return the following two factors:[1]

- *Size (market capitalization)*: small capitalization stocks have a size premium, that is they tend to outperform large capitalization stocks.
- *Price-to-Book Ratio (or its reciprocal that is, book value to price)*: low price to book (value) stocks have a premium to high price to book stocks; that is, value stocks outperform growth stocks.

Other research has both criticized these three factors and provided other market-oriented factors.

---

[1] Eugene F. Fama and Kenneth R. French, "The Cross-Section of Expected Stock Returns," *Journal of Finance* (June 1992), pp. 427-465.

Another theoretical construct called the APT (Arbitrage Pricing Theory), developed originally by Stephen A. Ross[2] and supported by empirical research,[3] specifies macroeconomic variables such as inflation and economic growth as the factors. The theory itself, however, neither specifies what the factors are or even how many there are.

Other research provides additional factors which attempt to specify stock portfolio returns. These factors are primarily of the following types:

- fundamental stock portfolio factors (the three factors mentioned above are of this type, but price to earnings ratio, dividends, and other fundamental factors have also been suggested).
- macroeconomic factors, primarily based on APT.

Only one conclusion about stock factor models can be made without controversy: "There is no model which has wide acceptance by academics and practitioners." Research and controversy continue.

ILLUSTRATION

This section provides a multi-factor model and a corresponding attribution analysis of a stock portfolio. The model and the corresponding attribution analysis was developed by BARRA and is part of their commercially provided U.S. Equity Version 3 (E3).[4] This factor model is based solely on fundamental stock market variables; there are no technical or macroeconomic variables.

The BARRA factor model and a corresponding attribution analysis of a stock portfolio is summarized in Exhibits 3, 4, and 5. Exhibit 6 provides an overall summary of this BARRA attribution analysis.

The attribution analysis provides quantitative measures of the amounts by which the various factors account for the components of the return on the managed portfolio, specifically the difference between the return on the managed portfolio and its benchmark (the active return).

As shown in Exhibit 3, the difference in the return between the managed portfolio and benchmark portfolio is called the *Total Active Return*. As indicated in Exhibit 3, the Total Active Return is +0.36 (= +20.60% − 20.24%). It is this total active return which is attributed to the BARRA factors.[5] The Total Active Return is then divided into two components.

---

[2] Stephen A. Ross, "The Arbitrage Theory of Capital Asset Pricing," *Journal of Economic Theory* (December 1976), pp. 341- 360.

[3] Richard Roll and Stephen A. Ross, "An Empirical Investigation of the Arbitrage Pricing Theory," *Journal of Finance* (December 1980), pp.1073-1103.

[4] *United States Equity, Version 3 (E 3, Risk Model Handbook*, BARRA, Berkeley, CA, 1996.

[5] Technically, the risk-free return could be subtracted from both the managed portfolio return and the benchmark return to provide the excess returns for the managed portfolio and the benchmark. However, when the excess benchmark return is subtracted from the excess total managed portfolio return, the risk-free returns cancels out and the total active return is the same.

Exhibit 3: BARRA Stock Portfolio Factor Model

Returns

Total Managed Portfolio (+20.60%)		Benchmark (+20.24%)

Total Active
(+0.36%)

Expected Active* (-0.42%)		Total Exceptional Active (+0.78%)		

	Market Timing (-0.64%)	Risk Indices (+2.69%)	Industries (+0.09%)	Asset Selection (-1.37%)

* $(B_p-1) \times 6.0\% = -0.42\%$ where B_p, the portfolio beta equals 0.93, and where 6.0% is the expected excess market return (that is, in excess of the risk free rate). See footnote 6 for the derivation.

Decomposition of Total Active Return

The Total Active Return is composed of the *Expected Active Return* and the *Total Exceptional Active Return*. We discuss each below.

Expected Active Return

The Expected Active Return is the expected or average amount by which the portfolio return is expected to exceed the average market return given the portfolio beta (β) and the average market excess return ($R_m - R_p$). Specifically, the Expected Active Equity Return is:[6]

---

[6] The Active Equity Return is derived as follows. We begin with the CAPM:

$$R_p - R_{RF} = \beta(R_m - R_{RF}) + \alpha$$

where

R_p = the portfolio return
R_{RF} = the risk free rate
R_m = the market return
β = beta
α = alpha

then

$$R_p = R_{RF} + \beta R_m - \beta R_{RF} + \alpha$$

$$R_p = R_{RF} (1 - \beta) + \beta R_m + \alpha$$

$$R_p - R_m = R_{RF} (1 - \beta) + R_m (\beta - 1) + \alpha$$
$$= (1 - \beta) (R_{RF} - R_m) + \alpha$$
$$= (\beta - 1) (R_m - R_{RF}) + \alpha$$

In this equation, $R_p - R_m$ is the Expected Active Return where β is the portfolio beta and $R_m - R_{RF}$ is the Expected Excess (above risk free) Market Return (i.e., expected excess return above the risk-free return).

The beta for this portfolio is 0.93 and the Expected Excess Market Return is currently approximately 6%. In this case,

Expected Active Return = $(0.93 - 1)$ $(6\%) = (-0.07)$ $(6\%) = -0.42\%$

Exhibit 4: Decomposition of Total Exceptional Active Return (0.7790)

Market Timing (-0.6370%)

- Average Active Equity Beta	-0.6030
- Active Equity Beta Variation	-0.0340
. Above Average Equity Beta	+0.0022
. Below Average Equity Beta	-0.0362
- Equity Beta Policy	-0.6370

Risk Indices (+2.6936%)

Size		-0.0416
Size	-0.1032	
Size Non-Linearity	0.0616	
Non-Est Universe	0.0000	
Growth/Value		2.0582
Growth	0.3940	
Earnings Yield	1.1492	
Value	0.6627	
Dividend Yield	-0.1477	
Risk		0.6772
Volatility	0.1754	
Momentum	-0.0575	
Trading Activity	0.0141	
Earnings Variation	0.2142	
Leverage	0.2634	
Currency Sensitivity	0.0676	
Total		2.6936

Industries (+0.0879%)

Sectors	
- Basic Mat'ls	-0.1496
- Energy	0.1658
- Cnsmr Non-cyclicals	0.1859
- Cnsmr Cyclicals	0.0603
- Cnsmr Services	0.2311
- Industrials	0.0705
- Utility	-0.3071
- Transport	-0.0565
- Health Care	-0.2740
- Technology	0.0522
- Telecommunications	0.0143
- Commercial Services	-0.0349
- Financial	0.1299
Total Sector	0.0879

(13 Sectors further subdivided into 52 Industries)

Asset Selection (-1.3656%)

- Assets Held in portfolio	-0.435
. Over-weighted Assets	-0.435
. Under-weighted Assets	+0.000
Benchmark Assets Not Held	-0.930
Total Asset Selection	-1.366

Exhibit 5: Sector/Industry Listing

Basic Materials	*Industry*	Mining & Metals
		Gold
		Forest Products & Paper
		Chemicals
Energy		Energy Reserves & Production
		Oil Refining
		Oil Services
Consumer Noncyclicals		Food & Beverages
		Alcohol
		Tobacco
		Home Products
		Grocery Stores
Consumer Cyclicals		Consumer Durables
		Motor Vehicles & Parts
		Apparel & Textiles
		Clothing Stores
		Specialty Retail
		Department Stores
		Construction and Real Property
Consumer Services		Publishing
		Media
		Hotels
		Restaurants
		Entertainment
		Leisure
Industrials		Environmental Service
		Heavy Electrical Equipment
		Heavy Machinery
		Industrial Parts
Utility		Electrical Utilities
		Gas Utilities
Transport		Railroads
		Airlines
		Trucking, Shipping, Air Freight
Health Care		Medical Providers & Services
		Medical Products
		Drugs
Technology		Electronic Equipment
		Semiconductors
		Computer Hardware & Office Equipment
		Computer Software
		Defense & Aerospace
Telecommunications		Telephones
		Wireless Telecommunications
Commercial Services		Information Services
		Industrial Services
Financial		Life & Health Insurance
		Property & Casualty Insurance
		Banks
		Thrifts
		Securities & Asset Management
		Financial Services

Exhibit 6: Attribution Analysis

Portfolio/Factor	Return	
Managed Portfolio	20.60	
Benchmark	20.24	
Active Return		0.36
Expected Active		-0.42
Exceptional Active		+0.78
Market Timing		-0.64
Risk Indices		+2.69
Industries		+0.09
Asset Selection		-1.37

$$R_p - R_m = (\beta - 1)(R_m - R_p) + \alpha$$

Given a portfolio beta of 0.93 and an assumed average market excess return of 6%, the Expected Active Return is:

$$(R_p - R_m) = (0.93 - 1.00)\ 6\% = -0.42\%.$$

Thus, the Expected Active Return is the under or outperformance which is expected due to the portfolio's average beta over the analysis period and the long-term equity risk premium. It is assumed that investing in equities will provide returns higher than those achieved by investing in risk-free instruments over a long horizon. The amount by which the portfolio is expected to outperform risk-free instruments is a function of the portfolio's beta and the equity risk premium (default is 6% in the BARRA software). If a portfolio has an average beta of 1.1, then a 6.6% outperformance (over cash) is expected. Because this amount of return is expected — or takes no skill to obtain — it is removed from the total active return and the manager's skill or value-added is analyzed net of it.

Total Exceptional Active Return

The Total Exceptional Active Return is the Total Active Return less the Expected Active Return. (Note that the Total Exceptional Return always denotes the Active Return net of the expected return from beta.) Given the Total Active Return of +0.36% and the Expected Active Return of -0.42%, the Total Exceptional Active Return is +0.78%. The Total Exceptional Active Return is the sum of four calculated factors, as shown in Exhibits 3 and 4. These four factors are defined below.

Thus, while there are different ways to evaluate football game films, there are also different types of stock portfolio return factor models. That is, stock portfolio factor models are non-unique. Even after selecting the factors, however, as discussed above, there are further decisions. For example, the BARRA model discussed below attributes the Total Exceptional Active Return to factors, whereas alternatively the Total Active Return could have been attributed to factors.

Market Timing Positive results from market timing are obtained by holding a higher than average beta when the market returns more than expected (as defined by the equity risk premium) or a lower than average beta when the market returns less than the expected premium. Negative returns from market timing result when the converse is true.

Risk Indices There are returns associated with being over or underexposed (relative to the benchmark) to the 13 risk indices in the BARRA risk model. The 13 risk indices are specified and defined below:

1. *Volatility* captures relative volatility using measures of both long-term historical volatility (such as historical residual standard deviation) and near-term volatility (such as high-low price ratio, daily standard deviation, and cumulative range over the last 12 months). Other proxies for volatility (log of stock price), corrections for thin trading (serial dependence), and changes in volatility (volume beta) are also included in this index.

2. *Momentum* captures common variation in returns related to recent stock price behavior. Stocks that had positive excess returns in the recent past are grouped separately from those that displayed negative excess returns.

3. *Size* captures differences in stock returns due to differences in the market capitalization of companies.

4. *Size nonlinearity* captures deviations from linearity in the relationship between returns and log of market capitalizations.

5. *Trading activity* measures the amount of relative trading in each stock. Stocks that are highly traded are likely to be those with greater institutional interest. Such stocks may display different return behavior compared with those that are not widely held by institutions.

6. *Growth* uses historical growth and profitability measures to predict future earnings growth.

7. *Earnings yield* combines current and historical earnings-to-price ratios with a measure of analyst-predicted earnings-to-price. Stocks with similar values of earnings yield behave in a similar fashion with respect to their returns.

8. *Value* distinguishes between value stocks and growth stocks using the ratio of book value of equity to market capitalization.

9. *Earnings variability* measures the variability in earnings and cash flows using both historical measures and analysts' predictions.

10. *Leverage* This risk index measures the financial leverage of a company.

11. *Currency sensitivity* measures the sensitivity of a company's stock return to the return on a basket of foreign currencies.

12. *Dividend yield* computes a measure of predicted dividend yield using the past history of dividends and the market price behavior of the stock.

13. *Non-estimation universe indicator* flags companies outside the estimation universe. It allows the linear factor model to be extended to stocks outside the U.S.-E3 estimation universe.

In general, the 13 risk indices are segmented into three styles as follows:

Size
• Size
• Size nonlinearity
• Non-estimation universe indicator

Growth/Value
• Growth
• Value
• Earnings yield
• Dividend yield

Risk
• Volatility
• Momentum
• Trading activity
• Earnings variability
• Leverage
• Currency sensitivity

Industries The return associated with over and underweighting industries relative to the benchmark. As indicated in Exhibits 4 and 5, there are 52 industries which are aggregated into 13 sectors.

Asset Selection The return associated with the particular stocks held in the portfolio. This return is residual or net of all the previous factor returns (i.e., beta, risk index, and industry-related returns). This return is not explained by the common factor exposures.

As shown in Exhibit 3, the Total Exceptional Active Return of +0.78% is composed of: (1) −0.64% due to Market Timing, (2) +2.69% due to the Risk Indices, (3) +0.09% due to Industries, and (4) −1.37% due to Asset Selection.

Each of these four components of Total Exceptional Active Return, in turn, have several components, as shown in Exhibit 4. The numbers in parentheses in Exhibits 3 and 4 are the returns attributed to these factors. Note that the attributed returns are additive, as summarized in Exhibit 6. That is, the Total Active Return of +0.36% is exactly attributed to the various factors in this BARRA factor model.

Beyond the attribution of return to these factors, detailed performance analysis also attributes risk to the factors. For example, the total active return (0.36%) for the portfolio just analyzed has an associated risk of 3.23%. This realized Active Return is quite modest, given the level of risk (a top quartile active manager will have an information ratio — ratio of return to risk — of at least 0.5). And risk attribution applies not only to Total Active Return but to each factor.

A related but distinct issue concerns statistics and significance. Is the return to a factor statistically significant, or could blind luck produce similar returns more than 5% of the time? Such risk and statistical significance measures are treated by the BARRA model but are not treated in this chapter.

What does this mean? We conclude this section with the answer to the following: Given the results of the attribution analysis provided in Exhibits 3 and 4, evaluate the managed portfolio's performance over this period.

The answer is as follows. The managed portfolio returned +20.60% over this period, outperforming the benchmark's +20.24% return by +0.36% (the Total Active Return). This +0.36% overperformance was composed of an underperformance of 0.42% in the Expected Active Return based on (1) the portfolio's beta (0.93) and the average excess market return (6%) and (2) an overperformance of 0.78% in the Total Exceptional Active Return.

The Total Exceptional Active Return is composed of the four components discussed above. The first component is Market Timing, in which there was an underperformance of 0.64%, almost all of which was due to the Average Active Equity Beta (0.60%). The remainder (0.04%) was due to an underperformance of 0.04% in below average equity beta — the above active equity beta outperformed by an insignificant 0.0022%.

The second component, the Risk Indices factor, was the largest positive contributor to Total Active Return with an outperformance of 2.69%. Of this, there was an overperformance of 2.06% due to the growth/value style factor. There was also an overperformance of 0.68% due to the Risk Index style factor and an underperformance of 0.04% due to the Size style factor. When decomposed into the 13 Risk Indices, the strongest and the weakest indices were as follows:

Strong		Weak	
Earnings Yield	1.1492	Yield	−0.1477
Value	0.6627	Size	−0.1032
Growth	0.3940	Momentum	−0.0575
Leverage	0.2634	Non-Estimation Universe	0.0000

Third, there was an overperformance of 0.09% due to the Industries factor. Among the 13 sectors, the three strongest and weakest sectors were as follows:

Strong		*Weak*	
Consumer Services	+0.2311%	Utility	−0.3071%
Consumer (non-cyclical)	+0.1859%	Health Care	−0.2740%
Energy	+0.1658%	Basic Materials	−0.1496%

The 13 sectors are divided into 52 industries as shown in Exhibit 5. While returns are attributed to the industries in the model, they are not included herein.

The fourth factor in the Total Exceptional Active Return is Asset Selection which provided an underperformance relative to the benchmark of 1.37%. This underperformance was caused by a 0.44% underperformance due to assets overweighted in the portfolio and an underperformance of 0.93% due to benchmark assets not held in the portfolio.

Overall, the rather small total active overperformance of +0.36% was the net effect of some much larger positive and negative performances as summarized in Exhibit 6 and as rank ordered below:

Risk Indices:	+2.69%
Industries	+0.09%
Expected Active	−0.42%
Market Timing	−0.64%
Asset Selection	−1.37%

The analysis suggests that this portfolio manager has been successful in "betting on" cheap earnings and book value (the Value and Earnings Yield Risk Indices) and unsuccessful in selecting individual stocks (Asset Selection) and market timing (Market Timing). This portfolio manager might be more successful if (1) more stocks were purchased to diversify and limit individual stock bets, (2) the portfolio beta was maintained to limit market timing, and (3) factors other than Value and Earnings Yield bets were controlled.

OVERVIEW

Calculating the return on a managed portfolio over a period of time (i.e., performance measurement) is the first step in evaluating the portfolio's performance. The second step is identifying a relevant benchmark for the portfolio whose performance or return provides a reasonable comparison for the portfolio. This benchmark depends on the nature of the managed portfolio. For example, the benchmark may be the S&P 500, the Russell 2000, or other indices. The return on the benchmark must be calculated over the same time period as the portfolio's return.

The third step is based on a return generating process which must be specified for the asset class. This return generating process is typically a linear equation with N independent variables — this type of model is called an N-factor model. The model is based on theory and empirical research.

The N-factor model can be made to specify quantitatively how the portfolio's Total Active Return (the amount by which the portfolio's return outperformed or underperformed the benchmark returns) was attributed to the various factors in the model. This decomposition of return is called attribution analysis. Thus, the Total Active Return of a managed portfolio relative to a benchmark answers the question, "How did the portfolio perform?" The resulting attribution analysis answers the question, "Why did the portfolio return perform relative to the benchmark as it did, that is, which factors contributed to its relative performance?" This question is answered relative to the factors in the N-factor return generating model.

Chapter 33

Fixed Income Attribution Analysis

Frank J. Jones, Ph.D.
Chief Investment Officer
Guardian Life Insurance

Leonard J. Peltzman
Analyst, Fixed Income Securities
Guardian Life Insurance

INTRODUCTION

Attribution analysis is *ex post* portfolio rate of return (ROR) analysis. Specifically, the *ex post* total ROR on a bond portfolio is "attributed" to the various risk factors of the bond portfolio; that is, portions of the ROR are associated with each of the risk factors. Attribution analysis, however, cannot be considered in isolation, but only in a broader structure of bond portfolio benchmarks, risk factors, strategies, and a wider set of portfolio return analyses, as summarized in Exhibit 1. This chapter considers attribution analysis in this broader analytical framework and provides an empirical example. The next sections discuss the benchmarks, performance measurement, risk factors, strategies, and portfolio return analysis as the basis for considering attribution analysis.

BENCHMARKS

To answer the question, "How big is big?" a frame of reference or benchmark (often called a "bogey") must be provided. A person who is 6'0" tall will be very big in the eighth grade (where the average height may be 5'4") but very small in the National Basketball Association (where the average height may be 6'5"). Is the benchmark for assessing someone's relative height the eighth grade or the NBA? Similarly, to evaluate bond portfolio returns, a benchmark must be provided. A return of 6% on a fixed income portfolio during a year when the bond market rallied might be very good if the portfolio was cash; but inferior if the portfolio was composed of long-term bonds. Similarly a given return may be good for a Treasury portfolio but weak for a non-investment grade corporate bond portfolio.

Exhibit 1: Portfolio Analysis

Benchmarks	Investment Managers by Benchmark	Risk Factors	Strategies	Portfolio Return Analysis*
Asset Group (e.g., Lehman Aggregate)	Mutual Funds	Duration	*Passive* (Replicate all or some risk factors).	Ex Ante
		Convexity	• Indexation	Sensitivity
			• Immunization	Analysis
Liability Driven ("Customized")	Pension Funds/ Insurance Cos.	Yield curve shape (Duration Buckets)	• Dedication	
		Sector Weightings • Macro (e.g. Corporate versus MBS) • Micro (e.g. Utilities versus Industrials in Corporates). • Security (e.g. Niagara Mohawk versus Florida P&L in Utilities)	*Active* (Actively deviate from one or more risk factors) • Trading • Market Timing	Ex Post Attribution Analysis
		Credit Rating		
		Short-Term Dislocations • Trading.		

* Returns calculated according to AIMR.

Fixed income benchmarks can be driven by either broad/aggregate fixed income asset classes or the liabilities related to the asset portfolio. Three investment banks have constructed broad and disaggregated bond indexes: Lehman Brothers, Inc. (the Lehman Aggregate); Salomon Brothers (the Salomon Broad Investment Grade (BIG)); and, Merrill Lynch (the Merrill Lynch Domestic Master). The subsets of the Lehman Aggregate are shown in Exhibit 2. A rate of return for the Aggregate and each subset can be calculated on a daily basis. Thus, from this list, portfolio managers may choose the Lehman Aggregate, the Lehman Corporate, or the Lehman Short Term (1-10 years), or High Grade (AAA/AA) Corporate Index as a benchmark, whichever is most appropriate, and compare the return on their portfolio to any of these indexes.

Most institutional investors, however, do not find a portfolio based on the composition of the broad market or a sector relevant to their needs, but instead want a portfolio which can fund their specific liabilities as a benchmark. In such cases, they develop their own "customized" benchmarks which reflect their liabilities. To develop their own benchmarks, they must determine the expected cash flows of their liabilities and specify the types of investments they wish to make (e.g. sectors, subsectors, credit ratings, etc.). They can then specify their own customized asset group and calculate the return on the benchmark from the returns on its components over a period of time.

Exhibit 2: Lehman Brothers Fixed Income Indices

January 1-31, 1997	Number Issues	Durat. ToWorst	Mod.Adj. Durat.	Coupon	Matur.	Price	Yield ToWorst	Market Value	% of Index	% of Aggregate
aggregate	5799	5.19	4.62	7.21	8.73	102.43	6.73	4710228	100.00	100.00
int. aggregate	4299	3.96	3.40	7.03	5.26	101.31	6.64	3803485		80.75
government/corporate	5085	5.35	5.06	7.13	9.51	103.34	6.50	3261687	100.00	69.25
int. gov/corp	3585	3.42	3.26	6.82	4.20	101.84	6.27	2354944	72.20	50.00
long gov/corp	1500	10.35	9.73	7.98	23.30	107.47	7.11	906743	27.80	19.25
governments	1387	4.99	4.76	6.97	8.44	103.85	6.31	2414134	74.01	51.25
int. governments	1247	3.13	2.97	6.64	3.78	101.79	6.13	1816375	55.69	38.56
long governments	140	10.61	10.20	8.04	22.58	110.72	6.87	597759	18.33	12.69
1-3 year govt.	423	1.75	1.70	6.30	1.88	100.80	5.88	913614	28.01	19.40
treasuries	170	4.94	4.79	7.05	8.27	105.14	6.26	2105810	64.56	44.71
int. treasuries	125	3.09	3.00	6.64	3.66	102.06	6.07	1579275	48.42	33.53
long treasuries	45	10.49	10.17	8.48	22.10	115.69	6.84	526535	16.14	11.18
20+ year treasuries	23	11.53	11.15	7.85	24.52	110.95	6.88	358185	10.98	7.60
agencies	1217	5.30	4.56	6.41	9.58	95.84	6.63	308324	9.45	6.55
int. agencies	1122	3.44	2.80	6.66	4.61	99.99	6.48	237100	7.27	5.03
long agencies	95	11.52	10.42	5.70	26.11	84.22	7.13	71224	2.18	1.51

January 1-31, 1997	Number Issues	Durat. ToWorst	Mod.Adj. Durat.	Coupon	Matur.	Price	Yield ToWorst	Market Value	% of Index	% of Aggregate
corporates	3698	6.39	5.91	7.57	12.57	101.91	7.05	847553	25.99	17.99
int. corporates	2338	4.40	4.24	7.40	5.61	102.01	6.74	538570	16.51	11.43
long corporates	1360	9.84	8.82	7.87	24.71	101.73	7.58	308984	9.47	6.56
industrials	1278	6.88	6.46	7.83	14.53	103.09	7.15	293681	9.00	6.23
int. industrials	706	4.38	4.23	7.64	5.67	102.77	6.78	161821	4.96	3.44
long industrials	572	9.96	9.20	8.06	25.41	103.49	7.61	131860	4.04	2.80
utilities	786	7.45	6.23	7.51	16.92	100.33	7.28	146809	4.50	3.12
int. utilities	391	4.48	4.26	7.11	5.72	100.97	6.76	68175	2.09	1.45
long utilities	395	10.02	7.93	7.85	26.62	99.78	7.73	78634	2.41	1.67
finance	1116	4.95	4.70	7.27	7.79	100.82	6.81	231461	7.10	4.91
int. finance	926	4.05	3.91	7.30	5.06	101.78	6.68	191109	5.86	4.06
long finance	190	9.22	8.44	7.14	20.73	96.53	7.43	40352	1.24	0.86
yankees	518	6.56	6.32	7.62	11.97	102.76	6.97	175603	5.38	3.73
int. yankees	315	4.97	4.80	7.42	6.36	101.98	6.77	117464	3.60	2.49
long yankees	203	9.77	9.40	8.02	23.29	104.39	7.39	58138	1.78	1.23

January 1-31, 1997	Number Issues	Durat. ToWorst	Mod.Adj. Durat.	Coupon	Matur.	Price	Yield ToWorst	Market Value	% of Index	% of Aggregate
AAA corporates	142	6.89	6.29	7.53	14.66	101.18	6.82	36824	1.13	0.78
int. AAA corporates	75	4.41	4.21	7.80	5.62	103.44	6.50	20325	0.62	0.43
long AAA corporates	67	9.95	8.86	7.21	25.79	98.54	7.21	16498	0.51	0.35
AA corporates	561	6.21	5.57	7.22	11.68	100.98	6.86	153793	4.72	3.27
int. AA corporates	365	4.42	4.25	7.00	5.64	101.27	6.59	105857	3.25	2.25
long AA corporates	196	10.17	8.50	7.71	25.01	100.33	7.47	47936	1.47	1.02
A corporates	1947	6.35	5.93	7.51	12.38	101.70	6.99	445976	13.67	9.47
int. A corporates	1251	4.33	4.18	7.39	5.46	101.98	6.70	285206	8.74	6.06
long A corporates	696	9.94	9.04	7.72	24.66	101.22	7.51	160770	4.93	3.41
BAA corporates	1048	6.50	6.05	7.98	13.26	103.18	7.32	210961	6.47	4.48
int. BAA corporates	647	4.56	4.40	7.72	5.91	102.50	6.99	127181	3.90	2.70
long BAA corporates	401	9.44	8.56	8.39	24.41	104.23	7.84	83780	2.57	1.78
asset backed	108	2.90	2.81	6.59	3.38	100.35	6.43	47342	100.00	1.01
charge/credit cards	73	3.25	3.15	6.71	3.83	100.42	6.49	37436	79.07	0.79
autos	28	1.56	1.51	6.15	1.68	100.08	6.20	9038	19.09	0.19
home equities	7	1.72	1.67	6.40	1.85	100.10	6.37	869	1.83	0.02

January 1-31, 1997	Number Issues	Durat. ToWorst	Mod.Adj. Durat.	Coupon	Matur.	Price	Yield ToWorst	Market Value	% of Index	% of Aggregate
mortgages	606	4.90	3.66	7.41	7.10	100.48	7.27	1401199	100.00	29.75
gnma	209	5.21	3.69	7.79	7.86	101.69	7.42	397521	28.37	8.44
gnma 15 yr	32	3.73	3.24	7.00	4.63	100.35	6.85	24155	1.72	0.51
gnma 30 yr	177	5.31	3.72	7.84	8.07	101.78	7.45	373366	26.65	7.93
fhlmc	208	4.70	3.63	7.22	6.69	100.02	7.20	468974	33.47	9.96
fhlmc 15 yr	47	3.75	3.20	6.82	4.64	99.66	6.88	118114	8.43	2.51
fhlmc 30 yr	112	5.32	3.97	7.46	7.89	100.18	7.40	316909	22.62	6.73
fhlmc balloon	49	2.32	2.00	6.40	2.59	99.77	6.49	33951	2.42	0.72
fnma	189	4.83	3.67	7.28	6.90	99.98	7.23	534703	38.16	11.35
fnma 15 yr	52	3.80	3.21	6.85	4.71	99.56	6.89	124513	8.89	2.64
fnma 30 yr	106	5.33	3.92	7.48	7.92	100.14	7.40	378228	26.99	8.03
fnma balloon	31	2.93	2.45	6.66	3.35	99.80	6.60	31962	2.28	0.68

TREASURY BELLWETHERS			Number Issues	Durat. ToWorst	Mod.Adj. Durat.	Coupon	Matur.	Price	Yield ToWorst	Market Value
3 month	0.000	5/01/1997	1	0.24	0.24	0.00	0.24	98.76	5.15	44459
6 month	0.000	7/31/1997	1	0.49	0.48	0.00	0.49	97.46	5.28	11311
1 year	0.000	1/08/1998	1	0.93	0.91	0.00	0.93	95.04	5.51	18340
2 year	5.875	1/31/1999	1	1.91	1.86	5.88	2.00	99.91	5.92	17491
3 year	5.875	11/15/1999	1	2.58	2.50	5.88	2.79	99.55	6.05	18653
5 year	6.250	1/31/2002	1	4.37	4.24	6.25	5.00	99.98	6.26	12502
10 year	6.500	10/15/2006	1	7.21	6.98	6.50	9.70	99.92	6.51	22871
30 year	6.500	11/15/2026	1	13.05	12.62	6.50	29.79	96.17	6.80	9757

Typically, mutual fund managers use asset-based benchmarks since they do not know the liabilities of their investors. However, companies which manage portfolios against the liabilities of a particular pension fund (which requires an actuarial analysis of the prospective obligations to retired and working lives) or an insurance company product (e.g., a single premium deferred annuity, a book of individual life insurance, or a book of universal life insurance) develop liability-based benchmarks. Since these liabilities relate to a specific company, they are individually developed and are called "customized benchmarks." The cash flows of the specific liabilities are then translated into collections of cash flows and these cash flows and desired credit risk parameters (and other risk parameters) are converted to desired fixed income asset classes to form a benchmark portfolio. The returns on this benchmark portfolio can then be calculated from the returns on its components.

PERFORMANCE MEASUREMENT

The objective of selecting an appropriate benchmark is to compare the rate of return (ROR) on the portfolio with the ROR on its benchmark and evaluate the difference. The ROR on the benchmark, or at least its components if a customized benchmark is chosen, is usually calculated by the sponsoring agency of the benchmark (e.g. Lehman Brothers, Salomon Brothers, and Merrill Lynch). If the benchmark is constructed from scratch on a security-by-security basis, the ROR on the benchmark will have to be calculated by the portfolio manager. In most cases, the ROR on the managed portfolio is calculated by the portfolio manager.

Calculating the ROR on a fixed income portfolio is no mean feat. Until recently, there was little standardization in calculating RORs. That is, by employing different methods, different RORs for the same portfolio over the same time period using the same security prices would be calculated. To standardize ROR calculations for pension fund portfolio managers, in 1993 the AIMR (Association for Investment Management and Research) developed and propagated "AIMR Standards" for calculating RORs.[1] Currently these standards are used for pension fund portfolio management and increasingly for other types of portfolio managers (e.g. the SEC has adopted standards for mutual fund performance reporting).

Specifying the prices of the securities in the portfolio is also essential to calculating the portfolio ROR. While the prices of some standard and liquid securities are readily available, the prices of other less "on-the-run," less liquid securities are not as commonly available.

Assume the ROR for the portfolio and the benchmark over a period of time are determined. The next step is to interpret and evaluate the portfolio performance. To do so requires an understanding of the original strategy of the portfolio manager. And to be able to interpret the strategy, the "risk factors" or "risk characteristics" of the type of portfolio managed must be understood and, in fact,

---

[1] A brief discussion of the AIMR standards is provided in the appendix.

measured. The next two sections consider the risk factors of a fixed income portfolio and the portfolio strategies that can be used based on these risk factors.

RISK FACTORS

The risk factors of a bond portfolio are shown in Exhibit 3. The risk factors of a common stock portfolio would be different, including the portfolio beta, the average market capitalization, the sector composition, etc. There is, however, comparability of risk factors between stocks and bonds. For example, the duration on a bond portfolio and the beta on a stock portfolio both measure exposure to market risk. Stocks, however, do not have a risk factor which is comparable to convexity for bonds.

Any fixed income portfolio and fixed income benchmark will have a set of risk factors. Thus, changes in market behavior may affect the performance of the portfolio and the benchmark differently due to their differences in risk factors. The specification measurement of a portfolio's risk factors and the benchmark's risk factors are critical in being able to compare the performance of the portfolio and benchmark due to market changes. Exhibit 3 provides the risk factors, the measurement of the risk factors, and types of market behavior which affect these risk factors. This chapter does not discuss the individual risk factors and measurements.

Exhibit 3: Risk Factors and Portfolio Performance

Risk Factors	Risk Factor Measurement	Market Changes which Affect Risk Factors
Market Risk	Duration	Change in Yield Levels-Parallel
Yield Curve Risk	Convexity/Distribution of Key Rate Durations (Bullet, Barbell, Ladder, et. al.)	Change in Slope and Shape of Yield Curve.
Exposure to Market Volatility	Convexity • Negatively convex assets (e.g., callables)/portfolios are adversely affected by volatility. • Positively convex assets (e.g., putables)/portfolios are benefited by volatility.	Market Volatility • Historical, based on past actual prices or yields. • Expected, as indicated by implied volatility of options.
Sector Allocation • Macro Sector • Micro Sector • Security Selection	Percent allocation to each macro sector, micro sector, and security and the option-adjusted spread (OAS) of each.	Change in option-adjusted spreads (OAS) of macro sectors, micro sectors, or individual securities.
Credit Risk	Average credit rating of portfolio and its sectors.	Changes in credit spreads (e.g. spread between Treasuries versus AAA corporates; or spread between AAA corporates versus BBB corporates). Also specific company rating changes.

Overall, however, two different portfolios or a portfolio and a benchmark which have different risk factors will experience different RORs due to identical market changes. The portfolio manager should calculate or measure the risk factor variable *ex ante* and either be aware of the differential response to the relevant market change or, if undesired, to change the risk factor by portfolio actions.

STRATEGIES

Having selected a benchmark, being aware of the risk factors of the portfolio, and having calculated the risk factors for the benchmark, the portfolio managers must decide whether or not they want their portfolio to replicate the risk factors of the benchmark or to deviate from them. Replicating all the risk factors is called a *passive strategy*; deviating from one or more of the risk factors is called an *active strategy*.

Of course, the portfolio manager could be passive with respect to some risk factors and active with respect to others — there is a large number of combinations given the various risk factors. Passive strategies require no forecast of future market changes — both the portfolio and benchmark respond identically to market changes. Active strategies are based on a forecast, since the portfolio and benchmark will respond differently to market changes. In an active strategy, the portfolio manager must decide in which direction and by how much the risk factor value of the portfolio will deviate from the risk factor value of the benchmark on the basis of expected market changes.

Thus, given multiple risk factors, there is a pure passive strategy. There is a pure active strategy and there are several hybrid strategies which are passive on some risk factors and active in others. Exhibit 4 summarizes some of the common passive and active strategies.

Exhibit 4: Passive and Active Strategies

Strategy	Description	Comment
Passive (in order of decreasing passivity)		
Indexation (pure passivity)	Replicate all risk factors in the "index" or benchmark.	The only certain way to accomplish this is to buy all the securities in the index in amounts equal to their weight in the index. While this can easily be done in the stock market, say for the S&P500 stock index by buying all 500 stocks in the appropriate amounts, it is difficult to do so in the fixed income market. For example, the Lehman Aggregate is based on approximately 5,694 bonds, many of them illiquid.
Dedication	Replicates the duration of the benchmark and also replicates all the cash flows (or key rate durations)	By replicating all the cash flows, the portfolio is not exposed to the risks of non-parallel shifts in the yield curve as well as parallel shifts in the yield curve. Dedication is a more expensive strategy.

Exhibit 4 (Continued)

Strategy	Description	Comment
Immunization	The duration of the portfolio is constructed to be the same as the duration of the benchmark.	There are many portfolios with the same duration which may have very different compositions of key rate durations and thus have different convexities. Immunized portfolios eliminate risk relative to the benchmark due to parallel shifts in the yield curve, but are exposed to risks due to non-parallel shifts in the yield curve. Dedicated portfolios have neither risk.
Active Strategies		
Market Timing	Deviate from duration of the benchmark.	If the portfolios has greater duration than the benchmark: • it outperforms the benchmark during market rallies; • it underperforms during market contractions; • and vice versa.
Yield Curve Trades	Replicate duration of the benchmark but vary the convexity and yield curve exposure by varying the composition of key rate durations.	Bullets outperform during yield curve steepenings; barbells outperform during yield curve flattenings.
Volatility Trades	Deviates from optionality of benchmarks: • callables are more negatively convex than bullets; • putables are more positively convex than bullets.	Volatility increases benefit putables (which are long an option) and negatively affect callables (which are short an option).
Asset Allocation/ Sector Trades: Overweights/ Underweights • Macro Sector • Micro Sector • Security	Deviate from macro sector, micro sector or security weightings of benchmark: • macro – overall sectors (Treasuries; agencies; corporates; MBS; ABS; municipals); • micro – components of a macro sector (e.g. utilities versus industrials in corporate sector); • Securities – overweight/underweight individual securities in a micro sector (e.g. Florida Power and Light versus Niagara Mohawk in corporate utility sector).	Deviations based on OAS of sectors, subsectors and securities relative to historical averages and fundamental projections. Can use break-even spreads (based on OAS) as a basis for deviations. On overweights, spread tightening produces gain; spread widening produces losses, and vice versa.
Credit Risk Allocations	Deviate from average credit rating of macro sector or micro sectors and composites thereof.	Credit spreads typically widen when economic growth is slow or negative. Credit spread widening benefits higher credit rating, and vice versa. Can use spread duration as basis for deviations.
Trading	Short-term changes in specific securities on the basis of short-term price discrepancies.	Often short-term technicals, including short-term supply/demand factors, cause temporary price discrepancies.

Exhibit 5: Spectrum of Strategies

Replicate all Risk Factors	Deviate from One or More but not all Risk Factors of Benchmark		
Pure Passive			Pure Active
Indexation (Replicate all risk factors of benchmark)	Dedication (Replicate only duration and duration buckets of risk factors of benchmark; deviate from other risk factors)	Immunization (Replicate only duration risk factor of benchmark; deviate from other risk factors)	Deviate from all risk factors of benchmark

The range of passive to active strategies can be regarded as a spectrum or continuum wherein a pure passive strategy replicates all the risk factors of the benchmark. A pure active strategy replicates none of the risk factors of the benchmark. Intermediate active/passive strategies replicate some but not all of the risk factors. This spectrum is depicted in Exhibit 5.

PORTFOLIO RETURN ANALYSIS

Changes in market values affect a portfolio's return marginally via its risk factors and thereby in aggregate determine the portfolio's total ROR. A portfolio model determines a portfolio's ROR given its risk factors (RF(i)) from the market variable changes as illustrated in Exhibit 6.[2] For example, RF(A) may be the portfolio's duration and MC(A) the change (in a parallel way) in the level of the yield curve.

The same portfolio model would apply to the benchmark portfolio given its specific risk factors, which may be the same (passive strategy) or different (active strategy) as the risk factors of the portfolio. If the model is well specified,

---

[2] The use of factor models to explain security or portfolio returns originated in the common stock literature. The concept was that common stock prices and returns could be described by an econometric model with a small number of explanatory variables. These variables are called factors (or attributes). In general, the equation would be:

$$y = a_1 + b_1 x_1 + b_2 x_2 + \dots + b_n x_n + e$$

where the x_i's are the factors and the b_i's are the sensitivities (to the factors). A model with N factors is called an "N-factor model." A "one factor model" for stocks would specify that the X is the return on the market and its sensitivity, b, is then the beta of the stock or portfolio of stocks. Additional factors might be specified as capitalization (size) and P/E (price-to-earnings ratio). The equivalent one-factor model for bonds specifies the factor as the percent change in the price of the bond market (say as measured by the Lehman Aggregate) and the b would be the (negative) relative duration of the bond or bond portfolio to that of the bond market. The Taylor series expansion of the bond price/yield equation would dictate that the second factor would be the square of the bond market price and the sensitivity of this factor would be the relative convexity of the bond or bond portfolio. Other factors could be added as discussed herein. See Frank J. Fabozzi, *Investment Management* (Englewood Cliffs, NJ: Prentice Hall, 1995), pp. 264-267 and pp. 488-503.

the actual market changes given the portfolio's risk factors will provide a calculated ROR which is very close to the actual portfolio ROR over the period of time.
The model is "fit" or specified by relating actual market changes and RORs in the
past, given the portfolio's risk factors via theoretical price/yield relationships.

Portfolio return models have been developed and are commercially available. Given a portfolio return model specified from past data, the model can then
be used in two major ways — sensitivity analysis and attribution analysis.

SENSITIVITY ANALYSIS (EX ANTE)

The portfolio return model depicted in Exhibit 6 is specified (that is the risk factors
are identified based on theory and practice) and fit (that is the coefficients of the
variable are estimated by using historical, data). Once the model is specified and fit,
it can be used for two types of simulations, one ex ante, that is "running" the model
the way the arrows are shown in the exhibit — this is *sensitivity analysis*. The other
type is *ex post*, that is "running" the model in the opposite direction of the arrows
between ROR and the market value changes — this is called *attribution analysis*.[3]

Sensitivity analysis uses projected or assumed market changes and calculates the portfolio ROR in response to these changes. Often only one variable is
changed, so the effect of that one variable, say the slope of the Treasury yield curve,
on the portfolio ROR can be determined. In addition, changes in a set of market values can be assumed. Specifically, a set of correlated market variables can be jointly
tested (e.g., Treasury yields increase the Treasury yield curve flattens, and corporate spreads widen). Sensitivity analysis can also be conducted on both the portfolio
and the benchmark and the resulting differences in the RORs determined.

A related form of sensitivity analysis is "cash flow testing" whereas
future portfolio cash flows (which may vary significantly due to prepayments)
rather than portfolio RORs in response to assumed changes in market variables
are analyzed. Multiple market variable changes can be assumed and statistical
studies of cash flow outcomes can be studied.

Exhibit 6: Portfolio Return Model

---

[3] This is similar to the way a Black-Scholes options pricing model (or any other option pricing model) can
be run either forward, that is using a volatility input to calculate the option price; or can be run backward,
that is using an assumed option price input to calculate the implied volatility consistent with this price.

Exhibit 7: Difference between Managed Portfolio and Benchmark

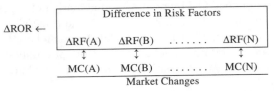

The portfolio return model depicted in Exhibit 6 can also be applied both to the managed portfolio and the benchmark portfolio, although they may have different risk factors. Of course, both portfolios will experience the same market variable changes. Applying the portfolio return model in Exhibit 6 to both the managed portfolio and the benchmark portfolio and subtracting the latter from the former provides the relationship in Exhibit 7, wherein ΔROR is the difference between the return on the managed portfolio and the benchmark, and $\Delta RF(I)$ is the difference in the Ith risk factor between the managed portfolios and the benchmark (for example, if the Ith risk factor is duration, $\Delta RFC(I)$ is the difference in their durations).

ATTRIBUTION ANALYSIS (EX POST)

Another way to utilize the portfolio return model is to run it backwards, that is to use the actual market changes $(MC(I))$ and the difference in the actual rates of return between the portfolio and the benchmark (ΔROR) to *attribute* this difference in returns to the differences in the various risk factors. For example, assume there are four risk factors, A, B, C, and D and the differences in these four risk factors between the managed portfolio and the benchmark are measured $(\Delta RF(A), \Delta RF(B), \Delta RF(C),$ and $\Delta RF(D))$. Assume the ΔROR is known and is 200 basis points (bp), that is the managed portfolio outperforms the benchmark by 2% during this period.

Attribution analysis permits answering an important question about this analysis. Why did this outperformance occur? Was it a market bet — that is, was the duration of the managed portfolio longer than the duration of the benchmark and yields declined? This outperformance would most likely reverse itself if yields increased. Or was it due to a correct allocation to MBS versus corporates; to expert allocation between utilities versus industrials in the corporate sector; or to expert issuer selection in the utility sector? Knowing which risk factor contributed to the return outperformance is very important in portfolio management evaluation. It serves as a quality control check on the investment process of a money manager. It can also be used to identify the strengths and weaknesses of money managers so they may improve their skills.

Exhibit 8 provides an example of attribution analysis for the case described above which had four risk factors and for which the managed portfolio outperformed the benchmark portfolio by 200 bp during the period in question. Of the 200 bp outperformance, 40 bp was due to risk factor A; 130 bp to risk factor B; 50 bp to risk factor D; and the managed portfolio underperformed the benchmark by 30 bp due to risk factor C. There was also a "residual" component of 10 bp of outperformance that could not be attributed to any risk factor.

As indicated, an attribution analysis system is simply one application of a portfolio return model. The requirements of developing an attribution analysis model include:

1. develop a general portfolio return model
   • define risk factors
   • measure risk factors
2. define a benchmark
   • measure risk factors
3. calculate the RORs on the managed portfolio and the benchmarks (according to AIMR standards)
   • requires data on portfolio composition and cash inflows and outflows for the portfolio.
4. requires data on market value changes and risk factors.

Attribution analysis packages are commercially available. The next section provides an example of one attribution analysis package.

ATTRIBUTION ANALYSIS — EXAMPLE

This example is based on a model developed by Global Advanced Technology (G.A.T.), a fixed income research, consulting, and analysis firm, that markets a return attribution model as part of its Integrative Bond System (I.B.S.), a PC-based fixed income portfolio management application.

This model, as in other commercially available models, decomposes a portfolio's return into a series of factors. These factors[4] are:

Total Return = Static Return + Interest Sensitive Returns
+ Spread Change Returns + Trading Return + Residual (error)

Exhibit 8: Attribution Analysis Example

Risk Factor	Return Outperformance Due To Risk Factor (bp)
A	40
B	130
C	−30
D	50
Residual	10
	200

These factors allow a user to identify the sources of return. The factors are defined as follows:

Static Return:	The portion of a portfolio's return that is due to "rolling down the yield curve." It calculates how much is earned assuming a static (meaning zero volatility) world, where the yield curve evolves to its implied forward curve.
Interest Sensitive Return:	The portion of a portfolio's return that is due to changes in the level, slope and shape of the entire yield curve.
Spread Change Return:	The portion of a portfolio's return that is due to changes in both bond sector spreads and individual security richness/cheapness.
Trading Return:	The portion of a portfolio's return that is due to changes in the composition of the portfolio. This identifies the value added by changing the composition of the portfolio as opposed to applying a buy-and-hold strategy.
Residual:	An error term that represents the part of the return that is not attributable to any of the above factors.

---

[4] These factors provide a more general level of detail. Each factor can be further decomposed to reveal more information. The more detailed model decomposition is as follows:

Static Return = Risk-Free Return + Accrual of OAS Return

Risk-Free Return is the return earned from rolling down the yield curve if the portfolio consisted of zero-coupon Treasuries.

Accrual of OAS Return is the return earned from being invested in assets other than zero-coupon Treasuries while rolling down the yield curve

Interest Sensitive Returns = Effective Duration Return + Convexity Return

where Effective Duration Return = Key Rate Return 1 + Key Rate Return 2 +... + Key Rate Return 11

Effective Duration Return is the return due to changes in the yield curve. It is measured by the sum of the *Key Rate Returns*. A *Key Rate Return* is the product of the *Key Rate Duration* (a measure of portfolio sensitivity to changes in one *key rate* on the yield curve) and the difference between the actual spot rate at the end of the period and the rate it would have evolved to if the yield curve evolved to its implied forward rate.

Convexity Return is the return that is due to the changes in the duration of a portfolio. As the yield curve changes its slope, shape, and level, a portfolio's duration changes as well and this has an impact on its return.

Spread Change Return = Delta OAS Return + Delta Rich/Cheap Return

Delta OAS Return is the return due to the widening and tightening of the sector OAS.

Delta Rich/Cheap Return is the return due to the widening and/or tightening of a security's specific spread.

G.A.T.'s software, as in many others, can apply the attribution model to various cross sections of a portfolio. The attribution model can be applied to a portfolio's benchmark index as well. A portfolio and its benchmark can both be "sliced and diced" according to a variety of risk factors. This makes possible an evaluation of the different bets that a portfolio manager puts on versus a benchmark. Examples of the possible segmentations that could be made are by bond type (i.e., Treasuries, corporates, mortgages, municipals, etc), by credit rating (i.e., AAA, AA, A, etc.), by effective duration (i.e., 0-2 years, 2-4 years, 4-6 years, etc.). These breakdowns answer the following questions "How and why did the portfolio outperform (underperform) its bogey?"

In the example that follows, an attribution performed on a portfolio of corporate securities during the month of September 1996 is considered as summarized in Exhibit 9. The bogey to which the portfolio is compared is the Merrill Lynch Corporate Index. During the month of September 1996, the yield curve shifted downward in almost a parallel fashion which led to a significant rally in the bond market.

Portfolio A outperformed its bogey by 23 bps during September. This makes intuitive sense since its duration is longer than its bogey and the market rallied during September. The Merrill Lynch Corporate Index returned 1.95%. The sector allocation of Portfolio A, which is what is being evaluated in Exhibit 9, is different than that of the benchmark — it is overweighted in industrials, utilities, telephones, oils, and internationals while being underweighted in agencies and Financials. This allocation reflects the portfolio manager's view of the market.

Overall, the portfolio manager did well with sector allocations. All of the sectors had positive returns. Compared to the benchmark, the bets on industrials, telephones, and internationals were successful, as they outperformed the bogey by 20, 11, and 15 bps, respectively. The bets on utilities and oil companies were not successful at all, as they underperformed the benchmark by 186 and 156 bps, respectively. The Financials outperformed the bogey's financials by 31 bps, though it was underweighted in the portfolio by 22%.

Considering the model decomposition of the total portfolio, the source of returns becomes more clear. (See Exhibit 10.) The static returns were quite good for both Portfolio A and the bogey (about 45 bps). The larger duration of the portfolio led to a higher interest sensitive return for the portfolio versus the benchmark (1.813% versus 1.433%). The spread change return was very small for the portfolio and for the benchmark, though it seems that there was evidence of some spread widening in Portfolio A (spread change return of −8 bps) compared to spread tightening in the benchmark (spread change return of +10 bps). Trading return was very small (less than 1 bp) because the portfolio's size and composition did not change very much over the month. Residuals are also very small (1 bp for Portfolio A and −3 bps for the benchmark). From looking at this data, the main story here was that the beneficial change in interest rates was the biggest source of return for Portfolio A and contributed to its outperformance relative to the benchmark.

Exhibit 9: Performance Attribution Example

Portfolio A: $3.0 billion corporate bond portfolio with an effective duration of 7.09

Merrill Corporate Index: Benchmark index with a duration of 5.76

	% of Portfolio	Total Return	Static Return	Interest Sensitive Return	Spread Change Return	Trading Return	Residual
Portfolio Totals							
Portfolio A	100.000	2.187	0.453	1.813	−0.087	−0.003	0.011
Merrill Corporate	100.000	1.954	0.452	1.433	0.098	0.000	−0.029
Difference	0.000	0.233	0.001	0.379	−0.185	−0.003	0.040
Sector Analysis*							
Agencies							
Portfolio A	0.000	0.000	0.000	0.000	0.000	0.000	0.000
Merrill Corporate	12.044	2.083	0.476	1.918	−0.118	0.000	−0.193
Difference	−12.044	−2.083	−0.476	−1.918	−0.118	0.000	0.193
Industrials							
Portfolio A	31.480	2.325	0.459	1.924	−0.026	−0.059	0.027
Merrill Corporate	26.769	2.121	0.460	1.606	0.108	0.000	−0.053
Difference	7.711	0.204	−0.001	0.318	−0.134	−0.059	0.080
Financials							
Portfolio A	15.580	2.023	0.439	1.560	0.077	-0.057	0.004
Merrill Corporate	37.363	1.707	0.444	1.210	0.060	0.000	−0.008
Difference	−21.783	0.316	−0.006	0.350	0.017	−0.057	0.012
Utilities							
Portfolio A	15.900	0.310	0.528	−0.090	0.540	0.042	−0.711
Merrill Corporate	7.385	2.167	0.469	1.564	0.185	0.000	−0.051
Difference	8.515	−1.857	0.060	−1.654	0.356	0.042	−0.660
Telephones							
Portfolio A	17.080	2.439	0.439	1.843	0.027	0.144	−0.014
Merrill Corporate	4.440	2.331	0.447	1.723	0.201	0.000	−0.040
Difference	12.640	0.108	−0.008	0.120	−0.174	0.144	0.026
Oil							
Portfolio A	4.940	0.562	0.467	2.035	−1.939	0.000	0.000
Merrill Corporate	1.670	2.123	0.462	1.513	0.194	0.000	−0.047
Difference	3.270	−1.561	0.004	0.522	−2.133	0.000	−0.047
Internationals							
Portfolio A	14.180	2.264	0.443	1.891	−0.079	0.021	−0.011
Merrill Corporate	10.022	2.118	0.446	1.597	0.095	0.000	−0.021
Difference	4.158	0.147	−0.004	0.294	−0.174	0.021	0.010
Miscellaneous							
Portfolio A	0.000	0.000	0.000	0.000	0.000	0.000	0.000
Merrill Corporate	0.308	0.796	0.416	0.384	−0.025	0.000	0.021
Difference	0.308	−0.796	−0.416	−0.384	0.025	0.000	−0.021

* In the sector analyses, we are comparing the constituents of Portfolio A that fall into a particular sector to the constituents of the benchmark that fall into the same sector. For example, the industrials from Portfolio A are being evaluated against the industrials from the Merrill Corporate Index.

Source: G.A.T. Integrative Bond System

Exhibit 10: Summary of Return Attribution Analysis

Risk Factor	Portfolio A Returns (bps)	Merrill Corporate Index Returns (bps)	Difference	% of Total Return Difference
Static Return	45.3	45.2	0.1	0.4%
Interest Sensitive Return	181.3	143.3	37.9	162.7%
Spread Change Return	−8.7	9.8	−18.5	−79.4%
Trading Return	−0.3	0.0	−0.3	−1.3%
Residual	0.1	−2.9	4.0	17.2%
Total	218.7	195.4	23.3	100%

The next step in the process is to try to understand what caused the various sectors to perform the way they did. Static returns are not significant except for utilities (a 6 bp outperformance), which could be explained by higher coupons which led to a more favorable roll down along the yield curve. The interest sensitive returns for all sectors, except for utilities (a 165 bps underperformance), show good outperformance. A possible explanation for the utilities' significant underperformance would be the presence of negative convexity associated with the call options present in many utility bonds (bond rallies make the call option on callable corporate bonds more in-the-money for the issuer and therefore, more likely to be called, which has a negative effect on callable corporate bond performance). The other sectors are less callable and longer in duration and therefore performed better in a bond rally. Spread change returns reveal a more mixed bag of results. In Portfolio A, we see evidence of spread widening in industrials, oils, and internationals and tightening in financials and utilities. Relative to the benchmark, spreads moved more favorably for the industrials, oils, and telephones in the bogey than they did in Portfolio A, while they moved more favorable for financials and utilities in Portfolio A than they did for the bogey. Trading returns do not reveal much except for telephones, where during the month, it shows that the portfolio manager added value by shifting the portfolio into the telephones sector. Note that trading return for the benchmark is zero in all cases. This is the case because during a month the benchmark constituents do not change.

This type of analysis can be extended to almost any risk factor. A portfolio can be sliced and diced according to the effective duration distribution, credit rating distribution, or its coupon distribution and then compared to its benchmark to see how much value was added and from where the added value came. Any bet that the portfolio manager can put on can be analyzed in the attribution process. This type of analysis adds to a portfolio manager's knowledge of his/her own strengths (are they good "sector pickers," or are they better at placing bets on yield curve movements?) and is designed to assist them in the investment decision making process.

OVERVIEW

Knowing only whether a portfolio outperformed its benchmark or not, and by how much, does not provide complete information for the evaluation of the portfolio manger and the portfolio management process. Was it due to having a long duration during a rally; a barbell duration bucket composition during a yield curve flattening environment; macro or micro asset allocation; expert security selection; or some other reason? Attribution analysis answers these questions and provides for a more comprehensive and detailed evaluation of portfolio management. Understanding and applying attribution analysis requires a thorough understanding of all the risk factors which affect bond pricing. All the concepts and practices in understanding bond market performance, which are discussed in other chapters in this book, come together in attribution analysis.

APPENDIX
AIMR PERFORMANCE CALCULATION METHODOLOGIES

In 1993, the Association for Investment Management and Research (AIMR) codified a set of standards for presenting performance results. AIMR's intent was to protect the users of performance data, namely, the investor community, by "keeping the investment managers honest." These standards call for full disclosure and fair representation by investment managers in reporting their investment results. They also call for uniformity in both the calculation and reporting of performance results so that investors can more directly compare among investment managers.

When an investment manager is said to be "AIMR compliant," it means the performance results he/she is providing are prepared and presented in such a way as to conform with these standards. There are different levels of compliance which reflect the degree to which the manager is complying with the standards. Some aspects are mandatory and some aspects are recommended. One should note that there is no legal statute compelling investment managers to comply with the AIMR standards. However, being in compliance provides a degree of comfort to an investor who is utilizing or seeking to utilize the services of a manager. Also, the investment management industry as a whole does not want to invite further regulation on the part of the Securities and Exchange Commission (SEC) or even worse, Congress, so these standards are a way for the industry to show that it can police itself.

Minimum Requirements

The AIMR standards stipulate that there should be some uniformity in the methodology used to calculate return. These apply to both the equity world as well as the fixed income world. Listed below are some of the more important requirements for calculating total rates of return. Total returns must:

1. Include realized and unrealized capital gains and losses plus income.
2. Include accrued interest
3. Be *time weighted* at least quarterly, then geometrically linked
4. Account for cash balances
5. Reflect *reasonable* pricing for all assets

Of these, the requirement that returns must be time weighted is important enough to warrant further attention. A time weighted return answers the question *"What happened to my first dollar of investment?"* Time weighting neutralizes the impact of cash flows not under the discretion of the portfolio manager. These "cash flows" can come in the form of a cash contribution or withdrawal or a security contribution or withdrawal. This is important because it reflects how much value was added to or subtracted from the portfolio by the actions of the portfolio manager only.

Reasonable pricing of all assets is also very important and is a bigger issue for fixed income securities portfolios than for equity portfolios. This is due primarily to the fact that the equity market is more efficient than the fixed income market. Stocks are bought and sold on an exchange where there is a great deal of liquidity which is evidenced by the very tight bid-asked spreads. Stocks are traded every day, so the last trade price provides the best estimate of a stock's value at the close of trading. The exchange also facilitates access to the final closing prices for each and every stock.

The fixed income market, in contrast, is an over-the-counter market, where, except for U.S. Treasuries, there is no consistent liquidity among different bond types. Bid-asked spreads can vary considerably by bond type (i.e., private placements versus public corporates) and are on the whole much wider than in the equity market. Also, not every bond trades every day, which forces investment managers to rely on sophisticated pricing matrices utilized by the various pricing services to estimate the value of their bonds. All of these structural issues in the fixed income market make it very cumbersome to value a bond portfolio daily. Certainly, there are many more sources of error in the calculations of performance for bonds than for stocks.

Calculations

There are many mathematical approaches to calculating performance. However, only the three that are acceptable to AIMR will be discussed. The three approaches are ranked from best to worst in terms of the exactness of the performance results generated by them. These methods can be applied equally to both equity and fixed income portfolios. The three approaches are:

1. Daily valuation method
2. Unit valuation method
3. Modified Dietz method (linked dollar-weighted internal rate of return (IRR))

Daily Valuation Method

The *daily valuation method* is the most accurate method available. The portfolio is valued at the close of every business day and by using the formula below, the daily total rate of return can be calculated:

$$R_{Daily} = \frac{\text{Market Value}_{End of Day}}{\text{Market Value}_{Beginning of Day}} - 1$$

Income that was earned and accrued as well as any amortized principal are included in the market value of the portfolio. If there are any cash or security contributions or withdrawals these are included in the following day's beginning market value.

To get a return for a longer period of time, like a week or a month, the following formula shows the linking process:

$$R_{n\,Days} = [(1 + R_{Daily_1}) \times (1 + R_{Daily_2}) \times \dots \times (1 + R_{Daily_n})] - 1$$

For example, assume that a portfolio of publicly traded fixed income securities of a life insurance company has a market value of $10 million on 12/2. On 12/3, new premiums of $1 million are paid in that the manager must invest and on 12/5, expenses of $500,000 must be paid by the portfolio. Assuming that the market value end of day (pre flow) column below reflects the daily changes in the portfolio's market value, the interest income earned, realized and unrealized capital gains, and the daily accruing of interest, the weekly return is calculated as follows:

Date	Market Value Beginning of Day ($000)	Market Value End of Day (Pre Flow) ($000)	Inflow/ Outflow ($000)	Market Value End of Day (Post Flow) ($000)	Daily Returns	
12/2	10,000	10,150	0	10,150	10,150/10,000 =	1.50%
12/3	10,150	10,100	+1,000	11,100	10,100/10,150 =	−0.49%
12/4	11,100	11,500	0	11,500	11,500/11,100 =	3.60%
12/5	11,500	11,000	−500	10,500	11,000/11,500 =	−4.35%
12/6	10,500	10,750	0	10,750	10,750/10,500 =	2.38%

Linking daily returns gives the weekly return:

$$\text{Weekly Return} = [(1 + 0.015) \times (1 - 0.0049) \times (1 + 0.036) \times (1 - 0.0435)$$
$$\times (1 + 0.0238)] - 1$$
$$= 1.0246 - 1 = 2.46\%$$

The daily valuation method provides the highest degree of accuracy because there is a market value for each day. Returns are computed without the influence of contributions and withdrawals from the portfolio. (Note that the market value end of day (pre flow) is used as the numerator, not the market value end of day (post flow). The portfolio manager is evaluated on how much value was added based on his/her actions for the day.

Mutual funds are required to publish their net asset values (NAVs) daily, which requires them to price their portfolios daily. However, as mentioned above, the more illiquid the security, the more difficult it is to get a daily price and hence the more difficult it is to use this method to calculate performance. This is a problem faced by insurance companies that have large portions of their portfolios allocated to illiquid private placements. For them, using this method to calculate performance is impratical.

Unit Valuation Method

The next best approach is the *unit valuation method*. This method requires the valuation of the portfolio at each significant cash flow contribution/withdrawal date, instead of every day. The returns are then calculated for the subperiods between the cash flow dates using the following formula:

$$R_{\text{Subperiod}} = \frac{\text{Market Value}_{\text{Ending}}}{\text{Market Value}_{\text{Beginning}}} - 1$$

As was the case with the daily valuation method, income that was earned and accrued as well as any amortized principal are included in the market value of the portfolio. When a cash inflow or outflow occurs, it is added to the beginning market value of the next subperiod.

To compute a return for a longer time interval such as a month or quarter, the following formula shows the linking process:

$$R_{Subperiod} = [(1 + R_{Subperiod_1}) \times (1 + R_{Subperiod_2}) \times \cdots$$
$$\times (1 + R_{Subperiod_{n-1}}) \times (1 + R_{Subperiod_n})] - 1$$

With this approach, one needs to link the subperiod returns together.

For example, assume that a portfolio of publicly traded fixed income securities of a life insurance company has a market value of $10 million on 12/2. On 12/3, new premiums of $500,000 are paid in that the manager must invest, and on 12/5 and 12/13, expenses of $250,000 and $300,000, respectively, must be paid by the portfolio. Assuming that the market value end of subperiod (pre flow) column below reflects the changes in the portfolio's market value, the interest income earned, realized and unrealized capital gains, and the accruing of interest for each subperiod, the monthly return is calculated as follows:

Period	Market Value Beginning of Subperiod ($000)	Market Value End of Subperiod (Pre Flow) ($000)	Inflow/ Outflow ($000)	Market Value End of Subperiod (Post Flow) ($000)	Subperiod Returns	
12/02-12/10	10,000	10,150	+500	10,650	10,150/10,000 =	1.50%
12/10-12/13	10,650	10,509	-250	10,259	10,509/10,650 =	-1.32%
12/13-12/25	10,259	10,488	-300	10,188	10,488/10,259 =	2.23%
12/25-12/31	10,188	10,384	0	10,384	10,384/10,188 =	1.92%

Linking the subperiod returns gives the monthly return.

Monthly Return = $[(1+0.015) \times (1-0.0132) \times (1+0.0223) \times (1+0.0192)] - 1$
= $1.0436 - 1 = 4.36\%$

The unit valuation method is more practical than the daily valuation method because it requires less frequent pricing on the part of the investment manager. He/she only has to value the portfolio on days when there are significant cash flows. However, if there is significant cash flow activity in the portfolio, it may require frequent pricing of the portfolio which may become impractical.

Modified Dietz Method

To reduce the pricing problem significantly, the third and last method, the *modified Dietz method* was developed. This method, named after its developer, Peter Dietz, unlike the unit valuation method, does not require the valuation of the portfolio at each significant cash flow date. This approach is also called a *linked dollar-weighted internal rate of return* (IRR). It provides a return that is approximately the same as that provided by the unit valuation method. The returns are calculated for the entire period using the following formula:

$$R_{Period} = \frac{(MV_E - MV_B) - (\text{Gross Contributions}) \ OR \ + (\text{Gross Withdrawals})}{MV_B - (\text{Adjusted Contributions}) \ OR \ + (\text{Adjusted Withdrawals})} - 1$$

where MV_E and MV_B are the ending and beginning market values, respectively. The gross cash contributions (withdrawals) are added to (subtracted from) the numerator, while in the denominator an adjustment must be made for the number of days the cash flows were available to be invested.

To make the adjustment in the denominator for a contribution into the portfolio, the following formula is applied:

$$1 - \frac{\text{Number of days in the period before cash was invested in portfolio}}{\text{Total number of days in the period}}$$

This represents the percentage of the period that the cash contributed was available for investment. This number is then multiplied by the dollar amount of the contribution and subtracted in the denominator.

To make the adjustment in the denominator for a withdrawal from the portfolio, the following formula is applied:

$$1 - \frac{\text{Number of days in the period invested in portfolio}}{\text{Total number of days in the period}}$$

This represents the percentage of the period that the cash withdrawn was not available for investment. This number is then multiplied by the dollar amount of the withdrawal and added in the denominator.

The modified Dietz method is the most common method used today. It is easier to implement because the information requirements are much less demanding. Valuations of the portfolios are not needed more frequently than at the ends of months and the cash flows into and out of the portfolio are well known.

To illustrate this method, assume that a portfolio of publicly traded fixed income securities of a life insurance company has a market value of $10 million on 12/2. On 12/3, new premiums of $500,000 are paid in that the manager must invest and on 12/5 and 12/13, expenses of $250,000 and $300,000, respectively, must be paid by the portfolio. Assuming that the market values column below reflects the changes in the portfolio's market value, the interest income earned, realized and unrealized capital gains, and the accruing of interest for each subperiod, the monthly return is calculated as follows:

Date	Transaction	Market Values ($000)	# of Days in portfolio	% of Period Cash was/was not Available ($000)	Adjusted Cash Flow ($000)
12/1	Beginning MV	10,000			
12/10	Contribution	500	20	$1 - ((30 - 20)/30) = 66\%$	$0.66 \times 500 = 333$
12/13	Withdrawal	250	13	$1 - (13/30) = 56\%$	$0.56 \times 250 = 142$
12/25	Withdrawal	300	25	$1 - (25/30) = 16\%$	$0.16 \times 300 = 50$
12/31	Ending MV	10,384			

$$\text{Monthly Return} = \frac{(10{,}384 - 10{,}000 - 500 + 250 + 300)}{(10{,}000 + 333 - 142 - 50)}$$

$$= \frac{434}{10{,}141} = 4.28\%$$

Note that the difference between the results computed from both methods is only 8 bps (4.36% − 4.28%) which suggests that the modified Dietz method provides a very good approximation to the unit valuation method. However, when there are cash flows greater than 10% of the value of the portfolio, the approximation becomes worse. Clearly, the magnitude of the cash flows within the period is critical to the performance calculation. AIMR prefers the unit valuation method when there are cash flows greater than 10% into and out of the portfolio because it provides a better approximation since it utilizes more data than the modified Dietz method.

Performance By Security

The formula for calculating the return on a security, stock or bond, is similar to those formulas for calculating the return on a portfolio. However, with an individual security, the amount of income earned by the security must be included in the numerator. The formula below can be used for any time period:

$$R_{\text{Security}} = \frac{\text{Market Value}_{\text{Ending}} - \text{Market Value}_{\text{Beginning}} + \text{Income}}{\text{Market Value}_{\text{Beginning}}}$$

Summary

AIMR set out to establish standards for calculating and reporting total rates of return on portfolios. The goal was to create a level playing field for the investment management industry so that investors can feel comfortable about their comparisons of managers. This standardization addressed the reporting of performance results as well as calculating performance data.

Portfolio managers also need to see and understand their performance in order to develop strategies to keep adding value for their clients. There are three methods to calculating performance that are accepted by AIMR — the daily valuation method, the unit valuation method, and the modified Dietz method. All three methods arrive at acceptable total rate of return numbers although they differ as to the information required to get there. The daily valuation method provides the most accurate results and is the most rigorous in terms of the data required. The modified Dietz method is the least accurate of the three, but it is also the least stringent in terms of the information required. The unit valuation method lies somewhere between those two in terms of accuracy and information requirements.

Index

731

ROE. See Return on equity.
Rogalski, Richard J., 501
Roll, Richard, 166, 280, 499, 699
Roll down characteristics, 571
Rolldown return, 438
Rolling bellwether method, 446
ROR. See Rate of return.
Ross, S., 361
Ross, Stephen A., 166, 496, 499, 501, 699
Rostow, W.W., 305, 309
RROC. See Residual return on capital.
Rubinstein, M., 361
Rule-based systems, 52
Rule-induction systems, 49
Russell, Frank, 277
Russell 1000 index, 277
Russell 2000 index, 277
Russell 3000, 110

S

Sachs, Goldman, 259
Sail trimming strategies, 559
Sakura Global Capital, 44
Sale transactions, limitation, 478
Sales analysis, 236–239
    trends, 237
Sales breakdowns, 237–238
Sales finance, 486
Salomon Broad Investment Grade (BIG), 710
Salomon Brothers, 277, 593, 710. See RAM model.
Salomon Brothers Inc., 153
Salomon Brothers Non-U.S. Government Bond Index, 622
Salomon Brothers World Government Bond Index (WBFI), 593, 603
Salomon Brothers World Government Bond/Bond Performance Indices, 601
Salomon index, 76
Salomon Non-U.S. Government Bond Index, 594
Samak, Vele, 166
Samson, William D., 245
Samsung Electronics, 313
Sargent, T.J., 54
Savings and loan associations (S&Ls), 11
Scenario analysis, 430–431
Scenario factors, 176
Scenario forecasting, 365
Scenario interest rate path, present value calculation, 406–408
Scenario optimization methods, 52
Scenario prices, 673
Scenario score, 176, 178
Scheinkman, J.A., 50, 54
Scheinkman, Jose, 501, 527
Schlarbaum, Gary G., 275
Schleifer, A., 105

Scholes, M., 361
Schroder, M., 40
Schulman, Evan C., 77
Seabrook Nuclear Unit I, 482
Seasonality, 585
SEC. See Securities and Exchange Commission.
Secondary markets, 577
Secondary trade rationales, 581–584
Sector, 566–569, 591
    duration contribution, 566
    enhancements, 572–573
    percent, 566
    selection, 603
Sector bets, 559
Sector rotation, 573, 589
Sector spreads, 566
    risk, hedging, 686–688
Sector/credit/security selection, 601
Sector-rotation trades, 583
Securities
    in-depth analyses, 113
Securities and Exchange Commission (SEC), 16, 186–188, 190, 199, 206, 223, 712, 725
Securities Exchange Act of 1934, 188
Security, 475
Security analysis, 644–645
Security analysis, EVA usage, 249–271
Security price, 352
Security pricing, 140
Security returns, non-linear models, 48–50
Security selection, 621–622
Security valuation, 648
Segmentation algorithms, 47, 49
Segmented market, integrated approach, 130–132
Segment-specific model, 132
Self-reflective systems, 55
Sell disciplines, 654–655, 655
Sell/buy, 296
Sell-side analysts, 216–218
Semi-deviation, 366
Sensitivity analysis (ex ante), 717–718
Separation rule, 81–82, 82
Service-based industries, 306, 314
SFAS 90, 476
Shape return, 441
Share prices, 322, 489–490
    analysis, 581
    last-resort lenders, 29
Shareholder equity. See Balance sheet.
    return, 231
Shareholder reporting, tax reporting comparison, 220–223
Shareholders, 249
Shareholders' letter, 188
Sharpe, William F., 496, 497
Sharpe ratios, 427, 595, 629
Sharpe-Lintner-Mossin, 46

Sherrerd, Katrina F., 217
Shift, 433, 446
Shift returns, 439
Shiller, Robert J., 115
Shleifer, Andrei, 284
Short call, 348
Short selling, assumptions, 364
Shorter-term money market instruments, 25
Shortfalls probability, limit, 70–73
Short-sell candidates, 271
Short-term borrowing costs, 26
Short-term debt, 243, 477, 484
Short-term demand imbalances, 621
Short-term fluctuations, 492
Short-term forecasting, 48
Short-term funds, 204
Short-term gains, 95
Short-term interest rates, 43, 503–506, 555, 613
    differential, 614, 615
Short-term market interest rates, 26
Short-term nominal interest rates, 501
Short-term obligations, 208
Short-term overreaction, 140
Short-term real rate of interest, 501
Short-term solvency, 216, 240
    ratios, 240–242
Short-term tactical investment, 580
Shoven, J.B., 99, 104, 105
Siegel, Andrew F., 512
Siegel's paradox, 78
Sierra Pacific, 157
Simulation, usage. See Cash flows; Interest rates.
Singer, Brian D., 613, 630
Single factor model, 266
Sinking funds, 477, 587–588
    obligation, 588
Sinking-fund provisions, 479
Size, 490–491, 704, 705
Size nonlinearity, 704
Skiadas, C., 40
S&Ls. See Savings and loans associations.
Small-cap investors, 273
Small-cap market segment, 140
Small-cap portfolios, 120
Small-cap stocks, 111, 137, 294
Small-capitalizations managers, 130
Small-caps, 117
Sobel, Robert, 190
Solnik, Bruno, 630
Sony, 313
Sorensen, Eric H., 152, 153, 166, 176, 182, 277
Sovereign credits, 643
Sovereign risk, 640–642
S&P500. See Standard & Poor's 500.
S&P/Barra Value and Growth indexes, 105
Specialized ratios, 236
Spoiler, 84

For Better Equity Trading

To maximize your profits from equity trading while minimizing your exposure to risk, you need the most powerful and convenient analytical tool available— **The BARRA Aegis System**. Aegis, offered in Windows and Windows NT, is a decision support tool used by brokers and traders alike to manage a variety of trading processes.

Drawing on BARRA's 20 years of risk modeling experience, Aegis uses the latest multiple factor risk technology to analyze and manage equity inventory risk. You can forecast the indirect costs of your trades, and construct baskets for hedging and arbitrage strategies. Better risk insight leads to better

The BARRA Aegis System™

planning of program trades and optimal sequencing of trades during book unloading. And you can characterize daily Value at Risk (VAR) for management control, reporting and regulatory needs.

BARRA is the world's leading provider of analytical tools for investment management and trading. Our models are used by over 1200 clients worldwide including a majority of the top 20 securities firms.

For further information or to arrange a demonstration please contact BARRA in Berkeley at 510.548.5442 or online at **www.barra.com**.

⑤ BARRA

Analytics | **Consulting** | **Investment Data** | **Trading Services** | **Asset Management**

BARRA...for your business

For Better Fixed Income Management

To maximize your profits from fixed income management while minimizing your exposure to risk, you need the most powerful and convenient analytical tool available–**The BARRA Cosmos System**. Cosmos, offered in Windows and Windows NT, is a decision support tool used by fixed income professionals worldwide to manage a variety of portfolio processes.

Drawing on BARRA's 20 years of risk modeling experience, Cosmos uses the latest multiple-factor risk technology to let you analyze and manage portfolios of bonds, derivatives and currencies across all major markets. Coverage of over 180,000 securities gives you unparalleled insight into multi-asset, multi-country exposures. Powerful optimization capabilities create tailored portfolios in seconds. And you can characterize Value at Risk (VAR) for management, reporting and regulatory needs.

BARRA is the world's leading provider of analytical tools for investment management and trading. Our risk and other models are used by over 1200 clients worldwide, including a majority of the top 100 asset management firms.

For further information or to arrange a demonstration please contact BARRA in Berkeley at 510.548.5442 or online at **www.barra.com**.

The BARRA Cosmos System™

 **BARRA**

Analytics | Consulting | Investment Data | Trading Services | Asset Management

Now the course comes to you!

HOW TO RESEARCH

ACTIVE STRATEGIES

Over 300 equity and fixed income investment managers, researchers, and analysts have taken this intensive, one-day course in the fundamentals of active portfolio management. Now BARRA, the world's leading provider of analytical investment and trading solutions, offers the same course material to view at your own pace. Each lecture is offered in one videotape and is accompanied by text, illustrations, and exercises in a companion workbook and textbook. The course cuts to the heart of the active portfolio management challenge through four main sections:

The Active Management Framework

- From business school to researching active strategies
- Risk modeling
- The information ratio
- Value added and optimality
- The fundamental law of active management
- Problems

Valuation and Expected Returns

- Dividend discount models
- Comparative valuation
- Returns-based analysis
- Arbitrage Pricing Theory
- Problems

Forecasting, Information Analysis

- Basic forecasting formula
- Combining information
- Information analysis
- Data mining
- Problems

Portfolio Construction and Transactions Costs

- Neutralizing signals
- Turnover and transaction costs
- Techniques for portfolio construction
- Value added versus turnover
- Problems

For more information or to order your copy of the "How to Research Active Strategies" Video Series please visit our website at **www.barra.com** or contact Mary Wang via e-mail at mary.wang@barra.com or call 510.548.4598.

How to Research **Active Strategies**

A One-day Training Course

Highlights

The investment community has acclaimed the book Active Portfolio Management by Grinold and Kahn (Irwin Publishing, 1995) for its thorough and comprehensive treatment of the process of active management. Now this material is available in a one-day training course.

This course covers in one day the most relevant material in the book. Each training course attendee will receive a copy.

Learn which investment ideas are most promising and classify the various approaches to forecasting returns. Learn how to measure the information content of different investment ideas, how to refine forecasts based on this content, and how to construct portfolios to best act upon information. Each session combines lectures and student exercises designed to reinforce concepts and provide hands-on experience with the details.

Prerequisites

This course is aimed at investment professionals with MBA-level training, or equivalent. Much of the material is quantitative, however, we will emphasize the intuition of the results. As to investment knowledge, the course is self-contained. Familiarity with a standard MBA-level course in investments would be useful. A hand-held calculator may help with some exercises.

Program

The Active Management Framework
- From business school to researching active strategies
- Risk modeling
- Focus on residual risk and return
- The information ratio
- Value added and optimality
- The fundamental law of active management
- Problems

Contact: **Mary Wang**
TEL: 510.649.4598 FAX: 510.548.4374
EMAIL: mary.wang@barra.com

Valuation and Expected Returns
- Dividend discount models
- Comparative valuation
- Returns-based analysis
- Arbitrage Pricing Theory
- Problems
- Case study, part A

Forecasting, Information Analysis
- Refining forecasts
- Basic forecasting formula
- Relation to regression
- Rule of thumb
- Two signals
- Information analysis
- The two-stage process
- Datamining
- Case study, part B
- Problems

Portfolio Construction and Transactions Costs
- Why is portfolio construction complicated?
- Pre-OPS
- Turnover and transaction costs
- Techniques for portfolio construction
- Implementation details
- Value added versus turnover
- Case study, part C
- Problems

Performance Analysis
- Goals
- Performance analysis
- Returns-based
- Portfolio-based
- Problems

 **BARRA**

To stay on top,
you need to know a lot
about key players in the
fixed-income market.
*Don't sweat the details,
use the Capital Access
Desk Reference Series.*

If you want to stay on top of the fixed-income
universe, you need comprehensive, reliable
information from an industry leader. Capital Access
International introduces its *Desk Reference Series*—
essential guides to the buyers and sellers of fixed-
income securities.

The Desk Reference Series provides you with
an inside look at the world of fixed-income. It
gives you detailed firm profiles that include
critical contact and asset information, as well
as structure preferences for an array of fixed-
income investment instruments.

These guides can help you assess your best
prospects—and peers—in each segment
of the market. They also take you a step
further, by providing essential information
to help you identify and reach key players.

**To find out more or to order copies
of the Desk Reference Series, contact us at
800-866-5987 or info@capital-access.com**

Capital Access
INTERNATIONAL

430 Mountain Avenue
Murray Hill, New Jersey 07974

**Tel. (908) 771-0800
Fax. (908) 771-0330
Toll Free: (800) 866-5987**

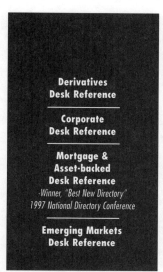

Derivatives
Desk Reference

Corporate
Desk Reference

Mortgage &
Asset-backed
Desk Reference
-Winner, "Best New Directory"
1997 National Directory Conference

Emerging Markets
Desk Reference

Mortgage &
Asset-backed
Desk Reference

U.S. Buyside &
Sellside Profiles

Corporate
Bond Desk
Reference

U.S. Buyside &
Sellside Profiles

Derivatives
Desk Reference

U.S. Buyside &
Sellside Profiles

Emerging
Markets
Desk Reference

Buyside &
Sellside Profiles

Each Desk Reference only $395.*

***Inquire about special package discounts.**

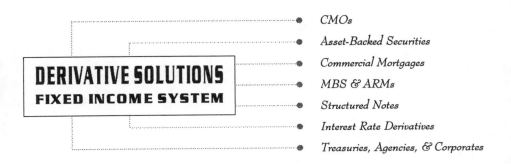

Bond Portfolio Management
Fixed Income Securities
Managing Fixed Income Portfolios
Selected Topics in Bond Portfolio Management
Valuation of Fixed Income Securities and Derivatives 3rd. Ed.
Valuation of Interest-Sensitive Financial Instruments
Advanced Fixed Income Analytics
Advances in Fixed Income Valuation Modeling and Risk Management
Treasury Securities and Derivatives
Managing MBS Portfolios
The Handbook of Investing in Corporate Debt Instruments
Corporate Bonds: Structures & Analysis
Collateralized Mortgage Obligations: Structures and Analysis
Asset-Backed Securities
The Handbook of Commercial Mortgage-Backed Securities 2nd Ed.
Handbook of Nonagency Mortgage-Backed Securities
Basics of Mortgage-Backed Securities
Inflation Protection Bonds
Perspectives on International Fixed Income Investing
The Handbook of Stable Value Investments
Trends in Commercial Mortgage-Backed Securities
Handbook of Emerging Fixed Income and Currency Markets
Handbook of Portfolio Management
Introduction to Quantitative Methods For Investment Managers
Measuring and Controlling Interest Rate Risk
Dictionary of Financial Risk Management
Risk Management: Framework, Methods, and Practice
Perspectives on Interest Rate Risk Management for Money Managers and Traders
Essays In Derivatives
Handbook of Equity Style Management - Second Edition
Active Equity Portfolio Management
Selected Topics in Equity Portfolio Management
Foundations of Economic Value-Added
Investing By The Numbers
Professional Perspectives on Indexing
Pension Fund Investment Management - Second Edition
Modeling the Market: New Theories and Techniques
Securities Lending and Repurchase Agreements
Credit Union Investment Management

For more information visit our web site: www.frankfabozzi.com